THE
SALVATION ARMY
YEAR BOOK

2013

INTERNATIONAL
MISSION STATEMENT

The Salvation Army, an international movement, is an
evangelical part of the universal Christian Church.
Its message is based on the Bible. Its ministry is motivated by the
love of God. Its mission is to preach the gospel of Jesus Christ and
to meet human needs in his name without
discrimination.

THE SALVATION ARMY
INTERNATIONAL HEADQUARTERS
101 QUEEN VICTORIA STREET, LONDON EC4V 4EH, UNITED KINGDOM

**Dedicated to the glory of God
in whose name and by whose grace
the work described in this volume
has been accomplished**

Annual reports in this edition mostly cover the period 1 May 2011 to 30 April 2012.

International appointments published on 1 October 2012, to take effect on 1 January/February/March 2013, have been included.

Staff lists and details of centres of work are generally accurate to 31 October 2012.

Statistics are those recorded on 1 January 2012.

First published 2012

Copyright © 2012 The General of The Salvation Army

ISBN *978-0-85412-849-5*

Editor: Lieut-Colonel Jayne Roberts

Cover design and colour maps: Berni Georges
Colour photo design: Jooles Tostevin

Published by Salvation Books
The Salvation Army International Headquarters
101 Queen Victoria Street, London EC4V 4EH, United Kingdom

Printed in the United Kingdom by Page Bros Ltd, Norwich NR6 6SA
using paper from sustainable sources

Contents

Foreword by the General 1

Articles of special interest

Kroc Centers USA..................................Commissioner Carol Seiler....................3

Salvos Legal ....Luke Geary..5

Preparing for the Worst ....Jonathan Hibbert-Hingston..................7

The Salvation Army - facts and figure

The Doctrines of The Salvation Army 10
Founders of The Salvation Army...11
The High Council 12
Generals Elected by a High Council 13
Significant Events 2011-2012 17
Countries where The Salvation Army is at work....................................18
International Statistics...20
Salvation Army Periodicals 22
Books Published 2011-2012 23
Ministries and Fellowships 25
Salvation Army Honours 27

International Headquarters - Information and Statistics

International Headquarters 30
   International Social Justice Commission 33
   International College for Officers and Centre for Spiritual Life Development 34
   The Africa Development Centre 35
   International Administrative Structure...36
   The Salvation Army International Trustee Company.............................37
   Reliance Bank Limited 37
   Overseas Service Funds 38
   Community Development Projects 40

Angola 41
Australia
   National Secretariat.................43
   Eastern.....................................44
   Southern 50
Bangladesh..................................58
Brazil 61
Canada and Bermuda..................65
Caribbean....................................74
Congo (Brazzaville)....................79
Democratic Republic of Congo ...83
Denmark 87
Eastern Europe............................90
Finland and Estonia 94
France and Belgium....................97
Germany and Lithuania 102
Ghana...106
Hong Kong and Macau 109
India:
National Secretariat 114
   Central 115
   Eastern 120
   Northern 123
   South Eastern 127
   South Western 131
   Western....................................134
Indonesia....................................138
Italy and Greece.........................142
Japan 144
Kenya East..................................147
Kenya West 150
Korea 153
Latin America North 158
Liberia..163
Malawi..165
Mali...167

Mexico 169
Middle East.................................173
Mozambique 175
Netherlands and Czech
   Republic 177
New Zealand, Fiji and Tonga 182
Nigeria 187
Norway, Iceland and
   the Færoes 191
Pakistan......................................195
Papua New Guinea 199
Philippines 202
Portugal......................................206
Rwanda and Burundi 208
Singapore, Malaysia and
   Myanmar 211
South America East 215
South America West...................219
Southern Africa 225
Spain 229
Sri Lanka 231
Sweden and Latvia 234
Switzerland, Austria and
   Hungary.................................238
Taiwan 243
Tanzania......................................245
Uganda..248
United Kingdom 250
USA
   National 257
   Central 259
   Eastern.....................................264
   Southern 272
   Western....................................278
Zambia...288
Zimbabwe 292

Abbreviations..295
Glossary of Salvation Army terms..296
Salvation Army History (chronological table)...298
Biographical Information...304
Retired Generals and Commissioners 335
Retirements from Active Service 344
Promotions to Glory 350
Index 356
List of territories, commands, regions and World Map 370

Moving Forward Together

Foreword by General Linda Bond
International Leader of The Salvation Army

**General Linda Bond with young
Salvationists from the Brazil Territory
mission team during the London Olympics**

*'I see a God-raised, Spirit-filled Army of the 21st century,
convinced of its calling, moving forward together into the world of
the hurting, broken, lonely, dispossessed and lost, reaching them
in love by all means with the transforming message of Jesus,
bringing freedom, hope and life.'*

The familiar logo, which captures the vision of *One Army
One Mission One Message*, is seen all around The Salvation
Army world in many languages. An innovative spirit has taken hold
of it so that now, along with posters and power points, the logo is on
t-shirts, mouse pads, key chains and mugs. It is not only attractive in
its design but more importantly it communicates our identity and
purpose clearly and succinctly.

But ultimately, it is not what is seen or what is said that will
matter. It will be what is done. That is why when the International

Conference of Leaders was held in Toronto, Canada on 7-14 July 2012, it was more than presentations, group discussions or plenary sessions. Delegates not just recommended what International Headquarters must do to honour the mission priorities but determined their course of action in their individual territories and commands and committed themselves to do it.

So much is being done in these priority areas already. This *Year Book* tells those stories in words and pictures. You will see an Army at prayer and an Army moving forward together in love. The transformation is taking place as we enter new countries and commence new work. Many of these initiatives have come through a Macedonian call (Acts 16:9-10), a cry of need to the Army to come over and help.

Yet it is not always a cry of need that calls us to move forward. Sometimes we forge ahead with 21st century ministry through the vision of others. Read Commissioner Carol Seiler's account of Joan Kroc's awesome donation to The Salvation Army in the United States, which has resulted in community centres that are mission-focused.

Luke Geary captured the Founder's vision when he created a modern version of the 'Poor Man's Lawyer'. What incredible work is being done through Salvos Legal, Australia Eastern Territory, to stand for and serve the marginalised. Lives and families are being transformed. Freedom and justice are hallmarks of this ministry.

The Salvation Army is committed to moving forward together into the world of the hurting, broken, lonely, dispossessed and lost. Every one of these descriptive words could be applied to people in communities that have experienced natural disasters. We are there during and after the emergency. Jonathan Hibbert-Hingston explains how we are now helping people who live in danger zones to take preparatory action to reduce the risk to themselves, their families and their possessions.

Though cultures and languages differ and our programmes are diverse, there is a unity in The Salvation Army that can only be explained by the blessing of the Holy Spirit who unites our hearts in allegiance to our Lord's message and mission.

Kroc Centers USA – 27 Mission Opportunities

Commissioner Carol Seiler, USA

In 1997, Joan Kroc, the widow of Ray Kroc who founded McDonald's, toured a district of San Diego, California that was in great need with few resources. She asked her friend, a former mayor of San Diego, whom she could trust with the funds and her vision to build a community center in that part of town. Her friend immediately replied, 'The Salvation Army'.

During the next few years Joan Kroc worked with the Army in San Diego to build a multifaceted facility with a theatre, library, classrooms and music rooms, an ice rink, pools and fitness facilities. Joan Kroc also matched endowment funds intended to subsidise the running costs, so that membership and class fees would not be too high for the community. Her total gift then was a staggering $80 million dollars.

Just two years after the center in San Diego opened, Joan Kroc developed cancer and died within months. She bequeathed a total of $1.6 billion dollars to provide centers throughout the four Salvation Army territories in the USA. By 2014, the last of 27 Salvation Army Ray and Joan Kroc Corps Community Centers will be completed. In each location the community has been engaged in fund-raising and in giving opportunities to families and individuals who have lacked access to such facilities.

From the San Diego experience have come Olympic contenders, theatre students, positive economic impact in the community, ministry and spiritual growth.

Ministry opportunities involve a holistic approach to body, mind and soul. There is an intentional focus on developing the abilities and assets of youth, investing in the future by strengthening the present. Values, skills and spiritual strength have become part of the internal and external assets created.

The centers are a safe haven for youth and adults, including vulnerable senior citizens, in communities affected by gangs and violence.

During the building of each Kroc Center, agreements put in place to employ local labor created 150-200 jobs during hard economic times. The centers are open seven days a week and this provides further employment opportunities to staff

The Hawaii Kroc Center, which opened in 2012

the various programmes offered.

Organizationally, The Salvation Army is conscious of keeping mission integrated in the ministry so that the 'center' is not separated from the 'corps'. Much work is done to build appropriate methods of operating, so that Kroc Centers can be self-sustaining and also not seen as the only expression of Army ministry in the community. Efforts to increase the standard of programming and evaluation for youth will be shared with other Salvation Army community centers.

One intentional strategy has been to keep the fitness elements open during worship opportunities; for example broadcasting the holiness meeting and music on televisions throughout the building or having Bible studies visible in a room beside a pottery class. People who have participated and seen Salvationists during the week in gym clothes also see them 'exercising their faith', and have attended worship as well.

In six months in one territory, six centers saw more than 325 people come to know Jesus Christ. On one evening 24 children accepted Christ as their Savior and friend.

On a daily basis between 800 and 1,700 people encounter Salvation Army ministry in each Kroc Center. People of all ages can eat, swim, play, learn, read, work or rest in a sanctuary where God's presence is woven through every part.

Commissioner Seiler is the Territorial President of Women's Ministries in the USA Central Territory.

SALVOS LEGAL
Luke Geary, Australia

'The moment you set about dealing with the wants of the people, you discover that many of their difficulties are not material, but moral. There never was a greater mistake than to imagine that you have only to fill a man's stomach, and clothe his back in order to secure his happiness. Man is much more than a digestive apparatus, liable to get out of order. Hence, while it is important to remember that man has a stomach, it is also necessary to bear in mind that he has a heart, and a mind that is frequently sorely troubled by difficulties, which, if he lived in a friendly world would often disappear. A man, and still more a woman, stands often quite as much in need of a trusted adviser as he or she does of a dinner or a dress.'
In Darkest England and the Way Out   William Booth, 1890

In late 2010, the Australia Eastern Territory answered William Booth's call and launched its very own law firm for the disadvantaged and marginalised, Salvos Legal Humanitarian. At the same time, it launched a separate law firm – Salvos Legal – to specialise in property and transactional commercial law for private clients as a means to fund the work of Salvos Legal Humanitarian.

Today, Salvos Legal Humanitarian has more than 120 employed and volunteer lawyers, migration agents and paralegals practising across eight offices throughout the territory. More than 260 clients are seen free of charge each fortnight. The caseload includes:

- Criminal law
- Family and children's law
- Debt
- Housing
- Social security law
- Migration and refugee law

To date, more than 5,000 clients have received assistance, people who could not otherwise afford or access a lawyer to act for them.

The commercial model adopted means that income from Salvos Legal completely funds the operational costs of Salvos Legal Humanitarian. Thus this 'Poor Man's Lawyer' such as William Booth envisioned in 1890 is not dependent upon any State or Federal Government funding, nor any other stream of Salvation Army funds.

Salvos Legal Humanitarian operates in a variety of local Salvation Army premises, both corps and territorial buildings. This gives access to other Salvation Army social services to assist with meeting the multi-dimensional needs of many clients. Counselling for drug and alcohol abuse, crisis accommodation, financial management, pastoral care, education and job training, as well as psychological counselling are available, according to need.

The use of Salvationist lawyers and a dedicated chaplain means that all Salvos Legal Humanitarian clients have the opportunity of being ministered to and hearing the gospel message of Jesus Christ.

One client recently said 'Freedom and justice are words I heard since I was a child. But I did not experience freedom and justice in my life. I thought I had been forgotten by God. Salvos Legal helped me to change my situation for the better. I had to work very hard. There were risks and it wasn't easy. In the end, freedom, justice and dignity won.'

That client was a victim of human trafficking. Salvos Legal Humanitarian sued the traffickers and won a substantial victory in court. The woman – formerly of the Islamic faith – is now a uniformed Salvationist, committed to Christ.

Luke Geary has been the Managing Partner of Salvos Legal and Salvos Legal Humanitarian since its inception in 2010

Luke Geary speaking at the launch of a new development of the service offered – the Salvos Legal Inhouse Pro Bono Desk in October 2012

PREPARING FOR THE WORST

by Jonathan Hibbert-Hingston

The reflection of the tamarind trees flickered in the swirls of the floodwaters that lapped against their trunks. As Martha watched from the roof of her water-logged house, she pondered the devastation the floods had brought. How would she feed the family now the rice had gone? How would her husband rebuild his small shop? The children, now cut off from school, would certainly miss their exams...and the baby? Her little daughter had suffered from diarrhoea for nearly a week and her life was ebbing away. The family had just enough to eat from the aid agencies but Martha wondered what they would do next month.

Martha's story might sound extreme but it is one that is all too common across the world. Whether an earthquake, drought or conflict, these are the hazards that face many of us. Martha, however, was particularly vulnerable because she was poor. Her family's wealth was tied into their crops and a shop for which they had no insurance and none of their cash was kept in the bank. Martha could not afford proper building materials and did not know how to raise her house above the floods.

The local government could not afford to keep petrol in their one fire engine and there was no sophisticated early warning system. Martha, her household, community and government were not prepared for the flooding and, as a result, they faced a disaster which left them poorer and more vulnerable than they were before.

Is Martha's situation inevitable? The Salvation Army does not believe that a hazard has to become a disaster. By helping communities and families plan with the government for hazards we support them in doing the following:

• Creating appropriate educational materials and early warning systems.
• Linking people to experts who can advise them on building design and materials.
• Strengthening incomes and encouraging practices that will reduce vulnerability to hazards.
• Putting together a plan so that the whole community are mobilised to help one another in times of hazard.

An army without body armour for its soldiers is vulnerable to the predictable injuries of war and relies on trained medics to help the injured. Similarly, an unprepared family or community is vulnerable to the damage of hazards, and may be beyond the help of our Emergency Services when disaster strikes.

There are many examples of how The Salvation Army is responding to this challenge. In Bangladesh and Pakistan communities are helped to form disaster management committees to prepare for, plan and coordinate during hazardous events. These committees also talk to families about easy steps they can take to reduce their vulnerability. Corps members take an active part in these initiatives in a number of ways and the corps building is often at the heart of the plans as a refuge. This builds relationships with non-Christians and opens opportunities to extend the kingdom of God.

Another example is from the USA, where The Salvation Army has published booklets to help communities prepare for the worst. These contain advice as simple as storing identity papers in safe places, recording important contact numbers in advance, and being aware of government systems of early warning. With steps such as these, families like Martha's could reduce the risk that hazard will turn into long-term disaster.

If you would like to know more about The Salvation Army's work in this area, or how you could begin to help your community consider these issues and prepare, please contact IHQ Projects or Emergency Response (email addresses below) which are working together to raise awareness and develop resources in this area.

Jonathan Hibbert-Hingston is the Community Development Coordinator: South Asia and SPEA Zone, in the International Projects and Development Services Section of the Programme Resources Department at IHQ.

IHQProjects@salvationarmy.org
IHQEmergency@salvationarmy.org

Left: **In Pakistan TPWM Colonel Marguerite Ward** (left) **participates in a hazard-mapping exercise as part of disaster management**

Below: **A donkey and cart are distributed in Hyderabad as part of a relief programme, following severe floods in 2010**

THE DOCTRINES OF THE SALVATION ARMY

We believe that the Scriptures of the Old and New Testaments were given by inspiration of God, and that they only constitute the Divine rule of Christian faith and practice.

We believe that there is only one God, who is infinitely perfect, the Creator, Preserver and Governor of all things, and who is the only proper object of religious worship.

We believe that there are three persons in the Godhead – the Father, the Son and the Holy Ghost, undivided in essence and co-equal in power and glory.

We believe that in the person of Jesus Christ the Divine and human natures are united, so that he is truly and properly God and truly and properly man.

We believe that our first parents were created in a state of innocency, but by their disobedience they lost their purity and happiness, and that in consequence of their fall all men have become sinners, totally depraved, and as such are justly exposed to the wrath of God.

We believe that the Lord Jesus Christ has by his suffering and death made an atonement for the whole world so that whosoever will may be saved.

We believe that repentance towards God, faith in our Lord Jesus Christ, and regeneration by the Holy Spirit, are necessary to salvation.

We believe that we are justified by grace through faith in our Lord Jesus Christ and that he that believeth hath the witness in himself.

We believe that continuance in a state of salvation depends upon continued obedient faith in Christ.

We believe that it is the privilege of all believers to be wholly sanctified, and that their whole spirit and soul and body may be preserved blameless unto the coming of our Lord Jesus Christ.

We believe in the immortality of the soul; in the resurrection of the body; in the general judgment at the end of the world; in the eternal happiness of the righteous; and in the endless punishment of the wicked.

FOUNDERS OF THE SALVATION ARMY

William Booth

The Founder of The Salvation Army and its first General was born in Nottingham on 10 April 1829 and promoted to Glory from Hadley Wood on 20 August 1912. He lived to establish Salvation Army work in 58 countries and colonies and travelled extensively, holding salvation meetings. In his later years he was received in audience by emperors, kings and presidents. Among his many books, *In Darkest England and the Way Out* was the most notable; it became the blueprint of all The Salvation Army's social schemes. It was reprinted in 1970.

Catherine Booth

The Army Mother was born in Ashbourne, Derbyshire, on 17 January 1829 and promoted to Glory from Clacton-on-Sea on 4 October 1890. As Catherine Mumford, she married William in 1855. A great teacher and preacher, she addressed large public meetings in Britain with far-reaching results, despite ill health. Her writings include *Female Ministry* and *Aggressive Christianity*.

William Bramwell Booth

The eldest son of the Founder, and his Chief of the Staff from 1880 to 1912, Bramwell (as he was known) was born on 8 March 1856. He was largely responsible for the development of The Salvation Army. His teaching of the doctrine of holiness and his councils with officers and young people were of incalculable value. In 1882 he married Captain Florence Soper (organiser of the Women's Social Work and inaugurator of the Home League), who was promoted to Glory on 10 June 1957. During his time as General (1912-1929), impetus was given to missionary work. Published books include *Echoes and Memories* and *These Fifty Years*. He was appointed a Companion of Honour shortly before his promotion to Glory from Hadley Wood on 16 June 1929.

THE HIGH COUNCIL

THE High Council was originally established by William Booth in 1904 as a safeguard to allow the removal from office of an incumbent General who had become, for whatever reason, unfit to continue to exercise oversight, direction and control of The Salvation Army. Should such an allegation be made and receive significant support from officers of the rank of commissioner, a High Council would be called to decide upon the matter and to appoint a successor should the General be found unfit.

The Founder intended, however, that the normal method of appointment would be for the General in office to select his or her successor, but only one General – Bramwell Booth in 1912 – was ever selected in this way.

By November 1928, Bramwell Booth had been absent from International Headquarters for seven months on account of illness, and a High Council was called. The 63 members, being all the commissioners on active service and certain territorial commanders, gathered at Sunbury Court near London on 8 January 1929 and eventually voted that the General, then aged 73, was 'unfit on the ground of ill-health' to continue in office. On 13 February 1929 the High Council elected Commissioner Edward Higgins as the Army's third General.

Subsequently, a commissioners' conference agreed to three major constitutional reforms later passed into law by the British Parliament as the Salvation Army Act 1931, namely:

i. the abolition of the General's right to nominate his or her successor, and the substitution of the election of every General by a High Council;

ii. the fixing of an age limit for the retirement of the General;

iii. the creation of a trustee company to hold the properties and other capital assets of the Army, in place of the sole trusteeship of the General.

The High Council is currently constituted under provisions of the Salvation Army Act 1980 as amended by deeds of variation executed in 1995, 2005 and 2010.

Since 1929, High Councils have been held in 1934 (electing General Evangeline Booth), 1939 (General Carpenter), 1946 (General Orsborn), 1954 (General Kitching), 1963 (General Coutts), 1969 (General Wickberg), 1974 (General Wiseman), 1977 (General Brown), 1981 (General Wahlström), 1986 (General Burrows), 1993 (General Tillsley), 1994 (General Rader), 1999 (General Gowans), 2002 (General Larsson), 2006 (General Clifton) and 2011 (General Bond).

High Councils are normally called by the Chief of the Staff and have usually met at Sunbury Court but can meet anywhere in the United Kingdom. Since 1995 the High Council has been composed of all active commissioners except the spouse of the General, and all territorial commanders. All TPWMs now attend.

GENERALS ELECTED BY A HIGH COUNCIL

Years in office are shown immediately below each General's name. The place and date at the beginning of an entry denote the corps and the year from which the General entered officer service.

Edward J. Higgins
1929–34

Reading, UK, 1882. General (1929-34). b 26 Nov 1864; pG 14 Dec 1947. Served in corps and divisional work, British Territory; at the International Training Garrison, as CS, USA; as Asst Foreign Secretary, IHQ; Brit Comr (1911-19); Chief of the Staff (1919-29). CBE. Author of *Stewards of God*, *Personal Holiness*, etc. m Capt Catherine Price, 1888; pG 1952.

Evangeline Booth
1934–39

b 25 Dec 1865; pG 17 Jul 1950. The fourth daughter of the Founder, at 21 years of age she commanded Marylebone Corps, its Great Western Hall being the centre of spectacular evangelistic work. As Field Commissioner this experience was used to advantage throughout Great Britain (1888-91). The Founder appointed her to train cadets in London (1891-96); then as TC, Canada (1896-1904); Commander of The Salvation Army in the United States of America (1904-34). Author of *Toward a Better World*; *Songs of the Evangel*, etc.

George L. Carpenter
1939–46

Raymond Terrace, Australia, 1892. b 20 Jun 1872; pG 9 Apr 1948. Appointments included 18 years in Australia in property, training and literary work; at IHQ (1911-27) for the most part with General Bramwell Booth as Literary Secretary; further service in Australia (1927-33), including CS, Australia Eastern; as TC, South America East (1933-37); TC, Canada (1937-39). Author of *Keep the Trumpets Sounding*; *Banners and Adventures*, etc. m Ens Minnie Rowell, 1899; pG 1960. Author of *Notable Officers of The Salvation Army*; *Women of the Flag*, etc.

Albert Orsborn
1946–54

Clapton, UK, 1905. b 4 Sep 1886; pG 4 Feb 1967. Served as corps officer and in divisional work in British Territory; as Chief Side Officer at ITC (1925-33); CS, New Zealand (1933-36); TC, Scotland & Ireland (1936-40); Brit Comr (1940-46). CBE, 1943. Writer of many well-known Army songs. Author of *The House of My Pilgrimage*, etc. m Capt Evalina Barker, 1909; pG 1942. m Maj Evelyn Berry, 1944; pG 1945. m Comr Mrs Phillis Taylor (née Higgins), 1947; pG 1986.

Wilfred Kitching
1954–63

New Barnet, UK, 1914. b 22 Aug 1893; pG 15 Dec 1977. Served in British Territory corps, divisional and NHQ appointments, then as CS, Australia Southern (1946-48); TC, Sweden (1948-51); Brit Comr (1951-54). Composer of many distinctively Salvationist musical works. Hon LLD (Yonsei, Seoul, Rep of Korea), 1961; CBE, 1964. Author of *Soldier of Salvation* (1963) and *A Goodly Heritage* (autobiography, 1967). m Adjt Kathleen Bristow (Penge, 1916), 1929; pG 1982.

Generals of The Salvation Army

Frederick Coutts
1963–69

Batley, UK, 1920. b 21 Sep 1899; pG 6 Feb 1986. Served in British Territory in divisional work (1921-25) and as corps officer (1925-35); for 18 years in Literary Dept, IHQ; writer of *International Company Orders* (1935-46); Editor of *The Officers' Review* (1947-53); Asst to Literary Secretary (1947-52); Literary Secretary (1952-53); Training Principal, ITC (1953-57); TC, Australia Eastern (1957-63). Author of *The Call to Holiness* (1957); *Essentials of Christian Experience* (1969); *The Better Fight* (1973); *No Discharge in this War* (1975), *Bread for My Neighbour* (1978); *The Splendour of Holiness* (1983), etc. Order of Cultural Merit (Rep of Korea), 1966; Hon Litt D (Chung Ang, Rep of Korea), 1966; CBE, 1967; Hon DD (Aberdeen), 1981. m Lt Bessie Lee, BSc, 1925; pG 1967. m Comr Olive Gatrall (Thornton Heath, 1925), 1970, pG 1997.

Erik Wickberg
1969–74

Bern 2, Switzerland, 1925. b 6 Jul 1904; pG 26 Apr 1996. Served as corps officer in Scotland; in Germany as Training (Education) Officer, and Private Secretary to CS and TC (1926-34); at IHQ as Private Secretary to IS and Asst to Under Secretary for Europe (1934-39); in Sweden as IHQ Liaison Officer (1939-46) and DC, Uppsala (1946-48); as CS, Switzerland, (1948-53); CS, Sweden (1953-57); TC, Germany (1957-61); Chief of the Staff (1961-69). Commander, Order of Vasa, 1970; Order of Moo Koong Wha (Rep of Korea), 1970; Hon LLD (Rep of Korea), 1970; Grand Cross of Merit, Fed Rep of Germany, 1971; King's Gold Medal (Grand Cross) (Sweden), 1980. Author of *Inkallad* (*Called Up*) (autobiography, Swedish, 1978; English, 2012) and *Uppdraget* (*The Charge – My Way to Preaching*) (1990).

m Ens Frieda de Groot (Berne 1, Switz, 1922), 1929; pG 1930. m Capt Margarete Dietrich (Hamburg 3, Ger, 1928), 1932; pG 1976. m Major Eivor Lindberg (Norrköping 1, Swdn, 1946), 1977.

Clarence Wiseman
1974–77

Guelph, Ont, Canada, 1927. b 19 Jun 1907; pG 4 May 1985. Served in Canada as corps officer and in editorial work; chaplain with Canadian forces overseas (1940-43); Senior Representative, Canadian Red Shield Services Overseas (1943-45); back in Canada as divisional commander (1945-54), Field Secretary (1954-57) and CS (1957-60); as TC, East Africa (1960-62); Training Principal, ITC (1962-67); TC, Canada & Bermuda (1967-74). Order of Canada, 1976, Hon LLD, Hon DD (Yonsei, Seoul, Rep of Korea). Author of *A Burning in My Bones* (1980) and *The Desert Road to Glory* (1980). m Capt Jane Kelly (Danforth, Ont, Can, 1927), 1932; pG 1993. Author of *Earth's Common Clay*; *Bridging the Year*; *Watching Daily*.

Arnold Brown
1977–81

Belleville, Canada, 1935. b 13 Dec 1913; pG 26 Jun 2002. Served in Canada in corps, editorial, public relations and youth work (1935-64); as Secretary for Public Relations at IHQ (1964-69); Chief of the Staff (1969-74); TC, Canada & Bermuda (1974-77). MIPR, Hon LDH (Asbury, USA); Freeman, City of London; Hon DD (Olivet, USA), 1981; Officer, Order of Canada, 1981. Author of *What Hath God Wrought?*; *The Gate and the Light* (1984); *Yin – The Mountain the Wind Blew Here* (1988); *With Christ at the Table* (1991); *Occupied Manger – Unoccupied Tomb* (1994). m Lt Jean Barclay (Montreal Cit, Can, 1938), 1939. Author of *Excursions in Thought* (1981).

Generals of The Salvation Army

Jarl Wahlström
1981–86

Helsinki 1, Finland, 1938. b 9 Jul 1918. pG 3 Dec 1999. Served in corps, youth and divisional work in Finland; as Second World War chaplain to Finnish armed forces; in Finland as a divisional commander (1960-63), Training Principal, Secretary of Music Dept (1963-68) and CS (1968-72); as CS, Canada & Bermuda (1972-76); TC, Finland (1976-81); TC, Sweden (1981); Knight, Order of the Lion of Finland, 1964; Order of Civil Merit, Mugunghwa Medal (Rep of Korea), 1983; Hon DHL (W Illinois), 1985; Paul Harris Fellow of Rotary International, 1987; Commander, Order of the White Rose of Finland, 1989. Author of *Pilgrimage Song* (autobiography, Finnish/Swedish, 1989; English, 2012). m Lt Maire Nyberg (Helsinki 1, 1944).

Eva Burrows
1986–93

Fortitude Valley, Qld, Australia Eastern, 1951. b 15 Sep 1929. Appointed to corps in British Territory, before post-graduate studies; served at Howard Institute, Zimbabwe (1952-67), Head of Teacher Training (1965), Vice-Principal (1965-67); as Principal, Usher Institute (1967-70); Asst Principal, ICO (1970-74), Principal (1974-75); Leader, WSS (GBI) (1975-77); TC, Sri Lanka (1977-79); TC, Scotland (1979-82); TC, Australia Southern (1982-86). BA (Qld); M Ed (Sydney); Hon Dr of Liberal Arts (Ehwa Univ, Seoul, Rep of Korea), 1988; Hon LLD (Asbury, USA), 1988; Paul Harris Fellow of Rotary International, 1990; Hon DST (Houghton), 1992; Hon DD (Olivet Nazarene Univ), 1993; Hon Dr Philosophy (Qld), 1993; Hon Dr of University (Griffith Univ), 1994; Companion of Order of Australia, 1994; Living Legacy Award from Women's International Center, USA, 1996.

Bramwell Tillsley
1993–94

Kitchener, Ont, Canada, with wife née Maude Pitcher, 1956. b 18 Aug 1931. Served in Canada in corps, youth, training college and divisional appointments, including Training Principal USA E (1974-77), Provincial Commander in Newfoundland (1977-79) and DC, Metro Toronto (1979-81); as Training Principal, ITC (1981-85); CS, USA Southern (1985-89); TC, Australia Southern (1989-91); Chief of the Staff (1991-93). Resigned from the office of General in 1994. BA University of Western Ontario. Has written extensively for SA periodicals. Author of *Life in the Spirit*; *This Mind in You*; *Life More Abundant*; *Manpower for the Master*.

Paul Rader
1994–99

Cincinnati Cit, USA Eastern, with wife née Frances Kay Fuller, BA (Asbury), Hon DD (Asbury Theol Seminary) 1995, Hon LHD (Greenville) 1997, 1961. b 14 Mar 1934. Served in corps prior to transfer to Korea in 1962; in Korea in training work (1962-73), as Training Principal (1973), Education Secretary (1974-76), Asst Chief Secretary (1976-77) and CS (1977-84); in USA Eastern as Training Principal (1984-87), DC, Eastern Pennsylvania (1987-89) and CS (1989); as TC, USA Western (1989-94). BA, BD (Asbury); MTh (Southern Baptist Seminary); D Miss (Fuller Theological Seminary); Hon LLD (Asbury); 1984 elected to board of trustees of Asbury College; 1989 elected Paul Harris Fellow of Rotary International; Hon DD (Asbury Theol Seminary), 1995; Hon LHD (Greenville), 1997; Hon DD (Roberts Wesleyan), 1998.

Generals of The Salvation Army

John Gowans
1999–2002

Grangetown, UK, 1955. b 13 Nov 1934. Served in British Territory as corps officer, divisional youth secretary, National Stewardship Secretary and divisional commander; as Chief Secretary, France (1977-81); in USA Western as Programme Secretary (1981-85) and DC, Southern California (1985-86); TC, France (1986-93); TC, Australia Eastern and Papua New Guinea (1993-97); TC, UK (1997-99). Paul Harris Fellow of Rotary International; Hon DLitt (Yonsei, Seoul, Rep of Korea); Freedom of the City of London (2000). Songwriter. Author of *O Lord!* series of poetry books and *There's a Boy Here* (autobiography, 2002). Co-author with John Larsson of 10 musicals. m Lt Gisèle Bonhotal (Paris Central, France, 1955) 1957.

John Larsson
2002–2006

Upper Norwood, UK, 1957. b 2 Apr 38. Served in corps; at ITC; as TYS (Scotland Territory); NYS (British Territory); CS, South America West (1980-84); Principal, ITC (1984-88); Assistant to Chief of the Staff for UK Administrative Planning, IHQ (1988-1990); TC, UK (1990-93); TC, New Zealand and Fiji (1993-96); TC, Sweden and Latvia (1996-99); Chief of the Staff (1999-2002). BD (London). Author of *Doctrine without Tears* (1964); *Spiritual Breakthrough* (1983); *The Man Perfectly Filled with the Spirit* (1986); *How Your Corps Can Grow* (1989); *Saying Yes to Life* (autobiography, 2007). Composer of music and co-author with John Gowans of 10 musicals. m Capt Freda Turner (Kingston-upon-Thames, UK, 1964) 1969.

Shaw Clifton
2006–2011

Edmonton, UK, with wife née Helen Ashman, 1973. b 21 Sep 45. Served as corps officer in British Territory; in Literary Department, IHQ (1974); in Zimbabwe as Vice Principal, Mazoe Secondary School (1975-77) and CO, Bulawayo Citadel (1977-79); in further BT corps appointments (1979-82, 1989-92); at IHQ as Legal and Parliamentary Secretary (1982-89); in UK as DC (1992-95); in USA Eastern as DC, Massachusetts (1995-97); as TC, Pakistan (1997-2002); TC, New Zealand, Fiji & Tonga (2002-04); TC, UK (2004-06). LLB (Hons), AKC (Theol), BD (Theol) (Hons), PhD. Freedom of the City of London (2007). Author of *What Does the Salvationist Say?* (1977); *Growing Together* (1984); *Strong Doctrine, Strong Mercy* (1985); *Never the Same Again* (1997); *Who are these Salvationists?* (1999); *New Love – Thinking Aloud About Practical Holiness* (2004), *Selected Writings, vols 1 and 2* (2010). Ww Comr Helen Clifton, pG 2011.

Linda Bond
2011–present

St James, Winnipeg, Canada, 1968. b 22 Jun 46. Served as corps officer in Canada and Bermuda Territory (1969-78) (1987-89); at the Training College (1978-82) (1989-91), Secretary for Candidates (1982-87); Divisional Secretary (1991-93); divisional commander (1993-95) and Chief Secretary (1999-2002); in UK as divisional commander (1998-99); at IHQ as Under Secretary for Personnel (1995-98); Secretary for Spiritual Life Development & International External Relations (2005-08); TC/TPWM USA Western (2002-04) and Australia Eastern (2008-11). B Relig Ed, MTS, Hon DD (Tyndale University College, Canada) 2012.

SIGNIFICANT EVENTS 2011-2012

2011
September
IHQ: The Worldwide Prayer Meeting launched on 1 September by General Linda Bond.

October
IHQ: General Linda Bond launched the International Vision 'One Army, One Mission, One Message'.

November
IHQ: The Salvation Army's International Programme Resources Consultancy Group, involving representatives from nine countries and International Headquarters convened in London from 31 October to 4 November.

SPEA Zone: The formal 'Opening Fire' weekend of The Salvation Army's work on the **Solomon Islands**, led by territorial commanders from Papua New Guinea and both Australian territories.

2012
January
IHQ: The Salvation Army's daily reading book, *Words of Life*, was made available in electronic format as a Kindle e-book.

February
Europe Zone: In **Hungary** the country's parliament granted The Salvation Army legal recognition as a church.

March
IHQ: The Salvation Army's international website, www.salvationarmy.org was relaunched with improved search facilities and content from Flickr, Twitter, Google Maps and Issuu (online versions of *All the World* and *Revive* magazines).

IHQ: International Doctrine Council held at the International College for Officers and Centre for Spiritual Life Development, London.

June
United Kingdom: General Linda Bond addressed Salvationists at the I'll Fight Congress at the Royal Albert Hall, held to commemorate General William Booth's last public appearance in 1912.

July
Canada: The Salvation Army's International Conference of Leaders (ICL) took place from 7-14 July in Toronto under the leadership of General Linda Bond, with the theme of the International Vision 'One Army, One Mission, One Message'.

August
Europe Zone: Salvation Army work expanded to 125 countries as work commenced in **Greenland** (8 August).

IHQ: The Salvation Army's International Moral and Social Issues Council (IMASIC) met under the leadership of Colonel Geanette Seymour, Director of the ISJC.

London: 20 August marked the centenary of the promotion to Glory of General William Booth, Founder of The Salvation Army on 20 August 1912.

September
IHQ: The ICO and CSLD hosted the first-ever International College for Soldiers from 10-24 September.

Emergency Responses
During the year under review local Salvation Army teams and IHQ personnel have responded with emergency relief and long-term assistance in situations including the following:

Civil unrest: Democratic Republic of Congo (Burundi, Rwanda and Uganda also assisted Congolese refugees).

Drought and famine: Kenya; Uganda.

Earthquake: Christchurch, New Zealand.

Floods: Australia; Central America; Fiji; Georgia, Eastern Europe; Indonesia; Nigeria; Philippines; USA.

Hurricanes and tornadoes: Caribbean and USA.

Severe cold weather: Ukraine.

Wildfires: Colorado and Texas, USA.

COUNTRIES WHERE THE SALVATION ARMY IS AT WORK

THE Salvation Army is at work in 125 countries. A country in which the Army serves is defined in two ways:

(i) Politically - see a, b, c below.

(ii) Where the General has given approval to the work, thus officially recognising it, ensuring it has legal identity and a Deed Poll is published to acknowledge this.

As far as political status is concerned, for the Army's purposes, three categories are recognised:

(a) Independent countries, eg USA and New Zealand;

(b) Internally independent political entities which are under the protection of another country in matters of defence and foreign affairs, eg The Færoes, Isle of Man, Puerto Rico;

(c) Colonies and other dependent political units, eg Bermuda, French Guiana, Guernsey, Jersey.

Administrative subdivisions of a country such as Wales and Scotland in the UK are not recognised as separate countries for this purpose. The countries fulfilling the quoted criteria, with the date in brackets on which the work was officially recognised, are as follows:

Angola ....(1985)
Antigua ....(1903)
Argentina ....(1890)
Australia..............(1881)
Austria ....(1927)

Bahamas..............(1931)
Bangladesh..........(1971)
Barbados ....(1898)
Belgium ....(1889)
Belize ....(1915)
Bermuda..............(1896)
Bolivia ....(1920)
Botswana ....(1997)
Brazil ....(1922)
Burundi ....(2007)

Canada ....(1882)

Chile....................(1909)
China ....(1916)
Colombia ....(1985)
Congo, Republic of
    (Brazzaville) ....(1937)
Congo, Democratic
    Republic of (Kinshasa)
    ....(1934)
Costa Rica ....(1907)
Cuba....................(1918)
Czech Republic ..(1919)
    ....(reopened 1990)

Denmark ....(1887)
Dominican Republic
    ....(1995)

Ecuador ....(1985)

El Salvador ....(1989)
Estonia ....(1927)
    ....(reopened 1995)

Færoes, The ....(1924)
Fiji ....(1973)
Finland ....(1889)
France ....(1881)
French Guiana ....(1980)

Georgia ....(1993)
Germany ....(1886)
Ghana..................(1922)
Greece ....(2007)
Greenland............(2012)
Grenada ....(1902)
Guam ....(1994)
Guatemala ....(1976)

Countries where The Salvation Army is at work

Guernsey ....(1879)
Guyana...............(1895)

Haiti ....(1950)
Honduras ....(2000)
Hong Kong ....(1930)
Hungary ....(1924)
............(reopened 1990)

Iceland ....(1895)
India ....(1882)
Indonesia ....(1894)
Ireland, Republic of
  (Eire) ....(1880)
Isle of Man..........(1883)
Italy ....(1887)

Jamaica ....(1887)
Japan ....(1895)
Jersey ....(1879)

Kenya..................(1921)
Korea ....(1908)
Kuwait ....(2008)

Latvia..................(1923)
............(reopened 1990)
Lesotho ....(1969)
Liberia ....(1988)
Lithuania ....(2005)

Macau ....(2000)
Malawi................(1967)
Malaysia..............(1938)
Mali ....(2008)
Marshall Islands..(1985)
Mexico ....(1937)
Micronesia ....(1993)
Moldova..............(1994)
Mongolia.............(2008)
Mozambique ......(1916)

Myanmar ....(1915)

Namibia ....(1932)
............(reopened 2008)
Nepal ....(2009)
Netherlands, The (1887)
New Zealand ......(1883)
Nicaragua............(2010)
Nigeria ....(1920)
Norway ....(1888)

Pakistan ....(1883)
Panama................(1904)
Papua New Guinea
............................(1956)
Paraguay ....(1910)
Peru ....(1910)
Philippines, The ..(1937)
Poland ....(2005)
Portugal ....(1971)
Puerto Rico ....(1962)

Romania..............(1999)
Russia..................(1913)
............................(1991)
Rwanda ....(1995)

St Christopher Nevis
  (St Kitts) ....(1916)
St Helena ....(1884)
St Lucia ....(1902)
St Maarten ....(1999)
St Vincent ....(1905)
Sierra Leone........(2010)
Singapore............(1935)
Solomon Islands (2011)
South Africa........(1883)
Spain ....(1971)
Sri Lanka ....(1883)
Suriname ....(1924)
Swaziland............(1960)

Sweden................(1882)
Switzerland ....(1882)

Taiwan ....(1965)
Tanzania..............(1933)
Togo....................(2011)
Tonga..................(1986)
Trinidad and Tobago
............................(1901)
Turks and Caicos
  Islands..............(2011)

Uganda................(1931)
Ukraine ....(1993)
United Arab Emirates
............................(2010)
United Kingdom (1865)
United States of
  America ....(1880)
Uruguay ....(1890)

Venezuela ....(1972)
Virgin Islands ....(1917)

Zambia................(1922)
Zimbabwe ....(1891)

19

INTERNATIONAL STATISTICS
(as at 1 January 2012)

Countries and territories where SA serves
(at 30 September 2012, see pp 18-19) 125
Languages used in SA work, including
  some tribal languages....................175
Corps, outposts, societies, new
  plants and recovery churches....15,765
Goodwill centres................................223
Officers 26,321
  Active...17,117
  Retired..9,204
Auxiliary-captains..............................222
Envoys/sergeants/non officer personnel,
  full-time.......................................3,273
Cadets 1,188
Employees...................................110,360
Senior soldiers 1,148,426
Adherent members 188,727
Junior soldiers 384,694
Corps cadets..................................53,560
Senior band musicians..................26,703
Senior songsters..........................105,608
Other senior musical group
  members....................................91,591
Senior and young people's
  local officers 136,751
Women's Ministries (all groups) –
  members 620,744
League of Mercy – members......145,949
SAMF – members............................8,374
Over-60 clubs – members..........103,963
Men's fellowships – members......66,535
Young people's bands –
  members 22,712
Young people's singing
  companies – members..............86,240
Other young people's music
  groups – members....................84,071
Sunday schools – members........635,232
Junior youth groups
  (scouts, guides, etc, and clubs) –
  members....................................754,873

Senior youth groups –
  members 120,104
Corps-based community development
  programmes..............................10,721
  Beneficiaries/clients 641,749
Thrift stores/charity shops
  (corps/territorial) 2,473
Recycling centres 13

Social Programme
Residential
Hostels for the homeless 421
  Capacity 23,729
Emergency lodges............................391
  Capacity 20,325
Children's homes 221
  Capacity 9,274
Homes for elderly persons 152
  Capacity 10,048
Homes for disabled persons...............50
  Capacity 1,569
Homes for blind persons 6
  Capacity 158
Remand and probation homes.............36
  Capacity 864
Homes for street children..................29
  Capacity 596
Mother and baby homes.....................50
  Capacity 1,372
Training centres for families 13
  Capacity 480
Care homes for vulnerable people 75
  Capacity 1,941
Women's and men's refuge
  centres 61
  Capacity 1,959
Other residential care
  homes/hostels 171
  Capacity 6,024

Day Care
Community centres............................626

Early childhood education centres....106
    Capacity 7,166
Day centres for the elderly................100
    Capacity 3,954
Play groups...75
    Capacity 1,319
Day centres for the hearing
    impaired 43
    Capacity 1,241
Day centres for street children 19
    Capacity 651
Day nurseries 533
    Capacity 18,235
Drop-in centres for youth..................103
Other day care centres 490
    Capacity 66,103

Addiction Dependency

Non-residential programmes 55
    Capacity 3,559
Residential programmes....................204
    Capacity 13,144
Harbour Light programmes 20
    Capacity 1,922
Other services for those with
    addictions 76
    Capacity 3,229

Service to the Armed Forces

Clubs and canteens...............................24
Mobile units for service personnel......41
Chaplains 72

Emergency Disaster Response

Disaster rehabilitation schemes 187
    Participants 1,299,878
Refugee programmes –
    host country 8
    Participants 11,365
Refugee rehabilitation programmes....19
Participants 14,343
Other response programmes..............566
    Participants 44,165

Services to the Community

Prisoners visited......................... 240,415
Prisoners helped on discharge....149,845
Police courts – people helped 191,986
Missing persons – applications......7,136

Number traced...........................4,435
Night patrol/anti-suicide –
    number helped......................439,184
Community youth programmes 3,701
    Beneficiaries 396,862
Employment bureaux –
    applications 78,879
    initial referrals......................108,268
Counselling – people helped......408,378
General relief – people
    helped 14,673,141
Emergency relief (fire, flood,
    etc) – people helped............1,190,524
Emergency mobile units 19,517
Feeding centres 126
Restaurants and cafes 1,390
Thrift stores/charity shops
    (social) 962
Apartments for elderly 745
    Capacity 9,788
Hostels for students, workers, etc.......60
    Capacity 1,642
Land settlements (SA villages,
    farms etc) 11
    Capacity 2,001
Social Services summer camps 266
    Participants 27,808
Other services to the community
    (unspecified) 1,113
    Beneficiaries 3,028,846

Health Programme

General hospitals 22
    Capacity 2,502
Maternity hospitals..............................23
    Capacity 378
Other specialist hospitals 6
    Capacity 307
Specialist clinics..................................76
    Capacity 983
General clinics/health centres 129
    Capacity 2,450
Mobile clinics/community health
    posts 63
Inpatients.....................................290,619
Outpatients 1,756,848
Doctors/medics 5,386

Non medical staff............................3,717
Invalid/convalescent homes................22
   Capacity 4,028
Health education programmes
   (HIV/Aids, etc) 50
   Beneficiaries............................609,053
Day care programmes...........................6

Education Programme
Kindergarten/sub primary..................954
Primary schools 1,247
Upper primary and middle schools ..133
Secondary and high schools..............274

Colleges and universities....................10
Vocational training schools/centres ..151
Pupils..599,350
Teachers 18,650
Schools for blind students (included in
   above totals)....................................18
Schools for disabled students (included
   in above totals)................................15
Boarding schools (included in
   above totals)....................................63
Staff training, development study and
   distance learning centres 14

SALVATION ARMY PERIODICALS
by territory/command

International Headquarters: *All the World*, *Revive*, *The Officer*

Australia National: *Kidzone*, *Warcry*

Australia Eastern: *Creative Ministry*, *Pipeline*, *Venue*, *Women in Touch*

Australia Southern: *On Fire*

Brazil: *O Oficial*, *Rumo* and *Ministério Feminino* – *Devocionais* (Women's Ministries magazines)

Canada and Bermuda: *Edge for Kids*, *Faith & Friends*, *Foi & Vie*, *Salvationist*

Caribbean: *The War Cry*

Congo (Brazzaville): *Le Salutiste*

Democratic Republic of Congo: *Echo d'Espoir*

Denmark: *Krigsråbet (The War Cry)*, *Vision-Mission*

Eastern Europe: *Vestnik Spaseniya* (*The War Cry*), *The Officer* (both Russian)

Finland and Estonia: *Krigsropet* (Swedish), *Nappis*, *Sotahuuto* (both Finnish)

France and Belgium: *Avec Vous*, *Le Bulletin de la Ligue du Foyer*, *Le Fil*, *Le Magazine*, *L'Officier*, *Quand Même*

Germany and Lithuania: *Danke*, *Heilsarmee-Forum*, *Heilsarmee-Magazin*

Ghana: *Salvationist Newsletter*

Hong Kong and Macau: *Army Scene*, *The War Cry*

India National: *The War Cry* (English)

India Central: *Home League Magazine*, *Udyogasthudu*, *Yovana Veerudu*, *Yudha Dwani*

India Eastern: *Sipai Tlangau* (*The War Cry*), *The Officer*, *Young Salvationist*, *Chunnunpar*, *Naupang Sipai* (all Mizo)

India Northern: *Home League Yearly* (Hindi and English), *Mukti Samachar* (Hindi and Punjabi), *The Officer*, *Yuva Sipai* (both Hindi)

India South Eastern: *Chiruveeran*, *Home League Quarterly*, *Poresathan*, *The Officer* (all Tamil)

India South Western: *Home League Quarterly* (Malayalam/English), *The Officer*, *Youdha Shabdan*, *Yuva Veeran* (all Malayalam)

India Western: *Home League Quarterly*, *The Officer*, *The War Cry*, *The Young Soldier* (all Gujarati and Marathi)

Indonesia: *Berita Keselamatan* (*The War Cry*), *Cakrawala* (*Waves of Hope*), *Medical Fellowship Bulletin*, *Oasis Fajar* (Daily Devotions)

Italy: *Il Bollettino del Dipartimento Società*

e Famiglia, Il Grido di Guerra

Japan: *Home League Quarterly, The Officer, The Sunday School Guide, Toki-no-Koe, Toki-no-Koe Junior*

Kenya East: *Sauti ya Vita* (English and Kiswahili)

Kenya West: *Sauti ya Vita* (English and Kiswahili)

Korea: *Home League Programme Helps, The Officer, The War Cry*

Latin America North: *Voz de Salvación (Salvation Voice), Arco Iris de Ideas (Rainbow of Ideas)*

Mexico: *El Grito de Guerra (The War Cry), El Eslabón (The Link)*

Mozambique: *Devocionias para Encontros da Liga do Lar* (Home League resource manual)

The Netherlands and Czech Republic: *Dag in Dag Uit, Heils-en Strijdzangen, InterCom, Strijdkreet, Kans* (all Dutch), *Prapor Spásy* (Czech)

New Zealand, Fiji and Tonga: *War Cry*

Nigeria: *Salvationist, The Shepherd, The War Cry*

Norway, Iceland and The Færoes: *Krigsropet,* (Norwegian), *Herópid* (Icelandic)

Pakistan: *Home League Annual, The War Cry* (in Urdu)

Papua New Guinea: *Tokaut*

The Philippines: *The War Cry*

Portugal: *O Salvacionista, Ideias e Recursos* (for Women's Ministries)

Rwanda: *Salvationist News*

Singapore, Malaysia and Myanmar: *The War Cry*

South America East: *El Oficial, El Salvacionista*

South America West: *El Grito de Guerra, El Trébol* (for Women's Ministries)

Southern Africa: *Home League Resource Manual, The Reporter, The War Cry*

Sri Lanka: *Yudha Handa (The War Cry)*

Sweden and Latvia: *Stridsropet*

Switzerland, Austria and Hungary: *Espoir, Dialogue, Just 4 U, Trampoline* (all French), *Dialog, Klecks, Trialog* (all German), *IN* (French and German)

Taiwan: *Salvationist.tw, Reach-Out!, Live!*

Uganda: *Voice of Hope* (quarterly)

United Kingdom with the Republic of Ireland: *Kids Alive!, Salvationist, The War Cry*

USA National: *The War Cry, Women's Ministries Resources, Word & Deed – A Journal of Theology and Ministry, Young Salvationist*

USA Central: *Central Connection*

USA Eastern: *¡Buenas Noticias!, Cristianos en Marcha* (both Spanish), *Good News!* (English and Korean), *Priority!, Ven a Cristo Hoy* (Spanish)

USA Southern: *Southern Spirit*

USA Western: *Caring, New Frontier, Nuevos Fronteras* (Spanish)

Zimbabwe: *Zimbabwe Salvationist, ZEST*

Books Published during 2011-12

International Headquarters: *A Field for Exploits: Training Leaders for The Salvation Army* by Eva Burrows and Stephen Court; *A Pilgrim's Song* by Jarl Wahlström (autobiography, English edition); Classic Salvationist Texts: *Just a Moment, Lord* (revised) by Flora Larsson; *From Her Heart: Selections from the Preaching and Teaching of Helen Clifton,* by Helen Clifton, edited by Shaw Clifton; *Pages from the Story of my Life: Called Up* by Erik Wickberg (autobiography, English edition); *Reunited! The Fascinating Work of The Salvation Army Family Tracing Service* by Peter Willmott; *The Salvation Army Handbook of Doctrine* (French); *The Salvation Army Year Book 2012; Words of Life*

Books Published 2011-12

Australia Eastern: *Courtyard Legal* by Luke Geary; *Conversations on Prayer* (DVD) produced by Peter Farthing

Australia Southern: *Faith Alive* by Lucille Turfrey; *Giving to God* by Ian Southwell; *Leading Simply* by John Staite; *Mission Mandates* edited by Geoff Webb; *The Baby Jesus Story* by Sally Allchin; *Walter Wants Wings* by Rachael Castle and Nicholas Wight

Brazil: *O Exército de Salvação no Corpo de Cristo (The Salvation Army in the Body of Christ)*; *Chamados para Ser o Povo de Deus (Called to be God's People)* by Robert Street

EET: *Forty Day Spiritual Journey to a More Generous Life* by B. Kluth; *Never the Same Again* by Shaw Clifton; *Samuel Logan Brengle: Teacher of Holiness* by Alice R. Stiles; *Who are these Salvationists?* by Shaw Clifton (all Russian)

Finland: *Rakastakaa täsmärakkaudella (Love Right at the Heart)* by Robert Street; *Sacramental Army* (English) *En sakramental Armé* (Swedish) *Sakramentaalinen Armeija* (Finnish) by Vibeke Krommenhoek, Johnny Kleman and Antero Puotiniemi

Germany: *Gesichter und Geschichten* (the 125th anniversary of The Salvation Army in Germany) by Christine Schollmeier

India South Western: *The Salvation Army in the Body of Christ*

Italy: *Soup, Soap, Salvation oppure Salvati per Servire* by Francesca and Giovanni Colangelo

Japan: *William Booth – Apostle of Love for Mankind*

Korea: *The Story of Worship in The Salvation Army* by Colonel Park, Chong-duk; *Nine Lay-Salvationists who brought honour to The Salvation Army Korea Territory* by Lieut-Colonel Kim, Joon-chul, Major Lee, Deok-joong and Major Kang, Jong-kwon

United Kingdom: *Saved to Serve* by Stephen Grinsted

USA Eastern: *Mapping Our Salvationist DNA* by Steve Hedgren and Rob Lyle; *Powers of Salvation Army Officers* by Mrs Bramwell Booth; *9.11 – Helping the Heroes: A Salvation Army Story* by Linda Carlson Johnson

Published with the assistance of grants from the International Literature Programme, IHQ

Angola: *Called to be God's People* (Portuguese)

Brazil: *Servants Together* by Robert Street; *Discipleship Vision and Mission* (Portuguese)

Caribbean: *Adventurers*; *Discovery*; *Women's Ministries resources* (French)

Czech Republic: *The Soul Winner's Secret* by Samuel Logan Brengle (Czech)

Eastern Europe: *A Generous Life; The Privilege of all Believers;* (Russian) *Faith-based Facilitation;* (Georgian, Romanian, Russian) *Handbook of Doctrine; O and R for Officers;* (Romanian) *Samuel Logan Brengle: Teacher of Holiness* (Georgian, Russian)

Ghana: *International Bible Lessons for Children; Salvation Story*

India Eastern: *Bible Lessons; Discovery; Heroes of the Faith* by Derek Elvin; *Never the Same Again* by Shaw Clifton

India National: *New Hope in Christ* (Women's Ministries manual)

India South Eastern: *Never the same again* by Shaw Clifton

India South Western: *Discovery; International Bible Lessons for Children*

Kenya West: *Adventurers; Discovery; God's Grace is Sufficient*

Liberia: *Adventurers*

Nigeria: *Adventurers; Discovery; International Bible Lessons for Children*

South America West: *Adventurers; More Stories That are Seen* by Douglas G. Clarke; *O and R for Officers* (Spanish)

Sweden and Latvia: *Unwrap the Gift; Bible Study Notes* (Latvian)

Tanzania: *Do You Want to Remain Blessed?*

MINISTRIES AND FELLOWSHIPS

WOMEN'S MINISTRIES

THE ideal basic unit of society is the home and family, where women play a vital and definitive role. Furthermore, as natural providers of hope, women play an important part in shaping society. Therefore, any fellowship of women in which Christian influence is exerted and practical help given benefits not only the individual and the family, but also the nation.

Women's Ministries provide a programme of meetings and other activities based on the fourfold aim of the Army's international women's organisation, the Home League, which was inaugurated in 1907. Those aims are worship, education, fellowship, service. The motto of the Home League is: 'I will live a pure life in my house' (Psalm 101:2 *Good News Bible*).

The mission of Women's Ministries is to bring women into a knowledge of Jesus Christ; encourage their full potential in influencing family, friends and community; equip them for growth in personal understanding and life skills; address issues which affect women and their families in the world.

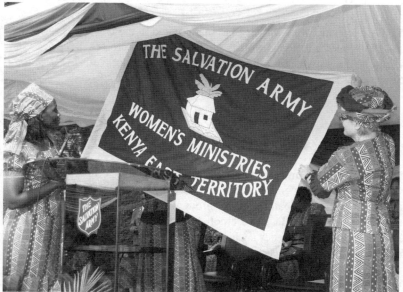

KENYA EAST: Commissioner Sue Swanson, then World President of Women's Ministries (right), **at the unfurling of a new Women's Ministries flag during 90th anniversary celebrations in November 2011**

THE LEAGUE OF MERCY AND COMMUNITY CARE MINISTRIES

THE League of Mercy began in 1892 in Canada and is made up of people of all ages whose mission is to engage in a caring ministry. The main objective of the League of Mercy is to respond to the spiritual and social needs of the community. The ministry is adapted according to the local situation, the size of its membership and the skill of its members, and endeavours to follow Christ's injunction, 'Inasmuch as ye have done it unto one of the least of these my brethren, ye have done it unto me' (Matthew 25:40 *Authorised Version*).

THE FELLOWSHIP OF THE SILVER STAR

THE Fellowship of the Silver Star, inaugurated in the USA in 1930 and extended worldwide in 1936, expresses gratitude to parents or other significant life mentors of Salvation Army officers.

THE SALVATION ARMY MEDICAL FELLOWSHIP

THE Salvation Army Medical Fellowship, instituted in 1943 by Mrs General Minnie Carpenter, is an international fellowship of dedicated medical personnel. Physical suffering in our world today challenges both the medical and the physical and emotional resources of medical personnel. The fellowship encourages a Christian witness and application of Christian principles in professional life while at the same time being involved with practical application in hospitals, clinics and various other places of medical care. The motto of the Fellowship is: 'If we walk in the light, as he is in the light, we have fellowship one with another' (1 John 1:7 *Authorised Version*).

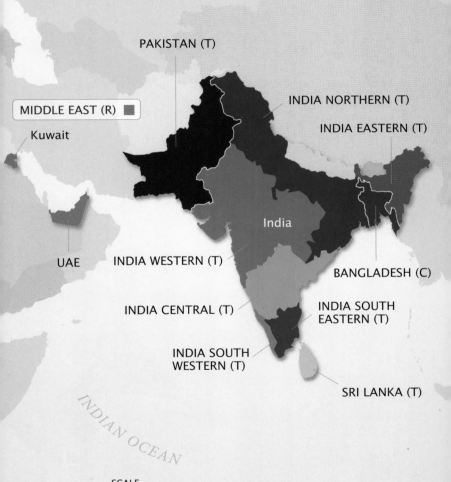

TERRITORIES (T)
COMMANDS (C)
REGIONS (R)

MIDDLE EAST (R) ▪

Kuwait

PAKISTAN (T)

INDIA NORTHERN (T)

INDIA EASTERN (T)

UAE

INDIA WESTERN (T)

India

BANGLADESH (C)

INDIA CENTRAL (T)

INDIA SOUTH
EASTERN (T)

INDIA SOUTH
WESTERN (T)

SRI LANKA (T)

INDIAN OCEAN

SCALE

0 km 1000 2000 3000 km

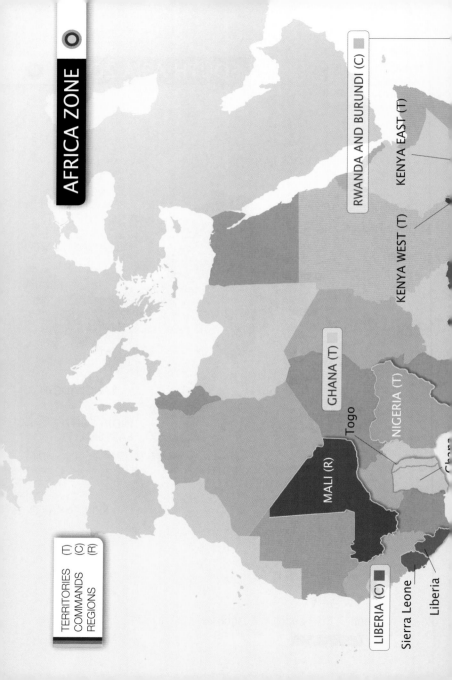

AFFRICA ZONE

○

TERRITORIES (T)
COMMANDS (C)
REGIONS (R)

RWANDA AND BURUNDI (C)

KENYA EAST (T)

KENYA WEST (T)

GHANA (T)

Togo

NIGERIA (T)

Ghana

MALI (R)

LIBERIA (C)

Sierra Leone

Liberia

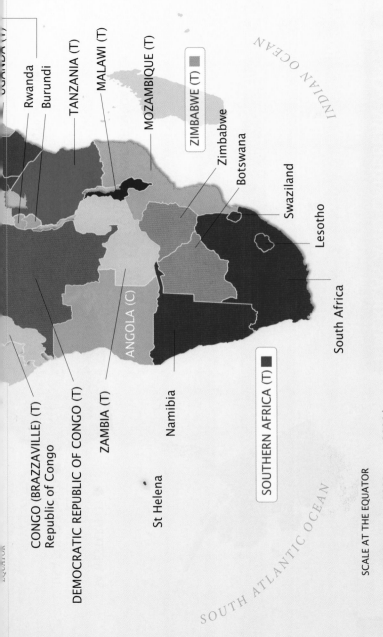

Rwanda
Burundi
TANZANIA (T)
MALAWI (T)
MOZAMBIQUE (T)
ZIMBABWE (T)
Zimbabwe
Botswana
Swaziland
Lesotho
South Africa

CONGO (BRAZZAVILLE) (T)
Republic of Congo
DEMOCRATIC REPUBLIC OF CONGO (T)
ZAMBIA (T)
ANGOLA (C)
Namibia
St Helena
SOUTHERN AFRICA (T)

INDIAN OCEAN
SOUTH ATLANTIC OCEAN

SCALE AT THE EQUATOR

0 km   1000   2000   3000 km

AMERICAS AND CARIBBEAN ZONE

TERRITORIES (T)
COMMANDS (C)

CANADA AND BERMUDA (T)

USA EASTERN (T)

USA CENTRAL (T)

USA WESTERN (T)

USA SOUTHERN (T)

Canada

United States of America

Bermuda

Guam, Marshall Islands
and Micronesia – 3000 km (approx)

CARIBBEAN (T)

SOUTH AMERICA EAST (T)

LATIN AMERICA NORTH (T)

SOUTH AMERICA WEST (T)

Hawaii

Virgin Islands
Dominican Republic
Puerto Rico
Venezuela
Guyana
Suriname
French Guiana
Haiti
Cuba
Belize
MEXICO (T)
Guatemala
Honduras
El Salvador
Nicaragua
Costa Rica
Panama
Colombia
Ecuador
Peru
Bolivia
BRAZIL (T)
Paraguay
Uruguay
Argentina
Chile

ATLANTIC OCEAN

SOUTH PACIFIC OCEAN

EQUATOR

SCALE AT THE EQUATOR

0 km   1000   2000   3000 km

Greenland (see small scale map)

NORWEGIAN SEA

FINLAND AND
ESTONIA (T) ■

Iceland

NORWAY, ICELAND AND THE FÆROES (T) ■

Norway

Sweden

SWEDEN AND LATVIA (T) ■

The Færoes

NORTH SEA

GERMANY AND LITHUANIA (T) ■
(Includes Poland)

United Kingdom

Lithuania

UNITED KINGDOM WITH
THE REPUBLIC OF IRELAND (T) ■

DENMARK (T) ■
(Includes Greenland)

Poland

Republic of Ireland

Netherlands

Germany

Czech Republic

THE NETHERLANDS AND
CZECH REPUBLIC (T) ■

Belgium

SWITZERLAND, AUSTRIA
AND HUNGARY (T) ■

Austria   Hungary

France

Switzerland

FRANCE AND BELGIUM (T) ■

Italy

ATLANTIC OCEAN

PORTUGAL (C)

SPAIN (C)

Canary Islands (part of Spain Command)

1000 km (approx)

ITALY AND GREECE (C) ■

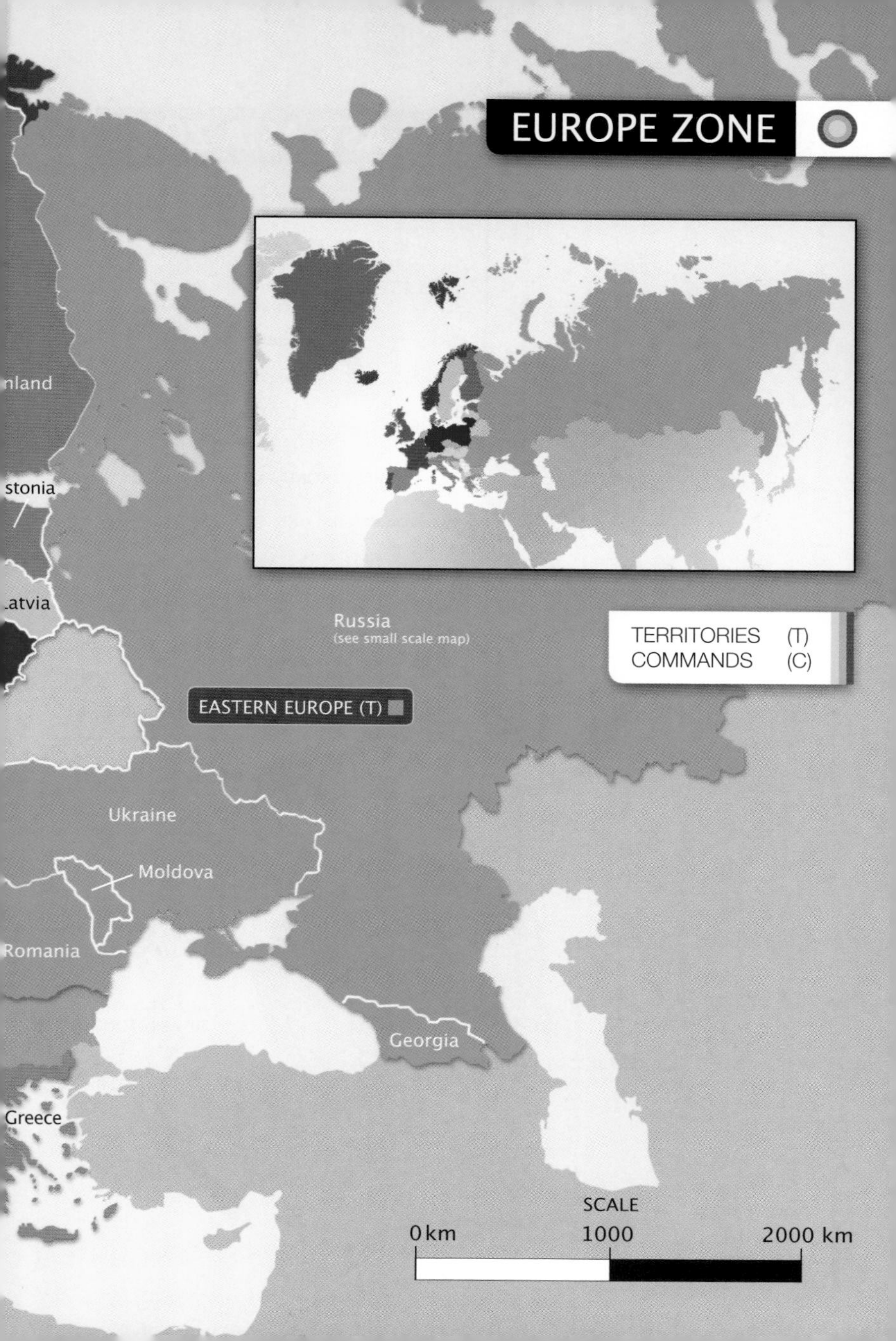
EUROPE ZONE
TERRITORIES (T)
COMMANDS (C)
nland
stonia
atvia
Russia
(see small scale map)
EASTERN EUROPE (T)
Ukraine
Moldova
Romania
Georgia
Greece
SCALE
0 km
1000
2000 km

SOUTH PACIFIC AND EAST ASIA ZONE

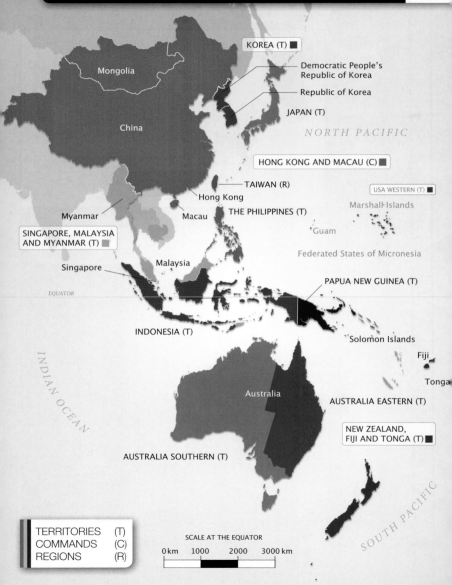

KOREA (T) ◼

Democratic People's Republic of Korea

Republic of Korea

JAPAN (T)

Mongolia

China

NORTH PACIFIC

HONG KONG AND MACAU (C) ◼

TAIWAN (R)

Hong Kong

Macau

THE PHILIPPINES (T)

USA WESTERN (T) ◼

Marshall Islands

Myanmar

SINGAPORE, MALAYSIA AND MYANMAR (T) ◼

Guam

Federated States of Micronesia

Singapore

Malaysia

EQUATOR

PAPUA NEW GUINEA (T)

INDONESIA (T)

Solomon Islands

Fiji

Tonga

INDIAN OCEAN

Australia

AUSTRALIA EASTERN (T)

NEW ZEALAND, FIJI AND TONGA (T) ◼

AUSTRALIA SOUTHERN (T)

SOUTH PACIFIC

TERRITORIES (T)
COMMANDS (C)
REGIONS (R)

SCALE AT THE EQUATOR

0 km   1000   2000   3000 km

SALVATION ARMY HONOURS

ORDER OF THE FOUNDER

Instituted on 20 August 1917 by General Bramwell Booth, the Order of the Founder is the highest Salvation Army honour for distinguished service.

IN 1917, five years after the death of William Booth, his son, General Bramwell Booth, inaugurated the Order of the Founder 'to mark outstanding service rendered by officers and soldiers such as would in spirit or achievement have been specially commended by the Founder'.

The first awards were made in 1920 to 15 officers and one soldier. Three years later, seven officers and one local officer were honoured, but since then the awards have been made much more sparingly and, to date, 158 officers and 95 lay Salvationists have been recognised with the Army's highest honour – a total of 253 in 92 years (1920-2012).

The first presentation was to a soldier, Private Herbert Bourne, for outstanding Christian witness and service during military service in the First World War. A few senior leaders such as Commissioner Henry Howard, General Evangeline Booth and Commissioner Catherine Bramwell-Booth have been recipients but, much more commonly, faithful and devoted service by less well-known personalities has been acknowledged.

Every nomination is carefully scrutinised by a panel of senior leaders at International Headquarters. Salvationists have every reason to be proud of those who have been awarded this outstanding recognition for meritorious Christian example, witness and service.

Recipients of the Order of the Founder 2011-12

Lieut-Colonel Kamla K. Parshad (India Northern Territory)
PRESENTED in recognition of her visionary, passionate, Christlike officer service, extending well past retirement. Lieut-Colonel Kamla K. Parshad's work in education, developing The Salvation Army's schools from pre-school to Senior Secondary Schools in Batala, has had an impact in her community, nationally and internationally.
Admitted to the Order of the Founder on 19 September 2011.

Lieut-Colonel Donald Thomas Woodland (Australia Eastern Territory)
CITED as a man of the people, serving beyond the call of duty, nationally and internationally, in the name of Jesus, bringing hope, compassion and relief to those affected by tragedy and trauma, at their point of need. Admitted to the Order of the Founder on 19 February 2012.

Dr Roger Green (USA Eastern Territory)

AWARDED in recognition of the sterling Salvationism of a committed soldier of Jesus Christ. Dr Roger Green has enriched the life and ministry of The Salvation Army through his writing, teaching, preaching and tireless efforts to encourage people in their Christian faith and personal commitment to Army service.
Admitted to the Order of the Founder on 2 June 2012.

Warren C. Johnson (USA Western Territory)
FOR outstanding and exemplary service above and beyond the call of duty, Warren C. Johnson has demonstrated commitment to evangelism and spiritual formation at corps, territorial and worldwide levels.
Admitted to the Order of the Founder on 8 June 2012.

General Linda Bond admits Warren C. Johnson, a soldier at Tustin Ranch Corps, California to the Order of the Founder at the USA Western Territory's congress, 'The Gathering', in June 2012

ORDER OF DISTINGUISHED AUXILIARY SERVICE

On 24 February 1941 General George Carpenter instituted this order to mark the Army's appreciation of distinguished service rendered by non-Salvationists who have helped to further its work in a variety of ways.

Recipients of the Order of Distinguished Auxiliary Service 2011-12

Baillieu Myer AC (Australia Southern Territory)
The Salvation Army honours Mr Baillieu Myer AC as a member and as the Chairman of the advisory board of the Australia Southern Territory and as patron of the NewLife08 Campaign. Mr Myer AC has demonstrated vision, leadership, generosity and compassion in his service to The Salvation Army over many years.
Admitted to the Order of Distinguished Auxiliary Service on 15 August 2011.

Mr Don Fry AO (Australia Eastern Territory)
In recognition of, and appreciation for, dedicated service and advocacy on behalf of The Salvation Army for more than 35 years. Mr Fry's service above self has resulted in many outstanding achievements which have enhanced the ministry of The Salvation Army in the Australia Eastern territory.
Admitted to the Order of Distinguished Auxiliary Service on 10 December 2011.

INTERNATIONAL HEADQUARTERS

The Salvation Army, 101 Queen Victoria Street, London EC4V 4EH, United Kingdom

Main entrance: Peter's Hill, London EC4

Tel: (020) 7332 0101 (national)

[44] (20) 7332 0101 (international);

email: websa@salvationarmy.org;

website: www.salvationarmy.org

General
LINDA BOND
(2 April 2011)

Chief of the Staff
COMMISSIONER ANDRÉ COX
(1 February 2013)

INTERNATIONAL Headquarters exists to support the General as she leads The Salvation Army to accomplish its God-given worldwide mission to preach the gospel of Jesus Christ and meet human need in his name without discrimination. In so doing, it assists the General:

- To give spiritual leadership, promote the development of spiritual life within the Army, and emphasise the Army's reliance on God for the achievement of its mission.
- To provide overall strategic leadership and set international policies.
- To direct and administer the Army's operations and protect its interests – by means of appointments and delegation of authority and responsibility with accountability.
- To empower and support the territories and commands, encourage and pastorally care for their leaders, and inspire local vision and initiatives.
- To strengthen the internationalism of the Army, preserve its unity, purposes, beliefs and spirit, and maintain its standards.
- To promote the development, appropriate deployment and international sharing of personnel.
- To promote the development and sharing of financial resources worldwide, and manage the Army's international funds.
- To promote the development and international sharing of knowledge, expertise and experience.
- To develop the Army's ecumenical and other relationships.

The General directs Salvation Army operations throughout the world through the administrative departments of International Headquarters, which are headed by international secretaries. The Chief of the Staff, a commissioner appointed by the General to be second-in-command, is the Army's chief executive whose function is to implement the General's policy decisions and effect liaison between departments.

The Christian Mission Headquarters, Whitechapel Road, became the Army's first International Headquarters in 1880. However, the Founder soon decided that a move into the City of London would be beneficial and in 1881 IHQ was moved to 101 Queen Victoria Street. Sixty years after this move the IHQ building was destroyed by fire during the Second World War. The rebuilt International Headquarters was opened by Queen Elizabeth, the Queen Mother, in November 1963.

When it was decided to redevelop the Queen Victoria Street site, IHQ took up temporary residence at William Booth College, Denmark Hill, in 2001. Three years later IHQ returned to 101 Queen Victoria Street and the new building was opened by Her Royal Highness The Princess Royal in November 2004.

Website of the Office of the General: www.salvationarmy.org/thegeneral

INTERNATIONAL MANAGEMENT COUNCIL

The International Management Council (IMC), established in February 1991, sees to the efficiency and effectiveness of the Army's international administration in general. It considers in detail the formation of international policy and mission. It is composed of all London-based IHQ commissioners, and meets monthly with the General taking the chair.

Secretary: Lt-Col Rob Garrad
Asst Secretary: Maj Lorraine Hart

GENERAL'S CONSULTATIVE COUNCIL

The General's Consultative Council (GCC), established in July 2001, advises the General on broad matters relating to the Army's mission strategy and policy. The GCC is composed of all officers who qualify to attend a High Council, and operates through a Lotus Notes database. Selected members also meet three times a year in London with the General taking the chair.

Secretary: Lt-Col Rob Garrad
Asst Secretary: Maj Lorraine Hart

ADMINISTRATION DEPARTMENT

The Administration Department is responsible for all matters with which the Chief of the Staff deals; for the effective administration of IHQ; for IHQ personnel; for international external relations; for providing legal advice; and for ensuring that the strategic planning and monitoring process is implemented and used effectively. The department also facilitates the sharing and appropriate deployment of personnel resources on a global basis; assists in the identification of officers with potential for future leadership; monitors training and development; registers and coordinates all offers for international service.

International Secretary to the Chief of the Staff

COMR WILLIAM COCHRANE (1 Jun 2009)

Under Sec for Administration:
Maj Peter Forrest
Under Sec for International Personnel:
Maj Mark Watts
Executive Sec to the General:
Lt-Col Rob Garrad
Private Sec to the General: Maj Lorraine Hart
Private Sec to the Chief of the Staff: Maj Christine Clement
Sec for International Ecumenical Relations:
Col Richard Munn
Sec for Spiritual Life Development:
Col Janet Munn
Director, International Social Justice Commission: Col Geanette Seymour
International Doctrine Council:
Chair: Comr William Francis
International Moral and Social Issues Council:
Chair: Col Geanette Seymour
IHQ Chaplain and City of London Liaison Officer: Maj Patricia Brown
International Statistician: Maj Juliet Nyakuswama
Legal Sec: Maj Patrick Booth
Medical Sec for Personnel: Lt-Col Wendy Leavey
Project Coordinator, The Salvation Army Song Book: Maj Christine Clement
Sec for Officer Development and Records:
Lt-Col Janet Read
2015 International Congress Coordinator:
Lt-Col Eddie Hobgood

WOMEN'S MINISTRIES
World President of Women's Ministries
COMR SILVIA COX (1 Feb 2013)

World President, SA Scouts, Guides and Guards
COMR SILVIA COX (1 Feb 2013)

Personal Asst to World President of Women's Ministries: Maj Julie Forrest

BUSINESS ADMINISTRATION DEPARTMENT

The Business Administration Department is responsible for international accounting, auditing, banking, property and related matters. The International Secretary for Business Administration has the oversight of the finance functions in territories and commands.

International Secretary for Business Administration

COMR ANN WOODALL (1 Mar 2008)

Finance Sec: Lt-Col Alan Read
Chief Accountant: Miss Karen Dare
Chief International Auditor: Lt-Col Edmund Chung
Auditors: Maj João Paulo Ramos (Asst Chief International Auditor) Maj Samuel Amponsah, Maj Alan Milkins, Maj Francis Nyakusamwa, Comr John Wainwright
Information Technology Manager: Mr Mark Calleran
Property Manager: Mr Howard Bowes
Travel Manager: Mr Mark Edwards

PROGRAMME RESOURCES DEPARTMENT

The mission of the Programme Resources Department is to participate with others in envisioning, coordinating, facilitating and raising awareness of programmes that advance the global mission of The Salvation Army.

International Secretary for Programme Resources

COMR GERRIT MARSEILLE (1 Sep 2011)

Under Sec: Maj Dean Pallant
International Emergency Services Coordinator: Maj Raymond Brown
International Health Services Coordinators: Majs Dean and (Dr) Eirwen Pallant
International Projects Officer: Capt Elizabeth Nelson

Mission Resources Secretary: Comr Eva Marseille
Communications Section:
  Communications Sec, Editor-in-Chief and Literary Sec: tba
  Book Production Specialist: Mr Paul Mortlock
  Editor *All the World*: Mr Kevin Sims
  Editor *Revive*: tba
  Editor *The Officer*: Maj Sandra Welch
  Editor *The Year Book*: Lt-Col Jayne Roberts
  International Literature Programme: Maj Martha Pawar
  Webmaster: Mr David Giles
  Writer *Words of Life*: Maj Beverly Ivany

ZONAL DEPARTMENTS

The zonal departments are the main administrative link with territories and commands. The international secretaries give oversight to and coordinate the Army's work in their respective geographical areas.

AFRICA
International Secretary
COMR JOASH MALABI (1 Jan 2013)

Under Secs: Lt-Col Margaret Wickings and Lt-Col Keith Conrad
Zonal Sec WM: Comr Florence Malabi

AMERICAS AND CARIBBEAN
International Secretary
COMR TORBEN ELIASEN (1 Jul 2012)

Under Sec: Maj Deborah Sedlar
Zonal Sec WM: Comr Deise Eliasen

EUROPE
International Secretary
COMR ROBERT STREET (1 Nov 2010)

COMR BIRGITTE BREKKE (from 1 Mar 2013)

Under Sec: Lt-Col Jonathan Roberts
Zonal Sec WM: Comr Janet Street
  Comr Dorita Wainwright (from 1 Mar 2013)

Officer for EU Affairs: Maj Germen Stoffers

SOUTH ASIA
International Secretary
COMR LALKIAMLOVA (1 Jan 2004)

Under Sec: Maj Suresh Pawar
Zonal Sec WM: Comr Lalhlimpuii

SOUTH PACIFIC AND EAST ASIA
International Secretary
COMR ALISTAIR HERRING (1 Apr 2011)

Under Sec: Lt-Col Jennifer Groves
Zonal Sec WM: Comr Astrid Herring

STATISTICS
Officers 84 **Employees** 73

International Social Justice Commission
221 East 52nd Street, New York, New York 10022, USA
Tel: [1] (212) 758-0763; website: www.salvationarmy.org/isjc
email: ihq-isjc@salvationarmy.org

Director: Colonel Geanette Seymour (1 Jul 2012)

The International Social Justice Commission (ISJC) with its secretariat in New York, is attached to the Administration Department of IHQ. The ISJC advises the General and other senior leaders at IHQ in matters of social justice. The director and staff are the Army's principal international advocate and adviser on social, economic and political issues and events giving rise to the perpetuation of social injustice in the world. They assist the Army in addressing social injustice in a systemic, measured, proactive and Christian manner.

The commission is also the secretariat to the work of the International Moral and Social Issues Council (IMASIC). The director of the ISJC chairs the IMASIC.

THE ISJC continues to develop resources to teach and explain social justice from theological, theoretical and best practice perspectives.

The Salvation Army's mission has always been marked by love for God, service among the poor and an invitation to believe and follow Jesus Christ. The mandate of the ISJC is to challenge Salvationists to harmonize their historic mission with God's call to pursue justice in today's world.

The ISJC seeks to fulfil this mandate through the implementation of a strategic plan to:

• Raise strategic voices to advocate with the world's poor and oppressed.

• Be a recognised centre of research and critical thinking on issues of global social justice.

• Collaborate with like-minded organisations to advance the global cause of social justice.

• Exercise leadership in determining social justice policies and practices of The Salvation Army.

• Live by principles of justice and compassion and inspire others to do likewise.

The Salvation Army is consistently engaged in the international arena at the UN and associated non-government organisations, and in the faith based community.

STATISTICS
Officers 6 **Employees** 5 (full-time 1 part-time 4)
Policy Interns 4

STAFF
Assistant Director: Maj Teresita Pacheco
Senior Policy Analyst (IMASIC):
Dr James E. Read
Senior UN Rep and Intern Trainer:
Maj Victoria Edmonds (New York)
UN Reps: Maj Sylvette Huguenin (Geneva);
Lt-Col Julius Mukonga (Nairobi);
Maj Heidi Oppliger (Vienna)

International College for Officers and Centre for Spiritual Life Development

The Cedars, 34 Sydenham Hill, London SE26 6LS, UK

Tel: [44] (020) 8299 8450; website: www.salvationarmy.org/ico

Principal: Colonel Richard Munn (1 Jul 2008)

During the International Congress held at the Crystal Palace, Sydenham, London, in 1904, Commissioner Henry T. Howard voiced what he saw as the young Salvation Army's need for leaders inspired with the aggressive spirit of Salvationism. William Booth took up the idea and the International Staff Training Lodge was opened at Clapton on 11 May 1905.

Following the purchase of The Cedars in Sydenham, the International Staff College started in 1950. Four years later it became the International College for Officers (ICO), with General Albert Orsborn declaring it to be 'an investment in the great intangibles without which our cogs and wheels would soon be rusty and dead'. To date, more than 5,000 officers have attended the ICO, which Commissioner Alfred Gilliard (Pricipal 1954-50) described as 'one of the Army's most brilliant long-term investments'.

In July 2008 the mission of the college was broadened to include aspects of spiritual life development and the college was renamed International College for Officers and Centre for Spiritual Life Development (CSLD).

ICO MISSION STATEMENT

The Salvation Army's International College for Officers exists to further develop officers by:
o **nurturing personal holiness and spiritual leadership**
o **providing opportunity to experience the internationalism of the Army**
o **encouraging a renewed sense of mission and purpose as an officer**

CSLD MISSION STATEMENT

The international Centre for Spiritual Life Development exists to facilitate the development of the spiritual lives of Salvationists by:
o **offering conferences and events that are spiritually enriching and that help form people in Christlikeness**
o **providing resources to cultivate spiritual life development**
o **encouraging implementation of intentional and systematic opportunities for spiritual growth throughout the international Salvation Army**

DURING 2011-12 the ICO hosted more than 100 officers in four sessions (212 – 215) including Spanish and Tamil translation sessions.

In May 2012, delegates participated in the UK Territory 'I'll Fight' Congress. Session 215 was a special 'Youth and Children' session with guest lecturers from around the world serving in residence with the delegates for two week terms.

The establishment of the Centre for Spiritual Life Development alongside the ICO has brought a strong emphasis on prayer, spiritual disciplines and Bible study.

ICO sessions now include an exploration of items from the International Spiritual Life Commission. During each session ICO delegates create practical strategies to nourish Salvationist spirituality in their home contexts. They facilitate spiritual life events in their home territories and become part of the expanding international network of spiritual life development personnel.

STATISTICS

Officers 5 **Employees** 6 **Interns** 2

STAFF

Associate Principal and Secretary for Spiritual Life Development: Col Janet Munn
Business Sec: Maj Daniel Kasuso
Personnel Sec: Maj Tracey Kasuso
Programme Sec: Maj Janet Robson

The Africa Development Centre
The Salvation Army Kabete Compound, Karbarsiran Avenue,
Nairobi, Kenya

On 17 April 2009, IHQ gave approval for the relocation of The Salvation Army Leadership Training College (SALT College) of Africa to Nairobi and the setting up of the Africa Development Centre, which was established on 1 January 2010.

The Centre was made up of three units: the SALT College of Africa, the Africa Programme Development Office and the Zonal Facilitation Resource Office. Later that year the Zonal Facilitation Resource Office and Africa Programme Development Office were combined, to form the Africa Development Office.

Since 1 July 2010 the Africa Development Centre has consisted of two units: the SALT College of Africa and the Africa Development Office, each unit a satellite office of the IHQ Africa Zone, reporting to the International Secretary for Africa.While each unit retains its individual identity and purpose, since August 2012 they have shared one building.

The Salvation Army Leadership Training College (SALT College) of Africa
Postal Address: PO Box 40575, Nairobi 00100 GPO, Kenya
tel: [254] (020) 221 2217

Prompted by the request of territorial leaders within Africa, The Salvation Army Leadership Training College of Africa was established in 1986.

Its purpose is to coordinate in-service training for local leaders across Africa through the provision or recommendation of distance-learning courses and seminars, monitored by an extension training officer in each territory.

An IHQ-sponsored education and training facility, SALT College offers distance learning to 21 countries across the African continent. Its students include officers, envoys, candidates, local officers and soldiers.

Principal: Col Gabriel Kathuri
Director of Special Services: Col Monica Kathuri
Director of Studies: Maj Julius Omukonyi
Office Administrator: Maj Gaudencia Omukonyi
email: leadcoll_africa@salvationarmy.org

The Africa Development Office
Postal Address:c/o Kenya East THQ
Box 24927, Karen 00502, Nairobi, Kenya

The Africa Development Office supports the territories, commands and regions of Africa in planning strategically for the future. It supports territorial facilitation teams to encourage Salvationists and communities to realise and utilise their own strength and capacity to build a deeper sense of fellowship and to work together to respond to concerns within the community.

The Africa Development Office gives support and training to territorial and command leaders and to project officers in project design, implementation and reporting. Also, in collaboration with the IHQ Africa Zone, the IHQ International Projects and Development Services and donor territory project offices, it provides follow-up for projects as required.

2011-12 has seen further development of territorial capacity to use Faith-Based Facilitation in all activities, encouraging the development of territorial teams to continue this work. The roll out of the health flip charts in Swahili speaking territories has continued, with many corps and communities now using the charts regularly. The Office continues to support the development of women leaders.

Programme Development Secretary:
Lt-Col Mary Capsey
Assistant Programme Development Secretary: Capt Lena Wanyonyi
email: IHQ-AfricaDev@salvationarmy.org

STATISTICS Officers 6 Employees 5

International Administrative Structure

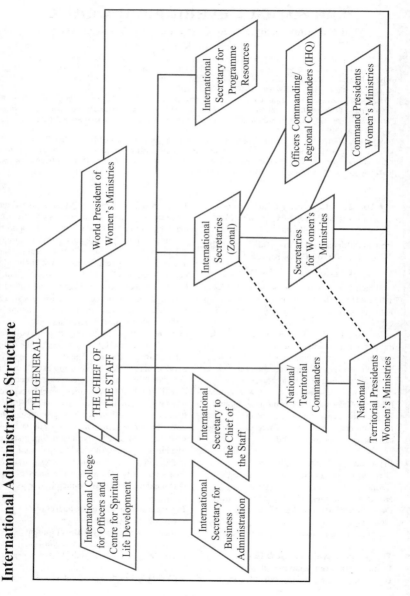

- THE GENERAL
- World President of Women's Ministries
- International College for Officers and Centre for Spiritual Life Development
- THE CHIEF OF THE STAFF
- International Secretary for Programme Resources
- International Secretary to the Chief of the Staff
- International Secretary for Business Administration
- International Secretaries (Zonal)
- Secretaries for Women's Ministries
- Officers Commanding/ Regional Commanders (IHQ)
- Command Presidents Women's Ministries
- National/ Territorial Commanders
- National/ Territorial Presidents Women's Ministries

The Salvation Army International Trustee Company

Registered Office: 101 Queen Victoria Street, London EC4V 4EH

Registration No 2538134. Tel: (020) 7332 0101

Company Secretary: Lieut-Colonel Alan Read

DIRECTORS: Comr Barry C. Swanson (Chair), Comr Ann Woodall (Managing Director and Vice Chair), Comr William Cochrane, Comr Torben Eliasen, Comr Alistair Herring, Comr Kenneth Hodder, Mr Andrew Justice, Mr David Kidd, Comr Lalkiamlova, Comr Amos Makina, Comr Gerrit Marseille, Lt-Col Alan Read, Comr Robert Street.

The company is registered under the Companies Acts 1985 and 1989 as a company limited by guarantee, not having a share capital. It has no assets or liabilities, but as a trustee of The Salvation Army International Trusts it is the registered holder of Salvation Army property both real and personal including shares in some of the Army's commercial undertakings. The company is a trust corporation.

Reliance Bank Limited

Faith House, 23-24 Lovat Lane, London EC3R 8EB

Tel: (020) 7398 5400; fax: (020) 7398 5401; email: info@reliancebankltd.com;
website: www.reliancebankltd.com

Chairman: Commissioner Ann Woodall

Managing Director: Trevor J. Smith, ACIB

Finance Director: Kevin Dare, BA(Hons), CIMA
Banking Lending Manager and Company Secretary: Paul Underwood, ACIB
Banking Services Manager: Andrew Hunt, ACIB
Business Development Manager: Nichola Keating

DIRECTORS: Comr Ann Woodall (Chairman), Comr William Cochrane, Lt-Col Alan Read, Col David Hinton, Lt-Col Ivor Telfer, Maj John Warner, Mr Trevor Smith, Mr Kevin Dare, Mr Philip Deer, Mr Gerald Birkett, ACIB, Mr Ian Scott ACIB.

Reliance Bank Ltd is an authorised institution under the Banking Act 1987, regulated by the Financial Services Authority and registered under the Companies and Consumer Credit Acts.

OWNED by The Salvation Army through its controlling shareholders – The Salvation Army International Trustee Company and The Salvation Army Trustee Company – Reliance Bank accepts sterling and foreign currency deposits, carries on general banking business, and provides finance for Salvation Army corporate customers and private and business customers.

The bank can grant residential and commercial mortgages, personal loans and overdrafts. It offers current accounts, together with a Reliance Bank Visa debit card, cheques, safe custody facilities, fixed deposits and savings accounts, including ISAs, and provides money transmission services both within the UK and abroad. Internet banking and telephone banking services are also offered.

The bank pays at least 75 per cent of its taxable profits by means of Gift Aid donation to its controlling shareholders.

Brochures are available on request, or visit www.reliancebankltd.com

STATISTICS Employees 21

OVERSEAS SERVICE FUNDS 2011–2012 INCOME

	International Self-Denial Contributions £	International Self-Denial Special £	Special Projects £	Donations via IHQ £	Total £
Angola	31,445				31,445
Australia Eastern	559,111		2,227,234	83,972	2,870,119
Australia Southern	604,939		704,246	366,702	1,675,888
Bangladesh	800				800
Brazil	24,405				24,405
Canada and Bermuda	1,252,093		859,098	180,674	2,291,864
Caribbean	42,208			3,006	45,215
Congo (Brazzaville)	76,434				76,434
Democratic Republic of Congo	51,523				51,523
Denmark	50,000		31,665	47,944	129,609
Eastern Europe	12,504			366	12,870
Finland and Estonia	52,595		42,909	46,933	142,437
France and Belgium	17,243		12,860	364	30,467
Germany and Lithuania	59,244			234,164	293,408
Ghana	14,878				14,878
Hong Kong and Macau	69,678		1,970,931	1,087,107	3,127,716
India Central	32,123			3,239	35,362
India Eastern	53,899			1,303	55,202
India Northern	19,567				19,567
India South Eastern	44,066				44,066
India South Western	24,836				24,836
India Western	24,210			520	24,730
Indonesia	45,830			6,004	51,834
Italy and Greece	11,362			5,110	16,472
Japan	87,423			31,149	118,571
Kenya East	34,667				34,667
Kenya West	45,282				45,282
Korea	59,134				59,134
Latin America North	11,864			1,441	13,304
Liberia	2,627				2,627
Malawi	3,816			305	4,121
Mali	689				689
Mexico	18,648			5,590	24,238
Mozambique	2,693				2,693
Netherlands and Czech Republic	184,197		797,481	106,432	1,088,110
New Zealand, Fiji and Tonga	441,223		182,768	80,913	704,904
Nigeria and Mali	15,481			500	15,981
Norway, Iceland and The Færoes	372,032		1,928,595	70,762	2,371,390
Pakistan	4,032			508	4,540
Papua New Guinea	7,159			2,000	9,159
Philippines	5,381			1,997	7,378
Portugal	2,163			2,103	4,266
Rwanda and Burundi	1,670				1,670
Singapore and Malaysia	96,285		38,621	53,782	188,687
South America East	13,760				13,760
South America West	23,957			501	24,458
Southern Africa	30,552			8,415	38,967
Spain	5,426			16,908	22,333
Sri Lanka	1,167				1,167
Sweden and Latvia	101,678		257,266	12,626	371,370
Switzerland, Austria and Hungary	648,941		2,153,383	70,897	2,873,221
Taiwan	3,876	-	-	20,513	24,390
Tanzania	4,386	-	-		4,386
Uganda	1,712	-	-		1,712
United Kingdom	1,728,494	-	1,476,058	209,633	3,414,185
USA Central	2,663,530		1,972,402	88,923	5,292,176
USA Eastern	2,884,011	567,322	2,056,536	709,160	5,789,311
USA Southern	2,862,829	139,604	2,181,268	131,162	5,446,319
USA Western	2,403,756	270,560	2,132,029	115,215	4,738,621
USA SAWSO		87,620	1,363,225	228,970	1,592,195
Zambia	51,686	-			51,686
Zimbabwe	287,981				290,345
		-			
	18,289,200	1,065,107	22,388,575	4,040,276	45,783,158

OVERSEAS SERVICE FUNDS 2011-2012 EXPENDITURE

	Support of Overseas Work	Special Projects	Donations via IHQ	Total
	£	£	£	£
Africa, General	492,688	-		492,688
Americas, General	955	-	11,852	12,807
Angola	61,925	516,250	22,441	600,616
Australia Eastern	-	4,592		4,592
Bangladesh	176,062	232,584	27,156	435,802
Brazil	677,521	600,600	23,377	1,301,498
Burundi	28,032	-		28,032
Caribbean	812,904	2,464,017	39,266	3,316,188
Congo (Brazzaville)	509,524	160,576	21,837	691,938
Czech Republic (Netherlands)	377,272		6,935	384,206
Democratic Republic of Congo	565,218	399,874	11,501	976,593
Eastern Europe	1,986,989	678,939	40,798	2,706,726
Estonia [Finland]	126,324	103,809	6,739	236,872
Europe, General	3,054	-	4,374	7,428
France and Belgium	-		3,832	3,832
Germany and Lithuania	142,130	9,045	5,572	156,747
Ghana	215,660	265,869	18,003	499,532
Greece (Italy)	28,421		7,055	35,476
Hong Kong and Macau	887	30,018	1,932	32,837
Hungary [Switzerland]	66,799	-	46	66,844
India National Secretariat	67,435	260,924	1,274	329,633
India Central	310,860	238,963	20,411	570,234
India Eastern	122,876	465,093	12,063	600,032
India Northern	326,491	292,687	16,965	636,143
India South Eastern	323,951	683,530	5,750	1,013,230
India South Western	360,582	156,721	25,720	543,023
India Western	282,890	94,415	24,932	402,237
Indonesia	72,262	496,974	33,405	602,640
Italy	195,124	151,207	7,162	353,493
Japan	-	2,661,589	15,015	2,676,604
Kenya East	378,638	939,831	41,703	1,360,172
Kenya West	431,964	290,552	26,149	748,665
Korea	3,375	56,657	5,333	65,365
Latin America North	690,595	548,964	26,803	1,266,362
Latvia [Sweden]	118,964	98,707	2,769	220,440
Liberia	185,055	97,854	10,689	293,598
Malawi	159,515	415,766	32,165	607,445
Mali	61,351		41	61,392
Mexico	416,507	488,677	16,113	921,297
Middle East Region	-	128,050	19,158	147,208
Mozambique	220,001	225,343	2,684	448,028
Myanmar [Singapore and Malaysia]	112,478	-	21,834	134,312
Netherlands and Czech Republic	-	95,814		95,814
New Zealand, Fiji and Tonga	-	1,265,184	99,742	1,364,926
Nigeria and Mali	222,064	216,208	24,914	463,185
Norway, Iceland and The Færoes	-	91,161		91,161
Pakistan	446,796	593,377	26,167	1,066,340
Papua New Guinea	456,839	405,315	24,444	886,598
Philippines	433,764	401,949	20,990	856,703
Poland [Germany]	136,045	-	41	136,085
Portugal	322,907	51,336	1,278	375,521
Rwanda	147,575	132,796	47,641	328,011
SALT College	49,784	-	43,538	93,321
Singapore & Malaysia	32,383	448,602	8,439	489,424
South America East	565,226	814,992	8,387	1,388,605
South America West	518,385	1,045,430	75,795	1,639,610
South Asia, General	-14,157	-	21,940	7,783
Southern Africa	254,579	883,879	32,125	1,170,583
SPEA, General	8,860	31,735	22,925	63,520
Spain	337,057	133,058	4,023	474,139
Sri Lanka	93,578	381,788	4,251	479,617
Switzerland, Austria and Hungary	-	59,703		59,703
Taiwan	55,201	117,310	121	172,631
Tanzania	172,670	287,050	32,242	491,962
Uganda	125,830	171,100	26,188	323,118
Zambia	415,403	156,395	14,534	586,331
Zimbabwe	515,478	345,722	24,111	885,311
Crisis Relief	-		3,236,283	3,236,283
Central Pension Scheme			369,943	369,943
Other International Operations	1,861,720		332,400	2,194,120
	18,271 265	22,388,575	5,123,317	45,783,158

COMMUNITY DEVELOPMENT PROJECTS

The Salvation Army thanks the donors listed below who, during 2011, assisted in its ministry to some of the world's most vulnerable people. This was accomplished through community development projects monitored by the International Projects and Development Services (IPDS) at IHQ. The projects included:

Combatting the HIV/Aids pandemic; developing savings and loans groups; promoting healthy communities; supporting educational services; improving access to safe water and sanitation; supporting social service programmes to the aged, the marginalised and the young; responding to disaster-hit areas.

Country	Donor	USD$*
Australia	Eastern Territory (AusAID)	1,003,709
Canada	CIDA	290,225
Denmark	*DANIDA (Denmark)	349,444
Netherlands	*Dutch Government MFS1 Programme	390,623
	*Goossens Trust	35,850
	*Langerer Trust	59,274
	*Van de Neut - de Vos Trust	265,380
	*Van Hoorn Legacy	306,344
Norway	(NORAD)	1,705,132
Sweden	*Disperse Foundation	115,000
	*Lakarmissionen	200,000
Switzerland	*Bread for All	276,266
	*Government grants	499,586
	*Government grants in kind	935,931
	*Swiss Solidarity	228,080
	*Various foundations	178,590
United Kingdom	*Conceptunet	8,147
	*Crown Agents (DFID)	265,551
	*Elizabeth Richards	211,833
	*Gwladys Bonsor	12,063
	*Individual charitable donations	100,974
	*Institute of Our Lady of Mercy	8,147
	*June Audrey Young	66,944
	*Lier Anne Rose	10,675
	*Roy William Armstrong	9,879
	*Sidney Hamilton	34,237
	*Spirax Sarco Group	12,212
USA	*NHQ (SAWSO)	3,569,345
	*USAID	1,372,622
TOTAL		**US$ 12,622,063**

*As per exchange rate at time amounts recorded by the IPDS at IHQ

ANGOLA COMMAND

Command leaders:
**Lieut-Colonels Célestin and
Véronique Pululu**

Officer Commanding:
Lieut-Colonel Célestin Pululu (1 Jul 2012)

General Secretary:
Major S. Edward Horwood (1 Jan 2011)

**Command Headquarters: Igreja Exército de Salvação,
Rua Olympia Macueira, Comuna de Palanca, Luanda, Angola**
Postal address: Caixa Postal 1656-C, Luanda, Angola
Tel: [00244] 928-570 867; email: ang_leadership@ang.salvationarmy.org

Salvation Army work in Angola was officially established in 1985. Having been part of the Congo (Kinshasa) and Angola Territory, it became a separate command on 1 March 2008.

In 1974, two officers originally from Angola but trained and serving in Congo (Kinshasa) entered Angola by Uige Province to commence Salvation Army meetings in that part of the country. In 1978, other Salvationists from Kinshasa met in Angola's capital, Luanda, and 'opened fire'. The Salvation Army was officially recognised by the Angola Government on 14 February 1992.

Zone: Africa
Country included in the command: Angola
'The Salvation Army' in Portuguese: Exército de Salvação
Languages in which the gospel is preached: Humbundu, Kikongo, Kimbundu, Lingala, Nchokwe, Ngangela,Portuguese

'ONE Army' was the focus for 2012 and events throughout the year brought Salvationists together to appreciate differences of language and culture.

A festival for timbrelists involved several corps and attracted a crowd of more than 400 people.

More than 1,000 women attended a Home League camp. During the Christmas season a Women's Ministries celebration attracted 500 women, including Junior Miss members. The all-day event included drama, singing, poetry, dance and timbrels. There was great joy as 110 women dedicated their lives to the Lord.

The International Day of Women featured a prominent march of witness in Luanda by Salvationists in their yellow, red and blue uniform clothing. More than 500 women gathered for a day of worship, fellowship and teaching.

During Holy Week, every corps in the command held daily meetings from Palm Sunday to Good Friday, followed by a special celebration on Easter Sunday. The two districts in Luanda joined together for a singing concert that involved young women from seven corps.

Angola Command

ANGOLA: A new corps opening at Makelele

Angola Command participated in the National Strategy for the Eradication of Polio. Hundreds of volunteers were trained to canvass their neighbourhoods encouraging new mothers to vaccinate their children and raising awareness of available treatments.

Angolan Salvationists are moving forward together as 'One Army', reaching their communities with the message of Jesus.

STATISTICS
Officers 44 (active 40 retired 4) **Cadets** 6
Envoys 8 **Employees** 34
Corps 19 **Outposts** 14 **Schools** 3
Senior Soldiers 3,063
Junior Soldiers 726

STAFF
Women's Ministries: Lt-Col Véronique Pululu
(CPWM) Maj Deborah Horwood (CSWM)
Maj Mamie Makuntima (HL)
Candidates: Maj Isabela Vuanza
Extension Officer: Capt Daniel Diantelo
Finance: Capt Sergio Nsumbu
Property: Capt Daniel Ngonga
Statistics: Capt Daniel Diantelo
Training: Maj Norbert Vuanza
Youth: Capt Timothée Lukanu
National BM: Sgt Raimond Nkuansambu
National SL: Sgt Kinavuidi

DISTRICTS
Luanda 1: Maj Joâo Mpembele;
 tel: (00244) 923-748074
Luanda 2: Maj Domingo Makuntima;
 tel: (00244) 923-742759

SECTIONS
Cabinda: Maj Antoine Kupesatel;
 tel: (00244) 924-868087
Uige: Capt Antonio Nsingi;
 tel: (00244) 924-118717
Zaire: Maj Joâo Batista Ndombele;
 tel: (00244) 934-657978

TRAINING COLLEGE
Rua Capola, Casa no 5/Bis, Q9/SAPU,
 Kilamba Kiaxi; tel: (00244) 926-842134

SECONDARY SCHOOL
Rua da Esquarda Intealao dos Moradores
 (Antigo Empromac), Bairo Hoji ha Yenda,
 Municipio do Cazenga;
 tel: (00244) 928-138191;
 Mr Paulo Mafuta (Director)

NZOANENE SCHOOL
Rua 21 de Janeiro, Bairo Rocha Pinto,
 Municipio de Maianga;
 tel: (00244) 923-607311;
 Sgt Nsumbu Mavug (Director)

SOCIAL SERVICES
Development and Emergencies
Moxico (vaccination and water supplies); Luena
1 Corps (polio project);Luao Corps (polio
project and water supplies)

AUSTRALIA NATIONAL SECRETARIAT

Offices: 2 Brisbane Ave, Barton, Canberra, ACT 2600

Postal address: PO Box 4256, Manuka, ACT 2603, Australia

Tel: [61] (02) 6273 3055

email: Kelvin.Alley@aue.salvationarmy.org

Two Christian Mission converts, John Gore and Edward Saunders, pioneered Salvation Army operations on 5 September 1880 in Adelaide. These were officially established on 11 February 1881 by the appointment of Captain and Mrs Thomas Sutherland. In 1921 the work in Australia was organised into Eastern and Southern Territories with headquarters in Sydney and Melbourne.

A National Secretariat serving the whole of Australia and funded jointly by both territories was established in 1987.

Periodicals: *Kidzone, Warcry*

THE Salvation Army's National Secretariat, strategically placed within view of the Parliament of Australia in Canberra, exists to represent the territorial commanders of the two Australian territories to ministers, members of parliament and officials of government departments. It also offers information and advice to Salvation Army leaders on government activities, especially in relation to social welfare policy.

During 2011/12, the National Secretary represented The Salvation Army in meetings on a variety of important issues. The reform of aged care, the introduction of carbon tax and possible implications for the charity sector, foreign aid funding, gambling reform, human trafficking and equal pay decisions impacting on welfare budgets were all addressed. Interaction with government focuses on the spiritual, moral, ethical and social welfare concerns and policy developments of both Salvation Army territories.

The National Secretary participates in national Salvation Army board meetings of Employment Plus – the Salvation Army's employment agency, 'Hope for Life' – suicide survivor support and the Indigenous Reference Group. Major Alley chairs the national public relations committee, which seeks to communicate 'one voice, one image' from The Salvation Army to the Australian people.

The Red Shield Defence Service continued its philanthropic support for personnel in the Australian Defence Services. Salvationists, known as 'Sallymen' served troops, going with them on manoeuvres – caring for their spiritual and material needs.

National Secretary: Maj Kelvin Alley

National Editorial Department:
95-99 Railway Rd, Blackburn, Vic 3130
(PO Box 479); tel: 03 8878 2303
National Editor-in-Chief: Capt Mal Davies

Red Shield Defence Services National HQ:
Gallipoli Barracks, Lloyd St, Enoggera Qld
4051 (PO Box 986, Ashmore City, Qld, 4214;
tel: (07) 3332 7788

Chief Commissioner: Lt Lyndley Fabre

AUSTRALIA EASTERN TERRITORY

Territorial leaders:
Commissioners James and Jan Condon

Territorial Commander:
Commissioner James Condon
(2 Apr 2011)

Chief Secretary:
Colonel Wayne Maxwell (1 Nov 2010)

Territorial Headquarters: 140 Elizabeth Street, Sydney, NSW 2000
Postal address: PO Box A435, Sydney South, NSW 1235, Australia
Tel: [61] (02) 9264 1711 (10 lines); website: www.salvos.org.au

Two Christian Mission converts having pioneered Salvation Army operations in Adelaide in September 1880, the work in Australia was organised into Eastern and Southern Territories in 1921, with headquarters for the Eastern Territory being set up in Sydney.

Zone: South Pacific and East Asia
States included in the territory: New South Wales, Queensland, The Australian Capital Territory (ACT)
Languages in which the gospel is preached: Cantonese, English, Korean, Mandarin
Periodicals: *Creative Ministry*, *Pipeline*, *Venue*, *Women in Touch*

THE territory embarked on a new mission strategy, Hubs, to unify all expressions of The Salvation Army within defined areas, under shared local leadership. Salvationists will be mobilised in holistic engagement with the community. Hub team leaders will oversee personnel as they work together in mission to bring the message of Jesus to their whole area.

In October 2011 at Parliament House, Canberra, the Army launched an initiative, 'Freedom Advocates' to improve Australia's response to human trafficking. Victims of human

trafficking who have been assisted by The Salvation Army in a safe house have become 'Freedom Advocates', trained to speak out and support other victims.

The territory produced a DVD, *'Still Standing'* and created a complementary website to support people who have been affected by recent natural disasters. The DVD tells the story of three Australians, each of whom was caught up in natural disasters and experienced heartbreaking loss as a result, but found a way to be 'still standing'. It is estimated that 30,000 free DVDs have already been distributed to households in affected areas and they will be an ongoing resource.

A new Salvation Army website called MySalvos provided reliable, up to date information on news events, resources and online interviews intended to assist people at the front line in ministry.

The outback flying service was developed through the donation of a second helicopter. The service operates from centres at Mt Isa in north Queensland and Dalby in south west Queensland. This ministry provides support to rural farmers and people in isolated settings.

The Salvation Army is meeting the challenge of multiculturalism with an initiative called 'Salvos plus Driving', an holistic driving school. Based at Auburn Corps in western Sydney, the school teaches driving skills, driver awareness and vehicle safety. Practical guidance is provided for residents new to Australia in how to buy a car and basic car maintenance. Clients of this programme not only learn to drive – they can also improve their language skills, learn about Australian society and hear about Jesus. This helps them engage with spiritual and faith issues.

Lieut-Colonel Don Woodland, a trauma-counselling pioneer, was awarded the Order of the Founder. As the Territorial Commander, Commissioner James Condon presented the award, he noted that the Colonel had previously received several other honours, including the Order of Australia for service including chaplaincy roles in military associations, including a 12-month deployment in Vietnam, the army reserve, fire brigade and the NSW fire service. He is the 19th person from the Australia Eastern Territory to receive the Order of the Founder.

Commissioner James Condon, TC, represented the territory at the official opening of The Salvation Army in the Solomon Islands. The two Australian territories are jointly contributing financially to the initial operations and partnering with Papua New Guinea Territory in mission, as PNG administers the Army's new work in the Solomon Islands.

STATISTICS

Officers 931 (active 531 retired 400)
  Cadets (1st Yr) 21 (2nd Yr) 22
  Employees 4,009
Corps 162 **Outposts/Plants/Missions** 21
  Social Centres/Programmes 271
  Community Welfare Services 185
  Thrift Stores/Charity Shops 236
Senior Soldiers 8,519
  Adherent Members 3,100
  Junior Soldiers 780
Personnel serving outside territory
  Officers 26 Layworkers 6

STAFF

Women's Ministries: Comr Jan Condon (TPWM)
  Col Robyn Maxwell (TSWM)
Business: Lt-Col Kerry Haggar
Personnel: Lt-Col David Godkin
Programme: Lt-Col Laurie Robertson
Territorial Legal Counsel: Maj Graeme Ross
Aged Care Plus: Ms Sharon Callister
Booth College: Maj Howard Smartt
Candidates: Majs David and Shelley Soper
Communications and Public Relations:
  Maj Bruce Harmer
Counselling Service: Maj Robyn Smartt
Emergency Services: Mr Norm Archer
Finance: Mr Ian Minnett
Information Technology: Mr Wayne Bajema

Mission and Resource Team:
Territorial Mission Directors (Corps):
Envoys Randall and Glenda Brown
Territorial Mission Director (Social): Maj
Paul Moulds
**Children's Ministry Team (Strategy
Development):** Capt Steven Smith
Property: Mr Peter Alward
Red Shield Defence Services: Lt Lyndley Fabre
**Salvation Army International Development
Office (SAID):** Maj John Rees
Salvationist Supplies: Mr Graham Lang
Salvos Stores: Mr Neville Barrett
Sydney Staff Songsters: S/L Graham Ainsworth

DIVISIONS

Australian Capital Territory and South NSW:
2-4 Brisbane Ave, Barton, ACT 2600;
PO Box 4224, Kingston, ACT 2604;
tel: (02) 6273 2211;
Lt-Cols Philip and Jan Cairns
Central and North Queensland: 54 Charles St,
North Rockhampton, QLD 4701; PO Box 5343,
Red Hill, Rockhampton, QLD 4701;
tel: (07) 4999 1999; Majs Kelvin and
Cheralynne Pethybridge
Newcastle and Central NSW: cnr of Union and
Parry Sts, PO Box 684, The Junction,
NSW 2291; tel: (02) 4926 3466;
Majs Gavin and Wendy Watts
North NSW: cnr Taylor and Beardy Sts,
PO Box 1180, Armidale NSW 2350;
tel: (02) 6771 1632; Majs Phillip and
Nancy McLaren
South Queensland: 342 Upper Roma St,
Brisbane QLD 4000; GPO Box 2210,
Brisbane, QLD 4001; tel: (07) 3222 6666;
Majs Mark and Julie Campbell
Sydney East and Illawarra: 61-65 Kingsway,
Kingsgrove NSW 2208; PO Box 740,
Kingsgrove, NSW 1480; tel: (02) 9336 3320;
Lt-Cols Peter and Jan Laws
The Greater West: 93 Phillip St, Parramatta,
NSW 2150; PO Box 66, Parramatta, NSW 2124;
tel: (02) 9635 7400; Majs Gary and Judith Baker

BOOTH COLLEGE

Bexley North, NSW 2207: 32a Barnsbury Grove,
PO Box 4063; tel: (02) 9502 0400

SCHOOL FOR OFFICER TRAINING

Bexley North, NSW 2207: 120 Kingsland Rd, PO
Box 4063; tel: (02) 9502 1777;

SCHOOL FOR CHRISTIAN STUDIES

Bexley North, NSW 2207: 32a Barnsbury
Grove, PO Box 4063; tel: (02) 9502 0432;

SCHOOL FOR LEADERSHIP TRAINING

Stanmore, NSW 2048: 97 Cambridge St;
tel: (02) 9557 1105; fax: (02) 9519 7319

SCHOOL FOR YOUTH LEADERSHIP

Lake Munmorah, NSW 2259: 42 Greenacre Ave;
tel: (02) 4358 8886; fax: (02) 4358 8882

HERITAGE PRESERVATION CENTRE

Bexley North, NSW 2207: 32a Barnsbury Grove,
PO Box 4063; tel: (02) 9502 0424;
email: AUEHeritage@aue.salvationarmy.org;
Maj Ken Sanz

EMPLOYMENT PLUS

National Support Office: Level 3, 10 Wesley Ct,
East Burwood, VIC 3151; tel: 136 123

TERRITORIAL MISSION AND RESOURCE TEAM – RECOVERY

Sydney: 140 Elizabeth St, Sydney, NSW 2000
(PO Box A435 Sydney South, NSW 1235)
tel: (02) 9212 4000; Maj David Pullen

BRIDGE PROGRAMME – ADDICTION RECOVERY
(Alcohol, other drugs and gambling)

Brisbane: Brisbane Recovery Services Centre
(acc men 73, women 13, detox unit 12,
halfway house 3)
Canberra: Canberra Recovery Services Centre
(acc men 38, halfway house 3)
Central Coast: Central Coast Recovery Services
Centre (acc women 36, halfway house 4)
Gold Coast: Recovery Services Centre,
(acc men 40, detox unit 11, women 16)
Hunter Region Recovery Services: Lake
Macquarie Recovery Services Centre:
Miracle Haven Bridge Programme (acc 78 men)
Endeavour Duel Diagnosis Bridge Programme
(acc 27 men)
Newcastle Bridge Youth and Family Drug and
Alcohol Support Programme (halfway house
acc 3 men)
Leura: Blue Mountains Recovery Services Centre,
(acc men 17, halfway house 3)
Nowra: Shoalhaven Bridge Programme
Sydney: William Booth House
Recovery Services Centre (acc men and
women 131)
Alf Dawkins Detoxification Unit (acc 10 men)
Townsville: Recovery Services Centre,
(acc men 30)
Recovery Services Women's out-Client
Service, Grace Cottage

SALVOS STORES

General Manager: Mr Neville Barrett
Head Office: 4 Archbold Rd, Minchinbury, NSW
2770; tel: (02) 9834 9030, fax: (02) 9677 1782
ACT and Monaro Area: (retail stores 8)
Brisbane Area: (retail stores 18)
Central Coast: (retail stores 5)
Eastern Sydney Area: (retail stores 18)
Gold Coast: (retail stores 13)
Illawarra Area: (retail stores 8)
Newcastle Hunter Area: (retail stores 11)
Townsville Area: (retail stores 3)
Western Sydney Area: (retail stores 19)

RURAL CHAPLAINS

ACT and South NSW; Atherton, Qld; Longreach,
QLD; Newcastle and Central NSW; North
NSW; South Queensland

AERIAL SERVICE

Flying Service Base: 10 Steelcon Pde,
Mt Isa, QLD 4825; tel: (07) 4749 3875;
South Queensland Flying Service: 7 Alfred St,
Dalby, QLD 4405: tel: (07) 4669 6393

CONFERENCE AND HOLIDAY HOUSES/UNITS

Collaroy, NSW 2097: The Collaroy Centre,
Homestead Ave, Collaroy Beach,
PO Box 11; tel: (02) 9982 9800 (office),
(02) 9982 6570 AH;
www.collaroycentre.org.au
Cairns, QLD 4870: 281-289 Sheridan St;
bookings through DHQ Rockhampton;
tel: (07) 4999 1999 (4 units)

*The folowing properties are booked through THQ
Property Dept contact: Elaine Whittaker; mob:
+61 4 11222905; email:
Elaine.Whittaker@aue.salvationarmy.org*
Budgewoi, NSW 2262: 129 Sunrise Ave;
(cottage acc 6)
Caloundra, QLD 4551: 4 Michael St, Golden
Beach; (house/sleeps 8)
Main Beach, QLD 4217: Unit 23 Ocean Park
Towers, 3494 Main Beach Pde;
(apartment/sleeps 4)
Margate, QLD 4019: 2 Duffield Rd;
(3 units/sleeps 3x6; 1x4)
Monterey, NSW 2217: 1/60 Solander St (acc 6)
Tugan, QLD 4224: 3/15 Elizabeth St;
(unit/sleeps 4)

RED SHIELD DEFENCE SERVICES

RSDS Administration: Queensland;
tel: (07) 3332 7788; mob: 0417 794 883

Adelaide Edinburgh Defence Precinct, SA
Darwin Robertson Barracks, NT
Gallipoli Barracks, Brisbane, QLD
Holsworthy Military Camp, Sydney, NSW
Lavarack Barracks, Townsville, QLD
Moorebank NSW School of Military Engineering
Puckapunyal Vic School of Armoured Trucks &
Artillery
Royal Military College, Duntroon, ACT
Singleton Infantry Centre, NSW

SOCIAL SERVICES
Residential Aged Care
Arncliffe, NSW (acc 114)
Balmain, NSW (acc hostel men 44)
Bass Hill, NSW (acc 104)
The Cairns Aged Care Centre, QLD
(acc 128)
Canowindra, NSW (acc 61)
Dee Why, NSW (acc 59)
Dulwich Hill, NSW (acc 63)
Erina, NSW (acc 169)
Goulburn, NSW (acc 103)
Merewether, NSW (acc 42)
Narrabundah, ACT (acc 67)
Parkes, NSW (acc 70)
Port Macquarie, NSW (acc 92)
Riverview, QLD (acc 167)
Rockhampton, QLD (acc hostel 50)

Independent Living Retirement Villages
Arncliffe, NSW (acc units 41)
Bass Hill, NSW (acc units 36)
Burwood, NSW (acc units 35)
Collaroy, NSW (acc units 108)
Erina, NSW (acc units 64)
Narrabundah, ACT (acc units 36)
Parkes, NSW (acc units 17)
Riverview, QLD (acc units 26)

Aged Care Respite and Day Care
Rivett, ACT (acc 15, respite day care 20)
Children's Services
(including Day Care and After School)
QLD; Carina, Gladstone, Slacks Creek
NSW: Macquarie Fields

Counselling Service
Head Office: Rhodes, NSW 2138:
15-17 Blaxland Rd, PO Box 3096;
tel: (02) 9743 4535
Batemans Bay, NSW; Brisbane, QLD;
Cairns, QLD; Campbelltown, NSW;
Canberra ACT; Cleveland, QLD; Goodna, QLD;
Gosford, NSW; Penrith, NSW; Stafford, QLD;
Sydney, NSW; Tuggeranong, ACT

THE SOLOMON ISLANDS: Fervent prayer is offered at an open-air meeting in February 2011, during a weekend of celebrations to mark the official opening of Army work on the islands

Moneycare Financial Counselling
Services: 22 Locations

Crisis and Supported Accommodation
(homelessness services)
Cairns North, QLD (acc men 29, women 20, women with children 10, patient transfer scheme men 5, women 5)
Campbelltown, NSW (women and children 4 units)
Carrington, NSW (acc men 21)
Faith Cottage, NSW (acc women and children 12)
Griffith, NSW (acc hostel 4, in community 6)
Leeton, NSW (acc family units 3)
Mount Isa, QLD (acc women and children 16)
Newcastle, NSW (acc single women, crisis hostel beds 8, community acc 24)
Oasis Youth Network, NSW
Southport, QLD (acc crisis beds women 20, women and children 7 units, single women medium-term 16)
Spring Hill, QLD (acc hostel 120 men, community units 9 men)
Spring Hill, QLD (acc 18 women)
Surry Hills, NSW 2010 (acc men's hostel 95 beds; IPU 30 beds; community housing 85) (acc women crisis hostel 10, medium-term beds 20, community units 10)
Tewantin, QLD (acc families, 16 places)
Toowomba, QLD (acc men's crisis and family community places)

Youth Services
Bundaberg, QLD (acc 6)
Canberra, ACT: Oasis Support Services, Oasis Youth Residential Service (acc crises 24)
Canley Vale, NSW
Fortitude Valley, QLD
Minchinbury, NSW
Newcastle, NSW: (acc 20)
Surry Hills, NSW (acc crises 13, medium-term 13, community 22)
Wyong, NSW

Intellectually Disabled Persons Services
Broken Hill, NSW
Toowong, QLD (acc in home community based lifestyle support 31 adults)
Toowoomba, QLD (acc 28)

Family Tracing Service
Brisbane, QLD 4000: 342 Upper Roma St, GPO Box 2210, Brisbane 4001; tel: (07) 3222 6661; fax: (07) 3229 3884
Sydney, NSW 2000: PO Box A435, Sydney South 1235; tel: (02) 9211 0277; fax: (02) 9211 2044
Special Search, tel: (02) 9211 6491; 1300 667 366 Australia Wide; fax: (02) 9211 2044

Telephone Counselling Service
Salvo Care Line: Five Dock, NSW; Brisbane, QLD

Crisis Line: 1300 36 36 22
Crisis Line: (07) 3831 9016

Counselling Service and Crisis Intervention
24hr Telephone Counselling Service:
  tel: (02) 8736 3297
Suicide Prevention and Crisis Intervention:
  tel: (02) 8736 3295
Salvo Youth Line and Crisis Intervention:
  tel: (02) 8736 3293

Domestic Violence Programme*
Chatswood, NSW

The territory also has 5 women's refuge centres which include accommodation for mothers and children.

Hostel for Students
Toowong, QLD (acc 66)

Employment Preparation and Skills Training
7 programmes

Court and Prison Ministry
6 programmes

Chaplains to Statutory Authorities
Fire and Rescue, NSW
New South Wales Rural Fire Service, NSW
Queensland Fire and Rescue Service, QLD

Community Welfare Service
22 locations

Campsie Corps, NSW, welcomes new soldiers to a growing fellowship which reflects the multi-cultural diversity of the community in this part of Australia Eastern Territory

AUSTRALIA SOUTHERN TERRITORY

Territorial leaders:
Commissioners Raymond and Aylene Finger

Territorial Commander:
Commissioner Raymond Finger
(1 Jul 2010)

Chief Secretary:
Colonel Peter Walker (1 Jul 2010)

Territorial Headquarters: 95-99 Railway Road, Blackburn 3130, Victoria

Postal address: PO Box 479, Blackburn 3130, Victoria, Australia
Tel: [61] (03) 8878 4500; email: Salvosaus@aus.salvationarmy.org;
website: www.salvationarmy.org.au

Two Christian Mission converts having pioneered Salvation Army operations in Adelaide in September 1880, the work in Australia was organised into Eastern and Southern Territories in 1921, with headquarters for the Southern Territory being set up in Melbourne.

Zone: South Pacific and East Asia
States included in the territory: Northern Territory, South Australia, Tasmania, Victoria, Western Australia
Languages in which the gospel is preached: Arabic and Nuer (Sudanese), Cantonese, English, Korean, Mandarin, local aboriginal languages
Periodicals: *On Fire*

THE Australia Southern Territory's mission intentions continued to be: transforming lives, caring for people, making disciples and reforming society.

The support of the general public was greatly appreciated, particularly after a number of local and international natural disasters at the beginning of 2011. Australians donated a total of nearly $4 million to five separate fundraising campaigns to support the Army's work in disaster relief. In May the annual Red Shield Neighbourhood Doorknock Appeal raised $4.5 million in the territory and tens of millions of dollars was donated by large corporations.

In June, a submission was made to a government inquiry into advertising standards. The Salvation Army strongly opposed the 'adultification and sexualisation of children' and 'the dehumanisation and objectification of women'. Such involvement in the formulation of government policy is clearly in accordance with the territory's stated mission intention 'to reform society'.

Also in June, Melbourne Staff Band toured the UK and played at a number of venues and also participated in celebrating the ISB's 120th anniversary. Highlights of the tour included playing at Buckingham Palace and the Royal Albert Hall.

On 14 August a large crowd gathered at 69 Bourke Street, Melbourne, when a fully restored and renovated Salvation Army building — home to Melbourne Corps Project 614 and formerly Melbourne City Temple Corps — was opened by Commissioner Raymond Finger, TC.

The building has been in use since 1894 and once served as the national headquarters for the Army's work throughout Australasia. The building houses the corps and a connected Life Centre, the territorial archives and heritage museum, the Melbourne Counselling Service and the Hamodava Café.

In September the territory launched a strategic business plan for the next four years. The key themes are 'strategy, strength and sustainability'. The plan offers the territory direction, alignment and focus, addressing the needs of social service programmes, corps, business units and administration.

October brought success as the Tasmania Division won top prize in the National Crime and Violence Prevention awards for its 'Safe From The Start' programme. The programme and accompanying resource kit is for those working with children aged 0-5 who have witnessed family or domestic violence and need help to deal with the trauma they have experienced.

In early December, the Friends of Christ session was commissioned and ordained as Salvation Army officers and they received their first appointments. On Saturday evening a concert called 'Our Christmas Gift' was enjoyed by more than 4,000 people, including many non-Salvationists. A nativity play featured live animals.

In March 2012, a new portrait of General Eva Burrows (Rtd) AC, by acclaimed portrait painter June Mendoza was unveiled. Ms Mendoza's first portrait of General Burrows was completed in 1993 to mark her retirement. The new portrait hangs at Melbourne Corps Project 614 where General Burrows soldiers and is active in corps life.

It was announced in April that a property had been purchased which will replace the present training college. Situated in Ringwood, close to THQ, the building will undergo extensive renovation. New accommodation units will be added during 2013. It is planned that the new college will be opened in 2014.

STATISTICS

Officers 929 (active 519 retired 410) **Cadets** (1st Yr) 19 (2nd Yr) 18 (10 in appointment) **Employees** 4,967

Corps 178 **Outposts** 9 **Social Centres/ Programmes** 253 **Salvos Stores** 213 **Community Support Centres** 149 **Outback Flying Service** 1

Senior Soldiers 7,759 **Adherent Members** 2,227 **Junior Soldiers** 1,185

Personnel serving outside territory Officers 23 Layworkers 1

STAFF

Women's Ministries: Comr Aylene Finger (TPWM) Col Jennifer Walker (TSWM)
Asst Chief Secretary: Lt-Col Ian Callander
Executive Support Officer: Capt Kerryn Roberts
Training Principal: Maj Geoff Webb
Catherine Booth College Co-ordinator: Maj James Weymouth
National Editor-in-Chief: Capt Malcolm Davies
Business Administration: Lt-Col Rodney Barnard
  Asst Sec for Business Admin and Overseas Development Secretary: Maj Sandra Maunder
  Asst Sec for Business and Territorial Legal Secretary: Capt Malcolm Roberts
  Audit: Mr Cameron Duck
  Communications and Fundraising: Maj Neil Venables
  Finance: Mr Gregory Stowe
  Information Technology: Mr Larry Reed
  Property: Mr David Sinden
  Salvationist Supplies: Mrs Karen Newton
  Salvos Stores: Mr Allen Dewhirst
Personnel: Lt-Col Vivien Callander
  Asst Sec for Personnel: Lt-Col Jennifer Barnard
  Candidates: Maj Judith Soeters
  Human Resources: Mr Stephen Webb
  Officer Development: Lt-Col Karyn Rigley
  Overseas Personnel: Maj Lorraine Hart
  Pastoral Care: Maj Graeme Faragher
Programme: Lt-Col Graeme Rigley
  Family Tracing: Maj Sophia Gibb
  Melbourne Staff Band: B/M Ken Waterworth
  Melbourne Staff Songsters: S/L Brian Hogg
  Mission Resources: Maj Bram Cassidy
  Social Justice: Maj Marion Weymouth
  Social Programme: Ms Netty Horton
  Spiritual Development: Maj Christine Faragher; Maj Marney Turner
  Youth: Capt Rowan Castle

DIVISIONS

Eastern Victoria: 347-349 Mitcham Rd, Mitcham, Vic 3132; tel: (03) 8872 6400; Majs Kelvin and Winsome Merrett
Melbourne Central: 1/828 Sydney Rd, North Coburg, Vic 3058; tel: (03) 9353 5200;
Northern Victoria: 65-71 Mundy Street, Bendigo, Vic 3550; tel: (03) 5440 8400; Majs John and Wendy Freind

South Australia: 39 Florence St, Fullarton, SA 5063; tel: (08) 8408 6900; Lt-Cols Ronald and Robyn Clinch
Tasmania: 27 Pirie St, New Town, Tas 7008; tel: (03) 6228 8400; Majs Richie and Gail Watson
Western Australia: 333 William St, Northbridge, WA 6003; tel: (03) 9260 9500; Maj Wayne Pittaway
Western Victoria: 102 Eureka St, Ballarat, Vic 3350; tel: (03) 5337 1300; Majs Bruce and Debra Stevens

REGION

Northern Territory: Level 2 Suite C, Paspalis Centre, 48-50 Smith St, Darwin, NT 0800; tel: (08) 8944 6000; Majs Gordon and Dianne Main

CATHERINE BOOTH COLLEGE

Parkville, Vic 3052: 303 Royal Parade; tel: (03) 9347 0299

SCHOOL FOR OFFICER TRAINING

Parkville, Vic 3052: 303 Royal Parade; tel: (03) 9347 0299

SCHOOL FOR CHRISTIAN STUDIES

Parkville, Vic 3052: 303 Royal Parade; tel: (03) 9347 0299

SCHOOL FOR LEARNING AND DEVELOPMENT

Blackburn Vic 3130: 95-99 Railway Road; tel: (03) 8878 4500
Parkville, Vic 3052: 303 Royal Parade; tel: (03) 9347 0299

ARCHIVES AND HERITAGE CENTRES

Melbourne, Vic 3000: Territorial Archives and Museum, 69 Bourke St, PO Box 18187, Collins St E, Melbourne, Vic 8003; tel: (03) 9639 3618
Nailsworth, SA 5083: Heritage Centre, 2a Burwood Ave; tel: (08) 8342 2545
Northbridge, WA 6003: Historical Society Display Centre, 3rd Floor, 333 William St; tel: (08) 9260 9500

CONFERENCE AND HOLIDAY CENTRES

Bicheno, Tas 7215: Holiday Home, 11 Banksia St; tel (03) 6228 8400
Busselton, WA 6280: Holiday Unit 2, 12 Gale St; tel: (08) 9260 9500

Retired General Eva Burrows, with a new portrait by June Mendoza, unveiled in March 2012

Cowes, Vic 3922: Holiday Unit,
2/28-30 McKenzie Rd; tel: (03) 5952 6497
Cullen Bay, NT: Holiday Unit, 602/26 Marina
Boulevard; tel: (08) 8944 6000
Daylesford, Vic 3460: Holiday Flat,
Unit 5/28, Camp St
Geelong, Vic 3219: Conference Centre, Adams
Court, Eastern Park; tel: (03) 5226 2121
George Town, Tas, 7253: Holiday Home,
36 Low Head Road; tel: (03) 6228 8400
Ocean Grove, Vic 3226: Holiday Home,
4 Northcote Rd
Victor Harbor, SA 5211:
Encounters Conference Centre,
22 Bartel Blvd;
tel: (08) 8552 2707
Weymouth, Tas 7252: Holiday Camp,
Walden St; tel: (03) 6331 6760 (acc 32)

EMPLOYMENT PLUS
National Office: Level 3, 10 Wesley Court,
Burwood, Vic 3151; tel: (03) 9847 8700;
Service Delivery Centres: New South Wales 25;
Queensland 16; South Australia 4;
Tasmania 3; Victoria 12; Western Australia 8
Enquiries: tel: 136 123

FLYING PADRE AND OUTBACK SERVICES
PO Box 43289, Casuarina, NT 0811;
tel: (08) 8941 2159 ; mob: 0428 342974
Capt David Shrimpton

RED SHIELD DEFENCE SERVICES
Edinburgh Defence Precinct Representative; tel:
(08) 8251 3834
Puckapunyal Representative;
tel: (03) 5793 1294
Robertson Barracks Representative;
tel: (08) 8935 6672

SALVOS STORES
Administration: 233-235 Blackburn Rd,
Mt Waverley 3149; tel: (03) 92105100
Stores: Northern Territory 6; South Australia
39; Tasmania 12; Victoria 110; Western
Australia 46

SOCIAL SERVICES
Aboriginal Ministry
Alice Springs, NT: Aboriginal Programme,
88 Hartley St; tel: (08) 8951 0207
Fullarton, SA: Divisional APY Lands Project,
39 Florence St; tel: (08) 8408 6900

Aged Care Non-Residential Services
Modbury, SA: Healthlink: 6 programmes

Alcohol, Other Drugs and Corrections
Adelaide, SA: Bridge Drug and Alcohol Outreach
Programme; All Victorious; Tea Tree Gully
(inc Police and Drug Court Diversion
Initiative)
Bendigo, Vic: Intensive Rehabilitation
Community Programme

Burnie, Tas: Drug and Alcohol Day Programme
with Outreach Geelong, Vic: Kardinia Alcohol
and Other Drugs (inc Geelong Withdrawal Unit)
Highgate, WA: The Bridge Programme, WA
Launceston, Tas: Bridge Outreach Service; Drug
and Alcohol Day Programme; Needle Syringe
Programme
New Town, Tas: Bridge Programme; Drug and
Alcohol Day Programme with Outreach;
XCELL Prison Support Service; Transitional
Housing Support for Prisoners
Stuart Park, NT: Drug and Alcohol Services

Asylum Seeker Support
Migrant and Refugee Services
Brunswick, Vic; Doveton, Vic

Bushfire Outreach Programme: Northern
Victoria Division
Seymour, Vic, Pathways Bushfire

Chaplaincy – Police, Fire and
Emergency Services
Perth, WA: FESA chaplain; tel: 0407 294 312
Winnellie, NT: Police, Fire and Emergency
Services Chaplain, tel: (08) 8999 4154

Child Care and Family Services
Balga, WA: Early Learning Centre
Ballarat, Vic: Karinya Occasional Childcare
Bendigo, Vic: Fairground Family Access
Programme
Blackmans Bay, Tas
Hobart, Tas: Communities for Children

Community Programmes
Adelaide, SA: Do Unto Others
Alice Springs, NT
Bendigo, Vic, Gravel Hill Community Garden
Bendigo, Vic, Hillskills Workshop; Berri, SA:
Riverland Community Services
Bordertown, SA: Thrift Shop
Darwin, NT: Darwin Life Centre
Hawthorn, Vic: Hawthorn Project, Homeless
Outreach Project; Community Connection
Project; Equity and Access Project
Mornington, Vic: PYFS, Reconnect Programme
Port Augusta, SA: Flinders and Riverland
Community Service
Rosebud, Vic: Peninsula Community Support

COMMUNITY SUPPORT SERVICES (CSS)
Northern Territory Region CSS
Alice Springs, Anula, Darwin, Katherine,
Palmerston

South Australia Division CSS
Adelaide, Berri, Cambelltown, Elizabeth East,
Gawler, Ingle Farm, Kapunda, Kilkenny,
Marion, Millicent, Modbury, Morphett Vale,
Mount Gambier, Murray Bridge, Noarlunga,
Norwood, Peterborough, Port Augusta, Port
Lincoln, Renmark, Seacombe Gardens, Tea
Tree Gully, Victor Harbour, Whyalla Norrie,
Wynn Vale

Tasmania Division CSS
('Doorway Centres')
Burnie, Clarence, Devonport, George Town,
Hobart, Launceston, Moonah, New Norfolk,
Scottsdale, Ulverstone

Victoria: Eastern Victoria Division CSS
Bairnsdale, Bentleigh, Berwick, Boronia,
Box Hill, Camberwell, Carrum Downs,
Cranbourne, Dandenong, Dingley Village,
Doncaster, Doveton, Ferntree Gully, Frankston,
Glen Waverley, Healesville, Leongatha, Moe,
Mooroolbark, Morwell, Noble Park, Oakleigh,
Pakenham, Ringwood, Rosebud, Rowville,
Sale, Traralgon, Warragul, Wonthaggi

Victoria: Melbourne Central Division CSS
Altona, Brunswick, Coburg North, Craigieburn,
Greensborough, Melbourne, Mill Park, Moonee
Ponds, Preston, Richmond, St Kilda, Sunbury,
Sunshine, Werribee

Victoria: Northern Victoria Division CSS
Beechworth, Benalla, Bendigo, Broadford,
Castlemaine, Echuca, Kyabram, Maryborough,
Mildura, Red Cliffs, Rochester, Seymour,
Shepparton, Swan Hill, Wangaratta, Wodonga

Victoria: Western Victoria Division CSS
Ballarat, Colac, Geelong, Hamilton,
Warrnambool

Western Australia Division CSS
(Doorways Centres)
Albany, Armadale, Balga, Bentley, Bunbury,
Busselton, Ellenbrook, Geraldton, Hamilton
Hill, Heathridge, Kalgoorlie, Karratha,
Kwinana, Mandurah, Merriwa, Morley,
Narrogin, Northam, Northbridge, Perth,
Rivervale, Rockingham
Swan View Inner City Financial Counsellors:
Balga, Morley, Perth, Rockingham

Court and Prison Services
Alice Springs, NT; Ballarat, Vic; Beechworth,

Vic; Bendigo, Vic; Broadmeadows, Vic;
Castlemaine, Vic; Dandenong, Vic; Deer Park,
Vic; Frankston, Vic; Geelong, Vic;
Hamilton, Vic; Heidelberg, Vic; Hobart, Tas;
Horsham, Vic; Korumburra, Vic; Latrobe
Valley, Vic; Launceston, Tas; Laverton North,
Vic; Manningham, SA; Melbourne, Vic;
Moorabbin, Vic; Northbridge, WA; Portland,
Vic; Ringwood, Vic; Sale, Vic; Sunshine, Vic;
Tatura (near Shepparton), Vic; Wangaratta,
Vic; Warrnambool, Vic; West Melbourne, Vic;
Wodonga, Vic; Yinnar, Vic

Crisis Services

Balga, WA: Family Accommodation Programme
Croydon, Vic: Gateways Crisis Services
Frankston, Vic: Peninsula Youth and Family
    Services Crisis Centre
Geraldton, WA: Family Crisis Accommodation
Ingle Farm, SA:
    Community Services Programme: Emergency
    Relief, Family Supported Accommodation,
    Youth Outreach Services, Substance Abuse
    Support Service For Youth, Communities For
    Children, Community Work Programme;
    Burlendi Youth Shelter; Muggy's
    Accommodation Service Youth Hostel and
    Outreach Services; Muggy's Accommodation
    (Southern Campus); Muggy's Country (Port
    Augusta, Port Pirie, Kadina, Port Lincoln,
    Whyalla, Wallaroo, Moonta Bay)
Leongatha, Vic: GippsCare Domestic Violence
    Outreach Service
New Town, Tas: SA Supported Housing
Perth, WA; Inner City Vulnerable Persons
    Programme
Rosebud, Vic: Crisis and Transitional Support
Salters Point, WA; Street to Home Programme
St Kilda, Vic: Access Health Service; Crisis
    Services

Drought Relief

Geraldton, WA; Horsham, Vic

Emergency Accommodation

Alice Springs, NT (acc service, single men, dual
    diagnosis)
Ballarat, Vic: Karinya (acc women with
    children 8)
Berri, SA: Riverland Community Services
    (acc 30)
Bunbury, WA (acc family units 2)
Burnie, Tas: Oakleigh House (acc 61)
Croydon, Vic: Gateways
Geelong, Vic: SalvoConnect (accommodation
    cross target 18)

Kardinia Women's Service (acc women
    with children 6)
Geraldton, WA (acc family units 3)
Horsham, Vic (acc family units 3, single 3)
Kalgoorlie, WA (acc family units 2)
New Town, Tas (acc 8, exit houses 4)
Sale, Vic (acc 6)

Emergency Family Accommodation

Berri SA: Riverland Community Services –
    Supported Accommodation for Families and
    Personal Support Programme
Burnie, Tas: Oakleigh House (acc 61)
Geelong, Vic: SalvoConnect
    (accommodation cross target 18)
Horsham, Vic: (acc family units 3, single 3)
New Town, Tas: McCombe House, Swanston St
    Family Units
Port Augusta, SA: (acc 65)
St Kilda, Vic: (acc 20)

Emergency Services

Darwin, NT; Eltham, Vic; Hobart, Tas; Malaga,
    WA; Pooraka, SA

Family Outreach (Community Programme)

Port Augusta, SA

Family Tracing Service

Adelaide, SA; tel: (08) 8408 6900
Darwin, NT; tel: (08) 8927 6499
Hobart,Tas; tel: (03) 6228 8404
Perth, WA; tel: (08) 9260 9500
Victoria and Inter-Territorial enquiries only:
    Blackburn, Vic; tel: (03) 8878 4500

Family Violence Services

Burnie, Tas
Darwin, NT: (acc 12)
Fullarton, SA: Bramwell House (acc 5 adults and
    children)
Geelong, Vic: Kardinia Women's Services;
Karratha, WA: (acc 16)
New Town, Tas: McCombe House
    (acc 12)
North Coburg, Vic: Crossroads (MAFVS)
Onslow, WA
Perth, WA: Graceville Centre (acc 43)
St Kilda, Vic: Crisis Services; Inner South
    Domestic Violence Services

Homeless or at Risk of Homelessness

Assertive Outreach Programme
Pathways Outreach Connections
Shepparton, Vic; Wangaratta, Vic
Wodonga, Vic

Hostels for Homeless Men
Abbotsford, Vic
Adelaide, SA: Towards Independence
  (acc 75)
Alice Springs, NT (acc 27)
Darwin, NT: Sunrise Centre (acc 26)
Mount Lawley, WA: Tanderra Hostel (acc 27)
North Melbourne, Vic: The Open Door
  (acc 45)
Perth, WA: Lentara (acc 55)
West Melbourne, Vic: Flagstaff Crisis
  Accommodation (acc 64)

Hostels/Housing for Homeless Youth
Fitzroy, Vic
Frankston, Vic: (4 houses residential youth
  services)
Kalgoorlie, WA (acc 12)
Karratha, WA (acc 8)
Lansdale, WA (acc 8)
Leongatha, Vic: GippsCare Cross-target
  Transitional Support
Mirrabooka, WA: Oasis House (acc 8)
Oaklands Park, SA: Muggy's
Pooraka, SA: Muggy's (acc 10)
Salisbury, SA: Burlendi (acc 8)
Shepparton, Vic:
  Brayton Youth and Family Services
St Kilda, Vic

Hostels for Intellectually Disabled Persons
Manningham, SA 5086: Red Shield Housing
  Network Services, (properties 310)

Mobile Ministry
Darwin, NT Flying Padre

Men's Support Service
Medina, WA

Parenting Partners Programme - Tasmania
Clarence, Moonah

Positive Lifestyle Counselling Services
Dandenong, Vic
Hobart, Tas
Ringwood, Vic

Red Shield Hostels
Alice Springs, NT (acc 27)
Darwin, NT (acc 64)

Rehabilitation Services
Adelaide, SA:

Bridge Drug and Alcohol Outreach
  Programme: 'IT' Futures Initiative (computer-
  based support programme) and Training
  Course; Sobering Up Unit; Supported
  Accommodation & Recovery Services (East);
  Supported Accommodation & Recovery
  Services (West); Co Morbidity Project and
  Warrondi Engage and Link (WEL) initiative)
Bendigo, Vic:
  Bendigo Bridge Intensive Community
  Rehabilitation Programme
Berrimah, NT: Drug and Alcohol Services (acc
  26); Sunrise Centre
Burnie, Tas: The Bridge Programme
Corio, Vic: Kardinia Alcohol and Other Drugs
  (inc Geelong Withdrawal Unit)
Gosnells, WA: Harry Hunter Adult Rehabilitation
Hawthorn, Vic: Aurora Women's
  Accommodation Service, Drug and Alcohol
  Counselling Programme; 4 Cs D&A
  Counselling
Highgate, WA: Bridge House (acc 27)
Launceston, Tas: The Bridge Programme
New Town, Tas: The Bridge Programme
Northbridge, WA: Bridge Non Residential
  Services
Preston, Vic: Bridgehaven (acc 15)
Ringwood, Vic: Drug Diversion Programme
St Kilda, Vic: The Bridge Centre
Swan Hill, Vic
The Basin, Vic: The Basin Centre
Warrnambool, Vic

Red Shield Housing Network Association
Hobart, Tas; Manningham, SA

Rural Outreach
Bendigo, Vic: Operation Living Waters,

Senior Citizens' Residences
Angle Park, SA (single units 90)
Clarence Park, SA (acc single units 10,
  double 4)
Footscray, Vic (acc 45)
Gosnells, WA (acc hostel 53, units 50)
Lenah Valley, Tas (acc units single 22, double 8)
New Town, Tas (acc res beds 77)

Social Housing – SASHS
Alice Springs, NT: Towards Independence
Anula, NT: Towards Independence Top End
Geelong, Vic: SalvoConnect
Hawthorn, Vic: EastCare Housing Services
Leongatha, Vic: Gippsland Region
Manningham, SA: Red Shield Housing Network
  Services

Morley, WA: Salvo Housing
New Town, Tas
Sunshine, Vic
Warragul, Vic
Warrnambool, Vic

Social Justice Advocacy
Adelaide, SA

Soup Run
Adelaide, SA
Marion, SA
Perth, WA

Telephone Counselling Service
Adelaide, SA: Financial Telephone Counselling;
    tel: 1800 025 539

Youth and Family Services
Adelaide, SA: Salvopsych
    (free counselling service)
Alice Springs, NT: Towards Independence
Box Hill, Vic:
    Intensive Case Management Service,
    Specialist Consulting and Assessment
    Service, Children in Residential Care

Education Support, Work and Recreation
    Programme with Education, Residential
    Youth Services, Leaving Care
    JJHIP (Juvenile Justice Housing Initiative
        Pathways)
Brunswick, Vic: Brunswick Youth Services
Hobart, Tas: Youth Therapeutic Residential Care
    Houses
Kew, Vic: The Hawthorn Project
Leongatha, Vic: GippsCare Adolescent
    Community Placement
Melbourne, Vic: Melbourne Counselling
Mornington, Vic:
    Peninsula Adolescent Community Placement,
    Peninsula High Risk Adolescent Programme,
    Peninsula Reconnect Programme
    Peninsula Home-based Care Services
Northbridge, WA
North Coburg, Vic: Transitional Support,
    Independent Living Programmes
    inc Youth Services, Transitional Support
    Accommodation for Youth (TSAY),
    Anger Management, Reconnect
Shepparton, Vic: Brayton Youth and Family
    Services

**These children are some of the first to participate in
Salvation Army activities in the Solomon islands**

BANGLADESH COMMAND

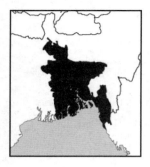

Command leaders:
Lieut-Colonels Alistair and Marieke Venter

Officer Commanding:
Lieut-Colonel Alistair Venter (1 Oct 2011)

General Secretary:
Major Leopoldo Posadas (1 Aug 2008)

Command Headquarters: House 365/2, Lane 6 (West), Baridhara DOHS, Dhaka 1216

Postal address: GPO Box 985, Dhaka 1000, Bangladesh

Tel: [880] (2) 8411755/6

email: banleadership@ban.salvationarmy.org

Work in Bangladesh began immediately after the Liberation War with Pakistan in 1971. Thousands of people moved from refugee camps in Calcutta, where Salvationists had served them, and a team of Salvationists accompanied them. A year earlier, relief operations had been carried out by The Salvation Army in East Pakistan (later Bangladesh) following a severe cyclone. On 21 April 1980, The Salvation Army was incorporated under the Companies Act of 1913. Bangladesh was upgraded to command status on 1 January 1997.

Zone: South Asia
Country included in the command: Bangladesh
'The Salvation Army' in Bengali: Tran Sena
Languages in which the gospel is preached: Bengali, English

2011 was a year of great celebration in Bangladesh. It marked 40 years of service and ministry for The Salvation Army and also 40 years of national independence. After a very difficult period for The Salvation Army in 2009 and 2010, the New Year brought a sense of joy and hope.

The highlight of the anniversary celebrations for the Army was the National Congress in September. The chief guests were Colonels Ross and Annette Gower (Zonal Under Secretary and Chaplain, IHQ). Held in Jessore, the congress was attended by more than 700 officers, soldiers, employees and friends of the Army. The theme for the congress and for the whole of 2011 was 'Rise Up', based on Isaiah 40:31. This reflected the prayers and hopes of Salvationists gathered to give thanks and celebrate God's goodness.

The congress included the retirement of and farewell salute to Lieut-Colonel Ethne Flintoff, who worked for many years in Bangladesh, the last nine as Officer Commanding. The Colonel served the people of Bangladesh tirelessly and with great wisdom. Her colleagues and friends will long remember her contribution to the mission of The Salvation Army in the command.

In October Lieut-Colonels Alistair and Marieke Venter were welcomed as Officer Commanding and Command President of Women's Ministries. The installation meeting was conducted by Commissioner Malcolm Induruwage, Territorial Commander, Sri Lanka.

Alongside evangelical work in Bangladesh, Salvation Army projects seek to address issues of major concern in the cities, towns and villages. These include human trafficking, adult literacy, economic empowerment, global warming, disaster preparedness and climate change. Many workshops and training events have taken place, aiming to empower people and equip communities to deal with the challenges of everyday life in Bangladesh.

Education and health remain high on the agenda, and while several schools continue to serve the poorest and most marginalised communities, the focus of health care is moving from formal clinic work to primary health care in communities.

Although Christians are in the minority in Bangladesh, Salvationists were privileged to gather with many thousands of fellow Christians for an Easter sunrise service to celebrate the resurrection of Jesus Christ. This joyful and exuberant gathering was held in the grounds of the Parliament building in Dhaka and Salvation Army officers participated in the service.

A highlight of 2012 was the annual officers' retreat, held at the BRAC Conference Centre during April. The 2012 theme, 'Build Together' based on Nehemiah 2:18 was launched at this event. It was a time of great fellowship, spiritual renewal, teaching and challenge for all the officers who serve in the command.

'Sally Ann', The Salvation Army's Trade for Hope initiative, continues to serve the communities of Bangladesh. More than 1,000 production workers throughout Bangladesh have been trained to produce high quality goods. These are mainly sold in other countries although there is a Sally Ann shop in Dhaka, with a coffee shop open to the public. Whilst Sally Ann encounters many challenges, its message of hope continues to make a difference to the people of Bangladesh.

STATISTICS
Officers 85 **Employees** 292
Corps 32 **Outposts** 12 **Institution** 1 **Schools** 4
  Clinics 3 **HIV/Aids Counselling Centres** 2
Senior Soldiers 1,885 **Adherent Members** 757
  Junior Soldiers 262

STAFF
Women's Ministries: Lt-Col Marieke Venter
  (CPWM) Maj Evelyn Posadas (CSWM)
Business Administration: Maj Cornelis
  de Ligt
Information Technology Development:
  Mr Palash (Paul) Baidya
Projects: Maj Jacoba de Ligt-Oosterheerd
Training: Maj Milon Dias
Youth and Candidates: Capt Stephen Baroi

DISTRICTS
Dhaka: House 365/2, Lane 6 (West), Baridhara
  DOHS, Dhaka 1216; tel: (0171) 1546012;
  Maj Alfred Mir

South Western: PO Box 3, By-Pass Rd, Karbala, Jessore 7400; tel: (0421) 68759; Maj Ganendro Baroi

TRAINING COLLEGE
Genda, Savar, Dhaka; tel: (02) 7712614

COMMUNITY WORK
Disaster Preparedness & Management Training Programme: South Western District
HIV/Aids Counselling Centres: Jessore, Old Dhaka
Income-generating Cooperatives: Jessore, Khulna
Training and Counselling Programme: Kalaroa, Satkhira

EDUCATIONAL WORK
Adult Education
Jessore, Khulna

Schools for the Hearing Impaired
Dhaka (acc 19); Jessore (acc 30)

Primary Schools
(pupils 610)
Jessore: Arenda, Bagdanga, Fatepur, Ghurulia, Kholadanga, Konejpur, Ramnagar, Sitarampur, Suro

Corps run Early Primary and Learning Centres
Gopalgonj: Bandhabari, Rajapur, Jessore: Arenda
Dinajpur: Shahargachchi
Joypurhat: Vanuikushalia, (total pupils 178)

Integrated Education for Sighted and Visually Impaired
Savar (pupils 346)

Vocational Training
Dhaka, Jessore, Khulna

MEDICAL AND DEVELOPMENT WORK
Urban Health and Development Project (UHDP)
Dhaka: Mirpur Clinic; Leprosy and TB Control Programmes

Community Health and Development Projects (CHDP)
Jessore
Khulna: Andulia Clinic
Village Clinics: Fatepur, Ghurulia, Konejpur, Ramnagar, Sitarampur

SOCIAL WORK
Integrated Children's Centre (ICC)
Savar (acc 42)

'SALLY ANN' PROGRAMME
'Sally Ann' Bangladesh Ltd (employees 26, production workers 980)
Managing Director: Lieut-Colonel Alistair Venter
General Manager: Mr Utpal Halder
Chair of Board: Maj Leopoldo Posadas
email: SallyAnn@ban.salvationarmy.com
website: www.sallyann.com
Shop: House 365/2, Lane 6 (West), Baridhara DOHS, Dhaka 1216;
Satu Barua (shop manager)

BANGLADESH:
A literacy programme gives these women the skills to improve life for their families

BRAZIL TERRITORY

Territorial leaders:
**Commissioners Oscar and
Ana Rosa Sánchez**

Territorial Commander:
Commissioner Oscar Sánchez
(1 Aug 2010)

Chief Secretary:
Lieut-Colonel Alex Nesterenko (1 Mar 2012)

**Territorial Headquarters: Rua Juá 264 - Bosque da Saúde,
04138-020 São Paulo-SP**

Postal address: Exército de Salvação; Caixa Postal 46036, Agência Saúde
04045-970 São Paulo-SP, Brazil

Tel: [55] (011) 5591 7070

email: BRA_Leadership@bra.salvationarmy.org;

website: www.exercitodesalvacao.org.br

Pioneer officers Lieut-Colonel and Mrs David Miche unfurled the Army flag in Rio de Janeiro on 1 August 1922. The Salvation Army operates as a national religious entity, Exército de Salvação, having been so registered by Presidential Decree 90.568 of 27 November 1984. All its social activities have been incorporated in APROSES (Assistência e Promoção Social Exército de Salvação) since 1974 and have had Federal Public Utility since 18 February 1991.

Zone: Americas and Caribbean
Country included in the territory: Brazil
'The Salvation Army' in Portuguese: Exército de Salvação
Language in which the gospel is preached: Portuguese
Periodicals: *O Oficial (The Officer)*, *Ministério Feminino – Devocionais*, *Rumo with Revista Salvacionista*

IN May 2011 many churches united in São Paulo for a great celebration of the anniversary of John Wesley's baptism in the Holy Spirit. The day was marked in the São Paulo State Legislative Assembly by the reading of a proclamation signed by church leaders, including Commissioner Oscar Sánchez, TC. The document called for the ideals of holiness and the pursuit of human dignity to be reflected in the promulgation of new laws, coupled with an emphasis on ethical conduct in political action. To conclude this special day The Salvation Army Territorial Band played the Brazilian national anthem at the Festival of Celebration in the Ibirapuera Stadium. Almost 10,000 people participated, giving thanks for the ministry and holiness teaching of John Wesley.

Young Salvationists from Torre Corps, North East Division, launched the film *'Rota sem Fim'(Unending Path)* after three and a half years of hard work and many challenges, including equipment being stolen on four occasions! The production involved 74 participants and a detailed script. The recording, available on YouTube, seeks to show the lifestyle of young people from marginalized communities and their opportunities to change direction in life.

The ministry of the Home League in the territory has helped many women to experience the grace of God. A compulsive gambler, heavily in debt, arrived at a local corps desperate for help. Another woman, learning of her husband's infidelity, threatened him with a gun. Since beginning to attend the Home League the lives of both women have been transformed and they have testified that God is at work in their personal situations.

A community care ministries team in Rio de Janeiro Division has engaged in ministry to sex workers on the streets around the corps premises. This year the team reached out with special invitations for them to attend a Christmas dinner in the corps hall. 'Legatto', a professional vocal group, presented a Christmas Cantata during this successful event.

Several corps in the territory have become increasingly aware of the need to be relevant in the context of Brazilian culture. For the past six years in the extreme south of Brazil two corps have joined in civic celebrations to commemorate Brazilian Independence Day on 7 September. Local people have welcomed The Salvation Army as the band from Livramento has participated in the march. This year Salvationist musicians were given the opportunity to train band members from a local government school and some of the children now attend Sunday school. Another corps in the division used regional music and food in an evangelistic campaign. One of the soldiers wrote, 'With Jesus in our hearts, we are making the most of all the opportunities that come our way to intertwine The Salvation Army and the Gaucho culture, to win souls and show the people that there is salvation in Christ'.

STATISTICS

Officers 178 (active 133 retired 45)
   Cadets (1st Yr) 7 (2nd Yr) 4
   Employees 338
Corps 43 **Outposts** 9 **Social Institutions** 32
Senior Soldiers 1,835 **Adherent Members** 96
   Junior Soldiers 495
Personnel serving outside territory Officers 6

STAFF

Women's Ministries: Comr Ana Rosa Sánchez (TPWM) Lt-Col Luz Nesterenko (TSWM) Maj Iolanda Camargo (TSAWM & TSLM)
Personnel: Maj Verônica Jung
Communications: Maj Téofilo Chagas
Editor-in-Chief: Maj Paulo Soares
Education: Majs Wilson and Nara Strasse
Finance: Capt Ricardo Iung
Legal/Property: Maj Giani Azevedo
Music: Maj Paulo Soares
National Band: B/M João Carlos Cavalheiro
National Songsters: S/L Vera Sales
Projects: Maj Joan Burton
Social: Mrs Marilene Oliveira
Training: Maj Wilson Strasse
   Maj Nara Strasse
Youth and Candidates: Maj Elisana Lemos

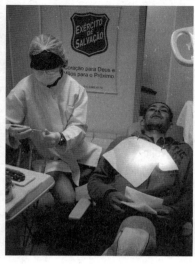

BRAZIL: During 2011 treatment was available at the Army's itinerant dental clinic 'Sorrindo com Cristo' which served needy communities

DIVISIONS

North East: Rua Conde de Irajá, nº 165, 50710-310 Recife – PE; tel: (81) 3228-4740; Majs Maruilson and Francisca Souza

Paraná and Santa Catarina: Rua Mamoré 1191, 80810-080 Curitiba, PR; tel/fax: (041) 3336-8624; Majs Alberto and Maria José Serem

Rio de Janeiro and Minas Gerais and Centre West: Rua Visconde de Santa Isabel no 20, salas 712/713, 20560-120, Rio de Janeiro – RJ; tel/fax: (21) 3879-5594; Majs Edgar and Sara Chagas

Rio Grande do Sul: Rua Machado de Assis 255, 97050-450, Santa Maria, RS; tel/fax: (55) 3026-1935; Majs Adão and Vilma Gonçalves

São Paulo: Rua Taguá 209, Liberdade 01508-010, São Paulo – SP; tel/fax: (11) 3207-3402; Majs Márcio and Jurema Mendes

TRAINING COLLEGE

Rua Juá 264, Bosque da Saúde, 04138-020, São Paulo – SP; tel: (11) 5071-5041

SOCIAL WORK
Centre for Street Children
São Paulo: Projeto Três Corações (acc 40)

Community Centres
These centres have after-school programmes for children at risk
Carmo do Rio Claro: 'Recanto da Alegria' (acc 40)
Cubatão: 'Vila dos Pescadores' (acc 300)
Curitiba: Socio-Educacional Support Unit for Children
Pelotas: Pelotas Integrated Centre (acc 45)
Prudente de Moraes: Arco Verde Integrated Family Centre (acc 40)
Recife: Torre Integrated Community Centre (acc 250)
Rio de Janeiro:
    Socio-educational Centre (acc 40)
    Nova Divinéia Community Centre (acc 50)
São Paulo: Projeto Três Corações (acc 40)
Uruguaiana: Integrated Centre Uruguaiana (acc 65)

Early Childhood Education Centres and Crechés
Carmo do Rio Claro: 'Recanto da Alegria' (acc 100)
Guarulhos: (acc 50)
Itaquaquecetuba: (acc 30)
Pelotas: Pelotas Integrated Centre (acc 15)
Recife: Torre Integrated Community Centre (acc 50)
São Gonçalo: 'Arca de Noé' (acc 150)

São Paulo: Ranchinho do Senhor (acc 60)
Suzano: Lar das Flores (acc 245)

Home for Street Children
Curitiba: (acc 11)

Mother and Baby Home (adolescent mothers)
São Paulo: (acc mothers 10, babies 10)

Old People's Home
Campos do Jordão: (acc 24)

Prison Work
Piraí do Sul and Carmo do Rio Claro

Social Services Centres
Cubatão, Curitiba, Guarulhos,Itaquaquecetuba, Joinville, Paranaguá, Pelotas, Porto Alegre, Prudente de Moraes, Recife: (acc 250), Rio de Janeiro: 2 centres, São Paulo, Uruguaiana

Students' Residence
Brasília: (acc 14)

Territorial Camp
Suzano: Rua Manuel Casanova 1061, 08664-000, Suzano – SP; tel: (11) 4746-3843

Thrift Stores
São Paulo: 2
Rio de Janeiro: 1

Vocational Training – Adolescents and Youth
Arco Verde: 'Arco Verde' Integrated Family Centre (acc 30)
Joinville: João de Paula Integrated Centre (acc 90)
Paranaguá: Honorina Valente Integrated Centre (acc 200)
Recife: Torre Integrated Community Centre (acc 120)

BRAZIL: The celebration in May 2011 when churches from the Wesleyan tradition, including The Salvation Army, united at a service in São Paulo

CANADA AND BERMUDA TERRITORY

Territorial leaders:
Commissioners Brian and Rosalie Peddle

Territorial Commander:
Commissioner Brian Peddle
(1 Jul 2011)

Chief Secretary:
Colonel Floyd J. Tidd (1 Mar 2010)

Territorial Headquarters: 2 Overlea Blvd, Toronto, Ontario M4H 1P4, Canada

Tel: [1] (416) 425-2111; email: can_leadership@can.salvationarmy.org;
websites: www.salvationarmy.ca; www.salvationist.ca

There are newspaper reports of organised Salvation Army activity in Toronto, Ontario, in January 1882, and five months later the Army was reported holding meetings in London, Ontario. On 15 July the same year, Major Thomas Moore, sent from USA headquarters, established official operations. In 1884 Canada became a separate command. The League of Mercy originated in Canada in 1892. An Act to incorporate the Governing Council of The Salvation Army in Canada received Royal Assent on 19 May 1909.

The work in Newfoundland was begun on 1 February 1886 by Divisional Officer Arthur Young. On 12 January 1896 Adjutant (later Colonel) Lutie Desbrisay and two assistant officers unfurled the flag in Bermuda.

Zone: Americas and Caribbean
Countries included in the territory: Bermuda, Canada
Languages in which the gospel is preached: Creole, English, French, First Nations languages (Gitxsan, Nisga'a, Tsimshian), Korean, Lao, Portuguese, Spanish, Thai
Periodicals: *Edge for Kids, Faith & Friends, Foi & Vie, Salvationist*

'CREATING the Compassionate Heart'– a territorial social services conference – was held in March 2011 in Mississauga, Ontario, as 355 Army delegates addressed issues such as human trafficking, affordable housing and restorative justice. Other significant conferences during the year included a Rural Ministries Conference in Nova Scotia and officers attended a Brengle Institute in Ontario, to study the doctrine of holiness.

In May, the territory emphasised the Dignity Project, a public awareness campaign to reinforce the principle that everyone deserves the fundamental right of human dignity. Declaring May as 'Dignity Month', the Army organized 'Dignity Speaks', at Toronto's Harbour Light Ministries, to showcase the Army's work with the marginalized. Also in May the Army re-opened The Homestead after a $3.5 million renovation. This facility is also known as the Alice M. Walter House residential recovery programme, for women struggling with substance abuse. During the year a variety of other innovative programmes were commenced including the New Hope Clinic for vulnerable people in downtown St John's, Newfoundland; Cedar Place Cèdre shelter for women and families in Sudbury, Ontario and a non-residential addictions counselling clinic in Chilliwack, British Columbia.

In June, the Ambassadors of Holiness Session was commissioned and ordained as Salvation Army officers in Winnipeg. The session comprised nine cadets from Canada and Bermuda Territory, and two from India Eastern Territory. At the newly named Booth University College, 41 degrees and certificates were conferred at spring convocation.

Booth University College also hosted a community forum in April called 'Homelessness in the City: Through the Eyes of Justice and Hope'. A similar event 'Let There be Light', held in Kingston, Ontario in May, included sessions on human trafficking. The guest speaker was Commissioner M. Christine MacMillan, the then Director of the International Social Justice Commission.

The Canadian Staff Band visited London, England in June, along with seven other staff bands to join with the International Staff Band to celebrate its 120th anniversary. The tour included a week long campaign in The Netherlands and Germany and a united march of witness to Buckingham Palace, London.

On 6 July at Jackson's Point Conference Centre, General Linda Bond installed Commissioners Brian and Rosalie Peddle as Territorial Commander and Territorial President of Women's Ministries. Commissioner Brian Peddle has made the International Vision statement, 'One Army, One Mission, One Message', the key priority as he leads the territory.

Jackson's Point was also the venue for the 43rd National Music Camp in August and featured guests Tom and Heather Hanton (USA Eastern Territory). Main studies were brass band, women's chorus, worship team, media and drama and other activities included creative writing, hip-hop dancing, social justice and timbrels.

In October 42 officers visited the Holy Land for a pilgrimage designed to promote the spiritual enrichment of officers and foster an increase in biblical knowledge.

The Holy Spirit breathed renewed hope, passion and commitment into Bermudian Salvationists during the divisional congress in November. The weekend was led by Commissioners Brian and Rosalie Peddle and focused on the doctrine of holiness. Salvationists shared the gospel through a march of witness.

In January, the Territorial Children and Youth Ministries Department launched 'Ready to Serve', a junior discipleship programme resourced through DVDs, classroom assignments and website interaction. It is hoped that 'Ready to Serve' will encourage young people in their faith and help them engage in mission.

STATISTICS

Officers 1,746 (active 817 retired 929) **Cadets** (1st Yr) 14 (2nd Yr) 18 **Employees** 9,217
Corps 312 **Outposts** 9 **Institutions** 118 **University College** 1
Senior Soldiers 18,090 **Adherent Members** 39,272 **Junior Soldiers** 2,533
Personnel serving outside territory Officers 33 Layworkers 5

STAFF

Women's Ministries: Comr Rosalie Peddle (TPWM) Col Tracey Tidd (TSWM)
Personnel: Lt-Col Sandra Rice
  Officer Personnel Dept: Maj Eddie Vincent
Leadership Development: Maj Mona Moore
Employee Relations: Mrs Josie DelPriore
Programme: Lt-Col Junior Hynes
Business: Lt-Col Neil Watt
Asst Chief Sec: Maj Alison Cowling
Corps Ministries: Maj Fred Waters
Editor-in-Chief and Literary Sec: Maj James Champ
Finance: Mr Paul Goodyear
Information Technology: Mr Robert Plummer
Legal: Mr Bryan Campbell
Music and Gospel Arts/Staff Band: Maj Kevin Metcalf
Property: Mr Michael Gilbert
Public Relations and Development: Mr Graham Moore
Recycling Operations: Mr John Kershaw
Social: Mrs Mary Ellen Eberlin
Supplies/Purchasing: Maj Michael LeBlanc
College for Officer Training: Maj James Braund
Booth University College – Principal: Dr Donald Burke
Youth & Candidates: Majs Keith and Shona Pike

DIVISIONS

Alberta and Northern Territories: 9618 101A Ave NW, Edmonton, AB T5H 0C7; tel: (780) 423-2111; Majs Ronald and Donna Millar
Bermuda: PO Box HM 2259, 76 Roberts Ave, Hamilton, HM JX Bermuda; tel: (441) 292-0601; Majs Shawn and Brenda Critch

British Columbia: 103-3833 Henning Dr, Burnaby, BC V5C 6N5; tel: (604) 299-3908; Majs Larry and Velma Martin
Maritime: 282-7071 Bayers Rd, Halifax, NS B3L 2C2; tel: (902) 455-1201; Majs Douglas and Jean Hefford
Newfoundland and Labrador: 21 Adams Ave, St John's, NL A1C 4Z1; tel: (709) 579-2022/3; Lt-Cols Alfred and Ethel Richardson
Ontario Central-East: 1645 Warden Ave, Scarborough, ON M1R 5B3; tel: (416) 321-2654; Lt-Cols Dirk and Susan van Duinen
Ontario Great Lakes: 371 King St, London, ON N6B 1S4; tel: (519) 433-6106; Lt-Cols Lee and Deborah Graves
Prairie: 204-290 Vaughan St, Winnipeg, MB R3B 2N8; tel: (204) 946-9101; Majs Wayne and Deborah Bungay
Quebec: 1655 Richardson St, Montreal, QC H3K 3J7; tel: (514) 288-2848; Majs Brian and Anne Venables

COLLEGE FOR OFFICER TRAINING

100-290 Vaughan St, Winnipeg, MB R3B 2N8; tel: (204) 924-5606

BOOTH UNIVERSITY COLLEGE

447 Webb Pl, Winnipeg, MB R3B 2P2; tel: (204) 947-6701/6702/6950

ETHICS CENTRE

447 Webb Pl, Winnipeg, MB R3B 2P2; tel: (204) 957-2412; email: ethics_centre@can.salvationarmy.org; Dr James Read

SALVATION ARMY ARCHIVES

Archives: 26 Howden Rd, Scarborough, ON M1R 3E4
Museum: 2 Overlea Blvd, Toronto, ON M4H 1P4; tel: (416) 285-4344
email: Heritage_Centre@can.salvationarmy.org
Col John Carew

NATIONAL RECYCLING OPERATIONS

2 Overlea Blvd, Toronto, ON M4H 1P4; tel: (416) 425-2111; fax: (416) 422-6167
Central & Southwestern Ontario Region: 2360 South Service Rd W, Oakville, ON L6L 5M9; tel: (905) 825-9208
Western Region: 1-111 Inksbrook Dr, Winnipeg, MB R2R 2V7; tel: (204) 953-1508

SOCIAL SERVICES (UNDER THQ)
Hospitals (public)
Rehabilitation

Montreal, QC H4B 2J5, Catherine Booth
Hospital, 4375 Montclair Ave;
tel: (514) 481-2070

General (B Class)

Windsor, ON N9A 1E1, Hotel-Dieu Grace
Hospital, 1030 Ouellette Ave;
tel: (519) 973-4444

Complex Continuing Care/ Rehabilitation/Palliative Care

Toronto, ON M4Y 2G5, Toronto Grace Health
Centre, 650 Church St; tel: (416) 925-2251

Family Tracing Services

2 Overlea Blvd, Toronto, ON M4H 1P4;
tel: (416) 422-6219

SOCIAL SERVICES (UNDER DIVISIONS)
Hospital Chaplaincy

Toronto, ON M1W 3W3 Scarborough Hospital,
3030 Birchmount Rd; tel: (416) 495-2536
Winnipeg, MB R3J 3M7 Winnipeg Grace
Hospital, 300 Booth Dr; tel: (203) 837-0515

Hospices

Calgary, AB T2N 1B8, Agape Hospice,
1302 8th Ave NW; tel: (403) 282-6588 (acc 20)
Regina, SK S4R 8P6, Wascana Grace Hospice,
50 Angus Rd; tel: (306) 543-0655 (acc 10)
Richmond, BC V6X 2P3, Rotary Hospice, 3111
Shell Rd; tel: (604) 244-8022 (acc 10)

Adult Services to Developmentally Handicapped

Fort McMurray, AB T9H 1S7, 9919 MacDonald
Ave; tel: (780) 743-4135
Hamilton, ON L8S 1G1, Lawson Ministries,
1600 Main St W; tel: (905) 527-6212 (acc 21)
Toronto, ON M4K 2S5, Broadview Village, 1132
Broadview Ave (Residential Living/Day
Programming for Developmentally
Handicapped Adults);tel: (416) 425-1052;
(acc 160)
Winnipeg, MB R3A 0L5, 324 Logan Ave;
tel: (204) 946-9418

Adult Services Mental Health

St John's, NL A1E 1C1, Wiseman Centre,
714 Water St; tel: (709) 739-8355/8 (acc 30)
Toronto, ON M8Z 6A4, Booth Support Services,
Unit 9A - 1020 Islington Ave,
tel: (416) 255-7070

CANADA: Ministries to young people (l) at Camp Starrigan and care for an elderly resident (r) at Dinsdale Personal Care Home

Toronto, ON M5A 2R5, Maxwell Meighen
Centre Primary Support Unit, 135 Sherbourne
St, tel: (416) 366-2733

Sheltered Workshops
Toronto, ON M8Z 6A4, Booth Packaging and
Supportive Services, Unit 9A - 1020 Islington
Ave, tel: (416) 255-7070
Toronto, ON M3A 1A3, PLUS Program,
150 Railside Rd; tel: (416) 693-2116 (acc 44)

Addictions and Rehabilitation Centres (Alcohol/Drug Treatment)
Men
Calgary, AB T2G 0R9, 420 9th Ave SE;
tel: (403) 410-1150 (acc 34)
Chilliwack, BC V2P 2M3, Fireside Addiction
Services, #17 – 45966 Yale Road (Cascade
Centre), tel: (604) 702-9879
Edmonton, AB T5H 0E5, 9611 102 Ave NW;
tel: (780) 429-4274 (acc 158)
Glencairn, ON L0M 1K0, PO Box 100;
tel: (705) 466-3435/6 (acc 35)
Halifax, NS B3K 3A9, 2044 Gottinggen St;
tel: (902) 422-2363 (acc 16)
Hamilton, Bermuda HM JX, PO Box HM 2238;
tel: (441) 292-2586 (acc 10)
Kelowna, BC V1X 2Z5, 200 Rutland Road S;
tel: (250) 860-3232
Kingston, ON K7L 1C7, 562 Princess St;
tel: (613) 546-2333 (acc 24)
Montreal, QC H3J 1T4, 800 rue Guy;
tel: (514) 932-2214 (acc 55)
Moose Jaw, SK S6H 0Y9, Hope Inn
175 – 1st Avenue NE;
tel: (306) 692-2844 (acc 4)
Ottawa, ON K1N 5W5, 171 George St;
tel: (613) 241-1573 (acc 25)
Sudbury, ON P3E 1C2, 146 Larch St;
tel: (705) 673-1175/6 (acc 45)
Toronto, ON M5B 1E2, 160 Jarvis St;
tel: (416) 363-5496 (acc 85)
Vancouver, BC V6A 1K8, 119 East Cordova St;
tel: (604) 646-6800 (acc 70)
Victoria, BC V8W 1M2, 525 Johnson St;
tel: (250) 384-3396 (acc 109)
Williams Lake, BC V2G 1R3, Non-Residential
Substance Abuse Program, 267 Borland St,
tel: (250) 392-2429
Winnipeg, MB R3N OJ8, 180 Henry Avenue;
tel: (204) 946-9401 (acc 32)

Women
Hamilton, New Choices, ON L8S 2H6, 431
Whitney Ave; tel: (905) 522-5556 (acc 15)
Toronto, ON M5R 2L6, The Homestead,

78 Admiral Rd; tel: (416) 921-0953 (acc 18)
Vancouver, BC V6P 1S4, The Homestead, 975
57th Ave W; tel: (604) 266-9696 (acc 32)

Residential Services (Hostels, Emergency Shelters)
Men
Barrie, ON L4M 3A5, Bayside Mission Centre,
16 Bayfield St; tel: (705) 728-3737 (acc 32)
Brampton, ON L6T 4X1, Wilkinson Road
Shelter, 15 Wilkinson Rd; tel: (905) 452-1335
(acc 85)
Brantford, ON N3T 2J6, Booth Centre,
tel: (250) 287-3720 (acc 27)
Chilliwack, BC V2P 2N4, 45746 Yale Rd;
tel: (604) 792-0001 (acc 11)
Fort McMurray, AB T9H 1S7, 9919 MacDonald
Ave; tel: (780) 743-4135 (acc 32)
Halifax, NS B3K 3A9, 2044 Gottingen St;
tel: (902) 422-2363 (acc 49)
Hamilton, ON L8R 1R6, Booth Centre,
94 York Blvd; tel: (905) 527-1444 (acc 99)
Langley, BC V3A 0A5, Gateway of Hope,
5787 Langley-By-Pass; tel: (604) 514-7375
(acc 55)
Miramichi, NB E1V 1Y6, 231 Pleasant St;
tel: (506) 622-7826
Montreal, QC H3J 1T4, Booth Centre,
880 rue Guy; tel: (514) 932-2214 (acc 195)
Nanaimo, BC V9R 4S6, 19 Nicol St;
tel: (250) 754-2621 (acc 31)
New Westminster, BC V3L 2K1, 32 Elliot St;
tel: (604) 526-4783 (acc 33)
Ottawa, ON K1N 5W5, Booth Centre,
171 George St; tel: (613) 241-1573 (acc 213)
Pembroke, Bermuda HM JX, 5 Marsh Lane;
tel: (441) 295-5310 (acc 83)
Penticton, BC V2A 5J1, 2469 South Main St;
tel: (250) 492-6494 (acc 20)
Prince Rupert, BC V8J 1R3, 25 Grenville Court;
tel: (250) 624-6180 (acc 20)
Quebec City, QC G1R 4H8, Hotellerie,
14 Côte du Palais; tel: (418) 692-3956 (acc 60)
Regina, SK S4P 1W1, 1845 Osler St;
tel: (306) 569-6088 (acc 75)
Regina, SK S4P 1W1, Waterston Centre,
1865 Osler St; tel: (306) 566-6088 (acc 40)
Richmond, BC V6X 2P3, Richmond House
Emergency Shelter, 3111 Shell Rd;
tel: (604) 276-2490 (acc 10)
Saint John, NB E2L 1V3, Centre of Hope,
36 St James St; tel: (506) 634-7021 (acc 75)
St Catharine's, ON L2R 3E7, Booth Centre,
184 Church St; tel: (905) 684-7813 (acc 21)
Saskatoon, SK S7M 1N5, 339 Avenue CS;
tel: (306) 244-6280 (acc 50)

Thunder Bay, ON P7A 4S2, CARS,
545 Cumberland St N; tel: (807) 345-7319
(acc 46)

Toronto, ON M5T 1P7, Hope Shelter,
167 College St; tel: (416) 979-7058 (acc 108)

Toronto, ON M5C 2H4, The Gateway,
107 Jarvis St; tel: (416) 368-0324 (acc 100)

Toronto, ON M5A 2R5, Maxwell Meighen
Centre, 135 Sherbourne St; tel: (416) 366-2733
(acc 378)

Toronto, ON M5B 1E2, 160 Jarvis St;
tel: (416) 363-5496 (acc 98)

Vancouver, BC V6A 1K7, James McCready
Residence, 129 East Cordova St;
tel: (604) 646-6800 (acc 44)

Vancouver, BC V6A 1K7, The Haven,
128 East Cordova St; tel: (604) 646-6800
(acc 40)

Windsor, ON N9A 7G9, 355 Church St;
tel: (519) 253-7473 (acc 111)

Women

Brampton, ON L6X 3C9, The Honeychurch
Family Life Resource Center, 535 Main St N;
tel: (905) 451-4115 (acc 73)

Montreal, QC H3J 1M8, L'Abri d'Espoir,
2000 rue Notre-Dame oust;
tel: (514) 934-5615 (acc 36)

Quebec City, QC G1R 4H8, Maison Charlotte,
14 Cote du Palais; tel: (418) 692-3956
(acc 25)

Toronto, ON M6P 1Y5, Evangeline Residence,
2808 Dundas St W; tel: (416) 762-9636
(acc 90)

Toronto, ON M6J 1E6, Florence Booth House,
723 Queen St W; tel: (416) 603-9800 (acc 60)

Vancouver, BC V5Z 4L9, Kate Booth House, PO
Box 38048 King Edward Mall;
tel: (604) 872-0772 (acc 12)

Mixed (male and female)

Abbotsford, BC V2S 2E8, 34081 Gladys Ave;
tel: (604) 852-9305 (acc 34)

Calgary, AB T2G 0R9, Centre of Hope,
420 9th Ave; tel: (403) 410-1111 (acc 295)

Courtney, BC V9N 2S2, 1580 Ftizgerald Ave
tel: (250) 338-5133 (acc 9)

Fort St John, BC, 10116 100th Ave;
tel: (250) 785-0506 (acc 20)

London, ON N6C 4L8, Centre of Hope,
281 Wellington St; tel: (519) 661-0343
(acc 253)

Maple Ridge, BC V2X 2S8, 22188 Lougheed
Hwy; tel: (604) 463-8296 (acc 43)

Medicine Hat, AB T1A 1M6, 737 8th St SE;
tel: (403) 526-9699 (acc 30)

Mississauga, ON L5A 2X3, Cawthra Road
Shelter, 2500 Cawthra Rd; tel: (905) 281-1272

Oakville, ON L6L 6X7, Lighthouse Shelter,
750 Redwood Sq; tel: (905) 339-2918 (acc 25)

Sudbury, ON P3A 1C2, 146 Larch St;
tel: (705) 363-5496 (acc 91)

Vancouver, BC V6A 4K9, Grace Mansion,
596 East Hastings St; tel: (778) 329-0674
(acc 85)

Vancouver, BC V6B 1K8, Belkin House,
555 Homer St; tel: (604) 681-3405 (acc 257)

Vancouver, BC V6B 1G8, The Crosswalk,
138-140 W Hastings St; tel: (604) 669-4349
(acc 35)

Winnipeg, MB R3B 0J8, Booth Centre Ministries,
180 Henry Ave; tel: (204) 946-9402
(acc 330)

Family

Mississauga, ON L5R 4J9, Angela's Place,
45 Glen Hawthorne Rd; tel: (905) 791-3887
(acc 80)

Mississauga, ON L4X 1L5, Peel Family Shelter,
1767 Dundas St. E; tel: (905) 272-7061

Montreal, QC H3J 1M8, L'Abri d'Espoir,
2000 rue Notre-Dame oust;
tel: (514) 934-5615 (acc 25)

Saskatoon, SK S7M 3A9, Mumford House,
341 Avenue T South; tel: (306) 986-2157

Youth

Moose Jaw, SK S6H 0Y9, Hope Inn
1st Avenue NE; tel: (306) 692-2894

Sutton, ON L0E 1R0, 20898 Dalton Rd,
PO Box 1087; tel: (905) 722-9076

Community and Family Services

Alberta: Calgary, Cranbrook, Drumheller,
Edmonton, Fort McMurray, Grande Prairie,
High River, Lethbridge, Lloydminster,
Medicine Hat, Peace River, Red Deer,
St Albert.

Bermuda: Hamilton.

British Columbia: Abbotsford, Campbell River,
Chilliwack, Courtenay, Dawson Creek, Duncan,
Fernie, Fort St John, Gibsons, Kamloops,
Kelowna, Maple Ridge, Nanaimo, Nelson,
New Westminster, North Vancouver, Parksville,
Penticton, Port Alberni, Powell River,
Prince George, Prince Rupert, Quesnel,
Richmond, Salmon Arm, Surrey, Terrace,
Trail, Vancouver, Vernon, Victoria,
White Rock, Williams Lake.

Manitoba: Brandon, Dauphin, Flin Flon,
Portage La Prairie, Thompson, Winnipeg (2).

New Brunswick: Bathurst, Campbelltown,

Canada and Bermuda Territory

Fredericton, Miramichi, Moncton, Saint John, Sussex.

Newfoundland and Labrador: Corner Brook, Gander, Grand Falls-Windsor, Labrador City/ Wabush, Pasadena, Springdale, St Anthony, St John's, Stephenville.

Nova Scotia: Bridgewater, Glace Bay, Halifax, Kentville, New Glasgow, Sydney, Truro, Westville, Yarmouth.

Ontario: Ajax, Belleville, Bowmanville, Brampton, Brantford, Brockville, Burlington, Cambridge, Chatham, Cobourg, Collingwood, Cornwall, Essex, Etobicoke (2), Fenelon Falls, Fort Frances, Gananoque, Georgetown, Goderich, Gravenhurst, Guelph, Hamilton, Huntsville, Ingersoll, Jackson's Point, Kemptville, Kenora, Kingston, Kirkland Lake, Kitchener, Leamington, Lindsay, Listowel, London, Midland, Milton, Mississauga (3), Napanee, New Liskeard, Newmarket, Niagara Falls, North Bay, North York (2), Oakville, Orillia, Oshawa, Ottawa, Owen Sound, Pembroke, Perth, Peterborough, Renfrew, Ridgetown, Sarnia, Sault Ste Marie, Scarborough, Simcoe, Smiths Falls, St Catharine's, St Mary's, St Thomas, Stratford, Strathroy, Sudbury, Thunder Bay, Tillsonburg, Toronto (3), Trenton, Wallaceburg, Welland, Whitby, Windsor, Woodstock.

Prince Edward Island: Charlottetown, Summerside.

Quebec: Montreal, Quebec City, Sherbrooke, St-Hubert, Trois-Rivieres.

Saskatchewan: Moose Jaw, Prince Albert, Regina.

Yukon Territory: Whitehorse.

Correctional and Justice Services
Community Programme Centres

Barrie, ON L4M 5A1, 400 Bayfield St, Ste 255; tel: (705) 737-4140

Chilliwack, BC V2P 2N4, 45742B Yale Rd; tel: (604) 792-8581

Corner Brook: PO Box 1018 Corner Brook, NL A2H 6J3; tel: (709) 639-1719

Guelph, ON N1L 1H3, 1320 Gordon St; tel: (519) 836-9360

Hamilton, ON L7R 1Y9, 2090 Prospect St; tel (905) 634-7977

Kingston, ON K7K 4B1, 472 Division St; tel: (613) 549-2676

Kitchener, N2H 2M4, 1-657 King St. E tel: (519) 742-8521

London, ON N6B 2L4, 281 Wellington St; tel: (519) 432-9553

Maple Creek, SK, S0N 1N0, 203 Maple St; tel: (306) 662-3871

Mapleridge, BC V2X 2S8, 22188 Lougheed Highway, tel: (604) 463-8296

Medicine Hat, AB T1A 0E7, 874 2 St E; tel: (403) 529-2111

Moncton, NB E1C 1M2, 68 Gordon St; tel: (506) 853-8887

Ottawa, ON K1Y K1N, 171 George St; tel: (613) 725-1733

Peterborough, ON K9H 2H6, 219 Simcoe St; tel: (705) 742-4391

Prince Albert, SK S6V 4V3, 900 Central Ave; tel: (306) 763-6078

Regina, SK S4P 3M7, 2240 13th Ave; tel: (306) 757-4711/2

Smiths Falls, ON K7A 4T2 243 Brockville St tel; (613) 283-3563

St Catharines, ON L2R 3E7, 184 Church St; tel: (905) 684-7813

St John's, NL A1C 4Z1, 21 Adams Ave; tel: (709) 726-0393

Swift Current, SK S9H 4M7, 780 1st Avenue; tel: (306) 778-0515

Thunder Bay, ON P7A 4S2, 268 Pearl St; tel: (807) 344-0683

Toronto, ON M5A 3P1, 77 River St; tel: (416) 304-1974

Trois-Rivieres, QC G8Y 3N8, 3885 De Landerneau; tel: (819) 840-3420

Winnipeg, MB R3A 0L5, 324 Logan Ave, 2nd Floor; tel: (204) 949-2100

Windsor, ON N9A 7G9, 355 Church St; tel: (519) 253-7473

Adult/Youth Correctional Residential Centres

Brampton, ON L6X 1C1, 44 Nelson St W; tel: (905) 453-0988 (acc 12)

Brantford ON, N3T 2E8, 187 Dalhousie St, tel: (519 753-4193

Calgary, AB T2G 0R9, 420-9 Avenue SE, (tel) (403) 410-1129

Dartmouth, NS B3A 1H5, 318 Windmill Rd; tel: (902) 465-2690 (acc 20)

Dundas, ON L9H 2E8, 34 Hatt St; tel: (905) 627-1632 (acc 10)

Kitchener, ON N2G 2M4, 657 King St E; tel: (519) 744-4666 (acc 21)

Milton, ON L9P 2X9, 8465 Boston Church Rd; tel: (905) 875-1775 (acc 10)

Moncton, NB E1C 8P6, 64 Gordon St, PO Box 1121; tel: (506) 858-9486 (acc 22)

Nanaimo, BC V9R 4S6, 19 Nichol St; tel: (250) 754-2621

Saskatoon, SK S7M 1N5, 339 Avenue C S; tel: (306) 244-6280 (acc 15)

Sudbury, ON P3A 1C2, 146 Larch St;

tel: (705) 363-5496 (acc 4)

Thunder Bay, ON P7A 4S2, 268 Pearl St;
tel: (807) 344-0683 (acc 4)

Toronto, ON M4X 1K2, 422 Sherbourne St;
tel: (416) 964-6316/967-6618 (acc 53)

Vancouver, BC V6B 1K8, Belkin House,
555 Homer St; tel: (604) 681-3405
(acc 30)

Victoria, BC V9A 7J6, Matson Sequoia
Residence, 554 Garrett Pl Ste 211;
tel: (250) 383-5821 (acc 30)

Whitehorse, YT Y1A 6E3, 91678 Alaska Hwy;
tel: (867) 667-2741 (acc 16)

Yellowknife, NWT X1A 1P4, 4927 45th St;
tel: (867) 920-4673 (acc 33)

Health Services
Long-Term Care/Seniors' Residences

Brandon, MB R7A 3N9, Dinsdale Personal
Care Home, 510 6th St; tel: (204) 727-3636
(acc 60)

Calgary, AB T3C 3W7, Jackson/Willan
Seniors' Residence, 3015 15 Ave SW;
tel: (403) 249-9116 (acc 18)

Edmonton, AB T5X 6C4, Grace Manor,
12510 140 Ave; tel: (780) 454-5484
(acc 100)

Kitchener, ON N2H 2P1, A. R. Goudie
Eventide Home, 369 Frederick St;
tel: (519) 744-5182 (acc 80)

Montreal, QC H4B 2J4, Montclair Residence,
4413 Montclair Ave; tel: (514) 481-5638
(acc 50)

New Westminster, BC V3L 4A4, Buchanan
Lodge, 409 Blair Ave; tel: (604) 522-7033 (acc
112)

Niagara Falls, ON L2E 1K5, The Honourable
Ray and Helen Lawson Eventide Home,
5050 Jepson St; tel: (905) 356-1221
(acc 100)

Ottawa, ON K1Y 2Z3, Ottawa Grace Manor,
1156 Wellington St; tel: (613) 722-8025
(acc 128)

Regina, SK S4R 8P6, William Booth Special
Care Home, 50 Angus Rd; tel: (306) 543-0655
(acc 81)

Riverview, NB E1B 4K6, Lakeview Manor,
50 Suffolk St; tel: (506) 387-2012/3/4 (acc 50)

St John's, NL A1A 2G9, Glenbrook Lodge,
105 Torbay Rd; tel: (709) 726-1575
(acc 114)

St John's, NL A1A 2G9, Glenbrook Villa,
107 Torbay Rd; tel: (709) 726-1575
(acc 20)

Toronto, ON M4S 1G1, Meighen Retirement

Residence, 84 Davisville Ave;
tel: (416) 481-5557 (acc 84)

Toronto, ON M4S 1J6, Meighen Manor,
155 Millwood Rd; tel: (416) 481-9449
(acc 168)

Vancouver, BC V5S 3T1, Southview Terrace,
3131 58th Ave E; tel: (604) 438-3367/8
(acc 57)

Vancouver, BC V5S 3V2, Southview Heights,
7252 Kerr St; tel: (604) 438-3367/8
(acc 47)

Victoria, BC V9A 4G7, Sunset Lodge,
952 Arm St; tel: (250) 385-3422 (acc 108)

Winnipeg, MB R2Y 0S8, Golden West
Centennial Lodge, 811 School Rd;
tel: (204) 888-3311 (acc 116)

Immigrant and Refugee Services

Toronto, ON M5B 1E2, 160 Jarvis St;
tel: (416) 360-6036

Women's Multi-Service Programmes (and unmarried mothers)

Hamilton, ON L8P 2H1, Grace Haven,
138 Herkimer St; tel: (905) 522-7336
(acc 12)

London, ON N6J 1A2, Bethesda Centre,
54 Riverview Ave; tel: (519) 438-8371
(acc 14)

Ottawa, ON K1Y 2Z3, Bethany Hope Centre,
1140 Wellington St; tel: (613) 725-1733

Regina, SK S4S 7A7, Gemma House,
2929 26th Ave; tel: (306) 352-1421 (acc 8)

Regina, SK S4S 7A7, Grace Haven,
2929 26th Ave; tel: (306) 352-1421
(acc 7)

Saskatoon, SK S7K 0N1, Bethany Home,
802 Queen St; tel: (306) 244-6758 (acc 15)

Child Day Care/Pre-schools

Barrie, ON L4V 5X5, Sonlight Child Care
Centre, 151 Lillian Cres; tel: (705) 737-1080
(acc 93)

Brampton, ON L6S 4B7, Noah's Ark Day Care
Centre, 9395 Bramalea Rd N;
tel: (905) 793-5610 (acc 46)

Chilliwack, BC V2P 1C5, Happy Hearts Day
Care, 46420 Brooks Ave; tel: (604) 792-5285
(acc 23)

Guelph, ON N1L 1H3, Salvation Army Nursery
School, 1320 Gordon St; tel: (519) 836-9360
(acc 121)

London, ON N6J 1A2, Cantara,
54 Riverview Ave; tel: (519) 438-8371 (acc 20)

London, ON N5W 2B6, The Salvation Army
Village Day Nursery, 1340 Dundas St E;

tel: (519) 455-8155 ext 308 (acc 75)

Medicine Hat, AB T1B 3R3, Rise and Shine Day Care, 164 Stratton Way SE; tel: (403) 529-2003 (acc 58)

Mississauga, ON L5L 1V3, Erin Mills Day Care, 2460 The Collegeway; tel: (905) 820-6500 (acc 32).

Mississauga, ON L5N 4W8, Gentle Guidance Day Care, 3025 Vanderbilt Rd; tel: (905) 785-0522 (acc 24)

Mississauga, ON L5A 2X4, Mississauga Temple Day Care, 3173 Cawthra Rd; tel: (905) 275-8430 (acc 82)

Moncton, NB E1E 4E4, Small Blessings, 20 Centennial Dr; tel: (506) 857-0588 (acc 95)

New Westminster, BC V3L 3A9, Kids Place Day Care, 325 6th St; tel: (604) 521-8223 (acc 20)

Owen Sound, ON N4K 2X9, Salvation Army Day Care, 365 14th St W; tel: (519) 371-9540 (acc 99)

Peace River, AB T8S 1E1, School Readiness, 9710-74 Ave; tel: (780) 624-2370 (acc 43)

Scarborough, ON M1W 3K3, Agincourt Temple Child Care, 3080 Birchmount Rd; tel: (416) 497-0329 (acc 94)

Scarborough, ON M1R 2Z2, Scarborough Citadel Child Care, 2021 Lawrence Ave E; tel: 416-759-5340 (acc 36)

Windsor, ON N8T 2Z7, Learning Corner Day Care Centre, 3199 Lauzon Rd; tel: (519) 944-4918 (acc 111)

Winnipeg, MB R3E 1E6, Weston Child Care, 1390 Roy Ave; tel: (204) 786-5066 (acc 59)

Parent Child Resource Centres

Courtney, BC V9N 2S2, 1580 Fitzgerald Ave; tel: (250) 338-6200

Kitchener, ON N2E 3T1, 75 Tillsley Dr; tel: (519) 745-335

CARRIBEAN: Salvation Army leaders wield their spades at the ground breaking ceremony for the new Delmas 2 facility, Port-au-Prince, Haiti in March 2012. (see report, page 72)

CARIBBEAN TERRITORY

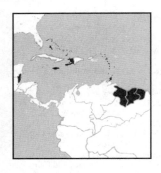

Territorial leaders:
Colonels Onal and Edmane Castor

Territorial Commander:
Colonel Onal Castor (1 May 2009)

Chief Secretary:
Lieut-Colonel Victor Leslie (1 Feb 2012)

Territorial Headquarters: 3 Waterloo Rd, Kingston 10, Jamaica

Postal address: PO Box 378, Kingston 10, Jamaica, WI

Tel: [1876] 929 6190/91/92; email: car_leadership@car.salvationarmy.org;

website: www.salvationarmycarib.org

In 1887 The Salvation Army 'opened fire' in Kingston, and thence spread throughout the island of Jamaica and to Guyana (1895), Barbados (1898), Trinidad (1901), Grenada (1902), St Lucia (1902), Antigua (1903), St Vincent (1905), Belize (1915), St Kitts (1916), Suriname (1924), Bahamas (1931), Haiti (1950), French Guiana (1980), St Maarten (1999) and the Turks and Caicos Islands (2011). The General of The Salvation Army is a Corporation Sole in Jamaica (1914), Trinidad and Tobago (1915), Barbados (1917), Belize (1928), Guyana (1930), the Bahamas (1936) and Antigua (1981).

Zone: Americas and Caribbean
Countries included in the territory: Antigua, Bahamas, Barbados, Belize, French Guiana, Grenada, Guyana, Haiti, Jamaica, St Kitts, St Lucia, St Maarten, St Vincent, Suriname, Trinidad and Tobago and the Turks and Caicos Islands.
'The Salvation Army' in Dutch: Leger des Heils; in French: Armée du Salut
Languages in which the gospel is preached: Creole, Dutch, English, French, Surinamese
Periodical: *The War Cry*

THE Salvation Army in the Caribbean Territory is a growing army, moving forward, united in purpose and mission, yet diverse in culture, language, geography and economy.

In June 2011 seven cadets of the Ambassadors of Holiness session were commissioned and ordained by Commissioner Larry Bosh with Commissioner Gillian Bosh (the then IS and ZSWM). Music was provided by the Caribbean Territorial Band and the Nassau Citadel Band, Bahamas.

Salvationists from Barbados Division presented the musical, *Brengle, My Life's Ambition*.

The British and Canadian High Commissioners, Salvation Army officers from International Headquarters and representatives of the Government of Jamaica and of Scotia Bank, gathered to give God thanks at the re-dedication of the William Chamberlain Drug Rehabilitation Centre. The centre provides accommodation and rehabilitation for 20 men.

In August 31 delegates attended a youth leaders conference. The territory also held a Youth Summit at which 85 delegates participated in a series of workshops aimed at developing their spiritual potential and implementing lifestyle Christianity.

Women's Ministries including weekly meetings, special programmes and social networks in the church and the community were highlighted in October, providing opportunities to nurture women in their faith and develop their spiritual experience As a result of the October campaign there has been a steady increase in membership and attendance. Women have been motivated to share the good news of Jesus within their families and in local communities.

In February 2012 the territorial leaders Colonels Onal and Edmane Castor (TC/TPWM) welcomed Lieut-Colonels Victor and Rose-Marie Leslie as Chief Secretary and Territorial Secretary for Women's Ministries respectively.

Friends, political dignitaries and local, territorial and international Salvation Army leaders gathered on 24 March 2012 to break ground for the new Salvation Army compound in Delmas 2, Port-au-Prince, Haiti. For more than 60 years this facility had marked the presence of The Salvation Army in the capital city. During the 2010 earthquake the buildings were damaged beyond repair. Colonel Castor (TC) dedicated the ground to the glory of God. The new compound will include a primary health care clinic, social services building, the Port-au-Prince Central Corps and College Verena, a school for 1,500 students. Partners from Kindernothilfe (KNH) and Salvation Army donor territories including Canada, Norway and SAWSO were invited to symbolically turn the soil – reaffirming the Army's passion to demonstrate the love of God through a commitment to recovery and redevelopment.

STATISTICS

Officers 321 (active 237 retired 84) **Cadets** (1st Yr) 9 (2nd Yr) 6 **Employees** 1,173
Corps 130 **Outposts** 50 **Institutions** 59 **Schools** 167
Senior Soldiers 10,646 **Adherent Members** 1,763 **Junior Soldiers** 3,279
Personnel serving outside territory Officers 12

STAFF

Women's Ministries: Col Edmane Castor (TPWM) Lt-Col Rose-Marie Leslie (TSWM) Lt-Col Hildegard Orsnes (TLOMS, TWAS)
Personnel: Lt-Col Dewhurst Jonas
Programme: Lt-Col Devon Haughton
Business: Lt-Col Bernt Olaf Orsnes
Coordinator for Disaster Services: Maj Selbourne Oates
Editor: Lt-Col Vevene Jonas
Leader Development: Lt-Col Verona Haughton
Pastoral Care: Lt-Col Raphael Mason
Prayer Coordinator: Lt-Col Vevene Jonas
Projects/Sponsorship: Maj Bruce Carpenter
Property: Lt-Col Sydney McKenzie
Public Relations Director: Maj Bruce Carpenter
Spiritual Life Development: Lt-Col Vevene Jonas
Territorial Music Director: Mr Terron Craig
Training: Lt-Col Verona Haughton
Youth and Candidates: Capt Sherma Evelyn

DIVISIONS

Antigua: PO Box 2, 36 Long St, St John's; tel: [1268] 462-0115; Majs Byron and Joycelyn Maxam
Bahamas: PO Box N 205, Nassau, NP; tel: [1242] 393-2340; Maj Lester and Capt Beverley Ferguson
Barbados: PO Box 57, Reed St, Bridgetown; tel: [1246] 426-2467; Maj Rosemarie Brown

Guyana: PO Box 10411, 237 Alexander St,
Lacytown, Georgetown;
tel: [592] 22 72619/54910;
Majs Emmerson and Carolinda Cumberbatch
Haiti: (temporary address) 65 Autoroute de
Delmas, Building Valerico Canez,
Port-au-Prince; tel: [509] 25 1036 71;
Majs Vilo and Yvrose Exantus
Jamaica Eastern: PO Box 153, Kingston;
153b Orange St, Kingston;
tel: [1876] 922-6764/0287;
Majs Stanley and Hazel Griffin
Jamaica Western: PO Box 44, Lot #949
West Green, Montego Bay, St James;
tel: [876] 952-3778;
Majs Darell and Joan Wilkinson
Trinidad and Tobago: 154a Henry St,
Port-of-Spain, Trinidad; PO Box 248,
Port-of-Spain; tel: [1868] 625-4120;
Majs Sinous and Marie Theodore

REGIONS

Belize: PO Box 64, 41 Regent St, Belize City,
Belize; tel: [501] 2273 365;
email: Belize HQ/BEL/CAR/SArmy;
Majs Joliker and Fidaliance Leandre
French Guiana: PO Box 329,97327 Cayenne
Cedex, French Guiana; tel: [594] 31-5832;
Majs Alisthene and Souvenie Simeon
Suriname: PO Box 317, Henck Arron Straat 172,
Paramaribo; tel: [597] 47-3310;
email: Suriname HQ/SUR/CAR/SArmy;
Maj Jean Miller and Capt Joan Cantave

COUNTRIES NOT IN DIVISIONAL
OR REGIONAL LISTS

Grenada: Grenville St, St George's, Grenada;
tel: [1473] 440-3299
St Kitts: PO Box 56, Cayon Rd, Basseterre,
St Kitts; tel: [1869] 465-2106
St Lucia: PO Box 6, High St, Castries, St Lucia;
tel: [1758] 452-3108
St Maarten: 59 Union Rd, Cole Bay,
PO Box 5184, St Maarten, Netherlands
Antilles; tel: [5995] 445424
St Vincent: Hall Melville St, PO Box 498,
Kingstown, St Vincent; tel: [1784] 456-1574;
Turks and Caicos Islands
Discovery Bay: PO Box 1093, Providenciales,
Turks and Caicos Islands, B.W.I;
tel: [649] 33-9711

TRAINING COLLEGE

GPO Box 437, 174 Orange St,
Kingston, Jamiaca;
tel: [1876] 922-2027

CITY WELFARE OFFICES
Bahamas: 31 Mackey St, Nassau NP
Jamaica: 57 Peter's Lane, Kingston

COMMUNITY CENTRES
Bahamas: Meadow and West Sts, Nassau
Barbados: Checker Hall, St Lucy; Wellington St,
Bridgetown; Wotton, Christchurch
Jamaica: Rae Town Goodwill Centre, 24 Tower
St, Kingston; tel: [1876] 928-5770/930-0028
Allman Town, 18-20 Prince of Wales St,
Kingston 4; tel: [1876] 92-27279

FEEDING CENTRES
Antigua: Meals on wheels
Bahamas: Mackey St and Grantstown, Nassau
Barbados: Reed St, Bridgetown
Belize: 9 Glynn St, Belize City (acc 50)
Guyana:
237 Alexander St, Georgetown;
Third Ave, Bartica;
Rainbow City, Linden
Haiti: Port-au-Prince (Nutrition Centre)
Jamaica:
Peter's Lane, Kingston; Jones Town,
Kingston; Spanish Town, St Catherine;
May Pen, Clarendon; St Ann's Bay, St Ann;
Port Antonio, Portland; Montego Bay,
St James; Savanna-La-Mar, Westmoreland
St Lucia: High St, Castries
Suriname: Gravenstraat 126, Paramaribo

For Children
Bahamas: Nassau, Mackey St
Grenada: St Georges
Guyana: Georgetown, Bartica, Linden
St Vincent: Kingstown

MEDICAL WORK
Haiti:
Bethel Maternity Home and Dispensary,
Fond-des-Negres
Bethesda TB Centre, Fond-des-Negres
Primary Health Care Centre and Nutrition
Centre, Port-au-Prince
Jamaica: Rae Town Clinic, 24 Tower St,
Kingston; tel: (876) 928-1489/930-0028

PRISON, PROBATION AND
AFTERCARE WORK
Antigua; Grenada; Guyana (Georgetown,
Bartica, New Amsterdam); Jamaica;
St Kitts; Suriname; Tobago; Trinidad

Prison Visitation Services
Belize: directed by Regional Commander

RETIRED OFFICERS' RESIDENCES
Jamaica: Francis Ham Residence,
57 Mannings Hill Rd, Kingston 8;
tel: (876) 924-1308 (acc 7)
Barbados: Long Bay, St Phillip
Guyana: East La Penitence

SOCIAL SERVICES
Blind and Handicapped
Adults
Bahamas: Visually Handicapped Workshop,
Ivanhoe Lane, PO Box N 1980, Nassau NP;
tel: (242) 394-1107 (acc 19)
Jamaica: Francis Ham Residence (Home for
Senior Citizens), 57 Mannings Hill Rd,
Kingston 8; tel: (876) 924-1308 (acc 37)

Children (schools)
Bahamas: School for the Blind,
33 Mackay St, PO Box N 205, Nassau NP;
tel: (242) 394-3197 (acc 15)
Jamaica: School for the Blind and Visually
Impaired, 57 Mannings Hill Rd, PO Box 562,
Kingston 8; tel: (876) 925-1362 (residential acc
120)

Women (vocational training)
Jamaica: Evangeline Residence, Kingston;
Port Antonio, Portland

SOCIAL SERVICES
Children
Day Care Centres (nurseries)
Barbados:
Wellington St, Bridgetown (acc 50)
Wotton, Christchurch (acc 50)
Grenada: St Georges (acc 25)
Jamaica:
Allman Town, Kingston (acc 40) Havendale,
Kingston (acc 16) Lucea, Hanover (acc 30)
Montego Bay, St James (acc 40)
St Lucia: Castries (acc 50)
St Vincent: Kingstown (acc 20)
Trinidad: San Juan (acc 20)

Homes
Antigua: St John's Sunshine Home (acc 12)
Haiti:
Bethany, Fond-des-Negres (acc 22)
La Maison du Bonheur, Port-au-Prince
(acc 52)
Jamaica:
Hanbury Home, PO Box 2, Shooter's Hill PO,
Manchester; tel: [1876] 603-3507 (acc 90)
The Nest, 57 Mannings Hill Rd, Kingston 8;
tel: [1876] 925-7711 (acc 45)
Windsor Lodge, PO Box 74,

Williamsfield PO, Manchester;
tel: [1876] 963-4222
(acc 80)
Suriname: Ramoth, Henck Arron Straat 172,
PO Box 317, Paramaribo; tel: [597] 47-3191
(acc 62)

Playgrounds
Jamaica: Rae Town, Kingston; Lucea, Hanover;
Montego Bay, St James
Suriname: Henck Arron Straat 126,Paramaribo
Schools
Basic (kindergartens)
Antigua: St John (acc 150)
Barbados: Checker Hall (acc 50)
Wellington St (acc 10)
Guyana: Bartica (acc 90)
Haiti:
Abraham (acc 63) Aquin (acc 112)
Arcahaie (acc 45) Balan (acc 30)
Bainet (acc 32) Bellamie (acc 35)
Bellegarde (acc 40) Belle Riviere (acc 24)
Bocolomond (acc 47) Bodoin (acc 17)
Brodequin (acc 64) Campeche (acc 43)
Cayot (acc 70) Couyot (acc 65)
Deruisseaux (acc 10) Dessources (acc 30)
Duverger (acc 77) Fond-des-Negres (acc 96)
Fort National (acc 26) Gardon (acc 40)
Gros-Morne (48) Guirand (acc 12)
Jacmel (acc 34) Kamass (acc 12)
L'Azile (acc 51) L'Homond (acc 75)
La Colline (acc 21) Laferonnay (acc 34)
Lafosse (acc 82) Lajovange (acc 35)
Le Blanc (acc 34) Lilette (acc 37)
Limbe (acc 20) Montrouis (30)
Moulin (acc 75) Perigny (acc 25)
Petit Goave (acc 53) Plaisance (acc 15)
Port-de-Paix (acc 14) Puit Laurent (acc 36)
Rossignol (acc 53) St Marc (acc 91)
Verena (acc 211) Vieux Bourg (acc 175)
Violette (acc 42)
Jamaica:
Bath (acc 25) Bluefields (acc 49)
Cave Mountain (acc 30) Cave Valley (acc 75)
Falmouth (acc 86) Great Bay (acc 40)
Kingston Allman Town (acc 150)
Kingston Havendale (acc 90)
Kingston Rae Town (acc 100)
Linstead (acc 65) Lucea (acc 200)
May Pen (acc 60) Montego Bay (acc 240)
Port Antonio (acc 50) St Ann's Bay (acc 36)
Savanna-la-mar (acc 110) Top Hill (acc 93)
St Kitts: Basseterre (acc 80)
St Lucia: Castries (acc 100)
Trinidad and Tobago: San Fernando (acc 80)
Scarborough, Tobago (acc 70)
Tragarete Rd, Port-of-Spain (acc 20)

Home Science
Barbados: Project Lighthouse (acc 12)
Haiti: Aquin; Carrefour; Desruisseaux;
Duverger; Fond-des-Negres, Gros Morne;
Vieux Bourg

Primary Schools
Belize: 12 Cemetery Road, Belize City;
tel: (501) 227-2156 (acc 250)
Haiti:
Abraham (acc 183) Aquin (acc 305) Arcahaie
(acc 212) Bainet (acc 150) Balan (acc 178)
Bas Fort National (acc 259) Bellamy (acc 215)
Bellegarde (acc 235) Belle Riviere (acc 203)
Boco Lomond (acc 255) Bodoun (acc 76)
Brodequin (acc 141) Campeche (acc 130)
Carrefour/Desruisseaux (acc 250) Cayot
(acc 273) College Verena (acc 486)
Couyot (acc 375) Dessources (acc 160)
Duverger (acc 265) Fond-des-Negres (acc 574)
Fort National (acc 259) Gardon
(acc 166) Gros Morne (acc 325) Guirand
(acc 206) Jacmel (acc 97) Kamass (acc 21)
L'Azile (acc 174) L'Homond (acc 209)
La Colline (acc 125) La Fosse (acc 367)
La Jovange (acc 255) La Zandier (acc 170)
Laferonnay (acc 215) Lilette (acc 130) Limbe
(acc 55) Luly (acc 182) Montrouis (acc 131)
Moulin (acc 180) Peirigny (acc 205) Petit
Goave (acc 165) Petite Riviere (acc118)
Plaisance (acc 174) Port-de-Paix (acc 315)
Puits Laurent (acc 195) Rossignol (acc 239)
St Marc (acc 222) Vieux Bourg (acc 617)
Violette (acc 133)

Evening Schools
Guyana: Happy Heart Youth Centre, New
Amsterdam (acc 20)
Haiti: Port-au-Prince (acc 83)

Secondary School
Haiti: Port-au-Prince (acc 450) Gros-Morne
(acc 325)

SOCIAL SERVICES
Men and Women
Centre for Homeless
Belize: Raymond A. Parkes Home,
18 Cemetery Rd, Belize City;
tel: [501] 207-4309
(acc 12)

Eventide Home
Trinidad: Senior Citizens' Centre,
34 Duncan St, Port-of-Spain;
tel: [868] 624-5883 (acc 13)

Men
Guyana: MacKenzie Guest House, Rainbow
City, PO Box 67, Linden Co-op MacKenzie,
Guyana; tel: [592] 444-6406 (acc 10)
Hostels and Shelters
Guyana:
Men's Hostel, 6-7 Water St, Kingston,
Georgetown; tel: [592] 226-1235 (acc 40)
Drug Rehabilitation Centre,
6-7 Water St, Kingston, Georgetown;
tel: [592] 226-1235 (acc 18)
Jamaica:
Men's Hostel, 57 Peter's Lane, Kingston;
tel: [1876] 922-4030 (acc 25)
William Chamberlain Rehabilitation Centre,
57 Peter's Lane, Kingston (acc 25)
Suriname: Night Shelter, Ladesmastraat 2-6,
PO Box 317, Paramaribo; tel: [597] 4-75108
(acc 70)

Women
Eventide Homes
Belize: Ganns Rest Home, 60 East Canal St,
Belize City; tel: [501] 227 2973 (acc 12)
Guyana: 69 Bent and Haley Sts, Wortmanville,
Georgetown; tel: [592] 226-8846 (acc 22)
Suriname:
Elim Guest House, Henck Arron
Straat 126, PO Box 317, Paramaribo;
tel: [597] 48-4325 (acc 15)
Emma House, Dr Nassylaan 76, PO Box 2402,
Paramaribo; tel: [597] 47-3890 (acc 22)

Hostels and Shelters
Bahamas: Women and Children's Emergency
Residence, Grantstown, PO Box GT 2216,
Nassau NP; tel: [242] 323-5608 (acc 21)
Jamaica: Evangeline Residence, 153 Orange St,
Kingston; tel: 1 (876) 922-6398 (acc 50)
Trinidad:
Geddes Grant House, 22-24 Duncan St,
Port-of-Spain; tel: 1 (868) 623-5700
(acc 34)
Josephine Shaw House, 131-133 Henry St,
Port-of-Spain; tel: 1 (868) 623623-2547
(acc 106)

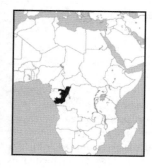

CONGO (BRAZZAVILLE) TERRITORY

Territorial leaders:
Colonels Joseph and Angélique Lukau

Territorial Commander:
Colonel Joseph Lukau (1 Dec 2010)

Chief Secretary:
Lieut–Colonel Daniel Moukoko
(1 Sep 2011)

**Territorial Headquarters: Rue de Reims, Brazzaville,
République du Congo**

Postal address: BP 20, Brazzaville, République du Congo

Tel: [242] 281144; email: congo_brazzaville_info@con.salvationarmy.org

In 1937 The Salvation Army spread from Léopoldville to Brazzaville, and in 1953 French Equatorial Africa (now Congo) became a separate command. Commissioner and Mrs Henri Becquet were the pioneers. The command was upgraded to a territory in December 1960.

Zone: Africa
Country included in the territory: The Republic of Congo
'The Salvation Army' in French: Armée du Salut; in Kikongo: Nkangu a Luvulusu; in Lingala: Basolda na Kobikisama; in Vili: Livita li Mavutsula
Languages in which the gospel is preached: French, Kikongo, Kituba, Lingala, Vili
Periodical: *Le Salutiste*

IN August 2011 more than 560 young people attended territorial music camp held at Kinkala in the Yangui Division. A farewell salute was held at Moungali Corps , for the then Lieut-Colonels Gerrit and Eva Marseille (CS/TSWM) as they were appointed to IHQ. In September the territory welcomed Lieut-Colonels Daniel and Arschette Moukoko as Chief Secretary and Territorial Secretary for Women's Ministries respectively.

A variety of Women's Ministries events held during the year included a residential camp at Yangui centre in August. This Army property had been abandoned in 1998 due to national political conflicts and so it was wonderful to gather there again. Every division sent delegates – almost 1,000 women Salvationists and officers attended – and 'A Joyful Heart' was the main theme of the camp. A divisional rally was held in October 2011 at Salle Centrale Corps in Pointe-Noire with the title 'On the road of faith'. More than 1,200 women met together and received teaching on 'the role of women in society' and personal health and hygiene. In November a territorial seminar for Women's Ministries was held in Gamboma

(North Division). Various subjects were presented and developed to equip and empower delegates to lead and teach in their communities.

January 2012 began with a full day of prayer at Moungali Corps when 700 women met together to pray for God's protection and guidance. In March, many World Day of Prayer meetings took place throughout the territory with the international theme 'Let Justice Prevail'. This event raised awareness of discrimination against women in the fields of education and employment and the situation of women in traditional societies who are often marginalised.

In October 2011 a special day of meetings was held at Moungali Corps to support the launching of Army work in Cameroon. The meeting commenced with prayers for the work to grow and become self-supporting. Donations were collected during the day to raise funds for the work in Cameroon .

In January 2012 the territorial theme, 'Let us work together and grow' was launched in meetings at Moungali, conducted by the territorial leaders. This theme was linked with the International Vision, 'One Army, One Mission, One Message' which was emphasised as the way forward for the territory.

Salvation Army medical personnel participated in many seminars organised by the Ministry for Public Health in 2011. Various subjects were addressed, including diabetes, tuberculosis, HIV and the provision of medication for those affected. The vaccination and monitoring of children aged 0-5 years was also emphasised. Salvation Army clinics gave care and treatment to an increasing number of patients throughout the year, particularly during an influenza epidemic and anti-malaria medicines were provided. Moukoundji-Ngouaka health clinic, a pilot centre, specialised in ophthalmological consultations and surgery to remove cataracts took place every week.

In March 2012 in Moungali, Salvationists welcomed 27 cadets of the Proclaimers of the Resurrection session for officer training. There are 13 couples and one single cadet. Colonel Lukau (TC) preached from Luke 14:25-35 on the subject of discipleship. More than 600 people were present at this inspiring gathering.

STATISTICS

Officers 336 (active 279 retired 57)
  Employees 178
Corps 108 **Outposts** 52 **Maternity Unit** 1
  Clinics 6 **Centres** 2 **Schools** 17
Senior Soldiers 22,174 **Adherent Members**
  1,251 **Junior Soldiers** 6,035
Personnel serving outside territory
  Officers 6

STAFF

Women's Ministries: Col Angélique Lukau
  (TPWM) Lt-Col Arschette Moukoko (TSWM)
  Lt-Col Monique Bakemba (THLS) Lt-Col
  Pauline Sakamesso (TJLS) Lt-Col Marie
  Jeannette Sonda (TLOMS)
Sec for Personnel: Lt-Col Prosper Bakemba
Sec for Programme: Lt-Col Alexis
  Sakamesso
Sec for Business Administration: Lt-Col Jean
  Pierre Sonda
Extension Training: Capt Prosper Komiena

Financial Administrator: Sgt Jean Mayandu
Health Services Coordinators: Majs Sebastien and Martine Diantezulua
Information Technology: M'Passi Loukeba Richard
Music: Wilfrid Milandou
Projects: Sgt Edy Seraphin Kanda
Property: Maj Bonaventure Bibimbou
Public Relations: Capt Guy Bonaventure Conckot
Social: Capt Blaise Kombo
Territorial Bandmaster: Sgt Sensa Malanda
Territorial Songster Leader: Wilfrid Milandou
Training: Maj Dieudonné Louzolo
Youth and Candidates: Capt Edith Dibanssa

DIVISIONS

Brazzaville 1: c/o THQ; tel: 05 536 43 19; Majs Victor and Emma Nzingoula
Brazzaville 2: c/o THQ; tel: 05 561 41 31; Majs François and Louise Mavouna
Lekoumou: c/o THQ; tel: 05 556 38 72; Majs Patrick and Clémentine Tadi
Louingui: c/o THQ; tel: 05 568 11 85; Majs Jean-Pierre and Odile Douniama
Mbanza-Ndounga: c/o THQ; tel: 05 547 12 86; Majs Gabin and Philomene Mbizi
Niari: BP 85, Dolisie; tel 05 558 41 36; Majs Urbain and Judith Loubacky
North: c/o THQ; tel: 05 535 53 21; Majs Antoine and Marianne Massiélé
Pointe Noire: BP 686, Pointe Noire; tel: 05 538 76 31; Majs Daniel and Angèle Taty
Yangui: BP 10, Kinkala; tel: 05 567 41 61; Majs Philippe and Rose Bonazebi

DISTRICTS

Bouenza: c/o THQ; tel: 05 553 83 75; Maj Alphonse Mayamba
Tchitondi: c/o THQ; tel: 05 547 17 95; Maj Aristide Samba

TRAINING COLLEGE

Nzoko: c/o THQ; tel: 56 95 72

SOCIAL AND EDUCATIONAL CENTRES

Day Care Centre
Ouenze Corps, Brazzaville

Guest Houses
Moungali: Auberge Makoumbou; (Brazzaville); Pointe-Noire: Auberge Nottingham
Home for the Visually Impaired

Yenge, Nzoko; c/o THQ

Institute for the Blind
INAC, Mansimou Brazzaville; c/o THQ

Primary and Secondary Schools
Bouansa: François Mananga Primary and Secondary School
Gamboma: Victor Makosso Primary School
Loua: John Swinfen Primary and Secondary School
Makelekele: Fred and Elaine Eardley Primary and Secondary School
Mfilou: Eugène Nsingani Primary School
Mpissa: Ime Akpan Nursery and Primary School
Moungali: Charles Houze Nursery, Primary and Secondary School
Ouenze: John Larsson Nursery, Primary and Secondary School
Nzoko: Véronique Makoumbou Nursery, Primary and Secondary School

HEALTH SERVICES

Health Clinic and Eye Treatment Centre
Moukoundji-Ngouaka: c/o THQ

Health Clinics
Loua: BP 20, Brazzaville
Moungali: BP 20, Brazzaville
Nkayi: BP 229, Nkayi Nkouikou, Pointe Noire

Health Clinics and Maternity Units
Dolisie: BP 235, Dolisie
Yangui c/o THQ

CONGO BRAZZAVILLE: A women's ministries group singing at their territorial seminar held in Gamboma, North Division

DEMOCRATIC REPUBLIC OF CONGO: In front of the Salvation Army hall at Kinigi, a new outpost in the territory

DEMOCRATIC REPUBLIC OF CONGO TERRITORY

Territorial Commander:
Commissioner Madeleine Ngwanga
(1 Dec 2009)

Chief Secretary:
Lieut-Colonel Lucien Lamartiniere
(1 Dec 2011)

**Territorial Headquarters: Ave Ebea 23, Kinshasa-Gombe,
Democratic Republic of Congo**

Postal address: Armée du Salut 8636, Kinshasa 1, Democratic Republic of Congo

Tel: [243] 997-526050; email: kin_leadership@kin.salvationarmy.org

The first Salvation Army corps was established in Kinshasa in 1934 by Adjutant (later Commissioner) and Mrs Henri Becquet. By decree of Léopold III, Armée du Salut was given legal status, with powers set out in a Deed of Constitution, on 21 February 1936. Work spread to Congo in 1937 and 16 years later it became a separate command, later being elevated to territory status. Congo (Kinshasa) and Angola Territory was renamed on 1 March 2008 when Angola became a command, then became Democratic Republic of Congo Territory on 1 June 2008.

Zone: Africa
Countries included in the territory: Democratic Republic of Congo
'The Salvation Army' in French: Armée du Salut; in Kikongo: Nkangu a Luvulusu; in Lingala: Basolda na Kobikisa; in Swahili: Jeshi la Wokovu; in Tshiluba: Tshiluila Tsha Luhandu
Languages in which the gospel is preached: Chokwe, French, Kikongo, Lingala, Swahili, Tshiluba, Umbundu
Periodical: *Echo d'Espoir*

THE Democratic Republic of Congo Territory has seen tremendous development in many aspects of its ministry during the year. Drama scripts and new songs have been created and Salvationists have participated in regular Bible studies in corps and institutions.

Large numbers of junior soldiers and senior soldiers have been enrolled. Almost 10,000 people have sought the Lord for the first time at the mercy seat. Four new corps and 18 outposts have been opened to the glory of God.

Salvation Army schools have seen a great increase in pupil numbers. The 256 primary schools have enrolled 67,659 pupils and 15 kindergartens have 800 young attendees. Christian education is a vital aspect of the curriculum in each school. Every year a special week called 'School for Christ' takes place and many children receive Christ as their Saviour.

The Army's social work in DRC is highly regarded. When the Kabila Foundation sponsored emergency relief for people in the eastern part of the country, the territorial social secretary was selected to be the chaplain in charge of the trauma counselling unit. The Salvation Army worked closely with Jeanette Kabila, daughter of the late President Kabila, to facilitate food distribution and other help to those in need during a period of six weeks.

The anti sex-trafficking programme continued to be successful. Practical help and prayer resulted in many people accepting Christ as their Saviour. Two women who were rescued began preparing to enter officer training and became accepted candidates for the 2012-2014 session.

The territory's medical services have continued to provide care and treatment for thousands of patients. Health centres, maternity hospitals, dental clinics and government hospitals under Army management have aided people suffering from a range of conditions. The health centres have been fully engaged in vaccination campaigns to promote child health care. Mother and baby clinics have provided valuable health education programmes, monitoring and advice.

Women's Ministries held many events during the year. Bible camps were held in the remote regions of Kasangulu and Lubumbashi. In Kinshasa conferences were organised on the subject of anti sex-trafficking.

Commissioner Madeline Nwanga (TC/TPWM) and Lieut-Colonel Marie Lamartiniere (TSWM) led World Day of Prayer meetings and also conducted nights of prayer in the territory.

STATISTICS
Officers 443 (active 360 retired 83) **Cadets** (1st Yr) 9 (2nd Yr) 6 **Employees** 4,478
Corps 182 **Outposts** 116 **Health Centres** 27 **Maternity Hospitals/Clinics** 6 **Other specialist hospitals** 1 **Other specialist clinics** (inc HIV/Aids, dental) 4 **Institutions** 5
Schools: Secondary 181 **Primary** 257 **Boarding** 2 **Kindergarten** 15 **University** 1
Senior Soldiers 28,759 **Adherent Members** 4,201 **Junior Soldiers** 14,169
Personnel serving outside territory Officers 16

STAFF
Women's Ministries: Comr Madeleine Ngwanga (TPWM) Lt-Col Marie Lamartiniere (TSWM) Capt Bibisky Nzila (THLS) Lt-Col Celestine Ngoy (LOM, Literacy) Maj Marie-Thérèse Mabwidi (Women's Dev/Anti-sex Trafficking) Lt-Col Lydia Matondo (JHLS, Officers' Children)
Sec for Business Administration: Lt-Col Gracia Matondo
Sec for Personnel: Lt-Col Hubert Ngoy
Sec for Programme: Lt-Col Jean-Baptiste Mata
Development and Emergency Services: Capt Dieudonné Tsilulu
Editorial/Literature: Maj Josué Leka
Extension Training: Lt-Col Joseph Bueya
Finance: Capt Barthélemy Nzila
Information Technology: Sgt Mbumu Muba Jean-Marc
Medical: Dr David Nku Imbie
Music and Creative Arts: Maj Philippe Mabwidi
 National Bandmaster: Sgt Jean-Marc Mbumu
 National Songster Leader: Sgt Joseph Nsilulu
 National Timbrel Leader: Sgt Pauline Matanu
Property: Maj Léon Tubajiki
Public Relations: Capt André Mulenda
Schools Coordinator: Maj Norbert Makala
Social: Maj Philippe Mabwidi
 HIV/Aids Section: Paul Kunzebiko
 Sponsorship: Maj Philippine Tsilulu
Training: Maj Sébastien Mbala
Youth: Maj Martin Buama
 Candidates: Maj Adolphe Masidiyaku

DIVISIONS

Bas-Fleuve/Océan: BP 123, Matadi;
Majs Antoine et Bernadette Toni
(mob: 0815107232)

Inkisi: Armée du Salut, Kavwaya, BP 45;
Majs Isidore and Marthe Matondo
(mob: 0990023962)

Kasaï-Occidental: BP 1404, Kananga;
Majs Esaïe and Marie-José Ntembi
(mob: 0991668909)

Kasangulu: BP 14, Kasangulu; Majs Emmanuel
and Madeleine Diakanwa
(mob: 0998336208)

Katanga: BP 2525, Lubumbashi; Majs Denis
and Modestine Mafuta (mob: 0994504967)

Kinshasa Central: BP 8636, Kinshasa;
Majs Alphonse and Bernadette Mayasi
(mob: 0998449971)

Kinshasa East: BP 8636, Kinshasa;
Maj Pascal Matsiona (mobile: 0998036399)

Kinshasa West: Lt-Cols Henri and Josephine
Nangi (mob: 0999371303)

Luozi: Armée du Salut, Luozi; Majs Clément and
Béatrice Ilunga (mob: 0998627937)

Mbanza-Ngungu: BP 160; Majs Pierre et
Marie-Josée Mukoko (mob: 0998277818)

Orientale (Kisangani): BP 412, Kisangani; Majs
William and Rose-Marie Ntoya
(mob: 0998277857)

DISTRICTS

Bandundu: Armée du Salut, Bandundu;
Maj André Mobubu (mobile: 0811620092)

Isiro: BP 135 (under supervision of THQ)

Plateau: Majs Emmanuel and Albertine Mpanzu
(mob: 0995662729)

Tanganyika: (under supervision of Katanga)

SECTIONS

Bukavu: Maj Pierre Masundu
(mobile: 0993187354)

Kwilu: Maj Germain Mbeni
(mobile: 0991302116)

TRAINING COLLEGE

BP 8636, Kinshasa

UNIVERSITY

William Booth University: BP 8636, Kinshasa;
Rector: Dr Mpiutu ne Mbodi Gaston

ATTACHED TO THQ

Conference Centre:
Mbanza-Nzundu

MEDICAL WORK

Health Centres

Bas-Congo: Kasangulu, Boko-Mbuba, Kifuma,
Kingantoko, Kingudi, Kinzambi, Kintete,
Nkalama, Shefu, Kavwaya, Kimayala,
Mbanza-Nsundi, Mbanza-Nzundu

Kananga: Moyo

Kinshasa: Amba (Kisenso), Bakidi (Selembao),
Bomoi, Bopeto (Ndjili), Boyambi (Barumbu),
Elonga, Esengo (Masina), Kimia (Kintambo),
Molende (Kingasani)

Kisangani: Libota, Dengue

Clinic

Maj Leka (Maluku/Kinshasa)

Dental Clinics

Boyambi (Barumbu), Elonga (Masuna),
Kasangulu (Bas-Congo)

Diabetic Clinic

Kananga

Foot Clinic

Boyambi

Maternity Units

Bomoi Kinshasa (acc 60); Kasangulu,
Bas-Congo (acc 13); Kavwaya, Bas-Congo
maternity and centre (acc 14); Maluku
Kinshasa (acc 12)

EDUCATION

Secondary Schools

Bandundu: Institut Elonga; Institut Kwango;
Institut Mabwidi; Institut Ngampo Maku;
Institut Ngobila; Institut Momwono;
Institut Nsele Mpibiri; Institut Wembe;
Institut Tomokoko; Institut Masamuna;
Institut Ngabidjo; 11 primary schools,
11 secondary schools

Bas-Congo: Institut Boyokani (Matadi);
Institut Diakanwa; Institut Kavwaya (Inkisi);
Institut Beti 1; Institut Beti 2;
Institut Kimbumba-Nord; Institut Bongo-Bongo;
Institut Kingudi; Institut Pédagogique Kasi;
Institut Dikal (Lufuku); ITP Kintete;
Institut Kimayasi; Institut Kinzadi 1;
Institut Kinzadi 2; CS Kimbongo;
Institut Kinzambi 1 (Kasangulu);
Institut Kinzambi 2 (Luozi);
Institut Lemba Diyanika; Institut Ludiazo;
Institut Mampemba; Institut Mikalukidi;

Institut Kitundulu; Institut Kivunda;
Institut Kumba Ndilu; ITS Kumbi; ITC Lovo;
Institut Maduma; Institut Manionzi;
Institut Matanda; Institut Mateso;
Institut Nkundi (Mbanza-Ngungu);
CS Nsanga-Mamba; ITC Mbanza-Nsanda; ITA
Mbanza-Nsundi; Institut Mbanza-Nzundu;
Institut Mwala-Kinsende; ITA Nsongi-Kialelua;
Institut Ndandanga; ITC Ngongolo;
Institut Shefu; Institut Sombala;
Institut Viaza; Institut Buetesa;
Institut Kimbata 1; Institut Landulu;
ITP Lukengo; Institut Mawangu;
Institut Miprosco; Institut Odeco;
Institut Sundi-Mamba;
Collège William Booth (Kasangulu);
64 primary schools, 1 kindergarten
Equateur: ITM Bukaka; Institut Obotela;
Institut Elonga; ITCA Lihau;
Institut Mambune; Institut Masobe;
Institut Mokuta; Institut Yambo;
ITA Yamwenga; Institut Yangola;
Institut Embonga; ITM Armée du Salut;
12 primary schools, 12 secondary schools,
2 kindergartens
Kasaï-Occidental (Kananga): Institut Bena-
Leka 1; Institut Bena-Leka 2;
ITAV Bena-Mbiye; Institut Bobumwe;
Institut Muzemba; Institut Mwanza-Ngoma;
Institut Tshibuayayi; ITC Bobumwe;
Institut Bukole; Institut Butoke;
Institut Kasende; Institut Katshimba;
Institut Kuetu; Institut Mande Muile;
ITAV Mfwamba; Institut Mpoyi;
Institut Mwanza-Ngoma; Institut Muyembe;
Institut Salut; ITAV Salut; Institut Tuelekeja;
Institut Tuende; 21 primary schools,
20 secondary schools
Kinshasa: Institut Bakidi; Collège Gabriel
Becquet (Selembao); Collège Bimwala;
ITC Bimwala; Institut Dianzenza; Institut Ilona;
ITC Kwamouth; Institut Lukabama;
Collège John Mabwidi; Institut Mabwidi; Lycée
Matonge; Lycée Technique de Matonge; ITS
Mbala; ITA Menkao;
Institut Mpiutu; ITC Ndjili-Kilambu; Institut
Ngizulu; Institut Nsemi; ITC Ntolani;
ITI Ntolani; Institut Rwakadingi;
Institut Wabaluku;
Institut Yanda Mayemba;
Institut Yimbukulu; 24 secondary schools,
38 primary schools
Province Orientale (Kisangani): Institut
Bonsomi; Institut Elikya; Institut Ilota; Institut

Ketele; Institut Wagenia; Institut Litoka;
Institut Yataka; Institut Afutami; Institut
Bagwasa; Institut Bakota; Institut Bambunze;
Institut Kambale; Institut Lisami; Institut
Lohale; Institut Lomongo; Institut Lotumbe;
Institut Lusa; Institut Yaengala; Institut
Yalokambe; Institut Yasaa; Institut Yasanga;
Institut Yawenda; 22 secondary schools, 42
primary schools, 2 kindergartens
Sud-Katanga (Lubumbashi): ITC Wokovu
(Katuba); ITC Tujenge; Institut Flambeau; 3
secondary schools, 5 primary schools,
1 kindergarten,

SOCIAL SERVICES
Children's Home and Community
Child Care
Kinshasa (acc 15 and 21)

Development and Emergencies
Impini; Kasungulu; Kavwaya; Mato;
Mbanza-Nzundu

Old People's Home
Kinshasa-Kintambo (acc 30)

Vocational Training Centres
Barumbu Kinshasa (acc 22); Ndjili Kinshasa
(acc 13); Sud-Katanga Lubumbashi (acc 10)

DENMARK TERRITORY

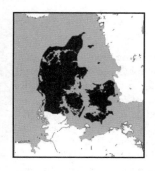

Territorial leaders:
**Colonels Knud David and
Lisbeth Welander**

Territorial Commander:
Colonel Knud David Welander
(1 March 2013)

Chief Secretary:
Lieut-Colonel Henrik Andersen
(1 Oct 2011)

**Territorial Headquarters: Frederiksberg Allé 9,
1621 Copenhagen V, Denmark**

Tel: [45] 33 31 41 92; email: Frelsens@den.salvationarmy.org;
website: www.frelsens-haer.dk

The work of The Salvation Army in Denmark commenced in Copenhagen on 8 May 1887, pioneer
officers being Majors (later Lieut-Colonels) Robert and Isabella Perry.

Zone: Europe
Countries included in the territory: Denmark, Greenland
'The Salvation Army' in Danish: Frelsens Hær
Language in which the gospel is preached: Danish
Periodicals: *Krigsråbet (The War Cry), Vision-Mission*

WHEN seven cadets were welcomed for officer training in the Proclaimers of the Resurrection session this took the total number of cadets to eight, the highest number in Denmark for 30 years. This was a source of joy and thanksgiving and a highly significant part of an encouraging new trend in the territory.

Work among marginalised families has developed during the past few years alongside the ever-present spiritual dimension of the Army's work. People have been encouraged on their faith journeys and they have made commitments to Christ and the Army through becoming junior and senior soldiers and adherent members. Although few in number, the trend is

clear and gives cause for much faith and expectancy.

Exciting breakthroughs have been experienced in work with young people. The teenage discipling programme 'Transformers' was held for a second year and mission teams of teenagers travelled to Moldova and Ukraine.

Record numbers of attendees were recorded at both the annual Bible camp and summer camp. Through these activities children and young people accepted Jesus Christ as Saviour and several of them have been enrolled as soldiers. One teenager, who participated in 'Transformers' and then the mission trip to Moldova made a commitment to Christ and decided to become a soldier. He was the first young person to be enrolled as a soldier at his corps for more than 20 years and the only soldier below the age of 70! Through him, with support of youth from neighbouring corps, a youth fellowship has been established and attracts unchurched young people from the town.

The Salvation Army continued to be the largest provider of Christmas aid to disadvantaged families in Denmark and thus enjoyed a high profile in the media. This gave The Salvation Army a voice in public affairs to speak for the marginalised and poor. In connection with the national election to the Danish parliament in September 2011, the Army published a special 'Election Newspaper'. It was distributed to all members of parliament as well as handed out on the streets throughout Denmark. The newspaper highlighted social issues in Danish society and politicians from all parties were challenged to govern responsibly in the light of these issues.

In January 2012 the Army recommenced its work in Sønderborg after more than 30 years absence. Through the Christmas Aid programme, contacts with many families already existed and they formed the nucleus for this new venture. It is hoped that in time there will be a new corps in Sønderborg.

The territory translated and published the booklet *30 Days with Samuel Logan Brengle*. Every soldier and adherent received a copy to use in their private devotions leading up to Easter.

Another publication, *Jesus and Justice*, emphasised the territory's commitment to work for social justice in the name of Jesus.

A multitude of challenges still face the Army in the highly secular and materialistic Danish culture, but there is also faith and optimism. Through the grace of God there is a growing sense of hope that God's Kingdom will be manifested in even greater ways in future years.

STATISTICS
Officers 73 (active 31 retired 42)
  Cadets (1st Yr) 7 (2nd Yr) 1
  Employees 263
Corps 29 **Outpost** 1 **Social Institutions** 11
  Community Centres 12
Senior Soldiers 905 **Adherent Members** 276
  Junior Soldiers 10
Personnel serving outside territory
  Officers 1

STAFF
Women's Ministries: Col Lisbeth Welander (TPWM) Lt-Col Lisbeth Andersen (TSWM)
Sec for Business Admin: Mr Lars Lydholm
  Chief Accountant: Ms Eva Haahr
  Property: Maj Terje Tvedt
  Public Relations and Information
    Technology: Mr Lars Lydholm
  Recycling: Mr Lars Lydholm
Sec for Personnel: Lt-Col Lisbeth Andersen
  Training: Maj Ingrid Larsen
Sec for Programme: Maj Joan Münch
  Candidates: Lt Elsebeth Jakshøj
  Child Sponsorship: Lt-Col
    Miriam Frederiksen
  Editor: Maj Levi Giversen
  Family: Maj Hanne Wahl
  Missing Persons: Cols Jørn and Nina
    Lauridsen
  Mission: Maj Ingrid Larsen
  Music and Development: Maj John Wahl
  Over-60s: Sgt René Jamrath
  Statistics: Lt-Col Miriam Frederiksen
  Vulnerable Adults: Maj Kurt Pedersen
  Youth: Lt Birgit Seier Jensen

SOCIAL INSTITUTIONS AND COMMUNITY CENTRES

Recycling Centres

6705 Esbjerg Ø, Ravnevej 2; tel: 75 14 24 22;
5000 Odense C, Roersvej 33; tel: 66 11 25 21;
9560 Hadsund, Mariagervej 3; tel: 98 57 42 48;
4900 Nakskov, Narviksvej 15; tel: 54 95 12 05

Secondhand shops

Head Office: Frederiksberg Alle 9, 1621
Copenhagen V; tel: 33 31 41 92
Shops: Århus, Brønderslev, Copenhagen (3),
Esbjerg (2), Nykøbing Falster, Grindsted,
Haderslev, Hadsund, Helsingør, Herning,
Hjørring, Kolding, Nakskov, Nyborg,
Odense (2), Ribe, Vejle.

Community Centres

1408 Copenhagen K, Wildersgade 66;
tel: 32 54 44 10 (acc 80)
1864 Frederiksberg C, Grundtvigsvej 17 st;
tel: 33 24 56 67
2200 Copenhagen N, Kalejdoskop,
Thorsgade 48 A; tel: 35 85 00 87
2500 Valby, Valby Langgade 83; tel: 36 45 67 67
2700 Brønshøj; tel: 33 31 41 92
3000 Helsingør, Strandgade 60, Regnbuen
Community Centre; tel: 49 21 10 06
4800 Nykøbing Falster, Jernbanegade 42,
Community Centre and Corps;
tel: 54 85 71 89
4900 Nakskov, Niels Nielsengade 6;
tel: 54 95 30 06 (acc 60)
5700 Svendborg, Lundevej 2; tel: 62 21 21 63
7100 Vejle, Midtpunktet, Staldgårdsgade 4;
tel: 75 82 78 38
9000 Aalborg, Skipper Clementsgade 11;
tel: 98 11 50 62
9560 Hadsund, Nørregade 10, Den Åbne Dør
Community Centre; tel: 23 26 19 15

Family Work

1621 Copenhagen, Frederiksberg Alle 9;
tel: 33 31 41 92
3000 Helsingør, Strandgade 60; tel: 30 17 94 41
5220 Odense, Peder Skrams Vej 31;
tel: 30 17 94 40
6700 Esbjerg, Skolegade 55; tel: 30 17 94 42
8000 Århus, Klostergade 54; tel: 30 17 94 32

Day Nurseries

9900 Frederikshavn Humlebien, Knudensvej 1B;
tel: 98 42 33 27 (acc 40)
2000 Frederiksberg, Melita, Mariendalsvej 4;
tel: 38 87 01 48 (acc 58)
2650 Hvidovre, Kastanjehuset, Idrætsvej 65A;
tel: 36 78 40 23 (acc 33)
2650 Hvidovre, Solgården, Catherine Booth vej
22; tel: 36 78 07 71 (acc 100)

Emergency Shelters for Families

2650 Hvidovre, Svendebjerggård, Catherine
Booth vej 20; tel: 36 49 65 77
(acc 25)
1754 Copenhagen V, Hedebygade 30,
Den Åbne Dør; tel: 33 24 91 03 (acc 15)
4700 Næstved, Østergade 13; tel: 55 77 22 70
(acc 6)

Rehabilitation Centre

Hørhuset, 2300 Copenhagen S, Hørhusvej 5;

tel: 32 55 56 22 (acc 64)

Project for Long-term Unemployed

Nørholmlejren, Oldenborrevej 2, 9000 Aalborg;
tel: 98 34 18 10 (acc 10)

Eventide Nursing Centre

2200 Copenhagen N Aftensol, Lundtoftegade 5;
tel: 35 30 55 00 (acc 43)

Students Residence

2100 Copenhagen Ø, Helgesengade 25;
tel: 35 37 74 32 (acc 41)

Summer Camps

9000 Aalborg, Nørholmlejren, Oldenborrevej 2;
tel: 98 34 18 10 (acc 50)
8700 Horsens, Hjarnø; tel: 75 68 32 24
(acc 25)
5450 Otterup, Rømhildsminde, Ferievej 11-13,
Jørgensø; tel: 64 87 13 36

Holiday Home and Conference Centre

2791 Dragør, Baggersminde, Fælledvej 132;
tel: 32 53 70 18; fax: 32 53 70 98
(acc 80)
5500 Middelfart, Lillebælt, Nørre Allé 47, Strib;
tel: 64 40 10 57; fax: 63 40 02 82 (acc 30)

News Update: The Salvation Army commenced work in Greenland on 8 August 2012
under the supervision of the Denmark Territory. Newly-commissioned Danish officers will
pioneer the work. Photos from Denmark are included in the colour pages.

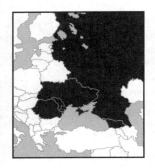

EASTERN EUROPE TERRITORY

Territorial leaders:
Colonels Kenneth and Paula Johnson

Territorial Commander:
Colonel Kenneth Johnson (1 Mar 2010)

Chief Secretary:
Lieut-Colonel Rodney Walters (1 Aug 2012)

Territorial Headquarters: Krestiansky Tupik 16/1, Moscow

Postal address: Russian Federation, 109044 Moscow, Krestiansky Tupik 16/1

Tel: [7] (495) 911 2600/2956 email: Russia@eet.salvationarmy.org;

website: www.thesalvationarmy.ru

Work was initiated in Russia in 1910 by Colonel Jens Povlsen of Denmark but circumstances necessitated his withdrawal after 18 months. Army operations then recommenced in St Petersburg in 1913 as an extension to the work in Finland. After the February 1917 revolution the work flourished, Russia became a distinct command and reinforcements arrived from Sweden. As a result of the October revolution they had, however, to be withdrawn at the end of 1918, leaving 40 Russian and Finnish officers to continue the work under extreme hardship until the Army was finally proscribed in 1923.

Salvation Army activities were officially recommenced in July 1991, overseen by the Norway, Iceland and The Færoes Territory with the arrival of Lieut-Colonels John and Bjorg Bjartveit. It became a distinct command in November 1992. Under the leadership of Commissioner Reinder J. Schurink, the work was extended to Ukraine (1993), Georgia (1993) and Moldova (1994). The Army commenced work in Romania in 1999. On 1 June 2001 the command was redesignated the Eastern Europe Command. It was elevated to territory status on 1 March 2005. The final stage of registering 'the Moscow Branch of The Salvation Army' was completed in April 2009.

Zone: Europe
Countries included in the territory: Georgia, Moldova, Romania, Russian Federation, Ukraine
'The Salvation Army' in Georgian: Khsnis Armia; in Moldovan/Romanian: Armata Salvarii; in Russian: Armiya Spaseniya; in Ukrainian: Armiya Spasinnya
Languages in which the gospel is preached: Georgian, Moldovan, Romanian, Russian, Ukrainian
Periodicals: *Vestnik Spaseniya* (*The War Cry*), *The Officer* (both Russian)

IN 2011 the territory commemorated 20 years since The Salvation Army reopened work in Eastern Europe. More than 700 Salvationists and invited guests travelled to the city of Kiev, Ukraine in May to mark this milestone of ministry and mission. Using the theme 'Celebrate the Past ...

Claim the Future!' those who gathered reflected on what the Army, by the grace of God, has accomplished in the territory. There was opportunity for Salvationists to reaffirm their commitment to God and dedicate themselves to his service for future years. The then Chief of the Staff (Commissioner

GEORGIA: Salvation Army personnel assessing damage caused by severe floods

Barry C. Swanson) and World President of Women's Ministries (Commissioner Sue Swanson) were the guest leaders. God poured out blessings in abundance as present day Salvationists joined with former Salvation Army leaders in praise and worship.

The energy and enthusiasm of this event sparked a resurgence in evangelistic zeal across the territory. Strong statistical growth was reported in almost every Army programme and it was particularly encouraging to see the increase in enrolments of senior and junior soldiers.

During the celebration weekend seven cadets were commissioned and ordained as Salvation Army officers. The territory also welcomed eight new cadets for officer training. This session will include a new distance-learning programme to assist with the practical aspects of training requirements.

Poverty and injustice remained great challenges for the citizens of Eastern Europe. The Salvation Army continued to reach out to the marginalised through generous funding supplied by other territories around the world. There was a particular focus on the migration of Roma people from Romania, which has had an impact in various countries in Europe. The Eastern Europe Territory joined with Norway, Iceland and the Færoes Territory to assist migrants who took up residence in Oslo and the surrounding communities. There were also preliminary discussions between The Salvation Army and the Romanian Government on ways in which their needs can be addressed.

Financing The Salvation Army's work in this part of the world remained a challenge. As the population emerges from decades of Soviet domination, the concept of philanthropy remains foreign to most people. Research has commenced on self-funding schemes and collaborative work continues between the EET and surrounding territories on innovative opportunities for micro businesses. The Fretex programme from Norway and the ReShare programme from the Netherlands remain key potential schemes for fundraising.

When the European Football Championship 2012 took place in Ukraine, local Salvationists seized the mission opportunities this presented. In a working partnership with the International Migration Organization, Salvationists were integral in the development and training of workers to combat the human trafficking that was expected to escalate during this event. Seminars were held at a number of corps, where community leaders and volunteers developed strategies to help the victims of human trafficking. This training will also equip Salvationists for opportunities when the 2014 Winter Olympic Games take place in Sochi, Russia.

The territory has a long-range strategic plan for the future, addressing the key areas of corps programme development, leadership development and financial stability. This plan may have been devised several years ago but it reflects the International Vision Statement launched by General Linda Bond in 2011. The five countries which comprise the territory are moving forward together and trusting God for greater things.

STATISTICS

Officers 122 (active) **Envoys** 5 **Cadets** 8
Employees 136
Corps 53 **Corps Plants** 3
Rehabilitation Centres 2
Senior Soldiers 1,660 **Adherent Members** 829
Junior Soldiers 323

STAFF

Women's Ministries: Col Paula Johnson (TPWM)
Lt-Col Wendy Walters (TSWM)
Sec for Business Administration: Lt-Col Gary Haupt
Sec for Personnel: Col Paula Johnson
Sec for Programme: Lt-Col Wendy Walters
Candidates: Capt Julia Dorofeeva
Editorial: Capt Elena Shulyanski
Education Secretary and Training Principal:
Capt Vitali Sidorov
Legal: Maj Alexander Kharkov
Projects Officer: Lt-Col Suzanne Haupt
Territorial Public Relations & Director for Resources: Capt Sophia Sidorova
Prayer Ambassador: Capt Vadim Kolesnik
Territorial Sergeant-Major: Envoy Yuri Gulyanitsky

DIVISIONS

Russia: 105120 Russia, Moscow, Khlebnikov Pereulok, 7 bld, 2; tel: 495 678 03 51;
Capts Alexander and Svetlana Sharov
Moldova: Chisinau, Petru Movila #19 ;
Postal address: Armata Salvarii, Moldova: Chisinau, 2004, PO Box 412; tel: (37322) 237972;
Majs Graham and Hélène Carey
Ukraine: 01033, Ukraine, Kiev, Shota Rustavely St 38, Suite 3
tel/fax: (380 44) 287 4598, 287 3705, 246 6689;
Maj Bobby and Capt Anne Westmoreland

REGIONS

Georgia: 16 Ikalto St, Tbilisi 0171, Georgia;
tel: (995 32) 33 37 85/86; fax: (995 32) 33 02 27;
Majs Bradley and Anita Caldwell
Romania: 722212 Bucharest, Sector 2,

Str Pargarilor Nr 2; tel: [10] (4037) 270 51 99;
Capts Valery and Victoria Lalac

MISSION TRAINING AND EDUCATION CENTRE – INSTITUTE FOR OFFICER TRAINING

Russia, Moscow, 105120 Karl Larsson Centre,
Khlebnikov Per 7/2; tel: (495) 678 55 14

SOCIAL SERVICES

Georgia

Corps based:
Children's After-school Programmes: Rustavi,
Samgory, Ponichala, Central, Batumi,
Lagodeki
Laundry Projects: Samgori, Rustavi, Didi
Digomi; Batumi
Senior Centres: Batumi, Samgori, Tbilisi;
Regional: Humanitarian Aid; Food Distribution;
Feeding Schemes, Back to School Aid

Moldova

After School Centres; Mobile Medical Clinic;
Rusca Women's Prison Project; 'Sally Ann'
Programme; Shoe Project; Humanitarian Aid
Distribution; Working Among Invalids:
Chimislia, Hincehsti

Romania

Bucharest Roma School Children Outreach;
Laundry Projects; After-school Programmes;
Support for Young Families

Russia

Kiev: Support group for children with cerebral palsy

Kirovograd: Programme for elderly and disabled
people; After-school programme
Moscow: Karl Larsson Centre, Unified Homeless
Services, Khlebnikov pereulok 7, bld 2;
tel: (495) 678 03 51
Feeding Programme; Food and Clothing
Distribution; First Aid
Murmansk Christian camp for children beyond
the Polar Circle
Rostov-on-Don:
The Bridge Programme, Lermontovskaya
St 229; tel/fax: (8632) 248-2410;
HIV+ Crisis Intervention; Group Services
St Petersburg:
Liteini Prospect # 44 B, 191104;
tel: (812) 273-9297; Project Hope – Medical
Clinic; HIV/Aids Outreach and Support
Corps based: Homeless Feeding Programme;
Food and Clothing Distribution;
Seniors' Support Group Programme

Ukraine

Kharkov Corps Social Centre: Ukraine,
Kharkov, Moskovsky prospect 122,
'Kalibr club'; tel: (380-57) 759-42-48;
email: Kharkiv_corps@ukr.net
Kirovograd Corps Social Centre:
25028 Ukraine, Kirovagrad, Volova St,
#15, SPTU #8;
tel: (380-52) 255-19-28;
email: armiyas@rambler.ru
Simferopol Children's Arts Centre: 95000
Ukraine, Simferopol, ulitsa Nekrasova, 22
office 1; tel: (380-652) 510-729

**UKRAINE: The new
divisional leaders
Major Bobby and
Captain Anne
Westmoreland
received traditional
gifts at their
welcome meeting**

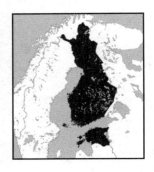

FINLAND AND ESTONIA TERRITORY

Territorial leaders:
Colonels Johnny and Eva Kleman

Territorial Commander:
Colonel Johnny Kleman
(1 Feb 2013)

Chief Secretary:
Lieut-Colonel Arja Laukkanen (1 Jun 2004)

Territorial Headquarters: Uudenmaankatu 40, 00120 Helsinki

Postal address: Post Box 161, 00121 Helsinki, Finland

Tel: [358] (09) 6812300; email: finland@pelastusarmeija.fi;
website: www.pelastusarmeija.fi

Work in Finland was commenced on 8 November 1889 in Broholm's Riding School, Helsinki, by four aristocratic Finns – Captain and Mrs Constantin Boije with Lieutenants Hedvig von Haartman and Alva Forsius. Within six months Hedvig von Haartman was appointed leader of the work in the country.

Work in Estonia first commenced in 1927 and continued until 1940 when it was closed due to the Second World War. It recommenced in the autumn of 1995 when three Finnish officers were assigned to start the work in Tallinn.

Zone: Europe
Countries included in the territory: Estonia, Finland
'The Salvation Army' in Estonian: Päästearmee; in Finnish: Pelastusarmeija; in Swedish: Frälsningsarmén
Languages in which the gospel is preached: English, Estonian, Finnish, Russian, Swedish
Periodicals: *Krigsropet* (Swedish), *Nappis* (Finnish), *Sotahuuto* (Finnish)

FOR the past 10 years the Roots Conference has been held during Midsummer weekend. In 2011 the theme was 'Rooted and Growing in Strength' with Lieutenants Rut and Peter Baronowsky, Latvian Regional Leaders as the guest speakers. A daytime programme of various lectures and workshops took place before an evening gathering for worship and

teaching. At the conclusion of each meeting, people moved forward for prayer, in response to the message.

In November 2011 General Linda Bond commissioned and ordained four cadets as Salvation Army officers during her visit. The General spoke powerfully and at the commissioning meeting young people from Finland and Estonia signified their willingness to serve as future officers. During Sunday meetings the mercy seat was lined with people making commitments to mission and service for God in the Army. A united band comprising Salvationists from Finland, Estonia and Switzerland gave musical support.

Renovation work on the 80 year-old Army hostel in Helsinki began in Autumn 2011. When the work is complete the residents, formerly homeless, will have individual accommodation within a modern complex. The territory plans to expand this level of provision and care for homeless people.

In February 2012, Commissioners Robert and Janet Street (IS/ZSWM, Europe) were the guest leaders at the annual 'Day before the Word'. They taught from the book *Love Right at the Heart*, written by Robert Street, which had just been published in Finnish. Their teaching had a powerful impact and as the author signed copies at this event, many Salvationists took the opportunity to purchase a copy.

The strategy of the territorial vision, 'Come join our Army' continued to be implemented. Corps-based integrated social outreach through 'Light House Church' services introduced a growing number of people to Christ. They have found a faith and are beginning to develop their spiritual life. Gradually, more and more people are attending Sunday meetings. The Salvationists of Finland and Estonia Territory are praying and trusting that this development will result in new soldiers and more workers in the Army, to the glory of God.

STATISTICS
Officers 153 (active 51 retired 102) **Cadets** 1 **Employees** 373
Corps 29 **Outposts** 8 **Goodwill Centres** 2 **Institutions** 18
Senior Soldiers 794 **Adherent Members** 95 **Junior Soldiers** 44

STAFF
Women's Ministries: Col Eva Kleman (TPWM)
Section Head for Programme: Maj Petter Kornilow
Sec for Programme: Maj Tella Puotiniemi
  Asst for Programme Section and Youth: Capt Natalia Penttinen
Section Head for Training and Education: Lt-Col Aino Muikku
  School for Officer Training: Lt-Col Aino Muikku
Section Head for Business Administration: Capt Rodrigo Miranda
  Property: Mika Tiittanen
  Recycling Industry: Harri Lehti
  Information Technology: Tapani Saaristo
Section Head for Personnel: Maj Marja Meras
Section Head for Communication: Maj Eija Kornilow
  The War Cry: Capt Toni Penttinen
  Public Relations: Maj Sirkka Paukku
  Missing Persons: Maj Kirsti Reponen
  Mission Sponsorships: Maj Camilla Rahkonen

SOCIAL CENTRES
Children's Day Care Centres
48100 Kotka, Korkeavuorenkatu 24; tel: 45 635 8085 (acc 36)
15140 Lahti, Hämeenkatu 28 A 5; tel: 3 878680 (acc 94)
06100 Porvoo, Joonaksentie 1; tel: 45 635 8089 (acc 54)
28100 Pori, Mikonkatu 19; tel: 45 635 8088 (acc 83)

Clothing Industry (Recycling Centres)
90580 Oulu, Ratamotie 22; tel: 44 757 7945
33500 Tampere, Itsenäisyydenkatu 25-27; tel: 44 757 7943
20100 Turku, Yliopistonkatu 5; tel: 44 757 7965
01260 Vantaa, Itäinen Valkoisenlähteentie 15; tel: 9 877 0270

Eventide Home
02710 Espoo, Viherlaaksonranta 19; tel: 9 84938410 (acc 60)

Finland and Estonia Territory

Family Support Centre
00530 Helsinki, Hedvig House, Castréninkatu
24-26 F; tel: 50 400 1708

Goodwill Centres
00530 Helsinki, Castréninkatu 25; tel: 44 757
7895
15140 Lahti, Hämeenkatu 28 B; tel: 44 757 7910
33230 Tampere, Pyynikintori 3; tel: 44 757 7941

Homes for Alcoholics and Homeless
68600 Pietarsaari, Permontie 34; tel: 44 757 7896
(acc 15)
28120 Pori, Veturitallinkatu 3; tel: 45 139 3292
(acc 25)
20500 Turku, Hämeenkatu 18; tel: 44 757 7897
(acc 37)

Hostels for Women
00530 Helsinki, Castréninkatu 24-26 A 41;
tel: 9 77431330 (acc 18)
00530 Helsinki, Castréninkatu 24-26 F 46
tel: 9 77431332 (acc 12)

Housing Unit for Men
00380 Helsinki, Pitäjänmäentie 12;
tel: 44 757 7999 (acc 111)

Reception Centre and Supported Living Unit
00550 Helsinki, Inarintie 8; tel: 44 756 2153
(acc 50)

Senior Citizens' Unit
00760 Helsinki, Puistolantie 6 (acc 75)

Service Centres
68600 Pietarsaari; Permontie 34; tel: 44 757 7938
20540 Turku, Karjakuja 1; tel: 44 757 7940

Shelters for Men
00550 Helsinki, Inarintie 8; tel: 44 757 7937
(acc 34)
28120 Pori, Veturitallinkatu 3; tel: 45 139 3292
(acc 25)

Summer Camp Centre
03100 Nummela, Hiidenrannatie 22
(acc 60)

Youth Camp
33480 Ylöjärvi, Sovelontie 91 (summer only)

ESTONIA REGION
Regional Headquarters: Kopli 8-3,
10412 Tallinn; tel: [372] 6413355

Regional Commander: Maj Daniel Henderson
Corps 5

Centres
Hope House (Lootusemaja): Laevastiku 1a,
10313 Tallinn; tel: 6561048
Camp: Ranna 24, Loksa; tel: 6031012

**FINLAND: Young
Salvationist musicians
from Finland, Estonia
and Switzerland unite
in playing at the 2011
commissioning
meetings held in
Helsinki**

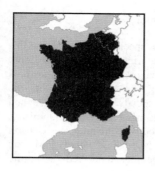

FRANCE AND BELGIUM TERRITORY

Territorial leaders:
Colonels Massimo and Jane Paone

Territorial Commander:
Colonel Massimo Paone (1 Feb 2011)

Chief Secretary:
Lieut-Colonel Sylvie Arnal (1 Feb 2011)

**Territorial Headquarters: 60 rue des Frères Flavien
75976 Paris Cedex 20, France**

Tel: [33] (1) 43 62 25 00; website: www.armeedusalut.fr

Since 'La Maréchale' (eldest daughter of William and Catherine Booth) conducted The Salvation Army's first meeting in Paris on Sunday 13 March 1881, Salvationist influence has grown and remarkable social and spiritual results have been achieved. French officers commenced work in Algeria in 1934 and this work was maintained until 1970.

In Belgium, Salvation Army operations were pioneered on 5 May 1889 by Adjutant and Mrs Charles Rankin and Captains Velleema and Hass. Most of the work in Belgium operates within the Francophone part of the country so, from 1 January 2009, the former Belgium Command became a region linked administratively to France under the newly created France and Belgium Territory.

Zone: Europe
Countries included in the territory: Belgium, France
'The Salvation Army' in French: Armée du Salut; in Flemish: Leger des Heils
Languages in which the gospel is preached: French, Flemish
Periodicals: *Avec Vous, Espoir, Le Bulletin de la Ligue du Foyer, Le Fil, Le Magazine, L'Officier, Quand Même*

THE territory welcomed eight cadets for officer training; six in France and two in Belgium. This brought a new sense of confidence for the Army's future in France and Belgium.

Sixty young people presented 'Spirit', an updated version of the original musical. Three presentations were held in theatres in Paris during Pentecost weekend 2011 and it was later performed in Belgium.

Following extensive renovation, Mulhouse Corps in the Alsace region was reopened in May 2011 and the band and songsters from Boulogne-Billancourt participated at this celebration. Ten years of 'Action Quartiers' Ministry – work with children from deprived areas in the region – was also highlighted.

In Paris, the large-scale refurbishment of the Army's 'Palais de la Femme' was completed and the opening ceremony was on 27 June 2011. This social centre has accommodation for 300 women and offers safety and stability to the guests as they rebuild their lives.

The Salvation Army scouts, known as 'Torchbearers' met in July for their 50 years anniversary camp at the Army's holiday centre in Chausse. Scouts from Portugal and the Netherlands also attended this event.

In September the Palais de la Femme was the venue for a day of thanksgiving meetings with guest leaders Commissioners Robert and Janet Street (IS/ZSWM, Europe). God's faithfulness during 130 years of Salvation Army work in France was the focus. During the afternoon meeting new cadets were welcomed for officer training. Translation equipment was provided for the cadets with funds raised by the Helping Hand project. This equipment will be used during future periods of training at William Booth College, London.

Fifty women gathered in Lyon for a training weekend with the theme 'Beyond Borders'. Having considered the importance of receiving from God before reaching out to others in love, a number of women came forward to the place of prayer in rededication

In October 50 youth leaders and workers met for a training weekend where the call of God to commitment and service was emphasised. By the conclusion, several young people had decided to become soldiers and others had expressed interest in Salvation Army officership.

When the managers of Army social centres and their assistants met in Montpellier they watched a video interview specially prepared for this event featuring General Linda Bond. The General answered questions regarding the motivation of the Army's social work worldwide and stated the need for holistic ministry. The Executive Directors met General Bond when she visited Paris on 23 November and led a public meeting that evening.

Commissioner Christine MacMillan, (Director of the ISJC) was the guest speaker at a territorial 'Social Justice' day held in Paris in March 2012. Officers and the managers of social centres in France and Belgium met together for the first time around a common theme. A rich time of sharing took place in the afternoon when groups divided into geographical regions to discuss how to work together for social justice.

The Territorial Band was invited to the Italy and Greece Command's 125th anniversary congress in April 2012. They gave several concerts and played in St Peter's Square, Rome, which delighted an attentive and curious audience.

Colonel Massimo Paone (TC) was among a group of church leaders who accompanied the French President on a visit to The Museum of the Desert near Ales. This site commemorates the historic persecution of Protestants in the Cevennes area.

Major Anne Thöni, THQ, received a medal (Knight in the National Order of Merit) for her hospital chaplaincy work in a multi-faith context. Her ministry is carried out in partnership with the Federation of

PARIS: Young people present the musical 'Spirit' during Pentecost weekend 2011

French Protestant Churches.

Throughout the year strategic plans for future years were discussed. The motto chosen for 2012 was 'The mission continues – let us dare for God!' A day of consecration was held in January in all corps and this gave soldiers and comrades the opportunity to renew their commitment to God.

STATISTICS
Officers 172 (active 67 retired 105)
Employees 2,218
Corps 37 **Outposts** 3 **Institutions** 56
Senior Soldiers 1,177 **Adherent Members** 287
Junior Soldiers 160
Personnel serving outside territory Officers 9

THE SALVATION ARMY CONGREGATION – FRANCE

BOARD OF DIRECTORS
Col Massimo Paone, Col Jane Paone,
Lt-Col Sylvie Arnal, Maj Bernard Fournel,
Maj Ruth Moratto, Maj Patrick March

STAFF
Women's Ministries: Col Jane Paone (TPWM)
Maj Danièle César (TSWM)
Candidates: Col Jane Paone

Education and Prisons: Maj Jean-Paul Thöni
Field: Majs Bernard and Claire-Lise Fournel
Finance: Mr Alain Raoul
Retired Officers: Majs Christian and Joëlle
Exbrayat
Territorial Band: B/M Mrs Arielle Mangeard

THE SALVATION ARMY FOUNDATION – FRANCE

BOARD OF DIRECTORS
President: Col Massimo Paone
Secretary: Lt-Col Sylvie Arnal
Treasurer: Mr Olivier Ponsoye
Members: Mr Patrick Audebert, Mr Bernard
Westercamp, Maj Pascale Glories

STAFF
Director General: Mr Alain Raoul
Director of Social Exclusion Programme:
Mr Olivier Marguery
**Director of Care, Handicap and Dependence
Programme:** Mr Eric Yapoudjian
Director of Youth Programme: Mr Samuel
Coppens
Director of Projects and Property Programme:
Mr Bernard Guilhou
Communications: Mr David Germain
Director of Finance and Administration: Mrs
Martine Dumont
Business Manager: Mr Bruno Fontaine
Missing Persons: Maj Dominique Glories
Spiritual Care: Capt Jean-Claude Ngimbi
Volunteers: Maj Dominique Glories

SUMMER COLONY FOR CHILDREN AND YOUTH CENTRE

30530 Chamborigaud: Chausse;
  tel/fax: (04) 66 61 47 08 (acc 100)

SOCIAL SERVICES

Centres for Men

57100 Thionville: 68 rte de Metz;
  tel: (03) 82 83 09 60 (acc 105)
59018 Lille Cedex: Les Moulins de l'Espoir,
  48 rue de Valenciennes, BP 184;
  tel: (03) 20 52 69 09 (acc 299)
75013 Paris: Palais du Peuple,
  29 rue des Cordelières; tel: (01) 43 37 93 61
  (acc 100)

Centres for Women (with or without children)

30900 Nîmes: Les Glycines (Home for Battered
  Wives), 4 rue de l'Ancien Vélodrome;
  tel: (04) 66 62 20 68 (acc 52)
75011 Paris: Le Palais de la Femme,
  94 rue de Charonne; tel: (01) 46 59 30 00
  (acc 300)
94320 Thiais: Résidence Sociale,
  7 blvd de Stalingrad; tel: (01) 48 53 57 15
  (acc 57)

Centres for Men and/or Women (with or without children)

27400 Louviers: Residence Henri Durand,
  51 ave Winston Churchill; tel: (02) 32 50 90
  60 (acc 90)
13003 Marseille: Residence William Booth;
  190 rue Félix Pyat; tel: (04) 91 02 49 37
  (acc 130)
68100 Mulhouse: Le Bon Foyer,
  24 rue de L'Ile Napoléon; tel: (03) 89 44 43
  56 (acc 113)
69006 Lyon: La Cité de Lyon,
  131 ave Thiers; tel: (04) 78 52 60 80
  (acc 147)
74560 Monnetier-Mornex: Les Hutins;
  3 chemin de la Vie de la Croix
  tel: (04) 50 36 59 52 (acc 16)
75011 Paris: Résidence Catherine Booth,
  15 rue Crespin du Gast; tel: (01) 43 14 70 90
  (acc 108)
75013 Paris: La Cité de Refuge/Centre Espoir,
  12 rue Cantagrel; tel: (01) 53 61 82 00
  (acc 215)
75020 Paris: Résidence Albin Peyron,
  60 rue des Frères Flavien; tel: (01) 48 97 54 50
  (acc 250)
76600 Le Havre: Le Phare, 191 rue de la Vallée;
  tel: (02) 35 24 22 11 (acc 265)

51100 Reims: Le Nouvel Horizon, 42 rue de
  Taissy; tel: (03) 26 85 23 09 (acc 184)
76005 Rouen: Residence du Vieux Marché;
  26 rue de Crosne; tel: (02) 35 70 38 00 (acc 97)
78100 St Germain en Laye: La Maison Verte,
  14 rue de la Maison Verte;
  tel: (01) 39 73 29 39 (acc 64)
81200 Aussillon: 23 blvd Albert Gaches;
  tel: (05) 63 98 23 95 (acc 16)
90000 Belfort: 7 rue Jean-Baptiste Colbert;
  tel: (03) 84 21 05 53 (acc 134)

Work Rehabilitation and Recycling Centre

43400 Le Chambon sur Lignon: Pause Café,
  Rte du Stade – Levée Ferrier;
  tel: 09 61 01 11 70

Emergency Accommodation

13015 Marseille: La Madrague, 110 chemin de
  la Madrague Ville; tel: (04) 91 95 92 31
  (acc 230)
75013 Paris: Centre d'accueil d'urgence,
  12 rue Cantagrel; tel: (01) 53 61 82 00
  (acc 58)
92200 Neuilly sur Seine: L'Amirale Georgette
  Gogibus, 14 quai du Général Koenig;
  tel: (01) 55 62 02 95

Emergency Day Centres with orientation services

75003 Paris: ESI Saint-Martin, Face au 31 bld
  St Martin; tel: (01) 40 27 80 07
75019 Paris: La Maison du Partage,
  32 rue Bouret; tel: (01) 53 38 41 30

Mother and Baby Home

75019 Paris: Résidence Maternelle les Lilas,
  9 ave de la Porte des Lilas;
  tel: (01) 48 03 81 90 (acc 77)

Children's Home

35400 Saint-Malo: Les enfants de
  Rochebonne, 23 ave Paul Turpin,
  tel: (02) 99 40 21 94 (acc 36)

Training Centres for Children and Young People

30000 Nîmes: La Villa Blanche Peyron,
  122 Impasse Calmette; tel: (04) 66 04 99 40
  (acc 10)
34093 Montpellier Cedex 5: Institut Nazareth,
  13 rue de Nazareth; tel: (0) 4 99 58 21 21
67100 Strasbourg: Le Foyer du
  Jeune Homme, 42 ave Jean Jaurès;
  tel: (03) 88 84 16 50 (acc 50)
68100 Mulhouse: Foyer Marie-Pascale Péan,

42 rue de Bâle; tel: (03) 89 42 14 77 (acc 38)

77270 Villeparisis: Domaine de Morfondé;
tel: (01) 60 26 61 61 (acc 67)

Centres for Children and Young People (Day Care)

69007 Lyon: L'Arche de Noé, 5 rue Félissent; tel:
(04) 78 58 29 66

Rehabilitation Centres for the Impaired

45410 Artenay: Château d'Auvilliers;
tel: (02) 38 80 00 14 (acc 68)

74560 Monnetier-Mornex: Résidence Leirens,
Chemin St Georges; tel: (04) 50 31 23 12
(acc 60)

93370 Montfermeil: MAS Le Grand Saule,
2 ave des Tilleuls; tel: (01) 41 70 30 40 (acc 50)

Eventide Homes

35400 Saint-Malo: Résidence Boris Antonoff,
12 rue du Tertre Belot; tel: (02) 99 21 08 70

42028 Saint-Etienne Cedex 01: La Sarrazinière,
Allée Amilcare Cipriani; tel: 04 77 62 17 92
(acc 137)

47400 Tonneins: Le Soleil d'Automne,
ave Blanche Peyron, Escoutet;
tel: (05) 53 88 32 00 (acc 50)

60500 Chantilly: L'Arc-en-Ciel, 5 blvd de la
Libération; tel: (03) 44 57 00 33
(acc 53)

67000 Strasbourg: Résidence Laury Munch, 8 rue
du Moulin à Porcelaine, tel: (03) 88 22 83 61

83230 Bormes les Mimosas,
Res Olive et Germain Braquehais,
66 chemin de la Queirade;
tel: (04) 94 02 37 00

Senior Housing

75014 Paris: 9 bis, Villa Coeur-de-Vey;
tel: (01) 45 43 38 75

93230 Romainville: 2 rue Vassou

Short-term Care Home and Services

07800 St Georges-les-Bains: Le Château;
tel: (04) 75 60 81 72 (acc 50)

Conference and Holiday Centre

30530 Chamborigaud: Chausse;
tel/fax: (04) 66 61 47 08
(acc 100)

BELGIUM REGION

Regional Headquarters: Place du Nouveau
Marché aux Grains, 34, 1000 Brussels;
tel: [32] (2) 513 39 04;
websites:
www.armeedusalut.be; www.legerdesheils.be

Regional Leader: Maj Noélie Lecocq
(RO/RSWM) (12 Jul 2012)

Finance: Capt Marc Dawans

SOCIAL SERVICES

Hostels for Men

Foyer Georges Motte, blvd d'Ypres 24,
1000 Brussels; tel: (02) 217 61 36 (acc 75)

'Le Foyer', Centre d'accueil, rue Bodeghem
27-29, 1000 Brussels; tel: (02) 512 17 92
(acc 70)

Family Aid (EU Food Distribution)

Service d'Aide aux familles: blvd d'Ypres 26,
1000 Brussels; tel: (02) 223 10 44

Guidance Centre (Housing Help and Debt Counselling)

102 rue de l'Église Ste Anne, 1180 Brussels;
tel: (02) 414 19 16

Refugee Centre

'Foyer Selah', blvd d'Ypres 28, 1000 Brussels;
tel: (02) 219 01 77 (acc 90)

Mother and Children's Home

Maison de la Mère et de l'Enfant,
Chaussée de Drogenbos 225, 1180 Brussels;
tel: (02) 376 17 01 (acc mothers 14,
children 25)

Children's Home

'Clair Matin', rue des Trois Rois 88,
1180 Uccle-Brussels; tel: (02) 376 17 40 (acc
41)

SHOPS

Antwerp: Ballaerstraat 94, 2018
Antwerpen; 03/237.28.68

Quaregnon: 82A rue Monsville 7390,
Quaregnon; 065/78.30.08

CONFERENCE AND YOUTH CENTRE

Villa Meyerbeer, route de Barisart 256,
4900 Spa; tel: (087) 77 49 00

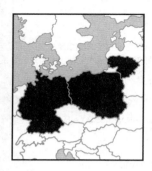

GERMANY AND LITHUANIA TERRITORY

Territorial leaders:
Colonels Patrick and Anne-Dore Naud

Territorial Commander:
Colonel Patrick Naud (1 June 2011)

Chief Secretary:
Lieut-Colonel Marsha-Jean Bowles
(1 June 2011)

Territorial Headquarters: 50677 Köln, Salierring 23-27, Germany

Tel: [49] (221) 20 8190; email: THQ@GER.salvationarmy.org;
website: www.heilsarmee.de

Salvation Army work in Germany began in Stuttgart on 14 November 1886 through the persistent sale of the Swiss *Kriegsruf* by Staff-Captain Fritz Schaaff who, after being converted in New York, was stationed in Switzerland and could not resist the call to bring the message over the border into his fatherland.

The Salvation Army was first registered as a limited company in Berlin in 1897 and was recognised throughout Germany as a church and public corporation on 10 October 1967 by law in Nordrhein-Westfalen. It is recognised as a religious association with public rights in the states of Berlin, Hessen, Schleswig-Holstein and Baden-Württemberg.

Salvation Army work in Lithuania having begun in 1998, the Germany Territory was redesignated the Germany and Lithuania Territory in September 2005. That same month, 'Project Warsaw' was launched to begin the Army's work in Poland (under IHQ) and on 1 July 2008 the Germany and Lithuania Territory took responsibility for this work when a regional office for Poland was established in Dresden.

Zone: Europe
Countries included in the territory: Germany, Lithuania, Poland
'The Salvation Army' in German: Die Heilsarmee; in Lithuanian: Isganymo Armija; in Polish: Armia Zbawienia
Language in which the gospel is preached: German, Lithuanian, Polish
Periodicals: *Danke, Heilsarmee-Forum, Heilsarmee-Magazin*

GUIDED by the Holy Spirit, the territory continued moving forward to realise the 'Vision 2030' strategy and goals, emphasising the mission statement 'The Salvation Army in Germany and Lithuania with the Poland Region – modern, strong, efficient – brings Christ to the people'.

Commissioners Robert and Janet Street (IS/ZSWM for Europe) installed Colonels Patrick and Anne-Dore Naud as Territorial Commander and President of Women's Ministries, and brought spiritual refreshment on a very hot day in June 2011. The new leaders confirmed their willingness to devote all they are and have to the Lord.

Also in June, the German Staff Band

hosted the Canadian Staff Band for two well-attended concerts before both bands travelled to London to participate in the International Staff Band 120th anniversary celebration weekend.

Throughout the year, an emphasis was placed on preparation as courses, seminars, events and retreats took place. In addition to skills training in youth work or corps ministry, many events had the purpose of spiritual formation and development.

'Leadership Weekend' was a time of personal challenge and corporate fellowship as officers with less than 10 years' service met in Cologne. 'All that I am', the conference for local officers was a spiritual highlight.

A mission team from USA Central Territory visited corps in Cologne, Guben and Warsaw. Children learned about spiritual freedom at the 'Alcatraz' Summer Camp – and they also learned to be creative with wood, saws, hammers and nails! Music camp was a highlight for the delegates with guest leader Major Kevin Metcalf (Canada and Bermuda). Family camp greatly benefitted families who needed quality time and fun together. 'As I have loved you', a spiritual retreat for retired officers, led by Majors Hugo and Esther Steiner (Switzerland) was appreciated just before Easter.

There were many opportunities for outreach through sport. The Territorial Sports Day involved activities at corps level and also united events such as the Football Cup. A small team of Salvationists used the EuroBasket 2011 (basketball tournament) held in Kaunas, Lithuania as a platform

BERLIN: The Salvation Army has an important ministry serving food and hot drinks at the annual 1 May demonstrations in the city.

to proclaim Christ.

As the territory looks to the future, the final part of its 'Vision 2030' strategy is the focus: 'We continually bring the ministry of our territory before God in prayer – personal and corporate – expecting his guidance in all plans, aims and intentions'.

STATISTICS

Officers 143 (active 72 retired 71) **Aux Capts** 4 **Field Sergeants** 8 **Employees** 703
Corps 48 **Outposts** 7 **Institutions** 40
Senior Soldiers 889 **Adherent Members** 484 **Junior Soldiers** 68

STAFF

Women's Ministries: Col Anne-Dore Naud (TPWM)
Territorial Evangelist and Director of Spiritual Life: Maj Frank Honsberg
Editor: Maj Alfred Preuß
Finance: Mr Hans-Joachim Bode
IT Manager: Maj Hartmut Leisinger
Property: Mr Rainer Wiebe
Communications and Marketing: Mr Andreas Quiring
Social: Maj Achim Janowski
Staff Band: B/M Heinrich Schmidt
Trade: Maj Heidrun Edwards
Training and Candidates: Maj Annette Preuß
Children and Youth: Lt-Col David Bowles

DIVISIONS

North-East: 12159 Berlin, Fregestr 13/14; tel: (0) 30-850 72980; email: DHQ_NordOst@GER.salvationarmy.org; Majs Reinhold and Ruth Walz
South-West: 45888 Gelsenkirchen, Hohenzollernstr 83; tel: (0) 0209-14908 546; email: DHQ_SuedWest@GER.salvationarmy.org; Majs Stephan and Andrea Weber

INVESTIGATION

Heckerstr 85, 34121 Kassel; tel: (0) 561 2889945; email: Suchdienst@GER.salvationarmy.org; Lt-Col Erika Siebel

SENIOR CITIZENS' RESIDENCES

12159 Berlin, Dickhardtstr 52-53 (acc apts 42)
45127 Essen, Hoffnungsstr 23 (acc apts 25)

44623 Herne, Koppenbergshof 2 (acc apts 11)
50858 Köln, Rosenweg 1-5 (acc apts 42)
68159 Mannheim, G3, 1 + 20 (acc apts 31)
68165 Mannheim, Augartenstr 43, Haus Marie Engelhardt (acc apts 19)
75175 Pforzheim, Pflügerstr 37-43 (acc apts 30)

SOCIAL SERVICES
Counselling

79110 Freiburg, Elsässer Str 7; tel: (0)761-89 44 92
20359 Hamburg, Counselling Centre, Talstr 11; tel: (0) 40-31 65 43
22117 Hamburg, Counselling Centre for Housing, Zum Seehafenbrücke 20; tel: (0) 40 3095360
22117 Hamburg, Counselling Centre 'Park-In', Oststeinbeckerweg 2 h; tel: (0) 40-713 65 64

Children's Day Nursery

12159 Berlin, Fregestr 13-14; tel: (0)30-850 729232 (acc 30)

Drop-in Cafés

Freiburg; Hamburg; Lübeck; Nürnberg

Hostels

60314 Frankfurt, Windeckstr 58-60; tel: (0) 69-49 74 33 (acc 40)
73033 Göppingen, Marktstr 58; tel: (0) 7161-7 42 17; (acc 33)
37073 Göttingen, Untere-Maschstr-Str 13b; tel: (0) 551-4 24 84 (acc 16)
23552 Lübeck, Engelsgrube 62-64; tel: (0) 451-7 33 94 (acc 37)
81369 München, Steinerstr 20; tel: (0) 89-26 71 49 (acc 50)
70176 Stuttgart, Silberburgstr 139; tel: (0) 711-61 09 67/68 (acc 40)
65189 Wiesbaden, Schwarzenbergstr 7; tel: (0) 611-70 12 68 (acc 191)

Nursing Homes

14163 Berlin, Goethestr 17-21; tel: (0) 30-3289000; (acc 51)
47805 Krefeld, Voltastr 50; tel: (0) 2151-93 72 60; (acc 63)

Therapeutic Rehabilitation Institutions

14197 Berlin, Hanauer Str 63; tel: (0) 30-8 20 08 40; (acc 30)
22453 Hamburg, Borsteler Chaussee 23; tel: (0) 40-514 314 0; email: HamburgJJH@GER.salvationarmy.org (acc 71)
34123 Kassel, Eisenacherstr 18; email: kasselsck@GER.salvationarmy.org (acc 85)

50825 Köln, Marienstr 116/118;
  tel: (0)221-955 6090 (acc 80)
90443 Nürnberg, Gostenhofer Hauptstr 47-49;
  tel: (0) 911-28 730; email:
  NuernbergSozWerk@GER.salvationarmy.org
  (acc 232)

Therapeutic Workshops

22453 Hamburg, Borsteler Chaussee 23;
  tel: (0) 40-514 314 35;
  90443 Nürnberg, Leonhardstr 17-21;
  tel: (0) 911 28730

Women's Hostels

34134 Kassel-Niederzwehren, Am Donarbrunnen
  32; tel: (0) 561-43113 (acc 7)
90443 Nürnberg, Gostenhofer Hauptstr 65;
  tel: (0) 911-272 3600 (acc 12)
65197 Wiesbaden, Königsteinerstr 24;
  tel: (0) 611-80 67 58 (acc 45)

CONFERENCE AND HOLIDAY CENTRE

24306 Plön, Seehof, Steinberg 3-4;
  tel: (0) 4522-5088200; email:
  seehof@GER.salvationarmy.org
  Conference and Holiday Home (acc 72 + 36)
  Youth Camp (acc 52) Camping Ground and
  3 holiday chalets and flats

LITHUANIA

Officer-in-Charge: Capt Susanne Kettler-
Riutkenen

Isganymo Armija, Lietuvoje, Tiltu 18, LT 91246
  Klaipeda; tel/fax: [370] 46-310634;
  email: klaipeda@isganymo-armija.org

POLAND

Regional Officer: Maj Patrick Granat

Warsaw Office: ul. Bialostocka 11 m. 21, 03-748
  Warszawa, Poland; tel: (0) 048 691 283 891;
  email: Warszawa@GER.salvationarmy.org
Starachowice Office: ul. Zakladowa 6 m 17,
  27-200 Starachowice, Poland;
  tel: (0) 048 60716 5903; email:
  starachowice@GER.salvationarmy.org

**LITHUANIA: Several new soldiers are enrolled at Klaipeda Corps
where the average age of senior soldiers is just 25 years**

GHANA TERRITORY

Territorial leaders:
Colonels Charles and Denise Swansbury

Territorial Commander:
Colonel Charles Swansbury (1 Mar 2011)

Chief Secretary:
Lieut-Colonel Samuel Kwao Oklah
(1 Jan 2011)

Territorial Headquarters: PO Box CT452 Cantonments, Accra, Ghana

Tel: [233] (21) 776 971; email: saghana@gha.salvationarmy.org

Salvation Army operations began in Ghana in 1922 when Lieutenant King Hudson was commissioned to 'open fire' in his home town of Duakwa. Ensign and Mrs Charles Roberts were also appointed to pioneer work in Accra. Work in neighbouring Togo was officially recognised on 1 April, 2011

Zone: Africa
Countries included in the territory: Ghana, Togo
'The Salvation Army' in Ga: Yiwalaheremo Asrafoi Le; in Fante and Twi: Nkwagye Dom Asraafo; in Ewe: Agbexoxo Srafa Ha La
Languages in which the gospel is preached: Bassa, Builsa, Dangme, English, Ewe, Fante, Frafra, Ga, Gola, Grushia, Twi
Periodical: *Salvationist Newsletter*

'FIGHTING for Right' based on 2 Corinthians 8:21 was the theme for 2012 in the Ghana territory.

In early 2012 anticipation was building for the 90th anniversary of the arrival of Lieutenant King Hudson. In 1922 he was appointed by General Bramwell Booth to 'open fire' in his hometown of Duakwa in the Central Region of the then Gold Coast. In recognition of this special anniversary, *Riches for Christ*, charting the history of the Ghana Territory from its humble beginnings, was published.

Two new buildings to support health centre services – at Duakwa and at Wenchi – were completed, along with a school classroom block at

Tongo in the Northern District. These properties, along with newly-built officers' quarters and continuing development of several hall properties, will be of lasting benefit in mission for many years.

The territory was blessed by the commitment of project partners to facilitate the continuation of health and vocational training centres and improvements to many school properties. Project teams visited and built relationships between donors and service recipients.

Progress has been made in both the reregistration of the Army's legal status in Ghana and the Army's religious status in neighbouring Togo.

The territory continued the initiative to encourage members to recognise their financial responsibilities through the publication in Twi of the teaching booklet, *A 40-day journey to a more generous lifestyle*. This emphasis was also seen as 'planned giving' was included within the remit of a newly-appointed Secretary for Spiritual Life Development.

For the first time in several years officers' councils were held; also a corps cadet and students union fellowship weekend took place. Other special events included a territorial business session and two women's local officers' retreats.

When Commissioner Amos Makina (IS for Africa) visited the territory, 40 senior soldiers were enrolled in recognition of the commissioner's 40 years' officer service.

During a weekend of celebration for the commencement of the work in Togo, 112 junior and 144 senior soldiers were enrolled. A Territorial Songster Brigade was formed, the Territorial Band relaunched and a Territorial Music Director appointed, inaugurating a new era of music ministry within the territory.

As the territory anticipates its 90th anniversary celebrations, the commissioning of 30 new officers, many new soldiers and improved facilities, there is a greater appreciation of the Army's mission and purpose within Ghana Territory. Everyone is poised to respond positively and enthusiastically to God-given opportunities to do what is right.

STATISTICS

Officers 238 (active 186 retired 52) **Cadets** 30 **Employees** 1,911
Corps 115 **Societies** 142 **Schools** 201 **Health Centres** 9 **Social Centres** 8 **Day Care Centres** 73
Senior Soldiers 19,237 **Junior Soldiers** 3,911
Personnel serving outside territory Officers 8

STAFF

Women's Ministries: Col Denise Swansbury (TPWM) Lt-Col Philomina Oklah (TSWM) Lt-Col Eva Danso (LOMS) Capt Emelia Asante Appiah (TJHLS)
Business Administration: Lt-Col Isaac Danso
Personnel: Lt-Col James Oduro
Programme: Lt-Col Eugene Dikalembolovanga
Candidates: Lt-Col Odile Dikalembolovanga
Communications and External Relations: Mr Kofi Sakyiamah
Extension Training: Capt Michael Eku
Finance: Capt Stephen Adu-Gyan
Human Resources: Lt-Col Elizabeth Oduro
Medical, Social and Community Services: Maj Heather Craig
Music: Capt Asare Bediako Tawiah
Projects and Child Sponsorship: Capt Margaret Amponsah
Property: Maj Richmond Obeng Appau
Public Relations: Maj Isaac Justice Incoom
Retired Officers: Lt-Col Elizabeth Oduro
Spiritual Life Development: Maj Graeme Craig
Territorial Band: B/M Emmanuel Hackman
Territorial Songsters: S/L Titus Ofori Arkoh
Trade Manager: Maj Beatrice Oyortey
Training: Lt-Col Samuel Baah
Youth : Capt Anthony Wiafe

DIVISIONS

Accra: PO Box 166 Tema; tel: (022) 215 530; Majs Godfried and Felicia Oduro
Akim Central: PO Box AS 283, Asamankese; tel: (081) 23 585; Majs Edward and Catherine Kyei
Ashanti Central: PO Box 15, Kumasi; tel/fax: (051) 240 16; Majs Samuel and Juliana Kyeremeh
Ashanti North: c/o PO Box 477, Mampong, Ashanti; Majs Stephen and Cecilia Boadu
Central: PO Box 62, Agona Swedru; tel: (041) 20 285; Majs Peter and Grace Oduro-Amoah
Nkawkaw: PO Box 3, Nkawkaw; tel: (0842) 22 208; Maj Jonas and Capt Constance Ampofo
Volta: PO Box 604, Ho, Volta Region;

Majs Edmund and Grace Abia

West Akim: PO Box 188, Akim Oda;
tel: (0882) 2 305; Maj Edward and Mercy
Addison

DISTRICTS

Brong Ahafo: PO Box 1454, Sunyani;
tel: (061) 23 513; Maj Ebenezer Danquah

East Akim: PO Box KF 1218, Koforidua E/R;
tel: (081) 22 580; Maj Modesto Kudedzi

Northern: PO Box 233, Bolgatanga;
tel: (072) 22 030; Capt Prosper Adua

Western: PO Box 178, Sekondi, C/R;
tel: (031) 23 763; Capt Alexander Siaw

TRAINING COLLEGE

PO Box CE 11991, Tema; tel: (022) 306 252/253

EXTENSION TRAINING CENTRE

PO Box CT 452, Cantonments, Accra;
tel: (021) 776 971

HEALTH CENTRES

Accra Urban Aid: PO Box CT 452,
Cantonments, Accra; tel: (021) 230 918
(acc 11, including maternity)

Accra Urban Aid Outreach: PO Box CT 452,
Cantonments, Accra; tel: (021) 246 764
(mobile outreach for street children)

Adaklu-Sofa: PO Box 604, Ho, V/R
(acc 4, including maternity)

Anum: PO Box 17, Senchi, E/R
(acc 11, including maternity)

Baa: PO Box 8, Baa, C/R (acc 4, including
maternity)

Begoro: PO Box 10, Begoro, E/R (acc 10,
including maternity)

Duakwa: PO Box 2, Agona Duakwa, C/R
(acc 30, including maternity)

Wenchi: PO Box 5, Wenchi, Akim Oda
(acc 8, including maternity)

Wiamoase: PO Box 14, Wiamoase, Ashanti;
tel: (051) 32 613

EDUCATION

Sub-primary Schools 73, Primary Schools 78,
Junior Secondary Schools 44, Senior
Secondary Schools 2

SOCIAL WORK

Adaklu-Sofa Vocational Training Centre

Anidasofie Street Girls' Training Centre, Accra;

Begoro Rehabilitation Centre

Child Care Training Centre, Baa

Malnutrition Centre, Agona Duakwa

Rehabilitation Centre, Wiamoase, Ashanti

Voluntary Counselling and Testing Centre, Accra

TOGO (UNDER THQ)

Officer-in-Charge: Capt Hervé Michel
Ahouyanganga

**GHANA:
Dressmaking
students from the
Sofa Vocational
Training Centre
perform a cultural
dance during
their graduation
ceremony in June
2011**

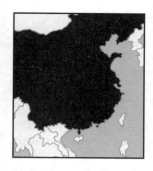

HONG KONG AND MACAU COMMAND

Command leaders:
Lieut-Colonels Samuel and Donni Pho

Officer Commanding:
Lieut-Colonel Samuel Pho (1 Jun 2009)

General Secretary:
Major On Dieu-Quang (1 Oct 2012)

**Command Headquarters: 11 Wing Sing Lane, Yaumatei,
Kowloon, Hong Kong**

Postal address: PO Box 70129, Kowloon Central Post Office, Kowloon, Hong Kong

Tel: [852] 2332 4531; email: Hongkong@hkt.salvationarmy.org;

website: www.salvation.org.hk

In March 1930, at a meeting held at Government House, Hong Kong, The Salvation Army was requested to undertake women's work in the crown colony, a work pioneered by Majors Dorothy Brazier and Doris Lemon. This work was directed from Peking until, in 1935, the South China Command was established in Canton to promote wide evangelistic and welfare operations. In 1939 Hong Kong became the Army's administrative centre. Later, the inclusion of the New Territories determined that the Command Headquarters move to Kowloon. Since 1951 the General of The Salvation Army has been recognised as a Corporation Sole. From 1993, disaster relief and community development projects have been carried out in mainland China. In 1999, a pioneer officer was appointed to the Special Administrative Region of Macau and Salvation Army work began there officially on 25 March 2000. In 2001, an officer was appointed to the North/North Eastern Project Office in Beijing.

Zone: South Pacific and East Asia
Regions included in the command: Hong Kong and Macau (Special Administrative Regions of the People's Republic of China) and Mainland China
'The Salvation Army' in Cantonese: Kau Sai Kwan; in Filipino: Hukbo ng Kaligtasan; in Putonghua: Jiu Shi Jun
Languages in which the gospel is preached: Cantonese, English, Filipino, Putonghua
Periodicals: *Army Scene, The War Cry*

WHEN Commissioners Alistair and Astrid Herring (IS/ZSWM for SPEA) visited the command and spoke in the united holiness meeting at the Grand Theatre, Heung Yee Kuk Building in October 2011 many people were encouraged to make commitments to Christ. Following the meeting, more than 50 young Salvationists held a praise meeting outside the theatre.

Commissioners Herring and Lieut-Colonels Samuel and Donni Pho (command leaders) visited the Beijing Office of the China Development Department. During a few days in China they also spent time with former Salvation Army officers and their families.

June 2011 saw the commissioning and ordination of four lieutenants from the Ambassadors of Holiness session. Three were appointed within the command and one to her home region, Taiwan.

Members of the 'Musical Force USA' Mission Team held a special concert in July 2011. This event glorified God and raised funds to enable the team to travel to the USA in August on a mission tour, led by Lieut-Colonels Samuel and Donni Pho. They participated in the San Francisco Chinatown Corps 125th anniversary celebration.

Kowloon East Corps organized an evangelical 'Musical Crusade' in February 2012 at the HKICC Lee Shau Kee School of Creativity in Hong Kong. Through a musical drama about overcoming challenges in life, the young people of the corps shared the gospel with an audience of more than 350 people.

Lieut-Colonels Samuel and Donni Pho and six other officers from the command participated in the 8th Chinese Congress on World Evangelization held in Bali, Indonesia in September 2011. With Chinese church leaders from many parts of the world, they shared a global vision for Chinese ministries.

Also in September, the Social Services department facilitated the first East Island young community leader training programme. Called 'Discover Gold in Rubbish', student leaders from six secondary schools collected classroom rubbish and reclaimed recyclable materials from the garbage. This helped to inform Hong Kong residents of the importance of sorting rubbish and recyling materials.

A new book, *Memoirs of Elder Trade Champions (II)* was published in April 2012 and 120 guests attended an event at Hong Kong Baptist University. The book launch was jointly organized by the Army's Yaumatei Multi-service Centre for Senior Citizens of the command and Lee Kau Yan Memorial School. The book is a collection of stories acknowledging the contributions the elderly have made to society through their working life. It provides a wealth of first-hand experiences to inspire younger generations..

The book launch of *Smiling Faces of the Northeast: A Memoir of the First Anniversary of the Japanese Earthquake* (東北の笑顔 – 日本大地震一周年紀念冊) was held in March 2012. All royalties were donated to the Hong Kong and Macau Command, in recognition of Salvationists' work following the earthquake in 2011.

STATISTICS

Officers 55 (active 43 retired 12) **Cadets** 1 **Employees** 2,459
Corps 18 **Outpost** 1 **Institutions** 20 **Schools** 6 **Kindergartens** 7 **Nursery Schools** 17 **Social Centres and Hotels** 81
Senior Soldiers 2,423 **Adherent Members** 31 **Junior Soldiers** 383

STAFF

Women's Ministries: Lt-Col Donni Pho (CPWM) Maj Ip Kan Ming-chun Connie (CSWM)
Business Administration: Ms Deirdre Ashe
China Development: Capt Lam Yin-ming Jeremy
Candidates: tba

Community Relations: Envoy Simon Wong
Editor/Literary: Capt Chan Tsui Heung-Ying Minny
Educational Services: Dr Cheng Kai Yuen Carl
Emergency Services Coordinator: Ms Karen Ng Wai-sze
Human Resources: Ms Eva Lau
Property: Envoy Daniel Hui Wah-lun
Sec for Personnel: tba
Sec for Programme: Capt Sara Tam Mei-shun
Business Administration: Deirdre Ashe
Social: Ms Irene Leung Pui Yiu
Trade: Ms Karen Ng Wai-sze
Training: tba

DIVISION

1 Lung Chu St, Tai Hang Tung, Kowloon, HK; tel: 2195 0222; fax: 2319 0670; Maj Susan Siu-suen Wun

OFFICER TRAINING COLLEGE AND GLOBAL CHINESE MINISTRY TRAINING CENTRE

1 Lung Chu St, Tai Hang Tung, Kln, PO Box 70129, Kowloon Central PO, Kln, HK; tel: 2195 0203; fax: 2319 1386

CHINA DEVELOPMENT

Hong Kong Head Office: tel: (852) 2783 2288; China Development Sec: Capt Jeremy Lam Yin-ming; tel: (852) 2783 2288; email: cdd@hkt.salvationarmy.org
North/Northeast Regional Project Office – Room 402, Unit 3, Building 5, Xin Yi Jia Yuan, Chong Wen District, Beijing 100062, China; tel: [86] (10) 6586 9331/2; email: nnerpo@hkt.salvationarmy.org
Yunnan Project Office – China: 6D, Unit 1, Block 8, Yin Hai Hot Spring Garden, Northern District, 173 Guan Xing Rd, Guan Shang, Kunming 650200, Yunnan, China; tel: [86] (871) 7166 111/222; email: ynpo@hkt.salvationarmy.org

EDUCATIONAL SERVICES

Kindergartens

Centaline Charity Fund: NT (acc 180) (acc 100 full-day)
Chan Kwan Tung: NT (acc 300) nursery (acc 56)
Hing Yan: Kln (acc 270) nursery (acc 108)
Ng Kwok Wai Memorial: NT (acc 360)
Ping Tin: Kln (acc 270) nursery (acc 42)
Tin Ka Ping: NT (acc 610, 2 sessions)

Crèches (1 month-2 years)

North Point: HK (acc 28 full-day)
Pak Tin: Kln (acc 16 full-day)

Nursery Schools (2-6 years)

Catherine Booth: Kln (acc 110 full-day)
Hoi Fu: Kln (acc 118 full-day)
Jat Min: NT (acc 168 full-day)
Kam Tin: NT (acc 104 full-day)
Lei Muk Shue:NT (acc 116)
Lok Man: Kln (acc 145)
Ming Tak: Kln (acc 126)
North Point: HK (acc 28)
Pak Tin: Kln (acc 104)
Sam Shing: NT (acc 104)
Tai Wo Hau: NT (acc 126)
Tai Yuen: NT (acc 100)
Tin Ping: NT (acc 116)
Tsuen Wan: NT (acc 183)
Wah Fu: HK (acc 126)
Wo Che: NT (acc 168)

Primary Schools

Ann Wyllie Memorial School (acc 984)

HONG KONG: The 'Musical Force USA' mission team from Hong Kong and local Salvationists outside San Francisco Chinatown Corps in August 2011

Centaline Charity Fund School (acc 1,011)
Lam Butt Chung Memorial School (acc 1,290)
Tin Ka Ping School (acc 1,040)

Secondary School
William Booth Secondary School, Kln;
   (acc 1,120)

Special School
Shek Wu School, Sheung Shui, NT
   (acc 200)

GUEST ACCOMMODATION
Booth Lodge, 7/F, 11 Wing Sing Lane, Yaumatei,
   Kln; tel: (852) 2771 9266;
   email: boothlodge@salvationarmy.org.hk

RECYCLING PROGRAMME
Logistic Centre: 7/F Tat Ming Industrial
   Building, 44-52 Ta Chuen Ping St,
   Kwai Chung, NT; tel: 2332 4433
   email: Recycling@hkt.salvationarmy.org

Family Stores
Hong Kong; Aberdeen Store, Mongkok Store;
   Nam Cheong Store; North Point Store; Shau
   Kei Wan Store; Stanley Store; Tin Hau Store;
   Wanchai Store; Western District Store;
   Yue Wan Store
Kowloon: City Store; Kwun Tong Store; Tai
   Hang Tung Store; Yaumatei Store
Macau Store

SOCIAL SERVICES
Camp Service
Bradbury Camp: 6 Ming Fai Rd,
   Cheung Chau, HK; (acc 108)
Ma Wan Youth Camp: Ma Wan Island, HK; (acc 40)

Children and Youth Centres
Chuk Yuen: Kln
Kwai Chung:NT
Lung Hang: Sin Sum House, Shatin, NT
Tai Wo Hau: Tai Wo Hau Community Centre,

Education and Employment Service
Education and Development Centre: 6 Salvation
   Army St, Wanchai, HK

Integrated Services for Young People
Chaiwan: Podium Level Market Bldg, HK
Tai Po: Tai Man House, NT
Tuen Mun: Hing Ping House, NT
Tuen Mun East: Ancillary Facilities Block, NT
Yaumatei: Block 4, Prosperous Garden, Kln

School Social Work Services
Tuen Mun: G/F, 13-24 Hing Ping House,
   Tai Hing Estate, Tuen Mun, NT

Services for Young Night Drifters
Tuen Mun: 5/F Ancillary Facilities Block,
   Fu Tai Estate, 9 Tuen Kwai Rd,
   Tuen Mun, NT

Youth Special Projects
'Flying High' Child Development Project: HK

Community Projects
Integrated Service for Street Sleepers: 1/F, GIC
   Bldg, 345A Shanghai St, Kln
Ngau Tam Mei Community Development
   Project: Kai Tak School, Wai Tsai Village,
   Yau Tam Mei, Yuen Long, NT
Sam Mun Tsai Community Development Project:
   31 Chim Uk Village, Shuen Wan, Tai Po, NT
So Uk Estate Community Service Team:
   G/F, 145-146 Azalea Hse, So Uk Estate,
   Shamshuipo, Kln
Urban Renewal Social Service Team: G/F,
   Shop C, 182 Fuk Wa Street, Shamshuipo, Kln

**Residential Care Service for Children and
Youth**
Tai Wo Hau Small Group Homes: NT:
   Home of Joy (acc 8)
   Home of Love (acc 8)
   Home of Peace (acc 8)
Ping Tin Small Group Homes: Kowloon:
   Home of Faithfulness (acc 8)
   Home of Goodness (acc 8)
   Home of Kindness (acc 8)
Hong Kong:
   Wan Tsui Home for Boys (acc 48)
   Yue Wan Boys' Hostel (acc 15)

Family Support Centre
Tung Chung: No. 4, G/F. Ying Yat House,
   Yat Tung Estate, Tung Chung, NT
Kowloon City: Flat C, 1/F. Po Shing Mansion,
   157-159 Kowloon City Road, Tokwawan
Shamshuipo Family Support Networking Team:
   Rm 69, 2/F Fuk Sing House,
   63-69 Fuk Wing St, Shamshuipo, Kln

Temporary Shelter
Sunrise House: 323 Shun Ning Rd, Cheung Sha
   Wan, Kln (acc 312)
Yee On Hostels: Unit 111-116, 1/F, Hoi Yu
   House, Hoi Fu Court, Mongkok, Kln;
   (acc 40)

Day Care Centres for Senior Citizens

Chuk Yuen: 141-150 Podium Level, Chui Yuen House, Chuk Yuen (South) Estate, Kln (acc 44)

Hoi Yu: G/F, Hoi Lam House, Hoi Fu Court, 2 Hoi Ting Rd, Mongkok, Kln (acc 44)

Tai Po: G/F. Wing B, Heng Yiu House, Fu Heng Estate, Tai Po, NT (acc 64)

Rehabilitation Homes

Cheung Hong: 2/F & 3/F Hong Cheung Hse, Cheung Hong Est, Tsing Yi, NT (acc 45)

Heng On Hostel: G/F, Heng Shan House, Heng On Estate, Ma On Shan, NT (acc 62)

Lai King Home: 200-210 Lai King Hill Rd, Kwai Chung, NT (acc 100)

Community Day Rehabilitation Services

Cheung Hong: 2/F & 3/F Hong Cheung Hse, Cheung Hong Est, Tsing Yi, NT (acc 45)

Shaukeiwan: 456 Shaukeiwan Rd, Shaukeiwan, HK (acc 40)

Tak Tin: G/F, Tak Yan House, Tak Tin Estate, Lam Tin (acc 53)

Integrated Home Care Service Teams

Kwun Tong: Unit 1-2, Wing B, G/F, Tak Lung House, Tak Tin Estate, Lam Tin, Kln

Sai Kung: 4/F, Po Kan House, Po Lam Estate, Tseung Kwan O, Kln

Tai Po: G/F, Wing A, Heng Yiu House, Fu Heng Estate, Tai Po, NT

Yau Tsim (Kowloon Central Office): G/F & 1/F, Chee Sun Building, 161-165 Reclamation St, Yaumatei

Yau Tsim (Yaumatei Office): 3/F, 11 Wing Sing Lane, Yaumatei, Kln

Elderly Special Projects

CADENZA Community Projects

CDSMP: Rm 105, 6 Salvation Army Street, Wan Chai, HK

Carer Project: 3/F, 11 Wing Sing Lane, Yaumatei, Kln

Palliative Care in Residential Care Homes for the Elderly: Rm 105, 6 Salvation Army Street, Wan Chai, HK

Promotional Scheme on Life and Death Journey: Rm 105, 6 Salvation Army Street, Wan Chai, HK

Senior Citizens Talent Advancement Projects

Kowloon: Tung Tau Centre; Kwun Tong Centre

Residences for Senior Citizens

Kowloon: Hoi Tai House (acc 98); Nam Ming Haven for Women (acc 38); Po Kan House (acc 105); Tak King House (acc 67)

NT: Bradbury Home of Loving Kindness (acc 136); Kam Tin (acc 15); Wing Sam House (acc 102)

Rehabilitation Special Projects

Share-Care Project: 200-210 Lai King Hill Rd, Kwai Chung, NT

Family Support Service for Persons with Autism: Room 201, 6 Salvation Army St, Wanchai, HK

Integrated Vocational and Rehabilitation Service

Heng On Integrated Vocational Rehabilitation Service: G/F, Heng Kong House, Heng On Estate, Ma On Shan, NT; tel: 2640 0656 (acc 285)

On the Job Training Programme for People with Disabilities: G/F, Heng Kong Hse, Heng On Est, Ma On Shan, NT; tel: 2640 0656 (acc 18)

Sunnyway – On the Job Training Programme for Young People with Disabilities: G/F, Heng Kong Hse, Heng On Est, Ma On Shan, NT; tel: 2640 0656 (acc 30)

Talent Shop: G/F, Heng Sing House, Heng On Estate, Ma On Shan, Shatin, NT; tel: 2633 7116

Social Enterprise

Digital Plus: Kln

Fitness Box: NT

Shatin Family Store: NT

Shatin Park Food Kiosk: NT

The WARM Project (Wheelchair and Assistive Device Re-engagement Movement): Kln

Tuen Mun Family Store: NT

INDIA NATIONAL SECRETARIAT

37 Lenin Sarani (1st Floor), Dharamtala St, PO Box 8994, Kolkata – 700 013, West Bengal, India

Tel: [91] (0) 33 2227 5780 /2249 7210 (O);
email:IND_Secretariat@ind.salvationarmy.org; website: www.salvationarmy.org/ind

India is The Salvation Army's oldest mission field. Frederick St George de Latour Tucker, of the Indian Civil Service, read a copy of *The War Cry*, became a Salvationist and, as Major Tucker (later Commissioner Booth-Tucker), took the Indian name of Fakir Singh and commenced The Salvation Army's work in Bombay on 19 September 1882. The adoption of Indian food, dress, names and customs gave the pioneers ready access to the people, especially in the villages.

In addition to evangelistic work, various social programmes were inaugurated for the relief of distress from famine, flood and epidemic. Educational facilities such as elementary, secondary, higher secondary and industrial schools, cottage industries and settlements were provided for the disadvantaged classes. Medical work originated in Nagercoil in 1895 when Captain (Dr) Harry Andrews set up a dispensary at the headquarters there. The medical work has grown from this. Work among the then Criminal Tribes began in 1908 at government invitation.

The Salvation Army is registered as a Guarantee Company under the Indian Companies Act 1913.

Publication: *The War Cry* (English)

THE National Secretariat for India serves the six Salvation Army territories within the country.

The Conference of Indian Leaders (COIL), established in 1989, meets annually to coordinate national Salvation Army affairs and give direction to the National Secretariat.

Several national offices had been established in earlier years, including the Editorial and Literary Office and the Audit Office. Since the establishment of The Salvation Army Health Services Advisory Council (SAHSAC) in 1986, a regionally based National Secretariat evolved to provide support to many aspects of Salvation Army work in India.

An administrative reorganisation took place in 2008. This led to all the secretariat departments being brought together in one building under the leadership of the National Secretary with the result that the

National Secretariat functions as a whole and not as separate departments.

THE SALVATION ARMY ASSOCIATION

Chairman: Comr M.C. James
National Sec: Lt-Col Davidson Varghese

Business Administration: tba
Editorial and Communication: Maj Samraj Babu
Human Resources Development and Education: Maj Hnamte Lalramliana
Social, Health and Emergencies: Maj Raj Paul Thamalapakula
Women's Advisory Council: Maj C. Lalhriatpuii

THE SALVATION ARMY CHRISTIAN RETREAT CONFERENCE CENTRE
'Surrenden', 15-18 Orange Grove Rd, Coonoor – 643 101, Nilgiris Dt, Tamil Nadu, S India; tel: (0423) 2230242

INDIA CENTRAL TERRITORY

Territorial leaders:
**Commissioners M.Y. Emmanuel and
T. Regina Chandra Bai**

Territorial Commander:
Commissioner M.Y. Emmanuel
(1 Dec 2006)

Chief Secretary:
Lieut-Colonel Edwin Masih (1 Mar 2012)

**Territorial Headquarters: 31 (15) Ritherdon Road, Vepery,
Chennai 600 007**

Postal address: PO Box 453, Vepery, Chennai 600 007, India

Tel: [91] (044) 2532 3148; email: ICT_mail@ICT.salvationarmy.org;

website: www.salvationarmy.org/ind

The India Central Territory comprises three regions – North Tamil Nadu (Madras-Chennai), Karnataka and Andhra Pradesh. Salvation Army work was commenced at Vijayawada in Andhra Pradesh in 1895 by Staff Captain Abdul Aziz, a person of Muslim background, with his friend Mahanada. Captain Abdul attended a revival meeting led by Captain Henry Bullard in 1884 at Bangalore and subsequently dedicated himself to be a Salvation Army officer. The territory was named the India Central Territory in 1992, with its headquarters at Madras (Chennai).

Zone: South Asia
States included in the territory: Andhra Pradesh, Karnataka, Tamil Nadu
'The Salvation Army' in Tamil: Ratchania Senai; in Telugu: Rakshana Sinyamu
Languages in which the gospel is preached: English, Tamil, Telugu
Periodicals: *Home League Magazine, Udyogasthudu, Yovana Veerudu, Yudha Dwani*

'COME near to God' was the territorial theme in 2012 and many revival meetings were held to emphasise this in various locations including Rajahmundry, Tanuku and Chennai. Many people responded and rededicated their lives to God. Fifteen families have joined a new corps which was opened at Repalli, Tenali Division in March 2012.

A Brengle seminar for officers, led by THQ staff, was conducted in each division in September 2011. Sessions based on the writings of Samuel Logan Brengle provided resources for deepening the spiritual life to the 750 officers in attendance.

A new Skill Training Centre at Chenneer Kuppam, Chennai was opened by Commissioners M.Y. and

T. Regina Chandra Bai Emmanuel, the territorial leaders.

USA Central Territory provided funding for 14 tricycles, which were distributed to physically challenged men in the territory and 48 bicycles were distributed to girls who live in remote areas to enable them to travel to Stuartpuram High School. A summer mission team, 15 young Salvationists from USA Central, visited the territory and encouraged young people and children to develop their lifeskills.

Children who are cared for in Salvation Army hostels gathered in Bapatla in February 2012 and 687 children participated at a spiritual get-together. A group of 50 young people participated in a discipling programme at the Youth Centre, also in Bapatla.

A prison ministry to children has commenced. Two officers visit detained children every Sunday in Chennai to distribute Bibles, offer counselling and lead spiritual and recreational programmes. This new ministry has been greatly appreciated by the 85 boys and 182 girls in the prison.

Women's Ministries held annual rallies in each district and division and more than 15,200 women attended, including some from other churches in the community. The Home League Helping Hand scheme raised 648,960 rupees. More than 4,000 seekers were recorded as women responded to the Bible messages and knelt in prayer.

STATISTICS
Officers 718 (active 540 retired 178) **Cadets** 31 **Employees** 520
Corps 281 **Outposts** 204 **Societies** 167 **Institutions** 14 **Schools and Colleges** 71 **Day Care Centres** 3 **Homes and Hostels** 20
Senior Soldiers 77,015 **Adherent Members** 8,936 **Junior Soldiers** 9,411

STAFF
Women's Ministries: Comr T. Regina Chandra Bai (TPWM) Lt-Col Sumita Masih (TSWM) Maj S. Vimalakumari (THLS) Lt-Col A. Yesu Rajaswari (TLOMS) Maj Yesamma (S&GSS) Maj Mercy Manjula (TWDO)
Business Administration: Lt-Col S.P. Abbulu
Editor: Capt I.D. Ebenezer
Education: Maj T.C.H. Abraham
Emergencies: Maj M. Prakasha Rao
Finance: Maj K. Yesudas
 Audit: Major K.Y. Dhana Kumar
Personnel: Lt-Col A. Nathaniel
 Human Resources Development: Capt G. Shanthi Babu
Programme: Lt-Col P. Samuel Rathan
 Evangelism and Outreach: tba
Property and Projects: Maj B. Joseph
Public Relations Officer: A. Sundar Singh
Social: Maj Chella Wyclif
Sponsorship: Mr Jeevan Roy
Trade: Maj V. Yesupadam
Training: Maj S. Jayananda Rao
 Candidates: Capt G. Shanthi Babu
Youth: Maj K. Prasad

DIVISIONS
Bapatla: Bapatla, Guntur District, 522 101; tel: (08643) 23931; Majs K. Samuel Raju and Raja Kumari
Chennai: 109 Gangadeeswara Koil St, Chennai 600 084; tel: (044) 2641 5021; Majs D. John Kumar & Mani Kumari
Eluru: Adivarapupet, Eluru, West Godavari District, 534 005; tel: (08812) 2237484; Majs D. Joshi & Leela Mani
Gudivada: Krishna District, 521 301; tel: (08764) 4243524; Majs K Suvarna Raju and Jhansi Bai
Hyderabad: 6D Walker Town, Padmarao Nagar, Secunderabad, 500 025; tel: (040) 27502610; Majs Dasari Daniel Raju and Baby Sarojini
Nellore: Dargamitta, Nellore, 524 003; tel: (0861) 2322 589; Majs K. Sundara Rao and Dasaratna Kumari
Rajahmundry: Mallayapet, East Godavari

**INDIA CENTRAL:
Tricycles provided
by the USA Central
Territory were
presented at Bapatla
to men with
disabilities**

District, 533 105; tel: (0883) 6579200;
Majs O. Philip Raju and Liliamma
Tanuku: West Godavari District, 534 211;
tel: 09989872902; Majs B.G. Prakash Rao and
Annamani
Tenali: Ithanagar, Tenali, Guntur District,
522 201; tel: (08644) 225949; Majs M.P.C.H.
Prasad and Krupamma
Vijayawada: nr Gymkhana Club,
Eastside H. No 26-191/2, Ghandi Nagar,
Vijayawada, 521 003; tel: (0866) 2575168;
Majs P. John William and Ratna Sundari

DISTRICTS

Bangalore: Karnataka Main Rd, J.P. Nagar,
Bangalore, 560 078, Karnataka State;
Maj J. Chelliadhas
Divi: PO Nagayalanka, Krishna District,
521 120; tel: (08671) 274991;
Maj Augustine
Machilipatnam: The Salvation Army,
Edepalli, Door No 15/344, Machilipatnam;
tel: (0867) 2224029; Maj J. Moshe
Mandavalli: Station Rd, Mandavalli, Krishna
District, 521 345; tel: (08677) 280503;
Maj D. Devadas
Prakasam: Stuartpuram, Guntur District, 522 317;
tel: (086432) 271131; Maj Chella Solomon Raju

EXTENSION AREAS
(under THQ)

Anantapur: The Salvation Army, H.No. 3616,
Jesus Nagar, Anantapur
Chittor: The Salvation Army, c/o Kamalamma
Samuel, D No 4 – 84, Balaji Nagar,
Greamspet, Chittor
Kadapa: The Salvation Army, c/o Mr M. Ajay
Kumar, D No 2/147 – 3, Balaji Nagar,
Kadapa, 515 003; tel: (098660) 77318
Khammam: The Salvation Army, c/o Ch.
Prabhakara Rao, D No 4-2-119, Sreenagar
Colony, nr Mamatha Medical College,
Khammam
Kurnool: The Salvation Army, c/o Y.A.
Evangeline, D No 40 – 448, A1A,
Gipson Colony, Kurnool; tel: (09391) 107852
Mahabub Nagar: The Salvation Army,
Venkateswara Colony, behind Jagadhamba
Temple, Laxmi Nager Colony, Mahabub Nagar
District
Medak: The Salvation Army, H. No. 4-7-
25/2/8/6, Plot No:64, Velugu Officer Rd,
Balajinagar Sangareddy, Medak
Nalgonda: The Salvation Army,
H No 7-1-155/D/19/4, Aruna Nilayam,
Srinagar Colony, Panagal Rd,
Nalgonda PO and District

Rangareddy: The Salvation Army, H No 20 – 45, Madhuranagar, Shamshebad, Rangareddy District

Vizianagaram: The Salvation Army, H No: 103, MIG -3, Phase - 3, Vuder Colony, Vizianagaram - 535 003

Warangal: The Salvation Army, H No 7 – 91, Gorry Kunta Crossroad, Labour Colony, Warangal

TRAINING COLLEGE

Dargamitta, Nellore, 524 003; tel: (0861) 2322687

EDUCATION
College (with hostel for boys and girls)
William Booth Junior College, Bapatla, Guntur District, 522 101; tel: (0864) 3224259

Community College
Virugambakkam, Chennai

High Schools (with hostels for boys and girls)
Bapatla: Guntur District, 522 101; tel: (0864) 3224282 (acc 300)
Stuartpuram: Prakasam District, 522 317; tel: (0864) 32271131 (acc 150)

Upper Primary School
Dargamitta, Nellore, Nellore District

Elementary Schools (Telugu Medium)
Bapatla Division: Bethapudi, Chintayapalem, Gudipudi, Kattivaripalem, Mallolapalem, MR Nagar, Murukondapadu, Valluvaripalem, Perlipadu, Pasumarthivaripalem, Pedapalli, Parli Vadapalem, Yaramvaripalem, Yazali
Eluru Division: Bhogapuram, Dendulur, Gopavaram, Gandivarigudem, Kovvali, Musunur, Pathamupparru, Surappagudem, Velpucharla
Gudivada Division: Chinaparupudi, Edulamadalli, Guraza, Gajulapadu, Gudivada, Kodur, Kancharlapalem, Kornipadu, Mandavalli, Narasannapalem, Pedaparupudi, Ramapuram
Nellore Division: Alluru, Buchireddipalem, Chowkacherla, Iskapalli, Kakupalli, Kanapartipadu, Mudivarthi, Modegunta, North Mopur, Pallaprolu, Rebala
Tenali Division: Annavaram, Burripalem, Chukkapallivaripalem, Duggirala, Danthuluru, Emani, Ithanagar, Kollipara, Kattivaram, Nambur, Nelapadu
Prakasam District: Cherukuru, Stuartpuram

Primary Schools (English Medium)
The Haven, 21 Thiru Narayanaguru Rd, Choolai, Chennai 600 112; tel: (044) 26612784
Teachers' Colony, Vijayawada 500 008, Krishna District; tel: (0866) 2479854
Hyderabad, 6D Walker Town, Padmarao Nagar PO, Secunderabad 500 025 (with day care)

English Medium High School
Teachers' Colony, Vijayawada 500 008; tel: (0866) 2479854

English Medium Matriculation School
The Haven, 21 Thiru Narayanaguru Rd, Choolai, Chennai 600 112; tel: (044) 26612784

English Medium Upper Primary School
B.H. Puram, Mangalagir Post, Vijayawada

Residential School
Tissot Sunrise School, PB9 Bapatla, 522 101; tel: (086432) 23336 (acc 125)

Vocational Training Centre
Adivarpet, Eluru, West Godivari District, 534 005 (with boys' hostel); tel: (08812) 550070

MEDICAL WORK
Evangeline Booth Hospital: Nidubrolu, Guntur District, 522 123; tel: (08643) 2522124 (acc 100)
Evangeline Booth Hospital (with home for the aged), Bapatla, Guntur District, 522 101; tel: (086432) 24134 (acc 75)

HIV/Aids Programme c/o THQ, Chennai

SOCIAL WORK
Children's Homes and Hostels

Boys' Hostels
Mallayyapet, Rajahmundry (acc 40)
Stuartpuram, Bapatla Mandal (acc 40)
Virugambakkam, Chennai (acc 80)

Girls' Hostels
Adivarpet, Eluru (acc 45)
Catherine Booth Girls' Hostel, Tenali (acc 30)
Dorcas Girls Hostel, Nagayalanka (acc 24)
Gudivada, Krishna District (acc 25)
'Haven', Virugambakkam, Chennai (acc 35)
'Home of Peace', Tanuku (acc 30)
Miriam Girls' Hostel, Kaikaluru, Mandavalli

(acc 30)

'Emma' Girls' Hostel, Nellore (acc 40)

'Stuart Girls Hostel', Stuartpuram, Bapatla
  Mandal (acc 40)

Home for the Aged

Virugambakkam, Chennai; tel: (044) 23770400
  (acc 70)

Working Women's Hostel

Catherine Booth Working Women's Hostel
  No: 82, Nungambakkam High Road,
  Chennai 600 034; tel: 30060325

Red Shield Guest House

15/31 Ritherdon Rd, Vepery, Chennai 600 007;
  tel: (044) 2532 1821 (acc 60)

**Waste Paper and Free Feeding
  Programme**

6D Walker Town, Secunderabad 500 025, AP

**INDIA EASTERN: A number of new soldiers were enrollled
at an outpost in Arunachal Pradesh outreach area**

INDIA EASTERN TERRITORY

Territorial Commander:
Colonel Lalngaihawmi (1 Jan 2011)

Chief Secretary:
Lieut-Colonel Lalramhluna (1 Jan 2011)

Territorial Headquarters: PO Box 5, Aizawl 796001, Mizoram, India

Tel: [91] 389 2322290 (EPABX)/2321864

email: IET_mail@IET.salvationarmy.org; website: www.salvationarmy.org/ind

Work in the region commenced on 26 April 1917 when Lieutenant Kawlkhuma, the first Mizo officer commissioned in India, returned to start the Army work. He was then joined by a group of earnest believers who shared his vision of an 'Army like a church, very much in line with The Salvation Army'. India Eastern became a separate command on 1 June 1991 and became a territory in 1993. Work was officially opened in Nepal on 26 April 2009.

Zone: South Asia

States included in the territory: Arunachal Pradesh, Assam, Manipur, Meghalaya, Mizoram, Nagaland, Sikkim, Tripura, West Bengal; also the Federal Democratic Republic of Nepal (part)

'The Salvation Army' in Mizo: Chhandamna Sipai Pawl

Languages in which the gospel is preached: Adhibasi, Bengali, Bru, English, Hindi, Hmar, Manipuri (Meitei), Mizo, Nagamese, Nepali, Paite, Pali, Simte, Thadou, Vaiphai

Periodicals: *Sipai Tlangau* (Mizo *War Cry*), *The Officer* (Mizo), *Young Salvationist* (Mizo), *Chunnunpar* (Mizo Women's Ministries magazine), *Naupang Sipai* (Mizo *Young Soldier*)

IN November 2011 the Territorial Youth Congress was held at Thenzawl. The theme was 'The Banquet is Ready', based on Matthew 22:4. More than 4,500 delegates enjoyed both physical and spiritual blessings during the event. Speakers included Commissioners Lalkiamlova and Lalhlimpuii (IS and ZSWM for South Asia), Colonel Lalngaihawmi (TC) and Major Cornell from the Sweden and Latvia Territory. They gave powerful and inspiring Bible messages. About 1,000 young people signed a purity pledge, promising to live a holy life and uphold Christian standards. A

special offering to build a Prayer Shed raised 37,200 rupees. The building was opened by the territorial commander the following month.

July 2011 brought severe flooding in Lakhimpur and Dhima Districts and Upper Assam. A medical team set up a free clinic to try and prevent disease and help those suffering from contaminated drinking water and food.

In September 2011 a new Territorial Council was inaugurated during a meeting at Bazar Corps. The members were dedicated to the service of God by the territorial commander, and their first meeting to discuss important issues was held the following day.

Community outreach ministries in many corps gave practical help to street dwellers. Spiritual counselling and prayer were also significant aspects of this work with people in need.

The commissioning and ordination of 21 cadets of the Friends of Christ session took place at Vengthar Corps, Kolasib, Western Division in March 2012. The new lieutenants also graduated with a Bachelor of Theology degree from Asia Theological Association, Bangalore and their parents received the fellowship of the Silver Star.

In April 2012 a Brengle Institute was held in Aizawl for 25 soldiers selected to attend. Lt-Colonel Janet Munn, Secretary for Spiritual Life Development, IHQ, was the main speaker. Many blessings were received as she taught about holiness.

STATISTICS

Officers 346 (active 277 retired 69) **Cadets** 14 **Employees** 138
Corps 299 **Societies/Outposts** 114 **Social Institutions** 13 **Schools** 18
Senior Soldiers 38,089 **Adherent Members** 889 **Junior Soldiers** 10,089

STAFF

Women's Ministries: Col Lalngaihawmi (TPWM) Lt-Col Kawlramthangi (TSWM) Maj Sailo Hmunropuii (THLS) Maj Zonunsangi (Dir, Special Services) Maj Ralte Thanzuali (LOM) Maj J Lalpianpuii (WDO) Maj Lalchhuanmawii (Fundraising) Maj Lalringliani (Retired and Pensioned Officers Fellowship) Maj Lalfakzuali (Literature) Maj Ramthanmawii (Officers' Children) Lt Lalnunmawii (Asst to TPWM)
Business Administration: Ter Env Joseph L.Vaikhuma
Community Health Action Network (CHAN): Maj Shamu Meitei

Editor and Literature Secretary: Maj K. Lalrinawma
Finance: Capt Ramdinthari Varte
Outreach: Maj Lianthanga
Personnel: Lt-Col Lalbulliana
Programme: Lt-Col Guite Khaizadinga
Projects and Sponsorship: Maj Saza Lalsangpuii
Property and Legal: Maj Tlau Lalhriatpuia
Public Relations: Maj Ralte Sangchhunga
Social Services: Maj Pachuau Lianhlira
Territorial Songsters: S/L K. Zohmingthanga
Territorial Band: B/M Territorial Envoy Joseph Lalrintluanga
Training: Maj Ralte Lalliankunga
Youth, Candidates and Education: Maj Chawnghlut Vanlalfela
Spiritual Life Development: Maj Hrahsel Vanlalthanga
Statistics: Lt-Col Lalnunhlui

DIVISIONS

Central North: PO Aizawl, 796 001, Mizoram; tel: (0389) 2317097; Majs Khiangte Zothanmawia and Thiak Vanlalnungi
Central South: PO Kulikawn, 796005, Aizawl – Mizoram; tel: (0389) 2300246; Majs Ngurte Lalhmingliana and Chawngthu Lalhlimpuii
Himalayan: 8 Bylane Zoo Narengi Rd, nr SBI Geeta Nagar Branch, PO Box 65, Guwahati – 781021, Assam; tel/fax: (0361) 2413405; Majs Chhangte Chawnghluna and Khawlhring Chhuanmawii
Manipur: Salvation Rd, PO Churachanpur, 795 128, Manipur; tel: (3874) 233188; Majs Ralte Laithanmawia and Tochhawng Lalbiaktluangi
Southern: PO Lunglei, 796 701, Mizoram; tel: (95372) 2324027; Majs Chhakchhuak Dawngliana and Hauhnar Manthangi
Western: PO Kolasib, 796 081, Mizoram; tel: (3837) 220037; Majs Sailo Biakliana and Hrangkhawl Biakmawii

UNDER THQ

Nepal: PO Box 8975, EPC-1677, Kathmandu, Nepal; tel: 00977-1-5537552; email: Lalsangliana/NEP/SArmy Majs Vuite Lalsangliana and Ralte Lalnunsangi
Kolkata: 72/3 SN Banerjee Road, 2nd Floor Suite No 17, Kolkata – 14; tel: 033-22654713; Maj Ralte Thangkhuma (Liaison Officer)

TRAINING COLLEGE
Kolasib Vengthar, PO Kolasib, 796 081,
Mizoram; tel: (3837) 220466

EDUCATION
Special Residential Schools for the Physically Challenged
Mary Scott Home for the Blind: Kalimpong,
West Bengal; tel: (3552) 255252;
email: sa_msh_kpg@yahoo.co.in (acc 80)
School for Deaf and Dumb Children:
Darjeeling, West Bengal;
tel: (354) 2252332/2257645
email: sadeaf@sify.com (acc 50)

Higher Secondary Schools
Children's Training Higher Secondary School:
Churachandpur, Manipur; tel: (3874) 235097
Modern English Higher Secondary School:
Aizawl, Mizoram; tel: (389) 2323248

High Schools
Blue Mount: Behliangchhip, Zampui, Tripura
Booth Tucker Memorial School: Gahrodpunjee,
Cachar
Hermon Junior: Moreh, Manipur
School for the Blind (Junior High School):
Kalimpong

Middle Schools
Booth Tucker: Thingkangphai, Manipur
Children's Education School: Zezaw, Manipur
Children's Training School: Singngat, Manipur
Hermon Junior: Moreh, Manipur
SA Middle School: Saikawt, Manipur
School for the Deaf: Darjeeling
Willow Mount: Durtlang, Mizoram

Primary School
Integrated Primary School: Kolasib

Outreach Schools: 27

SOCIAL WORK
Catherine Booth Home for the Aged, New
Serchhip (acc 10)

Homes for Boys and Girls
Mary Scott Home for the Blind: Kalimpong,
West Bengal
Hostel for the Deaf and Dumb: Darjeeling,
West Bengal

Homes for Boys
Hostel for the Blind: Kolasib, Mizoram;
tel: (3837) 220236 (acc 25)
Enna In: Kolasib; tel: (3837) 221419 (acc 30)
Kawlkhuma Home: Lunglei; tel: (372) 224420
(acc 25)
Muanna In: Mualpui, Aizawl; tel: (389) 2320426
(acc 30)
Manipur Boys' Home: Mualvaiphei,
Churachandpur; tel: (3874) 235469 (acc 25)
Saiha Orphanage; tel: (3835) 226140 (acc 15)
Silchar Home (acc 20)

Home for Girls
Hlimna In: Keifang, Mizoram;
tel: (389) 2862278 (acc 65)

Motherless Babies' Homes
Aizawl: Tuikal 'A', Aizawl, Mizoram;
tel: (389) 2329868 (acc 35)
Manipur: Mualvaiphei, Churachandpur, Manipur;
tel: (3874) 235469 (acc 10)

Community Caring Programme
Churachandpur, Manipur; tel: (3874) 235469

Deafness Reduction Programme
Darjeeling, West Bengal

HIV/AIDS PROGRAMME
Community Health Action Network (CHAN)
Kawlkhuma Bldg, Tuikal 'A', PO Box 5,
Aizawl 796001; tel: (389) 2320202/2327609;
fax: (389) 2326106;
email: chanaizawl@sancharnet.in

CENTENARY PRESS
PO Box 5, Tuikal 'A', Aizawl, Mizoram;
tel: (389) 2329626

MEXICO: Commissioner David Bringans (l), then TC, and General Linda Bond (r) with eight-year-old Rameses, who told a large congregation about the

One Army, united in prayer: (clockwise from top left) **in Canada at the International Conference of Leaders; Angola; India South Eastern; Zimbabwe at the All Africa Women Leaders Conference; India Central Hostel for Girls; Costa Rica; The Philippines** (centre)

One Army moving forward together in: **Zambia** on a united march of witness (above);
Angola where Salvationists make a bold witness on International Women's Day (below)

Finland – General Linda Bond commissions four cadets (above);
South America East Territory where The Salvation Army is marching forward in
Argentina, Paraguay and Uruguay (below)

One Army reaching them in love.with the transforming message of Jesus and practical care in: (clockwise from top left) **Kenya; Spain; Bamako, Mali; Georgia, EET; Copenhagen, Denmark**

INDIA SOUTH WESTERN: One of many enthusiastic young Salvationists welcoming the General in February 2012

INDIA NORTHERN TERRITORY

Territorial leaders:
Commissioners Kashinath and Kusum Lahase

Territorial Commander:
Commissioner Kashinath V. Lahase
(1 Jan 2006)

Chief Secretary:
Lieut-Colonel Daniel Raju Mathangi:
(1 Oct 2011)

Territorial Headquarters: H-15, Green Park Extension, New Delhi 110 016, India

Tel: [91] (11) 2651 2394; email: INT_mail@INT.salvationarmy.org;

website: www.salvationarmy.org/ind

Shortly after arriving in India in 1882, Booth-Tucker visited major cities in northern India, including Allahabad, Delhi, Lucknow, Benares and Kolkata (Calcutta). Rural work was established later and operations were extended to Bihar and Orissa. The boundaries of the India Northern Territory have changed over the years; there have been headquarters in Gurdaspur, Bareilly, Lucknow, Benares and Kolkata and, more recently, Delhi. In 1947, part of the territory became Pakistan. The present territory was established on 1 June 1991.

Zone: South Asia

States included in the territory: Bihar, Chattisgarh, Haryana, Himachal Pradesh, Jammu and Kashmir, Jharkhand, Odisha (Orissa), Punjab, Uttar Anchal, Uttar Pradesh, Uttara Khand, West Bengal; the Union Territories of Delhi, Chandigarh, and the Andaman and Nicobar Islands

'The Salvation Army' in Hindi, Punjabi and Urdu: Mukti Fauj

Languages in which the gospel is preached: Bengali, Burmese, English, Hindi, Kui, Nepali, Oriya, Punjabi, Santhali, Tamil, Urdu

Periodicals: *Home League Yearly* (Hindi and English), *Mukti Samachar* (Hindi and Punjabi), *The Officer* (Hindi), *Yuva Sipai* (Hindi)

THE commissioning and ordination of 45 cadets of the Friends of Christ session took place at Gurdaspur, Punjab in April 2012 conducted by Commissioners Lalkiamlova and Lalhlimpuii (IS and ZSWM for South Asia) with Commissioners Kashinath and Kusum Lahase, territorial leaders.

A new Burmese corps at Sitapuri, New Delhi, Chandigarh Division opened. It is attended by 21 families including 25 senior and 11 junior soldiers, with 20 children attending company meetings.

Mukerian District was upgraded to Mukerian Division and Pathankot

Extension was upgraded to Pathankot District on 1 September 2011.

The feeding programmes at Kolkata and New Delhi continued to serve hundreds of people. As they received meals they were also invited to attend church and some people have found faith in Jesus Christ.

Continued sponsorship for Veer Projects in these cities has enabled care and rehabilitation to be provided for many street children.

Women's ministry officers visited groups regularly, teaching about prenatal care, maternal health and provided health education. The issues of child labour and human trafficking were also regularly addressed.

Two tailoring centres, where women can develop and use their skills to earn some income, were opened. Many corps are now planning this kind of income generating programme to benefit women in their communities .

A Carpentry Training Centre was inaugurated by Commissioner K.V. Lahase, TC, in June 2011. The first intake of 17 young men has successfully completed training.

The Order of the Founder was presented to Lieut-Colonel Kamla Parshad on 19th September 2011 by the territorial leaders.

More than 5,000 women living below the poverty line were involved in 460 self help groups and 12 federations, enabling them to support their families through various schemes.

The Indian Northern Territory is moving forward with the transforming message of Jesus and reaching out to marginalised people.

STATISTICS

Officers 478 (active 386 retired 92) **Cadets** 47 **Employees** 276
Corps 164 **Outposts** 410 **Societies** 775 **Institutions** 23 **Schools** 9 **College** 1
Senior Soldiers 65,694 **Adherent Members** 2,867 **Junior Soldiers** 7,549

STAFF

Women's Ministries: Comr Kusum K. Lahase (TPWM) Lt-Col Rachel Mathangi (TSWM) Lt-Col Mariam Parkash (THLS)
Editor: Maj Robin
Education and Disasters: Maj Tarsem Masih
Personnel: Lt-Col Parkash Masih
Business Administration: Lt-Col Thomas Gera
Human Resources: Maj Raj Kumar
Legal and Community Development: Maj Robin Kumar Sahu
Music Ministry: Maj Swinder Masih
Programme: Lt-Col Joginder Masih
Projects: Capt Prakash Chandra Pradhan
Property: Maj Kashmir Masih
Public Relations/Fundraising: Maj George Patrick
Spiritual Development: Maj Vijayapal Singh
Training: Maj Yaqoob Masih
  Candidates: Maj Kailash Masih
Youth: Capt Thomson

DIVISIONS

Amritsar: 25 Krishna Nagar, Lawrence Rd, Amritsar 143 001, Punjab; Majs Piara and Grace Masih
Angul: Sikhayak Pada, Angul Post, Angul District 759 122, Odisha; tel: 06764-211271; Majs Dilip and Nivedita Singh
Bareilly: 220 Civil Lines, Bareilly 243 001, UP; tel: 05812-427081; Majs Baldev and Chandrika Nayak
Batala: Dera Baba Nanak Rd, Batala 143 505, Dist Gurdaspur, Punjab; tel: 01871-243038; Majs Makhan and Sunila Masih
Beas: Ajeet Nagar, Beas, Amritsar 143 201, Punjab; tel: 01853-273834; Majs Manuel and Anita Masih
Chandigarh: Surajpur Rd, Firojpur, PO Dhamala Via Pinjore, Dist Panchkula, Haryana 134 102; tel: 01733-654946; Majs Manga and Roseleen Masih
Dera Baba Nanak: Dist Gurdaspur, PO Dera Baba Nanak 143 604, Punjab;

INDIA NORTHERN: Twenty-one families meet for worship at the newly-opened Burmese corps in New Delhi

tel: 01871-247262; Majs Sulakhan and Sheela Masih

Gurdaspur: Jail Rd, Dist Gurdaspur 143 521, Punjab; tel: 01874-220622; Majs Gurnam and Razia Masih

Kolkata: 37 Lenin Sarani, Kolkata West Bengal 700 013; tel: 033-55101591; Capts Philip and Nayami Nayak

Moradabad: Kanth Rd, nr Gandhi Ashram PAC, Moradabad 244 001; tel: 09897-358114; Majs Salamat and Snehlata Masih

Mukerian: Rikhipura Mohalla, Dist Hoshiyarpur, Mukerian – 144 211, Punjab; tel: 01883-248733; Majs Daniel and Parveen Gill

DISTRICTS

Jasidih: Deoghar Rd, Ramchanderpur, Jasidih, Jharkand – 814 142; Maj Chotka Hembrom

Pathankot: Daulatpur Rd, Prem Nagar, nr FCI Godown, Pathankot – 145001, Punjab; tel: 09463-970566; Maj Salamat Masih

EXTENSION WORK

Ferozpur: c/o Vedparkash, Near 33 K.V. Power House, Gandhi Nagar, Ferozpur City-152002, Punjab; Captain Yusaf Masih

Patiala: Near Railway Fatak NO. 16, H. No. 116, Gali No. 1, Rasulpur Saidan, Patiala - 147001, Punjab; Maj Gurcharan Masih

Port Blair: Prothrapur, nr Atta Chakki, PO Garacharma, Port Blair – 744105,

Andaman Nicobar Islands; Lieut Jasbir Masih

Shahjahanpur and Lucknow: 43A Church Rd, Vishnupuri, Aliganj, Lucknow – 226 022, UP; tel: 0522-6540822 Capt Sanjay Robinson

Taran Taran: Sandhu Ave, nr Shota Kazi Kot Rd, Ward 11, Taran Taran – 143401, Dist Amritsar, Punjab; Maj Salamat Masih

Uttara Khand – Bajpur: Indira Colony, Baria Rd, Bajpur Udham Singh Nagar – 261 401, Uttara Khand; Maj Masih Dayal

TRAINING COLLEGE

Bareilly: 220 Civil Lines, Bareilly 243 001, UP; tel: 0581-2423304

MEDICAL WORK

Hospital

MacRobert Hospital: Dhariwal, Dist Gurdaspur 143 519, Punjab; tel: 01874-275152/275274 (acc 50)

Clinics

Social Service Centre: 172 Acharya Jagdish Chandra Bose Rd, Kolkata 700 014; tel: 033-22840441

Community Health Centre: 192-A, Arjun Nager, New Delhi 110 029; tel: 011-26168895

Eye Hospital: Surajpur Rd, Firojpur, PO Dhamala via Pinjore, Dist Panchkula, Haryana 134 102; tel: 01733-654946

HIV/Aids Clinic: 220 Civil Lines, Bareilly 243 001, UP; tel: 0581-2427081

EDUCATION
Senior Secondary School
Aliwal Rd, Batala 143 505, Dist Gurdaspur,
Punjab; tel: 01871-242593 (acc 900)

Extension Branch
Gurdaspur School: The Salvation Army DHQ
Compound, Jail Rd, Dist Gurdaspur,
Punjab; tel: 01874-20622

English Medium Schools
Andaman Nicobar Islands: Catherine Booth
School, Prothrapur, PO Garacharma, Port Blair
– 744105 (acc 25)
Behala: 671 D.H. Rd, Hindustan Park, Behala,
Kolkata 700034; tel: 033-23972692
Moradabad: Kanth Rd, opp Gandhi Ashram PAC,
Moradabad 244 001, UP;
tel: 0591-2417351/2429184 (acc 400)
William Booth Memorial School:
220 Civil Lines, Bareilly 243001, UP;
tel: 0581-2420007 (acc 200)

College
The Salvation Army College: Aliwal Rd, Batala
143 505, Dist Gurdaspur, Punjab;
tel: 01871-242593 (acc 300)

Non-residential Tailoring Units
Batala: Gurdaspur, Punjab
Dera Baba Nanak: Dist Gurdaspur, Punjab
Gumtala:Amritsar,Punjab
Kancharapada: West Bengal
New Delhi: H-15, Green Park Extn
Port Blair: Port Blair, Andaman

Skill Training Centre
Training Centre for young men (Carpentry)
Shahpur Goraya, District Gurdaspur, Punjab

SOCIAL WORK
Free Feeding Programmes
Kolkata: 172 Acharya Jagadish Chandra Bose Rd,
Kolkata 700 014 (beneficiaries 250)
New Delhi: 6 Malik Bldg, Chunamandi Paharganj,
New Delhi 110 055;
tel: 011-23588433 (beneficiaries 150)

Homes for the Aged
Bareilly: 220 Civil Lines, Bareilly 243 001, UP;
tel: 0581-2421432 (acc 20)
Dhariwal: MacRobert Hospital, Dhariwal,
Dist Gurdaspur 143 519, Punjab;
tel: 01874-275152/275274 (acc 20)
Kolkata: 172 Acharya Jagadish Chandra Bose Rd,
Kolkata 700 014 (acc 15)

Homes for Boys
Angul: Angul 759 122, Odisha;
tel: 06764-232829 (acc 25)
Batala: Aliwal Rd, Batala 143 505,
Dist Gurdaspur (acc 60)
Kolkata: 37 Lenin Sarani, Kolkata 700 013;
tel: 033-55124567 (acc 30)
Moradabad: Kanth Rd, Moradabad 244 001, UP;
tel: 0591-2417351 (acc 40)
Simultala: Simultala 811 316, Dist Jamui, Bihar
(acc 43)

Homes for Girls
Angul: Angul 759 122, Odisha; tel: 06764-232829
(acc 40)
Bareilly: 220 Civil Lines, Bareilly 243 001, UP;
tel: 0581-2421432 (acc 40)
Batala: Aliwal Rd, Batala 143505,
Dist Gurdaspur (acc 60)
Behala: 671 D.H. Rd, Hindustan Park, Behala,
Kolkata 700034; tel: 033-23972692
(acc 120)
Gurdaspur: Jail Rd, Dist Gurdaspur 143 521,
Punjab (acc 100)

Hostels
Blind (Men)
172 Acharya Jagdish Chandra Bose Rd, Kolkata
700 014 (acc 30)

Working Men and Students
172 Acharya Jagdish Chandra Bose Rd,
Kolkata 700 014; tel: 033-22840441
(acc 200)

Young Women
Bareilly: 220 Civil Lines, Bareilly 243 001, UP;
tel: 0581-2421432
Kolkata: 38 Lenin Sarani, Kolkata 700 013;
tel: 033-22274281 (acc 50)
Ludhiana: 2230, ISA Nagari, Ludhiana – 141 008,
Punjab

RED SHIELD GUEST HOUSE
Kolkata: 2 Saddar St, Kolkata 700 016;
tel: 033-22861659 (acc 80)

VEER PROJECT
Kolkata: 172 Acharya Jagadish Chandra Bose Rd,
Kolkata 700 014
New Delhi: 6 Malik Bldg, Chunamandi Paharganj,
New Delhi 110 055; tel: 011-2358 8433.

WASTE PAPER DEPARTMENT
6 Malik Bldg, Chunamandi Paharganj,
New Delhi 110 055; tel: 011-2358 8433

INDIA SOUTH EASTERN TERRITORY

Territorial leaders:
Commissioners M.C. and Susamma James

Territorial Commander:
Commissioner M.C. James (1 Dec 2006)

Chief Secretary:
Lieut-Colonel Gabriel Christian (1 Aug 2011)

**Territorial Headquarters: High Ground Road, Maharajanagar PO,
Tirunelveli – 627 011, Tamil Nadu, India**

Tel: [91] (462) 2574331/2574313; email: ISE_mail@ISE.salvationarmy.org;

website: www.salvationarmy.org/ind

The Salvation Army commenced operations in south-east India on 27 May 1892 as a result of the vision received by Major Deva Sundaram at Medicine Hill, while praying and fasting with three officers when the persecution in Southern Tamil Nadu was at its height. On 1 October 1970 the Tamil-speaking part of the Southern India Territory became a separate entity as the Army experienced rapid growth.

Zone: South Asia
States included in the territory: Pondicherry, Tamil Nadu
'The Salvation Army' in Tamil: Ratchaniya Senai; in Malayalam: Raksha Sainyam
Languages in which the gospel is preached: English, Malayalam, Tamil
Periodicals: *Chiruveeran* (Tamil), *Home League Quarterly*, *Poresatham* (Tamil), *The Officer* (Tamil)

IN October 2011 Salvationists and friends welcomed Colonels David E. and Sharron Hudson (CS and TSWM, USA Western Territory), whose ministry blessed many people during congress meetings.

Major Tim Foley, also from USA Western, a mission partner territory, conducted a Brengle Institute for the young people of the territory. It was a time of great spiritual refreshment.

The territorial theme for 2012, the international vision statement of 'One Army, One Mission, One Message'

was launched in January, just before the visit of General Linda Bond in February. Salvationists and dignitaries welcomed the General and bands played all along the route as the international leader travelled from the airport.

Large crowds attended every meeting and listened intently to the General's preaching. Many people responded to the invitation to pray at the mercy seat. The international leader's visits to institutions greatly encouraged the staff and residents.

Seven hundred new soldiers were recruited during the year. New Army work has commenced in Salem, Bhavani and Erode districts. Fund raising, including the women's ministries Helping Hand scheme, has helped to support these areas.

Commissioner Susamma James (TPWM) and her team from THQ conducted rallies for both junior and senior home league members. Seminars and retreats for women were a great source of spiritual strength and inspiration for holy living.

The first year cadets of the Proclaimers of the Resurrection session continued their training with corps placements during the summer, further equipping them for their life-time service as officers.

The industrial training school enabled young men to find employ-ment in the government once they have earned a diploma, or to acquire skills leading to self-employment.

A special campaign launched on Founders day emphasized personal visitation and special meetings for congregations, particularly in villages. The result is that many people have sought salvation and soldiers have deepened their spiritual lives.

STATISTICS
Officers 645 (active 474 retired 171)
Employees 593
Corps 310 **Outposts** 84 **Societies** 40
Schools 18 **Institutions** 34
Senior Soldiers 49,665
Adherent Members 17,944 **Junior Soldiers** 4,910
Personnel serving outside territory
Officers 18

STAFF
Women's Ministries: Comr L. Susamma James (TPWM) Lt-Col Indumati G. Christian (TSWM) Maj Retnam (THLS)
Sec for Business Administration: Lt-Col Appavoo Sam Devaraj
Finance and Audit: Maj Masilamony Stalin
Legal: Maj Swamidhas Nalladhas
Property and Projects: Maj G.F. Christopher Selvanath
Sponsorship: Maj Kezial
Supplies: Maj Retnam Aruldhas
Sec for Personnel: Lt-Col Arulappan Paramadhas
HRD: Maj Jeyaraj Daniel Jebasingh Raj
Training: Maj Yesuvadian Manoharan
Sec for Programme: Maj Tharmar Alfred
Church and Community Relations: Maj Abel Bailis
Health: Maj S.P. Simon
Editorial: Maj Caroline Aruldhas
Projects and Development: Mr Gnanadhas Benjamin Dhaya
Public Relations: Maj Abraham Jeyasekhar
Social: Maj Retnam Aruldhas
Youth: Maj Abraham Jeyasekhar

DIVISIONS
Azhagiapandipuram: KK Dist PO, 629 852; tel: (04652) 281952; Majs Perinbanayagam Suthananthadhas and Esther Evangelin
Kanyakumari: Kadaigramam, Suchindram PO, KK Dist 629 704; tel: (04652) 243955; Majs Sundaram Motchakan and Selvabai
Kulasekharam: Kulasekharam PO, 629 161 KK Dist; tel: (04651) 279446; Majs Chelliah Swamidhas and Joicebai
Marthandam: Pammam, Marthandam PO, 629 165; tel: (04651) 272492; Majs Nallathanbi Edwin Sathyadhas and Gnana Jessy Bell
Nagercoil: Vetturnimadam PO, Nagercoil 629 003; tel: (04652) 272787; Majs Jebamony Jayaseelan and Gnanaselvi
Palayamcottai: 28 Bell Amorses Colony, Palayamcottai 627 002; tel: (0462) 2580093; Majs Majs Jeyaraj Samraj and Jessie
Radhapuram: Radhapuram PO, 627 111; tel: (04637) 254318
Tenkasi: Tenkasi PO, 627 811; tel: (04633) 280774; Majs Yesuvadian Ponnappan & Pushpam
Thuckalay: Mettukadai, Thuckalay PO, 629 175; tel: (04651) 252443; Majs Devasundaram Samuel Raj and Kanagamony

INDIA SOUTH EASTERN: General Linda Bond greets young women in the enthusiastic crowds of people at a public meeting

Valliyoor: Valliyoor PO, 627 117;
tel: (04637) 221454; Majs Job William and Daisybai

DISTRICTS
Coimbatore: Dr Daniel Ngr, K. Vadamaduai PO, 641 017; tel: (0422) 2461277;
Maj Ponniah Ashok Sundar
Erode: 9 Sakthivinayagar Koil St, Thengapattakarar Lane, Railway Colony Post, Poondurai Road, Erode 638 002;
tel: (0424) 2283909; Maj Yacob Selvam
Madurai: TPK Rd, Palanganatham PO, 625 003; tel: (0452) 2370169;
Maj Geevanantham Kumaradhas
Trichy: New Town, Malakovil, Thiruvarumbur 620 013; tel: (0431) 2510464;
Maj Abel Yesudhas
Tuticorin: 5/254 G, Caldwell Colony, Tuticorin 628 008; tel: (0461) 2376841;
Maj Gnanabaranam Sam Singh

EXTENSION AREAS
Bhavani: No.770, Kalingarayan Palayam, Bhavani – 638301;
Pondicherry: opp Mahatma Dental College, Kamaraj Ngr, Goremedu Check Post, Pondicherry 605 006;
tel: (0413) 2271933;
Maj Gnanamony Moses
Salem: Near AVS College, Ramalingapuram, Salem -636 106;
Maj Jacob Vethamano

TRAINING COLLEGE
WCC Rd, Nagercoil 629 001;
tel: (04652) 231471

RED SHIELD HOUSE AND RETREAT CENTRE
Muttom, via Nagercoil 629 202;
tel: (04651) 238321

MEDICAL WORK
Catherine Booth Hospital: Nagercoil 629 001;
tel: (04652) 275516/7; fax: (04652) 275489;
Administrator: Maj S. P. Simon

Community Health and Development Programmes
Catherine Booth Hospital Campus,
tel: 04652 272068, email: benny@sachdp.com
Mr G. Benjamin Dhaya, Director
The Salvation Army Care and Support Project; Children Support Project; Community Empowerment Programme Adolescent Health and Development Project; People Empowerment for Holistic Community Health Actions and Network; Spirulina Farm; Community Action for Climate Change; Salvation Army Initiative for Integrated Dalit Development; Shaping Youth Towards Excellence; Housing Project; Learning and Resource Centre; Community Health Centre; Micro Finance; Micro Enterprises Development; District Resource Centre

EDUCATION
Higher Secondary School (mixed)
Nagercoil 629003; tel: (04652) 272647;

Matriculation Higher Secondary School
Nagercoil; tel: (04652) 272534;

Middle School (mixed)
Nambithoppu Middle School;

Noble Memorial High School
Valliyoor; tel: (04637) 220380;

Village Primary Schools: 9
**Nursery and English Medium Primary
Schools:** 4

SOCIAL SERVICES
Boys' and Girls' Homes
Boys' Home: Nagercoil(acc 72)
Noble Memorial Boys' Home: Valliyoor (acc 70)
Tucker Girls' Home: Nagercoil (acc 135)
Girls' Home: Thuckalay (acc 100)

Children's Home
Palayamcottai

Child Development Centres
Chemparuthivilai, Chemponvilai, Kadaigramam,
Madurai, Nagercoil, Pondicherry, Thuckalay,
Valliyoor

**Vocational Training Centre for the
Physically Disabled (Men and Boys)**
Aramboly 629 003; tel: (04652) 263133

**Vocational Training Centre for Women
and Home League Retreat Centre**
Nagercoil 629 003; tel: (04652) 232348

**Rural Development and Vocational
Training Centre**
Chemparuthivilai 629 166
tel: (04651) 253292

Vocational Training Institute
Kilkothagiri Junction, 643 216 Nilgris

Industrial Training School
Aramboly; tel: (04652) 262198

RETIRED OFFICERS' HOME
Catherine Booth Hospital, Nagercoil 629 001

**INDIA SOUTH WESTERN: General Linda Bond left the platform
to pray with seekers at the mercy seat**

INDIA SOUTH WESTERN TERRITORY

Territorial leaders:
Commissioners Samuel and Bimla Charan

Territorial Commander:
Commissioner Samuel Charan (1 Jan 2011)

Chief Secretary:
Lieut-Colonel Chelliah Moni (1 Jul 2012)

Territorial Headquarters: The Salvation Army, Kowdiar, Thiruvananthapuram, Kerala

Postal address: PO Box 802, Kowdiar, Thiruvananthapuram 695 003, Kerala State, India

Tel: [91] (471) 2314626/2723238; fax: [91] (471) 2318790;

email: ISW_mail@ISW.salvationarmy.org; website: www.salvationarmy.org/ind

Salvation Army work was commenced in the old Travancore State on 8 March 1896 by Captain Yesudasen Sanjivi, who was a high-caste Brahmin before his conversion. His son, Colonel Donald A. Sanjivi, became the first territorial commander from Kerala. The work spread to other parts of the state through the dedication of pioneer officers, including Commissioner P. E. George. The India South Western Territory came into being on 1 October 1970 when the Southern India Territory divided into two. The territory has its headquarters at Thiruvananthapuram and comprises the entire Malayalam-speaking area known as Kerala State.

Zone: South Asia
State included in the territory: Kerala
'The Salvation Army' in Malayalam: Raksha Sainyam; in Tamil: Ratchania Senai
Languages in which the gospel is preached: English, Malayalam, Tamil
Periodicals: *Home League Quarterly* (Malayalam/English), *The Officer* (Malayalam), *Youdha Shabdam* (Malayalam), *Yuva Veeran* (Malayalam)

MANY thousands of people were blessed through Spirit filled meetings held in the territory when General Linda Bond visited in February 2012. Salvationists were at the airport to accord the General an enthusiastic welcome with flags and shouts of hallelujah! The Honourable Minister for Transport, Sri. M. Sivakumar representing the State Government, received the international leader.

At one public meeting thousands of soldiers joined with the General in prayer for two young brothers suffering from a serious illness. The General addressed officers' meetings and visited Army institutions, bringing great joy to the residents.

Youth camps were held and inspired many young Salvationists to be faithful to God and the Army. Their spiritual fervour encouraged other young people locally. More than 8,000 young people attended the camps and many declared their intention to become Salvation Army officers.

The territorial youth department arranged vacation Bible schools for children with the theme 'We are stewards'. Many Hindu and Muslim children were welcomed by youth leaders and 12,000 children in total attended these programmes.

Career development courses have commenced throughout the territory and enabled young people to find employment with the Government, on completion of their training.

Senior and junior home league rallies were conducted in all divisions under the leadership of Commissioner Bimla Charan (TPWM). More than 4,000 senior home league members attended and an amount of 201,143 rupees was raised for Helping Hand projects. Development programmes have been arranged to teach income generating skills to women.

The Salvation Army in Trivandrum held a reception for the 'Red Ribbon Express' – a train which takes information regarding HIV/Aids throughout India. The state Government has recently accredited The Salvation Army to work in this field. A territorial team supported children affected by HIV/Aids through 'SMILE'; a life skills education programme implemented throughout Kerala. Another programme, 'Ready for War' equipped and informed Salvation Army officers on these issues

The number of self-help groups continued to grow, enabling women to improve the lives of their families.

Salvation Army personnel responded when flooding occurred in Thiruvananthapuram, providing help for bereaved family members.

STATISTICS
Officers 681 (active 432 retired 249) **Cadets** 18 **Employees** 174
Corps 333 **Societies and Outposts** 460 **Schools** 16 **Institutions** 20
Senior Soldiers 43,858 **Adherent Members** 15,383 **Junior Soldiers** 3,900
Personnel serving outside territory Officers 10

STAFF
Women's Ministries: Comr Bimla Charan (TPWM) Lt-Col Mallika Moni (TSWM) Maj Elizabeth Solomon (THLS) Maj Shylaja Babu (TLOMS) Maj Florence Charles (TSSFS)
Business Administration: Lt-Col K. M. Gabriel
Personnel: Lt-Col John Suseelkumar
Programme: Lt-Col K. M. Solomon
Editor and Literary Sec: Maj Charles V. John
Education: Maj Simson Samuelkutty
Finance: tba
HRD and Education: Maj Saju Daniel
Projects: Maj C. J. Bennymon
Property: Major P. S. Johnson
Social: Capt Roy Joseph
Territorial Evangelist, Church Growth and Sec for Spiritual Life Development: Maj Jacob George
Training: Maj John Samuel
Youth and Candidates: Maj O. P. John

DIVISIONS
Adoor: Adoor 691 523; tel: 0473-4229648; Majs Rajan K. John and Susamma Rajan
Cochin: Erumathala PO, Alwaye 683 105; tel: 0484-2638429; Majs D. Gnanadasan and D. I. Sosamma Gnanadasan
Kangazha: Edayirikapuzha PO, Kangazha 686 541; tel: 0481-2494773; Majs C. S. Yohannan and L. Rachel Yohannan
Kattakada: Kattakada 695 572; tel: 0471-2290484; Majs D. Sathiyaseelan and Aleyamma Sathiaseelan
Kottarakara: Kottarakara 691 506; tel: 452650; Majs M. Samuel and K. Thankamma Samuel
Malabar: Veliyamthode, Chandakunnu PO, Nilambur 679 342; tel: 2222824;

Majs Mathai Ezekiel and Kunjamma Ezekiel

Mavelikara: Thazhakara, Mavelikara 690 102; tel: 2303284; Majs Sam Immanuel and Rachel Immanuel

Nedumangadu: Nedumangadu 695 541; tel: 2800352; Majs T.J. Simon and Ammini Simon

Neyyattinkara: Neyyattinkara 695 121; tel: 2222916; Majs S. Samuelkutty and Lillybai Samuelkutty

Peermade: Kuttikanam PO, Peermade 685 501; tel: 232816; Majs Rajamani Christuraj and Mary Christuraj

Tiruvella: Tiruvella 689 101; tel: 2602657; Majs N.J. George and M.C. Ruth George

Thiruvananthapuram: Parambuconam, Kowdiar PO, Thiruvananthapuram 695 003; tel: 2433215; Majs Davidson Daniel and M.V. Estherbai Davidson

DISTRICTS

Kottayam: Manganam PO, Kottayam 686 018; tel: 0481-2577481; Maj D. Israel

Punalur: The Salvation Army, PPM PO, Punalur; tel: 0475-2229218; Maj V.D. Samuel

TRAINING COLLEGE

Kowdiar, Thiruvananthapuram 695 003; tel: 2315313

TERRITORIAL PRAYER CENTRE FOR SPIRITUAL EMPOWERMENT

Kowdiar PO, Thiruvanathapuram 695 003; tel: 0471-2723237

MEDICAL WORK
Hospitals

Evangeline Booth Community Hospital: Puthencruz 682 308; tel: Ernakulam 2731056

Evangeline Booth Leprosarium: Puthencruz 682 308; tel: Ernakulam 2730054 (acc 200) Administrator: Maj P.V. Stanley Babu

General Hospital: Kulathummel, Kattakada 695 572, Thiruvananthapuram Dist; tel: Kattakada 2290485 (acc 60)

Medical Centre

Kanghaza (acc 12)

EDUCATION
Higher Secondary School (mixed)

Thiruvananthapuram (acc 1,371)

Primary Schools:

15 (acc 2,640)

SOCIAL WORK
Boys' Homes

Kangazha (acc 30)
Kottarakara (acc 30)
Kowdiar, Thiruvananthapuram (acc 20)
Mavelikara (acc 25)

Community Development Centres

North: Trikkakara, Cochin
South: Konchira, Thiruvananthapuram

Girls' Homes

Adoor (acc 25)
Kowdiar, Thiruvananthapuram (acc 24)
Nedumangad (acc 30)
Peermade, Kuttikanam (acc 30)
Thiruvalla (acc 25)

Vocational Training Centre for Women

Nedumangad (acc 25)

Young Men's Training Centre

Thiruvananthapuram

Printing Press

Kowdiar, Thiruvananthapuram 695 003; tel: 0471 2725358

ITI and Computer Training Centre

Kowdiar, Thiruvananthapuram

Tailoring Centres

Adoor, Cochin, Kangazha, Kattakada, Kottarakara, Malabar, Neyyattinkara, Peermade

Young Women's Hostel (Goodwill Hostel)

Thiruvananthapuram (acc 20)

Working Women's Hostel

Thrikkakara, B.M.C. PO, Ernakulam

Youth Centre

Kowdiar, Thiruvananthapuram

RED SHIELD GUEST HOUSES

Kowdiar, Thiruvananthapuram 695 003; tel: 0471-2319926

Kovalam, Thiruvananthapuram; tel: 0471 2485895

RETIREMENT COTTAGES FOR OFFICERS

Thiruvananthapuram
(4 cottages)

INDIA WESTERN TERRITORY

Territorial leaders:
**Colonels Thumati Vijayakumar
and T.K. Manikyam**

Territorial Commander:
Colonel Thumati Vijayakumar:
(1 Aug 2011)

Chief Secretary:
Lieut-Colonel K.C. David (1 Jan 2011)

Territorial Headquarters: Sheikh Hafizuddin Marg, Byculla, Mumbai 400 008

Postal address: PO Box 4510, Mumbai 400 008, India

Tel: [91] (022) 2308 4705/2307 1140; fax: [91] (022) 2309 9245;

email: IWT_mail@iwt.salvationarmy.org; website: www.salvationarmy.org/ind

The Salvation Army began its work in Bombay (later Mumbai) in 1882 as a pioneer party led by Major Frederick Tucker and including Veerasoriya, a Sri Lankan convert, invaded India with the love and compassion of Jesus. Bombay (Mumbai) was the capital of Bombay Province, which included Gujarat and Maharashtra, and the first headquarters in India was in a rented building at Khetwadi. From these beginnings the work of God grew in Bombay Province. Various models of administration were tried for the work in Gujarat and Maharashtra until the India Western Territory was established in 1921.

Zone: South Asia

States included in the territory: Gujarat, Maharashtra, Madhya Pradesh, Rajasthan

'The Salvation Army' in Gujarati and Marathi: Muktifauj

Languages in which the gospel is preached: Gujarati, Hindi, Marathi, Tamil

Periodicals: *Home League Quarterly* (Gujarati and Marathi), *The Officer* (Gujarati and Marathi), *The War Cry* (Gujarati and Marathi), *The Young Soldier* (Gujarati and Marathi)

THE territorial theme for 2012 was 'That we may be one in Christ' and events and programmes through the year were planned to reflect this.

The Territorial Youth Camp in Maharashtra was a highlight for 450 young people who met together for three days. Praise and worship, Bible study, teaching about the Army and a cultural programme enriched the young delegates. Everyone who

attended rededicated their lives to serve God through the Army.

Each Thursday morning in THQ and in many other centres the territory participates in the 'Worldwide Prayer Meeting' following the General's invitation to all Salvationists to unite in this way. Every corps has formed an active prayer cell and a half night of prayer is held monthly. Encouraging reports of answers to prayer have been received. In one division 1,000 different subjects were covered in constant prayer. The prayer group leaders met together and shared experiences about the way God has answered prayer.

Senior and junior home league rallies were conducted in all divisions, districts and extension areas. and the number of women attending was encouraging. New home league members were enrolled and women presented cultural items in each rally.

A new project for street children was launched in Mumbai. Each morning and evening 50 children come to the centre to receive education and to share a meal. The project has been a great blessing and benefit to disadvantaged children in this city.

Outreach to the community continued through services for HIV/Aids sufferers. A shelter for the children of women working in local brothels provided food and care. Feeding programmes and other activities continued to help the poor and marginalised. The pupils at Salvation Army English medium schools in Maharastra and Gujarat have continued to achieve good exam results.

Young homeless men and women now living safely in Army hostels appreciated the encouragement received from the officers who manage these facilities. One former resident who has just completed his medical training wrote to thank the officer-in-charge for the care he has received.

India Western Territory continues its journey as part of one Army with one mission and one message, expecting great things from God in future days.

STATISTICS
Officers 623 (active 412 retired 211) **Cadets** 22 **Employees** 301
Corps 260 **Outposts** 275 **Institutions** 20 **Day Schools** 12
Senior Soldiers 39,920 **Adherent Members** 3,971 **Junior Soldiers** 10,052

STAFF
Women's Ministries: Col Keraham Manikyam (TPWM) Lt-Col G. Marykutty David (TSWM) Lt-Col Margaret Macwan (THLS - Gujarati) Lt-Col Leela R. Kale (THLS – Marathi); Lt-Col Vimla D. Sevak (LOMS – G) Lt-Col Ratnamala Randive (ROS – M) Maj Sunita J. Macwan (SSM – G) Lt-Col Ruth Mahida (ROS/JHLS – G
Sec for Business Administration: Lt-Col Jashwant D. Mahida
Finance: Capt Emmanuel Masih
Property: Maj Jashwant T. Macwan (Gujarat)
Property and Development: Maj J.P. Salve (Maharashtra)
Sec for Personnel Administration: Lt-Col David Sevak – G; Lt-Col Ratnakar D. Kale – M
Human Resources: Maj Jashi Daud (Gujarat); Maj Pramod Kamble (Maharashtra)
Sec for Programme Administration: Lt-Col Punjalal U. Macwan – G; Lt-Col Benjamin Randive – M
Editors: Maj Surendra Chopde (Marathi) ; Maj Ruth Macwan (Gujarati)
Projects: Maj Ashok Dushing
Training: Maj Yakub Macwan (Gujarat); Maj Vijay Dalvi (Maharashtra)
Youth: Maj Yusuf Daud (Gujarat) Maj Ravindra Kharat (Maharashtra)
Social: tba (Gujarat); Maj Sanjay Wanjare (Maharashtra)

DIVISIONS
Gujarat
Ahmedabad: Behrampura, Ahmedabad 380 022; tel: (079) 2539 4258; Majs Rasik and Ramila Paul
Anand: Amul Dairy Rd, Anand 388 001; tel: (02692) 240638; Majs Prabhudas and Persis Christian
Matar: Behind Civil Court, Matar District, Kheda 387 530; tel: (02694) 285482; Majs Purshottam and Dorothy Parmar

Nadiad: Nadiad, District Kheda 387 002;
tel: (0268) 2558856; Majs Viajy and
Pushpa Mahida
Panchmahal: Dohad, Panchmahal 389 151;
tel: (02673) 221771; Majs Paul and
Febiben Maganlal Christian
Petlad: Sunav Rd, Post Petlad,
District Anand 388 450; tel: (02679) 221527;
Majs Nicolas and Flora Damor
South Gujarat: Khambla Zampa, PO Vansda,
396 580 District Navsari; Majs Kantilal and
Eunice K. Parmar

Maharashtra
Ahmednagar: Fariabagh, Sholapur Rd,
414 001; tel: (95241) 2358194; Majs Ivor
Salve and Meena Salve
Mumbai: Sankli St, Byculla,
Mumbai 400 008; tel: (022) 2300 3990;
Majs Jagannath and Kusum Tribhuwan
Pathardi: Pathardi, District Ahmednagar
414 102; tel: (952428) 223116
Pune: 19 Napier Rd, 411 040;
tel: (9520) 2636 3198; Majs Gulab and
Meena Pathare
Satara: Satara, District Satara 415 001;
tel: (952162) 234006; Majs Ashok and
Sheela Mandgule
Shevgaon: Shevgaon, District Ahmednagar
414 502; tel: (952429) 223191;
Majs Bapusaheb Salvi and Vinodini Salvi
Shrirampur: District Ahmednagar 413 709,
Tal Shrirampur; Majs Bhausaheb and
Pushpa Magar

DISTRICT
Songadh: Maj Joseph Mahida

EXTENSION AREAS
Dharampur: Maj Rajesh Khristi
Kaprada: Maj Dhiraj Valji
Madhya Pradesh: Capt Savsing Bhabhor
Rajasthan: Maj James Solomon
Sangli: Maj Baban Borde

TRAINING COLLEGES
Gujarat: Anand 388 001, District Anand,
Amul Dairy Rd;
tel: (02692) 254801

Maharashtra: Fariabagh,
Ahmednagar 414 001;
tel: (95241) 2355950

EDUCATION
Boarding Schools (Boys and Girls)
William Booth Memorial Children's Home
and Hostel: Anand 388 001, District Anand,
Gujarat; tel: (2692) 255580 (acc 226)
William Booth Memorial Primary and High
Schools: Farlabagh, District Ahmednagar
414 001, Maharashtra;
tel: (022) 95241 2324267 (acc 513)

Day Schools
Anand:
William Booth Memorial High School,
Amul Dairy Rd; tel: (2692) 254901 (acc 276)
English Medium Primary and High
School Anand (acc 1,260)
William Booth Primary School (acc 476)
Ashakiran: Primary School, Satara; under DHQ
(acc 130)
Dahod: English Medium School (acc 210)
Pune: English Medium School, Vishrantwadi,
Pune 411 015; tel: (9520) 2669 2761 (acc 25)
Muktipur: PO Bareja 382 425, District
Ahmednabad; tel: 02718 233318 (acc 93)
Mumbai: Tucker English Medium School,
Sankli St, Byculla, Mumbai 400 008;
tel: (022) 307 7062 (acc 652)
Vadodara: English Medium School:
Chhani Rd, Vadodra; tel: (0265) 277 5361
(acc 150)

MEDICAL WORK
Emery Hospital: Amul Dairy Rd, Anand 388 001,
District Anand, Gujarat; tel: (2692) 253737
(acc 160)
Evangeline Booth Hospital: Ahmednagar 414 001,
Maharashtra; tel: (022) 95241 2325976 (acc 172)

HUMAN RESOURCES DEVELOPMENT CENTRES
Anand (Gujarat):
Faujabad Comp, Anand 388 001
Ahmednagar (Maharashtra):
tel: (022) 95241 2358489

SOCIAL WORK
CARE Programme Centre
Byculla, Mumbai:
Community-based Aids Programme;
Confidential Aids Counselling Clinic;
Aruna Children's Shelter;

Farm Colony
Muktipur 382 425, Post Bareja,
District Ahmedabad; tel: (02718) 33318

Feeding Programme
Mumbai (under King Edward Home)

Homes
Children
Mumbai: (acc 170)
Pune: Hope House (acc 50)

Elderly Men
Mumbai 400 008: 122 Maulana Azad Rd,
    Byculla; tel: (022) 23071346 (acc 15)

Industrial
King Edward Home: 122 Maulana Azad Rd,
    Byculla, Mumbai 400 008

Physically Handicapped Children
Joyland, Anand 388 001, District Anand,
    Gujarat; tel: (02692) 251891 (acc 20)

'Ray of Hope' Home
Vansda: under DHQ (acc 63)

Hostels
Blind Working Men
Ahmedabad: Locoshed, Rajpur-Hirpur,
    Ahmedabad, Gujarat; tel: (079) 2294 1217;
    (acc 15)
Mumbai 400 008: Sankli St, Byculla;
    tel: (022) 2305 1573 (acc 50)

Young Men
Satara: under DHQ; tel: (952162) 234006
    (acc 30)

Young Women
Anand: Gujarat (acc 50)
Baroda: Nava Yard
Mumbai: Concord House (acc 63)
Pune: c/o DHQ, Pune 411 040 (acc 16)

RED SHIELD HOTEL
30 Mereweather Rd, Fort, Mumbai 400 039;
    tel: (022) 2284 1824 (acc 450)

INDIA WESTERN: These children find safety and enjoy the activities provided at a shelter in Aruna

137

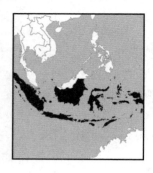

INDONESIA TERRITORY

Territorial leaders:
Commissioners Michael and Joan Parker

Territorial Commander:
Commissioner Michael Parker
(1 Jan 2013)

Chief Secretary:
Lieut-Colonel Jones Kasaedja (1 Jan 2013)

Territorial Headquarters: Jalan Jawa 20, Bandung 40117

Postal address: Post Box 1640, Bandung 40016, Indonesia

Tel: [62] (22) 4207029/4205056

website: www.salvationarmy.or.id

The Salvation Army commenced in Indonesia (Java) in 1894. Operations were extended to Ambon, Bali, East Kalimantan, Sulawesi (Central, North and South), Sumatra (North and South) Nias and East Nusa Tenggara, Aceh and Papua. A network of educational, medical and social services began.

Zone: South Pacific and East Asia
Country included in the territory: Indonesia
'The Salvation Army' in all Indonesian languages: Bala Keselamatan
Languages in which the gospel is preached: Indonesian with various dialects such as Batak, Daa, Dayak, Javanese, Ledo, Makassarese, Moma, Niasnese, Tado and Uma
Periodicals: *Berita Keselamatan* (*The War Cry*), *Cakrawala* (*Waves of Hope*), *Medical Fellowship Bulletin, Oasis Fajar* (Daily Devotions)

'VISION 2014' is the title of the territorial mission strategy. By 2014 the Indonesia Territory aims to have 40,000 mission-focused soldiers and to be financially independent. Progress towards this goal has been achieved.

A number of new buildings were made possible through corps raising the required funds themselves. Commissioner Kartodarsono (then TC) travelled by motor cycle or sailed in a small dinghy to access remote areas of Indonesia to open the new buildings and dedicate them to the glory of God.

A men's rally drew an attendance of 1,028. This was encouraging evidence of a growing outreach ministry to men.

The fourth National Youth Conference was led by Commissioners Alistair and Astrid Herring (IS and ZSWM for SPEA). This event brought 805 young people together to affirm their faith in Jesus Christ.

In one division in the territory, 694 senior soldiers and 430 junior soldiers were enrolled in a single meeting.

The Indonesia Territory had a special international focus when the Global Christian Forum was held in Manado.

This event was attended by 267 delegates from 65 countries.

The commissioning and ordination of new officers was led by Commissioners Hans and Marja van Vliet, TC and TPWM, Netherlands and Czech Republic. Thirteen lieutenants of the Ambassadors of Holiness session received their first appointments.

During a visit to Indonesia, Commissioner Christine MacMillan, the then Director of the Salvation Army International Social Justice Commission, spoke on social justice and met with the Social Welfare Minister and Unicef representative at the United Nations office .

The territorial theme for 2012 was 'Jesus Hope for the World'. This was expressed in many ways as the territory sought to serve suffering humanity. During the Muslim holiday of Ramadan, The Salvation Army distributed food and drinking water to homeless people and provided a mobile health clinic.

Earthquakes and mudslides are disasters that regularly hit the Indonesian islands in the 'ring of fire.' To resource officers and soldiers who deal with these emergencies, a number of post trauma counselling workshops were held.

During the past year The Salvation Army's Indonesia Health Foundation has been established, in response to a statutory requirement. The territory remains united in its vision and integrated mission is at the heart of all the Army's work.

STATISTICS

Officers 717 (active 582 retired 135) **Cadets** (1st Yr) 28 (2nd Yr) 25 **Employees** 1,850
Corps 281 **Outposts** 110, **Schools** 77 **Technical High School** 1 **Theological University** 1 **Hospitals** 6 **Clinics** 16 **Academies for Nurses** 1 **William Booth Medical College** 1 **Social Institutions** 20 **Kindergartens** 14
Senior Soldiers 28,464 **Adherents** 14,493 **Junior Soldiers** 6,528 **Officers serving outside territory** 2

STAFF

Women's Ministries: Comr Joan Parker (TPWM) Lt-Col Mariyam Kasaedja (TSWM)
Sec for Business Administration: tba
Finance: Maj Sri Widajati Goni
  Chief Auditor: Mr Anton Priyono
  Property: Maj Immanuel Supardi
  Information Technology: Kadek White
Sec for Programme: Lt-Col I Wayan Widyanoadi
Social Services: Maj Ernie Lasut
  Corps Growth: Maj Benjamin Goni
  Legal and Parliament: Maj Sasmoko Hertjahjo
  Youth and Children's Ministries: Capt Sabar Siagian
Sec for Personnel: tba
  Spiritual Life Development Sec: Lt-Col Herlina Widyanoadi
Candidates: Maj Murgiati Mardiyudi
Literature and Editorial: Maj Sasmoko Hertjahjo
Projects: Maj William Barthau

DIVISIONS

Jawa and Bali: Jalan Dr Cipto 64b, Kelurahan Bugangan, Semarang 50126, Jateng; tel: (024) 355 1361; Majs Gidion and Lidia Rangi
Kulawi: Bala Keselamatan Post Office, Kulawi 94363, Sulteng; tel/fax: (0451) 811 017; Majs Indra and Helly Mangiwa
Manggala (West Palu, Central Sulawesi): c/o Jalan Miangas 1-3, Palu 94112; Majs Imanuel and Henny Duhu
Palu Timur (East Palu): Jalan Miangas 1, Kantor Pos Palu 94112; tel: (0451) 426 821; fax: (0451) 425 846; Majs Yusak and Widiawati Tampai
Palu Barat (West Palu): Jalan Miangas 1-3, Palu 94112, Sulteng; mobile: 0816 4304498; Majs I. Made Sadia and Syastiel Lempid
Regional East Indonesia: Jl Dr Sutomo No 10, Makasar; tel/fax: (0411) 312 919; Majs Spener and Rai Tetenaung

INDONESIA: Lively worship at the National Youth Conference

Sulawesi Utara (North Sulawesi): Jalan A. Yani 15, Manado 95114; tel/fax: (0431) 864 052; Majs I. Made and Margaretha Petrus

Sumatera Utara: Jl. Sei Kera 186 Medan 20232, Sumatera Utara; tel: (061) 4510284; Majs Marthen and Yulin Pandorante

DISTRICTS

Under Jawa and Bali Division
East Kalimantan: Maj Ezra Mangela
Central Java: Maj Yohanis Diyo
East Java: Maj Philemon Ngkale
West Java: Maj Agustinus Sarman

Under East Palu Division
Kamarora: Maj Yosren Soekaryo
Maranatha: Maj Jantje Kasumba
Palolo: Maj Sakius Salogi
Palu: Maj Hesron Mpapa

Under West Palu Division
Dombu: Maj Robert Sumbasubu
Pakawa: Capt Bambang Tadewatu
Porame: Maj I. Ketut Darto Yasa
Rowiga: Capt Sopani Laia
Wawugaga: Capt Johnmboge Rusadama

Under Manggala Division
Lalundu: Capt Samuel Pene
Malino: Capt Resman Manurung
North Mamuju: Capt Albert Silinawa

Under Kulawi Division
Gimpu: Maj I. Ketut Putrayasa
Kantewu: Maj Jusuf Tarusu
Karangana: Maj Janji Rusanto

Kulawi: Maj Nogerto Mariono
Lindu: Maj Arsan Sukarmin
Tobaku: Maj Derens Lodju

Under North Sumatera Division
Nias: Maj Sopani Laia

OFFICER TRAINING COLLEGE
Jalan Kramat Raya 55, Jakarta 10450, PO Box 3203, Jakarta 10002; tel: (021) 310 8148

EDUCATION
Central Sulawesi: 75 schools (acc 7,118), 1 theological university (acc 223)
East Kalimantan: 1 school (acc 52)
Jawa: 13 schools (acc 1,110)
Kalawara: 3 schools (acc 400)
North Sumatra: 2 schools (acc 62)
South Sulawesi: 3 schools (acc 106)

MEDICAL WORK
General Hospitals (Jawa)
Bandung: Bungsu Hospital (acc 49) (poli-clinic attached)
Palu: Woodward Hospital (acc 110)
Semarang: William Booth Hospital (acc 100) (eye and general clinic attached)
Surabaya: William Booth Hospital (acc 171) (poli-clinics attached)
Turen: Bokor Hospital (acc 100) (poli-clinic attached)
Maternity Hospital
Makassar, Sulawesi Selatan: Catherine Booth Mother and Child Hospital (acc 53)

Clinics

Bandung (Specialist Clinic Under Bungsu Hospital)

Central Java (Under William Booth Semarang): Mangunharjo

Central Sulawesi: Gimpu, Kantewu, Kulawi, Mamu, Manusi Ampera, Panii

East Kalimantan: Long Merah, Muara Batuq, Muara Mujan

North Sulawesi: Amurang, Kumelembuai, Makasili

Regional East Indonesia: Ambon

Academy for Nurses' Training

Palu: under Woodward Hospital (acc 345)

William Booth Medical College

Surabaya: under William Booth Hospital (acc 155)

SOCIAL WORK

Babies' and Toddlers' Home

Surabaya: (acc 60)

Boys' Homes

Bandung: Maranatha (acc 80)

Denpasar, Bali: William Booth Home (acc 200)

Kalawara: Bahagia (acc 60)
Medan: William Booth Home (acc 90)
Semarang: Betlehem (acc 80)
Tompaso: Wisma Anugerah (acc 80)
Yogyakarta: Tunas Harapan (acc 32)

Children's Homes

Bandung: William Booth Home (acc 90)
Denpasar: Anugerah (acc 60)
Jakarta: Catherine Booth Home (acc 90)
Malang: Elim (acc 80)
Manado: Bukit Harapan (acc 60)
Medan: Evangeline Booth Home (acc 80)
Palu: Sejahtera (acc 80)

Eventide Homes

Bandung: Senjarawi (acc 100)
Semarang: Bethany (acc 60)
Turen: Tresno Mukti (acc 50)

Students' Hostels

Bandung: Jalan Dr Cipto 7 (acc 32)
Bandung: Jalan Jawa 18 (acc 32)
Medan: Jalan Samanhudi 27 (acc 30)
Surabaya: Jalan Gatotan 36 (acc 24)
Yogyakarta: Jalan Kenari 7 (acc 8)

ITALY: The Chief of the Staff and WPWM, Commissioners Barry C. and Sue Swanson (l) with Lt-Cols Daniel and Eliane Naud (r), command leaders, and the 125th anniversary cake in April 2012

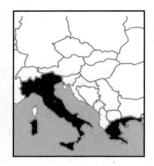

ITALY AND GREECE COMMAND

Command leaders:
Lieut-Colonels Daniel and Eliane Naud

Officer Commanding:
Lieut-Colonel Daniel Naud (1 Sep 2009)

General Secretary:
Major David Cavanagh (1 Sep 2011)

Command Headquarters: Via degli Apuli 39, 00185 Rome, Italy

Tel: [39] 06 447406300/06 4941089

email: Italy_Command@ity.salvationarmy.org; website: www.esercitodellasalvezza.org

The Salvation Army flag was unfurled in Italy on 20 February 1887 by Major and Mrs James Vint and Lieutenant Fanny Hack, though subsequent difficulties necessitated withdrawal. In 1890 Fritz Malan (later lieut-colonel) began meetings in his native village in the Waldensian Valleys. In 1893 Army work was re-established. In a decree of the President on 1 April 1965, The Salvation Army was recognised as a philanthropic organisation competent to acquire and hold properties and to receive donations and legacies. It received legal status as a religious body/church on 20 March 2009.

On 8 October 2007 The Salvation Army began operations in Greece, the work being linked to the Italy Command with the command leadership giving guidance and support to future development. Thessaloniki was identified as the centre of the new undertaking and Captains Polis Pantelidis and Maria Konti-Galinou, UK officers of Greek nationality, were entrusted with the task of launching the Army's mission in their home country. Greece was recognised as part of the command on 2 Feb 2011.

Zone: Europe
Countries included in the command: Greece, Italy
'The Salvation Army' in Italian: Esercito della Salvezza; in Greek: O Stratos Tis Sotirias
Languages in which the gospel is preached: Greek, Italian
Periodicals: *Il Bollettino del Dipartimento Società e Famiglia, Il Grido di Guerra*

THE Italy and Greece Command received eagerly-awaited reinforcements when three cadets of the Ambassadors of Holiness session were commissioned and ordained in London in July, 2011.

In 2011 five Italian cadets from Naples, Rome and Turin corps were received at the training college at the Army's headquarters compound in Rome. (For the past 52 years Italian cadets have been trained outside Italy.) On 24 September 2011, former cadets of the last session to be trained in Italy (now retired officers) were present at Rome Corps as the Proclaimers of the Resurrection session marched in to music from a specially formed National Band. Commissioners Robert and Janet Street, (IS and ZSWM for Europe) led the congregation, representative of the whole command, as the cadets were welcomed for officer training.

Traditional summer camps were held at Army sites and an innovative regional music camp took place. The closing concert presented in Faeto, southern Italy was well-attended.

Ariano Irpino Corps and Rome Corps held holiday clubs for children during July. Attendance at Family Camp on Forio d'Ischia Island increased and after each daily Bible study there was an eager response from people seeking to deepen their spiritual lives.

The 'Ri-Shop', a second-hand shop staffed by volunteers, opened at Torre Pellice. This project attracted new people and proved effective in spreading the Gospel as volunteers attended Sunday worship at the corps. The first three junior soldiers in more than 30 years were enrolled at the corps.

Atena Lucana, Brienza and Braide, introduced new activities. An English language course and a series of seminars raising awareness of depression were well received.

In April, the National Congress with the theme 'Thy Kingdom Come' was led by the then Chief of the Staff, Commissioner Barry C. Swanson, and the World President of Women's Ministries, Commissioner Sue Swanson, in Rome. Meetings were held to celebrate 125 years of Salvation Army work in Italy.

In Greece, Captains Pantelidis moved from Thessaloniki to pioneer Army work in Athens.

In Thessaloniki, newly-commissioned Lieutenants Totsios continued community service ministries launched by their predecessors and have started soldiers' classes.

STATISTICS

Officers 45 (active 21 retired 24) **Auxiliary-Captains** 2 **Auxiliary-Lieutenants** 1 **Cadets** 5 **Employees** 18
Corps 16 **Outposts** 17 **Institutions** 7
Senior Soldiers 240 **Adherent Members** 106 **Junior Soldiers** 33

STAFF

General's Personal Representative to the Vatican: Lt-Col Daniel Naud
Women's Ministries (and Youth and Resources): Lt-Col Eliane Naud (CPWM) Maj Elaine Cavanagh (CSWM)
Finance: Capt Emmanuel Gau
Property: Maj David Cavanagh
Social and PR Coordinator: Major Paolo Longo
Training: Lt-Col Eliane Naud/Maj David Cavanagh
Family Tracing: Maj Angela Dentico
Candidates: Maj Lidia Bruno

SOCIAL WORK

Centre for the Homeless

Centro Virgilio Paglieri, Via degli Apuli 41, 00185 Roma; tel: 06 44740601 (acc 200)

Workers' Lodge

Villa Speranza, Contrada Serra 57a, 85100 Potenza; tel: 0971 51245 (acc 6)

Holiday Centres

Le Casermette, Via Pellice 4, 10060 Bobbio Pellice (To); tel: 0121 957728
email: lecasermette@esercitodellasalvezza.org; www.centrovacanzebobbio.com (acc 206)

Concordia, Via Casa di Majo 36, 80075 Forio d'Ischia (Na); tel: 081 997324
email: concordia@esercitodellasalvezza.org (acc 55)

L'Uliveto, Via Stretta della Croce 20, 84030 Atena Lucana (Sa); tel: 0975 76321 (acc 80)
email: ulivetto@esercitodellasalvezza.org

Guest Houses

Florence: Villa delle Rose, Via Aretina 91, 50136 Firenze; tel/fax: 055 660445 email: villadellerose@esercitodellasalvezza.org (acc 13)

Rome: Foresteria, Via degli Apuli 41, 00185 Roma; tel: 06 44740601;
email: foresteriaroma@esercitodellasalvezza.org (acc 70)

GREECE

Defkalionos 9-11, GR – 11254 Athens, Greece; 0030/ 2111 821 846; www.salvationarmy.gr;
Capts Polycarpos Pantelidis and Maria Konti-Galinou

JAPAN TERRITORY

Territorial leaders:
Commissioners Jiro and Keiko Katsuchi

Territorial Commander:
Commissioner Jiro Katsuchi (1 Jan 2013)

Chief Secretary:
Lieut-Colonel Kenji Fujii (1 Jan 2013)

**Territorial Headquarters: 2-17 Kanda-Jimbocho,
Chiyoda-ku, Tokyo 101-0051, Japan**

Tel: [81] (03) 3237 0881; website: www.salvationarmy.or.jp

In 1895 a small group of pioneer officers from Britain arrived in Japan at Yokohama to start operations. In spite of great difficulties, work was soon established. Of several outstanding Japanese who were attracted to The Salvation Army, the most distinguished was Commissioner Gunpei Yamamuro OF, prominent evangelist and author, whose book *The Common People's Gospel* has been reprinted more than 500 times.

Zone: South Pacific and East Asia
Country included in the territory: Japan
Language in which the gospel is preached: Japanese
Periodicals: *Home League Quarterly*, *The Officer*, *The Sunday School Guide*, *Toki-no-Koe*, *Toki-no-Koe Junior*

'MOVE towards God's Kingdom' was the territorial theme in 2011 with an emphasis on bringing the gospel to the world.

Six cadets of the Proclaimers of the Resurrection session were welcomed in April 2011 for officer training. The Army in Japan has been aware of the need for more officers and these cadets are an answer to the prayers of Salvationists.

Following the severe earthquake and tsunami of 11 March 2011, Salvationists in the territory have been fully involved in relief work. The Salvation Army responded immediately, providing food and other essen-

tials to people in the north-east part of Japan. Emergency services continued with assistance from IHQ personnel and SAWSO supplied an emergency canteen vehicle.

The Government supplied temporary shelters for thousands of people evacuated from their former homes. The Salvation Army worked with the authorities in evaluating needs and supplying items such as mattresses, refrigerators and heaters.

Medium and long-term needs were addressed in due course, especially those of local people for whom the fishing industry provided their main income. It was reported that 22,000 boats were swept away in the disaster. The Salvation Army supplied 30 boats to one fishing village where 90 per cent of 150 boats had been lost.

Another aspect of recovery work was facilitating the provision of temporary shops, a crucial factor for the recovery of towns and villages. The Army enabled the building of three temporary shopping malls.

Fulfilling the vision of 'One Army' Salvationists have offered practical help, pastoral care and spiritual support to people in need. The Army has had many opportunities to show God's love and care through this long period of recovery.

In Japan, where soldier making is not easy, one new soldier is a cause for great rejoicing. One corps officer led a man to Christ during his hospital ministry and enrolled him as a soldier only weeks before his promotion to Glory.

Lieut-Colonels Graham and Rhondda Durston (Australia Eastern Territory) were the guest speakers at a Brengle Institute for officers of the territory. The teaching was recorded on CD and sent to those who were unable to attend.

A highlight of the year for the Japan Staff Band was the visit to the United Kingdom to participate in the ISB 120 celebrations. The Japanese musicians were welcomed into the Royal Albert Hall with a standing ovation from the large congregation.

The theme for 2012 was 'The Year of the Family' as Salvationists focused on sharing the gospel with their family members, seeking to encourage people to return to God.

STATISTICS

Officers 174 (active 77 retired 97) **Cadets** (1st Yr) 6 (2nd Yr) 1 **Employees** 1,105 **Corps** 47 **Outposts** 12 **Institutions** 20 **Hospitals** 2
Senior Soldiers 2,811 **Adherent Members** 27 **Junior Soldiers** 84

STAFF

Women's Ministries: Comr Keiko Katsuchi (TPWM) Lt-Col Chiaki Fujii (TSWM)
Business Administration: tba
Candidates: Maj Kyoko Yoshida
Editor: Sis Keiko Saito
Literary: Maj Kazumitsu Higuchi
Medical: tba
Music: B/M Hajime Suzuki
Personnel: Maj Chieko Tanaka
Programme: Maj Kazumitsu Higuchi
Social: Maj Tamotsu Nishimura
Staff Band: B/M Hajime Suzuki
Staff Songsters: S/L Mikako Ebara
Training: Maj Tsukasa Yoshida
Youth: Capt Kazuyuki Ishikawa

DIVISIONS

Hokkaido: 5-1-5, Kita-22-jo-Nishi, Kita-ku, Sapporo-shi, Hokkaido 001-0022; tel: (011) 788 5352; Majs Kojiro and Yumi Tokunaga
Kanto-Tohoku: 5 Yorai-cho, Takasaki-shi, Gunma Ken 370-0822; tel: (027) 323 1337; Majs Haruhisa and Hiromi Ota
Nishi Nihon: 3-6-20 Tenjinbashi, Kita-ku, Osaka-shi 530-0041; tel: (06) 6351 0084; Majs Nobuhiro and Yasuko Hiramoto
Tokyo-Tokaido: 4-11-3 Taihei, Sumida-ku, Tokyo 130-0012; tel: (03) 5819 1460; tba

TRAINING COLLEGE

1-39-5 Wada Suginami-ku, Tokyo 166-0012; tel: (03) 3381 9837

MEDICAL WORK

Booth Memorial Hospital: 1-40-5 Wada, Suginami-ku, Tokyo 166-0012; tel: (03) 3381 7236 (acc hospital 179, hospice 20)
Kiyose Hospital: 1-17-9 Takeoka, Kiyose-shi, Tokyo, 204-0023; tel: (042) 491 1411/3 (acc hospital 117, hospice 25)

SOCIAL WORK
Alcoholic Rehabilitation Centre
Tokyo: Jiseikan (acc 50)

Rehabilitation Centre (Men)
Tokyo (acc 15)

Social Service Centre (Men) (Bazaar)
Tokyo

Working Men's Homes
Tokyo:
Jijokan (acc 35)
Shinkokan (acc 40)

Women's Homes
Tokyo:
Fujinryo (acc 40);
Shinseiryo (acc 70)

Children's Homes
Hiroshima:
Aikoen (acc 30); Toyohama-Gakury (acc 60)
Osaka:
Kibokan (acc 65)
Tokyo:
Kiekoryo (acc 35)
Sekoryo (acc 50)

Day Nurseries
Kure-shi: Kure Hoikusho (acc 60)
Sapporo-shi:
Kikusui Kamimachi Hoikuen (acc 90)
Shiseikan Hoikuen (acc 120)
Soen Hoikusho (acc 60)
Sano-shi: Sano Hoikuen (acc 126)

Home for the Aged
Tokyo: Keisen Home (acc 50)

Hostel
Kyoto: Kyoto Hostel (acc 16)

Senior Citizens' Housing and Care Centre
Tokyo: Grace (acc 100)

Care House
Tokyo: Izumi (acc 32)

RETIRED OFFICERS' APARTMENTS
Olive House: 1-39-12 Wada, Suginami-ku, Tokyo 166-0012
Osaka Central Hall 5F: 3-6-20 Tenjinbashi, Kita-ku, Osaka 530-0041
Tokiwa House: 1-17-12 Takeoka, Kiyose-shi, Tokyo 204-0023

JAPAN: The enrolment of a new soldier is a very significant event at a small outpost in the territory

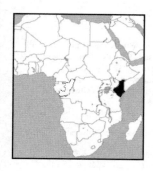

KENYA EAST TERRITORY

Territorial Commander:
Commissioner Vinece Chigariro
(1 Jan 2013)

Chief Secretary:
Lieut-Colonel Nahashon Njiru
(1 Jan 2013)

Territorial Headquarters: Marist Lane, Karen, Nairobi, Kenya

Postal address: Box 24927, Karen 00502, Nairobi, Kenya

Tel: [254] (020) 240-3260

In 1896 three Salvationists went to Kenya to work on the building of a new railway and made their witness while based at the Taru Camp. The first official meetings were held in Nairobi in April 1921, led by Lieut-Colonel and Mrs James Allister Smith. The first cadets were trained in 1923. On 1 March 2008, the Kenya Territory was divided into two and Kenya East Territory and Kenya West Territory were created.

Zone: Africa
Country included in the territory: Kenya
'The Salvation Army' in Kiswahili: Jeshi La Wokovu
Languages in which the gospel is preached: English, Kiswahili and a number of regional languages
Periodicals: *Sauti ya Vita* (*The War Cry,* English and Kiswahili)

'FAN the Flame', the territorial theme, inspired a rigorous consultation process for members of the Executive Council as Lieut-Col Mary Capsey (Africa Development Office) facilitated a two-day strategic planning retreat. Further planning took place at a workshop, territorial officers' councils, and a residential conference in November 2011. This process culminated in the publication of a mission plan for focused ministry for the next three years.

Salvationists from Kenya and beyond gathered in Nairobi for the 90th anniversary of Salvation Army

work and worship in Kenya. The then Chief of the Staff, Commissioner Barry C. Swanson. and World President of Women's Ministries, Commissioner Sue Swanson, led Salvationists and friends in the thanksgiving weekend celebrations.

Commissioners Swanson conducted the cadets' farewell meeting, officers' councils and joined the large congregations for the men's and women's rallies. New flags for the men's fellowship and women's ministries were unveiled in these special meetings.

The anniversary meetings were held at Nyayo National Stadium and focused first on 'Looking Back with Gratitude'. A celebration festival followed with the theme 'Looking forward with confidence'. The Holy Spirit's presence was felt throughout the weekend and more than 100 people knelt at the mercy seat in each gathering.

The Vice-President of Kenya, Stephen Kalonzo Musyoka, was present. He commended the Army's efforts to improve educational standards in Kenya through its early childhood centres, primary and secondary schools and vocational training centres and told the congregation of 6,000 people. 'Nothing liberates the mind and whole societies as much as education. Add Christian values to that and you have the best recipe for wholesome education.'

On the Sunday morning 51 cadets of the Friends of Christ session were commissioned and ordained. Both Kenya East and Kenya West territories received newly appointed lieutenants. After the Bible message, 70 people responded to the challenge to make themselves available for Salvation Army officership.

Various presentations throughout the weekend from songster brigades, Army-sponsored special schools, children's, youth, men's and women's groups had the resonating theme of thanksgiving to God and prayers for a future fully focused on him.

STATISTICS

Officers 559 (active 480 retired 79) Cadets 25
Employees 119
Corps 347 Outposts 351

Pre-primary Schools 159 Primary Schools 162 Secondary Schools 44 Institutions 13
Senior Soldiers 72,055
Junior Soldiers 72,385
Personnel serving outside the territory:
Officers 8

STAFF

Women's Ministries: Comr Vinece Chigariro (TPWM) Lt-Col Zipporah Njiru (TSWM)
Business Administration: tba
Personnel: Lt-Col Isaac Kivindyo
Programme: Lt-Col Encok Lufumbu
Audit: Maj Matthew Wangubo
Candidates: Maj Thomas Musyoki
Finance: Maj Joshua Kitonyi
Education: Capt Haron Wanyonyi
Extension Training: Maj Raymond Makali
Information Technology: Mrs Naum Juma
Projects: Cadet Richard Bradbury
Property: Mr John Kamau
Social: Capt Samuel Opuka
Education: Capt John Mutune
Property: Capt Samuel Kang'ara
Public Relations: Maj Daniel Kiama
Social: Lt-Col Beatrice Lufumbu
Spiritual Life Development: Maj Ann Kiama
Territorial Band: B/M Samuel Odiara
Territorial Songsters: S/L Joshua Rwolekya
Trade: Mr Joshua Mugera
Training Pricipal: Maj Samson Mwangi
Youth: Capt Martin Kimeu
Children: Capt Jane Kimeu

DIVISIONS

Coast: PO Box 98277, Mombasa;
tel: 041-490629; Majs Gideon and Lucy Nako
Embu: PO Box 74, Embu; tel: 068-20107;
Majs Lucas and Agnes Kithome
Kangundo: PO Box 324, Kangundo;
tel: 044-21049; tba
Kibwezi: PO Box 428, Sultan Hamud;
tel: 044-52200; Majs Peter and Annah Mutuku
Machakos: PO Box 160, Machakos;
tel: 044-21660; Majs Simon and Zippora Mbuthu
Nairobi: PO Box 31205, Nairobi;
tel: 020-767208; Majs Richard and Eunice Mweemba
Thika: PO Box 809, Thika; tel: 067-22056;Maj Joyce Mbungu

Westlands: PO Box 25240, Nairobi;
  Maj Sarah M'tetu
Yatta: PO Box 29 Kithimani; Majs Boniface
  and Esther Munyekhe

DISTRICTS

Kathiani: PO Box 2, Kathiani; Maj Ibrahim
  Lorot
Kilome: PO Box 85, Nunguni; Capt Joseph
  Muindi
Kirinyaga: PO Box 21, Kerugoya;
  Capt Kenneth Muriithi
Makueni: PO Box 40, Wote; tel: 044-77 Makueni;
  Capt Phineas Karanja
Matungulu: PO Box 422, Tala;
  Maj Emmanuel Mtepe
Meru: PO Box 465, Nkubu, Meru; tel: 064-51207;
  Capt Newton Madegwa
Mwala: PO Box 19, Mwala; Maj Wellington
  Ongaya
Nakuru: PO Box 672, Nakuru; tel: 051-212455;
  Capt Titus Kyengo

TRAINING COLLEGE

PO Box 4467, Thika; tel: 0733-629411

EDUCATIONAL WORK

SA Sponsored Primary Schools: 15
**SA Sponsored and Managed Secondary
Schools:** 26

Special Schools
Schools for the Visually Handicapped
Thika High School (acc 163)

Likoni Primary School (acc 120)
Thika Primary School (acc 297)

**Physically Disabled
Schools**
Joytown Primary School (acc 215)
Joytown Secondary School (110)

Multi-Handicapped Special Units
Joytown: (acc 22)
Njoro Special School
Thika Primary School:

SOCIAL SERVICES
Children's Homes
Kabete: Sarit Centre (acc 114)
Mombasa (acc 40)
Thika: Karibu Children's Centre

Community Centre
Kibera: Nairobi
Dandora Phase V: Nairobi

Lions Girls' Hostel
Nairobi: PO Box 31354, Nairobi;
  tel: 020-765750

Health Clinic
Kithituni: PO Box 482, Sultan Hamud 90132;
  tel: 020-136492

Vocational Training Centres
Variety Village: Thika
Nairobi Girls' Centre (acc 60)

KENYA EAST: Lt-Col David Shakespeare, then Assistant Chief Secretary (centre) **officiates at the presentation and dedication of a new vehicle for Kilome District in July 2012.**

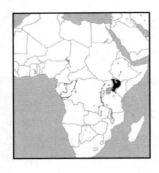

KENYA WEST TERRITORY

Territorial leaders:
**Commissioners Kenneth G. and
Jolene K. Hodder**

Territorial Commander:
Commissioner Kenneth G. Hodder
(1 Jan 2013)

Chief Secretary:
Lieut–Colonel Johnstone Wolayo
(1 Jan 2013)

Territorial Headquarters: Kisumu – Mumia Highway Rd, Kakamega, Kenya

Postal address: PO Box 660, Kakamega 50100, Kenya

In 1896 three Salvationists went to Kenya to work on the building of a new railway and made their witness while based at the Taru Camp. The first official meetings were held in Nairobi in April 1921, led by Lieut-Colonel and Mrs James Allister Smith. The first cadets were trained in 1923. On 1 March 2008, the Kenya Territory was divided into two and Kenya East Territory and Kenya West Territory were created.

Zone: Africa
Country included in the territory: Kenya
'The Salvation Army' in Kiswahili: Jeshi La Wokovu
Languages in which the gospel is preached: English, Kiswahili and a number of tribal languages
Periodicals: *Sauti ya Vita* (English and Kiswahili)

THIS has been a challenging year as the nation was involved in conflict following the abduction of aid workers and tourists from Kenya. Salvationists have united in prayer for all those caught up in this situation.

The territory praised God for opportunities for Kenyan officers to serve in Malawi. Kenya also has officer-couples serving in Australia, Burundi, IHQ (Nairobi), Uganda, and Zambia.

Three separate workshops for head teachers were conducted; one for those in charge of secondary schools, one for primary school head teachers and the third for divisional district education officers and chaplains. These have proved fruitful.

A one-day consultation meeting was held at the Rondo Retreat Centre. All the divisional and district leaders and the THQ cabinet met under the leadership of Commissioners Joash and Florence Malabi, the then territorial leaders, for a day of discussion and strategic planning. All those present were united in seeking to do their best in serving God and the people of Kenya.

The Women's Ministries leaders gathered for a three-day spiritual retreat.

International Emergency Services

facilitated a secondary school project in Turkana, the 'Food for Fees' project. Other communities received water supplied by Salvation Army bowsers – a lifesaving service to drought-stricken areas.

Salvationists from Kenya West travelled to Nairobi, Kenya East, for the last joint commissioning of cadets and to celebrate the 90th anniversary of the Army in Kenya. It was also a joy to witness 43 captains promoted to the rank of major after 15 years of faithful officer service.

There was construction and reorganisation within the THQ building. A central service desk has been established to ensure the efficient management and administration of mission assets and resources.The building was reopened on 3 January 2012. In the opening ceremony Commissioner Malabi encouraged all staff to begin the year by portraying God's love to one another and to trust in the Lord always.

STATISTICS

Officers 729 (active 498 retired 231) **Cadets** 21
Envoys/Employees 170
Corps 357 **Outposts** 1,016
  Pre-primary Schools 131 **Primary Schools**
  280 **Secondary Schools** 45 **Institutions** 3
Senior Soldiers 113,409
  Junior Soldiers 112,486

STAFF

Women's Ministries: Comr Jolene K. Hodder (TPWM) Lt-Col Linnet Wolayo (TSWM)
Business Administration: Lt-Col Timothy Mabaso
Personnel: tba
Programme: Lt-Col Herman Mbakaya
Audit: Maj Fanuel Maube.
Editor: Maj Rosemary Matunde
Education: Maj Wycliffe Ambuga
Finance: Maj Jacob Olubwayo

Information Technology: Capt Brown Musasia
Projects: Capt Isaac Siundu
Property: Mr Moses Maruti
Public Relations: Capt Timothy Kwalanda
Social: Lt-Col Lucia Mbakaya
Sponsorships: Capt Jane Wanyama
Statistics: Maj Lucy Maube
Youth: Capt Pelegi Wanyama
  Candidates: Capt Catherine Alemba

DIVISIONS

Bungoma: PO Box 1106, Bungoma; tel: 055-30589; Lt-Col Sarah Wanyama
Eldoret: PO Box 125, Eldoret; tel: 053-22266; Lt-Cols Tirus and Mebo Mbaja
Kakamega: PO Box 660, Kakamega; tel: 331-20344; Majs Moses and Gladys Shavanga
Kitale: PO Box 548, Kitale; tel:054-30259; Majs Fredrick and Leah Omuzee
Mbale: PO Box 80, Maragoli; tel: 056-51076; Majs Harun and Beatrice Chepsiri
Musudzuu: PO Box 278, Seremi; tel: 056-45055; Lt-Cols Peter and Jescah Dali
Shigomere: PO Box 125, Khwisero; tel: 056-20260; Majs Isaack and Rose Liviala
Tongaren: PO Box 127, Tongaren; Majs John and Mary Olewa

DISTRICTS

Bunyore: PO Box 81, Bunyore; Capt Reuben Malaba
Elgon: PO Box 274, Malakisi; tel: 055-20443; Capt Henry Changalwa
Kapsabet: PO Box 409, Kapsabet; Maj James Mukubwa
Kimilili: PO Box 220, Kimilili; Capt Bernard Shiraho
Kisumu: PO Box 288, Kisumu; tel: 057-2025632; Maj Meshack Wanjia
Lugari: PO Box 15, Matete; Capt Amos Malabi
Madzuu: PO Box 381, Vihiga; Maj James Mwanga
Migori: PO Box 59, Suna, Migori; Capt Paul Kyalo
Sabatia: PO Box102, Wodanga; Maj Nathan Musieni
Turkana: PO Box 118-30500, Lodwar; tel: 054-21010; Maj Peter Masaka
Webuye: PO Box 484, Webuye; Capt Samson Maweu

Kenya West: Many communities in the territory have self-help groups such as this one, based at Matete Corps. Members produce eggs and beef to sell and this provideds income for their families

EDUCATIONAL WORK
SA Sponsored Kindergartens: 131

SA Sponsored Primary Schools: 280

SA Sponsored and Managed Secondary Schools: 33

Special Schools
Schools for Visually Impaired
Kibos Primary School: PO Box 477, Kisumu (acc 230)
Kibos Secondary School: PO Box 77, Kisumu tel: 057-43135

Schools for Physically Impaired
Joyland Primary School: PO Box 1790, Kisumu; tel: 057-41864/50574 (acc 230)
Joyland Secondary School: PO Box 19494, Kisumu (acc 174)

School for Hearing Impaired
Chekombero Primary School: PO Box 93, Wodanga via Maragoli (60 pupils)

School for Mentally Challenged
Madegwa Primary School: PO Box 52, Maragoli (55 pupils)

Inclusive School
Joy Valley Primary School – Kimatuni: PO Box 1293, Bungoma (236 pupils)

SOCIAL SERVICES
Feeding Programmes for Destitutes
Kisumu: PO Box 288, Kisumu; tel: 057-4151
Shinoyi Community Centre

Health Centre
Kolanya: PO Box 88, Malakisi via Bungoma

Workshop
Kibos: PO Box 477, Kisumu (acc 12)

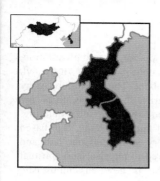

KOREA TERRITORY

Territorial leaders:
Commissioner Park, Man-hee and Commissioner Kim, Keum-nyeo

Territorial Commander:
Commissioner Park, Man-hee
(1 Oct 2010)

Chief Secretary:
Colonel Park, Chong-duk (1 Oct 2010)

**Territorial Headquarters: The Salvation Army Building,
5th and 6th floors, 476 Choong Chung Ro 3-ga, Sudaemun Ku,
Seoul 120-837, Republic of Korea**

Postal address: The Salvation Army, Central PO Box 1192, Seoul 100-709, Republic of Korea

Tel: [82] (2) 6364 4000

email: korea@kor.salvationarmy.org; website: www.salvationarmy.or.kr

Responding to a request while visiting Japan in 1907, the Founder despatched Commissioner George Scott Railton to survey prospects on the Korean peninsula. As a result, in October 1908 Colonel and Mrs Robert Hoggard (née Annie Johns) arrived with a group of officers to 'open fire' in Seoul. During the Korean conflict, which took place from 1950 to 1953, one Korean officer and a corps sergeant-major were martyred and three other Salvationists listed as missing, believed to be martyred.

Outreach work in Mongolia was officially commenced in October 2008.

Zone: South Pacific and East Asia
Countries included in the territory: Republic of Korea (South Korea), Democratic People's Republic of Korea (North Korea), Mongolia
'The Salvation Army' in Korean: (pronounced) 'Koo Sei Goon'
Languages in which the gospel is preached: Korean, Mongolian
Periodicals: *Home League Programme Helps*, *The Officer*, *The War Cry*

THE territorial theme for 2011 was 'The Year of the Soldier' based on Isaiah 60:1 – 'Arise, shine, for your light has come' which greatly inspired Korean Salvationists in their service. The 16th Territorial 'Strategy for Growth' Rally held at the Territorial Retreat and Conference Centre, Mount Paekhwasan, echoed the theme,

with enthusiastic attendance and participation by the delegates.

A new publication, *Nine Lay Salvationists who Brought Honour to The Salvation Army Korea Territory,* recognised the outstanding devotion and effort of nine comrades during the past century of ministry on the Korean peninsula.

Training was introduced in all divisions for Salvationists who are commissioned as local officers in the role of sergeant-major. The new course is designed to equip comrades as they serve alongside corps officers in implementing the Territorial Vision '2028 Hope Project'. During 2011, 219 soldiers completed this training and 45 were commissioned as corps sergeant-majors.

Other evidence of growth and development in ministry was especially related to social justice. The Switzerland, Austria and Hungary Territory joined with the Korea Territory in providing 100 tons of potatoes for shipment to the Sinuiju area of North Korea. In that region 300,000 people were suffering the effects of severe flooding and starvation. The Director of the Development Ministries Programme organised the shipment in June 2011.

Five professionally-run centres in larger cities of the territory assisted women who were victims of, or engaged in, the sex trade. Various counselling centres for women and the 'Sally Home' in Pusan (Busan) provided private consultation, legal and medical aid in an effort to intervene and support. The aim is to eradicate human trafficking and restore human dignity to its victims. During the year, as a result of these ministries, many women were saved from being forced into prostitution.

One woman had not been able to cover hospital expenses following surgery. She was forced into prostitution, made no money and was ill-treated. Hearing about The Salvation Army centre nearby, she managed to escape and found shelter, understanding, safety and nutritious food. She based her recovery on the Christian faith and was restored to physical and spiritual health. She is now an enthusiastic soldier at a corps.

Government permission was given for The Salvation Army to conduct an extra Christmas Kettle Appeal in Seoul in 2011. This raised funds for emergency relief in Japan following a devastating earthquake and tsunami. Funds were also sent for anti-malaria projects throughout Africa and provided education for Zambian children.

Women's Ministries also reported gradual expansion throughout the year. The influential leadership and active participation of women Salvationists, inspired by the territory's theme, resulted in souls saved. Some 1,459 new converts were won and 492 new home league members gained as a result of these efforts. The Women's Ministries department also launched the 'Planting Hope in the World' project and funding was raised to support grant-aided territories in their social service programmes.

STATISTICS

Officers 790 (active 622 retired 166) **Cadets** (1st Yr) 15 (2nd Yr) 18 **Employees** 1,076

Corps 254 **Outposts and Societies** 22 **Institutions** 23

Senior Soldiers 43,877 **Adherent Members** 9,277 **Junior Soldiers** 8,874

Personnel serving outside territory Officers 15

STAFF

Women's Ministries: Comr Kim, Keum-nyeo (TPWM) Col Yoon, Eun-sook (TSWM) Lt-Col Yeo, Keum-soo (THLS) Lt-Col Lee, Ok-kyung (TLMS) Maj Kim, Mi-kyung (TSAMFS) Maj Park, In-hwa (TSSS)

Sec for Personnel: Lt-Col Lim, Young-sik
  Editor and Education: Maj Park, Sang-yeon
  Literary Sec: Maj Kim, Jong-sun
  Director, Development Ministries:
    Capt Yun, In-jae
  Overseas Service Bureau: Capt Lee, Bo-tak

Sec for Programme: Lt-Col Kim, Nam-sun
  Church Growth Sec: Maj Han, Jai-oh
  Social Sec: Maj Lee, Soo-keun
  Youth: Maj Kim, Byoung-moo
  Music: Capt Kim, Hai-du

Sec for Business: Lt-Col Kim, Un-ho
  Territorial Auditor: Maj Kim, Young-tae
  Financial Sec: Capt Hwang, Kyu-hong
  Information Technology: Maj Lee, Hyun-hee
  Property: Maj Han, Sea-jong
  Public Relations: Maj Hong, Bong-shik
  Child Sponsorship: Maj Hong, Bong-shik
  Trade: Capt Kim, Sook-yung

Director, Territorial Heritage Centre: Lt-Col Hwang, Sun-yup

Training: Lt-Col Lim, Hun-taek

DIVISIONS

Choong Buk: 704 Doosan Hansol 1 cha Apartments 101 dong, 447-15 Kaeshin Dong, Heungduk Ku, Chung Ju, Choong Book 361-746; tel: (043) 276 1634; fax: (043) 263 6387; Maj Kim, Young-tae and Maj Kim, Choon-yun

Choong Chung: 603 Oosung Apartments 126 dong,162-15 Jeonglim suh Ro Suh ku, Taejon, Choong Nam Do 302-795; tel: (042) 584 2891; fax: (042) 584 2892; Maj Kim, Jong-koo and Maj Kim, Kye-suk

Choong Saw: 401 Hyundai Apartments 3-cha 302 dong, 208 Choongmoo Ro (Ssangyong dong), Suh Buk Ku, Chonan, Choong Nam Do 330-091; tel: (041) 572 0855; fax: (041) 578 0855; Maj Kang, Jik-koo and Maj Kim, Chong-sook

Chulla: 117-30 Song San Il Kil, Chung Eup, Chun Buk 580-200; tel: (063) 536 1190; fax: (063) 536 1191; Maj Ahn, Guhn-shik and Maj Yang, Shin-kyong

Kyung Buk: #901 Doosan We've Apartments 102 dong, Dang San Ro 82, Dahl suh ku, Taegu 704-082; tel: (053) 322 3695; fax: (053) 322 3694; Maj Shin, Jae-kook and Maj Cho, Hwa-soon

Kyung Nam: #1306 Green Core Apartments 301 dong, Deok Cheon Ro 234, Buk ku, Pusan, Kyung Sang Nam Do 616-782; tel: (051) 337 0789; fax: (051) 337 2292; Maj Kim, Pill-soo and Maj Choi, Sun-hee

Seoul: The Salvation Army Office Building, #705, 69 Saemoonan Gil Chongno gu, Seoul 110-061; tel: (02) 720 9543; fax: (02) 720 9546; Lt-Col Yang, Tae-soo and Lt-Col Chun, Ok-kyung

Seoul South: 602, Soojung Hanyang Apartments 235-dong, 1086 Sunboo 3-dong, Danwon Ku, Ansan, Kyunggi-do 425-765; tel: (031) 413 7811; fax: (031) 413 7812; Lt-Col Chun, Joon-hong and Lt-Col Shin, Myung-ja

Suh Hae: 301 Dongshin Apartments 204 dong, (Eupnae Dong Daelim Dongshin), 47 Buk Choon 2 Ro, Sosan, Choong Nam 356-758; tel: (041) 667 2580; fax: (041) 667 2576; Maj Lee, Ki-yong and Maj Kim, Sun-ho

MONGOLIA OFFICE

64th - 10 District 5, Bayanzurkh, Ulaanbaatar, Mongolia; tel: (976) 7016 5355; mobile: (976) 9191 7261; Maj Lee, Min-ho and Maj Chang, Mi-hyun

CONFERENCE CENTRES

Territorial Retreat and Conference Centre: Paekhwasan (Mount Paekhwa) (acc 1,000)
Choong Chung Div: Taejon Central Corps, Taejon (acc 400)
Seoul Div: Ah Hyun Corps, Kangwondo (acc 300)
Seoul Div: Youngwol Corps (acc 50)

OFFICER TRAINING COLLEGE

83-2 Chungang-dong, Kwachun, Kyunggi-do 427-010; tel: (02) 502 9505/2927; fax: (02) 502 7160

RETIRED OFFICERS' RESIDENCE

'Victory Lodge' Silver Nursing Home (acc 50)

SCHOOL

Inpyung Technical High School (acc 1,340)

TERRITORIAL HERITAGE CENTRE

1st and 2nd floors A,
The Salvation Army Central Hall,
1-23 Chung dong, Choong Ku, Seoul 100-120

THE SALVATION ARMY BUILDING

476 Choong Chung Ro 3-ga, Sudaemun Gu, Seoul 120-837

KOREA: Enthusiastic participants gathered at the territory's Mount Paekhwasan Conference Centre, for the 'Strategy for Growth' Rally

THE SALVATION ARMY CENTRAL HALL

1-23 Chung dong, Choong Ku, Seoul 100-120

THE SALVATION ARMY OFFICE BUILDING (THE SAOB)

69 Saemoonan Gil, Chongno Ku, Seoul 110-061

SOCIAL MINISTRIES

Adult Rehabilitation Centre (ARC)
Iljook (acc 50)

Bridge Centres (drop-in centres)
Seoul (acc 550)

Centres for the Handicapped
Kunsan:
   Catherine Centre for the Handicapped (acc 60)
   Day Care Centre for the Handicapped (acc 20)
Suwon:
   Support Centre for the Handicapped (acc 5)
   Rehabilitation Centre for the Handicapped
     (acc 20)
   Day Care Centre for the Handicapped
     (acc 15)

Children's Homes
Kunsan (acc 75), Seoul Broadview (acc 100),
   Taegu (acc 61), Taejon No 1 (acc 50),
   Taejon No 2 (acc 75), Sarangsaem (acc 7)

Community Centres
Community Centres: Hapchong, Hongeun,
   Kang Buk, Myung Chun, Non Hyun (Incheon
   city) Samyang Dong, Suh San Suklim, Youngwol
Corps Welfare Centres: An Sung Gongdo,
   Booyuh, Cheju, Mosan, Najoo, Seogwipo,
   Taegu, Suh An Sung Home Helper Centre
   for the Elderly, Taegu Chil Kok Centre for
   the Elderly, Yoju
Self-Support Training Centres: Asan, Bohryung,
   Nonsan, Sosan, Tai An

Corps Day Care Centres
Bahnyawol, Boo Nam, Chin Chang, Chun Kok,
   Hap Duk, Kang Buk, Keumbit Namoo
   (Hongeun), Kim Chon, Kwachun, Masan
   (Moonwha), Mindalae, Mosan, Myung Chun,
   Osan Saetbyeol (Star), San Kok, Sharon,
   Sok Cho, Suhdaemun, Suh Taegu, Suh San
   Suk Lim, Taegu, Wonju, Yul Mok

Counselling and Friendship Centres
Chonan Counselling Centre for Women, Donui-dong, Tong Taegu, Taegu, Suh Taejon, Taejon

Family Welfare Centres
Bohryung Multicultural Family Support Centre

Food Banks, Food Markets and Distribution Centres
Asan, Bohryung, Cheju, Chun An, Kwachun, Mapo #1, Mapo #2 Nonsan, Seogwipo, Song Dong, Sosan, Sudaemun #1, Sudaemun #2, Suh Chung Ju, Taejon, Taian, Yea San, Yeoju

HIV/Aids Care and Prevention Programme Units
Pusan Shelter; Red Ribbon Centre, Seoul

Oori Jip (transitional housing for those leaving children's homes)
Choongdong (Seoul Broadview Children's Home) (acc 2), Chun Yun (acc 3)

Sarangbang Centres (hostels for the homeless)
Buk Ah Hyun Dong (acc 30), Iljook (acc 59), Mangu Dong (acc 75), Sudaemun (acc 50)

Self-Support Training Centres
Boryung, Nonsan, Taian

Senior Citizens' Services Residential
Ansung Nursing Home (acc 60), Ansung Peace Village Nursing Home (acc 70), Kwachun Home for the Elderly (acc 60), Kwachun Nursing Home (acc 20), Namdong Peace Village Nursing Home (acc 60), Pusan Home for the Elderly (acc 71), Sooyong, Sun Chang Welfare Centre for the Elderly (acc 30), 'Victory Lodge' Silver Nursing Home, Kwachun (acc 58), Sun Chang Welfare Centre for the Elderly (acc 30)

Day Care Centres
Hapjung Day Centre for the Elderly (acc 18), Hongjae Dong Day Care Centre for the Elderly (acc 34), Mooan 'Silver Centre' for the Elderly (acc 5), Najoo Day Centre for the Elderly (acc 10), Namdong Day Centre for the Elderly (acc 117),

Suhsansung Day Centre for the Elderly (acc 20), Suwon Day Care Centre for the Elderly (acc 15), Wolsung Day Care Centre for the Elderly (acc 18)

Long Term Care Centres
Yong Ho (acc 17), Tongnae, Muloori (acc 20)

Welfare Centres for Seniors
Ansung, Balggeun, Chung Sung, Dan Chun, Sunchang, Taian

Special Service and Relief Services
9 programmes, 5 vehicles

Students' Study Centres (and after-school programmes)
1318 Happy Zone (Cheju), 1318 Happy Zone (Onyang), Asan, Baesan, Buk Choon Chun, Buk Gumi, Cheonju, Chew Kok, Chin Hae, Chisan, Chun An, Daniel (Eonyak), Doriwon, Eden, Hongjae, Huimang (Uijeongbu), Kang Buk, Keumsan, Leewon, Majeon, Mil Yang, Oh Ka, Sae Chung Ju, Sae Sungnam, Sak Sun, Seogwipo, Seoul Broadview, Shim Chon, Shinchang, Soyang, Taegu, Taegu Chil Kok, Wadong, Yea San, Yong Dong, Yoju, Youngwol

Student Accommodation
Taejon (university students, acc 25)

Thrift Stores and Sally's Coffee
Ah Hyun, Seoul; Buk Ahyun, Seoul; Changdong, Seoul; Chungdong, Bucheon; Daehangno, Seoul; Mapo #2, Seoul; Sookmyung Women's University Shop, Seoul; Suhdaemun, Seoul

Vocational Training and Support Centres
Chung Daoon House, Taejon (acc 30); Sally Home, Pusan (acc 22)

Women's Homes
Chonan House of Hope (acc 24); Didimdol (acc 16), Doori Home, Seoul (acc 35); Taejon Women's Refuge Shelter (acc 45)

LATIN AMERICA NORTH TERRITORY

Territorial leaders:
Colonels Tito and Martha Paredes

Territorial Commander:
Colonel Tito Paredes (1 Aug 2010)

Chief Secretary:
Lieut-Colonel Josue Cerezo (1 Mar 2011)

Territorial Headquarters: Avenida 11, Calle 20, San José, Costa Rica

Postal address: Apartado Postal 125-1005, Barrio México, San José, Costa Rica

Tel: [506] 2257-7535; fax: [506] 2257-5291; email: lan_leadership@lan.salvationarmy.org

The Salvation Army's work commenced in the Isthmus of Panama (1904), Costa Rica (1907), Cuba (1918), Venezuela (1972), Guatemala (1976), Colombia (1985), El Salvador (1989), Dominican Republic (1995), Honduras (2000) and Nicaragua (2010).

Legal recognition was given to El Ejército de Salvación by the Republic of Panama (1946), Costa Rica (1975), Guatemala (1978), Colombia (1988), Dominican Republic (1995), El Salvador (1996) and Honduras (2001). The territory was formed on 1 October 1976, then reformed on 1 September 1998, when Mexico became a command.

Zone: Americas and Caribbean
Countries included in the territory: Colombia, Costa Rica, Cuba, Dominican Republic, El Salvador, Guatemala, Honduras, Nicaragua, Panama, Venezuela
'The Salvation Army' in Spanish: Ejército de Salvación
Languages in which the gospel is preached: English, Kaqchikel, Spanish
Publications: *Voz de Salvación (Salvation Voice), Arco Iris de Ideas (Rainbow of Ideas)*

IN March 2012 the territory was greatly blessed to welcome the cadets of the Proclaimers of the Resurrection session. The 13 cadets entered training from Colombia, the Dominican Republic, Guatemala and Venezuela. During their welcome meeting in Costa Rica, Colonel Tito Paredes (TC) preached a powerful message. The congregation was moved by the response from the young people of the future officers' fellowship.

Major Joao-Paulo Ramos (IHQ) conducted an audit in February 2012

and his visit was of great benefit and encouragement to the finance staff.

Majors Gillian Brown and Loriann Metcalf from Canada and Bermuda, a mission partner territory, visited various corps and sponsorship programmes in the Costa Rica and Panama divisions and the Dominican Republic Region during April 2012.

Divisional and regional youth secretaries were appointed and worked hard with young people during the year, encouraging them to answer God's calling in their lives. The youth department held the first candidates' seminar. At a youth leaders' seminar, personnel from the USA Eastern Territory provided training which was later shared in divisions and regions throughout the territory.

In Colombia and Cuba evangelism took place through open-air meetings, door-to-door visitation and Sunday school. Various projects provided educational, social and spiritual help to children. Six young Colombians graduated from the development centre.

In Costa Rica 51 children attended junior soldier camp led by Captain Loraine Medina (TYS).

El Salvador faced many challenges during the year but the officers and soldiers worked faithfully to minister to people in their communities.

Guatemala Division's 'Renewal Sunday' for senior soldiers began with prayer and fasting and great blessings were received.

In Honduras work opened in Comayagua and 53 people from the community attended a meeting where they were challenged to follow Jesus Christ.

Pioneer work also continued in Nicaragua where membership has increased. God is blessing the Latin America North Territory.

STATISTICS
Officers 145 (active 128 retired 17)
  Employees 200
Corps 59 **Outposts** 10 **Institutions** 8 **Schools** 9
  Day Care Centres 9 **Children's Development
  Centres** 8 **Vocational Training Centres** 4
  Feeding Centres 14 **Camps** 2
Senior Soldiers 3,170 **Adherent Members** 1,125
  Junior Soldiers 1,458

STAFF
Women's Ministries: Col Martha Paredes
  (TPWM) Lt-Col Ruth Cerezo (TSWM)
Business Administration: Lt-Col María Alarcón
Personnel: Maj Esteban Calvo
Programme: Maj Max Mayorga
Candidates and Youth: Capt Loraine Medina
Editorial: Maj Ileana Calvo
Education: Maj Ileana Calvo
Finance: Maj Julia Mayorga
Sponsorship: Maj Max Mayorga
Social: Maj Max Mayorga
Training: Lt-Col David Alarcón

DIVISIONS
Colombia: Apartado Aéreo 17756 Santa Fe de
  Bogotá, Colombia; tel: (571) 263 2633; email:
  colombia.division@gmail.com;
  Majs José and Hilda Santiago
Costa Rica: Apartado Postal 6227-1000,
  San José, Costa Rica; tel: (506) 2221 8266;
  email: costarica.division@gmail.com;
  Majs Jorge and Idali Méndez
Cuba: Calle 96 Nª 5513 entre 55 Y 57,
  Marianao CP 11400, Ciudad de la Habana, Cuba;
  tel: (53) 7260-2171; email: ejdivcuba@enet.cu;
  Capts Julio and Leyanis Moreno
Guatemala: Apartado Postal 1881, Guatemala CA;
  2a Avenida 3-10, Sector A4 San Cristóbal 1,
  Zona 8 de Mixco, Guatemala;
  tel: (502) 2472-4868; email:
  guatemala.division@gmail.com
Panama: Apartado Postal 0843-01134 Balboa,
  Ancón Panamá, República de Panamá,
  Balboa Calle La Boca, Calle Julio Linares
  Edificio 0792, República de Panamá;
  tel: (507) 228-0148; email:
  panama.division@gmail.com

REGIONS
Dominican Republic: Residencial Antares
  casa N° B11, Ensanche Isabelita Sector Los
  Mameyes, Santo Domingo;
  tel: 1(809) 335 2678; email:
  republicadominicana.region@gmail.com;
El Salvador: Apartado Postal No 7,
  Centro de Gobierno, Calle 15 de Septiembre,
  N° 119 y N° 121 Barrio Candelaria,
  San Salvador; tel: (503) 2278 7071;
  email: elsalvador.region@gmail.com;
  Majs Walter and Lidia Gutierrez
Honduras (under THQ): Colonia Kennedy
  G14 B-49 # 3516. Tegucigalpa, M.D.C.,
  Apartado Postal 6590,
  tel: (504) 2230-6982/2230-7130;

email: honduras.region@gmail.com;
Capt Quelvin and Ana Cañas
Venezuela: Calle San Juan de Dios Melián, Entre
calle san Rafael y la Segunda de Cabudare
Riviera Departamento 1,
Cabudare-Barquisimento, Venezuela;
tel: (058) 251 261-6318;
email: venezuela.region@gmail.com;
Maj Pedro and Loraine López
Nicaragua: Reparto Miraflores de donde fue
el Restaurante Munich, 1 cuadra al Sur,
2 cuadras arriba y media cuadra al Sur
tel: (505) 2250 2527
email: nicaragua.region@gmail.com
Lts Israel y Lidia Polanco

TRAINING COLLEGE

Calle Puente de Piedra, 1 km norte del Puente
de Piedra, Barrio Los Angeles, San Rafael de
Heredia, Costa Rica; Postal address: Apartado
173-3015 San Rafael de Heredia, Costa Rica;
tel: (506) 2262 0061; fax: (506) 2262 0733

SOCIAL SERVICES
Institutions
Centre for Homeless

Costa Rica: Refugio de Esperanza: Avenida 9
Zona Roja, San José; tel: (506) 2233-2059
(acc 30)

Disabled Centre

Costa Rica: Hogar Sustituto 'Tierra Prometida',
Carretera Interamericana 100 metros sur de
Autos Mundiales, Pérez Zeledón;
tel: (506) 2771-2517 (acc 13)

Residential Homes for the Elderly

Cuba: William Booth Home, Calle 84
No 5525 e/55 y Lindero, Mariano, CP 11400,
Ciudad de la Habana; tel: (537) 260-1118
Panama: Hogar Jackson Home,
Avenida Amador Guerrero y Calle 3 No 2014,
Colón; tel: (507) 441-3371 (acc 30)

Residential Homes for Children

Panama: Hogar Dr Eno (Girls), Transísmica,
Sabanitas, Colón; tel: (507) 442-0371
(acc 20)
Venezuela: Hogar Nido Alegre, Calle 71 # 14
A63, Juana de Avila, Apdo Postal 1464
Maracaibo 4001; Estado de Zulia, Venezuela;
tel: (58-261) 798-3761 (acc 50)

Adult Rehabilitation Centres
Costa Rica:
Centro Modelo: Calle Naranjo, Concepción de

Tres Ríos, Cartago; tel: (506) 2273-6307
Refugio de Esperanza Liberia: Frente a la
Estación de Bomberos, Guanacaste;
tel: (506) 2666-5567
Cuba: Centro de Rehabilitación de Alcoholicos:
Carretera de Vertienes Km 3 #335, Reparto
Río Verde Camagüey CP 71200;
tel: (53) 3225-8230

EDUCATIONAL WORK
Kindergartens

Dominican Republic: Moca, Prolongación
Sánchez #12, Moca; tel: (1809) 578-9712
(acc 20)
Panama: Panamá Templo: Calle 25 y Avenida
Cuba-Este; tel: (507) 262-2545 (acc 30)

Kindergartens and Schools
Dominican Republic:
Cotui: Calle Duarte 62, Sector La Gallera
Provincia Sánchez Ramírez;
tel: (809) 585 3111 (acc 40)
Tres Brazos: Tres Brazos, Santo Domingo,
República Dominicana (acc 20)
Guatemala:
Chimaltenango: 7a Avenida y 1a Calle, Zona 1,
Villas del Pilar; tel: (502) 7839-6585
(acc 150)
Maya: Manzana #2, Lote 262, Zona 18,
Colonia Maya; tel: (502) 2260 1519
Mezquital: 4a Calle 3-99, Zona 12,
Colonia Mezquital; tel: (502) 2479-8443
(acc 150)
Tierra Nueva: Sector B-1, Manzana D, Lote 3,
Colonia Tierra Nueva 11, Chinautla;
tel: (502) 2484-1255 (acc 150)
Honduras: San Pedro Sula Montebello,
Chamelecón Casa 56, bloque 39m Residencial;
tel (504) 565 6488
Panama: Calle 11 y 1/2, La Pulida, Río Abajo;
tel: (507) 224-7480 (acc 40)

Kindergarten, Primary and Secondary School

Guatemala: Limón: Colegio William Booth,
Centro Communal 'El Limón' Costado
Derecho, Zona 18; tel: (502) 2260-0723
(acc 395)

Health Education in Hospitals
Honduras:
Avanzada de Tegucigalpa: Hospital Materno
Infantil (4 classrooms); tel: (504) 232-4927
Avanzada San Pedro Sula: Hospital Mario
Catarino Rivas (2 classrooms);
tel: (504) 565 5488

Latin America North Territory

Day Care Centres

Colombia: San Cristóbal Sur, Bogotá:
Calle 12 Sur # 11-71 Este, Barrio San Cristóbal
Sur, Santa Fe de Bogotá;
tel: (571) 333-0606/289-2672

Costa Rica:
Central Corps: Avenida 16, Entre Calle 5 y
7 San José; tel: (506) 2233-6850
(acc 35)
León XIII: Ciudadela León XIII, Detrás de la
Escuela de León XIII, San José;
tel: (506) 2222-3754 (acc 80)
Limón Central: Av 4 entre Calles 7 y 9;
tel: (506) 2758-0657 (acc 75)
Pavas: Villa Esperanza de Pavas, Contiguo
Al Instituto Nacional de Aprendizaje,
San José; tel: (506) 2231-1786 (acc 80)

Panama:
Templo Central: Calle 25 y Av Cuba-Este;
tel: (507) 262-2545 (acc 20)
Río Abajo: Calle 11 y 1/2 y la Pulida;
tel: (507) 224-7480 (acc 25)

Children's Development Centres

Colombia:
Armenia Outpost: Carrera 11 # 14-19 Barrio
Guayaquil; tel: (576) 736 9367
Nuevo Kennedy: Avda Calle 43 Sur #79 B47,
Barrio Nuevo Kennedy, Santa Fe de Bogotá,
Colombia; tel: (57) 1 264 9161
Ibague, Tolima: Carrera 4ta Sur # 20A-34,
Barrio Yuldaima, Apartado Aéreo 792;
tel: (578) 260-8032
Robledo, Medellín: Carrera 84B # 63-73,
Barrio Robledo, Medellín, Antioquía;
tel: (094) 234-8250
San Cristóbal Sur, Bogotá: Calle 12 Sur # 11-71
Este, Barrio San Cristóbal Sur,
Santa Fe de Bogotá;
tel: (571) 333-0606/289-2672

El Salvador:
Cuerpo Central: Calle 15 de Septiembre # 199
y # 121, Barrio Candelaria, San Salvador;
tel: (503) 270-5273 (acc 246)

Venezuela: Maracaibo: Calle 10 (99E) #62-09,
Barrio Simón Bolívar, Apartado postal 322,
Maracaibo 4001, Estado Zulia

Vocational Training Centres

Cuba:
Cuerpo Central: Computer Centre, Calle 96
Nª 5513 entre 55 y 57, Marianao 11400,
La Habana; tel: (53) 260-2171
Diezmero: Dressmaking, Calle 3ra Nª 25304
entre 2da y Martí Diezmero San Miguel

del Padrón, CP 130000 Guevara,
La Habana

Venezuela: Centro Vocacional – Carpenteria y
Costura, Calle 71 # 14 A-63, Cuartel Juana
de Acila, Apartado Postal 1464

Feeding Centres

Costa Rica:
Liberia: 500 mts Norte Estación de
Bomberos 100 Este y 50 Norte, Barrio San
Roque; tel: (506) 2666-3603 (acc 100)
Limón 2000: Barrio Limón 2000 frente al
Predio El Aragón, Alameda # 4;
tel: (506) 2797-1602 (acc 30)
Nicoya: Escuela de San Martín 900 al Oeste,
Barrio San Martín; tel: (506) 2685-5531
(acc 100)
Sagrada: Costado Este de la Escuela Carolina
Dent, Barrio Sangrada Familia
Salitrillos: Salitrillos de Aserri, de las
Prestaciones, 300 metros al sur;
tel: (506) 2230-4668 (acc 80)
San Isidro del General: Barrio Los Angeles,
Apartado Postal 7-8000;
tel: (506) 2770-6756 (acc 150)
Santa Cruz: Barrio Tulita Sandino,
300 este del IDA Guanacaste;
tel: (506) 2680-0724 (acc 100)

Colombia: Comedor de Ancianos, Carrera 5ta
Sur # 20A-34, Barrio Yulduima, Ibague,
Tolima

Cuba:
Comedor William Booth: Calle 96
No 5513 entre 55 y 57

Panama:
Colon: Avenida Amador Guerrero 14201,
Apartado 1163; tel: (507) 441-4570
(acc 75)
Chilibre: Transistmica, Lote No 175,
Chilibre; tel: (507) 216-2501 (acc 100)

Venezuela: Simón Bolívar, Calle 10 (99E) #62-09,
Barrio Simón Bolivar, Apartado postal 322,
Maracaibo 4001, Estado Zulia

Camps

El Salvador: Km 50, Carretera a la Herradura,
Caserio los Novios, Hacienda del Cauca;
tel: (503) 2354-4530 (acc 150)

Guatemala: Tecpán: Calle Tte Coronel Jack
Waters, Barrio Poromá, Colonia Iximché;
tel: (502) 2237 0269 (acc 100)

LATIN AMERICA NORTH: In Costa Rica young members of the future officers' fellowship participated with enthusiasm during the cadets' welcome meeting

LIBERIA:Captains John and Roseline Bundu (centre) **corps officers of Sierra Leone Freetown Corps distributing relief items to fire victims**

LIBERIA COMMAND

Officer Commanding:
Lieut-Colonel Festus Oloruntoba
(1 Jul 2010)

General Secretary:
Major Chatonda Joba Theu (1 Mar 2011)

Command Headquarters: 17th Street, Sinkor, Monrovia

Postal address: PO Box 20/5792, Monrovia, Liberia

The Salvation Army opened fire in Liberia in May 1988 as part of the Ghana and Liberia Territory, with Major and Mrs Leonard Millar as pioneer officers. This happened after more than 10 years of letters being written to International Headquarters by church pastors asking that they become part of the movement. Liberia was given separate command status on 1 January 1997. Neighbouring Sierra Leone became part of the command on 1 January 2010, with Captains John and Rosaline Bundu as pioneer officers.

Zone: Africa
Countries included in the command: Liberia, Sierra Leone
Languages in which the gospel is preached: Bassa, English, Gola, Krahn, Lorma

LIBERIA is enjoying relative peace after fourteen years of civil crisis. A second successful election after the ethnic war gave President Ellen Johnson Sirleaf a mandate to lead the country for a second term of six years. This political stability has given Liberians the opportunity to develop new infrastructures. The Salvation Army and other Christian churches have benefitted from this situation.

Captain Anthony Sio was a delegate to the International College for Officers in London; only the second officer to attend since Army work started in Liberia 25 years ago. Further training was undertaken by two officers who attended seminars at Kisumu, Kenya West Territory led by Lieut-Colonel Mary Capsey from the Africa Development Centre.

The Women's Ministries team led seminars throughout the command for home league local officers.

Leaders from Command Headquarters, district and sectional officers met to formulate a five year strategic plan which was introduced at officers' councils.

At the beginning of 2012 the first spiritual retreat for employees took place. The meetings included prayer and pastoral conversations. Mr Lawson Warbey, the command's accountant, was recognised for his hard work and faithfulness as one of the longest serving employees. He started as a security guard in 1992.

The school system also fulfilled the Army's mission through education. With funds from the Norway, Iceland and the Færoes Territory, two schools received new buildings.

A vehicle was purchased to facilitate regular inspections of schools. In the West Africa Examination Council's 2012 exam the three Salvation Army high schools achieved excellent results. John Gowans High School achieved the highest results in Bong county with 100 per cent pass rate.

The Salvation Army has opened fire in two new counties and in Sierra Leone centres have been opened at Dwarzark and Cocoa Yam farm.

The mobile clinic extended its service to Barnoe where people travel long distances to access medical services. An officer who is a trained nurse, started a home clinic for mothers and children in Arthington.

STATISTICS

Officers 53 **Auxiliary-Captains** 10 **Envoys** 1
Corps Leaders 4 **Cadets** 5 **Employees** 224
Corps 23 **Outposts** 21 **Schools** 12 (pupils 2,992)
Child Day Care Centres 6
Clinic 1 **Mobile Clinic** 1
Senior Soldiers 2,372 **Adherent Members** 86
Junior Soldiers 424

STAFF

Women's Ministries: Maj Joyce Theu (CSWM)
Maj Etta Gaymo (LOMS) Lt Georgina Snogba
(JMHLS)
Education Secretariat: Mr David Massaquoi
(Dir Education) Mr Elijah Sowen (Dep Dir
Education) Mr Julius Fayiah, Mr Christian
Smith (Education Officers)
Field: Maj Ben Gaymo
Finance: Maj William Mutungi
Projects: Maj William Mutungi
Sponsorship: Maj Florence Mutungi
Protocol and Communications: Envoy Momo
Douwee
Trade: Miss Maria Gee
Vocational and Technical Training Centre
Programme Coordinator: Mr Tweh Wesseh
Training/ETO: Capt Florence Pamacheche
Youth and Candidates: Lt Edwin Snogba

DISTRICT
Grand Bassa: c/o CHQ, PO Box 20/5792,
Monrovia; Capt Anthony Sio

SECTIONS
(c/o CHQ, PO Box 20/5792, Monrovia)
Bomi: Capt Amos Diah
Bong: Capt Lawrence Richardson
Buchanan City: Capt Jerry Duwah
Bushrod Island: Maj William Zogar
Compound Three: Maj Hilton Younger
Grand Gedeh: Capt Abraham Collins
Margibi: Capt Edwin Kpadebah
Monrovia City: Capt Phillip Boweh
Mount Coffee: Capt Moses Turey
Sinoe: Capt Broton Weah

TRAINING COLLEGE
17th Street, Sinkor, Monrovia

SCHOOLS AND COLLEGES
(c/o CHQ, PO Box 20/5792, Monrovia)
Salvation Army Vocational Technical and
Training College; Programme Coordinator:
Mr Tweh Wesseh BSc, LLB; Programme
Consultant: Mr Taweh Johnson MSc
William Booth High School; Principal:
Mr Prince Mulbah
John Gowans Junior and Senior High School;
Principal: Mr Morris Sargba BSc
Bill Norris Primary, Elementary and Junior High
School; Principal: Mr Joshua Q Roberts BTH, AA
Albert Orsborn Primary and Elementary School;
Principal: Ms Amelia Jallaht
Bramwell Booth Primary and Elementary School;
Principal: Mr Davison Paye
Len Millar Primary and Elementary School;
Mr Amu Q Roberts BTh
Len Millar Junior and High School; Mr Egbinda
F. Brima AA
Paul A. Rader Primary and Elementary School;
Principal: Mr Andrew Sagely
William Booth Primary and Elementary School;
Principal: Mr Lansana Kamara

CLINIC
William Booth Clinic: c/o CHQ, PO Box 20/5792,
Monrovia; Administrator: Mrs Korlu Smoke
Geh; Physician Asst: Mr Johannson David

SIERRA LEONE (under CHQ)
Officer-in-charge: Capt John Bundu
The Salvation Army, 39 Upper Brook St,
Freetown, Sierra Leone

Senior Soldiers 73 **Junior Soldiers** 128

MALAWI TERRITORY

Territorial leaders:
**Colonels Moses and
Sarah Wandulu**

Territorial Commander:
Colonel Moses Wandulu (1 Jan 2013)

Chief Secretary:
Lieut-Col Samuel Mkami (1 March 2011)

Territorial Headquarters: PO Box 51140, Limbe, Malawi
tel: [265] 1 917073 / 981142 email: MAL_Leadership@mal.salvationarmy.org

The Salvation Army began operations in Malawi on 13 November 1967 and was granted official government recognition on 2 October 1973. The Malawi Division was part of the Zimbabwe Territory until 1988, when it was integrated into the Zambia Command, which was given territorial status and became known as the Zambia and Malawi Territory. The Army's work in Malawi has grown and developed and on 1 October 2002 it became a separate region. Further growth and expansion of the work in Malawi resulted in the region being elevated to command status on 1 February 2004. The Malawi Command was elevated to territorial status on 1 March 2011.

Zone: Africa
Country included in the territory: Malawi
'The Salvation Army' in Chichewa: Nkhondo ya Chipulumutso
Languages in which the gospel is preached: Chichewa, English, Lomwe, Sena, Tumbuka

IN October 2011 General Linda Bond visited the Malawi Territory. A large crowd of Salvationists gathered at Robins Park Conference Hall, Blantyre, to witness the ordination and commissioning of the Friends of Christ session, conducted by the General. Her visit was received with enthusiasm and brought great inspiration and blessing to Salvationists. A large number of young people came forward to respond to the call for officership.

In November 2011, cadets of the Proclaimers of the Resurrection session were welcomed for officer training in Blantyre.

The Malawi Territorial Band travelled to Mocuba, Zambezia Province in the Mozambique Territory to support the sectional congress, led by the then territorial leaders, Colonels Torben and Deise Eliasen.

In February 2012, officers travelled great distances to attend officers' councils, conducted by Commissioners John and Dorita Wainwright (then TC and TPWM, Kenya East). The meetings were inspiring and challenging.

Following unprecedented flooding that submerged a number of villages in Shire Valley Division, The Salvation Army offered relief to hundreds of people. Tents, assorted foodstuffs and blankets were distributed.

Commissioner Brian Peddle (TC, Canada and Bermuda) and three other Salvationists from Canada, a mission partner territory, visited Malawi and led meetings at Lilongwe Corps and the training college. They also visited several projects in Central, Blantyre, Phalombe and Shire Valley divisions.

The cadets of the Proclaimers of the Resurrection session led a 10 day Easter campaign in Phalombe Division. There were wonderful results as many people made decisions for the Lord Jesus Christ, some for the first time.

STATISTICS

Officers 96 (active 90 retired 6) **Cadets** (1st year 14) **Employees** 78
Corps 50 **Outposts** 19 **Outreach Units and New Openings** 64
Senior Soldiers 6,534 **Junior Soldiers** 2,352
Personnel serving outside the territory
Officers 8

STAFF

Women's Ministries: Col Sarah Wandulu (TPWM) Lt-Col Mary Mkami (TSWM)
Finance: Capt Patrick Kimaswoch
Development Services: Narelle Gurney
Extension Training: Capt Oker Ntomba
Field: Maj Gerald Chimimba
Information Technology: Mr Aleck Chikopa
Property: Capt Stanley Phiri
Public Relations: Capt Luke Msikita
Sponsorship: Maj Ellen Chimimba
Youth and Candidates: Capt Fridah ` Kimaswoch

DIVISIONS

Blantyre: PO Box 51749, Limbe; tel: 01 655 901; Maj Effort and Capt Annet Paswera
Central: PO Box 40058, Kanengo, Lilongwe; tel: 01 716 869; Capts David and Grace Musyoki
Phalombe: PO Box 99, Migowi; tel: 01 481 216; Capts Paul and Doreen Kholowa
Shire Valley: PO Box 48, Chiromo; Capts Dickson and Chrissy Mpakula

DISTRICTS

Northern: PO Box 1129, Mzuzu: Maj Doricah Tulombolombo
Upper Shire: P/Bag 8, Ntcheu CDSS, Ntcheu; Capt Dyson Chifudzeni

OFFICER TRAINING COLLEGE AND EXTENSION TRAINING CENTRE

Ndirande Ring Rd, Chinseu, Blantyre; PO Box 51140, Limbe

COMMUNITY DEVELOPMENT PROGRAMMES
Adult Literacy
Blantyre, Central, Phalombe and Shire Valley Divisions, Northern District

Agriculture, Irrigation, Food Security Programme
Shire Valley Division

Child Advocacy
Central Division

Faith-Based Facilitation (FBF); FunctionalAdult Literacy; Micro-credit Schemes; Orphans and Vulnerable Children; Water, Sanitation and Hygiene
All divisions and districts

Feeding/Food for Work
Chikwawa, Migowi, Nguludi, Nsanje

HIV/Aids Home-based Care
Bangwe, Migowi, Nguludi, Nsanje

Rural Women Empowerment (inc boreholes)
Blantyre, Central and Shire Valley Divisions

Solar Power (Small Business) Enterprise
Blantyre Division

SOCIAL SERVICES
Hans Andersen Memorial Youth Centre for Child Anti-Trafficking: PO Box 167, Mchinji

MALI REGION

Regional leaders:
Majors Kapela and Rose-Nicole Ntoya

Regional Commander:
Major Kapela Ntoya (1 Nov 2011)

**Regional Headquarters: Armée du Salut,
Quartier Général Régional, Rue 360 Face Terrain Real de Bamako,
Hamdallaye, ACI 2000 Bamako, Mali**
Postal address: Armée du Salut Quartier Général, B.P. E 5249, Bamako, Mali

Following an invitation for the Army to establish a presence in Mali, registration was given on 29 November 2007. Work began under local leadership with oversight from Nigeria. In February 2008 officers were appointed. Mali was officially declared a separate region on 1 April 2011.

Zone: Africa
Country included in the region: Mali
'The Salvation Army' in Bambara: Kisili Kelebolo; in French: Armée du Salut
Languages in which the gospel is preached: Bambara, Dioula, French, Moré

FOLLOWING the pioneering work of Lieut-Cols Dikalembolovanga, Majors Kapela and Nicole Ntoya were installed as the regional leaders in Mali.

During New Year celebrations in Sogoniko Corps the regional theme 'One Wins One' was launched. Salvationists were urged to commit themselves to personal evangelism, to reach out to unchurched people so as to win souls for Christ. Activities such as evangelistic campaigns and door-to-door visitation led to the opening of three outposts at Kassela, Kati and Ouagadougou.

In March 2012, women from various churches flocked into The Salvation Army at Aci Corps for the World Day of Prayer. This was the first time most women had participated in this event. Previously Major Nicole Ntoya, (RPWM) had travelled to New York to represent The Salvation Army at a conference of the World Day of Prayer International Committee.

A successful feeding scheme in Bamako enabled Army personnel to reach out to vulnerable people facing hunger and poverty. This scheme reached street children, homeless people, mothers of infant twins – who face particular hardship, HIV/Aids sufferers, and sex-trafficking victims. Spiritual ministry was offered and their physical needs were met. As a result, new ministries developed among widows and mothers of infant twins.

In order to empower women to be financially independent, Major Nicole Ntoya (RPWM) conducted several income-generating workshops. Women were taught to make soap and dye fabric to make products which were then sold.

Commissioner Amos Makina (IS for Africa) visited in June 2012 and conducted the first ever review of Salvation Army work in the region.

STATISTICS
Officers 4
Corps 3 **Outpost** 1
   Senior Soldiers 74 **Adherent Members** 32
   Junior Soldiers 38
Vocational Training Centres 2

STAFF
Women's Ministries: Maj Rose-Nicole Ntoya (RPWM)

MALI: During an income-generating workshop, women learn how to make soap which can later be sold for profit

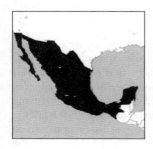

MEXICO TERRITORY

Territorial leaders:
Colonels Ricardo and Sonia Bouzigues

Territorial Commander:
Colonel Ricardo Bouzigues (1 Jul 2012)

Chief Secretary:
Lieut-Colonel Douglas Danielson
(1 Mar 2011)

**Territorial Headquarters: San Borja No 1456, Colonia Vértiz Narvarte,
Delegación Benito Juárez, México 03600, DF**

Postal address: Apartado Postal 12-668, México 03020, DF

Tel: [52-55] 5575-1042; 5559-5244/9625

email: mexico@mexsalvationarmy.org;

website: www.ejercitodesalvacionmx.org

In 1934, a group known as the Salvation Patrol was commenced in Mexico by Alejandro Guzmán. In October 1937, he was presented with a flag by General Evangeline Booth at the USA Southern Territory Congress in Atlanta, Georgia. The Salvation Patrol then became absorbed into the international Salvation Army, operating under the supervision of DHQ in Dallas, Texas, later becoming part of Latin America North Territory. On 1 September 1998 it was made a command and, on 1 October 2001, it became a territory.

Zone: Americas and Caribbean
Country included in the territory: Mexico
'The Salvation Army' in Spanish: Ejército de Salvación
Language in which the gospel is preached: Spanish
Publications: *El Grito de Guerra (The War Cry), El Eslabón (The Link)*

PRAISE God for every Salvation Army officer and soldier who has faithfully evangelized Mexico; through corps and social service ministry to needy people of all ages, in towns and cities throughout the country for the past 75 years.

More than 5,000 people accepted Jesus as their Saviour in 2011. Despite daily violence, deaths and fear instilled in the population by drug cartels, God's people fought on, claiming victory and peace in Jesus, as one by one, lives were transformed.

'Building the Future' was the theme for 2012, the 75th anniversary year. Two new halls were opened and dedicated to the glory of God by Commissioner David Bringans (then TC) at Matamoros in May 2011 and Hermosillo in February 2012.

Nine cadets of the Ambassadors of Holiness session were commissioned and ordained as officers in June 2011.

In September the 10 cadets of the Proclaimers of the Resurrection session were received for officer training.

From 12-30 October, an exciting and challenging outreach event was held in conjunction with the Pan-American Games in Guadalajara City, Jalisco State. Sixty-five Salvationists – officers, cadets and young people – were able to lead many people to Christ, pray with motorists at traffic lights and people on the streets, give out anti-human trafficking information, visit schools and hospitals and give public performances. Salvationists who participated testified to the event being a powerful spiritual experience in their lives. Some people who were contacted began attending The Salvation Army in Guadalajara.

The 'Future Officers' Fellowship' was held in January 2012, with a record 61 delegates attending from throughout Mexico. The enthusiastic delegates, Salvationists who feel that they are called by God to officership, participated in a weekend of personal interviews, practical workshops, spiritual meetings and ministry.

'The Seasons of Life' was the theme for two women's ministry camps. Coatzacoalcos in Sureste Region was the venue in early February and 45 women attended. Later in the month, 69 women from the Noroeste Division enjoyed time together in Hermosillo. The delegates were reassured that God was with them in every situation and were blessed as they ministered to each other through personal testimony and Bible study on the lives of Ruth, Naomi and Mary, the mother of Jesus.

The construction of the school for officer training accommodation blocks commenced early in 2011 but the site was shut down by Easter 2011 following local opposition from some Xochimilco residents and the Delegación (local government). Despite legal and other contacts made, no further work was permitted. God answered fervent prayers when, unexpectedly, the authorities asked for this building project, including the Training School, THQ and officer accommodation, to be completed. Construction was planned to begin again in June 2012 with all building permits granted.

In April 2012 cadets held successful evangelical Easter campaigns in Chihuahua, Torreón and Coatzacoalcos.

STATISTICS

Officers 168 (active 136 retired 32) **Auxiliary-Captains** 2 **Sergeants** 4 **Cadets** (1st Yr) 10 (2nd Yr) 9 **Employees** 45
Corps 48 **Outposts** 8 **Institutions** 25
Senior Soldiers 2,516 **Adherent Members** 704 **Junior Soldiers** 1,229

STAFF

Women's Ministries: Col Sonia Bouzigues (TPWM) Maj Verónica Tavares (TSWM)
Personnel: Maj Humberto García
Programme: Capt Luis Camarillo
Education and Editorial: Maj Leticia García
Finance: Maj Jannette Sáenz
Legal: Maj Humberto García
Property: Maj Marcos Tavares
Public Relations: Capt René Rodríguez
Social: Maj Jocabet Ramos
Training: Maj Víctor Vadés
Youth and Candidates: Capt Nohemí Camarillo

Mexico Territory

DIVISIONS
Capital: Alicante No 88, Colonia Alamos
Delegación Benito Juárez, México 03400, DF;
Apartado Postal 13-013, México, 03501 DF;
tel: [52-55] 5590-9220
Maj Guadalupe Galván

Noroeste: Tamborel No 601, Colonia Santa Rosa,
Chihuahua 31050, Chihuahua;
tel: [52-614] (614) 435-5968
Majs Facundo and Bersabé Vera

Río Bravo: Lombardo Toledano No 2709,
Colonia Alta Vista Sur, Monterrey 64740,
Nuevo León; tel: [52-81] (81) 8359-5711
Majs Manuel and Ana Campos

REGION
Sureste: Calle 19 No 116 x 22 y 24, Colonia
México, Mérida, 97128 Yucatán;
tel: [52-999] 944-6415; Maj Gilberto
Martínez

TRAINING COLLEGE
Calle Monte Albán No 510, Colonia
Independencia, México 03630, DF; tel: [52-55]
5672-7986

SOCIAL SERVICES
Adult Educational Support Programme
San Juan Ixhuatepec, Estado de México (acc 40)

Children's Day Care Centres
Ciudad Juárez, Chihuahua (acc 60)
Culiacán, Sinaloa (acc 27)
La Gloria, (Tijuana, Baja California) (acc 30)
Matamoros, Tamaulipas (acc 20)
México, DF Corps #1 (acc 30)
Nuevo Laredo, Tamaulipas (acc 20)
Reynosa, Tamaulipas (acc 25)
Saltillo, Coahuila Corps (acc 15)
San Luís Potosí (acc 30)
Tampico, Tamaulipas (acc 30)
Tapachula, Chiapas (acc 20)
Torreón, Coahuila (acc 20)

Children's Educational Support
Programmes
Ciudad Victoria, Tamaulipas (acc 40)
Genaro Vázquez, (Monterrey, Nuevo León) (acc 40)
Mexicali, Baja California (acc 40)
Monclova, Coahuila (acc 40)
Nogales, Sonora (acc 50)
Nueva Atzacoalco (México, DF) (acc 20)
Puerto Vallarta, Jalisco (acc 30)
Sabinitas, (Guadalupe, Nuevo León) (acc 60)
San Juan Ixhuatepec, Estado de México (acc 40)

Tuxtla Gutiérrez, Chiapas (acc 20)
Villahermosa, Tabasco (acc 15)

Children's Homes
Acapulco, Guerrero (acc 90)
Chihuahua, Chihuahua (acc 70)
Coatzacoalcos, Veracruz (acc 30)
Cuernavaca, Morelos (acc 45)
Culiacán, Sinaloa (acc 35)
Guadalajara, Jalisco (acc 100)
Matamoros, Tamaulipas (acc 35)
Mazatlán, Sinaloa (acc 40)
Mérida, Yucatán (acc 30)
México, DF (acc 120)
Nuevo Laredo, Tamaulipas (acc 40)
Puebla, Puebla (acc 35)
Reynosa, Tamaulipas (acc 45)
Saltillo, Coahuila (acc 35)
San Luis Potosí, San Luís Potosí (acc 30)
Tampico, Tamaulipas (acc 55)
Torreón, Coahuila (acc 50)
Veracruz, Veracruz (acc 50)
Villahermosa, Tabasco (acc 30)

Clinic and Dispensary
México DF: Clínica de Salud Mental

Feeding Centres
(Senior Citizens and Children)
Alvarado, Veracruz (acc 160)
Can Cún, Quintana Roo (acc 50)
Ciudad Madero, Tamaulipas (acc 40)
Ciudad Victoria, Tamaulipas (acc 40)
Cocotitlán, Estado de México (acc 25)
Durango, Durango (acc 100)
El Paso Texas, Mérida, Yucatán (acc 50)
El Porvenir (Can Cún, Quintana Roo) (acc 50)
Ensenada, Baja California (acc 30)
Genaro Vázquez, (Monterrey, Nuevo León)
(acc 40)
Hermosillo, Sonora (acc 50)
Mazatlán, Sinaloa (acc 40)
Mexicali, Baja California (acc 40)
México, DF Corps #3 (acc 20)
México, DF Corps #6 (acc 30)
Monclova, Coahuila (acc 40)
Monterrey, Nuevo León (acc 15)
Piedras Negras (acc 50)
Puerto Vallarta, Jalisco (acc 60)
Querétaro, Querétaro (acc 25)
Sabinitas, (Guadalupe, Nuevo León) (acc 60)
Saltillo, Coahuila (acc 35)
San Juan Ixhuatepec, Estado de México (acc 80)
Tapachula, Chiapas (acc 35)
Toluca, Estado de México (acc 25)

Mexico Territory

Tuxtla Gutiérrez, Chiapas (acc 20)
Xochitepec, Morelos (acc 40)

(Men)
Mexicali, Baja California (acc 50)
Nogales, Sonora (acc 50)

Night Shelters (Men)
México, DF La Esperanza (acc 125)

Monterrey, Nuevo León (acc 80)
Piedras Negras, Coahuila (acc 50)
Tijuana, Baja California (acc 150)

Vocational Training Centres
Cocotitlán, Estado de México (acc 6)
México, DF La Esperanza

Major Miguel Ruiz (r) offers counsel during Pan-American Games outreach

The triple treasures of Tampico's Children's Home, Israel, Ismael and Natanael

MIDDLE EAST REGION

Regional leaders:
Majors Stewart and Heather Grinsted

Regional Commander:
Major Stewart Grinsted
(1 January 2011)

**Regional Headquarters: The Salvation Army,
Ishbiliya, Block 4, Street 418, Villa 27, Flat 2**

Postal address; c/o The Lighthouse Church
National Evangelical Church Of Kuwait (Neck)
PO Box: 80 Safat 13001 Kuwait

The Salvation Army in the Middle East began with meetings held by ex-patriot Salvationists from Southern India who had moved to the Gulf coast countries for employment. After years of independent effort by local leaders, requests for official recognition were sent to IHQ. In August 2008 General Shaw Clifton appointed the first officers to Kuwait. Expansion continued in 2010 into the United Arab Emirates and the entire area, encompassing neighbouring countries, became a region officially on 1 April 2011.

Zone: South Asia
Countries included in the region: Kuwait, United Arab Emirates
Languages in which the gospel is preached: English, Tamil

IN the Middle East Region the challenge for The Salvation Army is to make the transition from being a spiritual home for a majority of transient members into something more permanent that can contribute to the wider community. During the past year the region's focus has been to engage more purposefully with both the expatriate and the indigenous people, to live with integrity and authenticity and to understand and relate to those of the Islamic faith.

In Kuwait the social care programme has grown and the Army has received donations and sponsorship from individuals and companies such as Chevron and Agility. Local and expatriate people worked together on a 'Trashion Show', where recycled clothing was sold and the proceeds used to help women in need. The average attendance at Saturday worship in 2011-12 was 90 people. Two Salvationist nurses newly arrived from India in 2012 have brought several friends to The Salvation Army.

The Booth House Shelter accommodated 40 domestic workers in distress and offered training in nutrition, English, craft and sewing.

A craft and care ministry to 50 domestic workers was held weekly in the Philippine Embassy. Other ministries included prison and hospital visitation and the distribution of winter coats to impoverished workers. Food, furniture and clothing was supplied to needy families and basic help with finance planning offered.

During the Christmas period 2,000 gift bags were given to runaway domestic workers sheltered in embassies and a deportation centre.

One Kuwaiti family was assisted in what was possibly the first family tracing or missing persons case in the Middle East.

Sharjah Corps, an established congregation in the UAE, met weekly in a room transformed into a Salvation Army hall with mercy seat, flag and musical support. There is a singing company and young people play a significant role in the corps.

In Bahrain around 35 people including 10 children met and each week after worship a meal was provided for camp labourers and poor families were given food parcels and clothes in December 2011. A medical camp where Salvationists with skills in health care can offer their services to labourers and poor people is planned.

In Oman, at Muscat and Salalah, Salvationists met weekly under local leadership.

STATISTICS
Officers 4
Senior Soldiers 288 **Junior Soldiers** 55
Congregations 6

STAFF
Women's Ministries: Maj Heather Grinsted (RPWM)
Assistant Regional Officers:
Majs Mark and Tracy Bearcroft

MIDDLE EAST: Under the Army flag, Major Heather Grinsted (l) conducts the enrolment of senior soldiers in Kuwait

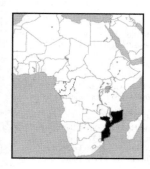

MOZAMBIQUE TERRITORY

Territorial leaders:
Colonels Ambroise and Alfonsine Zola

Territorial Commander:
Colonel Ambroise Zola
(1 Jul 2012)

Chief Secretary:
Lieut-Colonel Manuel Nhelenhele
(1 Jul 2012)

**Territorial Headquarters: Avenue Filipe Samuel Magaia, 860,
Maputo, Mozambique**

Postal address: PO Box 4099, Maputo, Mozambique

Tel: 843007490

The Salvation Army's evangelistic endeavours in Mozambique were pioneered in 1916 by Mozambican converts returning from South Africa. The work was recognised by the Mozambique government in 1986 and officially registered in June 2005. Previously part of the Southern Africa Territory, Mozambique became a separate command on 1 March 2008. It was elevated to a territory on 1 March 2011.

Zone: Africa
Country included in the territory: Mozambique
'The Salvation Army' in Portuguese (the official language): Exército de Salvação
Languages in which the gospel is preached: Portuguese, Chona, Chopi, Gitonga, Makhuwa, Ndau, Sena,
    Tchewa, Tsonga, Tswa
Periodicals: *Devocionias para Encontros da Liga do Lar* (Home League resource manual)

IN August 2011, more than 100 young Salvationists gathered for the first territorial school of music in Maputo, Capital Division. Majors Adonias and Maria de Souza, retired officers from Brazil, were the guest leaders and shared their skills in music and craft respectively. By the end of music school the first Army band in Mozambique was playing! During the same period, Women's Ministries members enjoyed learning new skills.

In September the territory hosted the Zonal Leaders' Conference for Africa, led by the General. Mozambican Salvationists gathered to welcome General Linda Bond, thrilled to witness the first visit by the international leader to the territory.

A spirit of revival was experienced when the conference delegates led Sunday meetings in Capital Division and when the General opened a new hall and inaugurated the site of a planned divisional headquarters in Maxixe, South Division.

A sectional congress in the Central North Division was held in November 2011, led by Colonels Torben and Deise Eliasen (then TC and TPWM), and 40 new soldiers were enrolled. The Malawian Territorial Band supported the congress and brought great blessing through their music.

The Easter Congress in April 2012 saw both a number of converts and a high level of giving to the Lord's work. New leaders were appointed to the territory, to be installed in July; Colonels Zola and Lieut-Cols Nhelenhele. The territory is moving forward, thanking God for leaders who established and developed the work and trusting him for greater things.

STATISTICS
Officers 51 **Cadets** 16 **Employees** 20
Corps 41 **Outposts** 59 **Day Care Centres** 5
HIV Home-based Care and OVC Projects 4
Adult Literacy Projects 50
Senior Soldiers 3,769 **Junior Soldiers** 1,437

STAFF
Women's Ministries: Col Alfonsine Zola (TPWM) Lt-Col Irene Nhelenhele (TSWM)
Education: Maj Maria Gutierrez

Finance: Maj Mário Nhacumba
Development and Projects: Maj Mário Nhacumba
Property: Capt Felix Nhaduate
Sponsorship: Col Alfonsina Zola
Training: Maj Hugo Gutierrez
Youth and Candidates: Capt Celeste Nhacumba

TRAINING COLLEGE
Rua no 5514 (do Hospital), 1360 Bagamoio, Maputo; tel:(258) 843986476
Training Principal: Maj Hugo Gutierrez
Education Officer: Maj Maria Gutierrez

DIVISIONS
Capital Division
  Province and City of Maputo
  Rua no 5514 (do Hospital), 1360 Bagamoio, Maputo; tel: (258) 843012023
  Majs Bishow and Pamela Samhika
Central-North Division
  Provinces of Nampula, Zambezia, Tete, Manica and Sofala
  Rua Dom António Barroso, 3272 Pioneiros, Beira: tel: (258) 843986478
  Capts Laurindo and Luisa Nombora
South Division
  Provinces of Inhambane and Gaza
  Rua Ngungunhane, talhão 100 Chambone, Maxixe; tel: (258) 843986491
  Capts José and Adélia Nharugue

MOZAMBIQUE: Easter Congress meeting in Capital Division

THE NETHERLANDS AND CZECH REPUBLIC TERRITORY

Territorial leaders:
Commissioners Hans and Marja van Vliet

Territorial Commander:
Commissioner Hans van Vliet (1 Jun 2010)

Chief Secretary:
Colonel Hannelise Tvedt (1 Feb 2013)

Territorial Headquarters: Spoordreef 10, 1315 GN Almere, The Netherlands

Tel: [31] (36) 5398111; fax: [31] (36) 5331458; email: ldhnl@legerdesheils.nl; websites: www.legerdesheils.nl; www.armadaspasy.cz

Captain and Mrs Joseph K. Tyler, English officers, and Lieutenant Gerrit J. Govaars, a gifted Dutch teacher, commenced Salvation Army work in the Gerard Doustraat, Amsterdam, on 8 May 1887. Operations soon spread throughout the country and reached Indonesia (then The Netherlands East Indies) in 1894. Further advances were made in 1926 in Surinam and in 1927 in Curaçao.

Salvation Army operations in Czechoslovakia commenced in 1919, the pioneer being Colonel Karl Larsson. Evangelistic and social activities were maintained until suppressed in June 1950. After the opening of the central European borders, The Salvation Army's work was re-established and The Netherlands Territory was asked to take charge of the redevelopment. By the end of 1990 centres were reopened in Havirov, Prague, Brno and Ostrava and the work has grown steadily since then.

On 1 February 2002 the territory was renamed The Netherlands and Czech Republic Territory.

Zone: Europe
Countries included in the territory: Czech Republic, The Netherlands
'The Salvation Army' in Dutch: Leger des Heils; in Czech: Armáda Spásy
Languages in which the gospel is preached: Czech, Dutch
Periodicals: *Dag In Dag Uit*, *Heils-en Strijdzangen*, *InterCom*, *Strijdkreet*, *Kans,* (all Dutch), *Prapor Spásy* (Czech)

IN May 2012 the territory celebrated the 125th anniversary of Salvation Army work in The Netherlands, which commenced on 8 May 1887. More than 150 veteran officers, envoys and soldiers gathered on Tuesday 8 May at the Army's 50|50 Hotel Belmont in Ede for a 'Veterans' Day'.

On Friday 11 May three days of national celebration began at the Westergasfabriek Park in Amsterdam. An officers' meeting was followed by a high tea for retired officers. The 125th anniversary celebrations were led by General Linda Bond who inspired the congregation and touched many hearts during the weekend's meetings. The General spoke about The Salvation Army's life-changing mission and called on Dutch Salvationists to pray, 'Above all, be a praying Army'. Numerous people rededicated their lives to Christ.

At the Major Bosshardt Gala on Friday evening – attended by Her Majesty Queen Beatrix of The Netherlands – the General presented the annual Major Bosshardt Award to Dutch TV host Lucille Werner, in recognition of her work to integrate disabled people into Dutch society. The General met with Queen Beatrix and special guests representing a wide range of Salvation Army work.

On Saturday afternoon Dutch Salvation Army bands marched through Amsterdam in a relay that started at Gerard Doustraat, from the building where The Salvation Army held its first meeting. Thousands of people lined the route through the city.

A music festival in the evening included contributions from the Amsterdam Staff Band and Staff Songsters, a youth choir and a large festival choir. A laser show at the start of the festival depicted the history of The Salvation Army and violinist Anne Roos (Almere Corps) played the violin that was used by Lieutenant Gerrit Govaars in the first meeting in 1887. Guest soloist was the Indian-born Salvationist and concert pianist Julian Clef.

The Salvation Army Church in The Netherlands enrolled new soldiers, adherent members and junior soldiers and accepted new candidates for officership. It was decided to extend the 'Revive the Church' strategy for a further three years to develop a more stable basis for the future of Army ministry and mission in the territory.

The Salvation Army in the Czech Republic – The Armáda Spásy – opened a newly-built hostel for men in the industrial city of Ostrava. It was provided by European Union funding and replaced a building in very poor condition.

The Armáda Spásy began the process to become a registered church. This initiative has motivated people to become recognised members of Army congregations, which has significantly increased membership. A 'Day for Women' was launched in March and women from northern Moravia gathered for fellowship, fun and worship.

In Prerov, a small Moravian town, the local Armáda Spásy started a successful programme for Roma men. A new musical group was formed called 'The Drom (Journey) of Life' which has been involved in evangelism in Roma communities.

STATISTICS
Officers 312 (active 113 retired 199)
  Cadets (1st Yr) 2 **Employees** 5,596
Corps 48, **Outposts** 16,
  Business Units 12 (251 local service centres)
Senior Soldiers 4,234 **Adherent Members** 1,212
  Junior Soldiers 443

STAFF
The Salvation Army Church
Women's Ministries: Comr Marja van Vliet (TPWM) Col Hannelise Tvedt (TSWM)

The Netherlands and Czech Republic Territory

Field: Lt-Col Johannes den Hollander
Mission Development: Mr Adiel Vader
Field Programme Support (inc Youth and Adult Ministries): Mr Alex van Zoeren
Candidates: Maj Tineke van de Wetering
Education: Maj Ria Scholtens
Training: (pro tem) Comrs Wim and Netty van der Harst
Family Tracing: Maj Jaap de Ruiter
Finance: Cadet Harm Slomp
Dataprocessing/Accounting: Mr Bert Barink
International Projects: Mr Hans de Graaf
Communications: Capt Robert Paul Fennema
Literary: Maj Simon M. van der Vlugt
Music: Mr Roel van Kesteren

DIVISIONS

Central: Piccolostraat 13, 1312 RC Almere;
tel: (36) 536 51 06; Maj Elsje Klarenbeek
North/East: Gein 27, 8032 BB Zwolle;
tel: (38) 452 67 13; fax: (38) 452 67 19;
Majs Teunis and Hendrika Scholtens
South: Hoeker 20, 2991 DC Barendrecht;
tel: 0180 5320877; Maj Ans Wimmers

THE SALVATION ARMY MAIN FOUNDATION
Board of Administration
Chairman: Comr Hans van Vliet (TC)

Staff
Secretary: Col Pieter Dijkstra (CS)*
Financial Sec and Managing Director:
Cadet Harm Slomp

THE SALVATION ARMY SERVICES FOUNDATION
Board of Administration
Chairman: Comr Hans van Vliet (TC)
Vice-Chairman: Col Pieter Dijkstra (CS)*
Official (non-voting) Sec: Cadet Harm Slomp
Members: Mr G. L. Telling,
Mrs L. M. Welschen-van der Hoek,
Mr P. Visser

Staff
Managing Director: Envoy Ed Bosma
Policy Worker: Mrs Martine Sloezarwij
Central Purchasing: Mr Egbert Oostra
Communications: Capt Robert Paul Fennema
Finance and Accounting: Mr Joop Rozema
Fundraising and Marketing:
Mr Will van Heugten
Human Resources: Capt Richard de Vree
Information Technology: Mr Friso van den Berg

Leger des Heils ReSHARE (Recycling Services)
Koopvaardijweg 15, 4906 CV Oosterhout;
tel: (0900) 9900099
Depot: Hattem
Director Operations: Mr Simon Smedinga

THE SALVATION ARMY FUNDRAISING FOUNDATION
Board of Administration
Chairman: Comr Hans van Vliet (TC)
Vice-Chairman: Col Pieter Dijkstra (CS)*
Official Sec: Cadet Harm Slomp RA
Members: Mrs J.W. Immink, Mrs N.C. de Waard,
Mr. A.G.C. van de Haar, Mr. P. Stigter

Staff
Managing Director: Envoy Ed Bosma
Director Operations: Mr Will van Heugten
All activities of the Foundation are to be executed by The Salvation Army Services Foundation.

THE SALVATION ARMY FOUNDATION FOR WELFARE AND HEALTH CARE
Care for the Homeless (total acc 4,059): night shelter (acc 511); day care (acc 713); 24-hour shelter (acc 601); care for vulnerable people (acc 1,092); young people (acc 267); supervised living (acc 832); preventative homelessness projects, ambulatory programs (267 FTE)
Substance Misuse Services (total acc 43): residential (acc 13); supervised living (acc 30); ambulatory programs (4 FTE)
Probation Services: ambulatory programmes (173 FTE); day training centres (acc 56)
Health Care and Care for the Elderly (total capacity 862): permanent stay (acc 370); hospice care (acc 19); temporary stay (inc medical care of homeless) (acc 156); day care (acc 30); ambulatory programmes (inc home care) (55 FTE); supervised living (acc 200); psychiatric clinic (acc 87)
Custody Care (total pupils 2,337): ambulatory programmes (141 FTE)
Care for Children and Young People: residential care (acc 450); day care (acc 47)
Prevention and Social Rehabilitation Services (total acc 624): community centres (392); ambulatory programmes (acc 373 FTE); work coaching (acc 232)

Board of Administration
Chairman: Comr Hans van Vliet (TC)

Queen Beatrix (centre) **and Commissioner Hans van Vliet, TC** (back, 2nd left) **with young Dutch Salvationists at The Major Bosshardt Gala**

Vice-Chairman: Col Pieter Dijkstra (CS) *
Sec/Treasurer: Cadet Harm Slomp
Members: Mrs G. W. van Montfrans-Hartman, Mr D. J. Rutgers, Mrs M. Trompetter, Mrs M.F.D. Waling-Huijsen, Mr J. Wienen

Staff
Managing Director: Envoy Cornel Vader
Deputy Director: Mr Hermanus M. van Teijlingen
Executive Sec: Mr Jeroen Hoogteijling
Business Administration: Mr Ruud de Vries
Risk Management and Internal Control: Mr Piet van Keulen
Main Office: Spoordreef 10, 1315 GN Almere; tel: (36) 539 82 50; fax: (36) 534 07 10

CENTRES FOR LIVING, CARE AND WELFARE
Central Region
Managing director: Mr Harrie de Heer
Information: Aïdadreef 8, 3561 GE Utrecht; tel: (30) 274 91 21
Northern Region
Managing director: Mr Pieter Plantinga
Information: Kwinkenplein 10-A, 9712 GZ, Groningen; tel: (50) 317 26 70
South-Western Region
Managing director: Mrs Joanne Blaak-van de Lagemaat
Information: Kromhout 110, 3311 RH Dordrecht; tel: (78) 632 07 00

Gelderland
Managing director: Mr Jan Jans
Information: Hoenderloseweg 108, 7339 GK Ugchelen; tel: (55) 538 03 33
Flevoland
Managing director: Mr Evert Dijkstra
Information: Spoordreef 12, 1315 GN Almere; tel: (36) 549 68 00
Northern Holland
Managing director: Mr Dik van den Hoek
Information: Mariettahof 25, 2033 WS Haarlem; tel: (23) 553 39 33
Overijssel
Managing director: Mr Elzo Edens
Information: Eiffelstraat 1 – 117, 8013 RT Zwolle; tel: (38) 467 19 40
Limburg/Brabant
Managing director: Mr Hans Martin Don
Information: Kolonel Millerstraat 67, 6224 XM Maastricht; tel: (43) 350 33 84
Amsterdam Goodwill Centres
Managing director: Envoy Henk Dijkstra
Information: Rode Kruisstraat 24b, 1025 KN Amsterdam; tel: (20) 630 11 11
The Hague Goodwill Work
Managing director: Mr Gert-Jan Freeke
Information: St Barbaraweg 4, 2516 BT Den Haag; tel: (70) 311 55 40
Rotterdam Centres for Social Services
Managing director: Mr Johan Koeman
Information: Kooikerweg 28, 3069 WP Rotterdam; tel: (10) 222 98 88

The Netherlands and Czech Republic Territory

Probation Services and Leger des Heils Youthcare
Managing director: Mr Bert Sprokkereef
Central Office: Zeehaenkade 30, 3526 LC Utrecht; tel: (88) 090 10 00

HOTEL AND CONFERENCE CENTRE
'Belmont', Goorsteeg 66, 6718 TB Ede;
tel: (31) 848 23 65 (50 twin-bedded rooms;
14 conference rooms acc varying 12-375)

* Colonel Pieter Dijkstra, is the Chief Secretary of the territory and Vice Chairman of the Salvation Army Foundations at the time of going to press.

CZECH REPUBLIC
Officer-in-charge: Maj Mike Stannett (1 May 2008)
National Headquarters: Armáda Spásy Petrzilkova 2565/23, 158 00 Praha 5;
tel: (00420) 251 106 424;
fax: (00420) 251 106 442
email: info@armadaspasy.cz;
website: www.armadaspasy.cz

STATISTICS
Officers 21 (active 19 retired 2) **Envoys** 4
   Employees 366
Corps 9 **Outposts** 2 **Community Centres** 17
   Institutions 20
Senior Soldiers 70 **Adherent Members** 64
   Junior Soldiers 13

STAFF
Asst Officer-in-charge: Maj Ruth Stannett
Personal Assistant: Env Pavla Vopeláková
Nat Director Residential Social Services:
   Mr Jan Krupa
Nat Director for Corps and Community
   Centres: Maj Rein van Wagtendonk
Training: Capt Aleš Malach
Editorial: Maj Attie van Wagtendonk
Finance: Mr Jan Benda
Fundraising: Envoy Jakub Vopelak

CENTRES
Hostels for Men and Women/Night Shelters
Brno: Dům Josef Korbel Mlýnská 25,
   602 00 Brno; tel: 543 212 530 (acc 136)
Krnov: Csl armády 837 bcd, Opavské předměstí,
   794 01 Krnov; tel: 554 612 296 (acc 85,
   includes mothers and children)
Opava: Nákladní 24, 746 01 Opava;
   tel: 553 712 984 (acc 48)
Prague: Dům Bohuslava Bureš, Tusarova 60,
   170 00 Praha 7; tel: 220 184 000 (acc 220)

Hostels for Men and Night Shelters
Havířov: Hostel, Na spojce 2, 736 01 Havířov;
   tel: 596 810 197 (acc 53)
Karlovy Vary: Nákladní 7, 360 05 Karlovy Vary;
   tel: 353 569 267 (acc 45)
Opava: Nákladní 24, 746 01 Opava;
   tel: 553 712 984 (acc 48)
Ostrava: U Nových Válcoven 9,
   709 00 Ostrava-Mariánské Hory;
   tel: 596 620 650 (acc 114)
Šumperk: Vikyrovicka 1495, Šumperk-Luže;
   tel: 583 224 634 (acc 35)

Homes for Mothers and Children
Havířov: Dvoráková 21/235, 736 01 Havířov;
   tel: 596 810 221 (acc 18 mothers plus children)
Krnov: Csl armády 837 bcd, Opavské předměstí,
   794 01 Krnov; tel: 554 612 296 (acc 85,
   includes hostel for men and women)
Ostrava: Gen Píky 25, Ostrava-Fifejdy 702 00;
   tel: 596 611 962 (acc women 30, mothers 10,
   children 15-20)
Opava: Rybárská 86, 746 01 Opava;
   tel: 553 714 509 (acc mothers 11, children 33)
Přerov: 9 kvetna 2481/107, 750 02 Přerov;
   tel: 581 210 769 (acc 45)

Alternative Punishment Programme
Opava: Nákladní 24, 746 01 Opava;

Azylovy Dům for Families
Stankova 4, 602 00, Brno; tel: 543 212 530
   (acc 12 flats)

Elderly Persons Project
Domov Přistav: Holvekova 38, 718 00, Ostrava-
   Kunčičky; tel: 596 238 163 (acc 40)

Farm Rehabilitation Project
Strahovice č.16, 747 24 pošta, Chuchelná;
   mobile: 737 215 396 (acc 4)

Follow-up Care (for alcoholics)
Dům pod svahem, Pod Svahem 1, 736 01,
   Havířov-Šumbark; tel: 596 881 007

Prevention Project (against homelessness)
Palackeho 25, 702 00 Ostrava – Přívoz;
   tel: 596 133 417/112 009 (25 flats)

Prison Work
Šumperk: Štefánikova 1, 787 01, Šumperk;
   tel: 737 215 396

Youth Centre
Brno-Bystrc: Kubickova 23, 635 00 Brno-Bystrc;
   tel: 546 221 756

NEW ZEALAND, FIJI AND TONGA TERRITORY

Territorial leaders:
**Commissioners Donald C. and
Debora K. Bell**

Territorial Commander:
Commissioner Donald C. Bell (1 Mar 2009)

Chief Secretary:
Colonel Graeme Reddish (1 Mar 2009)

Territorial Headquarters: 204 Cuba Street, Wellington, New Zealand

Postal address: PO Box 6015, Wellington 6141, New Zealand

Tel: [64] (04) 384 5649; website: www.salvationarmy.org.nz

On 1 April 1883 Salvation Army activities were commenced at Dunedin by Captain George Pollard and Lieutenant Edward Wright. Social work began in 1884 with a home for ex-prisoners. Work was begun officially in Fiji on 14 November 1973 by Captain Brian and Mrs Beverley McStay, and in Tonga on 9 January 1986 by Captain Tifare and Mrs Rebecca Inia.

Zone: South Pacific and East Asia
Countries included in the territory: Fiji, New Zealand, Tonga
'The Salvation Army' in Maori: Te Ope Whakaora
Languages in which the gospel is preached: English, Fijian, Hindi, Korean, Maori, Rotuman, Samoan,
   Tongan and Vietnamese
Periodical: *War Cry*

THE Salvation Army in New Zealand, Fiji and Tonga continued to see fruit from its long-term pursuit of four strategic mission goals: to make dynamic disciples of Jesus; to increase the number of soldiers; to take significant steps to eradicate poverty and injustice; to be a streamlined and mission-focused Army.

In 2011, congregational worship attendance reached an all-time high since records began in the 1930s. An average of 8,000 people worship weekly at The Salvation Army.

The Salvation Army in Tonga celebrated 25 years of faithful and growing ministry at Easter 2011. God is doing great things in and through the lives of Tongan Salvationists. There was great joy as many young people became soldiers and leaders in the Army's local mission.

The Fiji Division has planted new corps at a steady rate.

Following a major earthquake that claimed 185 lives in Christchurch on 22 February 2011, Salvation Army personnel continued to serve as part of the city's recovery and rebuilding programmes. The Salvation Army's expertise and efficiency in emergency relief and sustainable recovery was in great demand by other agencies. The Army provided support for schools in the severely damaged eastern suburbs, where the needs of families came to light through their children. Continuing aftershocks in Christchurch affected the community and many people faced uncertainty over insurance claims and property repairs. Many middle-income families and elderly residents sought help. The Salvation Army received the financial support to meet people's needs quickly and efficiently.

When devastating floods struck Fiji in early 2012 The Salvation Army provided shelter and supplies as well as ongoing support to people who lost possessions and even their livelihood. The process of economic recovery will take a considerable time

Successful initiatives in the territory continued. A second 'Pacific Trafficking in Persons Forum' in December 2011 brought together government and non-governmental representatives to consider issues and responses to human trafficking.

A third 'Amplify' creative arts camp for people aged 15-30 was attended by 160 delegates in January 2012. Forty staff members provided tutorage in a range of areas. The aim of the week was to empower young Salvationists to use their creative abilities for mission purposes.

The Social Policy and Parliamentary Unit's fifth 'State of the Nation' report, released in February 2012, warned that a growing number of New Zealanders were being sidelined from mainstream economic and social life. The annual report tracked social progress across five critical areas: New Zealand's children, work and incomes, crime and punishment, social hazards, and housing.

A partnership between The Salvation Army and a Mongrel Mob gang chapter, to combat methamphetamine addiction, brought family groups together as a treatment community. In February and March 2012, participants attended a camp that incorporated Maori customs and traditions to further encourage positive life change. Graduates from two previous programmes provided valuable peer support.

The then Chief of the Staff, Commissioner Barry C. Swanson, and World President of Women's Ministries, Commissioner Sue Swanson, inspired Salvationists when they took part in commissioning weekends in Fiji and New Zealand in December 2011. The territory was also pleased to host the South Pacific and East Asia Zonal Conference in February 2012.

STATISTICS

Officers 549 (active 308 retired 241) **Cadets** (1st Yr) 18 (2nd Yr) 11 **Employees** 2,786
Corps 92 **Plants** 7 **Outposts** 2 **Recovery Churches** 10 **Institutions** 82
Senior Soldiers 5,358 **Adherent Members** 1,454 **Junior Soldiers** 828
Personnel serving outside territory Officers 15

New Zealand, Fiji and Tonga Territory

STAFF

Women's Ministries: Comr Debora K. Bell (TPWM) Col Wynne Reddish (TSWM)
Business Administration: Maj Bruce Vyle
  Audit: Mr Graeme Tongs
  Finance: Maj David Bateman
  Information Technology: Mr Mark Bennett
  Property: Mr Ian McLaren
  Public Relations: Maj Lindsay Chisholm
  Trade: Mr George Borthwick
  Communications: Maj Christina Tyson
Personnel: Lt-Col Andrew Westrupp
  Asst (Officer Resources): Lt-Col Yvonne Westrupp
  Asst (Overseas Service and Health): Maj Tanya Dunn
Human Resources: Mr Paul Geoghegan
Candidates: Lt-Col Yvonne Westrupp
Programme: Lt-Col Rod Carey
  Asst: Lt-Col Jenny Carey
  Corps Growth & Development: Maj Clive Nicolson
  Social Services/Community Ministries: Maj Pam Waugh
Creative Ministries: Jim Downey
  National Youth Bandmaster: Grant Pitcher
  Youth: Capt Rebecca Gane
  Planned Giving: Maj Wayne Jellyman
  SpiritSong: Vocal Leader Marie Downey
Children's Ministries: Maj Bronwyn Malcolm
Book Production: Maj Christina Tyson
Moral and Social Issues Council: Maj Garth Stevenson
Overseas Development Consultant: Maj Vyvyenne Noakes
Social Policy and Parliamentary Unit: Maj Campbell Roberts
Territorial Events Co-ordinator: Selena Thomson

DIVISIONS

Central: 204 Cuba St, Wellington 6011, PO Box 6421, Wellington 6141;
tel: (04) 384 4713;
email: cdhq@nzf.salvationarmy.org;
tba
Midland: 12 Vialou St, PO Box 500, Hamilton 3240; tel: (07) 839 2242;
fax: (07) 839 2282;
email: Midland_dhq@nzf.salvationarmy.org;
Majs Ian and Lynette Hutson
Northern: 691A Mt Albert Road, Royal Oak, Auckland, 1023, PO Box 24306, Royal Oak, Auckland 1345;
tel: (09) 639 1103

email: ndhq@nzf.salvationarmy.org;
Maj Heather Rodwell
Southern: 71 Peterborough St, Christchurch 8013, PO Box 25-207, Christchurch 8144;
tel: (03) 377 0799;
email: southern@nzf.salvationarmy.org;
Majs Majs Ivan and Glenda Bezzant

FIJI

PO Box 14412, Suva, Fiji; tel: [679] 331 5177;
Divisional leaders: Majs Iliesa and Litiana Cola;
email: dhq_fiji@nzf.salvationarmy.org
Corps 11 Outposts 4

TONGA REGION

Regional Headquarters:
Mosimani Building, cnr Hala Fatafehi and Mateialona, Nuku'alofa, PO Box 1035, Nuku'alofa, Tonga;
tel: (676) 23-760; fax (676) 28-731;
email: rhq_tga@nzf.salvationarmy.org

Regional leaders: Lieuts Bryant and Pauleen Richards
Corps 4 Outpost 1

BOOTH COLLEGE OF MISSION (BCM)

20 William Booth Grove, Upper Hutt 5018;
PO Box 40-542, Upper Hutt, 5140;
tel: (04) 528 8628
Principal, BCM and SFOT: Maj David Noakes
  School for Officer Training (SFOT)
  School for Officer Training, Fiji
  School for Bible and Mission
  Centre for Leadership Development
  Leadership Development, Fiji
  Plowman Resource Centre: (Library, Archives and Heritage Centre)

FARM

Jeff Memorial Farm, Kaiwera RD 2, Gore;
tel: (03) 205 3572

FAMILY TRACING SERVICE

tel: (04) 382 0710; fax: (04) 802 6257;
email: familytracing@nzf.salvationarmy.org

INDEPENDENT LIVING UNITS

Ashburton: Wilson Court, 251-255 Tancred St (units 3)
Auckland: 353 Blockhouse Bay Rd (units 21); 425 West Coast Road (units 14); Roy Douglas Place (units 11); Dewhurst Place (units 2); Ceasar Place (units 2)

New Plymouth: Bingham Court, 46 Murray St,
Bell Block (units 10)

Blenheim: 35 George St (units 7)

Carterton: 204 High St South (units 8)

Christchurch: 794 Main North Rd, Belfast
(units 10)

Gisborne: Edward Murphy Village,
481 Aberdeen Rd (units 30)

Hamilton: Nawton Village, 57 Enfield St
(units 40)

Kapiti: 41 Bluegum Rd, Paraparaumu Beach
(units 18)

Mosgiel: Elmwood Retirement Village,
22 Elmwood Dr (units 30); 17 Cedar Cres
(units 30)

Oamaru: Glenside, 9 Arthur St (units 12)

Papakura: 91 Clevedon Rd (units 6)

Wellington: Summerset Units, Newtown: 182a
Owen St (units 11); 210, 212, 214 Owen St
(units 3); 226 Owen St (units 9)

RETIRED OFFICERS' ACCOMMODATION (under THQ)

Auckland: Lang Court, 9 Willcott St (units 6);
6D Liston St, Northcote (unit 1);
19 Splendour Cl, Henderson (unit 1)

Wellington: 176, 176a, 178, 178a Queens Dr,
Lyall Bay (units 4)

YOUTH CAMPS AND CONFERENCE CENTRES

Blue Mountain Adventure Centre: RD 1,
Owhango 3989; tel: (07) 892 2630;
website: www.bluemountainadventure.co.nz

SOCIAL SERVICES (under THQ)
Addiction and Supportive Accommodation Services

National Office: Level 1, 691a Mt Albert Road,
Royal Oak, Auckland 1023, PO Box 24073,
Royal Oak, Auckland 1345;
tel: (09) 639 1135

National Director: Aux-Capt Gerald Walker;
email: gerry_walker@nzf.salvationarmy.org

Bridge Programme: Community and Residential Programmes (Treatment of Alcohol and Drug Dependency)

Auckland: Bridge Centre (acc 32 treatment 22
day clients 10)

Christchurch: The Bridge Programme (acc 26)

Dunedin: (acc 7)

Hamilton: Midland Regional Residential and
Detox Centre

Invercargill

Manukau: Bridge Centre

Waikato: The Bridge Programme

Waitakere: Bridge Centre

Wellington: (acc 24)

Whangarei

Oasis Centres: Treatment Centres for Gambling

Auckland; Christchurch; Dunedin; Hamilton;
Queenstown; Tauranga; Wellington

Community Addictions Programme

Invercargill; Kaitaia; Kaikohe: New Plymouth;
Palmerston North; Tauranga

Supportive Accommodation Services

Auckland: Epsom Lodge (acc men 90)

Christchurch: Addington Supportive
Accommodation Services Social Services
Centre (acc 70)

Invercargill (acc 35)

Temuka: Bramwell Booth House (Intellectual
Disability) (acc 18)

Wellington: (Intellectual Disability) (acc 12)

Reintegration Services

Christchurch; Hawkes Bay; Wellington

Employment Plus

National Office: 204 Cuba St, PO Box 6015,
Wellington 6141; tel: (04) 382 0714;
toll free: 0800 437 587

National Director: Mr Mark Pickering; email:
m.pickering@eplus-salvationarmy.org.nz

Regions

Bay of Plenty; Central; Lower South; Northern;
Upper South; Waikato

Home Care Services

National Office: 71 Seddon Rd, Hamilton 3204;
PO Box 9417, Hamilton 3240; tel: (07) 848 2157

National Director: Mr Meng Cheong;
email: homecare.hamilton@xtra.co.nz

Service Centres: Auckland, Hamilton, Paeroa,
Rotorua, Tauranga

SOCIAL SERVICES (under DHQ)
Community Ministries

Aranui; Auckland City; Blenheim; Carterton;
Christchurch; Dunedin; Feilding; Gisborne;
Gore; Hamilton: Community Ministries (The
Nest) incl Mary Bryant Family Home, (acc 8);

Hastings; Hornby; Hutt City; Invercargill; Levin;
Linwood; Motueka; Napier; Nelson; North

Shore; North Taranaki; Palmerston North; Porirua; Queenstown; Rotorua; South Auckland; Sydenham; Tauranga; Timaru; Tokoroa; Upper Hutt; Waitakere; Wellington; Whangarei;

Early Childhood Education Centres

Gisborne: 'Noah's Young Ones', (24 places)
Hamilton: The Nest Educare, (50 places)
Upper Hutt: William Booth Educare, (roll 25)
Waitakere: Kidz Matter 2US, (25 places)
Wellington: Britomart ECEC, (roll 28)
Wellington Bridge – Te Matua Tamariki Home-based ECE Service

COURT AND PRISON SERVICE

Alexandra; Ashburton; Auckland; Blenheim; Christchurch; Dunedin; Gore; Hamilton; Invercargill; Kaitaia; Manukau; North Shore; Lower Hutt/Upper Hutt; Palmerston North; Porirua; Rimutaka; Tauranga; Thames; Timaru; Waitakere; Wellington; Westport; Whangarei

FIJI DIVISION SOCIAL SERVICES

Community Ministries Offices

Eastern: Grantham Rd, Raiwai, Suva;
tel: (679) 337 2122

Family Care Centres

Labasa: (acc 12); Lautoka: (acc 16); Suva: (acc 18)

Court and Diversion Officers

Lautoka; Suva

Farm Project

Farm 80, Lomaivuna; (acc 10)

Girls' Home

Suva; (acc 20)

Raiwai Hostel

Hostel for young male tertiary students,
Grantham Rd, Suva (acc 20)

Red Shield House

Suva Hostel; tel: (679) 338 1347 (acc 9)

Sewing Skills Programmes

Labasa; Lautoka; Sigatoka; Suva

Tiny Tots Kindergartens

Ba (acc 15); Labasa (acc 15); Lautoka (acc 50); Lomaivuna (acc 15); Nadi (acc 15); Nasinu (acc 30); Suva Central (acc 30)

TONGA REGION

Social Services based at Regional Headquarters
Community Ministries
Court and Prison Work: Nuku'alofa
Addiction Programme (ADAC)
Heath Team (incl. Mobile Health Clinic:
Popua and Patangata Community)
Farming project – Vaini Corps

Kindergartens:

Sopu, Nuku'alofa (acc 30)
Kolovai (acc 25)

TONGA: A march of witness on New Year's Day 2012

The Chief of the Staff (r) and World President of Women's Ministries (l) Commissioners Barry and Sue Swanson, with happy junior soldiers at a meeting to celebrate 90 years of Army work in Kenya, in November 2011

One Army with one mission, expressed in different ways: in the UK, an emergency response unit at the scene of a fire (above); in Moldova, General Linda Bond (second right) presents a much-needed wheelchair (above right); in India, Salvationists share the gospel message in the open air (below right); in Cuba, a family is invited to the local Salvation Army (below)

You're never too young to get involved at The Salvation Army! (clockwise from top centre) in Latvia, young Gabriela with General Linda Bond; timbrelists in India SE; musicians in The Philippines; Christmas toy distribution in USA Southern; 'Children's Day' in Sri Lanka; at summer camp in Moldova; dancing at the Festival of Gospel Arts in USA Central (centre)

New beginnings of all kinds are pictured here: (clockwise from top left) **USA Western** – women from an ARC celebrate a new start at camp; a new band in Pelotas, Brazil; in Japan a new boat gives this man work again, following the 2011 tsunami; a Canadian man receives the key to his new home; in Mexico General Linda Bond enrols 94 new soldiers; in Moldova a new headquarters building is opened; Lieutenants Haraldsen are appointed to open new Army work in Greenland (centre)

...torial Band from France and Belgium, playing in Rome in May
...to celebrate 125 years of The Salvation Army's work in Italy.

NIGERIA TERRITORY

Territorial leaders:
Commissioners Mfon and Ime Akpan

Territorial Commander:
Commissioner Mfon Akpan (1 Dec 2010)

Chief Secretary:
Lieut-Colonel Godfrey Payne (1 Jul 2010)

Territorial Headquarters: 6 Shipeolu St, Onipanu, Shomolu, Lagos

Postal address: Box 3025, Shomolu, Lagos, Nigeria

Tel/fax: [234] (1) 774 9125;

email: nig_leadership@nig.salvationarmy.org; thq.nigeria@gmail.com

Salvation Army operations began in Nigeria in 1920 when Lieut-Colonel and Mrs George H. Souter landed in Lagos, to be followed later by Staff-Captain and Mrs Charles Smith with 10 West Indian officers. Following an invitation for the Army to establish a presence in Mali, with registration being given on 29 November 2007, a response was undertaken under local leadership. In February 2008 officers were appointed and it became a separate region on 1 April 2011.

Zone: Africa
Country included in the territory: Nigeria
'The Salvation Army' in Yoruba: Ogun Igbala Na; in Ibo: Igwe Agha Nzoputa; in Efik: Nka Erinyana; in Edo: Iyo Kuo Imienfan; in Urhobo: Ofovwi re Arhc Na; in Hausa: Soldiogi Cheta
Languages in which the gospel is preached: Calabari, Edo, Efik/Ibibio, English, Hausa, Ibo, Ijaw, Tiv, Urhobo, Yoruba
Periodicals: *Salvationist, The Shepherd, The War Cry*

IN May 2011 President Goodluck Jonathan was returned to office during one of the most peaceful elections in Nigeria, the country with the largest population in Africa.

A Brengle Institute was held in Benin City and 20 selected officers attended. The leaders, Majors Ray and Pat Brown, corps officers from the UK, brought spiritual challenge and clarity to the delegates. Commissioners Mfon and Ime Akpan (TC and TPWM) attended the final Sunday meeting.

Also in May the Territorial Advisory Council was inaugurated and held its first meeting, following the executive officers' conference.

The national elections delayed the planned visits to divisions and districts by the territorial leadership, encompassing the entire territory from the border with Benin in the west, to the riverine area bordering Cameroon in the south-east and Kano in the north.

Kano was a target, among other cities, for attacks from the terrorist organisation Boko Haram. Indiscriminate attacks left many dead or injured across much of the north and north-east of the country. There is a strong corps in the city but many of the soldiers fled early in 2012 owing to frequent explosions. In the city of Jos inter-tribal and sectarian killing affected the number of pupils attending the Army's schools, located in a predominantly Muslim area. Thankfully, Army personnel and property in the city were unharmed.

Commissioners Amos and Rosemary Makina, (IS and ZSWM for Africa) visited Nigeria in October to conduct a review and they attended the final festival of the territorial music camp held in Uyo, Akwa Ibom state. The music camp's special international leaders were Bandmaster Bill Rollins and his wife Valencia from the USA Eastern Territory.

Lieut-Colonels Ian and Sonja Southwell, retired officers from the Australia Southern Territory visited to conduct a review of the training curriculum for officers and help create a useful 'road map' for future training.

The strategic planning and implementation committee held its first meeting in November and further meetings followed in 2012.

In February officers' councils were held in three areas – the first councils for some years. The opportunities for worship, Bible teaching and fellowship were exciting and encouraging.

The cadets of the Ambassadors of Holiness session held a busy Easter campaign in the south-east of the country, which inspired many people.

The territory is grateful for the support it receives from donors, providing resources to extend the gospel through a small network of clinics and its corrective surgery centre at Oji River.

STATISTICS

Officers 366 (active 311 retired 55) **Cadets** 23 **Employees** 303
Corps 162 **Societies and Outposts** 158 **Institutions** 15 **Schools** 32 **Clinics** 8
Senior Soldiers 16,842 **Adherent Members** 952 **Junior Soldiers** 6,169
Personnel serving outside territory Officers 1

STAFF

Women's Ministries: Comr Ime Akpan (TPWM) Lt-Col Diane Payne (TSWM) Lt-Col Patience Akpan (THLS) Lt-Col Edinah Onyekwere (Junior Miss and Young Women's Sec) Maj Edith Uzoho (Medical Fellowship and Retd Officers Sec)
Business Administration: tba
Editor/Literary: Capt Ifesinachi Ijioma
Extension Training: Maj Michael Olatunde
Finance: Capt Loveth Onuorah
Programme: Lt-Col Paul Onyekwere
Personnel: Lt-Col Joseph U. Akpan
Property: Lazarus Akpadiaha
Public Relations: Ntiense Williams
Social: Maj Ebenezer O. Abayomi
HIV/Aids: Kikelomo Omolola
Sponsorship: Maj Comfort Abayomi
Training: Maj Gabriel O. Adepoju
Youth and Candidates: Maj Gabriel Ogungbenle

DIVISIONS

Akwa Ibom Central: PO Box 8, Afia Nsit Urua Nko, Nsit Ibom LGA, Akwa Ibom State; Majs Udoh and Esther Uwak
Akwa Ibom East: PO Box 20, Ikot Ubo, via Eket, Akwa Ibom State; Majs Samuel and Glory Edung
Akwa Ibom South West: c/o Abak PO Box 23, Abak; Majs Ezekiel and Eno Akpan
Akwa Ibom West: PO Box 47, Etinan, via Uyo, Akwa Ibom State; Majs Michael and Comfort Sijuade
Anambra East: PO Box 16, Umuchu, Anambra State; Majs Edwin and Agnes Okorougo
Anambra West: PO Box 1168, Boundary Road Housing Estate, Onitsha, Anambra State; Majs Friday and Glory Ayanam

Ibadan: PO Box 261, Ekotedo, Ibadan, Oyo State; Majs Patrick and Blessing Orasibe

Imo Central: c/o Orogwe PO, Owerri, Imo State; Majs Obed and Violet Mgbebuihe

Lagos City: 41 Ajao Road, PO Box 2640, Surulere, Lagos State; Majs Benson and Celine Mgbebuihe

Ondo/Ekiti: 34 Odokoyo Street, PO Box 51, Akure, Ondo State; Majs Raphael and Esther Ogundahunsi

Rivers: PO Box 1161, Port Harcourt, Rivers State; Maj Joseph and Ngozi Mbagwu

DISTRICTS

Abia: 2-8 Market Rd, PO Box 812, Aba, Abia State; Maj Michael Oyesanya

Cross River: 32 Goldie Street, PO Box 11, Calabar, Cross River State; tel: (087) 220284; Maj Friday Ekpo

Edo/Delta: 20 First Circular Road, PO Box 108, Benin City, Edo State; Maj Vincent Adejoro

Imo North: PO Box 15, Akokwa, Imo State; Maj Godspower Sampson

Lagos West: Mission Street, PO Box 28, Badagry, Lagos State; Maj Silas Olebunne

Northern: PO Box 617, Garki, Area 1, Abuja, Federal Capital Territory; Maj Simon Ekpendu

Ogun: PO Box 64, Ado Odo, Ogun State; Maj Bramwell Chukwunwem

SECTIONS

Akwa Ibom South East: PO Box 25, Ikot Abasi; Maj Maurice Akpabio

Enugu/Ebonyi: PO Box 1454, Enugu; 4 Moorehouse St, Ogui, Enugu State; Maj Martins Ujari

TRAINING COLLEGE

4 Shipeolu St, PO Box 17, Shomolu, Igbobi, Lagos; tel: (01) 774 9125

SOCIAL SERVICES

THQ-based Prison Ministry

Badagry Prison, Ikoyi Prison, Kirikiri Maximum Security, Kirikiri Minimum Security, Kirikiri Women's Prison

Corps-based Prison Ministry

Afaha Eket, Agbor, Badagry, Benin Central, Ibadan Central, Port Harcourt Corps Team

HIV/Aids Facilitation Team: (based at THQ), 6 Shipeolu Street, Onipanu, Lagos

HIV/Aids Action Centre and Voluntary Counselling and Testing Centre

11 Odunlami St, PO Box 125, Lagos

Medical Centres

Gbethromey Training and Medical Centre: Lagos State (acc 8)

Lagos Central Corps Clinic: Lagos State (acc 2)

Nda Nsit Clinic/Maternity: Akwa Ibom State (acc 2)

Oji River Eye Clinic: Enugu State (acc 65)

Umucheke Corps Clinic: Imo State (acc 4)

Social Centres/Institutions/Programmes

Akai Children's Home: Akwa Ibom State (acc 35)

Benin Rehabilitation Centre: Edo State (acc 21)

Oji River Rehabilitation Centre: Enugu State (acc 64)

Orphans/Vulnerable Children Centre/Orphans Psycho-Social Centre – Akai: Akwa Ibom State

SCHOOLS

Nursery

Catherine Booth School, Lagos;

and at Aba Corps, Agbor Corps, Akai Corps, Akokwa Corps, Amauzari Corps, Benin Corps, Ibughubu Corps, Ikot Inyang Eti, Ile Ife Corps, Ivue Corps, Jos Corps, Mpape Corps, Onitsha Corps, Osumenyi Corps, Somorika Corps, Suleja, Umucheke Corps, Umuchu Corps, Umudike Corps

Primary

Catherine Booth School, 4 Shipeolu Street, Shomolu, Lagos

and at: Aba Corps, Akai, Amauzari Corps, Benin Corps, Ile Ife, Ikot Inyang Eti, Ivue Corps, Jos Corps, Mpape Corps, Onitsha Corps, Somorika Corps, Suleja

Secondary

Ilesha Corps, Ile-Ife, Orogwe

VOCATIONAL TRAINING CENTRES

Catherine Booth School, Lagos;

and at Aba Corps, Agbor Corps, Akai Corps, Akokwa Corps, Amauzari Corps, Benin Corps, Ibughubu Corps, Ikot Inyang Eti, Ile Ife Corps, Ivue Corps, Jos Corps, Mpape Corps, Onitsha Corps, Osumenyi Corps, Somorika Corps, Suleja, Umucheke Corps, Umuchu Corps, Umudike Corps

NIGERIA: A self-help group building new homes at Ikot Ebo

NORWAY, ICELAND AND THE FÆROES TERRITORY

Territorial leaders:
Commissioners Dick and Vibeke Krommenhoek

Territorial Commander:
Commissioner Dick Krommenhoek
(1 Feb 2013)

Chief Secretary:
Colonel Jan Peder Fosen (1 Dec 2010)

Territorial Headquarters: Kommandør T I Øgrims plass 4, 0165 Oslo, Norway

Postal address: Box 6866, St Olavs Plass, 0130 Oslo, Norway

Tel: [47] 22 99 85 00; fax: [47] 22 20 84 49; email: nor.leadership@frelsesarmeen.no;
website: www.frelsesarmeen.no

Commissioners Hanna Ouchterlony and George Scott Railton with Staff-Captain and Mrs Albert Orsborn 'opened fire' in Oslo (Kristiania) on 22 January 1888. Work began in Iceland on 12 May 1895, pioneered by Adjutant Christian Eriksen, Captain Thorstein Davidsson and Lieutenant Lange, and spread to The Færoes in 1924.

Zone: Europe
Countries included in the territory: Iceland, Norway, The Færoes
'The Salvation Army' in Norwegian: Frelsesarmeen; in Icelandic: Hjälpraedisherinn; in Færoese: Frelsunarherurin
Languages in which the gospel is preached: English, Færoese, Icelandic, Norwegian
Periodicals: *Krigsropet,* (Norwegian), *Herópid* (Icelandic)

THE territorial vision of 'A vital Army – on bended knee; with pure hearts; with open senses; with outstretched hands; with heads held high' has been shared throughout the territory during the Annual Congress, Days with the Word, officers' councils and meetings at corps and institutions. The vision is rooted in Ezekiel: 37.

The Annual Congress brought great blessing. Salvationists met together to worship and bring glory to God, under the territorial leadership team of Commissioners Adams and Colonels Fosen. For the first time meetings were live-streamed and some Salvationists met in corps halls to enjoy the congress via the Internet. Many people also participated in a live chat online.

'Care Plus', a new concept in housing for senior citizens was opened in Oslo in May 2011 with 62 flats and a service centre providing 24-hour help.

On 8 June the annual 'Sober Day', focusing on how families and children suffer because of alcohol misuse, had press coverage on national TV and radio. Salvationists on the streets handed out fruit drinks and pamphlets about the Army's position on this issue and 40,000 people supported 'Sober Day' on Facebook.

On 22 July, a terrible tragedy affected Norway when 69 young people were gunned down and killed on an island near Oslo. The Salvation Army, along with other churches, immediately offered counsel and support. This continued in the difficult days that followed through Army halls staying open for people to come and talk or pray; taking part in 'rose marches'; showing love and concern; praying for injured victims and bereaved families.

The textile project, 'Fretex' – Norway's largest work-rehabilitation programme run and owned by The Salvation Army – organised a bicycle tour of Norway. Starting in May from Kirkenes in the north and ending in August, after cycling a total of 2,000 miles, various groups converged in Oslo. Employees, clients and Salvationists participated by cycling part of the way and en route Fretex displayed information.

In August, the Oslo Slumstation marked 120 years of service. A gathering attended by representatives of all political parties in Norway, recognized Army work in Oslo both in past years and through services which meet current needs.

In September at the Oslo Temple Corps 15 cadets were welcomed for officer training, nine from the territory and six from Denmark.

During the summer months in 2011, a number of bronze sculptures called 'Exhibition of Homelessness' were displayed in front of the Norwegian Parliament in Oslo. The Army hosted this display, helping people to focus on the 6,000 homeless people in Norway, of whom 400 are children.

Commissioners Robert and Janet Street (IS and ZSWM for Europe) visited in September for the opening of the Jeløy Resource Centre; the Training College, Jeløy Folk High School and the Co-worker School have been amalgamated.

The Norwegian Bible Society launched a new Bible translation in October, and the Army took the opportunity for a renewed focus on reading the Bible.

A New Year Youth Conference was held in Gothenburg, Sweden bringing together 200 young people from Sweden and Latvia with the Norway, Iceland and the Færoes territories.

The 'Days with the Word' series of meetings has a long tradition, and is well received. This year the guest speakers were Commissioners Dick and Vibeke Krommenhoek (then TC and TPWM, Finland and Estonia) who ministered in Iceland and throughout Norway.

On 6 March 2012 the General conducted officers' councils at the Jeløy Resource Centre followed by a lively public meeting at Oslo Temple Corps. Salvationists and friends filled the hall and many seekers came forward in prayer after the General's message. Praise God for the moving of his Spirit!

Norway, Iceland and The Færoes Territory

STATISTICS
Officers 379 (active 162 retired 217) **Cadets** 15
Employees 1,259
Corps 110 **Outposts** 326 **Institutions** 28 (incl
slum posts)
Industrial Centres/Second-hand Shops 44
Senior Soldiers 4,766 **Adherent Members** 1,515
Junior Soldiers 13
Personnel serving outside territory Officers 10

STAFF
Women's Ministries: Comr Vibeke
Krommenhoek (TPWM) Col Birgit T. Fosen
(TSWM) Lt-Col Brit Knedal (Home & Family)
Sec for Business Administration:
Lt-Col Thorgeir Nybo
Financial Sec: Maj Eli Nodland Hagen
Chief Accountant: Vegar Thorsen
Missionary Projects: Maj Magna Våje Nielsen
Property: Dag Tellefsen
Sec for Communication: Maj Jostein Nielsen
Section for Information and Marketing:
Andrew Hannevik
Editor: Hilde Dagfinrud Valen
Sec for Personnel: Maj Lise O. Luther
Asst Sec for Personnel: Maj Bjørn
Ove Frøyseth
Sec for Field and Programme: Maj Anne Lise
Undersrud
Asst Sec for Field and Programme:
Maj Solfrid Bakken
Music: Maj Jan Harald Hagen
Territorial Band: B/M Espen Ødegaard
Over 60s: Maj Leif-Erling Fagermo
Youth and Children: Maj Henrik Bååth
Mission Team: Janne Nielsen
Special Efforts: Lt-Col Jan Øystein Knedal
Sec for Social Services: Lindis Evja (pro tem)
Alcohol and Drug Rehabilitation: Maj Knut
Haugsvær
Children and Family Services: Anne Hernæs
Hjelle (pro tem)
Day Care Centres for Children: Anne-Dorthe
Nodland Aasen
Family Tracing: Maj Erling Levang
Welfare and Development: Elin Herikstad
Work Rehabilitation and Recycling (Fretex):
Trond Ivar Vestre

JELØY RESOURCE CENTRE:
1516 Moss, Nokiavn 30; Maj Jan Risan
(Director)
Training College: Strandpromenaden 179, 1516
Moss tel: 69 91 10 85
Maj Frank Gjeruldsen (Training Principal)
Jeløy Folk High School: 1516 Moss,

Strandpromenaden 173 ; tel: 69 91 10 70;
fax: 69 91 10 80; Maj Wenche Walderhaug
Midjord (Principal)
Co-worker School: 1516 Moss,
Strandpromenaden 179; Maj Jan Risan
(Principal)

DIVISIONS
Central: Nordregt, 25 A, 0551 Oslo;
tel: 23 24 49 20; Lt-Col Elisabeth Henne
Eastern: Kneika 11, PO Box 40, 3056
Solbergelva; tel: 32 87 12 90;
fax: 32 87 12 01; Majs Per Arne and
Lillian Pettersen
Iceland and The Færoes: Kirkjurstræti 2,
IS 121 Reykjavik; tel: (00354) 552 0788;
Majs Paul William and Margaret Marti
Northern: Bjørkvn 12, PO Box 8255 Jakobsli,
7458 Trondheim; tel: 73 57 14 20;
Comrs Peder and Janet Refstie
North Norway: Skolegt 6, PO Box 177,
9252 Tromsø; tel: 77 68 83 70;
Maj Gro-Merete Berg
Western: Kongsgt 50, PO Box 553,
4003 Stavanger; tel: 51 56 41 60;
Lt-Cols Odd and Grethe Berg

SOCIAL SERVICES
Head Office: 0165 Oslo, Kommandør T. I.
Øgrims plass 4; tel: 22 99 85 00

Children's and Youths' Homes
3018 Drammen, Hotvedtveien 57; tel: 23 69 19 90
3028 Drammen, Bolstadhagen 61; tel: 32 20 45 80
1441 Drøbak, Nils Carlsensgt 31; tel: 64 90 51 30
1112 Oslo, Nordstrandsvn 7; tel: 23 16 89 10
2021 Skedsmokorset, Flesvigs vei 4;
tel: 63 83 67 10
4011 Stavanger, Vidarsgt 4; tel: 51 52 11 49
7037 Trondheim, Øystein Møylas veg 20 B;
tel: 73 95 44 33,
1540 Vestby, Soldammen, Gjølstadveien 73;
tel: 64 98 04 70

Family Centre
0487 Oslo, Kapellvn 61; tel: 22 09 86 20,

Home-Start Family Contact
Avd Drammen: 3007 Drammen, Rådhusgt 19,
tel: 478 93 800
Avd Nedre Eiker: 3007 Drammen, Rådhusgt 19,
tel: 478 93 800
Avd Lillehammer: 2609 Lillehammer,
Fossvegen 15 B; tel: 40 24 66 38
Avd Gamle Oslo: 0561 Oslo, Heimdalsgt 14 B;
tel: 90 61 76 74

Norway, Iceland and The Færoes Territory

Avd Østensjø: 0686 Oslo, Vetlandsveien 99/100;
tel: 23 43 89 10

Old People's Welfare Centre
0661 Oslo, Malerhaugvn 10b; tel: 22 57 66 30;

Slum and Goodwill Centres
6005 Ålesund, Giskegt 27; tel: 70 12 18 05
5808 Bergen, Ladegårdsgt 21; tel: 55 56 34 70
0656 Oslo, Borggt 2; tel: 23 03 74 494004

Hostels
5812 Bergen, Bakkegt 7; tel: 55 30 22 85
8001 Bodø, Kongensgt 16; tel: 75 52 23 38
5501 Haugesund, Sørhauggt 215;
tel: 52 72 77 01
0561 Oslo, Heimen, Heimdalsgt 27 A;
tel: 23 21 09 60
0656 Oslo, Schweigaardsgt 70;
tel: 23 24 39 00
0354 Oslo, Sporveisgt 33; tel: 22 95 73 50
3111 Tønsberg, Farmannsvn 26;
tel: 33 31 54 09
7041 Trondheim, Furulund, Lade Allè 84
FO-100 Torshavn, N Winthersgt 3;
tel: (00298) 31 73 93; tel: 73 90 70 30

**Self-catering Accommodation for Female
Drug Addicts**
Bodø

**Work-rehabilitation Programme among
Alcohol and Drug Addicts (The Job)**
0650 Oslo, Schweigaardsgt 68;
2609 Lillehammer, Morterudveien 15;
6400 Molde, Spolertbakken 3

**Rehabilitation Homes for Alcohol and
Drug Addicts**
Stavanger; Ualand, Heskestad

**Day Care Centres (Alcohol and Drug
Addicts)**
Bodø; Egersund; Oslo; Sandvika, Trondheim

**Supervisons of Residence (Alcohol and
Drug Addicts)**
0561 Oslo, Heimdalsgt 27A;
tel: 23 121 09 73

Health Clinics for Drug Addicts
0650 Oslo, Borggt 2, tel: 22 08 36 70
0187 Oslo, Urtegt 16 A/C; tel: 22 67 43 45

Prison Work
Bergen; Oslo, (2); Stavanger

Home for Prisoners
Oslo

**Work Rehabilitation and Recycling
Centres (FRETEX)**
(including 44 second-hand shops)
6002 Ålesund, Korsegt 6; tel: 70 12 71 75
5852 Bergen, Sandalsringen 3; tel: 55 92 59 00
8013 Bodø, Notveien 17; tel: 75 21 03 50
3036 Drammen, Kobbevikdalen 71;
tel: 32 20 83 50
4110 Forsand, Myra Industriområde;
tel: 51 70 39 07
3550 Gol, Sentrumsvn. 63; tel: 32 07 98 80
9406 Harstad, Storgt 34; tel: 77 00 24 77
7080 Heimdal, Heggstadmyra 2; tel: 72 59 59 15
7550 Hommelvik, Havneveien; tel: 73 98 72 00
2050 Jessheim, Storgata 11; tel: 67 49 04 30
9900 Kirkenes, Pasvikvn 2; tel: 78 97 02 40;
2615 Lillehammer, Storgt 91; tel: 61 24 65 50
1515 Moss, Bråtengt; tel: 64 69 27 50 69
0668 Oslo, Ole Deviksvei 20; tel: 23 06 92 00
3208 Sandefjord, Basen, Bugårdsgata 7;
tel: 33 52 27 38
4315 Sandnes, Tornerosevn 7; tel: 51 95 13 00
3735 Skien, Bedriftsvn 58; tel: 35 59 89 44
9018 Tromsø, Skattøravn 39; tel: 77 67 22 88

Second-hand Shops
Ålesund (2), Bergen (5), Bodø, Bryne, Drammen,
Fredrikstad, Gol, Harstad, Haugesund,
Jessheim, Jørpeland, Kirkenes, Kristiansand,
Lillehammer, Lillestrøm, Lyngdal, Mandal,
Molde, Moss, Oslo (5), Sandnes (2), Sandvika,
Skien, Stavanger (3), Stjørdal, Tromsø,
Trondheim (5), Tønsberg, Voss

Art Galleri
Bergen

Cafe
3016 Drammen, Torget Vest Rådhusgata 2

ICELAND
Convalescent Home: Skólabraut 10, PO Box 115,
IS-172 Seltjarnarnes; tel: [354] 561 2090
Guest Home: PO Box 866, IS-121 Reykjavik;
tel: [354] 561 3203

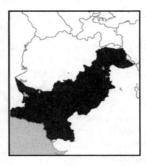

PAKISTAN TERRITORY

Territorial leaders:
Colonels Robert and Marguerite Ward

Territorial Commander:
Colonel Robert Ward (1 Feb 2008)

Chief Secretary:
Lieut-Colonel Yousaf Ghulam (1 Oct 2007)

Territorial Headquarters: 35 Shahrah-e-Fatima Jinnah, Lahore

Postal address: PO Box 242, Lahore 54000, Pakistan

Tel: [92] (042) 3758 1644/3756 9940

website:www.salvationarmy.org/pakistan

The Salvation Army began work in Lahore in 1883 and was eventually incorporated under the Companies Act of 1913 on 9 October 1968.

Zone: South Asia
Country included in the territory: Pakistan
Languages in which the gospel is preached: English, Pashto, Punjabi, Urdu
Periodicals: *Home League Annual, The War Cry* (in Urdu)

THERE was great joy in the territory at the development and growth experienced through an integrated approach in community programmes, flood relief, women's ministries and corps work. The international vision of 'One Army, One Mission, One Message' has strengthened the unified emphasis.

In the midst of inflation, internal armed conflict and political controversy, The Salvation Army in Pakistan continued to promote faith and unity. For the first time, retreats were held for officers, bringing spiritual refreshment and time for reflection.

Women's Ministries programmes had a strong influence. The annual 'Helping Hand' scheme raised an increased amount, which was allocated to community care.

Medical Fellowship members supported community programmes. The maternal and child programme was developed through community involvement in three more divisions.

At an Inner Wheel conference, Colonel Marguerite Ward (TPWM) spoke on 'The Empowerment of Women'. The delegates included more than 100 Muslim women which provided a wonderful opportunity for wider contacts.

Following severe flooding in 2010 the territory experienced a second year of community rehabilitation. Work continued to rebuild houses, replace livestock, restore livelihoods and

195

provide alternative sources of energy.

Heavy monsoon rains in the south caused further destruction. Financial assistance was provided through IHQ Emergency Services. Floods, earthquakes and displacement of people are common in Pakistan and the Army has worked at developing strategies and capacity to anticipate, prevent or mitigate the effects of future disasters.

The Sustainable Livelihood Development programme and other initiatives created cleaner, safer and more aware communities. Community Development Committees built capacity in disaster preparedness for the future.

Mission support funding from the United Kingdom Territory provided 14 new buildings, including a church hall and community centre for William Booth Village in Islamabad. The funds also supported music, children's and social programmes and provided education for children and further training for officers.

'Sally Ann', Pakistan, achieved registration as a private company after completing its third year of project funding. Part of the Army's 'Sally Ann' global network, the programme transforms poor communities by providing training and international markets for locally made products.

Permission was granted to build a centre in Peshawar that will serve as a base for emergency work, community development and worship.

The first youth leaders' conference for many years was held and Captain Mark Hall (TYS, Canada and Bermuda) was the guest speaker. This event inspired all who attended and provided the springboard for the development of divisional youth boards which meet regularly.

Fourteen cadets were welcomed to the Proclaimers of the Resurrection session for officer training.

The first annual Senior Soldiers' Day of Renewal was held and the stewardship programme continued to develop. Dr Jim Read and Colonel Geanette Seymour (ISJC) conducted a series of workshops on social justice issues.

The Pakistan Territory is grateful to God for the opportunities he provides for Salvationists to make a difference throughout the country.

STATISTICS

Officers 424 (active 326 retired 98)
Cadets (1st Yr) 16 **Employees** 166
Corps 134 **Societies** 516 **Institutions** 7
Schools 3
Senior Soldiers 52,643 **Adherent Members** 9,028 **Junior Soldiers** 14,783

STAFF

Women's Ministries: Col Marguerite Ward
(TPWM) Lt-Col Rebecca Yousaf (TSWM)
Projects: Col Marguerite Ward
National Project Director: Mr Asher David
'Sally Ann': Mr Faysal Yacoob
Secretary for Business Administration:
tba
Finance: Capt Amjad Sardar
Communications: Maj Saleem Yousaf
Property: Maj Yaqub Sardar
Secretary for Personnel: tba
Asst Sec for Personnel: Capt Diana Macdonald
Candidates: Capt Aneela Fahim
Mission Training and Education
Coordinator: Maj Rosemary Cowdery
Training Principal: Maj Colin Cowdery
Secretary for Programme: Maj Winsome
Mason

Prayer Coordinator: Maj Victoria Samuel
Social Services and Sponsorship: Lt-Col
Zarina Veru
Youth: Capt Fahim Asghar
Emergency Services and Public Relations:
Capt Macdonald Chandi

DIVISIONS

Faisalabad: Jamilabad Jamia Salfia Rd,
Faisalabad; tel: (041) 8783472; Majs Salamat
Masih and Grace Salamat
Islamabad: William Booth Village, Khana Kak
(Majaraj Plaza) Iqbal Town, Islamabad;
mobile: 0300 4805838; Capts Imran Ali Sabir
and Nighat Imran
Jaranwala: Water Works Rd, nr Telephone
Exchange, Jaranwala; tel: (041) 4312423;
Majs Michael Gabriel and Shamim Michael
Jhang: Yousaf Shah Rd, Jhang Saddar;
tel: (047) 7611589; Majs Samuel John and
Rebecca Samuel
Karachi: 78 NI Lines, Frere St, Saddar,
Karachi 74400; tel: (021) 3225460; Majs Javid
Yousaf and Surriya Javid
Khanewal: Chak Shahana Rd, Khanewal 58150;
tel: (065) 2553860; Maj Haroon Ghulam and
Capt Jennifer Haroon
Lahore: The Salvation Army, Bahar Colony,
Kot Lakhpat, Lahore; tel: (042) 35834568;
Majs Washington Daniel and
Azra Washington
Sahiwal: Karbala Rd, Sahiwal; tel: (040)
4466383; Capts Safdar Iqbal and Asia Safdar
Sheikhupura: 16 Civil Lines Rd, Qila,
Sheikhupura; tel: (056) 3786521; Majs
Samuel Barkat and Margaret Samuel

DISTRICT

Hyderabad: Bungalow No 9, 'E' Block,
Unit No 1-1, Latifabad 11, Hyderabad;
tel: (022) 3813445; Capts Raja Azeem Zia and
Nasreen Raja

TRAINING COLLEGE

Ali Bridge, Canal Bank Rd North, Tulspura,
Lahore; tel: (042) 36582450;
email: sacollege@cyber.net.pk

CONFERENCE CENTRE

Lahore: 35 Shahrah-e-Fatima Jinnah,
PO Box 242, Lahore 54000;
tel: (042) 37581644 ext 338

MISSION TRAINING AND EDUCATION CENTRE

35 Shahrah-e-Fatima Jinnah, PO Box 242, Lahore
54000; tel: (042) 37581644

SOCIAL SERVICES
Boarding Hostels
Boys: Jhang (acc 50)
Girls: Lahore (acc 50)

Children's Homes
Karachi Boys' Home (acc 50)
Joyland Girls' Home: Lahore (acc 50)
Sheikhupura Children's Home (acc 50)

EDUCATION
Schools
Azam Town Secondary School
Shantinagar Educational Institute
Tibba Coaching Centre: Shantinagar, Khanewal

REHABILITATION CENTRES FOR DISABLED

Karachi: Manzil-e-Umead, PO Box 10735,
Site Metroville, Karachi 75700;
tel: (021) 36650434
Lahore: Manzil-e-Shifa, 35 Shahrah-e-Fatima
Jinnah, PO Box 242, Lahore 54000;
tel: (042) 37582391

COMMUNITY DEVELOPMENT PROGRAMMES

'Advance Islamabad': Islamabad;
Faisalabad; Hyderabad; Jhang; Karachi;
Khanewal; Lahore; Peshawar; Sahiwal;
Sheikhupura

**PAKISTAN: Flood relief continued
throughout the year as communities were helped to rebuild
their lives** (see also article on page 9)

PAPUA NEW GUINEA:
(above) **Lavohoroi
Home League members
with their hand-crafted
mats**

(left) **Salvation Army
officers using local
transport en route to a
territorial event**

PAPUA NEW GUINEA TERRITORY

Territorial leaders:
Colonels Neil and Christine Webb
(1 Feb 2013)

Territorial Commander:
Colonel Neil Webb

Chief Secretary:
Lieut-Colonel Miriam Gluyas (1 Feb 2013)

Territorial Headquarters: Angau Dr, Boroko, National Capital District

Postal address: PO Box 1323, Boroko, NCD, Papua New Guinea

Tel: [675] 325-5522/5507; fax: [675] 323 3282; website: www.png.salvationarmy.org

The Salvation Army officially commenced in Papua New Guinea on 31 August 1956 and the first meeting was conducted on Sunday 21 October at the Royal Police Constabulary Barracks in Port Moresby. The first officers appointed there were Major Keith Baker, Mrs Major Edna Baker and Lieutenant Ian Cutmore. On 4 July 1994, after 38 years as part of the Australia Eastern Territory, Papua New Guinea became an independent command and on 9 December 2000 was elevated to territory status. Work began in The Solomon Islands in 2010 and was officially recognised on 1 February 2011.

Zone: South Pacific and East Asia
Countries included in the territory: Papua New Guinea, Solomon Islands
Languages in which the gospel is preached: English, Hiri Motu, Pidgin and many local languages
Periodicals: *Tokaut*

FOLLOWING the Army officially opening fire in the Solomon Islands on 1 February 2011, formal opening meetings took place in November 2011. Commissioner Andrew Kalai, (then TC) with Lieut-Cols Neil and Christine Webb (then CS and TSWM), travelled to conduct a weekend of dedication and celebration.

The territorial leaders of both Australian territories – who are financing this initiative – along with members of Brisbane City Temple Band also gave support. A prayer meeting, an open-air meeting, and a holiness meeting – in which more than 20 senior soldiers were enrolled and three local officers were commissioned – took place.

In September 2011 the Salvationists of Port Moresby united with other Christians in a five-mile march of witness to celebrate the 400th anniversary of the printing of the King James Bible. Christians in Papua New Guinea see this as significant because it was the publication of the Bible in the English language which led to the gospel being brought to them. More than 100 Salvationists joined with 600 other Christians in a march of witness and open-air meeting.

Fifteen cadets of the Friends of Christ session were commissioned and ordained. Eight students from the SALT college graduated and were appointed as cadet-lieutenants, adding vital resources to the ongoing development of the Army's work.

In an attempt to reach the poorest section of society an officer was appointed to begin work amongst the 'submerged tenth'. This involved much research and currently an action plan is emerging. A huge area of need has been discovered, which represents a significant challenge for the Army. Education through the Army's schools thrived, with good numbers of students. The Lae Primary school continued to develop and a number of its students have gone into mainstream education. Literacy training helped people throughout the territory.

A Social Justice Conference was held in December 2011, led by Commissioner Christine MacMillan (then Director, the ISJC). Many delegates from other faith-based organisations attended part of the conference.

The generosity of mission partners and other donors has provided new accommodation for officers, repairs to the training college, a new vehicle for the community health workers' training school and a new hall in Boregaina. A number of rural water and sanitation supplies projects were completed, providing much-needed fresh water to remote rural communities. Training opportunities made possible by funding from AusAid have enhanced and strengthened the territory.

An 'emerging leaders' course held in November 2011 helped 18 officers to consider leadership issues at depth and in ways which it is hoped will enable their accelerated development into more senior roles.

Divisional congresses were held around the territory. The North Coastal divisional event in Lae was led by Commissioners Alistair and Astrid Herring (IS and ZSWM for SPEA).

Support was given by the emergency services team who responded following several national disasters, including the sinking of a ferry when more than 300 lives were lost, a landslide which engulfed an entire rural community, and a plane crash.

STATISTICS

Officers 252 (active 224 retired 28) **Cadets** (1st Yr) 10 (2nd Yr) 10 **Employees** 462
Corps 58 **Outposts** 82 **Institution** 1
    Motels 2 **Schools** 10 **Health Centre and Sub Centres** 5 **Community Health Posts** 18
    Counselling Centres 4 **Staff Clinic** 1
Senior Soldiers 9,925 **Adherent Members** 7,754 **Junior Soldiers** 3,010

STAFF

Women's Ministries: Col Christine Webb (TPWM) Lt-Col Miriam Gluyas (TSWM)
Business Administration: Maj Philip Maxwell
Personnel: Maj Iveme Yanderave
Programme: Maj Rex Johnson
Leadership Development: Maj Bugave Kada
Editorial/Literature: Maj Deslea Maxwell
Property: tba
Projects: Maj Curtiss Hartley
Public Relations and Planned Giving:
    Capt Bernard Kila
SALT: Maj Kabona Rotona
Training: Maj Tilitah Goa
Youth Resources Co-ordinator:
    Capt Kila Apa

Papua New Guinea Territory

DIVISIONS

North Coastal: PO Box 667, Lae,
Morobe Province; tel: 472 0905;
fax: 472 0897; Capts David and Rita Vele

North Eastern: PO Box 343, Kainantu,
Eastern Highlands Province; tel: 537 1220;
tel/fax: 537 1482; Capts Jackson and
Lennie Suave

North Western: PO Box 365, Goroka,
Eastern Highlands Province; tel: 532 1382;
fax: 532 1218; Majs Nani and Serah Memeto

Sepik: PO Box 184, Wewak, East Sepik
Province; tel/fax: 456 1642;
Maj Vari and Capt Nellie Burava

South Central: PO Box 4227, Boroko,
National Capital District; mobile: 7285 0568;
fax: 321 6008; Capt Andrew Maino

South Eastern: PO Box 49, Kwikila, Central
Province; 2-way Radio Cell call no: 8564;
tel: 329 5008; Majs David and
Doreen Temine

DISTRICT

Gulf District Office: PO Box 132, Kerema, Gulf
Province; tel/fax: 648 1384;
Majs Leo and Susan Naua

OFFICER TRAINING COLLEGE

PO Box 5355, Boroko, National Capital District;
tel: 323 0553; fax: 325 6668

SALT COLLEGE

PO Box 343, Kainantu, Eastern Highlands
Province; tel/fax: 537 1125

EDUCATION SERVICES

Mary and Martha Child Care Centre, Koki
(acc 40)
Boroko Primary School (acc 759)
Lae Primary School (acc 689)
Goroka Elementary School (acc 167)
Kainantu Elementary School (acc 210)
Kerowagi Elementary School (acc 94)
Tamba Elementary School (acc 91)
Koki Secondary School (acc 337,
Grades 9 to 12)
Boroko FODE Centre (acc 689) (inc Boroko
Driving School)
Kimbe Computer School (acc 31)

Community Health Workers Training School

Private Mail Bag 3, Kainantu, Eastern Highlands
Province; tel/fax: 537 1404 (acc 52)

SOCIAL PROGRAMME
Community Services and HIV/Aids

Courts and Prison Ministry, Missing Persons,
Welfare Feeding Projects
House of Hope: Ela Beach Care and
Counselling Centre; tel: 320 0389
Jim Jacobsen Centre: PO Box 901, Lae,
Morobe Province; tel/fax: 472 1117

DEVELOPMENT SERVICES

Onamuga Development Project:
Private Mail Bag 3, Kainantu,
Eastern Highlands Province
Literacy Programmes: each division

HEALTH SERVICES PROGRAMMES

Gulf District: PO Box 132, Kerema,
Gulf Province; tel/fax: 648 1384
Community Health Posts (acc 2)

North Coastal: PO Box 667 Lae, Morobe
Province; tel: 472 0905, fax 472 0897
Community Health Posts (acc 3)

North Eastern: Private Mail Bag 3, Kainantu,
Eastern Highlands Province; tel/fax: 537 1279
Community Health Centres (acc 35)

North Western: PO Box 365, Goroka,
Eastern Highlands Province;
tel: 532 1382; fax: 532 1218
Community Health Centres (acc 4)

South Central: PO Box 4227, Boroko,
National Capital District;
tel: 321 6000; fax: 321 6008
Community Health Centres (acc 5)

South Eastern: PO Box 49, Kwikila,
Central Province Community Health Centres:
(acc 11)

MOTELS

Goroka: PO Box 365, Goroka, Eastern Highlands
Province; tel: 532 1382; fax: 732 1218
(family units 2, double units 4, house 1)
The Elphick: PO Box 637, Lae,
Morobe Province; tel: 472 2487;
(double rooms 22)

THE PHILIPPINES TERRITORY

Territorial leaders:
Colonels Lalzamlova and Nemkhanching, Nu–i

Territorial Commander:
Colonel Lalzamlova
(1 Apr 2011)

Chief Secretary:
Lieut–Colonel Bob Lee (1 Feb 2013)

**Territorial Headquarters: 1843 Leon Guinto Sr St,
1004 Malate, Manila**

Postal address: PO Box 3830, Manila 1099, The Philippines

Tel: [63] (2) 524 0086/88; (2) 524-2550

email: saphl1@phl.salvationarmy.org

The first Protestant preaching of the gospel in The Philippines was done by Major John Milsaps, a chaplain appointed to accompany US troops from San Francisco to Manila in July 1898. Major Milsaps conducted open-air and regular meetings and led many into a saving knowledge of Jesus Christ.

The advance of The Salvation Army in The Philippines came at the initiative of Filipinos who had been converted through contact with The Salvation Army in Hawaii, returned to their homeland and commenced meetings in Panay, Luzon, Cebu and Mindanao Islands during the period 1933-37. On 6 June 1937 Colonel and Mrs Alfred Lindvall officially inaugurated this widespread work.

The Salvation Army Philippines was incorporated in 1963 as a religious and charitable corporation under Company Registration No 24211. The Salvation Army Social Services was incorporated in 1977 as a social welfare and development corporation under Company Registration No 73979 and The Salvation Army Educational Services was incorporated in 2001 as an educational corporation under Company Registration No A200009937.

Zone: South Pacific and East Asia

Country included in the territory: The Philippines

'The Salvation Army' in Filipino: Hukbo ng Kaligtasan; in Ilocano: Buyot ti Salakan

Languages in which the gospel is preached: Antiqueño (Kinaray-a), Bagobo, Bicolano, Cebuano, English, Filipino (Tagalog), Hiligaynon (Ilonggo), Ilocano, Korean, Pangasinan, T'boli, Waray

Periodical: *The War Cry*

'FROM strength to strength we grow' was the territorial theme. Evangelism and discipleship training took place in each of the four divisions, funded by mission support from the USA Central Territory.

Commissioners James and Caroline Knaggs (TC and TPWM, USA Western) were the guest leaders during the commissioning and ordination of eight cadets of the Ambassadors of Holiness session in April 2011. Many young people present made a commitment to serve God, which gave a sense of hope for the future of the Army in The Philippines.

In May new territorial leaders Colonels Lalzamlova and Nemkhanching, Nu-i, were installed by Commissioners Alistair and Astrid Herring (IS and ZSWM for SPEA) at Manila Central Corps.

When floods and typhoons hit The Philippines the International Emergency Services responded. Working with local teams Salvationists assisted 5,775 families in Cagayan de Oro, Iligan and the surrounding areas. In Mindanao Island, Obando, Calumpit and Guguinto Bulacan food packs were distributed to 4,620 families.

A 6.9 magnitude earthquake struck La Libertad town in February 2012 and destroyed houses, commercial buildings, roads and electric power. More than 550 families lost their homes and 52 deaths were reported. The Army supplied mosquito nets and food in partnership with local government.

Women's ministries groups raised 150,000 pesos for projects in Bangladesh. Also, through their outreach 61 soldiers were enrolled and 96 new young people attended The Salvation Army.

A gospel arts camp was held at Camp Jabez, Cavite City in April. Majors Rick Carroll and John Stewart (USA Central Territory) were guest facilitators and 139 young people attended.

Officers, cadets and employees in the territory benefitted from training in building deeper relationships using faith-based facilitation.

STATISTICS

Officers 229 (active 177 retired 52) **Cadets** 15 **Envoys/Field Sgts** 7 **Employees** 51
Corps 79 **Societies, Outposts and Outreaches** 69 **Institutions** 2 **Social Programmes** 23
Senior Soldiers 7,154 **Adherent Members** 4,186 **Junior Soldiers** 1,470
Personnel serving outside territory
Officers 5 Layworker 1

STAFF

Women's Ministries: Colonel Nemkhanching, Nu-i (TPWM) Lt-Col Wendy Lee (TSWM)
Sec for Business Administration: tba
  Finance: Maj Allain Nietes
  Christian Books and Supplies: Lt-Col Maria Luisa Menia
  Property: Mr Alfredo Agpaoa Jr
Sec for Personnel Administration: Lt-Col Priscilla Nanlabi
  Candidates: Maj Nelia Almenario
  Training and Development: Maj Ruby Casimero
Sec for Programme Administration: Lt-Col Virgilio Menia
  Social Programme: Maj Susan Tandayag
  Corps Programme: Maj David Casimero
  Training Principal: Maj Linda Manhardt
  Training and Development/Education Services: Maj Ruby Casimero
  Editor and Literary Sec: tba
  Gospel Arts Coordinator: Mr Nicanor Bagasol
  Legal Consultant: Mr Paul Stephen Salegumba
  Public Relations Sec: Maj Miguel Tandayag
  Territorial Planned Giving Director: Maj Miguel Tandayag

DIVISIONS

Central Philippines: 20 Senatorial Dr, Congressional Village, Project 8, Quezon City; tel: (02) 929 6312; email: Central@phl.salvationarmy.org; Majs David and Elsa Oalang
Mindanao Island: 344 NLSA Rd, Purok Bayanihan, San Isidro, Lagao 9500 General Santos City; tel: (083) 302 3798; email: Mid@phl.salvationarmy.org; Majs Joel and Susan Ceneciro

Northern Luzon: Doña Loleng Subd.,
Nancayasan 2428 Urdaneta Pangasinan City;
tel: (075) 656 2383;
email: Northern@phl.salvationarmy.org;
Majs Alexander and Jocelyn Genabe
Visayas Islands: 731 M. J. Cuenco Ave,
Cebu City; tel: (032) 505 6972/6054;
email: Vid@phl.salvationarmy.org;
Majs Edward and Arlene Manulat

TRAINING COLLEGE
Pantay Rd, Sitio Bukal Brgy, Tandang Kutyo,
Tanay, Rizal; tel: (02) 654 2909

UNDER THQ
Sponsorship/Scholarship Programme;
Missing Persons/Family Tracing Service;
Emergency Disaster Relief

SOCIAL SERVICES
Residential Social Centres
Abused girls/children
Bethany Home: Quezon City (acc 25)

Street children in need of protection
Joyville Home: Rizal
(acc 30-40)

Learning Centres
Asingan Educational Services Inc: Pangasinan;
Caloocan; Cebu; La Paz: Iloilo City; Tondo;
Manila

Child Care Centres
Davao; General Santos; Laoag; Mariveles:
Bataan; Olongapo; Quezon City;
Signal Village: Manila

Nutrition, Feeding
Acala Corps: Pangasinan
Antipolo Outreach: Sitio San Lorenzo Ruiz
San Roque, Antipolo City
Aringay Outreach: Barangay Aringay, La Union
Bagong Silang: Bagong Silang Tala,
Caloocan City
Bautista Corps: Pangasinan
Bella Luz: Isabela
Butuan Corps: Butuan City
Camanggaan Corps: Tarlac
Davao Corps: Davao City
Fatima Outpost: General Santos City
Lake Sebu: South Cotabato
Lamsine Corps: Surallah South Cotabato
Lebe Corps: Kiamba Saranggani Province
Manila Central Corps: Ermita, Manila
Palmera Outreach: Del Monte City, Bulacan

Polomolok Corps Plant: South Cotabato
Quezon City 1: Quezon
Sun Valley Corps: Parañaque City
Urdaneta Corps: Pangasinan

Dormitories for Students and
Working Women
Baguio: (acc 50); Makati: (acc 12);
Quezon City (acc 12); Olongapo: (acc 12);
San Jose Mindoro: Occidental Mindoro
(acc 12)

Programmes for Minorities
Bulalacao: Bulalacao, 5214 Oriental Mindoro
Lake Sebu: 9512 Poblacion, Lake Sebu South
Cotabato
Lamsine: Lamsine, T'boli town South Cotabato
Palawan: Tabun, Quezon, Puerto Princesa
Wali: Bo Wali, Maitum, Saranggani Province

Skills Training
Lapu-lapu City

Livelihood Support
Ansiray; Badipa; Bautista; Caguray; Isabela;
Malingao; Nasukob; Orani; Ozamis;
Pahanocoy; Palili; Patnongon; Signal Village:
Manila (2 programmes)

Agricultural Assistance
Bautista; Cabayaoasan; Camanggaan; Diffun;
Isabela; Maiting; Nasukob; Palili;
Santa Wali

Micro-Credit Enterprise Projects
Ansiray: Bulalacao; Caguray; Dagupan;
Magsaysay; Malingao; Nasukob; Ozamis;
Palili; Patnongon

Anti-Human Trafficking Projects
Bansalan; Butuan; Davao; Fatima; General
Iligan; Kiamba; Lake Sebu; Lamsine; Lebe;
Malingao; Maitum; Ozamis; Polomolok;
Santos; Wali

Combat & Care Anti-Trafficking Project
Mindanao

Drop-in Centre for Trafficking Survivors
Davao

HEALTH
San Jose Occidental Mindoro: 3090 Roxas St,
Doña Consuelo Subd

THE PHILIPPINES: The Chief of the Staff gives enthusiastic leadership during a youth rally in Manila in June 2012

PORTUGAL: Lieutenant Marta Governo (l) **with her proud mother** (centre) **who has just received her Silver Star from Lieut-Colonel Susan Daly,**(r) **(CPWM), following her daughter's commissioning as a Salvation Army officer**

PORTUGAL COMMAND

Command leaders:
Lieut-Colonels Gordon and Susan Daly

Officer Commanding:
Lieut-Colonel Gordon Daly
(1 Oct 2010)

Command Headquarters: Rua Capitão Roby, 19

1900-111 Lisboa

Postal address: Apartado 14109, 1064-002 Lisboa, Portugal

Tel: [351] (21) 780 2930; email:Portugal_Command@POR.salvationarmy.org

website: www.exercitodesalvacao.pt

On 25 July 1971, official recognition was given to the first corps established in Portugal. The work was started in the northern city of Porto by a group of evangelical Christians. On 28 January 1972, Major and Mrs Carl S. Eliasen arrived in Lisbon to start work there and to supervise the existing activities.

On 4 July 1974 The Salvation Army was recognised by the Ministry of Justice as a religious and philanthropic organisation. All social activities are incorporated in Centro Social do Exército de Salvação which was constituted in Portugal on 26 March 1981 (Public Utility Register 16/82 dated 10 March 1982). On 8 March 2007 The Salvation Army was registered as a Collective Religious Person (the legal term for a church) and on 10 September 2009 became an Established (*Radicada*) Collective Religious Person, by decree from the Minister of Justice.

Zone: Europe
Country included in the command: Portugal
'The Salvation Army' in Portuguese: Exército de Salvação
Language in which the gospel is preached: English, Portuguese
Periodicals: *O Salvacionista*, *Ideias & Recursos* (for Women's Ministries)

THE Salvation Army was honoured to receive the annual citizenship award from the Beato district of Lisbon City in May 2011. This was in recognition of the social work carried out among the homeless and the elderly over a number of years.

Successful camps were held during the summer for women, junior soldiers, children and musicians. A group of scouts from Portugal took part in a summer camp in France and a young musician and an officer were delegates to the Territorial Music Institute of the USA Southern Territory.

The command was blessed by the visit in June of Commissioners Robert and Janet Street (IS and ZSWM for Europe). The commissioners met with officers and professional staff of social services and made visits to corps and social institutions in Lisbon and Sintra.

Signs of spiritual growth were seen in the enrolment of several senior and junior soldiers and recruits in various corps.

In December, the commissioning in São Paulo, Brazil, of a Portuguese officer-couple brought welcome reinforcements to the command. Lieutenants Gildo and Marta Governo returned to take up their first appointment in Portugal.

After several months of discussion and planning, the command formulated a strategic plan for 2012-14. All officers prayerfully signed copies of the document. When the plan was presented in corps, congregations were invited to add their names as a sign of their commitment to the plan.

The economic crisis in Portugal has placed added demands on social services and government funding. It was with great sadness that Picheleira day care and home help centre for the elderly was closed at the end of 2011 after 22 years of service in the community. However, as part of the command's strategic plan, each corps is finding new ways to serve their respective communities and reach out with the love of Christ.

There are great challenges for The Salvation Army in Portugal but there is also a great awareness of God's never-failing provision and constant guidance.

STATISTICS
Officers 14 Employees 109
Corps 5 Institutions 6
Senior Soldiers 66 Adherent Members 35
Junior Soldiers 28
Personnel serving outside command Officers 6

STAFF
Women's Ministries: Lt-Col Susan Daly (CPWM)
Finance: Dr Rui Kunzika
Social: Dra Sandra Martins Lopes

SOCIAL SERVICES
Children's Home
Centro de Acolhimento Novo Mundo,
  Ave Desidério Cambournac, 14,
  2710-553 Sintra; tel: 219 244 239;
  (acc 14)

Clothing and Food Distribution Centre
Rua Escola do Exército, 11-B, 1150-143 Lisboa;
  tel: 213 528 137

Thrift Shops
Chelas: Rua Rui de Sousa, Lote 65-A Loja C,
  1900-802 Lisboa
Rua D Jerónimo de Azevedo, 640-Loja,
  4550-241 Porto; tel: 22 6172769

Day Centres for the Elderly and Home Help Services
Colares: Av dos Bombeiros Voluntários,
  Várzea de Colares, 2705-180 Colares;
  tel: 219 288 450
Porto: Av Vasco da Gama, 645, Lojas 1 e 2,
  Ramalde, 4100-491 Porto; tel: 226 172 769

Eventide Homes
Nosso Lar: Av dos Bombeiros Voluntários,
  Várzea de Colares, 2705-180 Colares;
  tel: 219 288 450; (acc 30)
Marinel: Rua das Marinhas, 13, Tomadia, Praia
  das Maçãs, 2705-313 Colares;
  tel: 219 288 480; (acc 50)

Night Shelter for the Homeless
Rua da Manutenção, 7 (Xabregas) – 1900-318
  Lisboa; tel: 218 680 908; (acc 75)

HOLIDAY AND CONFERENCE CENTRES
Casa Marinel, Av José Félix da Costa, 9,
  Praia das Maçãs – 2705-312 Colares
  (information from CHQ)
Vivenda Boa Nova, Rua do Vinagre, 9,
  2705-354 Colares; tel: 214 095 738
  (holiday bookings to CHQ)

RWANDA AND BURUNDI COMMAND

Command leaders:
Lieut-Colonels Francis and Jamiya Nyambalo

Officer Commanding:
Lieut-Colonel Francis Nyambalo
(1 Mar 2011)

General Secretary:
Captain Jean Clénat (1 Apr 2010)

Command Headquarters: Plot 11737, Kibagabaga Road, Kimironko, Kimironko Sector, Kigali

Postal address: PO Box 812, Kigali, Rwanda

Tel: [250] 587639; email: Rwanda@rwa.salvationarmy.org

As a result of civil war and genocide in Rwanda, The Salvation Army became actively involved in relief work in September 1994. Operations were concentrated in Kayenzi Commune, part of the Gitarama Prefecture. Following mission work by officers from Zaïre, Uganda and Tanzania in 1995, officers were appointed from Congo (Brazzaville) to develop corps and mission work in Kayenzi Commune. Kayenzi Corps officially began its ministry on 5 November 1995. The Salvation Army was officially registered as a church in Rwanda on 15 September 2008.

In 1983, Justin Lusombo-Musese (a Congolese born in Burundi) was introduced by a friend to some of William Booth's writings and learned about The Salvation Army's early history. Justin and the friend were so enthused they decided to become members of the Army. Over the ensuing years they persistently requested International Headquarters to start Army operations in Burundi, and on 5 August 2007 the work was officially recognised with the warranting of Justin Lusombo-Musese and his wife Justine Fatouma as auxiliary-captains. The Rwanda Region was redesignated Rwanda and Burundi Region in October 2008 and upgraded to command status on 1 April 2010.

Zone: Africa
Countries included in the command: Burundi, Rwanda
The Salvation Army in Kinyarwanda: Ingabo Z'Agakiza
Languages in which the gospel is preached: English, French, Kinyarwanda, Kirundi, Kiswahili
Periodical: *Salvationist News*

THE work of God continues to grow in Rwanda and Burundi Command. The Burundi congress held in August 2011 saw the largest ever gathering of Salvationists and friends at an Army event. Fifty soldiers and officers from Rwanda travelled to Burundi to support and encourage their comrades. The theme 'Let us start building' was emphasised through various meetings and activities which included an open-air meeting, soldiers' and youth rallies; men's and women's meetings.

Young people participated and particularly enjoyed the opportunity to play musical instruments donated by the Army in The Netherlands through a fundraising project.

In October Commissioners Amos and Rosemary Makina (IS and ZSWM for Africa) visited the command and were received with great joy.

Officers, cadets and corps leaders received training on faith-based facilitation in November and learned useful skills to equip them for ministry and mission. Various seminars for local officers and soldiers, executive meetings and spiritual days for officers also took place.

Youth councils were held in December at Kayenzi Corps. The theme was 'God's Plan for us' and 416 young people attended.

During the year, remarkable development in Women's Ministries was seen, both in junior and senior home league programmes. New members were enrolled and a 'Helping Hand' collection was received from all groups.

In March 2012, the command welcomed Majors Robert and Anna-Maria Tuftström from the Sweden and Latvia Territory as the project officer and sponsorship secretary respectively.

During 2012 two houses adjacent to command headquarters were built and a further house was purchased through donations from the Australia Eastern and Southern territories. The first Salvation Army building in Burundi, at Kamenge, has been provided through support from mission partner territories.

STATISTICS
Officers 19 **Corps Leaders** 10 **Employees** 19
Corps 12 **Outreach Units** 3 **Outposts** 12
  Societies 3 **Pre-School Facilities** 2 (acc 170)
Senior Soldiers 1,858 **Adherent Members** 1,479
  Junior Soldiers 908
Personnel serving outside command:
  Officers: 2 Auxiliary-captains: 2

STAFF
Women's Ministries: Lt-Col Jamiya Nyambalo (CPWM) Capt Elianise Clénat (CSWM) Capt Dyna Namugisha Tungo (JHLS)
Accountant: Albine Batamuliza
Education and Extension Training: Capt Dancille Mukafuraha Ndagijimana
Finance: Mr John Evans
Information Technology: Mr Pascal Igiraneza
Projects: Maj Robert Tuftström
Public Relations: Capt Emmanuel Ndagijimana
Social: tba
Sponsorship: Maj Anna-Maria Tuftström
Training: Maj Bente Gundersen
Youth and Candidates: Capt Obed Tungo

DIVISION
Kamonyi: PO Box 812, Kigali; Majs Joseph and Alice Wandulu

SECTIONS
all c/o PO Box 812, Kigali
Kayenzi: Capt Jean Damascene Turikumana
Kigali: c/o PO Box 812, Kigali
Muhanga: Capt Theobald Kabagema
Nyagatare: Capt André Nsengiyaremye
Rukoma: Corps Leader Vedaste Rushingabigwi

BURUNDI
Ruhero II, Boulevard de l'Independence, Parcelle No 1416, Bujumbura, Burundi; Majs Japhet and Maureen Agusiomah

RWANDA: A Salvationist from Sweden (second right) **and officers from the command share conversation on a visit to a sponsorship project**

SINGAPORE, MALAYSIA AND MYANMAR: Major Lynn Gibbs (r) with young people in Melaka, Malaysia

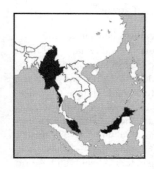

SINGAPORE, MALAYSIA AND MYANMAR TERRITORY

Territorial Commander:
Colonel Gillian Downer (1 Jul 2010)

Chief Secretary:
Lieut-Colonel Lyndon Buckingham
(1 Feb 2013)

Territorial Headquarters: 20 Bishan St 22, Singapore 579768

Postal address: Ang Mo Kio Central, PO Box 640, Singapore 915605

Tel: [65] 6555 0188; fax: [65] 6552 8542; website: www.salvationarmy.org.sg

In May 1935 Salvation Army work began in Singapore. It spread to Penang (1938), Melaka and Ipoh (1940), Kuching (Sarawak) (1950), Kuala Lumpur (1966) and Kota Kinabalu (Sabah) (1996).

'The General of The Salvation Army' is a 'corporation sole' by The Salvation Army Ordinance 1939 in the Straits Settlements; by The Salvation Army (Incorporation) Ordinance 1956 in the Federation of Malaya; and by the Missionary Societies Order 1957 in the Colony of Sarawak.

Adjutant Taran Das (Reuben Moss), who was attached to the Lahore headquarters in India, was appointed to open the work in Burma (now Myanmar) by Commissioner Booth Tucker in January 1915. Myanmar Salvationists have, since 1966, developed their witness and service despite the restriction on reinforcements from overseas. In 1994 Myanmar was joined to the Singapore and Malaysia Command. The command was elevated to territory status on 1 March 2005.

Zone: South Pacific and East Asia
Countries included in the territory: Malaysia, Myanmar, Singapore
'The Salvation Army' in Chinese: (Mandarin) Chiu Shi Chen, (Cantonese) Kau Shai Kwan, (Amoy, Hokkien) Kiu Se Kun; Bahasa: Bala Keselamatan; Myanmar: Kae Tin Chin Tat; Tamil: Retchania Senai Languages in which the gospel is preached: Burmese, Chin (Mizo, Zahau, Dai), Chinese (Amoy, Cantonese, Hokkien, Mandarin), English, Bahasa, Malay, Tamil, Telegu
Periodical: *The War Cry*

'INTENTIONAL in Worship, Holiness, Prayer, Discipleship and Mission' was the territorial theme for the year under review in Singapore, Malaysia and Myanmar. Following the launch of the international vision the territory also emphasised 'One Army with one mission and one message' in all corps and centres.

In June 2011 the women's ministries 'Helping Hand' scheme raised S$77,872.54 for Papua New Guinea settlement villages to provide housing for people in need. More than 200 women gathered in Upper Myanmar for the women's ministries camp. The theme was 'Women's Wellbeing' and teaching was given in primary health, emotional and spiritual care.

Youth camps in Malaysia and Singapore also took place in June and a total of 185 young people attended.

It was a great joy to see nine young people respond to the call to Salvation Army officership.

The Salvation Army's Peacehaven Nursing Home became a founding member of the Eastern Health Alliance; together with Changi General Hospital, St Andrews Community Hospital and SingHealth Polytechnics. This partnership will provide a complete health care service for the population of eastern Singapore, from transitional to long-term care. The Institute of Technical Education and Nanyang Polytechnic continued to place nursing and occupational therapy students for their clinical attachment at Peacehaven, demonstrating confidence in the quality of service provided by the Army.

In Bedok, the Multiservice Centre programmes (for elderly citizens) are at the forefront of elderly rehabilitative care in the region and were visited by leading service providers.

The Red Shield Appeal luncheon was held in July and the President of Singapore, Mr. S.R. Nathan, attended. The emphasis was on the ageing population of Singapore and the Army's response to this demographic. Their Excellencies, the British, Philippines and Finnish ambassadors were also present.

In east Malaysia the Kota Kinabalu Corps day care programme had an increased number of children attending. The 60 children, having 'stateless' status, have no access to government education and The Salvation Army provides schooling for them.

In west Malaysia, Melaka Hopehaven Centre launched a sensory room, funded by a donation from the Ronald McDonald House Charities. This facility provides multi-sensory environment therapy and rehabilitation for children with developmental disabilities.

Commissioners Alistair and Astrid Herring (IS and ZSWM for SPEA) conducted a territorial review and visited some of the ministries in Singapore and east Malaysia. Their visit to Upper Myanmar brought encouragement to the cadets during a spiritual day. The commisioners also conducted officers' councils.

In Myanmar, the first Mizo fellowship commenced in the southern district and 29 senior soldiers were enrolled in the region.

Colonel Gillian Downer (TC) commissioned and ordained five cadets of the Friends of Christ session.

A campaign called 'Go Forth – The Uniform of Change' is planned for August 2012 to recruit candidates for officer training. An envoy training programme was also introduced in the territory.

STATISTICS
Officers 154 (active 139 retired 15) **Cadets** 14
Employees 690
Corps 59 **Outposts** 26 **Institutions** 17
Kindergartens 2 **Day Care Centres** 17
Senior Soldiers 2,677 **Adherent Members** 464
Junior Soldiers 381

STAFF
Women's Ministries:
Col Gillian Downer (TPWM) Lt-Col Bronwyn Buckingham (TSWM)

Finance: Mdm Koh Guek Eng
Human Resources: Mrs Toh-Chia Lai Ying
Literary Sec: Maj Lynn Gibbs
Programme: Maj Raelton Gibbs
  Asst Programme Sec: Maj Lynn Gibbs
Property: Mr John Ng
Public Relations: Angeline Tan
Projects: tba
Training: tba
Youth and Candidates: Capt Zane Haupt

SCHOOL FOR OFFICER TRAINING
(Singapore and Malaysia)
500 Upper Bukit Timah Rd, Singapore 678106;
  tel: 6349 5333

SINGAPORE
Children's Homes
Gracehaven: 3 Lorong Napiri (off Yio Chu
  Kang Rd), Singapore 547528; tel: 6488 1510
  (acc 160)
The Haven: 350 Pasir Panjang Rd,
  Singapore 118692; tel: 6774 9588/9
  (acc 50)

Day Care Centres for Children
Ang Mo Kio Child Care Centre: Blk 610 Ang Mo
  Kio Ave 4, #01-1227 Singapore 560610;
  tel: 6452 4862 (acc 89)
Bukit Batok East Child Care Centre: Blk 247
  Bukit Batok East Ave 5, #01-86 Singapore
  650247; tel: 6562 4976 (acc 73)
Bukit Panjang Child Care Centre: Blk 402
  Fajar Rd, #01-217 Singapore 670402;
  tel: 6760 2624 (acc 82)
Tampines Child Care Centre: Blk 159
  Tampines St 12, #01-95 Singapore 521159;
  tel: 6785 2976 (acc 90)

Day Care Centres for the Elderly
Peacehaven Bedok Daycare Centre
  Blk 121, #01-161/163 Bedok North Rd,
  Singapore 460121; tel: 6445 1630 (acc 60)
Bedok Rehabilitation Centre: Blk 121,
  #01-163 Bedok North Rd,
  Singapore 460121; tel: 6445 1630 (acc 35)

Family Support Services
Blk 42, Beo Cresc, #01-95 Singapore 160042;
  tel: 6273 7207

Hostels
Peacehaven Nurses' Hostel: 9 Upper Changi Rd
  North, Singapore 507706; tel: 6546 5678
  (acc 100)

Young Women's Hostel: The Haven,
  350 Pasir Panjang Rd, Singapore 118692;
  tel: 6774 9588/9 (acc 10)

Retreat Centre
Praisehaven, 500 Upper Bukit Timah Rd,
  Singapore 678106; tel: 6349 5302 (acc 210)

Nursing Home
Peacehaven, 9 Upper Changi Rd North,
  Singapore 507706; tel: 6546 5678 (acc 401)

Prison Support Services – Kids In Play
7 Upper Changi Rd North,
  Singapore 507706;
  tel 6546 5868 (130 families)

Red Shield Industries
309 Upper Serangoon Rd, Singapore 347693;
  tel: 6288 5438

Youth Development Centres
WBC Bukit Panjang Youth Hub Centre: Fajar Rd,
  #01-267 Singapore 670404; tel: 6763 0837
  (acc 70)
Riverpoint Youth Development Centre: Blk 65
  Kallang Bahru, #01-305 Singapore 330065;
  tel: 6291 6303; under Balestier Corps

EAST MALAYSIA
Boys' Home
Kuching Boys' Home: Jalan Ban Hock,
  93100 Kuching; PO Box 547, 93700 Kuching,
  Sarawak, Malaysia; tel: (082) 24 2623 (acc 30)

Children's Home
Kuching Children's Home: 138 Jalan Upland,
  93200 Kuching; PO Box 106, 93700 Kuching,
  Sarawak, Malaysia; tel: (082) 24 8234
  (acc 60)

Kindergarten
Kuching Kindergarten: Sekama Rd,
  93300 Kuching, Sarawak, Malaysia;
  PO Box 44, 93700 Kuching, Sarawak,
  Malaysia; tel: (082) 333981 (acc 100)

Corps Community Services
Bintulu Corps and Community Services:
  S/Lot 1362, 1st Floor Tanjung Batu
  Commercial Centre, Jalan Tun Razak,
  97000 Bintulu; Sarawak; tel: (086) 315 843
Kota Kinabalu Corps and Community Services:
  Lot 1, Taman Seri Kiansom Lorong Seri
  Kiansom, Inanam, Kota Kinabalu, Malaysia;
  tel: (088) 433766

Kuching Corps and Community Services:
Sekama Rd 93300, Kuching, Sarawak,
Malaysia; PO Box 44, 93700 Kuching, Sarawak,
Malaysia; tel: (082) 333981

WEST MALAYSIA

Liaison and Public Relations Office:
26-1 Jalan Puteri, 4/2 Bandar Puteri,
47100 Puchong, Selangor Darul Ehsan,
Malaysia; tel: (06) 8061 4929

Boys' Home

Ipoh Boys' Home: 4367 Jalan Tambun,
31400 Ipoh; PO Box 221, 30720 Ipoh,
Perak, Malaysia; tel: [60] (05) 545 7819
(acc 60)

Centre for Special Children

Hopehaven Centre for Special Children:
321 Jalan Parameswara, 75000 Melaka,
Malaysia; tel: [60] (06) 283 2101 (acc 100)

Children's Homes

Ipoh Children's Home: 255 Kampar Rd,
30250 Ipoh, Perak, Malaysia;
tel: (05) 254 9767; fax: (05) 242 9630
(acc 50)
Melaka Lighthouse Children's Home:
404 Taman Sinn, Jalan Semabok 75050,
Melaka, Malaysia; tel: (06) 283 2101 (acc 25)
Penang Children's Home: 8A Logan Rd,
10400 Penang, Malaysia; tel: (04) 227 0162
(acc 60)

Day Care Centre for Children

Banting Day Care Centre: 30 Jalan Cendana 15,
Taman Mihhibah, Banting 42700 (acc 50)

Kindergarten

Batang Melaka Kindergarten: J7702 Main Rd,
Batang Melaka 77500, Selandar, Malaysia;
tel: (06) 446 1601 (acc 50)
Kuala Lumpur Kindergarten: 1 Lingkungan
Hujan, Overseas Union Garden, 58200 KL,
Malaysia; tel: (03) 7782 4766 (acc 60)

Homes for the Aged

Joyhaven Home for the Elderly: 1 Jalan 12/17,
Seksyen 12, 46200 Petaling Jaya, Selangor,
Malaysia; tel: (03) 7958 6257
(acc 25)
Perak Home for the Aged: Jalan Bersatu,
Jelapang, 30020 Ipoh, Perak, Malaysia;
tel: (05) 526 2108 (acc 50)

Corps Community Services

Banting Corps Community Services: 30 Jalan
Cendana 15, Taman Mihhbah, Banting 42700
(acc 50)
Kuala Lumpur Community Services: 26-1 Jalan
Puteri 4/2, Bandar Puteri 47100, Puchong,
Selangor, Malaysia; tel: (03) 8061 4929
(acc 50)
Penang Corps Community Services: 53 Perak Rd,
10150 Penang, West Malaysia;
tel: (04) 2290921

Social/Community Services

Melaka State Community Services: 321 Jalan
Parameswara, 75000 Melaka, Malaysia;
tel: (06) 283 1203

MYANMAR REGION

Headquarters: 176-178 Anawrahta St,
Botahtaung, East Yangon 11161, Myanmar;
Postal address: GPO Box 394, Yangon,
Myanmar; tel: [95] (1) 294267/293307;
fax: [95] (1) 298067
Regional Officer: Maj Amaro Pereira
(1 May 2012)

DISTRICTS

Central: District Office, Mandalay
Kalaymyo: District Office, D-group, Tahan,
Kalemyo; tel: [95] (73) 21396
Tamu: District Office, Kanan Corps, Kanan
Township

SCHOOL FOR OFFICER TRAINING

50 Byaing Ye O Zin St, Tarmway, Yangon,
Myanmar; tel: [95] (1) 543694

Boys' Home

406 Banyadala Rd, Tarmway, Yangon,
Myanmar; tel: [95] (1) 541462 (acc 50)

Children's Home

50 Bago Rd, Pyu, Myanmar (acc 50)

Girls' Home

50 Byaing Ye O Zin St, Tarmway, Yangon,
Myanmar; tel: [95] (1) 543961
(acc 50)

Day Care Centre for Children

Tarmway Corps

SOUTH AMERICA EAST TERRITORY

Territorial Commander:
Colonel Susan McMillan (1 May 2010)

Chief Secretary:
Lieut-Colonel Ricardo Fernández
(1 Jul 2012)

**Territorial Headquarters: Avda Rivadavia 3257 (C1203AAE),
Buenos Aires, Argentina**

Postal address: Casilla de Correo 2240 (C1000WAW) Buenos Aires, Argentina

Tel/fax: [54] (11) 4864-9321/9348/9491/1075; email: ejersaljefatura@SAE.salvationarmy.org;
website: www.ejercitodesalvacion.org.ar

Four officers, who knew no Spanish, established The Salvation Army in Buenos Aires in 1890. Operations spread to other South American nations, of which Paraguay (1910), Uruguay (1890) and Argentina now comprise the South America East Territory.

The Salvation Army was recognised as a juridical person in Argentina by the Government Decree of 26 February 1914 (No A 54/909); in Uruguay by the Ministry of the Interior on 17 January 1917 (No 366537); and in Paraguay by Presidential Decree of 28 May 1928 (No 30217).

Zone: Americas and Caribbean
Countries included in the territory: Argentina, Paraguay, Uruguay
'The Salvation Army' in Spanish: Ejército de Salvación
Languages in which the gospel is preached: Spanish, Korean, Guaraní
Periodicals: *El Oficial, El Salvacionista*

GENERAL Linda Bond was the special guest for the territorial congress held in Huerta Grande, Argentina, in October 2011 and her preaching was challenging and inspiring. The event began with councils for officers and local officers. The Buenos Aires Division presented the musical *Brengle: My Life's Ambition.* Lieut-Colonel Eddie Hobgood, (USA Southern) the author and composer, visited and played the role of Commissioner Samuel L. Brengle. The congress included workshops, children's congress events, youth, men's and women's ministries meetings.

In the final meeting many people rededicated their lives to the Lord.

In January 2012 youth and children's programmes took place. These included summer camps for underprivileged children, the Territorial Youth Institute (training for young leaders) and the Territorial Music Institute. Captain Juan Guadalupe, (USA Southern Territory), returned as special guest for the youth institute and challenged the young people to be leaders now.

The music institute welcomed international guests from the USA: Dorothy Gates, Thomas Scheibner and

Major Elizabeth Roby (USA Eastern), and Melinda Ryan, Wendy Hood, Jonathan Renfroe and Adely Charles (USA Southern). The musical *Brengle: My Life's Ambition* was presented during the week and the final concert showed the excellence of the work done at the institute. The theme was 'A Holy Army' and during the concluding holiness meeting many delegates renewed their commitment to serve God.

In March 2012 the five-year plan 'Acting to Grow' concluded and the territorial consultative council evaluated its implementation. This process and consultation at divisional level will inform the next five-year plan.

Also in March, Commissioner Larry Bosh (then IS for the Americas), conducted a territorial review and participated in the territorial consultative council and the welcome meeting for the Disciples of the Cross session.

An advisory board was inaugurated in Paraguay, with 11 community members who are committed to generating support for the Army.

A new building was opened at the Viñas Cué Outpost in Asunción, Paraguay. This facility was funded through donations from Norway and Canada. The inauguration was attended by 120 people and on the opening day Salvationist musicians announced that the new building was going to be dedicated to the glory of God.

The Refuge ('El Refugio'), a men's shelter, celebrated 100 years of service in Buenos Aires in April 2012. The work began in a rented facility, moved to its present site in 1912 and has faithfully served men who have little choice but life on the street. The centennial celebration was attended by civic officials, local artists and Salvationists; music for the event was provided by the Patricios Corps Band and a local entertainer performed Argentine folk music.

In May 2012, Colonel and Mrs Paul Kim, retired officers from Korea living in the USA, conducted a series of evangelistic meetings at the Korean outpost in Buenos Aires.

STATISTICS

Officers 157 (active 126 retired 31) **Cadets** 13
   Employees 181
Corps 43 **Outposts** 14 **Institutions** 28
Senior Soldiers 1,843 **Adherent Members** 860
   Junior Soldiers 429

STAFF

Women's Ministries: Col Susan McMillan
   (TPWM) Lt-Col Mirtha Fernández (TSWM)
Personnel: Maj Raúl Bernao
Programme: Maj Danton Moya
Business Administration: Maj Pablo Nicolasa
Education: Capt Lucy Viera
Finance: Mr Sergio Cerezo (Chief Accountant)
Legal: Mr Rene Menares
Literature and Editor: tba
Music and Gospel Arts: B/M Omar Pérez
Projects/Sponsorship/Missing Persons:
   Mrs Claudia Franchetti
Property: Maj Eduardo Villarroel
Red Shield/Thrift Store Operations:
   Maj Miguel Del Bello
Spiritual Formation: Maj Marjorie Barrault
Training: Maj Estela Nicolasa
Youth: Capt Luis Viera

Candidates: Capt Lucy Viera

DIVISIONS

Buenos Aires: Avda Rivadavia 3257 – Piso 2
   (C1203AAE), Buenos Aires, Argentina;
   tel: (011) 4861 1930/9499; Majs Roberto and
   María Juárez
Central Argentina: Urquiza 2142, (S2000AOD)
   Rosario Pcia de Santa Fe, Argentina;
   tel: (0341) 425 6739; Majs Rafael and
   Karina Giusti

At Rayito de Luz
(Little Ray of Light)
Programme, which
serves the
community in
Asunción,
Paraguay

Uruguay: Avda Agraciada 3567 (11700)
Montevideo, Uruguay;
tel: (00598) (2) 409 7581; Majs Hugo and
María del Luján Ramos

DISTRICTS
Central West Argentina: Felix Frías 434/6,
(X5004AHJ) Córdoba, Argentina;
tel: (351) 423-3228; Maj Osvaldo Corazza
North East Argentina: Brignole 126,
(H3500BOF) Resistencia, Prov De Chaco,
Argentina; tel: (3722) 466-529;
Maj Cristina Escudero
Paraguay: Héroes de la Independencia y Vietnam,
Casilla 2008, (CP 2160) San Lorenzo, Paraguay;
tel/fax: 595 (21) 577 082; Maj Thore Paulsen
Southern Argentina: Moreno 759 (B8000FWO),
Bahía Blanca, Pcia de Buenos Aires;
tel/fax: (291) 4533 642; Capt Diego Barth

TRAINING COLLEGE
Avda Tte Gral Donato Álvarez 465/67,
(C1406BOC) Buenos Aires;
tel/fax: (011) 4631 4815

CONFERENCE CENTRES AND
YOUTH CAMP
Argentina
Parque General Jorge L. Carpenter, Avda
Benavídez 115, (Paraguay y Uruguay)
(B1621) Benavídez, Pcia de Buenos Aires;
tel: (03488) 458644
Parque El Oasis, Ruta 14 Km 1 Camino a
Soldini – Zona Rural– Perez (Santa Fe);
tel: (341) 495 0003

COMMUNITY AND DAY CARE
CENTRES
Argentina: Carlos Pellegrini 376, (E3200AMF
Concordia (Entre Ríos); tel: (345) 421 1751
(acc 20)
Uruguay: Sarandí 1573, (60,000) Paysandú;
tel: (72) 22709
(acc 84)

SOCIAL SERVICES
Counselling and Labour Exchange
Argentina: Loria 190, (C1173ACD)
Buenos Aires; tel: (11) 4865 0074

Children's Homes (mixed)
Paraguay: El Redil, Dr Hassler 4402 y
MacArthur, Asunción; tel: [595] (21) 600 291
(acc 40)
Uruguay: El Lucero, J. M. Blanes 62,
(50,000) Salto; tel: (00598732) 32740
(acc 30)

Eventide Homes
Argentina
Catalina Higgins Home, Calle Mitre,
54 No 2749, (1650) Villa Maipú, San
Martín, Pcia de Buenos Aires;
tel: (11) 4753 4117 (acc 54)
Eliasen Home, Primera Junta 750,
(B1878IPP) Quilmes, Pcia de Buenos Aires;
tel: (011) 4254 5897 (acc 37)
Uruguay: El Atardecer, Avda Agraciada 3567,
(11800) Montevideo;
tel: (00598) (2) 308 5227 (acc 75)

South America East Territory

Recycling Operations
Argentina
Avda Hipólito Irigoyen 4750, (B1814ABQ)
Lanús Oeste, Buenos Aires; tel: (11) 42414756

Avda Sáenz 580, (C1437DNS) Buenos Aires;
tel: (11) 4911 7561/0781/7585

Avda Sánchez de Bustamante 1023 Gerli,
Lanús Este, Buenos Aires

Calle 93 # 883 Barrio Aeropuerto, Villa Elvira,
La Plata, Buenos Aires;
tel: (0221) 486 6654

Calle 4 Nº 711, (B1900) La Plata, Buenos Aires;
tel: (0221) 483-6152

Cañada de Gómez 2322, (1440EGV) Buenos
Aires

Gral Juan O'Brien 1260, (1137ABD)
Buenos Aires; tel: (011) 4305-5021

Einstein 705, (B1688DBO) Villa Santos Tesei,
Buenos Aires; tel: (011) 4450-3606

Barrio ULM, Cnel Bogado Nº 5, (H3730QA)
Charata, Chaco; tel: (03731) 421-292

Salta 3197, Barrio San Javier, (H3500BOF)
Resistencia, Chaco; tel: (03722) 466 529

Godoy Cruz 348, (M5500GOQ) Mendoza,
tel: (0261) 429-6113

Amenábar 581, (S2000OQK) Rosario;
tel: (0341) 482 0155

Génova 2592, (S2000AOD) Rosario, Provincia
de Santa Fe, Avenida del Rosario 867 (bis)
(S2001RNC) Rosario, Provincia de Santa Fe;
tel: (0341) 438-1898

Uruguay Félix Laborde 2577, (12000)
Montevideo; tel: (00598-2) 508-7766

Night Shelters (Men)
Argentina
Copahué 2032: (acc 75)
Maza 2258: (acc 86)

Night Shelters (Women and Children)
Argentina
José I. Rucci 1231: (acc 34)
O'Brien 1272: (acc 38)

Students' Homes
Argentina–7 homes: (acc 28); (acc 16);
(acc 15); (acc 6); (acc 20); (acc 6); (acc 14)
Paraguay–2 homes: (acc 12) (acc 10)
Uruguay–1 home: (acc 8)

Women's Residence
Argentina: Esparza 93, (C1171ACA)
Buenos Aires; tel: (11) 4861 3119 (acc 56)

Primary School
Argentina: EEGB No 1027 Federico Held,
Barrio ULM, (H3730BQA) Charata,
Pcia del Chaco; tel: (3731) 421 292 (acc 450)

Technical School
Argentina: 'Major Juan C. Costen and Friends of
Germany', Coronel Bogado s/n, Bo OLM,
(H3730BQA) Charata, Pcia del Chaco;
tel: (3731) 421 292

Health Centre
Argentina: Pcia del Chaco, Coronel Bogado 4,
Barrio ULM, (H3730BQA) Charata;
tel: (3731) 421 292

Medical Clinic
Paraguay: Héroes de la Independencia y
Vietnam, Villa Laurelty, San Lorenzo;
tel: [595] 21 577 082

General Linda Bond (r)
visited Tekokatu Clinic,
Asunción, Paraguay in
October 2011.

SOUTH AMERICA WEST TERRITORY

Territorial leaders:
Commissioners Jorge A. and Adelina Ferreira

Territorial Commander:
Commissioner Jorge A. Ferreira (1 Feb 2007)

Chief Secretary:
Lieut-Colonel William A. Bamford III (1 May 2010)

Territorial Headquarters: Avenida España No 44, Santiago, Chile

Postal address: Casilla 3225, Santiago, Chile (parcels/courier service: Avenida España No 44, Santiago Centro, Santiago, Chile)

Tel: [56] (2) 671 8237/695 7005; fax: [56] (2) 698 5560; email: saw_leadership@saw.salvationarmy.org

Salvation Army operations were commenced in Chile soon after the arrival of Brigadier and Mrs William T. Bonnet to Valparaíso on 1 October 1909. The first corps was opened in Santiago on 28 November, with Captain David Arn and Lieutenant Alfred Danielson as officers. Adjutant and Mrs David Thomas, with Lieutenant Zacarías Ribeiro, pioneered the work in Peru in March 1910. The work in Bolivia, started in December 1920, was planned by Brigadier Chas Hauswirth and established by Adjutant and Mrs Oscar E. Ahlm. Quito was the location of the Army's arrival in Ecuador on 30 October 1985 under the command of Captain and Mrs Eliseo Flores Morales.

Zone: Americas and Caribbean
Countries included in the territory: Bolivia, Chile, Ecuador, Peru
'The Salvation Army' in Aymara: Ejercitunaca Salvaciananaca; in Quechua: Ejercituman Salvacionman; in Spanish: Ejército de Salvación
Languages in which the gospel is preached: Aymara, Quechua, Spanish
Publications: *El Grito de Guerra* (*The War Cry*), *El Trébol*

THE Lord blessed the South America West Territory as new facilities were opened in each of its four countries.

In September 2011 the renovated Harry Williams Hospital in Cochabamba, Bolivia was dedicated to the glory of God by the then Chief of the Staff, Commissioner Barry C. Swanson, and World President of Women's Ministries, Commissioner Sue Swanson. The medical ministry at this hospital is a beacon of hope and a model of integrated mission in the community.

Through funds raised at their youth councils, the young people of the USA Eastern Territory helped to fund a new building for Guamote Corps in Ecuador. The facility will enable the soldiers to meet for worship and also serve the community.

The Chile Central Division opened six media-aguas (prefabricated housing units) in the earthquake-stricken area of Talca. Officers, divisional and territorial leaders joined with local authorities, as the chosen recipients were presented with the keys to their new homes.

January 2012 commenced with a challenge to all officers and soldiers to continue participating in the General's worldwide prayer meeting each Thursday, and to hold a monthly day of prayer and fasting.

In March 2012, 10 cadets of the Disciples of the Cross session were welcomed for officer training. Praise God for his leading in the lives of those called to serve in The Salvation Army.

Also in January a territorial women's camp was held in Huampaní, Peru. Celebrating the international theme 'Come and See', 329 women from Chile, Peru, Bolivia and Ecuador joined together in worship, education, fellowship and training for service under the leadership of Commissioners Adelina Ferreira (TPWM) and Gillian Bosh (then ZSWM). It was the first event of this kind to be held in Peru.

The Chile South Division held its first Brengle Institute for soldiers in July. Each of the 35 delegates appreciated the opportunity to grow spiritually under the ministry of guest leaders, Majors Andres and Norma Lugo (USA Eastern).

In the Bolivia Central Division the first Junior Home League Rally was held and the young women who joined in worship and fellowship had a wonderful time. A series of local leader training institutes was also held in Bolivia.

In October 2011 Lieut-Colonel Geanette Seymour, then assistant director of the International Social Justice Commission, visited Chile and participated in several events to raise awareness of human-trafficking.

The territory continues to implement its five-year theme, 'Your Word challenges us to grow, to be united and to make an impact'. South America West is working for growth in outreach, unity in Christ and sharing God's love.

STATISTICS

Officers 300 (active 264 retired 36) **Cadets** (1st Yr) 10 (2nd Yr) 8 **Employees** 1,122
Corps 89 **Outposts** 18 **Schools and Vocational Institutes** 13 **Day Nurseries** 34 **Community Centres** 41 **Hospital** 1 **Health Centre** 1 **Mobile Clinic** 1 **Community Health** 1 **Pre-Primary Schools** 2 **Institutions** 34
Senior Soldiers 4,868 **Adherent Members** 557 **Junior Soldiers** 2,041

STAFF

Women's Ministries: Comr Adelina de Ferreira (TPWM) Lt-Col G. Lorraine Bamford (TSWM)
Business Administration (Legal): Maj Manuel Márquez
Personnel: Lt-Col Cecilia Bahamonde
Programme: Maj Paulina Márquez
Editor and Literary: Maj Víctor García
Education: Maj Eliseo Flores
Enterprise Development: Maj Jaime Herrera
Finance: Maj Pedro Sánchez
League of Mercy/Golden Age: Maj Paulina Márquez
Property and Public Relations: Maj Manuel Márquez
Social: Maj Raquel Sánchez
Sponsorship: Maj Raquel Sánchez
Trade: Maj Pedro Sánchez
Training: Maj Eliseo Flores
Candidates: Maj Paulina Márquez

DIVISIONS

Bolivia Altiplano: Calle Cañada Strongest 1888, Zona San Pedro, Casilla 926, La Paz, Bolivia; tel: 591 (2) 249 1560; Majs Sixto and Aída Alí
Bolivia Central: Calle Rico Toro 773 Zona Queru Queru, Casilla 3594, Cochabamba, Bolivia; tel: 591 (4) 445 4281/468 1147; Majs Javier and Maria Obando
Chile Central: Agustinas 3020, Casilla 3225,

SOUTH AMERICA WEST: Bolivian women attending a community development programme at Harry Williams Hospital, Cochabamba

Santiago, Chile; tel: 56 (2) 681 4992/5277;
Majs Hernán and Glenda Espinoza
Chile South: Av Caupolicán 990, Casilla 1064,
Temuco, Chile; tel: 56 (45) 215 850;
Majs Antonio and Lilian Arguedas
Ecuador: Tomás Chariove 149-144 y Manuel
Valdivieso, El Pinar Bajo, Casilla 17.10.7179,
Quito, Ecuador; tel: 593 (2) 243 5422/
244 7829; Maj Maria Flores
Peru: Calle Zaragoza 215, Urbanización Parque
San Martín, Pueblo Libre, Lima 21,
Apartado 690, Lima 100; tel: 51 (1) 653
4965/6; Maj Deisy Costas

DISTRICT

Chile North: Sucre 872, Casilla 310, Antofagasta,
Chile; tel: 56 (55) 280 668/224 094;
Capt Orestes Linares

TRAINING COLLEGE

Coronel Souper 4564, Estación Central,
Casilla 3225, Santiago, Chile;
tel: 56 (2) 776 2425/5153

SALVATION ARMY CAMP GROUNDS
Bolivia
'Chapare', Población Chimoré, Chapare;
tel: 591 7642 8777
'Eben-Ezer', Puente Villa, Comunidad Tarila,
Provincia Nor Yungas
Chile
Complejo Angostura, Panamericana Sur km 55,

Paine, Región Metropolitana, Casila 3225,
Santiago; tel: 591 (2) 825 0398
Villa Frontera, Parcela 16, Calle San Martín,
Villa la Frontera, Arica

EDUCATIONAL WORK
Vocational Institutes
Bolivia
'Lindgren' Murillo 4364, Barrio Central Viacha,
La Paz; tel: 591 (2) 280 0969 (acc 200)
'William Booth' – Oruro, Sucre 909, Oruro;
tel: 591 (2) 525 1369

Aymara Bible Institute
Bolivia
La Paz, Prolongación Illampu 1888, Zona San Pedro

Schools
Bolivia
'William Booth' – Villa Cosmos: Uraciri
Patica 2064, Barrio Cosmos 79, Unidad
Vecinal C, La Paz; tel: 591 (2) 288 0118
'William Booth' – Oruro: Sucre 909, Oruro;
tel: 591 (2) 525–1369; (acc 800)
'William Booth' – Viacha: Murillo 4364, Barrio
Central, Viacha; tel: 591 (2) 280 0969
(acc 200)

Chile
Arica: Av Cancha Rayada 3839, Segunda Etapa
Población Cardenal Silva Henríquez,
Casilla 203; tel: 56 (58) 211 100 (acc 678)

Calama:
    Aníbal Pinto 2121, Casilla 62, Calama;
    tel: 56 (55) 311 216/345 802
    Catalina Booth – Calama, Irene Frei 2875,
    Villa Esmeralda, Casilla 347, Calama;
    tel: 56 (55) 360 458 (acc 800)
Osorno: William Booth, Zenteno 1015,
    Casilla 317, Osorno; tel: 56 (64) 247 449;
    (acc 879)
Puerto Montt: Naciones Unidas – Antuhue,
    Presidente Ibáñez 272, Casilla 277;
    tel: 56 (65) 286 236 (acc 1,207)
Ejército de Salvación, Séptimo de Línea 148,
    Población Libertad, Casilla 277;
    tel: 56 (65) 254 047/251 918 (acc 363)
Santiago: Ejército de Salvación, Herrera 185,
    Santiago; tel: 56 (2) 681 7097 (acc 400)

Peru

Eduardo Palací, Av Progreso 1032, Urb San
    Gregorio, Vitarte, Lima; tel/fax: 51 (1) 356 0461
    (acc 500)
Miguel Grau, Av 29 de Diciembre 127, Trujillo;
    tel/fax: 51 (44) 255 571 (acc 300)

Ecuador

Ejército de Salvación – Cayambe, Calle H 1
    393 Morales, Urbanización Las Orquídeas,
    Cayambe, Casilla 17.10.7179, Quito;
    tel: 593 (2) 211 0196 (acc 150)
Ejército de Salvación – Manta, Avenida 201,
    entre Calles 116 y 117, Barrio, La Paz;
    tel: 593 (5) 292 0147 (acc 40)

Pre-Primary Schools
Chile

Santiago:
    El Bosque, Las Vizcachas 858, Población
    Las Acacias, Comuna de El Bosque;
    tel: 56 (2) 529 4242 (acc 45)
    Ejército de Salvación N°1619, Pudahuel
    (and Initial Grades of Primary) Mapocho
    9047, Comuna de Pudahuel, Santiago;
    tel: 56 (2) 643 1875
    (acc 160)

MEDICAL WORK
Bolivia

Harry Williams Hospital: Av Suecia 1038-1058,
    Zona Huayra K'assa, Casilla 4099,
    Cochabamba; tel: 591 (4) 422 7778/474 5329/
    447 45612 (30 beds)
Community Extension Programme: Av Suecia
    1038-1058, Zona Huayra K'assa, Casilla 4099,
    Cochabamba; tel: 591 (4) 422 7778/
    474 5329/447 45612

SOCIAL WORK
Emergency and Social Welfare Office:

Chile Central, Mapocho 4130, Comuna de
    Quinta Normal, Casilla 3225 Santiago;
    tel: 56 (2) 775 1566

Men's Shelters
Bolivia

Calle Prolongación Illampu 1888,
    Zona San Pedro, Casilla 926, La Paz;
    tel: 591 (2) 231 1189 (acc 100)

Chile

Villagrán 9, Casilla 1887, Valparasío;
    tel: 56 (32) 221 4946 (acc 170)

Peru

Calle Colón 138/142, Apartado 139, Callao;
    tel: 51 (1) 429 3128 (acc 24)

Transit House (Women)
Chile

Calle Zenteno 1499, Casilla 3225, Santiago;
    tel: 56 (2) 554 1767 (acc 15)

Pregnant Teens Refuge
Ecuador

Av 201, entre calles 116 y 117, Barrio La Paz,
    Casilla 13-05-149, Manta; tel: 593 (5) 292 0147
    (acc 20)

Student Residence Halls
Bolivia

Cochabamba: 'Tte - Coronel Rosa de Nery' (Girls),
    Calle Lanza S-0555, Casilla 3198,
    Cochabamba; tel: 591 (4) 422 6553 (acc 30)
La Paz: 'Remedios Asín' (Girls), Cañada
    Strongest 1888, Casilla 926, La Paz;
    tel: 591 (2) 248 0502 (acc 20)
Oruro: 'Tte - Coronel Jorge Nery Torrico' (Boys),
    Calle Junin 459, entre 6 de Octubre y Potosí;
    Casilla 86, Oruro; tel: 591 (2) 528 6885
    (acc 24)

Chile

Santiago: 'El Faro' (Boys), Santiago Concha 1333,
    Casilla 3225, Santiago; tel: 56 (2) 555 3406
    (acc 24)

Peru

Lima: 'Catalina Booth' (Girls), Jirón
    Huancayo 245, Apartado 690, Lima 100;
    tel: 51 (1) 433 8747
    (acc 20)
San Martín: 'Las Palmeras' – Tarapoto, Jirón
    Amoraca 212, Distrito Morales, Apartado 88,
    Tarapoto, San Martín; tel: 51 (42) 527 540
    (acc 20)

Children's Homes
Bolivia
Cochabamba:
'Evangelina Booth' (Girls), Francisco
Viedma 1054, Villa Montenegro, Casilla 542;
tel: 591 (4) 424 1560 (acc 60)
'Oscar Ahlms' (Boys), Km 19.5 Carretera a
Oruro cruce San Jorge, Calle Boliviar s/n,
Comunidad de San Jorge, Vinto, Casilla 542;
tel: 591 (4) 435 6264 (acc 48)
La Paz: 'María Remedios Asín' (Boys),
Murillo 434, Barrio Central Viacha,
Casilla 15084; tel: 591 (2) 280 0404 (acc 50)
Potosí: Hogar de Ninos (AS) Wasinchej
'Cerca del Cielo' Zona Villa Canteria,
Calle Final Canada Strongest
tel: 591 (7)063 3659 (acc 48)

Chile
Llo Lleo: 'El Redil' (Boys), Arzobispo
Valdivieso 410, Casilla 61, Llo Lleo;
tel: 56 (35) 282 054 (acc 52)

Eventide Home
Chile
'Otoño Dorado', Av La Florida 9995, La Florida,
Casilla 3225, Santiago; tel: 56 (2) 287 5280;
tel/fax: 56 (2) 287 1869 (acc 48)

Day Care Centres for the Aged
Chile
'Los Lagos', Berlín 818, Población Los Lagos,
Angol; tel: 56 (45) 712 583 (acc 20)

Ecuador
Cayambe, Calle Montalvo 220, Las Orquideas,
Cayambe; tel: 593 (2) 236 1273 (acc 60)

Day Nurseries
Bolivia
Cochabamba:
'Catalina Booth', Lanza S-0555, Zona Central,
Casilla 542; tel: 591 (4) 422 7123 (acc 150)
La Chimba, Av Cañada Cochabamba 2572,
Zona La Chimba, Casilla 542;
tel: 591 (4) 428 3079 (acc 75)
'Mi Casita' – El Temporal, Calle J. Mostajo s/n,
Zona El Temporal,Casilla 542;
tel: 591 (4) 445 0809 (acc 50)
'Wawasninchej' – Huayra K'assa,
Av Suecia 1083, Zona Huayra K'assa,
Casilla 542; tel: 591 (4) 422 4808 (acc 50)
La Paz: 'Refugio de Amor', Villa 8 de Diciembre,
Calle Rosendo Gutiérrez 120, Barrio Alto
Sopocachi, Casilla 926; tel 591 (2) 241 0470
(acc 25)

Santa Cruz:
'Gotitas de Amor', Calle Corumba 2360
(esq Calle Cañada Larga), Barrio Lazareto,
Casilla 2576; tel: 591 (3) 346 3531 (acc 40)
'La Roca', Calicanto, Comunidad La Serena
Calicanto, Kilómetro 8, Carretera antigua a
Santa Cruz, Casilla 542; tel: 591 (4) 433 8338
(acc 35)

Chile
Antofagasta: Lautarito, Castro 5193, Población
Lautaro, Casilla 581; tel: 56 (55) 380 719
(acc 70)
Concepción: Catalina Booth, Hipólito Salas 760;
tel: 56 (41) 223 0447 (acc 24)
Copiapó: Gotitas, Av Carlos Condell 1535,
Los Salares, Casilla 436; tel: 56 (52) 216 099
(acc 32)
Iquique: Las Estrellitas, Esmeralda 862,
Casilla 134; tel: 56 (57) 421 325 (acc 38)
Rancagua: Hijitos de Dios, Iquique 24
(esquina Bolivia), Población San Francisco;
tel: 56 (72) 239 028 (acc 20)
Santiago:
Arca de Noé, El Fundador 13678, Población
Santiago de la Nueva Extremadura,
La Pintana, Casilla 3225; tel: 56 (2) 542 4523
(acc 58)
La Estrellita, Maipú 284, Maipú, Casilla 3225;
tel: 56 (2) 531 2638 (acc 40)
Las Acacias, Las Vizcachas 858, Población
Las Acacias, El Bosque, Casilla 3225;
tel: 56 (2) 529 4242 (acc 52)
Marta Brunet, Montaña Adentro 01650,
Puente Alto, Casilla 3225,
tel: 56 (2) 572 9340 (acc 50)
Neptuno, Los Aromos 833, Lo Prado,
Casilla 3225; tel: 56 (2) 773 5154
(acc 40)
Puente Alto, Soldaditos de Jesús, Santo
Domingo 90, Puente Alto, Casilla 3225;
tel: 56 (2) 419 0110/850 3331 (acc 86)
Rayitos de Sol, Av Brasil 73, Casilla 3225;
tel: 56 (2) 699 3595; fax: 56 (2) 688 4755
(acc 90)
Temuco: Padre Las Casas, Los Misioneros 1354,
Comuna de Padre Las Casas, (acc 20)
Valdivia: Rayito de Luz, Picarte 1894;
tel: 56 (63) 214 404 (acc 120)
Valparaíso: Faro de Ángeles, Calle Santa
Martha 443, Cerro Playa Ancha, Casilla 1887;
tel: 56 (32) 228 1160 (acc 76)
Ecuador
Guayaquil: Nueva Esperanza, Av Martha de
Roldós km 5½, Vía Daule, Casilla
09.01.10478; tel: 593 (4) 383 0351 (acc 60)

Manta: Arca de Noé, Av 201, entre calles
116 y 117, Barrio La Paz, Casilla 13-05-149;
tel: 593 (5) 292 0147 (acc 30)
Quito: El Ranchito: Manzana 44, Lote 801-802,
Rancho Alto, Casilla 7110.7179;
tel 593 (2) 338 2408/9 (acc 50)
Gotitas de Miel: Montalvo 220, Cayambe,
Casilla 17.10.7179; tel: 593 (2) 236 1273
(acc 100)
La Colmena:Calle Pomasqui 955 y Pedro Andrade,
La Colmena, Casilla17.01.1120;
tel: 593 (2) 258 1081/228 4776 (acc 60)
Mi Casita: Apuela S 25-182 y Malimpia,
Santa Rita, Casilla 17.107179;
tel: 593 (2) 284 5529 (acc 40)
Mi Hermoso Redil: Urbanización Sierra
Hermosa, Calle 5, lotes 237-239, Parroquia de
Carapungo; tel: 593 (2) 282 6835 (acc 100)

Food Aid Programmes
Chile:
Calle Ejército casa 721, Pobl Oscar Bonilla 2,
Ancud; tel: 56 (65) 622 045 (acc 80)
Avanzada Bonilla, Río Lauca 1162, Pobl Bonilla,
Antofagasta; tel: 56 (55) 761 312

Peru
Chiclayo: PP.JJ. Sto Toribibio de Mogrovejo
MZ A Lote 17, Chiclayo;
tel: 51 (74) 208 216 (neighbour) (acc 100)
El Porvenir: Calle Synneva Vestheim 583,
Cacerío El Porvenir, Provincia Rioja,
Dpto San Martín (acc 50)

Development Integral Centres and Nutritional Centres
Bolivia
Achachicala, La Paz (acc 150)
Corqueamaya, La Paz (acc 70)
El Tejar, La Paz (acc 245 journey)
Lacaya, La Paz (acc 75)
Nueva Vida, Santa Cruz (acc 250)
Potosí (acc 30)
Tiahuanacu, La Paz (acc 200)
Yaurichambi, La Paz (acc 75)
Villa Cantería, Potosí (acc 50)
Villa Cosmos, La Paz (acc 250)
Villa Fátima, La Paz (acc 50 journey)
Villa 8 de Diciembre, La Paz (acc 90)
Viacha, La Paz (acc 250 journey)
Zona Este de Oruro, Oruro
(acc 150 journey)
Ecuador
Bastión Popular, Guayaquil (acc 100)
El Rancho, Quito (acc 100)
Mi Casita, Quito Sur (acc 120)

Nido Alegre, La Colmena, Quito (acc 150)
Nueva Esperanza, Guayaquil (acc 160)
Pedacito de Cielo, Esmeraldas (acc 200)
William Booth, Cayambe (acc 150)

Peru
Moquegua (acc 60)

Day Care Centre (without corps/outposts)
Chile
Nido Alegre, Santiago (acc 40)

Community Day Centres/School-age Day Care Centres (attached to corps/outposts)
Bolivia
Batallón Colorados, Sucre (acc 60)
El Temporal, Cochabamba (acc 75)
'El Vergel', Chapare (acc 60)
Fortín del Niño, Uspha Ushpha, Santa Cruz
(acc 100)
Huayra K'assa, Cochabamba (acc 50)
La Chimba, Cochabamba (acc 80)
La Roca, Calicanto, Santa Cruz (acc 25)
Pacata, Cochabamba (acc 200)
Parotani, Cochabamba (acc 60)
Pockonas, Sucre (acc 50)
Primero de Mayo, Santa Cruz (acc 300)
Tarija (acc 50)

Peru
Buenos Aires, Trujillo (acc 50)
La Esperanza, Trujillo (acc 40)
San Martín de Porras, Lima (acc 40)
Tacna (acc 60)
Vitarte, Lima (acc 80)

Workshop
Ecuador
Tailoring Workshop and Sewing Centre:
Calle Apuela S25-182 y Malimpia,
Santa Rita, Casilla 17.10.7179, Quito;
tel: 593 (2) 284 5529

Enterprise Development
Warehouse: Coronel Souper 4564,
Estación Central, Casilla 3225, Santiago,
Chile; tel: 56 (2) 764 1917

SOUTHERN AFRICA TERRITORY

Territorial leaders:
**Commissioners William and
Thalitha Langa**

Territorial Commander:
Commissioner William Langa (1 May 2012)

Chief Secretary:
Lieut-Colonel Robert Donaldson
(1 May 2012)

**Territorial Headquarters: 119-121 Rissik Street,
Braamfontein, Johannesburg 2001**

Postal address: PO Box 1018, Johannesburg 2000, South Africa

Tel: [27] (011) 718 6700

email: CS_SouthernAfrica@SAF.salvationarmy.org; website: www.salvationarmy.co.za

On 4 March 1883 Major and Mrs Francis Simmonds with Lieutenant Alice Teager 'opened fire' in Cape Town. Other officers were sent to the island of St Helena in 1886 to consolidate work commenced (in 1884) by Salvationist 'Bluejackets'. Social services began in 1886. The Salvation Army's first organised ministry among the African people was established in 1888 in Natal and, in 1891, in Zululand. Work in Swaziland was commenced in 1960. Having previously been in Namibia from 1932 to 1939, the Army re-established a presence in the country in January 2008 and was given official recognition on 11 March 2008.

Zone: Africa

Countries included in the territory: Lesotho, Namibia, Island of St Helena, South Africa, Swaziland

'The Salvation Army' in Afrikaans: Die Heilsleër; in IsiXhosa: Umkhosi wo Sindiso; in IsiZulu: Impi yo Sindiso; in SeSotho: Mokhosi oa Poloko; in SiPedi: Mogosi wa Pholoso; in Tshivenda: Mbi ya u Tshidza; in Tsonga: Nyi Moi Yoponisa

Languages in which the gospel is preached: Afrikaans, English, IsiXhosa, IsiZulu, SeSotho, Shangaan, SiPedi, Tshivenda, Tsonga, Tswana

Periodicals: *Home League Resource Manual, The Reporter, The War Cry*

THE year under review was one of progress and change for the Southern Africa Territory. The territorial strategic plan guided the territory towards increased mission effectiveness. There were leadership changes and positive developments in several areas.

The strategic plan highlighted aspects of Salvation Army life that were deeply affected by the past. An important step of reconciliation was achieved in July 2011 during the first territorial officers' councils to be held for 24 years.

The then Chief of the Staff, Commissioner Barry C. Swanson, and World President of Women's Ministries, Commissioner Sue Swanson, visited and contributed to a reconciliation process that was a highly significant spiritual event for the officers of the territory.

There was an emphasis on the development of the Army's mission and ministry to young people and children. A divisional youth secretary was appointed to seven of the eight divisions; their focus was to train, resource, equip, support and encourage officers and local officers in work with young people.

Important progress was made in strengthening and developing the leadership and management of the territory, through improved support and administrative systems, policy and resource development and mission focused monitoring and evaluation systems.

A transitional model for officer training was implemented to facilitate leadership development and introduce a new model of training, to commence in 2013. This aims to integrate the three key components of officer training – spiritual formation, theological knowledge and ministry skills – in a manner consistent with key adult education principles.

Competencies in 'faith-based facilitation' to support community engagement goals were developed.

Territorial leaders Commissioners André and Silvia Cox, took up new appointments in the United Kingdom in April 2012. Their leadership in Southern Africa set a new direction through the development of the territorial strategic plan, which has had an impact on all aspects of Salvation Army mission and ministry. This influence was gratefully acknowledged during a farewell meeting.

Commissioners William and Thalitha Langa, South African officers, were warmly welcomed and installed as the territorial leaders in a colourful and energetic meeting in May 2012.

STATISTICS

Officers 260 (active 161 retired 99) **Auxiliary-Captains** 14 **Cadets** 7 **Employees** 532
Corps 168 **Societies, Outposts and Corps Plants** 80 **Hospitals** 2 **Institutions** 14 **Day Care Centres** 20
Senior Soldiers 22,252 **Adherent Members** 1,654 **Junior Soldiers** 3,325

STAFF

Women's Ministries: Comr Thalitha Langa (TPWM) Lt-Col Janine Donaldson (TSWM) Lt-Col Fikile Khoza (THLS)
Business Administration: Capt Garth Niemand
   Chief Accountant: Mr Leon Viljoen
   Financial Consultant: Mr John Pugsley
   Property and Projects: Mr Handre du Toit
Development and Donor Relations:
   Capt Keith Holmes
Public Relations: Maj Carin Holmes
   Trade: Mr Gavin Blackwood
Personnel: Lt-Col Jabulani Khoza
   Asst Sec for Personnel : Maj Rasoa Khayumbi
   Human Resources: Mr Leon Schmahl
   Retired Officers: Comr William Mabena
Programme: Maj Luka Khayumbi
   Anti Human-Trafficking:
     Maj Margaret Stafford
   Child Sponsorship: Capt Leanne Browski
   Family Tracing: Maj Margaret Strydom
   Statistician: Capt Magdeline Phore
   Candidates: Capt Darren Huke
   Youth: Capt Ananias Nhandara
Social Programme: Capt Patti Niemand
   Community Care Ministries: Lt-Col Fikile Khoza
   Medical Ministries: Capt (Dr) Felicia Christians
Training Principal: Maj Lenah Jwili
Extension Training Officer: Capt Colleen Huke
Editorial and Literary: Capt Wendy Clack

DIVISIONS

Central: PO Box 756, Rosettenville,
Johannesburg 2130; tel: (011) 408-6400;
Majs Shadrack and Rosannah Ntshangase

Eastern Cape: PO Box 12514, Centralhill,
Port Elizabeth 6006; tel: (041) 585-5363;
Capts Themba and Nokuthula Mahlobo

Eastern Kwa Zulu/Natal: PO Box 1267,
Eshowe 3815; tel: (035) 474-1132;
Majs Albert and Peggy Shekwa

Limpopo: PO Box 3549, Makhado 0920; tel/fax:
(015) 516-6658; Majs Thomas and Doris Dlamini

Mid Kwa Zulu/Natal: PO Box 100061,
Scottsville, Pietermaritzburg 3209;
tel: (033) 386-3881;
Majs Solomon and Mercy Mahlangu

Mpumalanga/Swaziland: PO Box 1571,
Nelspruit 1200; tel: (013) 741-2869;
Majs Herbert and Elizabeth Ngcobo

Northern Kwa Zulu/Natal: PO Box 923,
Vryheid 3100; tel: (034) 982-3113;
Capts Thataetsile and Noluntu Semeno

Western Cape: PO Box 18179, Wynberg,
Cape Town 7824; tel: (021) 761-8530/6;
Capts Stephen and Theresa Malins

St Helena: The Salvation Army, Jamestown,
Island of St Helena, South Atlantic Ocean;
tel: 09 (290) 2703;
email: salvationarmy@cwimail.sh;
Envoy Coral Yon

THQ OUTREACH – NAMIBIA

The Salvation Army, PO Box 26820,
Windhoek, Namibia; tel: [00] (264) 61223881;
mobile: 264 813087518;
email: salvationarmy@iway.na;
Capts Robert and Felicia Hendricks

COLLEGE FOR OFFICER TRAINING

PO Box 32902, Braamfontein 2017,
Johannesburg; tel: (011) 718 6762

CHILD AND YOUTH DAY CARE CENTRES

Central: Benoni, Bridgman Jabavu Crèche, Carl
Sithole Crèche, Galashewe, Katlehong,
Lethlabile, Mangaung
Eastern Kwa Zulu Natal: Inkonisa
Mpumalanga/Swaziland: Barberton, Pienaar
Mid Kwa Zulu/Natal: Hammarsdale, Imbali, Kwa
Mashu, Umlazi
Northern: Thohoyandou
Northern Kwa Zulu/Natal: Nongoma, Ulundi
Western Cape: Bonteheuwel, Mitchells Plein,
Manenburg

DAY CARE CENTRES FOR SENIOR CITIZENS

Central: Benoni
Western Cape: Goodwood

GOODWILL CENTRES

Benoni: PO Box 17299, Benoni West 1503
Family Mission Centre: PO Box 351,
Krugersdorp 1740

HEALTH SERVICES

Booth Hospital: 32 Prince St, Oranjezicht, Cape
Town 8001; tel: (021) 465-4896/46 (acc 84)
Mountain View Hospital: PO Box 1827
Vryheid, KZN; tel: (034) 982-6014
(acc 88) (with Mountain View Mobile Clinic)
Msunduza Community and Primary Health Care
Centre and Mbuluzi Clinic: Box 2543, Mbabane,
Swaziland; tel: (268) 404-5243

RETIRED OFFICERS RESIDENCES

Citadel Court: Vrede St Gardens, Cape Town 8001
Emmarentia Flats: PO Box 85214, Emmarentia
2029, Johannesburg; tel: (011) 646-2126
Ephraim Zulu Flats: PO Box 49, Orlando 1804,
Soweto; tel: (011) 982-1084

SOCIAL SERVICES

Crèches

Bridgman Crèche: PO Box 62, Kwa Xuma 1868;
88, 3b White City, Jabavu 1856;
tel: (011) 982-5574 (acc 140)
Carl Sithole Crèche: Carl Sithole Centre,
PO Box 180, Orlando 1804; tel: (011) 986-7417
(acc 40)

Child and Youth Care Centres

Bethany: Carl Sithole Centre, Klipspruit,
PO Box 180, Orlando 1804;
tel: (011) 986-7417 (acc 110 children 6-18 yrs)
Bethesda: Zodwa's House, Carl Sithole Centre,
PO Box 180, Orlando 1804, Soweto (acc 32
children 2-6 yrs)
Ethembeni (Place of Hope): 63 Sherwell St,
Doornfontein, Johannesburg 2094;
tel: (011) 402-8101 (acc 60 children 0-3 yrs)
Firlands: Fourth Ave, PO Box 44291,
Linden 2104; tel: (011) 782-5556/7 (acc 60
children 3-18 yrs)
Joseph Baynes House: 89 Trelawney Rd,
Pentrich, PO Box 212275, Oribi 3205, Natal;
tel: (033) 386-2266 (acc 72 children 0-18 yrs)
Strathyre: Eleventh Ave, Dewetshof,
PO Box 28240, Kensington 2101,
Johannesburg; tel: (011) 615-7327/7344
(acc 50 children 3-18 yrs)

Community Programme

Thusanong/Osizweni: Home-based Community Care and Counselling Programme, Carl Sithole Centre, Klipspruit, Soweto, PO Box 180, Orlando 1804; tel: (011) 986-7417

Msunduza: Orphans/Vulnerable Children and Home-based Community Care Programme, Swaziland

Eventide Home (men)

Beth Rogelim: Cape Town 8005, 22 Alfred St; tel: (021) 425-2138 (acc 52)

Eventide Homes (men and women)

Emmarentia: Johannesburg, PO Box 85214, Emmarentia 2029, 113 Komatie Rd; tel: (011) 646-2126 (acc 40)

Ephraim Zulu Senior Citizen Centre: Orlando 1804, PO Box 49; tel: (011) 982-1084 (acc 100)

Thembela: Durban 4001, 68 Montpelier Place; tel: (031) 321-6360 (acc 53)

Homes for Abused Women

Beth Shan, PO Box 19713, Pretoria West 0117, Pretoria (acc 15 women)

Care Haven: PO Box 38186, Gates Ville 7766, Cape Town; tel: (021) 638-5511; email: careaid@iafrica.co.za (acc 18 women, 60 children)

Men's Hostel

Beth Rogelim: 22 Alfred St, Cape Town 8005; tel: (021) 425-2138 (acc 100)

Rehabilitation Centres

Hesketh King Treatment Centre: PO Box 5, Elsenburg 7607, Cape; tel: (021) 884-4600 (acc 60)

Residential Psychiatric Care

Mountain Lodge: PO Box 168, Magaliesburg 2805; tel: (+27) 082 855 0382 (acc 60)

Captain Nokuthula Mahlobo, Southern Africa Territory (centre) participates in drama at the All Africa Women Leaders' Conference in Zimbabwe

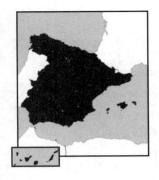

SPAIN COMMAND

Command leaders:
Lieut-Colonels Luis E. and Aída A. Castillo

Officer Commanding:
Lieut-Colonel Luis E. Castillo
(1 Jul 2008)

Command Headquarters: Hermosilla 126 Lc 1, 28028 Madrid

Postal address: Ejército de Salvación, c/ Hermosilla, 126 Local 1, 28028 Madrid, Spain

Tel: [34] 91 356 6644; email: Spain_Command@SPA.salvationarmy.org;

website: www.ejercitodesalvacion.es

Following the appointment of Captain and Mrs Enrique Rey to La Coruña on Ascension Day 1971, it was announced on 24 December 1971 that The Salvation Army had been granted the status of a Legal Person, enjoying full legal rights in the country and permitted to carry on its work without let or hindrance.

Zone: Europe
Country and autonomous communities included in the territory: Canary Islands, Mallorca, Spain
'The Salvation Army' in Spanish: Ejército de Salvación
Languages in which the gospel is preached: English (Mallorca, Denia), Filipino, Spanish

THE Salvation Army in Spain continued to grow in spite of a severe economic crisis. Officers redoubled their efforts through feeding programmes to serve the largest ever numbers of people in need.

The financial crisis also affected many Salvationists. Corps officers seeking resources to provide food for people have faced challenging situations, but they have proved the grace of God.

Each day, as officers and volunteers distributed food to people in need, they shared the gospel and invited them to spiritual programmes offered by The Salvation Army. Some of those reached in this way accepted the invitation and have received Jesus

Christ as their personal Saviour. Several people were enrolled as soldiers. Glory to God!

Although the significant increase in meeting attendance was welcome, it meant that sometimes Army halls exceeded their capacity and breached government regulations. In one location the Army met in a large marquee to accommodate the expanding congregation.

The ministry of the Army in Spain was recognized by civil, governmental and evangelical representatives on 'Reformation Day' when The Salvation Army received an award.

The visit of Commissioners Robert and Janet Street (IS and ZSWM for Europe) in October 2011 was encouraging and challenging.

A new programme called 'Básico' brought great blessing. Young Salvationists from the Madrid area brought together different art ministries, such as brass band, timbrels, mime and worship band. Their enthusiastic expression of their faith has had a great impact.

The Spain Command responded to the General's call to pray. Every corps participated in the Army's worldwide prayer meeting on Thursdays.

In November 2011 the General visited the Spain Command. More than 200 people gathered at a public welcome meeting. Salvationists in Spain were challenged by General Linda Bond to be 'One Army with One Mission and One Message'.

STATISTICS
Officers 28 (active 26 retired 2) **Employees** 32
Corps 11 **Outposts** 3 **Thrift Shops** 10
Senior Soldiers 596 **Adherent Members** 38
Junior Soldiers 89

STAFF
Women's Ministries: Lt-Col Aída Castillo (CPWM)
Business Administration: Maj Ambrosio Aycón
Programme and Evangelism: Maj Miguel Aguilera
Training: Maj Angélica Aguilera

SOCIAL SERVICES
Food and/or Clothing Distribution Centres
Alicante 03006: c/ Deportista César Porcel, 11 Bajo
Barcelona 08024: c/ del Rubí 18
Denia, Alicante 03700: c/ San José 14 B
La Coruña 15010: c/ Francisco Añón 9
Las Palmas 35014: Plaza de los Ruiseñores, Local 8 alto, Miller Bajo
Madrid 28028: c/ Hermosilla, 126, Local 4
Madrid 28038: Avda Rafael Alberti, 18 Bis
Mallorca 07015: Cala Mayor, Avda Joan Miró 285
Mallorca 07015: Palma Nova, c/ Jardiel Poncela 2
Tenerife 38006: c/ Marisol Marín 10
Valdemoro-Madrid 28340: c/ Bretón de los Herreros 10

Emergency Feeding Kitchens
Barcelona 08024: c/ del Rubí 18
La Coruña 15010: c/ Francisco Añón 9

Homeless Day Care Centres
La Coruña 15010: 'Sen Teito' c/ Francisco Añón 9 (acc 25)
Madrid 28028: c/ Hermosilla, 126, Local 4

Social Emergency Apartments
La Coruña 15010: c/ Francisco Añón 9 (acc 25)

CONFERENCE, RETREAT AND HOLIDAY CENTRE
Camp Sarón, Partida Torre Carrals 64, 03700 Denia, Alicante; tel: 96 578 2152; website: www.campsaron.com (acc 60)

SPAIN: Distribution of food gives opportunities for evangelism

SRI LANKA TERRITORY

Territorial leaders:
**Commissioners Malcolm and
Irene Induruwage**

Territorial Commander:
Commissioner Malcolm Induruwage
(1 April 2011)

Chief Secretary:
Lieut-Colonel William Mockabee
(1 Oct 2010)

Territorial Headquarters: 53 Sir James Peiris Mawatha, Colombo 2

Postal address: PO Box 193, Colombo, Sri Lanka

Tel: [94] 011 232 4660/232 2159; website: www.sri.salvationarmy.org

Salvation Army work began in Ceylon (now Sri Lanka) on 26 January 1883 under the leadership of Captain William Gladwin. 'The General of The Salvation Army' is a corporation Sole by Ordinance No 11 of 1924.

Zone: South Asia
Country included in the territory: Sri Lanka
'The Salvation Army' in Sinhala: Galaveeme Hamudaava; in Tamil: Ratchaniya Senai
Languages in which the gospel is preached: English, Sinhala, Tamil
Periodical: *Yudha Handa* (*The War Cry*)

THE Sri Lanka Territory had the theme 'Go on to Victory' as it marched forward sharing the gospel through corps ministries and institutions throughout the island.

The Army was strengthened when 12 cadets of the Proclaimers of the Resurrection session were commissioned and ordained as officers. They joined the ranks of Sri Lankan officers who continued to serve with the priority of leading people into a right relationship with the Lord. There were 12 accepted candidates.

There was a special emphasis on officer development commencing in April 2012 as 21 officers attended a 'Leadership Institute' conducted by Lieut-Colonel William Mockabee, (CS). Six one-day sessions held at monthly intervals gave delegates the tools to develop their ministry.

Women's Ministries held six seminars for female officers. Using the theme 'Walking Worthy' these two-day sessions were designed to motivate and encourage the delegates to be all that God has called them to be, while learning how to balance all that is required of them.

Officers also met together for three days to study the topic of holiness. All these seminars brought great blessing and the territory believes that great spiritual growth will result.

Livelihood programmes to assist people to develop skills and achieve the goal of becoming self-sufficient continued. Sewing classes were held for groups of 25 women who attended for six months. At the end of the course women were able to generate income for their families.

The mobile medical clinics assisted those who have no health care. Doctors and nurses visited many villages regularly. The 'Foster Child Care' programme continued to support many families, enabling children to be clothed and fed properly.

In 2012 Sri Lanka was chosen to host the South Asia College for Officers, from 15 February to 13 March, and the Regional Technology Exchange Conference for the South Asia Zone, 26-29 March.

Salvationists and officers in Sri Lanka are committed to work with passion, to lead people to know Jesus as their Saviour.

STATISTICS

Officers 142 (active 96 retired 46) **Cadets** 12 **Employees** 105
Corps 44 **Corps Plants** 13 **Social Homes and Hostels** 11 **Community Centres** 2 **Day Care Centres** 2 **Corps-based Child Care Centres** 4 **Health Centre** 1 **Conference Centre** 1
Senior Soldiers 4,024 **Adherent Members** 923 **Junior Soldiers** 586

STAFF

Women's Ministries: Comr Irene Induruwage (TPWM) Lt-Col Debra Mockabee (TSWM) Lt-Col Rohini Hettiarachchi (THLS & WDO)
Business Administration: Lt-Col Alister Philip
Candidates: Capt Anoma Wijesinghe

Editorial: Maj Chandra Jayaratnasingham
Finance: Capt Felix Kumaravel
Information Technology: Miss Coojanie Heendeniya
Personnel: Maj Packianathan Jayaratnasingham
Programme: Lt-Col Nihal Hettiarachchi
Projects: Capt Sharon Dannock
Property: Capt Jason Dannock
Training: Lt-Col Nilanthi Philip
Youth: Capt Wijenama Wijesinghe

DIVISIONS

Rambukkana: Mawanella Rd, Rambukkana; tel: 035 226 5179; Majs Ranjith and Vijayashri Senaratne
Western: 11 Sir James Peiris Mawatha, Colombo 2; tel: 011 232 4660 ext 214; Majs Newton and Ajantha Fernando

DISTRICTS

Kandy: 26 Srimath Bennet Soysa Veediya, Kandy; tel: 08 223 4804; Maj Kokila Muthusamy
Northern: Kandy Rd, Kaithady; tel: 0213 217450; Maj Newton Jacob

SECTIONS

Eastern: 135 Trincomalee St, Batticaloa; tel: 65 222 4558; Maj M. Puvanendran
Southern: Weerasooriya Watte, Patuwatha-Dodanduwa; tel: 091 227 7146; Maj Shelton Fernando

TRAINING COLLEGE

77 Ananda Rajakaruna Mawatha, Colombo 10; tel: 011 268 6116; email: sritraining.college@sri.salvationarmy.org

SOCIAL SERVICES
Children's Homes

Batticoloa Girls' Home: 135 Trincomalee St, Batticaloa; tel: 65 222 4558 (acc 16)
Dehiwela Girls' Home: 12 School Ave, Dehiwela; tel: (11) 271 7049 (acc 50)
Rajagiriya Boys' Home: Obeysekera Rd, Rajagiriya; tel: (11) 286 2301 (acc 30)
Shalom Children's Home and Centre: Kandy Rd, Kaithady, Jaffna; tel: (21) 3 210779 (acc boys 6, girls 12, remandees 17)
Sunshine Home: 127 E. W. Perera Mawatha, Colombo 10 (acc remandees 50)
Swed Lanka Boys' Home: South Pallansena Jaya Mawatha, Kochchikade; tel: 031 227 7964 (acc 22)
The Haven: 127, E. W. Perera Mawatha, Colombo 10; tel: (11) 269 5275 (acc babies 13, children 10)

SRI LANKA: Women participants in a livelihood development project

Hostels

Dehiwela Eventide Home for Women: 8 School Ave, Dehiwela; tel: (11) 272 8542 (acc 34)

Hope House Home for Employed Disabled Men: 11 Sir James Peiris Mawatha, Colombo 2; tel: (11) 232 4660 ext 200 (acc 12)

Ladies' Hostel (1): 18 Sri Saugathodaya Mawatha, Colombo 2; tel: (11) 311 7783 (acc 84)

Ladies' Hostel (2): 30 Union Pl, Colombo 2; tel: (11) 311 7735 (acc 84)

Rajagiriya Elders' Home and Iris Perera Home: 1700 Cotta Rd, Rajagiriya; tel: (11) 288 5947 (acc men 20, women 24)

Rajagiriya Young Men's Hostel: Obeysekera Rd, Rajagiriya; tel: (11) 286 2301 (acc 10)

Rawathawatte Hostel for Women: 14 Charles Pl, Rawathawatte, Moratuwa; tel: (11) 264 7209 (acc working girls 24)

The Haven: 127 E. W. Perera Mawatha, Colombo 10; tel: (11) 264 7209 269 5275 (acc unwed mothers 13, elderly women 10, rehabilitation 8)

Community Centres

Hope House: 11 Sir James Peiris Mawatha, Colombo 2; tel: 011 232 4660 ext 200

Rambukkana: Mawanella Rd, Rambukkana; tel: 035 226 5179

Child Day Care Centres

Kudagama: Kudagama, Dombemada; tel: (35) 3950 261

Hewadiwela: Halwatte, Hewadiwela; tel: (35) 226 6785

Talampitiya: Talampitiya, Mahagama, Kohilegedera, Talampitiya; tel: (37) 223 8278

Wattegama: 34 Nuwaratenne Rd, Wattegama; tel: (81) 380 3319

HEALTH SERVICES

Physiotherapy Unit: Colombo; tel 011 232 4660 ext 204

CONFERENCE CENTRE

Rambukkana Conference Centre for Camp: Mawanella Rd, Rambukkana; tel: 035 2265179

KALUTARA ESTATE AND CAMP CENTRE

Galapatha, Kalutara; tel: (34) 3944041

SWEDEN AND LATVIA TERRITORY

Territorial Commander:
Commissioner Marie Willermark
(1 Feb 2011)

Chief Secretary:
Lieut-Colonel Daniel Sjogren
(1 Feb 2013)

Territorial Headquarters: Nybrogatan 79B, 114 41, Stockholm, Sweden

Postal address: Box 5090, SE 102 42 Stockholm, Sweden

Tel: [46] (08) 562 282 00; fax: [46] (08) 562 283 91; email: fralsningsarmen@fralsningsarmen.se;
website: www.fralsningsarmen.se

Commissioner Hanna Ouchterlony, inspired by the first Army meeting held on Swedish soil in Värnamo in 1878 led by the young Chief of the Staff, Bramwell Booth, began Salvation Army work in a Stockholm theatre on 28 December 1882. The first women's home and a men's shelter were opened in 1890. Work among deaf and blind people was inaugurated in 1895. The Salvation Army was re-established in Latvia on 18 November 1990 and two months later, on 23 January 1991, The Salvation Army in Latvia became a juridical person. On 15 November 1994 the Sweden Territory was renamed the Sweden and Latvia Territory.

Zone: Europe
Countries included in the territory: Latvia, Sweden
'The Salvation Army' in Swedish: Frälsningsarmén; in Latvian: Pestíšanas Armija; in Russian:
   Armiya Spaseniya
Languages in which the gospel is preached: Latvian, Russian, Swedish
Periodical: *Stridsropet*

'WHERE are you Going?' was the theme of the territorial congress in July 2011. Led by the then Chief of the Staff, Commissioner Barry C. Swanson and the World President of Women's Ministries, Commissioner Sue Swanson, the focus was on the Army's identity and mission. Salvationists from Latvia and songsters from Riga participated. Two Swedish cadets were commissioned and ordained as officers. Children and young people also played a special part in the congress.

Involvement with The Salvation Army internationally included 'Check-In', a discipleship training course with seven weeks of practical work and mission outreach in Nagercoil, India.

Ten Salvationists from Vasakåren Corps, Stockholm, visited a water project funded by the corps in Mizoram, India Eastern Territory.

The International Development Office at THQ produced *Go Global,* a DVD on issues including global justice and fighting poverty.

The Secretary for Spiritual Life Development and her team visited 16 corps to conduct prayer weekends. Five prayer sergeants were appointed.

The territory rejoiced that more new soldiers were enrolled in both Sweden and Latvia than for many years past.

During one week in January 2012 all Salvation Army units in the city of Gothenburg united for an outreach and exhibition event in a large shopping centre. Leading chefs cooked the 'soup of the day', there was live music, a 'thought for the day' and a place available for prayer and counselling.

During severe winter temperatures in February-March 2012 the social service day centre in Stockholm opened an emergency night shelter for homeless people. There was an increase in migrants from other European countries looking for work; an issue that was debated in March with leading politicians and The Salvation Army.

In April, the plight of homeless children was emphasised by 'The Pillow Fight'. One morning just after dawn in Stockholm, pink and blue pillows with a printed message were placed around the city centre to draw attention to the situation.

The Army's Högaberg Camp provided holidays for disadvantaged children referred by social services.

Positive media attention was received when an officer, the director of a social centre, featured in a series of programmes about people in Sweden and their religion. Captain Carolina Nilsson was filmed at work and in her family setting.

Sunday schools at corps used new resources produced ecumenically, entitled *The Treasure*.

Young people had a great start to 2012 with the Nordic New Year Conference, 'So Much Greater', attended by 250 participants.

In Latvia the first ever training course for local officers took place.

The authorities in Riga closed the Leontine Gorska's Orphanage and the building now houses the school for officer training.

In December 2011 advisory board members secured permission for a Christmas Kettle collection at the Riga Dome during the Lucia Concert and a large amount was raised.

In February 2012 a one-year project with EU funding commenced to offer life skills to young people and prepare them for employment. Young people met for discussion with General Linda Bond when she visited Riga.

The Salvation Army served an estimated 90,000 meals during the year to Latvian people in great need.

STATISTICS

Officers 335 (active 139 retired 196)
   Cadets (1st Yr) 5 (2nd Yr) 5
   Employees 1,146
Corps (incl Community and Family Services)
   114 **Outposts** 20 **Hotel** 1 **Guest Home** 1
Senior Soldiers 4,098 **Adherent Members** 784
   Junior Soldiers 159
Personnel serving outside territory Officers 9

STAFF

Women's Ministries: Comr Marie Willermark
   (TPWM) Lt-Col Rebecca Sjogren (TSWM)
Sec for Business Administration: Capt
   Elisabeth Beckman
   Editor-in-Chief: Maj Bert Åberg
   Fundraising: Mr Mats Wiberg
   Legacies: Maj Margaretha Andersson
Sec for Personnel: Maj Sonja Blomberg
   Training College: Capt Mattias Nordenberg

Candidates Sec: Maj Veronica Wahlström
People's High School: Mr Magnus Wetterberg
Sec for Programme: tba
Development Officers: Maj Marianne
Lennermo-Ljungholm, Maj Christel
Lindgren, Maj Gunilla Olausson,
Maj Christina Paulsson
Area Experts:
Corps Development: Maj Mia-Lisa Alhbin
Home and Family: Col Kristina Frisk
Institutions: Maj Leif Öberg
Social Work: Maj Ywonne Eklund
Spiritual Life Development: Maj Mona
Stockman
Youth: tba
International Development: Mr Christian Lerne
Child Sponsorship: Mrs Anna-Carin Wiberg Löw
Missing Persons: Mrs Kristine Falk
'Sally Ann' – Trading Programme:
Sally Ann Sverige AB:
email: sallyann@fralsningsarmen.se
website: www.sallyann.se
Manager: Mr Lars Beijer
Shop: Hornsgatan 98, 118 21 Stockholm

TRAINING
Training College
Frälsningsarméns Officersskola, Ågestagården,
Bonäsvägen, 5, 123 52 Farsta;
tel: (08) 562 281 50

People's High Schools
Ågesta Folkhögskola: Bonäsvägen 5,
123 52 Farsta; tel: (08) 562 281 00
Älvsjö Bransch: Älvsjö Gårdsväg 9,
125 30 Älvsjö; tel: (08) 647 52 77

CONFERENCE CENTRE/GUEST HOMES
Smålandsgården, Örserum, 563 91 Gränna;
tel: (0390) 300 14; fax: (0390) 304 17 (acc 67)
'Lännerstahemmet', Djurgårdsvägen 7,
132 46 Saltsjö-Boo; tel: (08) 715 11 58;

SOCIAL SERVICES
Work Among Alcoholics
Treatment Centre for Substance Abusers
'Kurön', 178 92 Adelsö; tel: (08) 560 518 80;
(acc 63)

Rehabilitation Centres
Göteborg: 'Lilla Bommen' (acc 63)
Göteborg: 'Nylösegården' (acc 20)
Örebro: 'Gnistan' (acc 11)
Stockholm: 'Värtahemmet' (acc 42)
Stockholm Tyresö: 'Källan' (acc 20)

Sundsvall: 'Klippangården' (acc 16)
Uppsala: 'Sagahemmet' (acc 26)

Night Shelters
Örebro: 'Gnistan' (acc 10)
Stockholm: 'Midsommarkransen' (acc 27)
Sundsvall: 'Klippangården'
Uppsala: 'Sagahemmet' (acc 10)

Drop-in Centre
Stockholm

Harbour Light Corps
Göteborg: 'Fyrbåkskåren'

Advisory Services
Stockholm: 'Eken' Counselling Centre,
Hornsgatan 98, 118 21 Stockholm;
tel: (08) 55 60 80 76
Uppsala: 'Brobygget', S:t Persgatan 20,
753 20 Uppsala; tel: (018) 71 05 44

Work Among Children and Families
Pre-Schools
Jönköping: 'Vårsol' (acc 17)
Umeå: 'Krubban' (acc 18)
Västra Frölunda: 'Morgonsol' (acc 34)

Work Among Mother and Children
Stockholm: Frälsningsarméns Mamma
barnarbete, Gotlandsgatan 73 C,
116 38 Stockholm; tel: (08) 21 47 92

School and Treatment Centre for Adolescents
Svartsjö: 'Sundsgården' (acc 27)

Treatment Centre for Families
Fristad 'FAM-Huset' (acc adults 8, babies 8)

Emergency Diagnostic and Short-term Treatment Centre
Jönköping: 'Vårsol' (acc 6)

Group Homes for Adolescents
Jönköping: 'Vårsols Ungdomsboende' (acc 6)
Stockholm: 'Locus' (acc 14)

Family Centres with Advisory Service
Jönköping: 'Vårsols Familjecenter'
Stockholm: 393: Familjecenter

Refugee Aid
Jönköping SARA väster: V:a Storgatan 21,
553 15 Jönköping; tel: (036) 17 32 75

Jönköping SARA söder: S:t Larsgatan 16, 553 38
  Jönköping tel: (036) 17 32 55, (036) 16 74 58

Vacation Centres for Children
Gävle: 'Rörberg', Hedesundavägen 89,
  818 91 Valbo; tel: (026) 330 19 (acc 15)
Luleå: 'Sunderbyn', Sunderbynvägen 323,
  954 42 Södra Sunderbyn;
  tel: (0920) 26 57 25 (acc 15)
Malmö: 'Kotten', Klockarevägen 20,
  236 36 Höllviken; tel: (040) 45 05 24 (acc 15)

Centre for Elderly People
'Dalen', Kapellgatan 14, 571 31 Nässjö;
  tel: (0380) 188 11 (acc 20)

Recreation Centre for Elderly People
Malmö: 'Furubo', Klockarevägen 22, 236 36
  Höllviken; tel: (040) 45 39 13

Multicultural Ministries
'Akalla', Sibeliusgången 6, 164 73 Kista;
  tel: (08) 750 62 16

Women's Emergency Residence
Stockholm: 'Skogsbo', Box 112,
  132 23 Saltsjö Boo; tel: (08) 21 47 92

Second-hand Shops
Head office: Stensätravägen 3B,
  127 39 Skärholmen; tel: (08) 563 169 50;
Shops: Borås, Eskilstuna, Falun, Gävle,
  Göteborg, Halmstad, Jönköping, Karlstad,
Linköping, Luleå, Malmö (2), Norrköping,
Örebro, Skellefteå, Skövde, Stockholm (9),
Sundbyberg, Sundsvall, Trollhättan, Umeå,
Uppsala (2), Västerås,

LATVIA REGION (under THQ)
Regional Headquarters: Bruninieku iela 10A,
  LV 1001 Riga; tel: [371] 673 10037;
  email: info@pestisanasarmija.lv;
  website: www.pestisanasarmija.lv

Regional leaders: Lts Peter and Rut
  Baronowsky

STATISTICS
Officers 17 (active 16 retired 1) **Cadets** (1st Yr)
  8 **Envoys** 2 **Employees** 2
Corps 7 **Outposts** 4 **Institutions** 1
Senior Soldiers 209 **Adherent Members** 232
  Junior Soldiers 22

SOCIAL SERVICES
Bruninieku iela 10A, LV 1001 Riga;
  tel: [371] 672 71384
'Patverums' Day Centre for Children at Risk:
  Bruninieku iela 10 A, LV 1001 Riga;
  tel: [371] 731 14 63
Skangale School Home: Liepa pag,
  Césu rajons, LV 4128 Liepa;
  tel: [371] 641 02220

SWEDEN: A Salvationist volunteer and a willing donor to the Christmas Kettle appeal

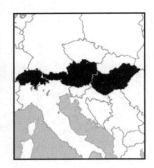

SWITZERLAND, AUSTRIA AND HUNGARY TERRITORY

Territorial leaders:
Commissioners Franz Boschung and Hanny Boschung-Abderhalden

Territorial Commander:
Commissioner Franz Boschung
(1 Sep 2011)

Chief Secretary:
Lieut-Colonel Massimo Tursi
(1 Sep 2011)

Territorial Headquarters: Laupenstrasse 5, Bern, Switzerland

Postal address: Die Heilsarmee, Postfach 6575, 3001 Bern, Switzerland

Tel: [41] (31) 388 05 91; fax: [41] (31) 388 05 95; email: info@swi.salvationarmy.org

websites: www.heilsarmee.ch; www.armeedusalut.ch; www.salvationarmy.ch

On 10 December 1882 Salvation Army operations were commenced in the Salle de la Réformation, Geneva, by the Maréchale, Catherine Booth, and Colonel Arthur S. Clibborn. Bitter opposition was encountered but now the Army is recognised as an evangelical and social force throughout the Confederation. The Salvation Army's constitution consists of Foundation Salvation Army Switzerland; Cooperative Salvation Army Social Organisation; Salvation Army Immo Ltd.

Work first commenced in Austria on 27 May 1927 in Vienna. Unofficial meetings had been held earlier, but the official opening was conducted by Lieut-Commissioner Bruno Friedrich and Captain Lydia Saak was the officer-in-charge. 'Verein der Heilsarmee' was legally recognised by the Austrian Federal Ministry on 8 May 1952.

The Salvation Army's operations in Hungary were commenced on 24 April 1924 by Colonel Rothstein with two German female officers. The evangelistic and social activities were maintained until suppressed in 1950. After the opening of the central European borders, The Salvation Army was officially re-established on 3 November 1990 by General Eva Burrows.

Zone: Europe

Countries included in the territory: Austria, Hungary, Switzerland

'The Salvation Army' in German: Die Heilsarmee; in French: Armée du Salut; in Hungarian:
Üdvhadsereg; in Spanish: Ejército de Salvación

Languages in which the gospel is preached: French, German, Hungarian, Spanish

Periodicals: *Espoir* (French), *Dialog* (German), *Dialogue* (French), *IN* (French and German), *Just 4 U* (French), *Klecks* (German), *Trampoline* (French), *Trialog* (German)

THE territory continued its strategy with an emphasis on the theme 'To worship, to win, to grow and to serve' as corps were encouraged to strengthen their integrated mission. In social services a comprehensive review examined whether the services offered corresponded with the needs of society. However professional and skilled The Salvation Army's work, the public perception is of an ageing organisation. Thus in Switzerland the territory launched a new marketing concept accompanied by a rebranding process with the red shield as the key image. A community-related approach supports marketing on every level.

'What's the purpose of life?' was the question considered during the 'Leben mit Vision' (The Purpose Driven Life) campaign lasting 40 days. Salvationists invited members, friends and employees to join a cell group and seek answers to the question 'What on earth am I here for?' Each Sunday a major spiritual topic was raised and the cell groups explored these subjects and connected with members of the group. As a result participants were encouraged to dedicate their lives to God. The number of small groups increased.

In society and family ministries a wide range of programmes was offered. 'PEP4Kids' was launched to help parents educate their children and balance everyday life.

'Neuland' (New Land) was an adventurous year of discipleship for young adults. Three participants worked three days per week in a corps and studied for two days at the college for officer training, accompanied by a mentor.

In social services new ways of treating alcoholics in institutions for homeless people and those with poor life skills were explored. A pilot project, in partnership with a teaching hospital, was launched to find alternatives to the strict sobriety that often proves difficult for recovering addicts.

During the year 68 junior and 120 senior soldiers were enrolled and 137 adherent members were welcomed.

The government in Vienna, Austria, fosters innovative alternatives to shelter homeless people. The Salvation Army opened a new service offering individual accommodation which reflects this approach.

In September 2011 The Salvation Army in Hungary celebrated the opening of 'Fény Háza (House of Light). A wonderful new building provides accommodation, counselling and rehabilitation for mothers and children who have experienced domestic violence.

General Linda Bond visited the territory in December 2011. At a meeting in Berne she urged Salvationists to take mission seriously saying, 'The world needs our redeemer offering freedom, hope and life'.

STATISTICS
(Switzerland and Austria)

Officers 390 (active 164 retired 226) **Cadets** 5 **Employees** 1,690
Corps 62 **Outposts** 28 **Institutions** 40 **Thrift Stores** 20
Senior Soldiers 2,670 **Adherent Members** 1,088 **Junior Soldiers** 336
Personnel serving outside territory Officers 18 Layworkers 4

STAFF

Dept of Evangelisation: Maj Fritz Schmid
  Society and Family: Comr Hanny Boschung-Abderhalden (TPWM) Lt-Col Anne-Florence Tursi-Cachelin (TSWM) Maj Brigitta Heiniger (Women's Ministries & Seniors Sec) Maj Barbara Bösch (Family Work)
  Music and Gospel Arts: Mr Micael Dikantsa
  Youth: Maj Thomas Bösch
Dept of Social Work: Mr Daniel Röthlisberger
  Social French Part: Mr Didier Rochat

Social German Part: Mr Christian Rohrbach
Prison Work: Maj Urs Meyner
Family Tracing: Maj Martha Mosimann
Refugees: Mr Paul Mori
Thrift Stores: Mr Jakob Amstutz
Dept of Personnel: Maj Marianne Meyner-
Stettler
Candidates: Maj Daniela Zurbrügg-Jäggi
Training: Maj Jean-Marc Flückiger
Personnel Administration: Sgt Christian Hefti
Dept of Finance and Business Administration:
Sgt Andreas Stettler
Finance Controlling Evangelisation:
Maj Peter Zurbrügg
Finance Controlling Social: Mr Michael
Lippuner
Finance Controlling THQ: Sgt Kenneth Hofer
Property: Mr Marc Hendry
Mission and Development: Mr Jacques
Miaglia
Dept of Communication: Sgt Martin Künzi
Editor-in-Chief: Mrs Gabrielle Keller
Fundraising: Sgt Christoph Bitter
Information Technology: Mr Martin Schweizer
Museum and Archives: Maj Corinne Gossauer
Trade Shop: Mrs Hanni Butler

DIVISIONS

Bern: Gartenstrasse 8, 3007 Bern;
tel: (031) 380 75 45; fax: (031) 380 75 42;
Majs Bernhard and Regina Wittwer
Division Romande: Rue de l'Ecluse 16,
2000 Neuchâtel; tel: (032) 729 20 81;
Majs Jacques and Claude-Evelyne Donzé
Nordwestschweiz: Breisacherstrasse 45,
4057 Basel; tel: (061) 691 11 50;
fax: (061) 691 12 59; Majs August and
Ruth Martin
Ost-Division: Eidmattstrasse 16, 8032 Zürich;
tel: (044) 383 69 70; fax: (044) 383 52 48;
Majs Hervé and Deborah Cachelin

SCHOOL FOR OFFICER TRAINING

4012 Basel, Habsburgerstrasse 15, Postfach 54,
CH-4012 Basel; tel: (061) 387 91 11

SOCIAL WORK
Social Services Advice Bureaux

4053 Basel: Frobenstrasse20A; tel: (061) 270 25 00
3007 Bern: Gartenstrasse 8; tel: (031) 380 75 40
2503 Biel-Bienne: Kontrollstrasse 22;
tel: (032) 322 53 66
1018 Lausanne: Rue de la Borde 22;
tel: (021) 646 46 10
8400 Winterthur: CASA, Wartstrasse 9;
tel: 052 202 77 80

8032 Zürich: Eidmattstrasse 16; Postfach 1610; tel:
044 383 69 70
8005 Zürich: Luisenstrasse 23; tel: 044 273 90 01

Adult Rehabilitation Centres

1201 Genève: Centre-Espoir, Rue Jean-Dassier
10; tel: (022) 338 22 00 (acc 108)
3098 Köniz: Buchseegut, Buchseeweg 15;
tel: (031) 970 63 63 (acc 40)
(with gardening and workshop)
1003 Lausanne: Foyer Féminin,
Ave Ruchonnet 49; tel: (021) 310 40 40
(acc 22)
1005 Lausanne: La Résidence, Place du Vallon 1a;
tel: (021) 320 48 55 (acc 32)
5022 Rombach (Aarau): Obstgarten,
Bibersteinstrasse 54; tel: (062) 839 80 80
(acc 34)
2024 St-Aubin: Le Devens, Socio-medical Home;
tel: (032) 836 27 29 (acc 34)
9205 Waldkirch: Hasenberg; tel: (071) 434 61 61
(acc 48) (agriculture and workshop)

Community Centres

Hochfeld, Bern; Eidmattegge, Zürich; Open
Heart, Zürich; Genève.

Emergency Shelters

1201 Genève: Accueil de Nuit, Rue Jean-Dassier
10; tel: (022) 388 22 00 (acc 40)
1005 Lausanne: La Marmotte, Rue du Vallon 17;
tel: (021) 311 79 12 (acc 31)

Holiday Flats

3715 Adelboden: Chalet Bethel;
tel: (033) 673 21 62 (acc 20)

Homes for the Aged

3013 Bern: Lorrainehof, Lorrainestrasse 34-38;
tel: (031) 330 16 16 (acc 50 + 10 flats)
1814 La Tour-de-Peilz: Le Phare-Elim,
Ave de la Paix 11, case postale 444;
tel: (021) 977 33 33 (acc 44)
1201 Genève: Résidence Amitié, Rue Baudit 1;
tel: (022) 919 95 95 (acc 52)
2000 Neuchâtel: Le Foyer, Rue de l'Ecluse 18;
tel: (032) 729 20 20 (acc 30)

Homes for Children

8344 Bäretswil: Sunnemätteli Home for
Handicapped Children, Wirzwil,
Rüggenthalstrasse 71; tel: (044) 939 99 80 (acc
16)
4054 Basel: Kinderhaus Holee,
Nenzlingerstrasse 2; tel: (061) 301 24 50 (acc
26)

SWITZERLAND: 'Alive', a dynamic youth choir, express their Christian faith in song during the General's visit to Berne

8932 Mettmenstetten: Kinderheim Paradies;
   tel: (044) 768 58 00 (acc 24)
3110 Münsingen: Kinderheim Sonnhalde,
   Standweg 7; tel: (031) 721 08 06 (acc 28)

Hostels for Men
4058 Basel: Rheinblick, Rheingasse 80;
   tel: (061) 666 66 77 (acc 53)
8004 Zürich: Dienerstrasse 76; tel: (044) 298 90 80
   (acc 26)
8005 Zürich: Geroldstrasse 27;
   tel: (043) 204 10 20 (acc 24)

Hostels for Men and Women
3006 Bern: Passantenheim, Muristrasse 6;
   tel: (031) 351 80 27 (acc 43)
2503 Biel: Passantenheim, Jakob-Strasse 58;
   tel: (032) 322 68 38 (acc 24)
3600 Thun: Passantenheim, Waisenhausstrasse
   26; tel: (033) 222 69 20 (acc 17)
8400 Winterthur: Wartstrasse 42;
   tel: (052) 208 90 50 (acc 34)
8026 Zürich: Molkenstrasse 6; Postfach 1669
   tel: (044) 298 90 00 (acc 85)

Hostel for Women
4058 Basel: Frauenwohnheim,
   Hagentalerstrasse 6; tel: (061) 681 34 70
   (acc 37)

Young Women's Residence
4059 Basel: Schlössli, Eichhornstrasse 21;
   tel: (061) 335 31 10 (acc 14)

Refugee Work
Main Office: 3008 Bern, Effingerstrasse 67;
   tel: (031) 380 18 80 (12 centres, 6 offices)

Social Flats
3012 Bern: Begleitetes Wohnen,
   Waldheimstrasse 16; tel: (031) 302 02 35

HOTELS
4055 Basel: Alegria B&B, Habsburgerstrasse
   15; tel: (061) 387 91 10
1204 Genève: Bel' Espérance,
   Rue de la Vallée 1; tel: (022) 818 37 37;
   (acc 39 beds)
3852 Ringgenberg: Guesthouse, Hauptstrasse
   125; tel: (033) 822 70 25 (acc 22 beds)

YOUTH CENTRES
Under THQ
3715 Adelboden (acc 75)
Under DHQ
Nordwestschweiz: 4462 Rickenbach, Waldegg
   (acc 100)
Division Romande: 1451 Les Rasses (acc 150)
Ost-Division: 8712 Stäfa (acc 55)

AUSTRIA

City Command: AT-1020 Vienna
Salztor-Zentrum, Grosse Schiffgasse 3;
tel: [43] (1) 890 3282 2266;
City Commander: Maj Hans-Marcel Leber
www.heilsarmee.at

Hostel for Men

SalztorZentrum, AT-1020 Vienna:
Grosse Schiffgasse 3; tel: [43] (1) 214 48 30 27
(acc 60)

Residential Home for Men

Haus Erna, AT-1210 Vienna
Moritz-Dreger-Gasse 19
tel: [43] (1) 890 3282 2017 (acc 60)

Prison Chaplaincy
Missing Persons Bureau

at above address; tel: 890 3282 2264
Vienna Corps:at above address (entrance in
Oswald-Redlich-Strasse 11a)
mobile tel: [43] (664) 163 67 23

HUNGARY REGION

Regional Headquarters: Bajnok utca 25,
1063 Budapest, Hungary;
tel: +36-1-332-3324;
email: kozponti@swi.salvationarmy.org;
website: www.udvhadsereg.org
Regional Officer: Capt Andrew Morgan

STATISTICS

Officers 13 (active 10 retired 3) **Cadets** 2
Employees 57
Corps 4 **Outpost** 1 **Institutions** 3
Senior Soldiers 35 **Adherent Members** 17
Junior Soldiers 6

STAFF

Asst Regional Officer: Capt Darlene Morgan
Administrative Assistant: Laura Halmaghi
Finance: Zsuzsa Kübler

SOCIAL WORK
Hostel for Men

'Új Remenység Háza', 1086 Budapest,
Dobozi utca 29; tel: +36-1-314-2775 (acc 98)

Rehabilitation Home for Women

'Válaszút Háza', 1171 Budapest,
Lemberg utca 38-42; tel: +36-1-259-1095
(acc 24)

Refuge for Maltreated Women and Children

'Fény Házá', Budapest
(acc 40, inc mothers with children)

Adult Day Drop-In Centre

1171 Budapest, Lemberg utca 38-42; tel: +36-1-
259-1095 (acc 50)

Day Nursery

1086 Budapest, Dobozi utca 31; tel: +36-20-572-
9656 (acc 7)

Feeding Programmes

1086 Budapest, Dobozi utca 29;
tel: +36-1-314-2775 (250 meals daily)
1171 Budapest, Lemberg utca 38-42;
tel: +36-1-259-1095 (150 meals daily)
4034 Debrecen, Ruyter utca 23;
tel: +36-52-534-616 (100 meals daily)

HUNGARY: Major Ruth Tschopp, a Swiss officer who pioneered work with women who were victims of domestic violence, returned to Budapest for the opening of the new refuge,'Fény Háza'. Pictured with her is a boy for whom 'Fény Háza' is a safe place to live

TAIWAN REGION

Regional leaders:
Majors Michael and Annette Coleman

Regional Commander:
Major Michael Coleman (1 May 2008)

Regional Headquarters: 3/F, 273 Dun Hua South Road, Section 2, Da-An District, Taipei 106

Postal address: PO Box 44-100, Taipei, Taiwan

Tel: [886] (02) 2738 1079/1171

email: taiwan@taw.salvationarmy.org: website: www.salvationarmy.org.tw

Pioneered in 1928 by Colonel Yasowo Segawa, Salvation Army work in Taiwan was curtailed by the Second World War. Following initiatives by an American serviceman, operations were officially re-established in October 1965 by Colonel and Mrs George Lancashire. Taiwan has been a separate region since 1997.

Zone: South Pacific and East Asia
Country included in the region: Taiwan
'The Salvation Army' in Taiwanese (Hokkien): Kiu Se Kuen; in Mandarin: Chiu Shih Chun
Languages in which the gospel is preached: English, Mandarin, Taiwanese (Hokkien)
Periodicals: *Salvationist.tw, Reach-Out! Live!*

THE focus of 2011 was on building for the future. A number of initiatives commenced and others were planned by the end of the year.

The region worked on projects including income-generating businesses, new social programmes, social justice advocacy and evangelism. Morale was high as greater viability in financial, structural, evangelistic and spiritual aspects were developed.

In August 2011 the Taipei University Mission began an evangelistic outreach to students on three campuses at the southern end of Taipei City. A network of about 20 students was established; the nucleus

of a group of converts and the potential for a future leadership team.

Training events and other activities throughout the year emphasised a greater mission focus and included: faith-based facilitation training (a specific community development model); mission training for soldiers and the development of 'Building a Strong Foundation' – bi-lingual material aimed at establishing the principles by which corps can become effective in their communities and can grow.

A four-day training event for all officers and a seminar on corps growth principles also took place.

A major research project into the

status of the alcohol and other drugs service sector was carried out for internal planning purposes.

An evaluation of the effectiveness of the case management of homeless persons was published. A community consultation in Si Wei public housing community, resulted in recommendations for the local ministries and service going forward.

In July, a music ministry team from the Australia Southern Territory conducted workshops, open-air meetings and a regional family day.

One of the spiritual highlights of the year was the 'Discover Officership' weekend, conducted by Captains Craig and Donna Todd (Australia Eastern). Eighteen young people with potential for officership were invited and affirmed a continuing interest in leadership in The Salvation Army.

In December the Army partnered with a number of other organisations to campaign against the hosing of homeless people in public parks and metro stations. When actual footage of homeless people being hosed, and of a local politician advocating the action, was shown on YouTube the issue was reported by national and international media. The practice was stopped the same day, and the politician released a public apology within two days.

The Taiwan Salvation Army began talks with two other territories to set up a network in 2012 to help women who have been trafficked into Taiwan and are returning home after being rescued.

STATISTICS
Officers 18 (active 16 retired 2)
Corps with Community Centres 5 **Social Services Centres** 3 **University Outreach Mission** 1
Senior Soldiers 171 **Adherent Members** 97 **Junior Soldiers** 33

STAFF
Women's Ministries: Maj Annette Coleman (RPWM) Maj Mary Tsou (WMO)
Administration Officer: Maj Stephen Tsou **Finance:** Mr Fred Lee
Human Resources: Ms Yvonne Tsai
Regional Mission and Resource Officers: (Programme Development) Maj Robert Duncan (Social Programmes) Maj Leanne Duncan

SOCIAL SERVICES
Homeless
Taipei Homeless Caring Centre: c/o 1/F, No 42, Lane 65, Jin Si St., Taipei 103

Youth
Puli Youth Services Centre: No 192 Pei Hwang Rd, Puli Town, Nantou County 545 (acc 60)

COMMUNITY SERVICES
Puli Community Development Centre: c/o No 62-1, Shueitou Rd, Puli Town, Nantou County 545

TANZANIA TERRITORY

Territorial leaders:
Colonels Lindsay and Lynette Rowe

Territorial Commander:
Colonel Lindsay Rowe (1 Feb 2012)

Chief Secretary:
Lieut-Colonel Seth Appeateng (1 Jul 2011)

Territorial Headquarters: Kilwa Road, Dar es Salaam

Postal address: PO Box 1273, Dar es Salaam, Tanzania

Tel/fax: [255] (22) 2850468/2850542

Adjutant and Mrs Francis Dare began Salvation Army work in Tabora, Tanzania (formerly known as Tanganyika), in November 1933, as part of the East Africa Territory. In 1950, at the request for assistance from the Colonial Governor, The Salvation Army set up Mgulani Camp, where the Tanzania Headquarters is now located. Tanzania became a separate command on 1 October 1998 and was elevated to territory status on 1 February 2008.

Zone: Africa
Country included in the territory: Tanzania
'The Salvation Army' in Kiswahili: Jeshi la Wokovu
Languages in which the gospel is preached: Kiswahili and various tribal languages

INSPIRED by the theme 'Forward Together' the territory continued to grow, despite financial challenges.

Bukine and Tabora sections became districts and Ilembo Section and Coastal and Serengeti districts were elevated to divisional status.

The territory helped many girls rescued from human trafficking. In May 2011 eight young women aged 14-18 were reunited with their families. Ten girls began the residential programme at Kwetu Counselling Centre. Others aged 6-13, housed at Mbagala Girls' Home, were successfully placed with foster families. An income-generating seminar was attended by the foster carers who then received loans to enable them to start new businesses. In August a new rehabilitation programme for 30 rescued girls was funded by the United Kingdom Territory.

Tanzania's commitment to Stop Human Trafficking was strengthened by a project in Mwanza District, supported by the Denmark Territory. Community-based activities combat trafficking by improving the social, psychological and economic well-being of young people aged 12-25, rescued from the streets.

At Matumaini School, personnel from West Midlands Fire Service

(UK) worked for two weeks to transform the physiotherapy room and also built ramps for wheelchair access.

A Salvation Army team from Canada renovated two boys' dormitories and the sewing room, enabling classes in tailoring to be provided.

Eight officers were selected to preach on TBC television and radio stations. The programmes went out live from Mgulani Corps, Dar es Salaam, in August 2011.

The territory gratefully acknowledges the support of mission partners in enabling Salvationists to serve the people of Tanzania.

STATISTICS

Officers 138 (active 133 retired 5) **Cadets** (Ist Yr) 9 **Employees** 188 **Corps** 78 **Outposts** 79 **Schools** 2 **Day Care Centres** 17 **Hostel** 1 **Senior Soldiers** 6,408 **Junior Soldiers** 3,794

STAFF

Women's Ministries: Col Lynette Rowe (TPWM) Lt-Col Janet Appeateng (TSWM) Maj Tamali Mwalukani (LOMS/ SAMF)
Candidates: Capt Peter Tingo
Education and Officer Development: Maj Joy Paxton
Editor: Maj Esther Mwita
Field: Maj Wilson Mwalukani
Finance: Maj Francis Amakye
Projects: Mr Frederick Urembo
Property: Maj Samson Ngocho
Public Relations: Maj Esther Mwita
Social Services: Capt Josephat Nyerere
Sponsorship: Major Jemima Amakye
Training: Maj Lynda Levis
Youth and Children: Capt Pamela Tingo

DIVISIONS

Coastal: PO Box 7622, Dar es Salaam; tel: (022) 2860365; Majs James and Yustina Gitang'ita
Ilembo: PO Box 2545, tel: (0255) 0752 820045; Majs Japhael and Aliyinza Madoki
Mbeya: PO Box 1214, Mbeya; tel: (025) 2560009; Majs Musa and Esther Magaigwa

Tarime: PO Box 37, Tarime; tel: (028) 2690095
Serengeti: PO Box 28, Mugumu; tel: (028) 2621434; Majs Christopher and Mary Ighoty

DISTRICTS

Bukine: Maj Julius Lackson
Mwanza: PO Box 11267, Mwanza; tel: (028) 40123; Maj Fanuel Ndabila
Tabora: PO Box 1, Tabora tel: (026) 2604728) Maj Daniel Simwali

TRAINING COLLEGE
PO Box 1273, Dar es Salaam

AGRICULTURE DEVELOPMENT PROGRAMME
PO Box 1273, Dar es Salaam

EDUCATIONAL WORK
College for Business Management and Administration
Shukrani International College for Business Management and Administration, PO Box 535, Mbeya; tel: (00255) (0)25 2504404

Primary School for Disabled Children
Matumaini School, PO Box 1273, Dar es Salaam; tel: (022) 2851861 (acc 175)

Secondary School
Itundu School, PO Box 2994, Mbeya

SOCIAL SERVICES
Kwetu Counselling and Psycho-Social Support Services: PO Box 1273, Dar es Salaam
Mbagala Girls' Home: PO Box 1273, Dar es Salaam
Mgulani Hostel and Conference Centre: PO Box 1273, Dar es Salaam; tel: (022) 2851467 (acc 110)
Vocational Training Workshop: PO Box 1273, Dar es Salaam

Anti-Human Trafficking Programmes

Rehabilitation and Reunification Services for Orphans and Vulnerable Children

PROJECTS
Community counselling, Gardening and farming activities, Goat banks schemes, Home-based care services, Literacy classes, Micro-credit schemes, Nutrition programmes, Primary health care, Training and economic empowerment for rural women, Water and sanitation programmes

TANZANIA: Visiting officers try out a new borehole which will provide clean safe water for many people

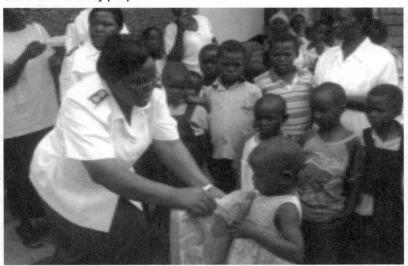

UGANDA: Colonel Grace Mnyampi (TPWM) distributes mosquito nets which will help protect young children from malaria

UGANDA TERRITORY

Territorial leaders:
Colonels Benjamin and Grace Mnyampi

Territorial Commander:
Colonel Benjamin Mnyampi (1 Jan 2013)

Chief Secretary:
Lieut-Colonel Eugene Bamanabio
(1 Mar 2011)

Territorial Headquarters: Plot 78-82 Lugogo Bypass, Kampala

Postal address: PO Box 11776, Kampala, Uganda

Tel: [256] 41 533901; Kampala mobile: [256] 752 375782

The Salvation Army opened fire in Uganda in 1931 when Captain and Mrs Edward Osborne unfurled the flag in Mbale, as part of the East Africa Territory. In September 1977 the Army's religious teaching was banned and in June 1978 its ministry, including social work, was proscribed. In 1980 Majors Leonard and Dorothy Millar began work with the persecuted Salvationists to re-establish The Salvation Army. Uganda became a separate command on 1 November 2005 and was elevated to territorial status on 1 March 2011.

Zone: Africa
Country included in the territory: Uganda
'The Salvation Army' in Kiswahili: Jeshi La Wokovu; in Luganda: Ejje Elyobulokozi
Languages in which the gospel is preached: English, Kiswahili, Luganda and a number of tribal languages
Periodicals: *Voice of Hope* (quarterly)

IN response to the steady increase of soldiers in Uganda two new districts, Busulwa and Lwakhakha, were formed. There was an emphasis on mission and expansion.

More than 90 people applied for candidateship and 70 officers enrolled in academic programmes to further equip them for ministry.

Practical and prayerful support from mission partners has been appreciated. A team from Georgia Division (USA Southern) has visited on several occasions during the past five years. Under the leadership of Major William Mockabee (now CS, Sri Lanka) and

Jim Arrowood their caring spirit has encouraged Ugandan Salvationists.

An increase in self-denial and harvest festival contributions during 2011 was the positive response to Bible teaching on the subject of giving.

The women's ministries department was active in training and empowering women's groups. Income was generated through exporting hand-crafted beadwork to the Australia Eastern Territory. 'Naomi' groups brought fresh hope and encouragement to widows.

A new programme to support orphans and vulnerable children was launched in September 2011, funded by USAID. During the next five years it is planned to assist 1,800 children.

Heavy rain storms followed by prolonged drought led to famine in many parts of the country. The Salvation Army International Emergency Response unit provided relief. Eleven boreholes providing safe water were dug in eastern Uganda.

Commissioners Amos and Rosemary Makina (then IS and ZSWM for Africa) conducted a review of Salvation Army work in Uganda.

In April 2012 28 members of international emergency response teams met at Graceland Motel in Kampala, Uganda for an assessment and training conference, led by Commissioner Gerrit Marseille (IHQ). The delegates' visit to Bududa landslide resettlement camp in western Uganda provided opportunity to review and learn from the methods used in the management of this situation.

STATISTICS

Officers 82 (active 78 retired 4) Envoys 2 Corps leaders 91 Cadets 24 Employees 86
Corps 75 Outposts and Outreach Centres 69 Pre-primary Schools 2 Day Care Centre 1 Primary Schools 11 Vocational Centres 3 Institutions 3
Senior Soldiers 10,634 Junior Soldiers 7,134
Personnel serving outside the territory Officers 4

STAFF

Women's Ministries: Col Grace Mnyampi (TPWM) Lt-Col Brigitte Bamanabio (TSWM) Maj Nolega Imbiakha (CCMS/Retired Officers Sec) Maj Miriam Walimbwa (JHL)
Field: Maj Daniel Imbiakha
Finance: Maj Patrick Sithole
Projects: Maj Emmanuel Sichibona
Property: Maj Moses Ndeke
Social Services: Maj Rose Ndeke
Statistics: Capt Jesline Sithole

Training: Capt Alfred Banda
Youth/Candidates: Maj Grace Walukano

DIVISIONS

Central: PO Box 11776, Kampala; Majs Jamin and Topista Wasilwa
Eastern: PO Box 168, Tororo; Majs Peter and Elizabeth Soita
Mbale: PO Box 2214, Mbale; Majs Esau and Margaret Wekala
Southern: PO Box 2012, Busia; Majs Moses and Achola Itwalume
West: PO Box 73, Kigumba via Masindi; Majs Bramwell and Margaret Simiyu

DISTRICTS

Busulwa: PO Box 33, Magale via Mbale; Maj Vincent Nazeba
Lwakhakha: PO Box 33, Magale via Mbale; Maj Augustus Webaale
Mulimani: PO Box 168, Tororo; Maj George Musamali
Sebei: PO Box 2214, Mbale; Maj Esau Wekala

TRAINING COLLEGE

Jinja: PO Box 133, Jinja

SOCIAL SERVICES
Children's Home

Tororo: PO Box 48, Tororo; tel: 045-45244 (acc 54)

Community Centre

Kampala: PO Box 11776, Kampala; tel: 041-532517

Home for Children with Physical Disabilities

Home of Joy, PO Box 1186, Kampala; tel: 041-542409 (acc 30)

Vocational Training Workshops

Kampala (carpentry, catering, tailoring): PO Box 11776, Kampala
Lira (carpentry, tailoring, building): PO Box 13, Lira
Mbalala: Kasenge Vocational Training (carpentry, tailoring): PO Box 11776, Mbalala

'Score' Project for vulnerable children and their households: PO Box 11776, Kampala; tel: 041-533113

WORTH Programme

Income Generation for Women: PO Box 2214, Mbale; tel: 045-79295

UNITED KINGDOM TERRITORY WITH THE REPUBLIC OF IRELAND

Territorial leaders:
Commissioners Clive and Marianne Adams

Territorial Commander:
Commissioner Clive Adams (1 Feb 2013)

Chief Secretary:
Colonel David Hinton (1 Jul 2011)

Territorial Headquarters: 101 Newington Causeway, London SE1 6BN, UK

Tel: [44] 20 7367 4500; email: thq@salvationarmy.org.uk;
website: www.salvationarmy.org.uk

The foundation of the territory dates from the earliest formation of The Salvation Army – prior to the adoption of that title in 1878 – when in July 1865 the Founder, William Booth, took charge of a mission to the East End of London. Certain UK corps were first established as Christian Mission stations.

Throughout the Army's history its work in this geographical area has been organised in a variety of forms and territories, but before 1990 these were all part of International Headquarters administration. However, on 1 November 1990 a restructuring occurred so that now the United Kingdom Territory is separate from International Headquarters and under a single command similar to that of the Army's other territories.

Zone: Europe
Countries included in the territory: Channel Islands, Isle of Man, Republic of Ireland, United Kingdom of Great Britain and Northern Ireland
Languages in which the gospel is preached: Czech, English, Korean, Urdu, Welsh
'The Salvation Army' in Welsh: Byddin Yr Iachawdwriaeth; in Czech: Armáda Spásy
Periodicals: *Kids Alive!*, *Salvationist*, *The War Cry*

CONTINUED financial uncertainty affected many communities in the United Kingdom Territory with the Republic of Ireland. Yet through God's provision and under his guidance, the territory committed £2 million to planting initiatives, to save souls, grow saints and serve suffering humanity. A 'Vision to Plant' conference brought together divisional leaders and teams to pray, reflect and plan strategically for future mission opportunities.

Four regional 'ROOTS' events took place; in Edinburgh, Birmingham, Doncaster and London. These events explored what it means to be a prophetic witness in the face of social injustice and Salvationists were challenged to take seriously the call to social action and justice.

'Change4Change' and 'Kids in Action' were child-led initiatives through which children put their belief into action to make positive differences in local, national and global situations.

ALOVE UK continued its mission to youth; calling a generation to dynamic faith, radical lifestyle, adventurous mission and a fight for justice, by delivering discipleship resources, events and training.

Discipleship was a key focus for all age groups and extensive resources were generated to support this. Spiritual life was developed through age-specific programmes and resources. The place of music in facilitating discipleship was evidenced by ISB 120 at the Royal Albert Hall in London; outstanding musical ability and skill was matched by outstanding ministry in this prestigious venue. A memorable march of witness along the major route in London leading to Buckingham Palace culminated in the eight staff bands from seven nations playing on the Palace forecourt. Despite the rain large crowds watched and listened.

Employment Plus continued William Booth's vision of 'Work for All', providing a 'hand up' rather than a 'hand out' for unemployed people, supporting them into sustained employment. Activities were offered from corps premises and this was a catalyst for integrated mission.

The territory responded to the needs of families by offering life skills programmes, parenting courses and direct practical methods such as food banks. Many corps community programmes received funding from local authorities in the form of grants, governed by service level agreements.

The Salvation Army continued to work with 10 subcontractors to deliver support to male and female victims of human trafficking, under the UK government's Ministry of Justice. The territory's 'safe house' and Lifehouses (residential facilities) played a major part in this work.

Homelessness services adopted a model of service delivery that places education, training and employment at the centre of its holistic approach to support services.

A service review was implemented to assess key performance indicators set for each element of the service offered. 'Supporting People' contracts to deliver homeless services figured prominently in the territory's ministry, although in the current economic climate all funding streams have been affected. A picture of needing to do more and of higher quality, with less financial and personnel resources, emerged from the review.

There was substantial investment in the upgrade of facilities at William Booth College for the training of cadets, officers and all Salvation Army personnel. From the outside the building was not significantly changed, due to its heritage status, but the interior has been transformed. A newly-revamped International Heritage Centre with interactive media and displays is also on-site. The

251

Young people enjoy discussion during a 'ROOTS' conference

"

William Booth Birthplace Museum in Nottingham has been extensively remodelled inside to portray life as it would have been during the Founder's earliest years.

THE SALVATION ARMY TRUSTEE COMPANY
Registered Office: 101 Newington Causeway, London SE1 6BN

THE SALVATION ARMY (REPUBLIC OF IRELAND)
Registered Office: 114 Marlborough St, Dublin 1, Republic of Ireland

STATISTICS
Officers 2,567 (active 1,149 retired 1,418)
Cadets (1st Yr) 26 (2nd Yr) 23 (+ 10 distance learning cadets) **Employees** 5,405
Corps/Outreach Centres/New Plants 697 **Social Services Centres** 106 **Red Shield Defence Services Clubs** 12 **Mobile Units for Service Personnel** 8
Senior Soldiers 28,771 **Adherent Members** 9,135 **Junior Soldiers** 3,946
Personnel serving outside territory Officers 80 Layworkers 5

STAFF
Women's Ministries: Comr Marianne Adams (TPWM) Col Sylvia Hinton (TSWM)
Asst Chief Sec: Lt-Col Carol Telfer

Executive Sec to Territorial Leadership: Col Sylvia Hinton
International Staff Band: B/M Dr Stephen Cobb
International Staff Songsters: S/L Mrs Dorothy Nancekievill
Sec for Business Administration: Lt-Col Ivor Telfer
Asst Sec for Business Admin (Risk and Research): Mr David Rice
Company Sec: Maj John Warner
Finance: Maj John Warner
Internal Audit: Mr Phil Goss
Property: Mr Keith Manners
SAGIC: Mr Gordon Dewar
Strategic Information: Mr Martyn Croft
Trade: Mr Trevor Caffull
Sec for Communications: Lt-Col Marion Drew
Assistant Secretary for Communications: Mr Julius Wolff-Ingham
Editor-in-Chief and Publishing Sec: Maj Martin Hill
Editors: *Salvationist*: tba
The War Cry: Maj Nigel Bovey
Kids Alive!: Mr Justin Reeves
Head of Media: Joanna Inskip
Head of Public Affairs Unit: Dr Helen Cameron
Territorial Ecumenical Officer: Maj John Read
International Heritage Centre: Maj Stephen Grinsted (Director)
Schools and Colleges Unit: Maj Stephen Grinsted (Director)
Marketing and Fundraising: Mr Julius Wolff-Ingham

Sec for Personnel: Lt-Col George Pilkington
  Asst Sec for Personnel: Maj Beverley McCombe
  Asst Sec for Personnel (Leadership Development) Maj Judith Payne
  Human Resources (Employees): Mr Ian Hammond
  Overseas Services Sec: Maj Pam Cameron
  Pastoral Care Unit: Maj Stephen Gowler
  Retired Officers Sec: Maj James Williams
  Safeguarding: Mr Dean Juster
Sec for Programme: Lt-Col Ian Barr
  Anti-Trafficking Response: Maj Anne Read
  Employment Plus: Mrs Helen Robinson
  Evangelism: Maj Drew McCombe
    Adult and Family Ministries: Maj Valerie Mylechreest
    Children's and Youth Ministries:
      Maj Drew McCombe
      Maj Denise Cooper
    Mission Development Unit: Maj Noel Wright
    Music Ministries: B/M Dr Stephen Cobb
  International Development: Maj Heather Poxon
  Family Tracing: Maj Paul Hardy
  Research and Development: Mrs Jacqui King
Social Services: Maj Ray Irving (SocS Sec);
  Maj Paul Kingscott (Deputy – Head of Operations); Homelessness Services:
  Mr Mitch Menagh;
  Older People's Services: Mrs Elaine Cobb
  Red Shield Defence and Emergency Services: Maj Muriel McClenahan
  Special Events: Mr Melvin Hart

WILLIAM BOOTH COLLEGE

Denmark Hill, London SE5 8BQ;
  tel: (020) 7326 2700
  Principal: Lt-Col Anthony Cotterill
  Directors of School for Officer Training:
    Training Programme: Maj Malcolm Martin
    Spiritual Programme: tba
  Director of School for In-Service Training and Development: Maj Gillian Jackson
  Territorial Candidates Director: Maj Mark Herbert

INTERNATIONAL HERITAGE CENTRE (including The William Booth Birthplace Museum, Nottingham) AND SCHOOLS AND COLLEGES UNIT

Denmark Hill, London SE5 8BQ;
  tel: (020) 7326 7801;
  email: heritage@salvationarmy.org.uk;
  Director: Maj Stephen Grinsted

SCOTLAND SECRETARIAT

12a Dryden Rd, Loanhead, Midlothian
EH20 9LZ; tel: (0131) 440 9100;
Scotland Sec: Lt-Col Alan Burns

DIVISIONS

Anglia: 2 Barton Way, Norwich NR1 1DL;
tel: (01603) 724 400; Maj David Jackson (DC)
Maj Joy Allchin (DDWM)

Central North: 80 Eccles New Rd, Salford,
Gtr Manchester M5 4DU; tel: (0161) 743 3900;
Majs Melvyn and Kathleen Jones

Central South: 16c Cowley Rd, Uxbridge,
UB8 2LT; tel: (01895) 208800;
Majs Paul and Jenine Main

East Midlands: Paisley Grove, Chilwell,
Nottingham NG9 6DJ; tel: (0115) 983 5000;
Lt-Cols Mike and Wendy Caffull

East Scotland: 12a Dryden Rd, Loanhead,
Midlothian EH20 9LZ;
tel: (0131) 440 9100;
Major Carol Bailey

Ireland: 12 Station Mews, Sydenham,
Belfast BT4 1TL; tel: (028) 9067 5000;
Majs Alan and Linda Watters

London Central: 1 Tiverton St, London SE1 6NT;
tel: (020) 7378 1021;
Lt-Cols Melvin and Suzanne Fincham

London North-East: Maldon Rd, Hatfield
Peverel, Chelmsford CM3 2HL;
tel: (01245) 383000;
Majs Norman and Margaret Ord

London South-East: 1 East Court, Enterprise Rd,
Maidstone ME15 6JF;
tel: (01622) 775000;
Lt-Cols Peter and Sandra Moran

North Scotland: Deer Rd, Woodside,
Aberdeen AB24 2BL;
tel: (01224) 496000;
Majs Denis and Olive Lomax

North-Western: 16 Faraday Rd, Wavertree
Technology Park, Liverpool L13 1EH;
tel: (0151) 252 6100;
Majs Michael and Lynn Highton

Northern: Balliol Business Park West,
Newcastle upon Tyne NE12 8EW;
tel: (0191) 238 1800;
Majs Darrell and Katrina Thomas

South and Mid Wales: East Moors Rd,
Ocean Park, Cardiff CF24 5SA;
tel: (029) 2044 0600;
Majs Derek and Susan Jones

South-Western: 6 Marlborough Court,
Manaton Close, Matford Business Park,
Exeter EX2 8PF; tel: (01392) 822100;
Majs Ian and Jean Harris

Southern: 6-8 Little Park Farm Rd, Segensworth, Fareham PO15 5TD; tel: (01489) 566800; Lt-Cols Graham and Kirsten Owen

West Midlands: 102 Unett St North, Hockley, Birmingham B19 3BZ; tel: (0121) 507 8500; Maj Samuel Edgar (DC) Maj Beverley Stringer (DDWM)

West Scotland: 4 Buchanan Court, Cumbernauld Rd, Stepps, Glasgow G33 6HZ; tel: (0141) 779 5000; Majs Russell and Catherine Wyles

Yorkshire: 1 Cadman Court, Hanley Rd, Morley, Leeds LS27 0RX; tel: (0113) 281 0100; Lt-Cols William and Gillian Heeley

CONFERENCE CENTRES

Carfax: Bath BA2 4BS; tel: (01225) 462089
St Christopher's: 15 Sea Rd, Westgate-on-Sea, Kent; tel: (01932) 782196
Sunbury Court (incl Recreation Centre and Log Cabin): Lwr Hampton Rd, Sunbury-on-Thames, Middlesex TW16 5PL; tel: (01932) 782196

CONFERENCE AND YOUTH CENTRE

Sunbury Court, Log Cabin and Recreational Centre: Lwr Hampton Rd, Sunbury-on-Thames, Middlesex TW16 5PL; tel: (01932) 782196

SELF-CATERING ACCOMMODATION

Caldew House: Sebergham, Cumbria; tel: (01225) 462089 (large house)
St Christopher's: Westgate-on-Sea, Kent; tel: (01932) 782196 (5 flats)
Sunbury Court, Log Cabin and Recreational Centre: Lower Hampton Rd, Sunbury-on-Thames, Middlesex TW16 5PL; tel: (01932) 782196

FAMILY TRACING SERVICE

101 Newington Causeway, London SE1 6BN; tel: (020) 7367 4747

FARM

Hadleigh: Castle Lane, Hadleigh, Benfleet, Essex; tel: (01702) 558550

HOTELS

Bath: Carfax Hotel, Gt Pulteney St, Bath BA2 4BS; tel: (01225) 462089
Bournemouth: Cliff House, 13 Belle Vue Rd, Southbourne, Dorset BH6 3DA; tel: (01202) 424701 (office); (01202) 425852 (guests)
Westgate-on-Sea: St Christopher's, 15 Sea Rd, Westgate-on-Sea, Kent CT8 8SA; tel: (01932) 782196

INSURANCE CORPORATION

The Salvation Army General Insurance Corporation Ltd, Faith House, 23-24 Lovat Lane, London EC3R 8EB; tel: 0845 634 0260

PASTORAL CARE UNIT

Administration (inc Trauma Care Programme): 101 Newington Causeway, London SE1 6BN; tel: (020) 7367 6580; After-office hours mobile: 0779 503 7651
Counselling Services: 1 Water Lane, Stratford, London E15 4LU; tel: (020) 8536 5480;
Pastoral Support:
London Central, London North-East, UKT personnel departing/arriving from overseas; tel: (020) 7367 6580; mobile: 0779 503 7651
Central South, London South-East, Southern, South-Western; tel: 0772 669 3390
Central North, North-Western, South and Mid Wales, West Midlands; tel: 07714 064987
Northern, Yorkshire, East Midlands, Anglia: tel: (0114) 24402304
Scotland and Ireland: tel: 07726 692605
Director: Maj Stephen Gowler

TRADE (SP&S)

Head Office (and shop): 66-78 Denington Rd, Denington Industrial Estate, Wellingborough, Northants NN8 2QH; tel: (01933) 445445 (mail order); fax: (01933) 445415
Shop: 1 Tiverton St, London SE1 6NT

TRADING (SA TRADING CO LTD)

66-78 Denington Rd, Denington Industrial Estate, Wellingborough, Northants NN8 2QH
Textile Recycling Division: tel: (01933) 441086 email: paul.ozanne@satradingco.org
Charity Shops Division: tel: (01933) 441807 email: reception@satradingco.org

SOCIAL SERVICES DEPARTMENT
Centres for Older People

Bath: Smallcombe House (acc men and women 32, sheltered flat 1)
Buxton: The Hawthorns (acc 34)
Coventry: Youell Court (acc 40)
Edinburgh: Davidson House (acc 40) Eagle Lodge (acc 33)
Glasgow: Eva Burrows Day Centre (places 112)
Hassocks: Villa Adastra (acc 40, day centre 20)
Holywood: The Sir Samuel Kelly Memorial Home (acc 39)

United Kingdom Territory with the Republic of Ireland

London:Alver Bank, Clapham (acc 30)
  Glebe Court, Lewisham (acc 42)
North Walsham: Furze Hill House
  (acc 40, day centre 22)
Nottingham: Notintone House (acc 40)
Prestwich: Holt House, (acc 31)
Sandridge: Lyndon, (acc 32)
Southend-on-Sea: Bradbury Home (acc 34)
Tunbridge Wells: Sunset Lodge (acc 20)
Weston-super-Mare: Dewdown House (acc 40)

Centres for Families (Residential)
Belfast:
  Belfast:Glen Alva (acc family units 20, max
  77 residents)
  Thorndale Parenting Assessment/Family
  Centre, (acc family units 34, single bedsits 4,
  max 125 residents)
Leeds: Mount Cross (acc flats 28,
  max 78 residents)
Portsmouth: Catherine Booth House
  (acc family units 21, max 40 residents)

Refuge from Domestic Abuse (women with children)
Birmingham: Shepherd's Green House;
  contact via West Midlands DHQ (acc 16
  families, 4 single women, max 44 residents)

Centres for People with Learning Difficulties
Kilbirnie: George Steven Centre
Stoke: Lovatt Court

Centres for the Single Homeless
Accrington: (acc 11)
Belfast: Centenary House (acc direct access 80)
  Calder Fountain (attached to Centenary
  House) (registered care 28, resettlement 12)
Birmingham: William Booth Centre (acc 74)
Blackburn: Bramwell House (acc 55)
Braintree: New Direction Centre,
  David Blackwell House (acc 14)
Bristol: Logos House (acc 69)
Cardiff: Crichton House Outreach Services,
  Dowlais Court
  Northlands (acc 26)
Coventry: Harnall (acc 80)
Dublin: Granby Centre (acc units 101)
Dundee: Strathmore Lodge (acc 25)
  Burnside Mill (acc 20)
Edinburgh: Ashbrook (acc 30)
  The Pleasance (acc 37)
Glasgow: Eva Burrows 1st Stop Project, Eva
  Burrows Centre (acc 32)
  Hope House (acc 40)

Wallace of Campsie House (acc 52)
  William Hunter House (acc 43)
Grimsby: The Booth Lifehouse (acc 35)
Hull: William Booth House (acc 113)
Huntingdon: Kings Ripton Court (acc 36)
Ipswich: Lyndon House (acc 39)
Isle of Man: David Gray House (acc 13)
Isle of Wight: Fellowship House (acc 27)
Leamington Spa: Eden Villa (acc 11)
Liverpool: Ann Fowler House (acc 38)
  Darbyshire House (acc 45)
  Green Lane Lifehouse (acc 23)
London: Booth House (acc 150)
  Cambria House (acc 48)
  Edward Alsop Court (acc 108)
  Hopetown (acc 118)
  Riverside House (acc 30)
  Springfield Lodge (acc 35)
Manchester: Wilmott St (acc 79)
Newcastle upon Tyne: City Rd (acc 69)
  Cedar House (acc direct access 18,
  resettlement flats 6)
Nottingham: Sneinton House (acc 70)
Perth: Skinnergate (acc 30)
Plymouth: Devonport House and Zion House
  (acc 72)
Reading: Willow House (acc 38)
St Helens: Salisbury House (acc 68)
Salford: Abbot Lodge (acc 20)
Sheffield: Charter Row (acc 56)
Skegness: Witham Lodge (acc 30)
Southampton: The Booth Centre (acc 46)
Stoke-on-Trent: Vale St (acc 60 + 4 training
  flats)
Sunderland: Swan Lodge (acc 65)
Swindon: Booth House (acc 50)
Warrington: James Lee House (acc 54)

Children's Homes/Centres (Residential)
Dublin: Lefroy Night Light (acc 7 overnight
  emergency beds)
  Lefroy Support Flats (acc 7)
Leeds: Spring Grove (acc 6 female care leavers)

Day Care, Early Years Education and Contact Centres for Children
Bath: The Mews Nursery (registered for 40 total)
Birmingham: Sally Ann's Pre-School and Out of
  School Club (registered for 64 total)
Leeds: Copper Beech Day Nursery and Rainbow
  After-School Club (registered for 62 total)

*There are a further 6 Day Nurseries, 24
Pre-schools/Playgroups, 2 Crèches, 9 Out-of-
School Clubs and 8 Child Contact Centres
attached to social centres and corps.*

Domiciliary Care (elderly)
Community Care Service (Angus) Forfar

Drop-in Centres
Edinburgh: Regener8+
London: No 10 Drop In
Norwich: Pottergate Arc
Southampton: H2O Project

Employment Training Centres
Hadleigh, Essex;
Norwich, Norfolk:

Outreach Teams
Bristol: Logos House, Bridge Project (acc 24)
Cardiff: Bus Project, Ty Gobaith
London: Faith House, King's Cross
York: Homeless Prevention/Resettlement,
    Gillygate

Prison Ministries
Prison Ministries Officer, THQ,
    101 Newington Causeway,
    London SE1 6BN; tel: (020) 7367 4866

Probation Hostel
Isle of Man: David Gray House (acc 9)

Red Shield Services
UK THQ: 101 Newington Causeway,
    London SE1 6BN; tel: (020) 7367 4851
Germany Regional Office: Arndt Strasse,
    Paderborn BFPO 22; tel: [49] (5251) 55763

Sheltered Housing
London: Alver Bank (acc single 6, double 2)
Tunbridge Wells: Charles Court (acc single 9,
    double 8)

Addiction Service
Bristol: Bridge Project (acc 24)
Cardiff: Bridge Project, Ty Gobiath, (acc 23)
Dublin: York House, Alcohol Recovery Unit
    (inc short-term intervention) (acc 80)
Highworth: Gloucester House (Residential
    Rehabilitation Centre), Swindon
    (acc 12, halfway house 3, day programme 5)
London: Greig House (acc 36)
    Riverside House 'Specialist' Homeless Centre
        for People with Addiction Issues
        (acc 31)
    Riverside House Harbour Recovery
        Project (inc detoxification)
        (acc 40)
    Stirling: Harm Reduction Service,
        SA Hall, Drip Rd, FK8 1RA;
        tel: (01786) 448923

Offering Hope to Trafficked Women
The Jarrett Community c/o THQ

Biomedical Services
Biomedical Support Services are
    provided across social work
    disciplines in partnership with the
    University of Kent, Canterbury

A poster designed by Berni
Georges (IHQ) and published
as a call to prayer for victims
of human trafficking

THE UNITED STATES OF AMERICA

National leaders:
Commissioners William A. and Nancy L. Roberts

National Commander:
Commissioner William A. Roberts (1 Nov 2010)

National Chief Secretary:
Colonel William Harfoot (1 Aug 2011)

National Headquarters: 615 Slaters Lane, PO Box 269, Alexandria, VA 22313-0269, USA

Tel: [1] (703) 684 5500

website: www.salvationarmyusa.org

The Salvation Army began its ministry in the United States in October 1879. Lieutenant Eliza Shirley left England to join her parents who had migrated to America in search of work. She held meetings that were so successful that General William Booth sent Commissioner George Scott Railton and seven women officers to the United States in March 1880 to formalise the effort. Their initial street meeting was held on the dockside at Battery Park in New York City the day they arrived.

In only three years, operations had expanded into California, Connecticut, Indiana, Kentucky, Maryland, Massachusetts, Michigan, Missouri, New Jersey, New York, Ohio and Pennsylvania. By 1902 The Salvation Army was operating throughout the United States. Family services, youth, elderly and disaster services are among the many programmes offered in local communities throughout the United States, in Puerto Rico, the Virgin Islands, the Marshall Islands and Guam.

The National Headquarters was incorporated as a religious and charitable corporation in the State of New Jersey in 1982 as 'The Salvation Army National Corporation' and is qualified to conduct its affairs in the Commonwealth of Virginia.

Zone: Americas and Caribbean
Periodicals: *The War Cry, Women's Ministries Resources, Word & Deed – A Journal of Theology and Ministry, Young Salvationist*

SALVATION Army services and programmes touched the lives of approximately 30 million Americans, including thousands affected by catastrophic tornadoes in the Midwestern and Southern parts of the United States in May 2011. Donations of $1,073,017 towards relief services were received in Joplin, Missouri alone.

In June the annual Brengle Holiness Institute took place in Chicago, IL and welcomed 72 selected delegates from the four USA territories.

In August, the 42nd National Seminar on Evangelism, 'Amazing Grace', was attended by 145 delegates and 25 staff members. It was an encouraging and inspiring event.

In September the national leaders, Commissioners William and Nancy Roberts, joined General Linda Bond at Ground Zero in New York City to commemorate the 10th anniversary of the 9/11 terrorist attacks and recognise The Salvation Army's work in serving survivors and emergency responders.

The National Advisory Board's chairperson, Charlotte Jones

Anderson, facilitated The Salvation Army's 15th annual Red Kettle Kick-off half-time show at the Dallas Cowboys' Thanksgiving Day game featuring pop singer Enrique Iglesias.

The second 'Rock the Red Kettle' concert took place in Los Angeles. Hosted by The Salvation Army, this event encouraged volunteerism and philanthropy in young people. Popular artists such as Greyson Chance, Hanson, Cody Simpson, Drake Bell, Honor Society and Colbie Caillat performed for an audience of more than 17,000 at the venue and online. During 2011 Red Kettle Clubs commenced in high schools and many young adults collected donations for The Salvation Army.

A study called 'Growing up in a Downturn' reported that 81% of the Army's youth programmes saw an increase in demand during the year. A report from the US Census Bureau in September 2011 revealed that 46 million Americans are living in poverty. Despite this situation, The Salvation Army's Red Kettle Campaign raised a record-breaking $147.6 million, enabling Salvationists to meet the rising demand for services.

In April 2012, Commissioners William and Nancy Roberts travelled to Japan and witnessed SAWSO's international work first-hand during the first anniversary of the earthquake and tsunami that devastated Japan's Pacific coastline in 2011. Americans donated $9 million to The Salvation Army's recovery work, facilitating the construction of new marketplaces in some of Japan's most devastated fishing villages.

Also in April, during National Volunteer Week, The Salvation Army recognised the 3 million volunteers who have given their services during the past 132 years of Army work in the United States of America.

NATIONAL STATISTICS
(incorporating all USA territories)
Officers 5,330 (active 3,375 retired 1,955) **Cadets** (1st Yr) 170 (2nd Yr) 165 **Employees** 63,925 **Corps** 1,221 **Outposts** 25 **Institutions** 793 **Senior Soldiers** 83,979 **Adherent Members** 16,330 **Junior Soldiers** 24,196

STATISTICS
(National Headquarters)
Officers (active) 24 **Employees** 82

STAFF
Women's Ministries: Comr Nancy L. Roberts (NPWM); tel: (703) 684 5503; Col Susan Harfoot (NSWM, NRVAVS); tel: (703) 684 5514
Asst Nat Chief Sec: Maj Raymond Cooper III ; tel: (703) 684 5508
Nat Treasurer and Nat Sec for Business Administration: Lt-Col Sandra Defibaugh; tel: (703) 684 5507
Nat Sec for Personnel: Lt-Col Janet Banfield ; tel: (703) 684 5512
Nat Sec for Programme: Lt-Col Stephen Banfield; tel: (703) 684 5527
Nat Social Services Sec: Maj Betty A. Israel; tel: (703) 684 5533
Nat Community Relations and Development Sec: Maj George Hood; tel: (703) 684 5526;
Nat Director for Public Policy and Liaison for Emergency Disaster Services: Maj Darryl Leedom; tel: (703) 684 5521
Editor-in-Chief and Nat Literary Sec: Maj Allen Satterlee; tel: (703) 684 5523;
Salvation Army World Service Office (SAWSO): Lt-Col Joan Canning; tel: (703) 684 5524

ARCHIVES AND RESEARCH CENTRE
Email: Archives@usn.salvationarmy.org

USA CENTRAL TERRITORY

Territorial leaders:
Commissioners Paul R. and Carol Seiler

Territorial Commander:
Commissioner Paul R. Seiler
(1 May 2010)

Chief Secretary:
Colonel Merle Heatwole (1 Feb 2011)

Territorial Headquarters: 10 W Algonquin Rd, Des Plaines, IL 60016-6006, USA

Tel: [1] (847) 294-2000; fax: [1] (847) 294-2295; website: www.usc.salvationarmy.org

The Salvation Army was incorporated as a religious and charitable corporation in the State of Illinois in 1913 as 'The Salvation Army' and is qualified to conduct its affairs in all of the states of the territory.

Zone: Americas and Caribbean
USA states included in the territory: Illinois, Indiana, Iowa, Kansas, Michigan, Minnesota, Missouri, Nebraska, North Dakota, South Dakota, Wisconsin
'The Salvation Army' in Spanish: Ejército de Salvación; in Swedish: Frälsningsarmén
Languages in which the gospel is preached: English, Korean, Laotian, Russian, Spanish, Swedish
Periodical: *Central Connection*

MOVING mission forward in the USA Central Territory, Commissioners Paul R. and Carol Seiler (TC and TPWM) invited Salvationists to join them in creating a shared future through five core principles; pursue mission, ignite creativity, uplift consistently, serve vigorously and invest intentionally. Two pilot schemes were launched – an annual review process focused on engaging potential and 'Pathway of Hope', a social services approach to help families in crisis achieve sufficiency and stability.

Retired leaders General Paul A. Rader and Commissioner Kay Rader were inspiring guest speakers at the Festival of Gospel Arts during commissioning weekend in June 2011. Multifaceted meetings showcased a wide range of talent and expressions of creative worship. The winners of a territorial composition contest were announced by Bandmaster William Himes, who had just returned from a tour of the UK with the Chicago Staff Band (CSB) as part of the ISB120 anniversary celebration. He issued a challenge to every corps to have live music in worship by 2020.

The World Services/Self-Denial ingathering reached a record total of $7.6 million.

Eighteen cadets of the Ambassadors of Holiness session were commissioned and ordained. Three months later, the territory welcomed 35 Proclaimers of the Resurrection session for officer training.

Ray and Joan Kroc Corps Community Centers were opened in Green Bay, WI in August, Quincy, IL in September and South Bend, IN in January 2012 respectively. The Chicago, IL Kroc Center was planned to open later in 2012. Territorial plans to meet national youth asset development goals were launched at Kroc Centers in August 2011.

The distinguished musical career of CSB Deputy Bandmaster Peggy Thomas, a brilliant cornetist, was celebrated in a new CD, *Perspectives*. Three USA Central officers were included in the book *Called to Preach*, a sermon collection penned by 35 women officers from many countries.

A territorial men's camp in April attracted 1,000 enthusiastic delegates desiring Christ-centered lives. A social services conference was held in May to equip frontline workers and discuss issues such as human trafficking. The territorial social services department launched online training to meet 'Safe from Harm' abuse risk management standards for people working with children, youth and vulnerable adults.

A territorial jamboree in mid-July attracted more than 300 campers to Minnesota for outdoor fun and inspiration. In late July, the territorial Central Bible Leadership Institute held four mission-oriented workshops for adults in: youth development, urban mission, pastoral crisis intervention and immigrant ministry.

In August, the territory's first women-only adult rehabilitation centre opened in Michigan. Cultural competency was the aim of the territory's biennial Multicultural Ministries Conference in October. In February, a record 400 young adults met for the territorial 'Regeneration' conference.

Summer mission teams served in Argentina, India Central, Poland/Germany and Zimbabwe; young adults interned in Haiti, the Philippines and the Republic of Georgia. Adult global mission teams served in Congo (Brazzaville) and Jamaica.

Emergency disaster services responded in several states across the territory to severe floods and devastating tornadoes. Immediate and long-term care plans to meet physical and spiritual needs were provided by EDS and social services personnel. Long-term recovery efforts continued in Joplin, MO, a city decimated by a massive tornado in Spring 2011.

A landmark 1,000 EDS courses since 2004 have trained over 15,000 people in disaster response work.

STATISTICS

Officers 1,146 (active 716 retired 430) **Cadets** (1st Yr) 35 (2nd Yr) 33 **Employees** 10,248 **Corps** 261 **Institutions** 174 **Corps Plant** 1 **Senior Soldiers** 16,713 **Adherent Members**

2,321 **Junior Soldiers** 3,457
Personnel serving outside territory Officers 25

STAFF

Women's Ministries: Comr Carol Seiler (TPWM)
Col Dawn Heatwole (TSWM)
Maj Carol Wurtz (TCCMS)
Personnel: Lt-Col Jeffrey Smith
Programme: Lt-Col Richard E. Vander Weele
Business: Lt-Col Richard Amick
Adult Rehabilitation Centres: Maj Graham Allan
Audit: Maj David Clark
Candidates: Col Dawn Heatwole
Community Relations and Development: Maj
John Wilkins
Corps Mission and Adult Ministries: Maj
Phillip Aho
Evangelism and Corps Growth: Capt Carol J.
Lewis
Finance: Maj Randall Polsley
Information Technology: Mr Ronald E.
Shoults
Multicultural Ministries: Maj Mary Hammerly
Music and Gospel Arts: B/M William F.
Himes Jr, OF
Pastoral Care Officers: Majs Larry and Margo
Thorson
Property: Maj Cheryl Lawry
Resource Officer and Development: Lt-Col
Dorothy R. Smith
Resource Connection Dept: Mr Robert Jones
Risk Management: Mr Wesley Carter
Social Services: Mrs Maribeth Velasquez
Swanson
Training: Maj Paul Fleeman
Youth: Maj Gail Aho

DIVISIONS

Eastern Michigan: 16130 Northland Dr,
Southfield, MI 48075-5218;
tel: (248) 443-5500; Cols Dennis and
Sharon Strissel
Heartland: 401 NE Adams St, Peoria,
IL 61603-4201; tel: (309) 655-7220;
Maj Evelyn Diaz
Indiana: 3100 N Meridian St, Indianapolis,
IN 46208-4718; tel: (317) 937-7000;
Majs John and Theresa Turner
Kansas and Western Missouri: 3637 Broadway,
Kansas City, MO 64111-2503; tel: (816) 756-
1455; Majs Charles and Sharon Smith
Metropolitan: 5040 N Pulaski Rd, Chicago,
IL 60630-2788; tel: (773) 725-1100;
Lt-Cols Ralph and Susan Bukiewicz
Midland: 1130 Hampton Ave, St Louis, MO

63139-3147; tel: (314) 646-3000;
Majs Lonneal and Patty Richardson
Northern: 2445 Prior Ave, Roseville,
MN 55113-2714; tel: (651) 746-3400;
Lt-Cols Daniel and Rebecca Sjögren
Western: 3612 Cuming St, Omaha,
NE 68131-1900; tel: (402) 898-5900;
Majs Paul and Renea Smith
Western Michigan and Northern Indiana:
1215 E Fulton, Grand Rapids, MI 49503-3849;
tel: (616) 459-3433; Majs Thomas and
Jacalyn Bowers
Wisconsin and Upper Michigan: 11315 W
Watertown Plank Rd, Wauwatosa, WI
53226-0019; tel: (414) 302-4300; Majs Robert
E. and Nancy Thomson, Jr

COLLEGE FOR OFFICER TRAINING

700 W Brompton Ave, Chicago, IL 60657-1831;
tel: (773) 524-2000

UNDER THQ
Conference Centre
10 W Algonquin, Des Plaines, IL 60016-6006

SOCIAL SERVICES
Adult Rehabilitation Centres

Chicago (Central), IL 60654: N Des Plaines St;
tel: (312) 738-4367 (acc 201)
Chicago (North Side), IL 60614: 2258 N
Clybourn Ave; tel: (773) 477-1771 (acc 140)
Davenport (River Valley), IA 52806: 4001 N
Brady St; tel: (563) 323-2748 (acc 86)
Des Moines, IA 50309-4897: 133 E 2nd St;
tel: (515) 243-4277 (acc 58)
Flint, MI 48506: 2200 N Dort Highway;
tel: (810) 234-2678 (acc 121)
Fort Wayne, IN 46802: 427 W Washington Blvd;
tel: (260) 424-1655 (acc 75)
Gary, IN 46402: 1351 W 11th Ave;
tel: (219) 882-9377 (acc 110)
Grand Rapids, MI 49507-1601: 1491 S Division
Ave; tel: (616) 452-3133 (acc 115)
Indianapolis, IN 46202-3915: 711 E Washington
St; tel: (317) 638-6585 (acc 103)
Kansas City, MO 64106: 1351 E 10th St;
tel: (816) 421-5434 (acc 132)
Milwaukee, WI 53202-5999: 324 N Jackson St;
tel: (414) 276-4316 (acc 94)
Minneapolis, MN 55401-1039: 900 N 4th St;
tel: (612) 332-5855 (acc 125)
Omaha, NE 68131-2642: 2551 Dodge St;
tel: (402) 342-4135 (acc 95)
Rockford, IL 61104-7385: 1706 18th Ave;
tel: (815) 397-0440 (acc 72)

USA Central Territory

Romulus, MI 48174-4205: 5931 Middlebelt;
  tel: (734) 729-3939 (acc 111)
St Louis, MO 63108-3211: 3949 Forest Park
  Ave; tel: (314) 535-0057 (acc 101)
South Bend, IN 46601-2226: 510-18 S Main St;
  tel: (574) 288-2539 (acc 60)
Southeast, MI 1627: W Fort St, Detroit,
  MI 48216; tel: (313) 965-7760;
  toll-free: 1-(800) SA Truck (acc 360)
Springfield, IL 62703-1003: 221 N 11th St;
  tel: (217) 528-7573 (acc 85)
Waukegan, IL 60085-6511: 431 S Genesee St;
  tel: (847) 662-7730 (acc 100)

UNDER DIVISIONS
Emergency Lodges
Alton, IL 62002: 525 Alby
Alton, IL 62002: 14-16 E 5th St
Ann Arbor, MI 48108: 3660 Packard Rd
Belleville, IL 62226: 4102 W Main St
Benton Harbor, MI 49022: 645 Pipestone St
Bloomington, IL 61701: 601 W Washington St
Champaign, IL 61820: 2212 N Market St
Chicago, IL 60640: 800 W Lawrence
Columbia, MO 65203: 602 N Ann St
Davenport, IA 52803-5101: 301-307 W 6th St
Decatur, IL 62523: 137 Church St
Detroit, MI 48208-2517: 3737 Humboldt
Detroit, MI 48208-2517: 3737 Lawton
Detroit, MI 48219: 20775 Pembroke
Grand Island, NE 68801-5828; 818 W 3rd St
Hutchinson, KS 67504-0310: 200 S Main
Independence, MO 64050-2664:
  14704 E Truman Rd
Indianapolis, IN 46204: 540 N Alabama St
Jefferson City, MO 65101: 907 Jefferson St
Kankakee, IL 60901: 148 N Harrison
Kankakee, IL 60901: 541 E Court Ave
Kansas City, KS 66102: 6721 State Ave
Kansas City, MO 64127: 6935 Bell Rd
LaCrosse, WI 54601: 223 N 8th St
Lafayette, IN 47904-1934: 1110 Union St
Lawrence, KS 66044: 946 New Hampshire St
Madison, WI 53703: E 630 Washington Ave E
Mankato, MN 56001-2338: 700 S Riverfront Dr
Milwaukee, WI 53205: 1730 N 7th St
Monroe, MI 48161: 815 E 1st St
O'Fallon, MO 63366-2938: 1 William Booth Dr
Olathe, KS 66061: 400-402 E Santa Fe
Omaha, NE 68131: 3612 Cuming St
Peoria, IL 61603: 417 NE Adams St
Peoria, IL 61603: 414 NE Jefferson St
Quincy, IL 62301: 400 Broadway
Rockford, IL 61104: 1706 18th Ave E
St Cloud, MN 56304: 400 Highway 10
St Joseph, MO 64501: 618 S 6th St

St Louis, MO 63132: 10740 W Page Ave
Sheboygan, WI 53081: 710 Pennsylvania Ave
Sioux Falls, SD 57103-0128: 800 N Cliff Ave
Somerset, WI 54025: 203 Church Hill Rd
Springfield, IL 62701: 100 N 9th St
Springfield, MO 65802: 636 N Boonville
Warren, MI 48091: 24140 Mound Rd
Waterloo, IA 50703: 218 Logan Ave
Waterloo, IA 50703: 229 Logan Ave
Waterloo, IA 50703: 603 S Hanchett Rd
Waukesha, WI 53188: 445 Madison St
Wichita, KS 67202-2010: 350 N Market

Senior Citizens' Residences
Chicago, IL 60607: 1500 W Madison
Columbus, IN 47201: 300 Gladstone Ave
Grandview, MO 64030: 6111 E 129th St
Indianapolis, IN 46254-2738: 4390 N High
  School Rd
Kansas City, KS 66112: 1331 N 75th St
Minneapolis, MN 55403-2116: 1421 Yale Pl
Oak Creek, WI 53154: 150 W Centennial Dr
Oak Creek, WI 53154: 180 W Centennial Dr
Omaha, NE 68131: 923 38th St
St Louis, MO 63118: 3133 Iowa St

Harbour Light Centres
Chicago, IL 60607: 1515 W Monroe St;
  tel: (312) 421-5753
Clinton Township, MI 48043: 42590 Stepnitz
Detroit, MI 48201: 3737 Lawton;
  tel. (313) 361-6136
Indianapolis, IN 46222: 2400 N Tibbs Ave;
  tel: (317) 972-1450
Kansas City, KS 66102: 6721 State Ave;
  tel: (913) 232-5400
Minneapolis, MN 55403: 1010 Currie Ave;
  tel: (612) 767-3100
Monroe, MI 48162: 3250 N Monroe
St Louis, MO 63188: 3010 Washington Ave

Substance Abuse Centres
Clinton Township, MI 48043: 42590 Stepnitz
Detroit, MI 48216: 3737 Humboldt
Grand Rapids, MI 49503: 72 Sheldon Blvd SE
Kansas City, MO 64127: 5100 E 24th
Minneapolis, MN 55403: 1010 Currie Ave
Monroe, MI 48162: 3250 N Monroe

Transitional Housing
Appleton, WI 54914: 105 S Badger Ave
Champaign, IL 61820: 502 N Prospect
Cheboygan, MI 49712: 444 S Main St
Clinton Township, MI 48043: 42590 Stepnitz
Detroit, MI 48216: 3737 Humboldt
Detroit, MI 48219: 20775 Pembroke
Duluth, MN 55806: 215 S 27th Ave W

Grand Haven, MI 49417: 310 N Despelder St.
Grand Island, NE 68801-5828: 818 W 3rd St.
Grand Rapids, MI 49503: 1215 E Fulton St
Green Bay, WI 54301: 626 Union Ct
Jefferson City, MO 65101: 907 Jefferson St
Joplin, MO 64801: 320 E 8th St
Kansas City, KS 66102: 6723 State Ave
Kansas City, MO 64111: 101 W Linwood Blvd
Lawrence, KS 66044: 946 New Hampshire
Minneapolis, MN 55403: 1010 Currie
Monroe, MI 48162: 3250 N Monroe
New Albany, IN 47151: 2300 Green Valley Rd
Olathe, KS 66061: 400 E Santa Fe
Omaha, NE 68131: 3612 Cuming St
Pekin, IL 61554: 243 Derby St
Pine Lawn, MO 63120: 4210 Peyton Ln
Rochester, MN 55906: 20 First Ave NE
Rockford, IL 61104: 416 S Madison
Steven's Point, WI 54481: 824 Fremont
St Louis, MO 63118: 2740 Arsenal
St Paul, MN 55108: 1471 Como Ave W
Sioux Falls, SD 57103-0128; 800 N Cliff Ave
Springfield, MO 65802: 10740 W Chestnut Expy
Waterloo, IA 50703: 149 Argyle St
Wausau, WI 54401-4630: 113 S Second St
Wichita, KS 67202-2010: 350 Market

Child Day Care

Benton Harbor, MI; Bloomington, IN;
    Chicago, IL; DeKalb, IL; Emporia, KS;
    Kansas City, KS; Kansas City, MO; Lansing,
    MI; Menasha, WI; Mishawaka, IN;
    Oak Creek, WI; Olathe, KS; Omaha, NE;
    Pekin, IL; Peoria, IL; Plymouth, MI;
    Rockford, IL; Royal Oak, MI;
    Sheboygan, WI; St. Paul, MN; Topeka, KS;
    Traverse City, MI

Youth Group Home

Omaha, NE 68131-1998: 3612 Cuming St

Emergency Shelter Care of Children

Kansas City, MO 64111: 101 W Linwood Blvd
North Platte, NE 69101: 704 S Welch Ave
Oak Park, IL 60302-1713: 924 N Austin
Omaha, NE 68131: 3612 Cuming St
St Paul, MN 55108-2542: 1471 Como Ave W
Wichita, KS 67202-2010: 350 N Market

Emergency Shelter of Young Adults

St. Paul, MN 55108-2542; 1471 Como Ave W

Head Start Programmes

Chicago, IL 60651: 4255 W Division
Chicago, IL 60644: 500 S Central
Chicago, IL 60651: 1345 N Karlov
Chicago, IL 60607: 1 N Ogden

Chicago, IL 60621: 945 W 69th St
Chicago, IL 60649: 1631 E 71st St
Saginaw, MI 48602: 2030 N Carolina St

Early Head Start

Omaha, NE 68131: 3612 Cuming St.

Homes (with facilities for unmarried mothers)

Grand Rapids, MI 49503: 1215 E Fulton St;
tel: (616) 459-9468 (teen-parent centre)
Omaha, NE 68131-1998: 3612 Cuming St

Latchkey Programmes

DeKalb, IL (2); Evanston, IL; Fort Wayne, IN;
    Gary-Merrillville, IN; Huntington, IN; Huron,
    SD; Indianapolis, IN; Jacksonville, IL; Newton,
    IA; North Platte, NE; Omaha, NE; Pekin, IL;
    Royal Oak, MI; Springfield, MO;
    St Louis, MO (2); Wyandotte, MI

Residential Services for Mentally Ill

Omaha, NE 68108: 819 Dorcas St

Permanent and/or Supportive Housing

Coon Rapids, MN 55433: 10347 Ibis Ave
Indianapolis, IN 46204: Barton Center,
    222 E Michigan St
Jefferson City, MO 65101: 907 Jefferson St
Joplin, MO 64801: 320 E 8th St
Kansas City, KS 66102: 6723 State Ave
Kansas City, MO 64111: 101 W Linwood
Mankato, MN 56001: 700 S Riverfront Dr
Minneapolis, MN 55403: 53 Glenwood Ave
Omaha, NE: 3612 Cuming St
Rochester, MN 55906: 120 N Broadway
St Louis, MO 63103: 205 N 18th St
St Louis, MO 63132: 10740 W Page Ave
St Paul, MN 55108: 1471 Como Ave W

Foster Care

Wichita, KS 67202: Koch Center, 350 N Marat

Medical/Dental Clinics

Grand Rapids, MI 49503: 1215 E Fulton St
Rochester, MN 55906: 120 N Broadway
Sheboygan, WI 53081: 710 Pennsylvania Ave

Legal Aid Clinic

Detroit, MI 48201: 3737 Lawton

In addition, fresh-air camps, youth centres, community centres, red shield clubs, day nurseries, family service and emergency relief bureaux are attached to corps and divisions

USA EASTERN TERRITORY

Territorial leaders:
Commissioners Barry C. and Sue Swanson

Territorial Commander:
Commissioner Barry C. Swanson
(1 Feb 2013)

Chief Secretary:
Colonel William R. Carlson (1 Aug 2010)

Territorial Headquarters: 440 West Nyack Road, PO Box C-635, West Nyack, New York 10994-1739, USA

Tel: [1] (845) 620-7200; website: www.salvationarmy-usaeast.org

The Salvation Army was incorporated as a religious and charitable corporation in the State of New York in 1899 as 'The Salvation Army' and is qualified to conduct its affairs in all of the states of the territory.

Zone: Americas and Caribbean
USA states included in the territory: Connecticut, Delaware, Kentucky, Maine, Massachusetts, New Hampshire, New Jersey, New York, Ohio, Pennsylvania, Rhode Island, Vermont
Other countries included in the territory: Puerto Rico, Virgin Islands
'The Salvation Army' in Korean: Koo Sei Kun; in Norwegian: Frelsesarmeen; in Spanish: Ejército de Salvación; in Swedish: Frälsningsarmén
Languages in which the gospel is preached: Creole, English, Korean, Laotian, Portuguese, Russian, Spanish, Swedish
Periodicals: *¡Buenas Noticias!* (Spanish), *Cristianos en Marcha* (Spanish), *Good News!* (English and Korean), *Priority!*, *Ven a Cristo Hoy* (Spanish)

DURING territorial officers' councils, Commissioner R. Steven Hedgren (then TC) shared his vision 'Army Essential/Essential Army' with more than 1,200 officers at Hershey, PA. The concept of the vision is a fundamental plan to save the lost and to bring them to the Lord. Commissioner Hedgren said the plan 'is rooted in the very DNA of every Salvationist. Every General from the Founder to our current leader has sought to lead us back to an ideal of first things – and forward to the practical effectiveness of our present reality.' He challenged officers to develop strategies and to set goals for their ministries, including Sunday school, senior and junior soldiership, ARC, adherent members, corps cadet classes, and 'Bible Bowl'. Each officer received a copy of the commissioner's newly-published book, *Mapping our Salvationist DNA: Beliefs, Values, Behaviors.*

The 42 cadets of the Ambassadors of Holiness session were commissioned and ordained as Salvation Army officers. The territorial commander challenged them to 'work hard, create harmony and live a holy life'.

The Ray and Joan Kroc Corps Community Centers continued to develop. In Philadelphia, 49 senior soldiers and 10 junior soldiers were enrolled. They included teachers, nurses, police officers, a beautician, a caterer, computer technicians, college students and retired people. In the centre's first year 8,661 members have enrolled in social service, recreational, and educational programmes. The Scholarship Member programme had 942 members and 140 staff team members worked to meet the needs of all age groups.

A capacity crowd filled Centennial Memorial Temple in New York City last September to welcome both the 39 cadets of the Proclaimers of the Resurrection session and General Linda Bond, on her first visit to the United States as the Army's international leader. The New York Staff Band, Eastern Territorial Songsters and a contemporary worship band participated during the event.

The Candidates' Seminar and Railton Preview Weekend in February drew more than 300 delegates – a record number. Keynote speakers, drama teams and invited guests vividly portrayed the theme 'Are You Ready?', describing the power of being willing to accept God's call to service.

The fourth Mission Advance Conference attracted 100 delegates. Training in either Natural Church Development or small group ministries was delivered to 170 corps.

The New York Staff Band (Bandmaster Ronald Waiksnoris) celebrated its 125th anniversary with a concert at New York's historic Carnegie Hall. The guest artistes were The King's Singers, a renowned British a cappella group; Salvationist Philip Cobb, principal trumpet of the London Symphony Orchestra; and Philip Smith, former staff bandsman and current principal trumpet of the New York Philharmonic.

STATISTICS
Officers 1,656 (active 1,031 retired 625)
    Cadets 76 **Employees** 9,668
Corps 369 **Outposts** 2 **Institutions** 75
Senior Soldiers 21,803
    Adherent Members 8,084
    Junior Soldiers 8,814
Personnel serving outside territory Officers 37
    Layworker 1

STAFF
Women's Ministries: Comr Sue Swanson (TPWM) Col Marcella Carlson (TSWM) Lt-Col Sharon Tillsley (TMFS) Maj Edelweiss G. Diaz (TCCM, TWAS) Capt Kathleen J. See (OCS)
Asst Chief Sec: Lt-Col Barbara Hunter
Personnel: Lt-Col Mark W. Tillsley
Programme: Lt-Col Kenneth W. Maynor
Business: Lt-Col James W. Reynolds
Territorial Ambassadors for Evangelism: Lt-Cols Howard and Patricia Burr
Territorial Ambassador for Holiness: Maj Young Sung Kim
Territorial Ambassador for Prayer/Spiritual Formation: Lt-Col Cheryl A. Maynor
ARC Commander: Lt-Col Timothy Raines
Audit: Maj John Cramer
Candidates: Maj Thomas M. Lyle
Community Relations/Development: Maj John Hodgson
Education: Maj Robin R. Lyle
Finance: Maj Glenn C. Bloomfield
Information Technology: Mr Paul Kelly

Legal: Maj Thomas A. Schenk
Literary: Linda D. Johnson
Mission and Culture: Maj Betty Pate
Music: B/M Ronald Waiksnoris
  New York Staff Band: B/M Ronald Waiksnoris
  Territorial Songsters: S/L Gavin Whitehouse
Officers' Services/Records: Maj Deborah K.
  Goforth
Pastoral Care and Spiritual Special:
  Maj David E. Antill
Property/Mission Expansion: Maj Jorge E. Diaz
Risk Management: Mr Samuel C. Bennett
Social Services: Maj Claranne Meitrott
Supplies/Purchasing: Maj Ronald Lugiano
Training: Maj Ronald R. Foreman
Youth: Maj James W. Betts, III

DIVISIONS

Eastern Pennsylvania and Delaware:
  701 N Broad St, Philadelphia, PA 19123;
  tel: (215) 787-2800; Lt-Cols Donald W. and
  Renée P. Lance
Empire State: 200 Twin Oaks Dr, PO Box 148,
  Syracuse, NY 13206-0148; tel: (315) 434-1300;
  Majs Donald D. and Arvilla Hostetler
Greater New York: 120 West 14th St, New
  York, NY 10011-7393; tel: (212) 337-7200;
  Lt-Cols Guy D. and Henrietta Klemanski
Massachusetts: 25 Shawmut Rd, Canton,
  MA 02021; tel: (339) 502-5934;
  Majs David E. and Naomi R. Kelly
New Jersey: 4 Gary Rd, Union, NJ 07083-5598,
  PO Box 3170, 07083; tel: (908) 851-9300;
  Majs Donald and Vicki Berry
Northeast Ohio: 2507 E 22nd St, Cleveland, OH
  44115-3202, PO Box 5847, 44101-0847;
  tel: (216) 861-8185; Cols Steven M. and Janice
  A. Howard
Northern New England: 297 Cumberland Ave,
  Portland, ME 04101, PO Box 3647, 04104;
  tel: (207) 774-6304; Majs James P. and Patricia
  J. LaBossiere
Puerto Rico and Virgin Islands: San Juan PR,
  00901-2235, PO Box 71523, 00936-8623;
  tel: (787) 999-7000; Maj Jorge L. and Capt
  Limaris Marzan
Southern New England: 855 Asylum Ave,
  Hartford, CT 06105, PO Box 628, 06142-0628;
  tel: (860) 543-8400; Majs David A. and
  Eunice M. Champlin
Southwest Ohio and Northeast Kentucky:
  114 E Central Parkway, Cincinnati, OH 45202,
  PO Box 596, 45201; tel: (513) 762-5600;
  Majs Hubert S. and Kathleen J. Steele
Western Pennsylvania: 700 N Bell Ave,
  PO Box 742, Carnegie, PA 15106;

tel: (412) 446-1500; Majs William H. and
Joan I. Bode

SCHOOL FOR OFFICER TRAINING
201 Lafayette Ave, Suffern, NY 10901-4798;
  tel: (845) 357-3501

THE SALVATION ARMY
RETIREMENT COMMUNITY
1400 Webb St, Asbury Park, NJ 07712;
  tel: (732) 775-2200; John Coolican
  (Residence Manager) (acc 32)

SOCIAL SERVICES
Adult Rehabilitation Centres
(*Includes facilities for women)
Akron, OH 44311: 1006 Grant St, PO Box 1743;
  tel: (330) 773-3331 (acc 83)
Albany, NY 12206: 452 Clinton Ave,
  tel: (518) 465-2416 (acc 90)
Altoona, PA 16602: 200 7th Ave,
  PO Box 1405, 16603;
  tel: (814) 946-3645 (acc 39)
Binghamton, NY 13904: 3-5 Griswold St;
  tel: (607) 723-5381 (acc 62)
Boston (Saugus), MA 01906: 209 Broadway
  Rte 1; tel: (781) 231-0803 (acc 125)
Bridgeport CT 06607: 1313 Connecticut Ave; tel:
  (203) 367-8621 (acc 50)
Brockton, MA 02301: 281 N Main St;
  tel: (508) 586-1187 (acc 56)
Brooklyn, NY 11217: 62 Hanson Pl;
  tel: (718) 622-7166 (acc 136)
Buffalo, NY 14217-2587: 1080 Military Rd,
  PO Box 36, 14217-0036; tel: (716) 875-2533
  (acc 90)
Cincinnati, OH 45212: 2250 Park Ave,
  PO Box 12546, Norwood, OH 45212-0546;
  tel: (513) 351-3457 (acc 150)
Cleveland, OH 44103: 5005 Euclid Ave;
  tel: (216) 881-2625 (acc 159)
Columbus, OH 43207: 1675 S High St;
  tel: (614) 221-4269 (acc 122)
Dayton, OH 45402: 913 S Patterson Blvd;
  tel: (937) 461-2769 (acc 72)
Erie, PA 16501: 1209 Sassafras St, PO Box 6176,
  16512; tel: (814) 456-4237 (acc 50)
Harrisburg, PA 17110: 3650 Vartan Way,
  PO Box 60095, 17106-0095;
  tel: (717) 541-0203 (acc 100)
Hartford, CT 06132: 333 Homestead Ave,
  PO Box 320440; tel: (860) 527-8106 (acc 110)
Hempstead, NY 11550: 194 Front St;
  tel: (516) 481-7600 (acc 100)
Jersey City, NJ 07302: 248 Erie St; PO Box 261
  07303; tel: (201) 653-3071 (acc 75)

Mount Vernon, NY 10550: 745 S Third Ave;
tel: (914) 664-0800 (acc 80)

Newark, NJ 07101: 65 Pennington St, PO Box 815;
tel: (973) 589-0370 (acc 125)

New Haven, CT 06511: 301 George St; tel: (203)
865-0511 (acc 45)

New York, NY 10036: 535 W 48th St;
tel: (212) 757-7745 (acc 140)

Paterson, NJ 07505: 31 Van Houten St,
PO Box 1976, 07509; tel: (973) 742-1126
(acc 89)

Philadelphia, PA 19128: 4555 Pechin St;
PO Box 26099, tel: (215) 483-3340 (acc 138)

Pittsburgh, PA 15203: 44 S 9th St;
tel: (412) 481-7900 (acc 127)

Portland, ME 04101: 30 Warren Ave,
PO Box 1298, 04104; tel: (207) 878-8555
(acc 70)

Poughkeepsie, NY 12601: 570 Main St;
tel: (845) 471-1730 (acc 50)

Providence, RI 02906: 201 Pitman St;
tel: (401) 421-5270 (acc 129)

Rochester, NY 14611: 745 West Ave;
tel: (585) 235-0020 (acc 135)

San Juan, PR 00903: ARC, Fernández Juncos Ave,
cnr of Valdés #104, Puerta de Tierra,
PO Box 13814, 00908; tel: (787) 724-2525
(acc 36)

Scranton, PA 18505: 610 S Washington Ave,
PO Box 3064; tel: (570) 346-0007 (acc 62)

Springfield, MA 01104: 285 Liberty St,
PO Box 1569, 01101-1569;
tel: (413) 785-1921 (acc 70)

Syracuse, NY 13224: 2433 Erie Blvd East;
tel: (315) 445-0520 (acc 100)

Toledo, OH 43602: 27 Moorish Ave,
PO Box 355 43697; tel: (419) 241-8231 (acc 60)

Trenton, NJ 08638: 436 Mulberry St,
PO Box 5011; tel: (609) 599-9801 (acc 86)

Wilkes-Barre, PA 18702: 163 Hazle St,
PO Box 728, 18703-0728; tel: (570) 822-4248
(acc 52)

Wilmington, DE 19801: 107 S Market St;
tel: (302) 654-8808 (acc 81)

Worcester, MA 01603: 72 Cambridge St;
tel: (508) 799-0520 (acc 115)

ATTACHED TO DIVISIONS
Adult Day Care

Buffalo, NY 14202: Golden Age Center,
Day Programme for Homeless People,
960 Main St; tel: (716) 883-9800

Lancaster, OH 43130: 228 W. Hubert Ave,
tel: (740) 687-1921, ext 111 (acc 50)

Syracuse, NY 13202: 749 S Warren St;
tel: (315) 479-1309

Extended In-home Service for the Elderly

Syracuse, NY 13202: 749 S Warren St;
tel: (315) 479-1309

Adult Rehabilitation

Kenmore, NY 14217: 1080 Military Rd;
tel: (716) 875-2533 (acc 90)

Day Care Centres

Akron, OH 44303: Child Development Center,
135 Hall St; tel: (330) 762-8177 (acc 74)

Boston, MA 02124: 26 Wales St;
tel: (617) 436-2480 (acc 70)

Bronx, NY 10451: 425 E 159th St;
tel: (718) 742-2346 (acc 45)

Bronx, NY 10457: 2121 Washington Ave;
tel: (718) 563-1530 (acc 69)

Brooklyn, NY 11212: 280 Riverdale Ave;
tel: (718) 345-2488 (acc 100)
Sutter Day Care; 20 Sutter Ave;
tel: (718) 773-3041 (acc 55)

Brooklyn, NY 11216: 110 Kosciusko St;
tel: (718) 857-7264 (acc 39)

Brooklyn, NY 11221: 1151 Bushwick Ave;
tel: (718) 455-0100 (acc 55)

Cambridge, MA 02139: 402 Massachusetts Ave,
PO Box 390647; tel: (617) 547-3400
(acc 28)

Cincinnati, OH 45202: 3501 Warsaw Ave;
tel: (513) 251-1451 (acc 112)

Danbury, CT 06813-0826: 15 Foster St,
PO Box 826; tel: (203) 792-7505 (acc 30)

Hartford, CT 06105: 121-123 Sigourney St;
tel: (860) 543-8488

Hartford, CT 06120: 100 Nelson St;
tel: (860) 543-8419

Jersey City, NJ 07034: 562 Bergen Ave,
PO Box 4237, Bergen Stn;
tel: (201) 435-7355 (acc 70)

Lexington, KY 40508: 736 W Main St;
tel: (859) 252-7709 (acc 80)

Meriden, CT 06450-0234: 23 St Casimir Dr,
PO Box 234; tel: (203) 235-6532 (acc 27)

Morristown, NJ 07960: 95 Spring St,
PO Box 9150; tel: (973) 538-0543 (acc 95)

New York, NY 10034: 3732 Tenth Ave;
tel: (212) 569-4300 (acc 60)

Philadelphia (Kroc), PA 19129: 4200
Wissahickon Ave; tel: (215) 717-1200 (acc 78)

Syracuse, NY 13202:
677 S Salina St; Cab Horse Commons,
tel: (315) 479-1113
South Salina Street Infant Care Center,
tel: (315) 479-1329;
749 S Warren St; School Age Day Care,
Cab Horse Commons, tel: (315) 479-1334

Wilmington, DE 19899: 107 W 4th St;
tel: (302) 472-0712 (acc 110)

Family Centres

Dorchester, MA 02125: The Salvation Army
Ray and Joan Kroc Corps Community Center,
650 Dudley Street; tel: (617) 318-6900

Newark, NJ 07102: Newark Area Services
Kinship Care and Legal Guardianship,
Grand Family Success Center,
699 Springfield Ave; tel: (973) 373-5062

Oil City, PA 16301: The Salvation Army
Dental Center, 217 Sycamore St;
tel: (814) 677-4056

Development Disabilities Services

Beaver Falls, PA 15010: Friendship Homes
Program for Developmentally Disabled,
414 16th St; tel: (724) 846-2330

Bronx, NY 10457: Topping Ave Residence,
1638-1640 Topping Ave; tel: (718) 466-1567
(acc 8)

Brooklyn, NY 11220: Centennial House,
426 56th St; tel: (718) 492-4415 (acc 9)

Brooklyn, NY 11237: Decade House,
315 Covert St; tel: (718) 417-1583 (acc 10)

Brooklyn, NY 11206: Millennium House,
13 Pulaski St; tel: (718) 222-0736 (acc 8)

Glendale, NY 11385: Glendale House,
71-29 70th St; tel: (718) 381-7329 (acc 10)

Jamaica, NY 11423: Family Care,
90-23 161st St; tel: (718) 206-9171 (acc 16)

Philadelphia, PA 19123: Developmental
Disabilities Program, 701 N Broad St,
Administrative Offices; tel: (215) 787-2804
(community homes 46, acc 100)

South Ozone Park, NY 11420: Hope House, 115-
37 133rd St; tel: (718) 322-1616 (acc 9)

Springfield, OH 45501: Hand N'Hand Activity
Center for Adults with Disabilities,
15 S Plum St; tel: (937) 322-3434

St Albans, NY 11412: Pioneer House, 104-14
186th St; tel: (718) 264-8350 (acc 12)

Evangeline Residence

New York, NY 10011: 123 W 13th St (Markle
Memorial Residence); tel: (212) 242-2400

Family Counselling

Boston, MA 02118: Family Service Bureau, 1500
Washington St; tel: (617) 236-7233;
fax: (617) 236-0123

Buffalo, NY 14202: Emergency Family Assistance,
Supervised Visitation Program; Conflict
Resolution/Anger Management Program;
960 Main St; tel: (716) 883-9800

Cincinnati, OH 45210: Cincinnati Family Service

Bureau, 131 E 12th; tel: (513) 762-5660

Cincinnati, OH 45224: Cincinnati Center Hill
Family Service Bureau, 6381 Center Hill Ave,
tel: (513) 242-9100

Cincinnati, OH 45205: Cincinnati West Side
Family Service Bureau, 3503 Warsaw Ave,
tel: (513) 251-1424

Newport, KY 41072: N Kentucky Family Service
Bureau, 340 W 10th St; tel: (859) 431-1063

Pittsburgh, PA 15206: Family Caring Center,
6017 Broad St; tel: (412) 362-0891

Rochester, NY 14604-4310: Rochester
Emergency and Family Services, 70 Liberty
Pole Way, PO Box 41210; tel: (716) 987-9540

San Juan, PR 00921-2118: Family Services for
Victims of Crime, 1327 Americo Miranda Ave,
PO Box 10601, 00922-0601;
tel: (787) 749-0027, 0029

Syracuse, NY 13202:
Family Services, 749 S Warren St;
tel: (315) 479-1369
Family Place Visitation Center, 350 Rich St;
. tel: (315) 474-2931

Foster Home Services

Allentown, PA 18109: Foster Care In-Home
Placement Services, Adoption Services and
Administrative Services, 425 Allentown Dr,
Suite 1; tel: (610) 821-7706

Group Home for Adolescents

Fall River, MA 02720: Gentle Arms of Jesus Teen
Living Center, 429 Winter St;
tel: (508) 324-4558 (acc 15)

Harbour Light Centres

Boston, MA 02118: Adult Women's Emergency
Shelter, 407-409 Shawmut Ave,
PO Box 180130; tel: (617) 536-7469 (acc 74)

Cleveland, OH 44115-2376: Harbor Light
Complex, 1710 Prospect Ave;
tel: (216) 781-3773 (acc 221)

Pittsburgh, PA 15233: 865 W North Ave;
tel: (412) 231-0500 (acc 50)

Hotels, Lodges, Emergency Homes

Akron, OH 44302: Booth Manor Emergency
Lodge, 216 S Maple St; tel: (330) 762-8481 ext
1113 (acc 62)

Allentown, PA 18102: Hospitality House,
344 N 7th St; tel: (610) 432-0128 (acc 65)

Bellaire, OH 43906: 315 37th St;
tel: (740) 676-6225 (acc 40)

Brooklyn, NY 11207: Bushwick Family
Residence, 1675 Broadway; tel: (718) 574-2701
(acc families 87)

Brooklyn, NY 11203: Kingsboro Men's Shelter,

681 Clarkson Ave; tel: (718) 363-7738 (acc 126)

Bronx, NY 10456: Franklin Women's Shelter and Referral, 1122 Franklin Ave; tel: (347) 417-8200 (acc 200)

Bronx, NY 10457: Anthony Annex (Franklin) tel: (347) 590-1508 (acc 49)

Buffalo, NY 14202: 960 Main St, Emergency Family Shelter; tel: (716) 884-4798 (acc 108)

Cambridge, MA 02139-0008: Day Drop-in Shelter for Men and Women/Night Shelter for Men, 402 Mass Ave, PO Box 390647; tel: (617) 547-3400 (acc 200/50)

Carlisle, PA 17013: Genesis House (Men's Emergency Housing), 24 E Pomfret St; tel: (717) 249-1411

Chester, PA 19013: Stepping Stone Program, 151 W 15th St; tel: (610) 874-0423 (acc 35)

Cincinnati, OH 45210: Emergency Shelter, 131 E 12th St, PO Box 238; tel: (513) 762-5655 (acc 24)

Cleveland, OH 44115: Zelma George Family Shelter, 1710 Prospect Ave; tel: (216) 641-3712 (acc 110)

Concord, NH 03301: McKenna House (Adult Shelter), 100 S Fruit St; tel: (603) 228-3505 (acc 26)

East Stroudsburg, PA 18301: 226 Washington St; tel: (570) 421-3050

Elizabeth, NJ 07201: 1018 E Grand St; tel: (908) 352-2886 (acc 45)

Elmira, NY 14902: 414 Lake St, PO Box 293; tel: (607) 732-0314 (24-hour Domestic Violence Hotline); Victims of Domestic Violence Safe House (acc 15)

Hartford, CT 06105: 225 S Marshall St; Family Shelter; tel: (860) 543-8423 Emergency Shelter; tel: (860) 543-8430

Jamaica, NY 11434: Springfield Family Residence, 146-80 Guy R. Brewer Blvd; tel: (718) 521-5090 (acc families 82)

Jamestown, NY 14702: Anew Center: Domestic and Rape Crisis Programs, PO Box 368; tel: (716) 661-3894; 24-hour Hotline tel: (800) 252-8748 (acc 13)

Johnstown, PA 15901: Emergency Shelter; tel: (814) 539-3110 (acc 24)

Laconia, NH 03246: The Carey House, 6 Spring St; tel: (603) 528-8086 (acc 30)

Lexington, KY 40508: Early Learning Center Families, 736 W Main St; tel: (859) 252-7706 (acc 129)

Montclair, NJ 07042-2776: 68 N Fullerton Ave; tel: (973) 744-8666 (acc 18)

Newark, OH 43055: 250 E Main St; tel: (740) 345-3289 (acc 60)

New Britain, CT 06050: 78 Franklin Sq; tel: (860) 225-8491 (acc 25 men)

Norristown, PA 19404: 533 Swede St; tel: (610) 275-9225 (acc 41)

Northport, NY 11768-0039: Northport Veterans' Residence, 79 Middleville Rd, Bldg 11, PO Box 300; tel: (631) 262-0601 (acc 41)

Perth Amboy, NJ 08862-0613: Seasonal Shelter for Men, 433 State St; tel: (732) 826-7040 (acc 20)

Philadelphia, PA 19107: Eliza Shirley House, 1320 Arch St; tel: (215) 568-5111 (acc 125)

Philadelphia, PA 19123: Red Shield Family Residence, 715 N Broad St; tel: (215) 787-2887 (acc 100)

Pittsburgh, PA 15206: Family Caring Center, 6017 Broad St; tel: (412) 362-0891 (acc 40)

Pottstown, PA 19464: Lessig-Booth Family Residence, 137 King St; tel: (610) 327-0836 (acc 32)

Queens (Jamaica), NY 11435: Briarwood Family Residence, 80-20 134th St; tel: (718) 268-3395 (acc 91)

Rochester, NY 14604-4310: Men's Emergency Shelter, Booth Haven, 70 Liberty Pole Way, PO Box 41210; tel: (585) 987-9500 (acc 39) Women's Shelter, Hope House, 100 West Ave, PO Box 41210; tel: (585) 697-3430 (acc 25) Safe Haven Emergency Shelter, 60 Liberty Pole Way, PO Box 21210; tel: (585) 987-9540 (acc 16)

San Juan, PR 00903: Homeless Shelter, Proyecto Esperanza, Fernández Juncos, cnr Valdés; tel: (787) 722-2370

Schenectady, NY 12305: Evangeline Booth Home and Women's Shelter, 168 Lafayette St; tel: (518) 370-0276 (acc 17)

Syracuse, NY 13202: Parenting Center, 667 S Salina St; tel: (315) 479-1330 (acc 30) Emergency Lodge, 749 S Warren St; tel: (315) 479-1332

Trenton, NJ 08601: Homeless Drop-in Center, 575 E State St; tel: (609) 599-9373

Waterbury, CT 06720: 74 Central Ave; tel: (203) 756-1718

West Chester, PA 19380: Railton House, 101 E Market St; tel: (610) 696-7434 (acc 17)

Wilmington, DE 19899: Booth Social Service Center, 104 W 5th St; tel: (302) 472-0764 (acc 52)

Wooster, OH 44691: 24-Hour Open Door Emergency Shelter, 433 S Market St; tel: (330) 264-4704 (acc 44)

Zanesville, OH 43701: 515 Putnam Ave; tel: (740) 454-8953 (acc 35)

HIV Services

Bronx, NY 10458: 601 Crescent Ave;
tel: (718) 329-5410
Newark, NJ 07102: 45 Central Ave;
tel: (973) 623-5959
New York, NY 10010: 340 East 24th St;
tel: (212) 585-6085

Homeless Youth and Runaways

Rochester, NY 14604-1210: Genesis House,
35 Ardmore St, PO Box 41210;
tel: (585) 235-2600 (acc 14)
Syracuse, NY 13205: Barnabas House,
1912 S Salina St; tel: (315) 475-9774 (acc 11)
Booth House and Host Home, 264 Furman St;
tel: (315) 471-7628 (acc 8)

Transitional Housing Programme

Allentown, PA 18101; Fleming Hospital House,
344 N 7th St; tel: (610) 432-0128
Arlington, MA 02474-6597: Wellington House,
6510, 8 Wellington St (Single Resident
Occupancy); tel: (781) 643-8120 (acc 20)
Carlisle, PA 17013; Stuart House, 20 E Pomfret St;
tel: (717) 249-1411 (acc 41)
Cleveland, OH 44103: Railton House, 6000
Woodland; tel: (216) 361-6778 (acc 56)
Cleveland, OH 44115: Pass Programme, 1710
Prospect Ave; tel: (216) 619-4722 (acc 75)
Project Share, 2501 E 22nd St;
tel: (216) 623-7492 (acc 29)
Lancaster, PA 17603: 131 South Queen St;
tel: (717) 397-7565 (acc 21)
Norristown, PA 19404; Faith and Bridge
Programmes, 533 Swede St; tel: (610) 275-4183

Perth Amboy, NJ 08862-0613: Care House
Transitional Residence, 433 State St;
tel: (732) 293-1400 (acc veterans 11,
homeless men 7)
Philadelphia, PA 19147: Reed House Permanent
Housing, 1320 S 32nd St; tel: (215) 755-6789
(acc 66)
Philadelphia, PA 19123: Shelter Plus Care
Program Permanent Housing,
tel: (215) 787-2978 (acc 60)
Pottstown, PA 19464: Transitional Housing,
137 King St; tel: (610) 326-1621
Syracuse, NY 13205:
Transitional Family Apartments, 1482 S State St;
tel: (315) 475-7663 (acc 10)
Transitional Living Project Apartments (youth),
1941 S Salina St; tel: (315) 475-9744
(acc 10)
Women's Shelter, 1704 S Salina St;
tel: (315) 472-0947
West Chester, PA 19380: William Booth Initiative,
101 E Market St; tel: (610) 696-8746 (acc 7)
Wilkes Barre, PA 18703: Kirby House;
17 S Pennsylvania Ave; tel: (570) 824-8741

Senior Citizens' Residences

Cincinnati, OH 45224: Booth Residence for the
Elderly and Handicapped, 6000 Townvista Dr;
tel: (513) 242-4482 (acc 150)
New York, NY 10025: Williams Residence,
720 West End Ave; tel: (212) 316-6000;
Philadelphia, PA 19139: Booth Manor,
5522 Arch St; tel: (215) 471-0500 (acc 102)
Philadelphia, PA 19131: Ivy Residence,
4051 Ford Rd; tel: (215) 871-3303 (acc 127)

**USA Central: At the
Quincy Kroc Center
young children enjoy
storytime**

USA Central: An EDS vehicle amidst devastation caused by tornadoes and floods in May 2011

USA Southern: A glimpse of commissioning – the Ambassadors of Holiness session in June 2011

USA Western: The territory welcomes 61 cadets for officer training – the Proclaimers of the Resurrection session in September 2011

USA SOUTHERN TERRITORY

Territorial leaders:
Commissioners David and Barbara Jeffrey

Territorial Commander:
Commissioner David Jeffrey
(1 Aug 2011)

Chief Secretary:
Colonel Bradford Bailey (1 Sep 2012)

Territorial Headquarters: 1424 Northeast Expressway, Atlanta, GA 30329-2088, USA

Tel: [1] (404) 728 1300; website: www.salvationarmysouth.org

The Salvation Army was incorporated as a religious and charitable corporation in the State of Georgia in 1927 as 'The Salvation Army' and is qualified to conduct all its affairs in all of the states of the territory.

Zone: Americas and Caribbean
USA states included in the territory: Alabama, Arkansas, Florida, Georgia, Kentucky, Louisiana, Maryland, Mississippi, North Carolina, Oklahoma, South Carolina, Tennessee, Texas, Virginia, West Virginia, District of Columbia
Languages in which the gospel is preached: English, Haitian-Creole, Korean, Laotian, Spanish, Vietnamese
Periodical: *Southern Spirit*

'FOLLOW Jesus' was the simple and direct instruction from Commissioners David and Barbara Jeffrey as they were installed as territorial leaders in the USA Southern Territory.

In June 2011 a new musical, *Our People,* was presented on the eve of the commissioning and ordination of the 38 cadets of the Ambassadors of Holiness session. Written and produced by Lieut-Colonel W. Edward Hobgood, the musical tells the amazing story of William and Catherine Booth, including their first meeting, courtship and marriage, Catherine's

debut as a preacher and their work in founding The Salvation Army.

In spring 2011 tornadoes, floods and other severe weather hit the southern United States. More than 300 people died and many more were left homeless and hungry. The territory's Emergency Disaster Services (EDS) team provided immediate material, emotional, and spiritual care for thousands of people. As the operation changed from response into long-term recovery, personnel in the divisions affected expended $6 million to alleviate the ongoing hardships faced by individuals and families.

In August, response plans were in place as Hurricane Irene made her way along the South Carolina coast. EDS teams from the North and South Carolina and the National Capital and Virginia divisions provided help and hope to people affected by the storm.

Three Ray and Joan Kroc Corps Community Centers were opened. The first in July in Augusta, GA is in an historic district and offers incredible facilities. The second was opened in September in Biloxi, MS near the Gulf coast and has an athletics track and football field. The Greenville Center, SC opened in October and has a tennis facility, reputedly one of the finest in the south east US.

A record result from the Annual Red Kettle Campaign in November and December provided assistance for many people during the Christmas season. It was possible to give online at www.onlineredkettle.org.

In January 2012 *Salvation Army Today*, the first regular Internet webcast of international Salvation Army news was launched. Researched and hosted by the USA Southern Territory, the weekly show is intended to appeal both to Salvationists and those who know very little about the Army. Previous episodes are on the *Salvation Army Today* YouTube channel.

In April, an Easter tour by the UK Territory's Bristol Easton Band brought great blessing through their high standard of musicianship and Salvationism. The band visited cities in Georgia, North and South Carolina, Virginia, the State Capital and Pennsylvania.

STATISTICS

Officers 1,406 (active 923 retired 483) **Cadets** (1st Yr) 37 (2nd Yr) 49 **Employees** 13,639
Corps 344 **Societies/Outposts** 10 **Institutions** 274
Senior Soldiers 23,338 **Adherent Members** 2,271 **Junior Soldiers** 6,505
Personnel serving outside territory Officers 15

STAFF

Women's Ministries: Comr Barbara Jeffrey (TPWM) Col Heidi Bailey (TSWM) Maj Susan Ellis (CCMS/Outreach)
Personnel: Lt-Col John Needham
Programme: Lt-Col Kelly Igleheart
Business: Lt-Col Samuel A. Henry
Adult Rehabilitation Centres Command: Lt-Col Mark Bell
Audit: Maj Eugene Broome
Community Relations and Development: Maj John Carter
Evangelism and Adult Ministries: Maj Otis Childs
Employee Relations: Murray Flagg PhD
Finance: Maj Stephen Ellis
Legal: Maj Larry Broome
Multicultural Ministries: Maj Vivian Childs
Music: Mr Nicholas Simmons-Smith
Officers' Health Services: Maj Jeanne Johnson
Property: Mr Robert L. Taylor
Retired Officers: Maj Karen Carter
Social Services: Maj John Jordan, MSW, ACSW
Supplies and Purchasing: Maj Robert Bagley
Training: Maj Allan Hofer
Youth: Maj Art Penhale
Candidates: Lt Dan Nelson

DIVISIONS

Alabama-Louisiana-Mississippi: 1450 Riverside Dr, PO Box 4857, 39296-4857, Jackson, MS 39202; tel: (601) 969 7560; Majs Ronnie L. and Sharon L. Raymer
Arkansas and Oklahoma: Broadway Executive Park 5, 6601 N Broadway Ext, Suite 300, PO Box 12600, 73157, Oklahoma City, OK 73116 tel: (405) 840 0735; Majs Stephen P. and Wendy J. Morris
Florida: 5631 Van Dyke Rd, Lutz, FL 33558, PO Box 270848, 33688-0848, Tampa, FL; tel: (813) 962 6611; Lt-Cols Vernon and Martha Jewett
Georgia: 1000 Center Pl, NW, 30093, PO Box 930188, 30003 Norcross, GA 30003;

tel: (770) 441-6200;
Majs James E. and Linda Arrowood

Kentucky and Tennessee: 214-216
W Chestnut St, Box 2229, 40201-2229,
Lt-Cols Mark and Carolee Israel

Maryland and West Virginia: 814 Light St,
Baltimore, MD 21230; tel: (410) 347 9944;
Majs Charles and Paula Powell

National Capital and Virginia: 2626
Pennsylvania Ave NW, PO Box 18658,
Washington, DC 20037; tel: (202) 756 2600;
Lt-Cols John R. and Arduth Jones

North and South Carolina: 501 Archdale Dr,
PO Box 241808, 28224-1808, Charlotte, NC
28217-4237; tel: (704) 522 4970;
Majs Willis and Barbara Howell

Texas: 6500 Harry Hines Blvd, PO Box 36607,
75235, Dallas, TX 75235; tel: (214) 956 6000;
Lt-Cols Kenneth and Dawn Luyk

SCHOOL FOR OFFICER TRAINING

1032 Metropolitan Pkwy, SW Atlanta, GA 30310;
tel: (404) 753 4166; fax: (404) 753 3709

ATTACHED TO DIVISIONS

Alcoholic Rehabilitation

Fort Worth, TX 76103: 1855 E Lancaster
(women only, acc 13)
Greenville, SC 29609: 417 Rutherford St (acc 40)
Mobile, AL 36604: 1009 Dauphin St (acc 30)

Child Care Centres

Austin, TX 78767: 4523 Tannehill Hill (acc 26)
Freeport, TX 77541-2620: 1618 Ave J (acc 85)
Jacksonville, FL 32202: 318 N Ocean St (acc 125)
Lakeland, FL 33801: 835 N Kentucky (acc 45)
Lynchburg, VA 24501: 2301 Park Ave (acc 40)
Naples, FL 34104: 3180 Estey Ave (acc 124)
Nashville, TN 37207: 631 Dickerson Rd
(acc 37)

Children's Residential Care

Birmingham, AL 35212: Youth Emergency
Services, 6001 Crestwood Blvd (acc 33)
St Petersburg, FL 33733: Children's Village,
PO Drawer 10909 (acc 24)
St Petersburg, FL 33733: Sallie House Group
Home, PO Drawer 10909 (acc 18)

Family Resident Programme

Aiken, SC 29801: 604 Park Ave (acc 32)
Alexandria, VA 22301: 2525 Mt Vernon Ave
(acc 40)
Albany, GA 31721: 304 W 2nd Ave (acc 41)
Amarillo, TX 79101: 400 S Harrison (acc 40)
Anderson, SC 29624: 106 Tolly St (acc 30)

Arlington, TX 76013: 711 W Border (acc 30)
Asheville, NC 28801: 204 Haywood St (acc 59)
Athens, GA 30606: 484 Hawthorne Ave (acc 52)
Atlanta, GA 30310: 400 Luckie St NW (acc 327:
men 156 women 64 Harbour Light 22)
Augusta, GA 30901: 138 Greene Street St (acc 118)
Austin, TX 78701: 501 E 8th St (acc 60)
Austin, TX 78767: 4523 Tannehill Ln (Women
and Children Shelter) (acc 26)
Baltimore, MD 21030: 1114 N Calvert St (acc 75)
Beaumont, TX 77701: 1078 McFadden (acc 10)
Bradenton, FL 34205: 1204 14th St W (acc 102)
Brunswick, GA 31520: 1620 Reynolds St (acc 24)
Cambridge, MD 21613: 200 Washington St
(acc 10)
Charleston, WV 25302: 308, 308A, 310,
312 Ohio St (acc 16)
Charlotte, NC 28206: 534 Spratt St (acc 270)
Charlottesville, VA: 207 Ridge St NW (acc 36)
Chattanooga, TN 37403: 800 McCallie Ave (acc 72)
Clearwater, FL 33756: 1527 E Druid Rd (acc 64)
Columbus, GA 31909: 1718 2nd Ave (acc 39)
Corpus Christi, TX 78401: 513 Josephine (acc 28)
Dalton, GA 30720: 1101A North Thorton Ave
(acc 24)
El Paso, TX: 79905: 4300 Paisano Drive (acc 106)
Enid, OK 73701: 223 W Oak (acc 8)
Fayetteville, NC 28301: 245 Alexander St (acc 52)
Florence, SC 29501: 2210 Hoffmeyer Rd (acc 12)
Ft Lauderdale, FL 33312: 1445 W Broward
Blvd (acc 251)
Ft Myers, FL 33901: 2163 Stella St (acc 134)
Fort Worth, TX 76103: 1855 E Lancaster Ave
(acc 62)
Gainesville, FL 32601: 639 E University Ave
(acc 24)
Gainesville, GA: 711 Dorsey St (acc 52)
Gastonia, NC 28052: 107 S. Broaad St (acc 65)
Greensboro, NC 27406: 1311 S. Eugene St
(acc 96)
Greenville, SC 27609: 417 Rutherford St (acc 90)
Griffin, GA 30224: 329 N 13th St (acc 32)
Hagerstown, MD 21740: 534 W Franklin St
(acc 30)
Harrisonburg, VA 22801: 895 Jefferson St
(acc 72)
Hickory, NC 28602: 780 Third Ave Place SE
(acc 75)
High Point, NC 27262: 301 W Green Dr (acc 54)
Hollywood, FL 33020: 1960 Sherman St
(acc 140)
Houston, TX 77004: 1603 McGowen (acc 42)
Jacksonville, FL 32201: PO Box 52508
(acc 123)
Lakeland, FL 33801: 835 N Kentucky Ave
(acc 166)

Louisville, KY 40203: 831 S Brook St (acc 18)
Lynchburg, VA 24501: 2215 Park Ave (acc 22)
Macon, GA 31206: 2312 Houston Ave (acc 131)
Melbourne, FL 32901: 1080 S Hickory St
 (acc 48)
Memphis, TN 38105: 696 Jackson Ave
 (acc 120)
Miami, FL 33142: 1907 NW 38th St (acc 266)
Nashville, TN 37207-5608: 631 Dickerson Rd
 (acc 53)
Newport News, VA 23602: 11931 Jefferson Ave
 (acc 30/scattered sites)
N Central Brevard, Cocoa, FL 32922:
 919 Peachtree St (acc 17)
Norfolk, VA 23502: Hope Village,
 5525 Raby Rd (acc 65)
Ocala, FL 34475: 320 NW 1st Ave (acc 121)
Orlando, FL 32804: 400 W Colonial Dr (acc 190)
Panama City, FL 32401: 1824 W 15th St (acc 48)
Parkersburg, WV 24740: 534-570 Fifth St (acc 56)
Raleigh, NC 27601: 215 S Person St (acc 34)
Richmond, VA 23220: 2 W Grace St (acc 52)
Rock Hill, SC 29730: 125 S Charlotte Ave
 (acc 15)
Rome, GA 30161: 317 E First Ave (acc 26)
San Antonio, TX 78212: 515 W Elmira 78212
 (acc 300)
Sarasota, FL 34236: 1400 10th St (acc 226)
Savannah, GA 31405: 3100 Montgomery St (acc
 120)
St Petersburg, FL 33733: PO Drawer 10909
 (acc 112)
Tampa, FL 33602: 1603 N Florida (acc 192)
Texarkana, TX 71854: 316 Hazel (acc 46)
Thomasville, GA 31792: 208 South St (acc 9)
Titusville, FL 32796: 1212 W Main (acc 16)
Tulsa, OK 74103: 102 N Denver (acc 100)
Tyler, TX 75701: 633 N Broadway 75702
 (15 rooms)
Valdosta, GA 31601: 317 Virginia Ave (acc 10)
Washington, DC 20009: 1434 Harvard St NW
 (acc 60)
Waycross, GA 31501: 977 Tebeau St (acc 11)
Wilmington, NC 28401: 820 N Second St
 (acc 52)
West Palm Beach, FL 33402: PO Box 789
 (acc 95)
Wheeling, WV 26003: 140 16th St (acc 32)
Winchester, VA 22603: 300 Ft Collier Rd
 (acc 48)
Winter Haven, FL 33882: PO Box 1069
 (acc 40)
Winston-Salem, NC 27101: 1255 N Trade St
 (acc 84)
Williamsburg, VA 7131: Merrimac Trail
 (acc 17/scattered sites)

Harbour Light Centres

Atlanta, GA 30313: 400 Luckie St (acc 324)
Dallas, TX 75235: 5302 Harry Hines Blvd
 (acc 309)
Houston, TX 77009: 2407 N Main St (acc 308)
Washington, DC 20002: 2100 New York Ave,
 NE (acc 207)

Homeless Shelters

Daytona Beach, FL 32114: 560 Ballough Rd
 (acc 84)
Gainesville, FL 32601: 639 E University Ave
 (acc 14)
Goldsboro, NC 27530: 610 N William St
 (acc 16)
North Charleston, SC 29405: 4248 Dorchester Rd
 (acc 24)
Pensacola, FL 32505: 1310 North S St
 (acc 28)
Titusville, FL 32796: 1212 W Main (acc 17)
West Palm Beach, FL 33402: PO Box 789
 (acc 95)

Senior Citizens' Centres

Arlington, TX 76013: 712 W Abrams
Brooklyn, MS: Carnes Rd
Dallas Cedar Crest, TX 75203:
 1007 Hutchins Rd
Dallas Oak Cliff, TX 75208: 1617 W Jefferson
 Blvd
Dallas Pleasant Grove, TX 75217-0728: 8341
 Elam Rd
Ft Worth, TX 76106: 3023 NW 24th St
Ft Worth, TX 76119-5813: 1909 E Seminary Dr
 (acc 121)
Houston Aldine/Westfield, TX 77093:
 2600 Aldine Westfield
Houston Pasadena, TX 77506:
 45/6 Irvington Blvd
Houston Temple, TX 77009: 2627
 Cherrybrook Ln 77502
Jacksonville, FL 32202: 17 E Church St
Lufkin, TX 75904: 305 Shands
San Antonio Citadel, TX 78201:
 2810 W Ashby Pl
San Antonio Dave Coy Center, TX 78202:
 226 Nolan St
San Antonio Hope Center, TX 78212:
 521 W Elmira
St Petersburg, FL 33713: 3800 9th Ave N

Senior Citizens' Residences

Atlanta, GA 30306: William Booth Towers,
 1125 Ponce de Leon Ave NE (acc 99)
Charlotte, NC 28202-1727: William Booth
 Gardens Apts, 421 North Poplar St (acc 130)

El Paso, TX: 79903-2840: Pleasant View Lodge, 3918 Bliss Ave (acc 22)

Fort Worth, TX 76119-5813: Catherine Booth Friendship House, 1901 E Seminary Dr (acc 157)

Gastonia, NC 28054: Catherine Booth Gardens Apts, 1436 Union Rd (acc 82)

High Point, NC 27263: William Booth Gardens Apts, 123 SW Cloverleaf Place (acc 77)

Houston, TX 77009: William Booth Gardens Apts, 808 Frawley (acc 62)

Ocala, FL 34470: Evangeline Booth Gardens Apts, 2921 NE 14th St (acc 64)

Orlando, FL 32801: William Booth Towers, 633 Lake Dot Circle (acc 168)

Orlando, FL 32801: Catherine Booth Towers, 625 Lake Dot Circle (acc 125)

Pasadena, TX 77502: Evangeline Booth, 2627 Cherrybrook Ln (acc 62)

San Antonio, TX 78201-5397: William Booth Gardens Apts, 2710 W Ashby Pl (acc 95)

San Antonio, TX 78201: Catherine Booth Apts, 2810 W Ashby Pl (acc 62)

Tyler, TX 75701: William Booth Gardens Apts, 601 Golden Rd (acc 132)

Tyler, TX 75701: Catherine Booth Apts, 602 Golden Rd (acc 75)

Waco, TX 76708-1141: William Booth Gardens Apts, 4200 N 19th (acc 120)

Waco, TX 76708-1141: Catherine Booth Appts, 2005 Steward Dr (acc 75)

Service Centres

Ada, OK 74820: 805 N. Broadway Ave.

Alexander City, AL 35010: 823 Cherokee Rd

Americus, GA 31709: 204 Prince St

Bainbridge, GA 39818: 600 Scott St

Bay City, TX 77414: 1911 7th St

Borger, TX 79007-2502: 1090 Coronado Center Cir 79008-1046, P.O. Box 1046

Boone, NC 28607: High Country 7979, Hwy 105 South High Country

Brownwood, TX 76801: 403 Lakeway

Buckhannon, WV 26201: 21 N. Spring Street (Upshur County)

Bushnell, FL 33513: PO Box 25 (Sumter County)

Canton, GA 30117: 121 Waleska Street

Carrollton, GA 30117: 115 Lake Carroll Blvd

Carthage, MS 39051: 610 Hwy 16 West, Suite A

Cleburne, TX 76031: 111 S Anglin St

Columbia, MD 21045: PO Box 2877 (Howard County)

Copperas Cove, TX 76522: 458 Town Square

Corinth, MS 38834: 1209 Hwy, 72 West

Covington, GA 30014: 5193 Washington St

Culpeper, VA 22701: 102 Main St, #304

Douglas, GA 31533: 110 S Gaskin Ave

Dublin, GA 31921: 1617 Telfair St

Easley, SC 29640: 501 Liberty Highway

East Pasco, Dade City, FL 33523: 14445 7th St

Eden, NC 27288: 314 Morgan Rd

Edinburg, TX 78539, 500 E. Cano

Elberton, GA 30635: 262 N McIntosh St

Elizabethtown, KY 42701: 1006 N Mulberry

Enterprise, AL 366331: 1919-B E Park Ave (Coffee County)

Fernandina Beach, FL 32034: 421 S 9th St (The Salvation Army Hope House)

Fort Payne, AL 35967: 450 Gault Ave N (Dekalb County)

Frankline, VA, 23851: Western Tidewater Svc Ctr, 50l N Main St

Fulton, MS 38843: 414 E Main St

Glen Burnie, MD 21061: 511 S Crain Hwy

Granite Falls, NC 28630: 4370 Hickory Blvd (Lenoir)

Guntersville, AL 35976: 1336 Gunter Ave (Marshall County)

Houma, LA 70363: 1414 E Tunnel Blvd.

Houston, MS 38851: 114 Washington St

Immokalee, FL 34142: 2050 Commerce Ave, Unit 3A

Jackson, GA 30233: 178 N Benton St (Jackson/Butts County)

Jasper, AL 35502: 207 20th St E (Walker County)

Kaufman, TX 75142: 5 Oak Creek Dr (mail PO Box 217)

LaBelle, FL 33935: 180 N Main St

Lake City, FL 32055: 303 NW Quinten Street

Lebanon, TN, 37087: 215 University Ave

Lewisburg, WV 24901: 148 Maplewood Ave (Greenbriar Valley)

Lewisville, TX 75067: 207 Elm St 75057

McDonough, GA 30253: 401 Race Track Rd

McGehee, AR 71654: 102 E Oak St (Desha County)

Milledgeville, GA 31061: 420 S Wilkinson St

Mocksville, NC 27028: 279 N Main St (Davie County)

Morganton, NC 28655: 420-B W Fleming Dr

Nacogdoches, TX 75963: 118 E Hospital Suite 101

New Braunfels, TX 78130: 617 S. Business IH 35

Newnan, GA 30264: 670 Jefferson St

Okmulgee, OK 74447-0123: 105-111 E 8th St

Oneonta, AL 35121: 333 Valley Rd (Blount County)

Opelika, AL 36801: 720 Columbus Pkwy (Lee County)

Oxford, MS 38655: 2617 W Oxford Loop, Ste 4

Ozark, AL 36360: 1177 Andrews Ave (Dale County)

Pleasanton, TX 78064: 2132 2nd St (mail PO Box 951)

Pontotoc, MS 38863: 187 Hwy 15 N

Putnam County, WV 25177: 720 N Winfield Rd, St Albans, WV

Sallisaw, OK: PO Box 292, Fort Smith, AR 72902

San Marcos, TX 78667: 1658 I-35 S

Scottsboro, AL 35768: 1501 E Willow St (Jackson County)

Spencer, WV 25276: 145 Main St (Roane County)

Starksville, MS 39759:39759: 407 A Industrial Parkway Rd

St Mary's, GA 31558: 1909 Osborne Rd

Tarpon Springs, FL 34689: 209 S Pinellas Ave

Thomasville, AL 36784: 122 W Wilson Ave

Tifton, GA 31793: 612 Love Ave

Troy, AL 36081: 509 S Brundidge St

Vidalia, GA 30475: 204 Jackson St

Warrenton, VA 20186: 26 S Third St

Wellsburg, WV 26070: 491 Commerce St

Westminster, MD 21157: 300 Hahn Rd

Yadkinville, NC 27055: 111 E Main St (Yadkin County)

Spouse House Shelters

Cocoa, FL: 919 Peachtree St 32922 (PO Box 1540, 32923) (acc 20)

Panama City, FL 32401: 1824 W 15th St (PO Box 540, 32412) (acc 46)

Port Richey, FL 34673: PO Box 5517 Hudson, FL 34674-5517 (acc 32)

Roanoke, VA 24016 815 Salem Ave, SW (acc 60)

Warner Robins, GA 31093: 96 Thomas Blvd (acc 18)

SOCIAL SERVICES
Adult Rehabilitation Centres (including industrial stores)

Alexandria, VA 22312: Northern Virginia Center, 6528 Little River Turnpike (acc 120)

Atlanta, GA 30318-5726: 740 Marietta St, NW (acc 132)

Austin, TX 78745: 4216 S Congress (acc 118)

Baltimore, MD 21230: 2700 W Patapsco Ave (acc 115)

Birmingham, AL 35234: 1401 F. L. Shuttlesworth Dr (acc 107)

Charlotte, NC 28204: 1023 Central Ave (acc 117)

Dallas, TX 75235-7213: 5554 Harry Hines Blvd (acc 137)

Fort Lauderdale, FL 33312-1597: 1901 W Broward Blvd (acc 99)

Fort Worth, TX 76111-2996: 2901 NE 28th St (acc 109)

Houston, TX 77007-6113: 1015 Hemphill St (acc 167)

Hyattsville, MD 20781: (Washington, DC, and Suburban Maryland Center) 3304 Kenilworth Ave (acc 151)

Jacksonville, FL 32246: 10900 Beach Blvd (acc 121)

Memphis, TN 38133-4734: 2649 Kirby Whitten Rd, 38133-4734 (acc 86)

Miami, FL 33127-4981: 2236 NW Miami Court (acc 134)

New Orleans, LA 70121-2596: 200 Jefferson Highway (acc 50)

Oklahoma City, OK 73106-2409: 2041 NW 7th St (acc 81)

Orlando, FL 32808-7927: 3955 W Colonial Dr (acc 105)

Richmond, VA 23220-1199: 2601 Hermitage Rd (acc 81)

San Antonio, TX 78204: 1324 S Flores St (acc 110)

St Petersburg, FL 33709-1597: Suncoast Area Center, 5885 66th St N (acc 119)

Tampa, FL 33613-2205: 13815 Salvation Army Lane (acc 131)

Tulsa, OK 74106-5163: 601 N Main St (acc 86)

Virginia Beach, VA 23462: Hampton Roads Center, 5560 Virginia Beach Blvd (acc 123)

In addition, 10 fresh-air camps and 347 community centres, boys'/girls' clubs are attached to the division

USA WESTERN TERRITORY

Territorial leaders:
Commissioners James M. and Carolyn R. Knaggs

Territorial Commander:
Commissioner James M. Knaggs
(1 Jul 2010)

Chief Secretary:
Colonel David E. Hudson (1 Aug 2011)

**Territorial Headquarters: 180 E Ocean Boulevard,
PO Box 22646 (90801-5646), Long Beach, California 90802-4709, USA**

Tel: [1] (562) 436-7000; website: www.usw.salvationarmy.org

The Salvation Army was incorporated as a religious and charitable corporation in the State of California in 1914 as 'The Salvation Army' and is qualified, along with its several affiliated separate corporations, to conduct its affairs in all of the states of the territory.

Zone: Americas and Caribbean
USA states included in the territory: Alaska, Arizona, California, Colorado, Hawaii, Idaho, Montana, Nevada, New Mexico, Oregon, Utah, Washington, Wyoming, Guam (US Territory)
Other countries included in territory: Republic of the Marshall Islands, Federated States of Micronesia
'The Salvation Army' in Cantonese: Kau Shai Kwan; in Japanese: Kyu-sei-gun; in Mandarin (Kuoyo): Chiu Shi Chuen; in Spanish: Ejército de Salvación
Languages in which the gospel is preached: Cantonese, Chamarro, Chuukese, English, Hmong, Korean, Laotian, Mandarin, Marshallese, Filipino, Pohnpeian, Portuguese, Spanish, Tlingit
Periodicals: *Caring, New Frontier, Nuevas Fronteras* (Spanish)

IN March 2011 the new Herberger Campus, a 78,000-square-foot complex including DHQ for the Southwest Division, social services and shelter facilities was dedicated to the glory of God in Phoenix, Arizona.

A Territorial Arts Ensemble was formed to develop arts ministry and train local artists at various venues.

In May, nearly 1,000 homeless people attended the fourth annual 'Homeless Connect', an event spon-

sored by the Army and other agencies.

William B. Flinn was installed as the new chair of the Crestmont Council, the educational authority for the college for officer training.

During May and June, '2nd Chance Kids' (a charity that provides for the medical needs of at-risk children) worked with The Salvation Army in San Bernardino, CA to offer visual, hearing, asthma and diabetes care.

Also in May, the first-ever territorial

women's ARC retreat was held at Camp Redwood Glen attended by 179 participants.

In June the territory commissioned and ordained 52 cadets of the Ambassadors of Holiness session. Lieut-Colonels Richard and Janet Munn (ICO/CSLD) were special guests and the weekend featured the musical *Brengle: My Life's Ambition*.

A new Salvation Army Veterans and Family Center opened in Beaverton, Oregon, providing expanded services in the Portland-Metro area.

In July, nearly 500 Target stores nationwide partnered with The Salvation Army in a one-day event for school students, providing an $80 Target gift card to purchase back-to-school supplies. Each of the 10 Army divisions participated

The San Francisco Chinatown Corps – the first Chinese Salvation Army corps in the world – celebrated its 125th anniversary in August. A 'Musical Mission Force' from Hong Kong visited the Oakland Chinatown Corps and made several appearances in the Greater Bay Area during the celebrations.

In September the 61 cadets of the Proclaimers of the Resurrection session were welcomed for officer training. Colonels David and Sharron Hudson were also welcomed as Chief Secretary and Territorial Secretary for Women's Ministries respectively.

The territory's newest camp, Pine Summit in Big Bear Lake, CA, Sierra Del Mar Division, was dedicated to the glory of God.

For the seventh consecutive year, the territory's Information Technology Department was featured in the 2011 Information Week 500, an annual listing of the nation's most innovative users of business technology.

San Francisco's transitional housing programme, Railton Place, marked three years of supporting some of the city's most vulnerable people in 110 transitional and permanent housing units.

In October the Western Territorial Band travelled to Anchorage, Alaska, where members led workshops, gave a concert and participated in Sunday worship.

The Matsiko World Orphan Choir sang at the Portland Tabernacle Corps.

Commissioner James Knaggs (TC) welcomed employees and officers alike to the first-ever THQ Missions Conference – a day designed to ensure that everyone understood the nature and scope of The Salvation Army's mission worldwide and in the territory.

For the 92nd consecutive year, a Salvation Army band marched in the Tournament of Roses Parade on New Year's Day 2012.

Commissioner Knaggs presided at the Ray and Joan Kroc Corps Community Center opening in Kapolei, West Oahu, Hawaii in February 2012.

From 26 March-2 April more than 100 cadets campaigned in 18 corps throughout the territory, witnessing and participating in the Army's ministries, thus sharing God's love in local communities.

STATISTICS

Officers 1,046 (active 652 retired 394) **Cadets** 105
Employees 7,931
Corps 247 **Outposts** 13 **Institutions** 284
Senior Soldiers 17,075 **Adherent Members**
3,654 **Junior Soldiers** 5,420
Personnel serving outside territory Officers 28
Lay Personnel 2

STAFF

Women's Ministries: Comr Carolyn R. Knaggs
(TPWM) Col Sharron Hudson (TSWM)
Personnel: Lt-Col Douglas G. O'Brien
  Asst Sec for Personnel Maj Eloisa Martin
Business: Lt-Col Victor R. Doughty
Programme: Lt-Col Edward Hill
  Asst Programme Sec for Corps Ministries:
  Maj Victoria Shiroma
  Asst Sec for Programme: Mr Martin Hunt
ARC Command: Maj Man-Hee Chang
Audit: Maj Joe Frank Chavez
Candidates and Recruitment: Maj John P.
Brackenbury
Community Care Ministries: Lt-Col Diane
O'Brien
Education: Maj Jeffrey A. Martin
Finance: Mr Tom Melott
Gift Services: Ms Kathleen Durazo
Human Resources: Mr Howard Yamaguchi
Information Technology: Mr Clarence White
Legal: Mr Michael Woodruff
Multicultural Ministries: Lt-Col Zoilo Pardo
Music: Mr Neil Smith
Officer Care and Development: Majs Harry and
Marina Lacey
Property: Maj Evelyn Chavez
Risk Management: Lt-Col Walter Fuge
Senior Housing Management: Mrs Susan
Lawrence
Social Services: Maj Lawrence Shiroma
Spiritual Life Development: Maj Steven D.
Bradley
Supplies and Purchasing: Mr Piers Fairclough
Training: Maj Timothy Foley
Western Bible Conference Sec: Maj Victoria
Shiroma
Youth: Captain Roy S. Wild

DIVISIONS

Alaska: 143 E 9th Ave, Anchorage,
AK 99501-3618 (Box 101459, 99510-1459);
tel: (907) 276-2515; Majs George L. and
Jeanne L. Baker
Cascade: 8495 SE Monterey Ave, Happy Valley,
OR 97086; tel: (503) 794-3200;
Lt-Col Judith E. Smith

Del Oro: 3755 N Freeway Blvd, Sacramento,
CA 95834-1926 (Box 348000, 95834-8000);
tel: (916) 563-3700; Majs William Jr. and Lisa
Dickinson
Golden State: 832 Folsom St, San Francisco,
CA 94107-1123 (Box 193465, 94119-3465)
tel: (415) 553-3500; Lt-Cols Stephen C. and
Marcia C. Smith
Hawaiian and Pacific Islands: 2950 Manoa Rd,
Honolulu, HI 96822-1798 (Box 620, 96809-
0620); tel: (808) 988-2136; Majs John and
Lani Chamness
Intermountain: 1370 Pennsylvania St, Denver,
CO 80203-2475 (Box 2369, 80201-2369);
tel: (303) 861-4833; Lt-Cols Daniel L. and
Helen Starrett
Northwest: 111 Queen Anne Ave N,
Suite 300, Seattle, WA 98109-4955 (Box 9219,
98109-0200); tel: (206) 281-4600; Majs
Douglas and Sheryl Tollerud
Sierra Del Mar: 2320 5th Ave, San Diego,
CA 92101-1679; tel: (619) 231-6000; Majs Lee
R. and Michele Lescano
Southern California: 180 E Ocean Blvd Ste 500,
Long Beach, CA 90802-4709 (Box 93002,
90809-9355); tel: (562) 264-3600;
Lt-Cols Douglas F. and Colleen R. Riley
Southwest: 2707 E Van Buren St, Phoenix,
AZ 85008-6039 (Box 52177, 85072-2177);
tel: (602) 267-4100; Lt-Cols Joseph E. and
Shawn L. Posillico

COLLEGE FOR OFFICER TRAINING

30840 Hawthorne Blvd, Rancho Palos Verdes,
CA 90275-5301; tel: (310) 377-0481;
fax: (310) 541-1697

SOCIAL SERVICES
Adult Rehabilitation Centres (Men)

Anaheim, CA 92805: 1300 S Lewis St;
tel: (714) 758-0414 (acc 145)
Bakersfield, CA 93301: 200 19th St;
tel: (661) 325-8626 (acc 57)
Canoga Park, CA 91304: 21375 Roscoe Blvd; tel:
(818) 883-6321 (acc 56)
Denver, CO 80216: 4751 Broadway;
tel: (303) 294-0827 (acc 98)
Fresno, CA 93721: 804 S Parallel Ave;
tel: (559) 490-7020 (acc 111)
Honolulu, HI 96817: 322 Sumner St;
tel: (808) 522-8400 (acc 77)
Long Beach, CA 90813: 1370 Alamitos Ave;
tel: (562) 218-2351 (acc 94)
Lytton, CA 95448: 200 Lytton Springs Rd,
Healdsburg, PO Box 668, Healdsburg, 95448;
tel: (707) 433-3334 (acc 75)

Oakland, CA 94607: 601 Webster St, PO Box 24054, 94623; tel: (510) 451-4514 (acc 131)

Pasadena, CA 91105: 56 W Del Mar Blvd; tel: (626) 795-8075 (acc 107)

Phoenix, AZ 85004: 1625 S Central Ave; tel: (602) 256-4500 (acc 142)

Portland, OR 97220: 6655 NE 82nd Ave (acc 76)

Riverside County, CA 92570: 24201 Orange Ave, Perris, PO Box 278, Perris 92572; tel: (951) 940-5790 (acc 125)

Sacramento, CA 95814: 1615 D St, PO Box 2948, 95812; tel: (916) 441-5267 (acc 91)

San Bernardino, CA 92408: 363 S Doolittle Rd; tel: (909) 889-9605 (acc 122)

San Diego, CA 92101: 1335 Broadway; tel: (619) 239-4037 (acc 132)

San Francisco, CA 94110: 1500 Valencia St; tel: (415) 643-8000 (acc 112)

San Jose, CA 95126: 702 W Taylor St; tel: (408) 298-7600 (acc 96)

Santa Monica, CA 90404: 1665 10th St; tel: (310) 450-7235 (acc 56)

Seattle, WA 98134: 1000 4th Ave S; tel: (206) 587-0503 (acc 117)

Stockton, CA 95205: 1247 S Wilson Way; tel: (209) 466-3871 (acc 80)

Tucson, AZ 85713: 2717 S 6th Ave; tel: (520) 624-1741 (acc 85)

Adult Rehabilitation Centres (Women)

Anaheim, CA 92805: 909 Salvation Pl; tel: (714) 758-0414 (acc 30)

Arvada, CO 80002: Cottonwood, 13455 W 58th Ave; tel: (303) 456-0520 (acc 30)

Fresno, CA 93704: Rosecrest, 745 E Andrews St; tel: (559) 490-7080 (acc 18)

Pasadena, CA 91107: Oakcrest Women's Program, 180 W Huntington Dr; tel: (626) 447-4264 (acc 14)

Phoenix, AZ 85003: Lyncrest Manor, 344 W Lynwood St; tel: (602) 254-0883 (acc 14)

San Diego, CA 92123: 2799 Health Center Dr; tel: (858) 279-1755 (acc 30)

San Francisco, CA 94116: Pinehurst Lodge, 2685 30th Ave; tel: (415) 681-1262 (acc 27)

Shoreline, WA 98155: The Marion-Farrell House, 17925 2nd Ave NE; tel: (206) 367-0697 (acc 15)

UNDER DIVISIONS
Anti-Human Trafficking Centres

Las Vegas, NV 89030: tel: (702) 639-0277 (acc 22)

Phoenix, AZ 85008: tel: (602) 267-4122

San Clemente, CA 92672-4272: tel: (949) 366-6652

Clinics

Kalispell, MT 59901: 110 Bountiful Dr; tel: (406) 257-4357

Oakland, CA 94601: Kerry's Kids, 2794 Garden Street; tel: (510) 437-9437

Oxnard/Port Hueneme, CA: Medical and Dental Clinic, 622 W Wooley Rd; tel: (805) 483-9235

Sacramento, CA 95814: 1200 B St, tel: (916) 442-0331

San Diego, CA 92123: Door of Hope, 2799 Health Center Dr; tel: (858) 279-1100

Prescott, AZ 86303; 237 S Montezuma St; tel (928) 778-0150

Family Services

Anacortes, WA 98221: 3001 'R' Ave Ste #100, tel: (360) 293-6682

Anaheim, CA 92801-4333; 1515 W north St; tel: (714) 491-1020

Anchorage, AK 99501: 1712 'A' St; tel: (907) 277-2593

Bellingham, WA 98225: 2912 Northwest Ave; tel: (360) 733-1410

Bremerton, WA 98337: 832 6th St; tel: (360) 373-5550

Centralia, WA 98531: 303 N Gold; tel: (360) 736-4339

Eastside (Bellevue), WA 98008: 911-164th Ave NE; tel: (425) 452-7300

El Cajon, CA 92021: 1011 E Main St; tel: (619) 440-4686Everett, WA 98201: 2525 Rucker Ave; tel: (425) 259-8129

Everett, WA 98201: 2525 Rucker Ave; tel: (425) 259-8129

Federal Way, WA 98198: 26419 16th Ave: S, Des Moines; tel: (253) 946-7933

Fresno, CA 93721: 1752 Fulton St; tel (559) 233-0138

Garden Grove, CA 92841-4216; West Orange County, 7245 Garden Grove Blvd #A; tel: (714) 901-1480

Grandview, WA 98930; 246 Division St; tel: (509) 882-2584

Grays Harbor (Aberdeen) WA 98520: 118 W Wishkah; tel: (360) 533-1062

Great Falls, MT 59405: 527 9th Ave S; tel: (406) 761-5660

Globe, AZ 85501-1944; Service Ctr, 161 E Cedar St; tel: (928) 425-4011

Havre, MT 59501: Service Ext, Social Service Center, PO Box 418; tel: (406) 265-6411

Helena, MT 59601: 1905 Henderson; tel: (406) 442-8244

Honokaa, HI 96727: Prevention Program, 45-511

Rickard Pl; tel: (808) 959-5855

Honolulu, HI 96819: 1931 N King St;
tel: (808) 841-5565

Honolulu, HI 96816: Family Treatment Services,
845 22nd Ave; tel: (808) 732-2802

Huntington Beach, CA 92647-5896; Coastal
Area, 17261 Oak Ln; tel: (714) 841-0150

Kalispell, MT 59901: 110 Bountiful Dr;
tel: (406) 257-4357

Kent, WA 98032: S King County Service Center,
1209 Central Ave #145;
tel (253) 852-4983

Kingman, AZ 86401-5835; Service Ctr, 309 E
Beale St; tel: (928) 718-2600 Lewiston, ID
83501; 1835 "G" St; tel: (208) 746-9653

Longview, WA 98632: 1639 10th Ave;
tel: (360) 423-3992

Los Angeles, CA 90001-2945: Siemon Family
Youth & Community Center, 7651 S. Central
Ave; tel: (323) 586-0288

Mesquite, NV 89048: Mesquite Service Center,
780 Hafen Ln #D; tel: (775) 751-8199

Missoula, MT 59802; 339 W Broadway St;
tel: (406) 549-0710

Modesto, CA 95354: 625 "I" St; tel (209) 523-7577

Monterey, CA 93942: 1491 Contra Costa: tel
831-899-4911

Moses Lake, WA 98837: Service Ext, Social
Service Center, 215 Broadway, PO Box 1000;
tel: (509) 766-5875

Oakland, CA 94607: 379 12th St;
tel: (510) 645 9710

Olympia, WA 98501: Tri-Cities Social Services,
824 5th Ave SE; tel: (360) 352-8596

Pasco, WA 99301: Social Services,
310 N 4th Ave; tel: (509) 547-2138

Phoenix, AZ 85034-2177: 2702 E Washington;
tel: (602) 267-4122

Port Angeles, WA 98362: 206 S Peabody St;
tel: (360) 452-7679

Puyallup, WA 98373: 4009 0th St SW;
tel: (253) 841-1491

Renton, WA 98055: Food Bank and
Multi-Service Center, 206 S Tobin St;
tel: (425) 255-5969

Riverside, CA 92501: 3695 1st; tel:
(951) 784-3571

Sacramento, CA 95838: 4350 Raley Blvd;
tel: (916) 678-4010

San Clemente, CA 92672-4272; South Orange
County, 626 S El Camino Real #82;
tel: (949) 366-6652

San Diego, CA 92101: Social Services;
tel: (619) 231-6000

San Diego, CA 92115: Kroc Family Service

Center, Kroc Pre-School, 6845 University Ave;
tel: (619) 269-1430

San Francisco, CA 94103: 520 Jesse St;
tel: (415) 575-4848

San Jose, CA 95112: 359 N 4th St;
tel (408) 282-1165

Santa Ana, CA 92704; 1710 W Edinger Ave;
tel: (714) 384-0481

Seattle, WA 98101-1923: Emergency Family
Assistance, 1101 Pike St;
tel: (206) 447-9944

Seattle Temple, WA 98103: 9501 Greenwood
Ave N; tel: (206) 783-1225

Seattle White Center, WA 98106:
9050 16th Ave SW; tel: (206) 767-3150

Spokane, WA 99207: 204 E Indiana;
tel: (509) 325-6821

Tacoma, WA 98405; 1501 6th Ave;
tel: (253) 572-8452

Tiyan, Guam: 613-615 E Sunset Blvd;
tel: (671) 477-3528

Tucson, AZ 85716: 3525 E 2nd St #1;
tel: (520) 546-5969

Vancouver, WA 98684: 7509 NE 47th Ave;
tel: (360) 448-2890

Walla Walla, WA 99362: Service Ext, Social
Service Center, 827 W Alder St;
tel: (509) 529-9470

Washougal, WA 98671; 1612 "I" St;
tel: (360) 835-3171

Wenatchee, WA 98801: 1205 Columbia St S; tel:
(509) 662-8864

Yakima, WA 98907: Social Services, 9 S 6th
Ave; tel: (509) 453-3139

Yuba City, CA 95991: 401 Del Norte Ave;
tel: (530) 216-4530

Yucca Valley, CA 92284: Service Ext, 56659
Twenty-nine Palms Hwy; tel: (760) 228-0114

Adult Care Centres

Anchorage, AK 99508: Serendipity Adult
Day Services, 3550 E 20th Ave;
tel: (907) 279-0501 (acc 35)

Henderson, NV 89015: 830 E Lake Mead Dr; tel:
(702) 565-9578 (acc 49)

Honolulu, HI 96817: 296 N Vineyard Blvd;
tel: (808) 521-6551 (acc 57)

San Pedro, CA 90731-2351: Sage House Adult
Day Center, 138 S Bandini;
tel: (310) 832-7228 (acc 30)

**Alcoholic and Drug Rehabilitation
Services**

Anchorage, AK 99503-7317: Box 190567,
99519-0567 Clitheroe Center;
tel: (907) 276-2898 (acc 58)

Bell, CA 90201-6418: Bell Shelter, 5600 Rickenbaker Rd 2a/b; tel: (323) 263-1206

Honolulu, HI 96816-4500: Women's Way/Family Treatment Services, 845 22nd Ave; tel: (808) 732-2802 (ext. 4938) (acc 41)

Honolulu, HI 96817: Addiction Treatment Services, 3624 Waokanaka St; tel: (808) 595-6371 (acc 80)

Honolulu, HI 96816: Therapeutic Living, 845 22nd Ave; tel: (808) 732-2802

Los Angeles, CA 90007: Hope Harbor, 3107 S Grand Ave; tel: (213) 744-8186

Los Angeles, CA 90073: The Haven-Victory Place, 11301 Wilshire Blvd, Bldg 212; tel: (310) 478-3711 ext 48761 (acc 200)

Marysville, CA 95901: The Depot Family Crisis Center, 408 J St; tel: (530) 216-4530

San Francisco, CA 94103-4405; 1275 Harrison St; tel: (415) 503-3000

Tiyan, GU 96921: Lighthouse Recovery Center, 155003 Corsair Ave, PO Box 23038, GMF GU 96921, E Agana; tel: (671) 477-7671

Child Day Care Centres

Aurora, CO 80011: Aurora After School Program, 802 Quari Ct, Box 31739, 80041-0739; tel: (720) 810-7304 (acc 123)

Boise, ID Booth, 83702: 1617 N 24th, Box 1216 83701; tel: (208) 343-3571 (acc 15)

Bozeman, MT 59715: 32 S Rouse, Box 1307, 59771-1307; tel: (406) 586-5813 (acc 13)

Broomfield, CO 80020: Broomfield After-School Program, PO Box 1058, 1080 Birch St; tel: (303) 635-3018

Colorado Springs, CO 80903-4023: Child Discovery Center, 709 S Sierra Madre; tel: (719) 955-8412 (acc 30)

Denver, CO 80205-4547: Denver Red Shield Tutor Program, 2915 High St; tel: (303) 295-2108 (acc 250)

Denver, CO 80219-1859: Denver Citadel Tutor Program, PO Box 280750, 80228-0750, 4505 W Alameda Ave; tel: (303) 922-4540

Globe, AZ 85501: Box 1743, 85502, 161 E Cedar St; tel: (928) 425-4011 (acc 59)

Honolulu 96816: (FTS-Therapeutic Nursery), 845 22nd Ave; tel: (808) 739-2802 (acc 24, 12)

Kailua-Kona, HI 96740: (Ohana Keiki) 75-223 Kalani St, Box 1358 96745; tel: (808) 326-7780 (acc 326)

Los Angeles, CA 90026: Alegria Day/After-School Care, 2737 Sunset Blvd; tel: (323) 454-4200 (acc 90)

Los Angeles, CA 90021: LA Day Care, 836 Stanford Ave; tel: (213) 623-9022 (acc 250)

Los Angeles, CA 90025: Bessie Pregerson Childcare, Westwood Transitional Village, 1401 S Sepulveda Blvd; tel: (310) 477-9539 (acc 64)

Los Angeles, CA 90001: Seimon Family Center, 7655 Central Ave; tel: (323) 277-0732 (acc 62)

Modesto, CA 95354: 625 'I' St, PO Box 1663, 95353 (mail); tel: (209) 342-5220 (acc 60)

Monterey, CA 93942: 1491 Contra Costa St, Seaside, PO Box 1884, 93955 (mail); tel: (831) 899-4911 (acc 114)

Oakland, CA 94601: Box 510, Booth Memorial CDC, 2794 Garden St; tel: (510) 535-5088 (acc 63)

Pomona, CA 91767: Box 2562, 91769, 490 E Laverne Ave; tel: (909) 623-1579 (acc 66)

Portland, OR 97296: 2640 NW Alexandra Ave; tel: (503) 239-1248 (acc 18)

Riverside, CA 92501: 3695 1st St; tel: (909) 784-4495 (acc 108)

Sacramento, CA 95817: 2550 Alhambra Blvd; tel: (916) 451-4230

San Francisco, CA 94103: Harbor House, 407 9th St; tel: (415) 503-3000 (acc 66)

Santa Barbara, CA 93111: Santa Barbara After-School Program, 4849 Hollister Ave; tel: (805) 964-8738

Santa Fe Springs, CA 90606: Infant/Pre-School and After-School Care, 12000 E Washington Blvd; tel: (310) 696-7175 (acc 57)

Seattle, WA 98103: Little People Preschool and Child Care, 9501 Greenwood Ave N, Box 30638, 98103-0638; tel: (206) 782-3142 (acc 65)

Tustin, CA 92680: Creator's Corner Pre-School, 10200 Pioneer Rd; tel: (714) 918-0659 (acc 90)

Tustin, CA 92680: Henley Youth Center and After-school Care, 10200 Pioneer Rd; tel: (714) 918-0659

Emergency Shelters, Hospitality Houses

Anchorage, AK 99501: Eagle Crest Transitional Housing, 438 E 9th Ave; tel: (907) 276-5913 (acc 70)

Bell, CA 90201: 5600 Rickenbacker; tel: (323) 263-1206 (acc 484)

Boise, ID 83702: 1617 N 24th St; tel: (208) 343-3571 (acc 24)

Cheyenne, WY 82001: Sally's House, 1920 Seymour St, PO Box 385, 82003 (mail); tel: (307) 634-2769 (acc 6)

Colorado Springs, CO 80909: Bridge House, 2641 E Yampa St; tel: (719) 635-1287 (acc 7)

Colorado Springs, CO 80909-4037:
2649 E Yampa St, Freshstart Transitional
Family Housing; tel: (719) 227-8773 (acc 61)

Colorado Springs, CO 80903-4023:
R.J. Montgomery Center, 709 S Sierra Madre;
tel: (719) 578-9190 (acc 210)

Colorado Springs, CO 80909: Freshstart
Transitional Family Housing, 918 Yuma St;
tel: (719) 635-1287

Denver, CO 80221-4115: Denver New Hope
(Lambuth) Family Center, 2741 N Federal
Blvd; tel: (303) 477-3758 (acc 84)

El Centro, CA 92244: 375 N 5th St;
tel: (760) 352-8462

Fresno, CA 93711-3705: Gabelcrest Women's
Transitional Home, 1107 W Shaw;
tel: (559) 226-6110 (acc 35)

Glendale, CA 91204-2053: Nancy Painter
Home, 320 W Windsor Rd;
tel: (213) 245-2424 (acc 19)

Grand Junction, CO 81502: Women's and Family
Shelter, 915 Grand Ave, PO Box 578, 0578
81501 (mail); tel: (907) 242-3343 (acc 10)

Grass Valley, CA 95945: Booth Family Center,
12390 Rough and Ready Hwy;
tel: (530) 272-2669 (acc 46)

Helena, MT 59601: Transitional Housing,
1905 Henderson; tel: (406) 442-8244 (acc 8)

Hilo, HI 96720: Interim Home for Youth,
1786 Kinoole St, Box 5085;
tel: (808) 959-5855 (acc 18)

Honokaa, HI 96727: Residential Group Home,
45-350 Ohelo St, PO Box 5085, Hilo,
HI 96720; tel: (808) 775-0241

Honolulu, HI 96816: FTS-Supportive Living, 845
22nd Ave; tel: (808) 732-2802 (acc 24)

Kahului, HI 96732-2256: Safe Haven Drop-in
Center, 45 Kamehameha St;
tel: (808) 877-3042

Kailua-Kona, HI 96740: Youth Shelter,
75-235 Kalani St, PO Box 5085, Hilo, HI 96720;
tel: (808) 331-1674 (acc 8)

Kodiak, AK 99615-6511: Kodiak, Beachcombers
Transitional Housing, 1855 Mission Rd;
tel: (907) 486-8740 (acc 10)

Las Vegas, NV 89030:
Safehaven Shelter, 31 W Owens Ave;
tel: (702) 639-0277 (acc 25)
Pathways, 37 W Owens Ave;
tel: (702) 639-0277 (acc 42)
Lied Transitional Housing, 45 W Owens Ave;
tel: (702) 642-7252 (acc 71)
Emergency Lodge, 47 W Owens Ave;
tel: (702) 639-0277 (acc 167)
PATH – Petaluma Area Transitional Housing,
33 W Owens Ave; tel: (702) 639-0277 (acc 25)

Horizon Crest Apts, 13 W Owens Ave;
tel (702) 639-0277 (acc 78)

Lodi, CA 95240-2128: Hope Harbor Family
Service Center, 622 N Sacramento St;
tel: (209) 367-9560 (acc 80)

Lodi, CA 95240: Hope Avenue,
331 N Stockton Ave (acc 26)

Los Angeles, CA 90015: Alegria (HIV/Aids
housing) Aids Project, Transitional Housing,
2737 Sunset Blvd; tel: (323) 454-4200
(acc 195); Emergency Shelter, 832 W James M
Woods Blvd; tel (213) 438-0933

Los Angeles, CA 90025-3477: Westwood
Transitional Housing, 1401 S Sepulveda Blvd;
tel: (310) 477-9539 (acc 60)

Marysville, CA 95901-5629: The Depot Family
Crisis Center, 408 'J' St; tel: (530) 216-4530
(acc 67)

Marysville, CA 95901: Transitional Living
Program, 5906 B Riverside Dr;
tel: (530) 216-4530 (acc 40)

Medford, OR 97501-4630: 1065 Crews Rd;
tel: (541) 773-7005 (acc 43)

Modesto, CA 95354: Berberian Shelter,
320 9th St; tel: (209) 525-8954 (acc 110)

Nampa, ID 83651: 1412 4th St South;
tel: (208) 461-3733 (acc 54)

Oakland, CA 94601: Family Emergency Shelter,
2794 Garden St, Box 510, 94604 (mail);
tel: (510) 437-9437 (acc 86)

Olympia, WA 98501: Hans K Lemcke Lodge,
808 5th Ave SE; tel: (360) 352-8596 (acc 58)

Phoenix, AZ 85008: Kaiser Family Center,
2707 E Van Buren, Elim House, PO Box
52177, 85072; tel: (602) 267-4122 (acc 50)

Portland, OR 97209: SAFES, Female Emergency
Shelter, 11 NW 5th Avenue; tel: (503) 227-8681

Portland, OR 97210: 2640 NW Alexandra Ave;
tel: (503) 239-1248 (acc 10)

Portland, OR 97208: Women and Children's
Family Violence Center, PO Box 2398;
tel: (503) 239-1254 (acc 53)

Redlands, CA 92374: Cold Weather Shelter
838 Alta Street; tel: 909-792-8818

Sacramento, CA 95814-0603: Emergency
Shelter, 1200 N 'B' St; tel: (916) 442-0331
(acc 134)

Salem, OR 97303:
1901 Front St NE; tel: (503) 585-6688 (acc 83)
105 River St NE; tel: (503) 391-1523 (acc 6)
1960 Water St NE; tel: (503) 566-7267 (acc 10)

San Bernardino, CA 92411: Hospitality
House, 925 W 10th St; tel: (909) 888-4880
(acc 78)

Sand City, CA 93955: Good Samaritan Center,
800 Scott St; tel: (831) 899-4988 (acc 60)

San Diego, CA 92101: STEPS, 825 7th Ave; tel: (619) 669-2200 (acc 30)

San Francisco, CA 94103: SF Harbor House, 407 9th St; tel: (415) 503-3000 (acc 52)

San Francisco, CA 94102: Railton Place (Permanent and Transitional Housing), 242 Turk St; tel: (415) 345-3142 (acc 110)

San Jose, CA 95112: Hospitality House, 405 N 4th St; tel: (408) 282-1175 (acc 78)

Santa Ana, CA 92701 (Orange County): 818 E 3rd St; tel: (714) 542-9576 (acc 52)

Santa Barbara, CA 93101: 423 Chapala St; tel: (805) 962-6281 (acc 40)

Santa Fe Springs, CA 90606: Transitional Living Center, 12000 E Washington Blvd, Box 2009, 90610; tel: (562) 696-9562 (acc 116)

Santa Rosa, CA 95404: Transitional Living Program; tel (707) 535-4271 (acc 33)

Seaside, CA 93955:
Casa De Las Palmas Transitional Housing, 535 Palm Ave; tel: (831) 392-1762 (acc 54)
The Frederiksen House, 1430 Imperial St; tel: (831) 899-1071 (acc 16)
Two-Step-Two Transitional Housing, 1430 Imperial St; tel: (831) 899-4988 (acc 16)

Seattle, WA 90101: Women's Shelter (Emergency Financial Assistance), 1101 Pike St, PO Box 20128; tel: (206) 447-9944 (acc 22)

Seattle, WA: Catherine Booth House (Shelter for Abused Women), Box 20128, 98102; tel: (206) 324-4943 (acc 37)

Seattle, WA 98134: William Booth Center – Emergency Shelter and Transitional Shelter/Living, 811 Maynard Ave S; tel: (206) 621-0145 (acc 171)

Seattle, WA 98136: Hickman House (Women), 5600 Fauntleroy Way SW, Box 20128, 98102; tel: (206) 932-5341 (acc 35)

Spokane, WA 99201:
Family Shelter, 204 E Indiana Ave, Box 9108, 99209-9108; tel: (509) 325-6814 (acc 90)
Sally's House (Foster Care Home), Box 9108, 99209-9108, 222 E Indiana; tel: (509) 392-2784 (acc 20)

Spokane, WA 99207-2335: Transitional Housing, 127 E Nora Ave; tel: (509) 326-7288 (acc 96)

Tacoma, WA 98405: Jarvie Family/Women's Emergency Shelter, 1521 6th Ave, Box 1254, 98401-1254; tel: (253) 627-3962 (acc 76)

Tucson, AZ 85705: Hospitality House 1021 N 11th Ave; tel: (520) 622-5411 (acc 91)

Tucson, AZ 85716: SAFE Housing, 3525 E 2nd St #1; tel: (520) 622-5411 (acc 117)

Ventura, CA 93001-2703: 155 S Oak St; tel: (805) 648-5032 (acc 51)

Watsonville, CA 95076-5048: Supportive Housing Program for Women, 232 Union St; tel: (831) 763-2701 (acc 60)

Harbour Light Centres

Denver, CO 80205: Denver Harbor Light, 2136 Champa St; tel: (303) 296-2456 (acc 80)

San Francisco, CA 94103-4405: 1275 Harrison St; tel: (415) 503-3000 (acc 85)

Homeless Centres

Anchorage, AK 99508: McKinnell House, 1712 'A' St; tel: (907) 276-1609 (acc 110)

Modesto, CA 95351 320-9th St; tel: (209) 529-7507) (acc 150)

Residential Youth Care and Family Service Centres

Anchorage, AK 99508: Booth Memorial Youth and Family Services, 8600 E 20th Ave; tel: (907) 279-0522 (acc 20)

Boise, ID 83702: Family Day Care Center, 1617 N 24th St, Box 1216, 83701; tel: (208) 343-3571 (acc 15)

Los Angeles, CA 90028: The Way In (teen counselling) Transitional Housing, 5941 Hollywood Blvd, Box 38668, 90038-0668; tel: (213) 468-8666 (acc 20)

Portland, OR 97210: 2640 NW Alexandra Ave, Box 10027; tel: (503) 239-1248 (acc 33)

San Diego, CA 92123: Door of Hope Haven, Transitional Living Center, 2799 Health Center Dr; tel: (858) 279-1100

San Francisco, CA 94102: Railton Place Foster Youth Housing, 242 Turk St; tel (415) 345-3400 (acc 27)

Adult Rehabilitation Programmes (Men)

Albuquerque, NM 87102: 400 John St SE, Box 27690, 87125-7690; tel: (505) 242-3112 (acc 36)

Anchorage, AK 99503: ARP, 660 E 48th Ave; tel: (907) 562-5408 (acc 61)

Chico, CA 95973: 13404 Browns Valley Dr; tel: (530) 342-2199 (acc 30)

Grand Junction, CO 81502: 903 Grand Ave, Box 578, 81502; tel: (970) 242-8632 (acc 32)

North Las Vegas, NV 89030:
211 Judson St, Box 30096; tel: (702) 399-2769
2035 Yale St; tel (702) 649-2374

Reno, NV 89512-1605: 2300 Valley Rd; tel: (775) 688-4570 (acc 70)

San Bernardino, CA 92410: Path to Prosperity, 730 W Spruce; tel: (909) 884-2364

San Diego, CA 92101-6304: STEPS, 825 7th Ave; tel: (619) 669-2200

Adult Rehabilitation Programmes (Women)

Chico, CA 95973: 13404 Browns Valley Dr;
tel: (530) 342-2199 (acc 20)

Grand Junction, CO 81502: Adult Rehabilitation
Program – Women's Residence, 915 Grand Ave,
PO Box 578, 0578-81501 (mail);
tel: (907) 242-8632 (acc 10)

North Las Vegas, NV 89030: 39 W Owens;
tel: (702) 649-1469

Senior Citizens' Housing

Albuquerque, NM: Silvercrest, 4400 Pan Am
Fwy NE, 87107; tel: (505) 883-1068 (acc 55)

Broomfield, CO 80020-1876: Silvercrest,
1110 E 10th Ave; tel: (303) 464-1994
(acc 85)

Chula Vista, CA 91910: Silvercrest, 636 3rd Ave;
tel: (619) 427-4991 (acc 73)

Colorado Springs, CO 80909-7507: Silvercrest I,
904 Yuma St; tel: (719) 475-2045 (acc 50)

Colorado Springs, CO 80909-5097: Silvercrest II,
824 Yuma St; tel: (719) 389-0329 (acc 50)

Denver, CO 80219-1859: Silvercrest, 4595 W
Alameda Ave; tel: (303) 922-2924 (acc 66)

El Cajon, CA 92020: Silvercrest, 175 S Anza St;
tel: (619) 593-1077 (acc 73)

El Sobrante, CA 94803-1859: Silvercrest,
4630 Appian Way #100; tel: (510) 758-1518
(acc 63)

Escondido, CA 92026: Silvercrest, 1303 Las
Villas Way; tel: (760) 741-4106 (acc 75)

Eureka, CA 95501-1264: Silvercrest,
2141 Tydd St; tel: (707) 445-3141 (acc 152)

Fresno, CA 93721-1041: Silvercrest,
1824 Fulton St; tel: (559) 237-9111 (acc 158)

Glendale, CA 92104: Silvercrest, 323 W Garfield;
tel: (818) 543-0211 (acc 150)

Hollywood, CA 90028: Silvercrest, 5940 Carlos
Ave; tel: (323) 460-4335 (acc 140)

Lake View Terrace, CA 91354: Silvercrest,
11850 Foothill Blvd; tel: (818) 896-7580
(acc 150)

Los Angeles, CA 90006: Silvercrest,
947 S Hoover St; tel: (213) 387-7278
(acc 120)

Mesa, AZ 85201: Silvercrest, 255 E 6th St;
tel: (480) 649-9117 (acc 82)

Missoula, MT 59801: Silvercrest, 1550 S 2nd
St W #125; tel: (406) 541-0464 (acc 75)

N Las Vegas, NV 89030: Silvercrest, 2801 E
Equador Ct; tel: (702) 643-0293 (acc 60)

Oceanside, CA 92056: Silvercrest, 3839 Lake
Blvd; tel: (760) 940-0166 (acc 67)

Pasadena, CA 91106: Silvercrest, 975 E Union St;
tel: (626) 432-6678 (acc 150)

Phoenix, AZ 85003: Silvercrest, 613 N 4th Ave;
tel: (602) 251-2000 (acc 126)

Portland, OR 97232: Silvercrest, 1865 NE Davis;
tel: (503) 236-2320 (acc 78)

Puyallup, WA 98373: Silvercrest, 4103 9th St SW;
tel: (253) 841-0785 (acc 41)

Redondo Beach, CA 90277: Mindeman Senior
Residence, 125 W Beryl St;
tel: (310) 318-2827/0582 (acc 54)

Reno, NV 89512-2448: Silvercrest,
1690 Wedekind Rd; tel: (775) 322-2050
(acc 59)

Riverside, CA 92501: Silvercrest, 3003 N Orange;
tel: (951) 276-0173 (acc 72)

San Diego, CA 92101: Silvercrest, 727 E St;
tel: (619) 699-7272 (acc 122)

San Francisco, CA 94133-3844: SF Chinatown
Senior Citizens' Residence, 1450 Powell St; tel:
(415) 781-8545 (acc 9)

San Francisco, CA 94107-1132: Silvercrest,
133 Shipley St; tel: (415) 543-5381 (acc 514)

Santa Fe Springs, CA 90670: Silvercrest, 12015
Lakeland Rd; tel: (562) 946-7717 (acc 25)

Santa Monica, CA 90401: Silvercrest,
1530 5th St; tel: (310) 393-5336 (acc 122)

Santa Rosa, CA 95404-6601: Silvercrest,
1050 3rd St; tel: (707) 544-6766 (acc 186)

Seattle, WA 98103, Silvercrest,
9543 Greenwood Ave N #105;
tel: (206) 706-0855 (acc 75)

Stockton, CA 95202-2645: Silvercrest,
123 N Stanislaus St; tel: (209) 463-4960
(acc 84)

Tulare, CA 93274: 350 North 'L' St;
tel: (559) 688-0704 (acc 65)

Turlock, CA 95380: Silvercrest, 865 Lander Ave;
tel: (209) 669-8863 (acc 82)

Ventura, CA 93004: Silvercrest, 750 Petit Ave;
tel: (805) 647-0110 (acc 130)

Wahiawa, HI 96786: Silvercrest Residence, 520
Pine St #116; tel: (808) 622-2785 (acc 159)

Senior Citizens' Nutrition Centres

Anchorage, AK 99501: Older Alaskans' Program
(OAP), 1712 'A' Street; tel: (907) 349-0613

Denver, CO 80205-4547: Denver Red Shield,
2915 High St; (tel): (303) 295-2107

Fresno, CA 93712-1041: 1824 Fulton St;
tel: (559) 233-0139

Glendale, CA 91204-2053; Home-Delivered Meals,
320 W Wundsir Rd; tel: (818) 2246-5586

Phoenix, AZ: Laura Danieli Senior Activity
Center, 613 N 4th Ave; tel: (602) 251-2005

Portland, OR 97232-2822: Rose Centre – Senior
Citizens' Program, 211 NE 18th Ave;
tel: (503) 239-1221

Redondo Beach, CA 90277-2056:
Home-delivered meals, 125 W Beryl St;
tel: (310) 318-2827

Salinas, CA 93906-1519: 2460 N Main St;
tel: (831) 443-9655

San Diego, CA 92101-1679: Senior Citizens'
Program (9 Locations), 2320 5th Ave;
tel: (619) 446-0212

San Francisco, CA 94107-1125: Senior Meals
Program, 850 Harrison St; tel: (415) 777-5350

San Jose, CA 95112: 359 N 4th St;
tel: (408) 282-1165

Tulare, CA 93274-4131: 314 E San Joaquin Ave;
tel: (559) 687-2520

Turlock, CA 95380-5815: 893 Lander Ave;
tel: (209) 667-6091

Veterans Centres

Beaverton, OR 97007: 14825 SW Farmington Rd;
tel: (503) 239-1259 (acc 143)

Casper, WY 8260: 625 So. Jefferson Street:
tel: (307) 234-1368

El Paso County, CO 80909: 910 Yuma Street;
tel: (719) 884-1060

Fort Collins, CO 80525: 3901 South Mason
Street; tel: (970) 207-4472

Los Angeles, CA 90073: The Haven:
Victory Place-Drug and Alcohol Rehab;
Naomi House For Women (Emergency
Shelter); Exodus for Mentally Ill (Emergency
Shelter); 1301 Wilshire Blvd, Bldg 212;
tel: (310) 478-3711 ext 48761
(acc 265)

Pueblo, CO 81003: 520 W 13th Street;
tel: 719-543-3656

*In addition there are 15 fresh-air camps and
36 youth community centres attached to divisions,
as well as 519 service units in the territory*

**June 2012: The Pasadena Tabernacle Youth Chorus visited International
Headquarters, London during a tour of the Finland and Estonia and UK
territories. The 60-strong choir was accompanied by USA Western Territory
leaders Commissioners Carolyn and James Knaggs** (standing extreme left, first
and second rows respectively)

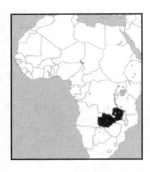

ZAMBIA TERRITORY

Territorial leaders:
Colonels Stephen and Grace Chepkurui

Territorial Commander:
Colonel Stephen Chepkurui (1 Mar 2011)

Chief Secretary:
Lieut-Colonel Christopher Mabuto
(1 Jul 2011)

Territorial Headquarters: 685A Cairo Road, Lusaka

Postal address: PO Box 34352, Lusaka 10101, Zambia

Tel: [260] 1 238291/228327; email: zamleadership@zam.salvationarmy.org

In 1922 emigrants from villages on the north bank of the Zambezi River working in a mica mine near Hurungwe were converted. They carried home the message of salvation to their chief and established meeting places in their villages. Two years later, Commandant Kunzwi Shava and Lieutenant Paul Shumba were appointed to command the new opening. The Zambia Division in the Rhodesia Territory became the Zambia Command in 1966. In 1988, the Malawi Division was transferred from the Zimbabwe Territory to form the new Zambia and Malawi Territory. The Zambia and Malawi Territory became the Zambia Territory on 1 October 2002 when Malawi became an independent region.

Zone: Africa
Country included in the territory: Zambia
Languages in which the gospel is preached: Chibemba, Chinyanja, Chitonga, English, Lozi

A SUCCESSFUL self-denial ingathering was held in July 2011 and many divisions and districts reported an increased amount of money raised. This meeting also marked the retirement of Lieut-Colonels Bislon and Melody Hanunka (CS and TSWM) from active service.

Regional congresses took place from August to October 2011 and were supported by the leadership team from THQ. Congress meetings were very well attended. At a gathering in Musamba, Central North District, Lieut-Colonels Christopher and Annah Mabuto were welcomed as Chief

Secretary and Territorial Secretary for Women's Ministries.

Zambia showed true democracy when the people went to the polls on 20 September. There was a smooth transition to a newly-elected government and a Salvationist from Chelstone Corps, the corps sergeant-major, became a member of parliament.

In November, 33 cadets were commissioned and ordained as Salvation Army officers by Commissioner Amos Makina (then IS for Africa). So many people attended the meeting that the hall was overflowing and crowds stood outside. During the same weekend Commissioner Rosemary Makina (then ZSWM for Africa) was the guest speaker for the women's ministries 'Helping Hand' ingathering. This inspiring meeting attracted large numbers of women, some of whom had travelled great distances to attend.

At Christmas the women's ministries and the public relations departments invited 556 impoverished children who live on the streets of Lusaka to a special meal at Libala Citadel. The children also received food and clothing to take with them. Business organizations and the government Minister for Community Development attended this event. The minister paid tribute to The Salvation Army 'for being a reliable partner in the development of the nation through many services rendered to society'.

In January 2012 a Brengle Institute was held at Chikankata Seminar Centre for 25 officers. Retired Commissioners Stuart and Hope Mungate from Zimbabwe were the guest speakers.

Thirty cadets of the Disciples of the Cross session were received for officer training in February 2012. During the meeting, the new training principal and director of special services, Majors Kenneth and Ann Hawkins, (from UKT) were welcomed by the territorial commander.

In March the World Day of Prayer was observed in all divisions, districts and at THQ. The theme was 'Let Justice Prevail' and Salvation Army home league members participated in ecumenical worship services with readings, singing and timbrel displays.

STATISTICS

Officers 258 (active 231 retired 27) **Cadets** 30 **Employees** 422
Corps 128 **Societies** 44 **Outposts** 156 **New Openings** 13 **Hospital** 1 **High School** 1 **Old People's Home** 1 **Farm** 1
Senior Soldiers 24,529 **Adherent Members** 3,157 **Junior Soldiers** 8,009
Personnel serving outside territory Officers 5

STAFF

Women's Ministries: Col Grace Chepkurui (TPWM) Lt-Col Annah Mabuto (TSWM) Maj Christine Chenda (THLS) Capt Esther Munkombwe (TJHLS) Maj Patricia Hangoma (TLOMS)
Sec for Personnel: Lt-Col Metson Chilyabanyama
  Extension Training: Capt Henry Shiridzinodya
  Human Resources: Maj Joster Chenda
Sec for Programme: Lt-Col Edward Shavanga
  Community Development, Faith-Based Facilitation and HIV/Aids Services: Maj Angela Hachitapika
  Education: Maj Brighton Hachitapika
  Men's Fellowships/Strategist: Maj Adeck Mwiinga
  Projects: Collins Sianjobo
  Public Relations Secretary: Capt Henry Shirizdinodya
  Social Secretary/ Micro Credit: Maj Ireen Hachamba
  Child Sponsorship: Elijah Hazemba
  Territorial B/M: Brave Hanunka
  Youth and Candidates: Capt Britius Munkombwe
Sec for Business Administration: Lt-Col Frazer Chalwe
  Finance and Audit: Maj Donald Hangoma
  Property: Maj Kennedy Mizinga
Spiritual Life Centre Manager: Maj Mary Mizinga
Trade: Maj Elison Cheelo
Training: Maj Kenneth Hawkins

DIVISIONS

Lusaka North West: PO Box 33934, Lusaka; Majs Clifford D. and Moudy Chikoondo
Lusaka South East: PO Box 34352, Lusaka; tel: (01) 221960; Majs Richard and Eunice Mweemba

Mapangazya: P Bag S2, Mazabuka;
Majs Casson and Mary Sichilomba
Mazabuka: PO Box 670017, Mazabuka;
tel: (032) 30420; Majs Bexter and
Jessie Magaya
Southern: PO Box 630537, Choma; Majs Elisha
and Alice Mankomba

DISTRICTS
Central North: Capt John Mweene
Copperbelt: PO Box 70075, Ndola;
tel: (02) 680302; Capt Aubey Hatukupa
Siavonga: PO Box 59, Siavonga;
tel: (01) 511362; Capt Victor Hamalala

SECTION (reporting to THQ)
Eastern: PO Box 510199, Chipata;
tel: (097) 881828; Maj Benson Champanga

TRAINING COLLEGE
PO Box 34352, Lusaka, 10101; tel: (260) 211 261
755; email: zsaotc@gmail.com

CHIKANKATA MISSION
P Bag S2, Mazabuka
Mission Director: Maj Benard Chisengele

CHIKANKATA HEALTH SERVICES
P Bag S2, Mazabuka; tel: (01) 222060;
email: administration@chikankata.com
Administration: Mr Simon Ledger
Business Manager: Maj Isaac Kauseni
**Manager/Community Health and
Development:** Mr Charles Mang'ombe
Manager/Nursing Education: Mrs Z. Ngalande
Hospital Chaplain: Maj Rotinah Sitwala
Chief Medical Officer: Dr Zairemthiamma
School of Nursing Matron: Maj Ruth Kauseni
Bio Medic School Matron: Maj Besnart
Chiwoya
Medical Clinics (under Chikankata)
Chaanga, Chikombola, Nadezwe, Nameembo,
Syanyolo

Youth Project (under Chikankata)
Chikombola

CHIKANKATA HIGH SCHOOL
P Bag S1, Mazabuka; tel: (01) 220820;
email: administration@chikankata.sch.zm
Headmaster: Mr Oscar Mwanza
Business Manager: Maj Wilson Chiwoya

OLD PEOPLE'S HOME AND VOCATIONAL TRAINING CENTRE
Mitanda Home for the Aged: PO Box 250096,
Kansenshi, Ndola; tel: (02) 680460;
email: mitanda@zamtel.zm:
Centre Manager: Maj Joyce B. Pierce

PRE-SCHOOL GROUPS
Chikankata, Chikanzaya, Chipapa, Chipata,
Chitumbi, Choma, Dundu, George, Hapwaya,
Ibbwe Munyama, John Laing, Kakole,
Kalomo, Kanyama, Kawama, Kazungula,
Lusaka Citadel, Maamba, Magoye, Mitchel,
Mukwela, Mumbwa, Ngangula, Njomona,
Nkonkola, Petauke, Peters, Siavonga,
Sikoongo, Sinazongwe, Situmbeko

COMMUNITY SCHOOLS
Chelstone, Chipata (Lusaka), Choma, George,
John Laing, Kanyama, Kasiwe, Kawama,
Luanshya, Maamba, Mbala, Monze,
Petauke

COMMUNITY WORK
Agriculture Projects: Chikankata, Chitumbi,
Dundu, Hamabuya, Malala, Ngamgula
Health Centres: George, John Laing
HIV/Aids Training, Counselling: Chikankata,
THQ
Micro-Credit Projects:
Eastern: Chipata
Lusaka North West: Mumbwa
Mapangazya: Chikankata
Mazabuka: Magoye, Monze, Nakambala,
Njomona

FARM (income-generating)
PO Box 250096, Kansenshi, Ndola;
tel: (02) 680460

ZAMBIA: A large crowd of women Salvationists attended the 'Helping Hand' ingathering in November 2011

ZIMBABWE: Commissioner Sue Swanson (seated, right) **joins in prayer at the mercy seat during the holiness meeting in Harare, March 2012**

ZIMBABWE TERRITORY

Territorial leaders:
**Commissioners Henry and
Catherine Nyagah**

Territorial Commander:
Commissioner Henry Nyagah
(1 Jan 2013)

Chief Secretary:
Colonel Wilfred Varughese
(1 Aug 2008)

Territorial Headquarters: 45 Josiah Chinamano Avenue, Harare

Postal address: PO Box 14, Harare, Zimbabwe

Tel: [263] (4) 736666/7/8, 250107/8; email: ZIMTHQ@zim.salvationarmy.org;

website: www.salvationarmy.org/Zimbabwe

A pioneer party led by Major and Mrs Pascoe set out from Kimberley, South Africa, on 5 May 1891 in a wagon drawn by 18 oxen, arriving in Fort Salisbury on 18 November. The then Rhodesia became a separate territory on 1 May 1931. Work spread to Botswana where The Salvation Army was officially recognised in 1997.

Zone: Africa
Countries included in the territory: Botswana, Zimbabwe
'The Salvation Army' in Ndebele: Impi yo Sindiso; in Shona: Hondo yo Ruponiso
Languages in which the gospel is preached: Chitonga, English, Ndebele, Shona, Tswana
Periodicals: *Zimbabwe Salvationist, ZEST* (women's magazine)

'ROOTED in Mission' was the theme of both residential officers' councils and divisional youth councils held in May 2011, conducted by the territorial leadership

The territorial Self-Denial ingathering took place in June. During this meeting, the women's ministries team donated vehicles to Tshelanyemba Hospital and the Kadoma and Midlands divisions. The Men's Mission Trust Fund presented a total of Z$478,970 from fundraising efforts.

Women's ministries staff donated items to inmates at Chikurubi Prison, including warm clothing, toiletries and farming equipment. Inmates at Khami Mlondolozi Female Prison in Matabeleland also received items. The prison authorities thanked The Salvation Army for such generous support.

More than 4,000 women gathered at Karimazondo in Marondera for a convention conducted by a team of officers from Malawi, led by the then Colonel Catherine Nyagah (TPWM).

The event was Spirit-filled, life-enhancing and encouraging.

In July men officers attended a retreat at a hotel in Zimbabwe where they received physical and spiritual refreshment and were encouraged in their family life and ministry.

Two conferences were held in July 2011 and January 2012 respectively, to appraise the implementation of the territorial strategic plan objectives.

The Salvation Army had a stand at the Agricultural Show Expo 2011 in August. The social and medical departments, in collaboration with Howard Hospital's Tariro Clinic, were featured and a puppet show was used by the 'Child First Project' to teach people about HIV/Aids risks and children's rights.

Commissioner Vinece Chigariro (then TC) commissioned and ordained 41 cadets of the Ambassadors of Holiness session in September.

The territorial men's congress was held at Gweru Showgrounds in Midlands Division in October.

On 18 November 2011, the territorial commander officiated at the groundbreaking ceremony for the Chingwena Clinic in Mudzi. Building materials worth Z$10,000 were donated through the Ministry of Home Affairs.

Also in November, 44 cadets of the Proclaimers of the Resurrection session were received for officer training and 19 delegates attended a servant leadership seminar at the training college.

In March 2012 Commissioner Sue Swanson (then WPWM) led a united holiness meeting in Harare, following the All Africa Women Leaders' Conference. She preached to a congregation of thousands declaring that 'no one is shut out of God's Kingdom'.

STATISTICS

Officers 615 (active 504 retired 111) **Cadets** 44 **Employees** 1,430
Corps 431 **Societies** 335 **Outposts** 217 **Institutions/Social Centres** 5 **Hospitals** 4 **Schools: Pre-Schools** 51 **Primary** 33 **Secondary** 13 **Boarding** 4 **Vocational Training** 7
Senior Soldiers 125,908 **Adherent Members** 7,829 **Junior Soldiers** 17,939
Personnel serving outside territory Officers 19

STAFF

Women's Ministries: Comr Catherine Nyagah (TPWM) Col Prema Wilfred (TSWM) Lt-Col Ellen Nyereyemhuka (TLOMS) Lt-Col Orlipha Ncube (THLS)
Sec for Business: Lt-Col Langton Zipingani
Sec for Personnel: Lt-Col Dubayi Ncube
Sec for Programme: Lt-Col Funny Nyereyemhuka
Audit: Maj Moyo Marasha
Development Services: Capt Criswell Chizengeya
Education: Maj Henry Chitanda
Finance: Maj Sheila Chitanda
Human Resources Development: Lt-Col Beauty Zipingani
Information Technology: Capt Jonathan Payne
Medical and Social: Maj Angeline Kapere
Property: Capt Tendai Kadzvatsva
Public Relations: Maj Itai Mutizwa
Sponsorship: Capt Joice Chizengeya
Statistics: Capt Susan Payne
Territorial Bandmaster: B/M M. Mtombeni
Territorial Songster Leader: S/L K.E. Mushababiri
Trade: Capt Tsaurai Mukwamuri
Training: Maj Trustmore Muzorori
Youth and Candidates: Maj Richard Makarawu

DIVISIONS

Bindura: PO Box 197, Bindura; tel: (071) 6689; Majs Yohana and Jesinala Msongwe

Chiweshe: PO Box 98, Glendale;
tel: (077) 214524; Maj Margaret Siamoya
Greater Harare: PO Box 1496, Harare;
tel: (04) 747359; Majs Onai and Deliwe Jera
Guruve: c/o Box 150, Guruve; tel: (058) 505;
Capts Taviringwa and Emmaculate Mupukuta
Harare Central: c/o Highfield Temple;
Stand # 3300, Old Highfield; tel: 663 159;
Majs Sammy and Ellen Nkoma
Harare Eastern: PO Box 26, Zengeza;
tel: (070) 22639;
Majs Eliud and Aidah Nabiswa
Harare West: c/o Dzivarasekwa Corps,
PO Box 37, Dzivarasekwa;
tel: (04) 216 293;
Maj Crisia Nyarubero
Hurungwe: PO Box 269, Karoi;
tel: (064) 629229;
Majs Final and Pfumisai Mubaiwa
Kadoma: PO Box 271, Kadoma;
tel: (068) 23338;
Majs Casman and Martha Chinyembe
Makonde: PO Box 33, Chinhoyi;
tel: (067) 2107;
Majs Frederick and Rosemary Masango
Masvingo: PO Box 314, Masvingo;
tel: (039) 63308;
Majs Isaac and Charity Mhembere
Matebeleland: PO Box 227 FM, Famona,
Bulawayo; tel: (09) 46934;
Majs Tineyi and Rumbidzai Mambo
Midlands: PO Box 624, Kwekwe;
tel: (055) 3992;
Majs Bigboy and Winnet Nkomo
Mupfure: PO Box 39, Mt Darwin;
tel: (076) 529;
Majs Clever and Daphine Kamambo
Semukwe: PO Box Maphisa Township,
Maphisa; tel: (082) 396;
Majs Joseph and Molly Madyanenzara

DISTRICTS

Manicaland: PO Box DV8, Dangamvura,
Mutare; tel: (020) 30014;
Maj Lovemore Chidhakwa
Murehwa: PO Box 268, Murehwa;
tel: (078) 2455; Maj Luckson Chimbalanga

AREAS

Hwange: PO Box 130, Dete; tel: 018 237;
Area Coordinator: Maj Peter Nikisi

TRAINING COLLEGE

PO Box CR95, Cranborne; tel: (04) 742298;

MASIYE TRAINING CAMP

PO Box AC800 Bulawayo; tel: (09) 60727;
Camp: tel: (0838) 222/261;
tel: (0838) 228;
emails: info@masiye.com (camp),
info@byo.masiye.com (town office)

EDUCATION
Boarding Schools
Bradley Secondary School (acc 516)
Howard High School (acc 908)
Mazowe High School (acc 670)
Usher Secondary School (acc 560)

MEDICAL
Bumhudzo Hospital Home: St Mary's Township,
PO Box ZG 48, Zengeza, Harare;
tel: (070) 24911; 'C' scheme hospital home
(acc 55); 'B' scheme residential (acc 55)
Howard Hospital: PO Box 190, Glendale;
tel: (0758) 2433; emails:
howard.hospital@africaonline.co.zw (acc 144)
Tshelanyemba Hospital: PO Tshelanyemba,
Maphisa; tel: (082) 254; email:
tshelanyemba.hosp@healthnet.zw (acc 103)

SOCIAL SERVICES
Bulawayo
Enterprise House (acc men 65)
Ralstein Home (acc mixed 30)
Harare
Braeside Social Complex (acc women 20,
men 64)
Arcadia Girls' Hostel (acc 28)
Howard
Weaving and Dressmaking School: PO Howard;
tel: (0758) 45921

Abbreviations used in *The Year Book*

A

(A) (active officer pG); Acc (Accommodation); Adj (Adjutant); Afr (Africa); Am (America); Ang (Angola); AO (Area Officer); Apt (Apartment); Appt (Appointment); ARC (Adult Rehabilitation Centre); Asst (Assistant); Aus (Australia); A/Capt, Aux-Capt (Auxiliary-Captain)

B

b. (born); Ban (Bangladesh); Belg (Belgium); B/M (Bandmaster); Braz (Brazzaville); Brig (Brigadier); Brz (Brazil); BT (British Territory)

C

Can (Canada and Bermuda); Capt (Captain); Carib (Caribbean); CIDA (Canadian International Development Agency); CO (Commanding Officer); Col (Colonel); Comr (Commissioner); Con (Congo); Con [Braz] (Congo Brazzaville); CoS (Chief of the Staff); CS (Chief Secretary); C/S (Corps Secretary); CSLD (Centre for Spiritual Life Development); CSM (Corps Sergeant-Major); C/T (Corps Treasurer); CPWM (Command President of Women's Ministries); Cze R (Czech Republic)

D

DC (Divisional Commander); Den (Denmark); DO (Divisional Officer); DR Con (Democratic Republic of Congo)

E

E Afr (East Africa); E Eur/EET (Eastern Europe); Ens (Ensign); Env (Envoy); ESFOT (European School for Officers' Training)

F

Fin (Finland and Estonia); Frce (France and Belgium)

G

Ger (Germany and Lithuania); Gha (Ghana); Grce (Greece); GS (General Secretary)

H

HK (Hong Kong and Macau); HL (Home League); Hun (Hungary)

I

ICO (International College for Officers); IHQ (International Headquarters); IHS (International Health Services); Ind C, E, etc (India Central, Eastern, etc); Ind M&A (India Madras and Andhra); Indon (Indonesia); Intnl (International); IPDS (International Projects and Development Services); IS (International Secretary); ISJC (International Social Justice Commission); It (Italy and Greece); ITC (International Training College)

J

JHLS (Junior Home League Secretary); Jpn (Japan)

K

Ken (Kenya); Kin (Kinshasa); Kor (Korea)

L

L Am N (Latin America North); Lat (Latvia); Lib (Liberia); Lt, Lieut (Lieutenant); Lt-Col, Lieut-Colonel (Lieutenant-Colonel); LOM (League of Mercy)

M

m (married); Maj (Major); Mal (Malawi); Mid E (Middle East); Mli (Mali); Mlys (Malaysia); Mol (Moldova); Moz (Mozambique); My (Myanmar)

N

Nat (National); NC (National Commander); Neth (The Netherlands and Czech Republic); NHQ (National Headquarters); Nor (Norway, Iceland and The Færoes); NZ (New Zealand, Fiji and Tonga)

O

OC (Officer Commanding); ODAS (Order of Distinguished Auxiliary Service); OF (Order of the Founder); O&R (Orders and Regulations)

P

Pak (Pakistan); pG (promoted to Glory); Phil (The Philippines); PNG (Papua New Guinea); Port (Portugal)

R

RC (Regional Commander); RDWM (Regional Director of Women's Ministries); ret (retired); RO (Regional Officer); ROS (Retired Officers Secretary); RPWM (Regional President of Women's Ministries); Rtd (Retired); Rus (Russia/CIS); Rwa (Rwanda and Burundi)

S

S/, Snr (Senior); S Afr (Southern Africa); SALT (Salvation Army Leadership Training); S Am E (South America East); SAMF (Salvation Army Medical Fellowship); S Am W (South America West); SAWSO (Salvation Army World Service Office); Sec (Secretary); Sen (Senior); SFOT (School for Officers' Training); Sgt (Sergeant); Sing (Singapore, Malaysia and Myanmar); S/L (Songster Leader); Soc S (Social Services); Sp (Spain); SP&S (Salvationist Publishing and Supplies); Sri Lan (Sri Lanka); Supt (Superintendent); Swdn (Sweden and Latvia); Switz (Switzerland, Austria and Hungary)

T

Tai (Taiwan); Tanz (Tanzania); tba (to be appointed); TC (Territorial Commander); tel (telephone); TCCMS (Territorial Community Care Ministries Secretary); THQ (Territorial Headquarters); TLWM, TPWM, TSWM (Territorial Leader of, President of, Secretary for Women's Ministries); TWMS (Territorial Women's Ministries Secretary)

U

Uga (Uganda); UK (United Kingdom); Uk (Ukraine); USA (United States of America); USA Nat, USA C, etc (USA National, Central, etc)

W

WI (West Indies); WPWM WSWM (World President of, Secretary for Women's Ministries); Ww (Widow/Widower)

Z

Zai (Zaïre); Zam (Zambia); Zimb (Zimbabwe); ZSWM (Zonal Secretary for Women's Ministries)

GLOSSARY OF SALVATION ARMY TERMS

Adherent Member: A member of The Salvation Army who has not made a commitment to soldiership.

Advisory Board: A group of influential citizens who, believing in the Army's programme of spiritual, moral and physical rehabilitation and amelioration, assist in promoting and supporting Army projects.

'Blood and Fire': The Army's motto; refers to the blood of Jesus Christ and the fire of the Holy Spirit.

Cadet: A Salvationist who is in training for officership.

Candidate: A soldier who has been accepted for officer training.

Chief of the Staff: The officer second in command of the Army throughout the world.

Chief Secretary: The officer second in command of the Army in a territory.

Citadel: A building used for worship and community service.

Colours: The tricolour flag of the Army. Its colours symbolise the blood of Jesus Christ (red), the fire of the Holy Spirit (yellow) and the purity of God (blue).

Command: A type of small territory.

Command leaders: A married officer couple appointed to a joint role of spiritual leadership, ministry, administration and pastoral care.

Commission: A document presented publicly, authorising an officer, or local officer to fulfil a specified ministry.

Congress: Central gatherings often held annually and attended by most officers and many soldiers of a territory, command, region or division.

Corps: A Salvation Army unit established for the preaching of the gospel and to provide Christian-motivated service in the community.

Corps Cadet: A young Salvationist who undertakes a course of study and practical training in a corps, with a view to becoming effective in Salvation Army service.

Corps Sergeant-Major: The chief local officer for public work who assists the corps officer with meetings and usually takes command in his/her absence.

Dedication Service: A public presentation of infants to the Lord. This differs from christening or infant baptism in that the main emphasis is upon specific vows made by the parents concerning the child's upbringing.

Division: A number of corps grouped together under the direction of a divisional commander (may also include social service centres and programmes), operating within a territory or command.

Divisional Commander: The officer in charge of the Army in a division.

Envoy: A Salvationist whose duty it is to visit corps, societies and outposts, for the purpose of conducting meetings. An envoy may be appointed in charge of any such unit.

General: The officer elected to the supreme command of the Army throughout the world. All appointments are made, and all regulations issued, under the General's authority (see under High Council – p 12).

General Secretary: The officer second in charge of the Army in a command (or, in some territories, a large division).

Halfway House: A centre for the rehabilitation of alcoholics or parolees (USA).

Harbour Light Centre: A reclamation centre, usually located in inner city areas.

High Council: See p 12.

Home League: See p 25.

International Headquarters (IHQ): The offices in which the business connected with the command of the worldwide Army is transacted. See p 30.

International Secretary: A position at IHQ with responsibility for the oversight and coordination of the work in a specific geographical zone or functional category, and for advising the General on zonal and worldwide issues and policies.

Junior Soldier: A boy or girl who, having accepted Jesus as their saviour, has signed the junior soldier's promise and become a Salvationist.

League of Mercy: Salvationists who visit prisons, hospitals and needy homes, in their own time, bringing the gospel and rendering practical aid (see p 26).

Local Officer: A soldier appointed to a position of responsibility and authority in the corps; carries out the duties of the appointment without being separated from regular employment or receiving remuneration from the Army.

Medical Fellowship: See p 26.

Mercy Seat or Penitent Form: A bench provided as a place where people can kneel to pray, seeking salvation or sanctification, or making a special consecration to God's will and service. The mercy seat is usually situated between the platform and main area of Army halls as a focal point to remind all of God's reconciling and redeeming presence.

Officer: A Salvationist who has has been trained, commissioned and ordained to service and leadership, in response to God's call. An officer is a recognised minister of religion.

Officer Commanding: The officer in charge of the Army in a command.

Order of Distinguished Auxiliary Service: See p 29

Order of the Founder: See p 27

Outpost: A locality in which Army work is carried out and where it is hoped a society or corps will develop.

Pastoral Care Council: Established in each corps for the care of soldiers, etc, and maintenance of the membership rolls.

Promotion to Glory: The Army's description of the death of Salvationists.

Ranks of Officers: Lieutenant, captain, major, lieut-colonel, colonel, commissioner, General.

Red Shield: A symbol saying 'The Salvation Army' in the local language, identifying personnel, buildings, equipment, mobile units and emergency services.

Red Shield Appeal: A financial appeal to the general public; also known as the Annual Appeal in some countries.

Red Shield Centre: A Salvation Army facility on military premises serving the physical and spiritual needs of military personnel and their families.

Salvation: The work of grace which God accomplishes in a repentant person whose trust is in Christ as Saviour, forgiving sin, giving meaning and new direction to life, and strength to live as God desires. The deeper experience of this grace, known as holiness or sanctification, is the outcome of wholehearted commitment to God and enables the living of a Christlike life.

Self-Denial Appeal: An annual effort by Salvationists and friends to raise funds for the Army's worldwide operations.

Sergeant: A local officer appointed for specific duty, usually in a corps.

Society: A company of soldiers who work together regularly in a district, without an officer.

Soldier: A converted person at least 14 years of age who has, with the approval of the pastoral care council, been enrolled as a member of The Salvation Army after signing the Soldier's Covenant.

Soldier's Covenant: The statement of beliefs and promises which every intending soldier is required to sign before enrolment. Previously called 'Articles of War'.

Territorial Commander: The officer in command of the Army in a territory.

Territorial leaders: A territorial commander and spouse in their joint role of sharing spiritual leadership and ministry, providing pastoral care and exemplifying the working partnership of officer couples. The chief secretary is the second-in-command of the territory.

Territory: A country, part of a country or several countries combined, in which Salvation Army work is organised under a territorial commander.

Young People's Sergeant-Major: A local officer responsible for young people's work in a corps, under the commanding officer.

CHRONOLOGICAL TABLE OF IMPORTANT EVENTS IN SALVATION ARMY HISTORY

1829 Catherine Mumford (later Mrs Booth, 'the Army Mother') born at Ashbourne, Derbyshire (17 Jan); William Booth born at Nottingham (10 Apr).

1844 William Booth converted.

1846 Catherine Mumford converted.

1855 Marriage of William Booth and Catherine Mumford at Stockwell New Chapel, London (16 Jun).

1856 William Bramwell Booth (the Founder's eldest son and second General of the Army) born in Halifax (8 Mar).

1858 William Booth ordained as Methodist minister (27 May). (Accepted on probation 1854.)

1859 *Female Teaching*, Mrs Booth's first pamphlet, published (Dec).

1860 Mrs Booth's first public address (27 May, Whit Sunday).

1865 **Rev William Booth began work in East London** (2 Jul); The Christian Mission, founded; Eveline (Evangeline) Cory Booth (fourth General) born in London (25 Dec).

1867 First Headquarters (Eastern Star) opened in Whitechapel Road, London.

1868 *The East London Evangelist* – later (1870) *The Christian Mission Magazine* and (1879) *The Salvationist* – published (Oct).

1874 Christian Mission work commenced in **Wales** (15 Nov).

1875 *Rules and Doctrines of The Christian Mission* published.

1876 *Revival Music* published (Jan).

1878 First use of the term 'Salvation Army' – in small appeal folder (May); 'The Christian Mission' became **'The Salvation Army'**, and the Rev William Booth became known as the General; deed poll executed, thus establishing the doctrines and principles of The Salvation Army (Aug); first corps flag presented by Mrs Booth at Coventry (28-30 Sep); *Orders and Regulations for The Salvation Army* issued (Oct); brass instruments first used.

1879 First corps in **Scotland** opened (24 Mar) and **Channel Islands** (14 Aug); cadets first trained; introduction of uniform; first corps band formed in Consett; issue No 1 of *The War Cry* published (27 Dec).

1880 First training home opened, at Hackney, London; first contingent of SA officers landed in the **United States of America** (10 Mar); SA work commenced in **Ireland** (7 May); children's meetings commenced at Blyth (30 Jul); SA work extended to **Australia** (5 Sep).

1881 Work began in **France** (13 Mar); *The Little Soldier* (subsequently *The Young Soldier*) issued (27 Aug); *The Doctrines and Disciplines of The Salvation Army* prepared for use at training homes for Salvation Army officers; Headquarters removed to Queen Victoria Street, London (8 Sep).

1882   The Founder's first visit to France (Mar); former London Orphan Asylum opened as Clapton Congress Hall and National Training Barracks (13 May); work began in **Canada** (21 May), **India** (19 Sep), **Switzerland** (22 Dec) and **Sweden** (28 Dec).

1883   Work begun in **Sri Lanka** (26 Jan), **South Africa** (4 Mar), **New Zealand** (1 Apr), **Isle of Man** (17 Jun) and **Pakistan** (then a part of India); first prison-gate home opened in Melbourne, Australia (8 Dec); *The Doctrines and Disciplines of The Salvation Army* published in a public edition.

1884   Women's Social Work inaugurated; *The Soldier's Guide* published (Apr); work began in **St Helena** (5 May); *The Salvation Army Band Journal* issued (Aug); *All the World* issued (Nov).

1885   Commencement of the Family Tracing Service, known as Mrs Booth's Enquiry Bureau; *Orders and Regulations for Divisional Officers* published (10 Jun); *The Doctrines of The Salvation Army* published; Purity Agitation launched; Criminal Law Amendment Act became law on 14 Aug; trial (began 23 Oct) and acquittal of Bramwell Booth – charged, with W. T. Stead, in connection with the 'Maiden Tribute' campaign.

1886   Work begun in **Newfoundland** (1 Feb); first International Congress in London (28 May-4 Jun); *The Musical Salvationist* issued (Jul); first Self-Denial Week (4-11 Sep); first slum corps opened at Walworth, London, by 'Mother' Webb (20 Sep); work began in **Germany** (14 Nov); *Orders and Regulations for Field Officers* published; the Founder first visited the United States and Canada.

1887   Work began in **Italy** (20 Feb), **Denmark** (8 May), **Netherlands** (8 May) and **Jamaica** (16 Dec); the Founder's first visit to Denmark, Sweden and Norway.

1888   Young people's work organised throughout Great Britain; first food depot opened, in Limehouse, London (Jan); work began in **Norway** (22 Jan); first junior soldiers' brass band (Clapton); the Army Mother's last public address at City Temple, London (21 Jun).

1889   Work begun in **Belgium** (5 May) and **Finland** (8 Nov); First edition of *The Deliverer* published (Jul).

1890   Work began in **Argentina** (1 Jan); *Orders and Regulations for Soldiers of The Salvation Army* issued (Aug); the Army Mother promoted to Glory (4 Oct); *In Darkest England and the Way Out*, by the Founder, published (Oct); work began in **Uruguay** (16 Nov); banking department opened (registered as The Salvation Army Bank, 1891; Reliance Bank Ltd, 28 Dec 1900).

1891   The Founder publicly signed 'Darkest England' (now The Salvation Army Social Work) Trust Deed (30 Jan); £108,000 subscribed for 'Darkest England' scheme (Feb); Land and Industrial Colony, Hadleigh, Essex, established (2 May); International Staff Band inaugurated (Oct); work began in **Zimbabwe** (21 Nov) and **Zululand** (22 Nov); the Founder's first visit to South Africa, Australia, New Zealand and India; the charter of The Methodist and General Assurance Society acquired.

1892   Eastbourne (UK) verdict against Salvationists quashed in the High Court of Justice (27 Jan); Band of Love inaugurated; League of Mercy begun in Canada (Dec).

1893   Grace-Before-Meat scheme instituted; *The Officer* issued (Jan).

1894   Second International Congress (Jul); work began in **Hawaiian Islands** (13 Sep) and **Java** (now part of **Indonesia**) (24 Nov); naval and military league (later red shield services) established (Nov); Swiss Supreme Court granted religious rights to SA (Dec).

1895   Work began in **British Guiana** (now **Guyana**) (24 Apr), **Iceland** (12 May), **Japan** (4 Sep) and **Gibraltar** (until 1968).

1896   Young people's legion (Jan) and corps cadet brigades (Feb) inaugurated; work began in **Bermuda** (12 Jan) and **Malta** (25 Jul until 1972); first SA exhibition, Agricultural Hall, London (Aug).

1897   First united young people's meetings (later termed 'councils') (14 Mar); first International Social Council in London (Sep); first SA hospital founded at Nagercoil, India (Dec).

1898   *Orders and Regulations for Social Officers* published; work began in **Barbados** (30 Apr) and **Alaska**; first united corps cadet camp at Hadleigh (Whitsun).

1899   First bandsmen's councils, Clapton (10 Dec).

Salvation Army History

1901 Work began in **Trinidad** (7 Aug).

1902 Work begun in **St Lucia** (Sep) and **Grenada**.

1903 Migration Department inaugurated (became Reliance World Travel Ltd, 1981; closed 31 May 2001); work began in **Antigua**.

1904 Third International Congress (Jun-Jul); Founder received by King Edward VII at Buckingham Palace (24 Jun); Founder's first motor campaign (Aug); work began in **Panama** (Dec).

1905 The Founder campaigned in the Holy Land, Australia and New Zealand (Mar-Jun); first emigrant ship chartered by SA sailed for Canada (26 Apr); opening of International Staff Lodge (later College, now International College for Officers) (11 May); work began in **St Vincent** (Aug). Freedom of London conferred on the Founder (26 Oct); Freedom of Nottingham conferred on the Founder (6 Nov).

1906 *The YP* (later *The Warrior*, then *Vanguard*) and *The Salvation Army Year Book* issued; Freedom of Kirkcaldy conferred on the Founder (16 Apr).

1907 Anti-Suicide Bureau established (Jan); Home League inaugurated (28 Jan); *The Bandsman and Songster* (later *The Musician*) issued (6 Apr); honorary degree of DCL, Oxford, conferred on the Founder (26 Jun); work began in **Costa Rica** (5 Jul).

1908 Work began in **Korea** (Oct).

1909 Leprosy work commenced in **Java** (now part of **Indonesia**) (15 Jan); SA work began in **Chile** (Oct).

1910 Work began in **Peru**, **Paraguay** and **Sumatra** (now part of **Indonesia**).

1912 Founder's last public appearance, in Royal Albert Hall, London (9 May); **General William Booth promoted to Glory** (20 Aug); **William Bramwell Booth appointed General** (21 Aug).

1913 Inauguration of life-saving scouts (21 Jul); work began in **Celebes** (now part of **Indonesia**) (15 Sep) and **Russia** (until 1923).

1914 Fourth International Congress (Jun).

1915 Work began in **British Honduras** (now **Belize**) (Jun) and **Burma** (now **Myanmar**); life-saving guards inaugurated (17 Nov).

1916 Work began in **China** (Jan until 1951), in **St Kitts** and in **Portuguese East Africa** (now **Mozambique**) (officially recognised 1923).

1917 Work began in **Virgin Islands** (USA) (Apr); chums inaugurated (23 Jun); Order of the Founder instituted (20 Aug).

1918 Work commenced in **Cuba** (Jul).

1919 Work began in **Czechoslovakia** (19 Sep until 1950).

1920 Work began in **Nigeria** (15 Nov) and **Bolivia** (Dec).

1921 Work began in **Kenya** (Apr); sunbeams inaugurated (3 Nov).

1922 Work began in **Zambia** (1 Feb), **Brazil** (1 Aug) and **Ghana** (Aug); publication of a second *Handbook of Salvation Army Doctrine*.

1923 Work began in **Latvia** (until 1939).

1924 Work began in **Hungary** (24 Apr until 1950), in **Surinam** (10 Oct) and **The Færoes** (23 Oct).

1927 Work began in **Austria** (27 May), **Estonia** (31 Dec until 1940) and **Curacao** (until 1980); first International Young People's Staff Councils (May-Jun).

1928 General Bramwell Booth's last public appearance – the stonelaying of the International (William Booth Memorial) Training College (now William Booth College), Denmark Hill, London (10 May).

1929 First High Council (8 Jan-13 Feb); **Comr Edward J. Higgins elected General**; General Bramwell Booth promoted to Glory (16 Jun); Army work began in **Colombia** (until 1965).

1930 Inception of goodwill league; Order of the Silver Star (now Fellowship of the Silver Star) inaugurated (in USA, extended to other lands in 1936); work began in **Hong Kong**; Commissioners' Conference held in London (Nov).

1931 Work began in **Uganda** and the **Bahamas** (May); The Salvation Army Act 1931 received royal assent (Jul).

1932 Work began in **Namibia** (until 1939).

1933 Work began in **Yugoslavia** (15 Feb until 1948), Devil's Island, **French Guiana** (1 Aug until closing of the penal settlement in 1952) and **Tanzania** (29 Oct).

1934 Work began in **Algeria** (10 Jun until 1970); second High Council elected Commander Evangeline Booth General (3 Sep); work began in **Congo (Kinshasa)** (14 Oct); **General Evangeline Booth took command of The Salvation Army** (11 Nov).

1935 Work began in **Singapore** (28 May).

1936 Work began in **Egypt** (until 1949).

1937 Work began in **Congo (Brazzaville)** (Mar), **The Philippines** (6 Jun) and **Mexico** (Oct).

1938 Torchbearer group movement inaugurated (Jan); *All the World* re-issued (Jan); work spread from Singapore to **Malaysia**.

1939 Third High Council elected Comr George Lyndon Carpenter General (24 Aug); **General George Lyndon Carpenter took command of The Salvation Army** (1 Nov).

1941 Order of Distinguished Auxiliary Service instituted (24 Feb); International Headquarters destroyed in London Blitz (10 May).

1943 Inauguration of The Salvation Army Medical Fellowship (16 Feb) (SA Nurses' Fellowship until 1987).

1944 Service of thanksgiving to mark centenary of conversion of William Booth (in 1844) held in St Paul's Cathedral, London (2 Jun).

1946 Fourth High Council elected Comr Albert Orsborn General (9 May); **General Albert Orsborn took command of The Salvation Army** (21 Jun).

1948 First Army worldwide broadcast (28 Apr).

1950 Work began in **Haiti** (5 Feb); first TV broadcast by a General of The Salvation Army; official constitution of students' fellowship; first International Youth Congress held in London (10-23 Aug); reopening of Staff College (later International College for Officers) (10 Oct).

1954 Fifth High Council elected Comr Wilfred Kitching General (11 May); **General Wilfred Kitching took command of The Salvation Army** (1 Jul).

1956 Work began in Port Moresby, **Papua New Guinea** (31 Aug); first International Corps Cadet Congress (19-31 Jul).

1959 Over-60 clubs inaugurated (Oct).

1962 Work began in **Puerto Rico** (Feb).

1963 Sixth High Council elected Comr Frederick Coutts General (1 Oct); Queen Elizabeth the Queen Mother declared International Headquarters open (13 Nov); **General Frederick Coutts took command of The Salvation Army** (23 Nov).

1965 Queen Elizabeth II attended the International Centenary commencement (24 Jun); Founders' Day Service held in Westminster Abbey, London (2 Jul); work

re-established in **Taiwan** (pioneered 1928) (Oct).

1967 Work began in **Malawi** (13 Nov).

1969 Seventh High Council elected Comr Erik Wickberg General (23 Jul); *The Salvation Army Handbook of Doctrine* new edition published (Aug); **General Erik Wickberg took command of The Salvation Army** (21 Sep); work began in **Lesotho**.

1970 Cyclone relief operations in East Pakistan (later **Bangladesh**) (25 Nov) lead to start of work in 1971.

1971 Work began in **Spain** (23 Jul) and **Portugal** (25 Jul).

1972 Work began in **Venezuela** (30 Jun).

1973 Work began in **Fiji** (14 Nov).

1974 Eighth High Council elected Comr Clarence Wiseman General (13 May); **General Clarence Wiseman took command of The Salvation Army** (6 Jul).

1976 Work began in **Guatemala** (Jun); **Mexico and Central America Territory** (now **Latin America North Territory** and **Mexico Territory**) formed (1 Oct).

1977 The ninth High Council elected Comr Arnold Brown General (5 May); **General Arnold Brown took command of The Salvation Army** (5 Jul).

1978 Fifth International Congress (Jun-Jul), with opening ceremony attended by HRH the Prince of Wales.

1979 The Salvation Army Boys' Adventure Corps (SABAC) launched (21 Jan).

1980 Inauguration of International Staff Songsters (8 Mar); The Salvation Army Act 1980 received royal assent (1 Aug); work began in **French Guiana** (1 Oct).

1981 Tenth High Council elected Comr Jarl Wahlström General (23 Oct); **General Jarl Wahlström took command of The Salvation Army** (14 Dec).

1984 International Conference of Leaders held in Berlin, West Germany (May).

1985 Work began in **Colombia** (21 Apr) and **Marshall Islands** (1 Jun); second Inter-national Youth Congress (Jul) held in Macomb, Illinois, USA; work began in **Angola** (4 Oct) and **Ecuador** (30 Oct).

1986 Work began in **Tonga** (9 Jan); *Salvationist* first issued (15 Mar); 11th High Council elected Comr Eva Burrows General (2 May); **General Eva Burrows took command of The Salvation Army** (9 Jul);

International Development Conference held at Sunbury Court, London (Sep).

1988 Work began in **Liberia** (1 May); International Conference of Leaders held in Lake Arrowhead, California, USA (Sep).

1989 Work began in **El Salvador** (1 Apr).

1990 Work began in **East Germany** (Mar), **Czechoslovakia** (May), **Hungary** (Jun) and re-established in **Latvia** (Nov); sixth International Congress held in London (Jun-Jul); **United Kingdom Territory** established (1 Nov).

1991 Restructuring of **International Headquarters** as an entity separate from UK Territory (1 Feb); work reopened in **Russia** (6 Jul); International Conference of Leaders held in London (Jul-Aug).

1992 Opening of new **USA National Headquarters** building in Alexandria, Virginia (3 May).

1993 The 12th High Council elected Comr Bramwell H. Tillsley General (28 Apr); **General Bramwell H. Tillsley took command of The Salvation Army** (9 Jul); work began in **Micronesia**.

1994 First International Literary and Publica-tions Conference held at Alexandria, Virginia, USA (Apr); General Bramwell H. Tillsley resigned from office (18 May); 13th High Council elected Comr Paul A. Rader General (23 Jul); **General Paul A. Rader took command of The Salvation Army immediately**; work began in **Guam**.

1995 International Conference of Leaders held in Hong Kong (Apr); all married women officers granted rank in their own right (1 May); work began in **Dominican Republic** (1 Jul); work reopened in **Estonia** (14 Aug); following relief and development programmes, work began in **Rwanda** (5 Nov).

1996 Work began in **Sabah (East Malaysia)** (Mar); first meeting of International Spiritual Life Commission (Jul).

1997 International Youth Forum held in Cape Town, South Africa (Jan); first-ever congress held in Russia/CIS; Salvation Army leaders in Southern Africa signed commitment to reconciliation for past stand on apartheid; work began in **Botswana** (20 Nov).

1998 International Conference of Leaders held in Melbourne, Australia (Mar), receives report of International Spiritual Life Commission; publication of a fourth Handbook of Doctrine entitled *Salvation Story* (Mar); International Commission on Officership opened in London (Oct).

1999 International Education Symposium held in London (Mar); work began in **Romania** (May); 14th High Council elected Comr John Gowans General (15 May); **General John Gowans took command of The Salvation Army** (23 Jul).

2000 International Commission on Officership closed and subsequent Officership Survey carried out (Mar-May); work began in **Macau** (25 Mar); The Salvation Army registered as a denomination in **Sweden** (10 Mar); International Conference of Leaders held in Atlanta, Georgia, USA (Jun); seventh International Congress held in Atlanta, Georgia, USA (28 Jun-2 Jul) (first held outside UK); work began in **Honduras** (23 Nov)

2001 International Conference for Training Principals held in London (Mar); International Theology and Ethics Symposium held in Winnipeg, Canada (Jun); International Music Ministries Forum held in London (Jul); International Poverty Summit held on the Internet and Lotus Notes Intranet (Nov 2001-Feb 2002)

2002 The 15th High Council elected Comr John Larsson General (6 Sep); **General John Larsson took command of The Salvation Army** (13 Nov)

2004 International Conference of Leaders held in New Jersey, USA (29 Apr-7 May); International Music and Other Creative Ministries Forum (MOSAIC) held in Toronto, Canada (Jun); New International Headquarters building at 101 Queen Victoria Street, London, opened by Her Royal Highness, The Princess Royal (9 Nov); IHQ Emergency Services coordinates disaster relief work after Indian Ocean tsunami struck (26 Dec)

2005 Eastern Europe Command redesignated Eastern Europe Territory; Singapore, Malaysia and Myanmar Command redesignated Singapore, Malaysia and Myanmar Territory (both 1 Mar); International Literary and Publications Conference held at Alexandria, Virginia, USA (Apr); European Youth Congress held in Prague, Czech Republic (4-8 Aug); All-Africa Congress held in Harare, Zimbabwe (24-28 Aug); work in **Lithuania** officially recognised by IHQ, and Germany Territory redesignated Germany and Lithuania Territory (Sep); 'Project Warsaw' launched to begin Army's work in **Poland** (23-25 Sep); East Africa Territory redesignated Kenya Territory, with Uganda Region given command status (1 Nov)

2006 The 16th High Council elected Comr Shaw Clifton General (28 Jan); **General Shaw Clifton took command of The Salvation Army** (2 Apr); Salvation Army Scouts and Guides World Jamboree held in Almere, Netherlands (Aug); 2nd International Theology and Ethics Symposium held in Johannesburg, South Africa (Aug)

2007 Website for Office of the General launched (Feb); first of General's pastoral letters to soldiers dispatched electronically (15 Mar); first International Conference of Personnel Secretaries held in London (27 May-3 Jun); International Social Justice Commission established (1 Jul), headed by an International Director for Social Justice; work began in **Burundi** (5 Aug) and **Greece** (1 Oct)

2008 Work recommenced in **Namibia** (3 Jan); new opening began in **Mali** (7 Feb); ICO renamed International College for Officers and Centre for Spiritual Life Development (Jul); first officers appointed to **Kuwait** (1 Aug); work began in **Mongolia** (13 Oct); first International Women Leader Development Programme held at Sunbury Court, UK (18 Nov-6 Dec)

2009 Official opening of work in **Nepal** (15 Apr); largest-ever assembly of SA leaders at International Conference of Leaders held in London, UK (7-13 Jul); first International Prayer Leaders Gathering held at CSLD, London (11-18 Sep)

2010 Work began in **Sierra Leone** (1 Jan); **Nicaragua** (1 Mar); **United Arab Emirates** (1 Jun); Sweden hosted 'Raised Up' World Youth Convention (15-18 Jul); first Salvation Army building opened in **Mongolia** (9 Sep)

2011 Work began in the **Turks and Caicos**

Islands (1 Jan); 17th High Council elected Comr Linda Bond 19th General (31 Jan); Work began in the **Solomon Islands** (1 Feb); **Greece** was recognised as part of Italy and Greece Command (2 Feb); Malawi, Mozambique and Uganda became territories (1 Mar); International Doctrine Council held in North Carolina, USA (23-26 Mar); Work began in **Togo**, Mali and Middle East were given regional status (all 1Apr);

General Linda Bond took command of The Salvation Army (2 Apr); ISB 120 celebrations in London (3-5 Jun)

Biographical Information

Based on information received by 31 October 2012

1. The following list contains the names of all active officers with the rank of lieut-colonel and above, and other officers holding certain designated appointments.

2(a) The place and date in parenthesis immediately following the name denote the place from which the officer entered Army service and the year of service commencement. Officers commissioned prior to 1 January 1973 have their active service dated from the conclusion of the first year of training. After 1 January 1973 active service begins at the date of commissioning following a two-year session of training.

(b) Details of married women officers' entry to active service are shown separately, including maiden name. If a wife was trained separately from her husband the word *and* joins the two entries, but if trained together the word *with* joins them.

(c) At the end of each entry of married officers a joint record of their service in other countries is given. Where applicable this includes countries each served in individually before marriage.

3. Where an officer is serving in a territory/command other than his/her own this is indicated by including the territory/command of origin after the corps from which he/she entered training. In all other instances the information given implies that the officer is serving in his/her home territory.

4. Details of appointments (where not given in this section) may be ascertained under the territorial or departmental headings.

5. A key to abbreviations is given on pages 295-296.

A

ABAYOMI, Ebenezer (Ife Ife, 1988); Maj, Nig. b 4 Apr 60; and
  ABAYOMI, Comfort (Ife Ife, 1990) m 1990; Maj, Nig. b 12 Dec 63.

ABEL, Bailis (Chenkody, 1980); Maj, Ind SE. b 20 Feb 53; and
  ABARANAM, Bailis (Chadayanvilai, 1972) m 1980; Maj, Ind SE. b 23 Aug 48.

ABBULU, Sankurati Pedda (Achanta, 1978); Maj, Ind C. b 2 Jan 50; with
  ABBULU, Vimala (née Kumari) m 1970; Maj, Ind C. b 10 Dec 53. Served in Tanz.

ABIA, Edmund (Somanya, 1993); Maj, Gha, b 14 Mar 62; with
  ABIA, Grace (née Awo) m 1991; Maj, Gha. b 15 Feb 69.

ADAMS, Clive (Claremont, S Afr, 1983); Comr, TC, UK. b 5 Jan 57; and
  ADAMS, Marianne (née Jokobsen) (Oslo 3, 1985) m 1990; Comr, TPWM, UK. b 10 Feb 60. Served in S Afr, UK, at IHQ and in Nor (CS/TSWM, TC/TPWM).

ADDISON, Edward (Swedru, 1981); Maj, Gha. b 24 Jan 54. Ww Lt Margaret, pG 1983; and
  ADDISON, Mercy (née Simpson) (Swedru, 1985) m 1985; Maj, Gha. b 4 Nov 60.

ADEPOJU, Gabriel (Ibadan, 1986); Maj, Nig. b 17 Jul 60. MSc, MA, BEd; and
  ADEPOJU, Comfort (Ibadan, 1994) m 1994; Maj, Nig. b 15 Aug 70.

AHN, Guhn-shik (Oh Ka, 1985); Maj, Kor. b 23 Dec 57; and
  YANG, Shin-kyong (Sudaemun, 1984) m 1985; Maj, Kor. b 5 Jul 54.

AKPAN, Joseph (Calabar, 1980); Lt-Col, Nig. b 30 Sep 58; with
  AKPAN, Patience m 1978; Lt-Col, Nig. b 15 May 62.

AKPAN, Mfon Jaktor (Igbobi, 1969); Comr, TC, Nig. b 21 Jul 49; and
  AKPAN, Ime Johnnie (née Udo) (Ikot Udobia, 1974) m 1974; Comr, TPWM, Nig. b 8 Nov 53. Served in Con (Braz) (CS/TSWM, TC/TPWM).

ALARCÓN, David (Punta Arenas, 1980); Lt-Col, L Am N. b 24 Jun 56; and
  ALARCÓN, María (née Arredondo) (Rancagua, 1984) m 1982; Lt-Col, L Am N. b 3 Mar 55. Served in S Am W.

ALÍ, Sixto (El Tejar, 1990); Maj, S Am W. b 28 Mar 63; with
  ALÍ, Aída (née Cáceres) m 1988; Maj, S Am W. b 8 Mar 68.

ALLAN, Graham (Kokomo, IN, 1975); Maj, USA C. b 24 Feb 49. BA (Counselling/Bus Adm), AA (Bus); with
  ALLAN, Vickie (née Hardebeck) m 1969; Maj, USA C. b 26 Jan 50.

ALLCHIN, Joy (néeMuskett) (Aylsham, 1981); Maj, UK. b 13 Feb 60; and
  ALLCHIN, Clifford (Gravesend, 1981) m 1982; Maj, UK. b 26 Feb 58.

ALLEMAND, Carolyn (née Olckers) (Cape Town Citadel, S Afr, 1980); Lt-Col, UK. b 4 Oct 55. Served in S Afr, at IHQ and in S Am E. m 1989; Lt-Col Gustave, ret 2006.

ALLEY, Kelvin (Belconnen, Aus E, 1987); Maj, Aus Nat and Aus E. b 3 Apr 54. BA (Admin), BDiv, DMin; with

Biographical Information

ALLEY, Julie (née Stewart) m 1975; Maj, Aus E. b 19 Jun 56. Dip Min. Served in PNG.

ALM, Britt-Marie (née Johansson) (Hisingskåren, 1970); Lt-Col, Swdn. b 28 Dec 45.

AMAKYE, Francis (Achiase, 1995); Maj, Tanz. b 25 Jul 65; with
AMAKYE, Jemima (née Agyei Yeboah) m 1992; Maj, Tanz. b 3 May 65. Served in Gha.

AMBITAN, Harold (Manado 1, 1973); Lt-Col, Indon. b 9 May 49; and
AMBITAN, Deetje (née Malawau) (Bandung, 1972) m 1975; Lt-Col, Indon. b 8 Jun 49.

AMICK, Richard (Hutchinson, KS, 1978); Lt-Col, USA C. b 24 Nov 54. BA (Bus Adm); and
AMICK, Vicki (née Anderson) (Grand Haven, MI, 1978) m 1979; Lt-Col, USA C. b 29 Jun 55.

AMPOFO, Jonas (Asiakwa, 1981); Maj, Gha. b 6 Oct 1950; W w Maj Agnes pG 2000 and
AMPOFO, Constance (née Nyamekye) m 2004; Capt, Gha. b 14 Apr 57.

ANDERSEN, Henrik (Lyngby, 1986); Lt-Col, CS, Den. b 30 Aug 61; with
ANDERSEN, Lisbeth (née Bjarkam) m 1984; Lt-Col, TSWM, Den. b 17 Apr 64. Served in Latvia and UK.

APPAVOO, Sam Devaraj (Muttacaud, 1976); Maj, Ind SE. b 23 Jun 51; and
KANAGARETNAM, Sam Devaraj (Anducode, 1975) m 1977; Maj, Ind SE. b 19 Oct 54.

APPEATENG, Seth (Manso, 1989); Lt-Col, CS, Tanz. b 19 Oct 62; with
APPEATENG, Janet (née Nkansah) m 1987; Lt-Col, TSWM, Tanz. b 12 Dec 67. Served in Gha.

ARGUEDAS, Antonio (Callao, Peru, 1974); Maj, S Am W. b 9 Sep 53; and
ARGUEDAS, Lilian (née Sánchez) (Lima Central, 1981) m 1981; Maj, S Am W. b 24 Nov 58.

ARNAL, Sylvie (Alès, 1977); Lt-Col, CS, Frce and Belg. b 13 Apr 53. Served in Zaï and Con (Braz).

ARROWOOD, James (Winston-Salem Central, NC, 1983); Maj, USA S. b 23 Jan 56; with
ARROWOOD, Linda (née Portis) m 1975; Maj, USA S. b 16 Feb 57.

ARULAPPAN, Paramadhas (Elanthiady, 1972); Lt-Col, Ind SE. b 11 May 54; and
ARULAPPAN, Retnam Paramadhas (Changaneri, 1974) m 1976; Lt-Col, Ind SE. b 30 May 51.

ASIRVATHAM, Devadhas (Palliyady, 1971); Maj, Ind SE. b 20 May 51; and
JOTHI, Vasanthabai Devadhas (Manakarai, 1973) m 1973; Maj, Ind SE. b 11 Apr 53

AYANAM, Friday S. (Akai, 1988); Maj, Nig. b 2 Oct 64; with
AYANAM, Glory m 1986; Maj, Nig. b 28 Apr 64. Served in Zimb.

B

BAAH, Samuel (Duakwa, Gha, 1987); Lt-Col, Gha. b 13 Mar 63; with
BAAH, Theresa (née Kumi) m 1984; Lt-Col, Gha. b 10 Sep 64. Served in Nig.

BAHAMONDE, Cecilia (Lo Vial, 1983); Maj, S Am W. b 23 Mar 63.

BAILEY, Carol (Greenock, 1977); Maj, UK. b 13 May 57.

BAILEY, F. Bradford (Kansas City [Westport Temple], MO, USA C, 1982); Col, CS, USA C. b 4 May 58. BS (Soc Work); with
BAILEY, Heidi J. (née Chandler) m 1978; Col, TSWM, USA C. b 17 Jul 54. Served in USA C, Sp (OC/CPWM) S Am W (CS/TSWM) and at IHQ.

BAKEMBA, Prosper (Mabenga, 1982); Lt-Col, Con (Braz). b 21 Oct 49; with
BAKEMBA, Monique (née Mafoua) m 1980; Lt-Col, Con (Braz). b 28 Jun 52.

BAKER, Gary (Nundah, 1976); Maj, Aus E. b 23 Sep 48; with
BAKER, Judith (née Wells) m 1969; Maj, Aus E. b 3 Jun 49.

BAMANABIO, Eugene (Mfilou, Con (Braz), 1990); Lt-Col, CS, Uga. b 10 Jul 62; with
BAMANABIO, Brigitte (née Locko-Oumba) m 1988; Lt-Col, TSWM, Uga, b 13 Dec 1963. Served in Con (Braz) and Rwa.

BAMFORD, William A. III (Quincy, MA, USA E, 1989); Lt-Col, CS, S Am W. b 11 Jun 57. BS (Pharm), MS (Org Ldrshp); with
BAMFORD, G. Lorraine (née Brown) m 1980; Lt-Col, TSWM, S Am W. b 25 Jul 53. BA (Mod Langs). Served in USA E.

BANDA, Alfred (Kaning'a 1997); Capt, Mal. b 10 Aug 71; with
BANDA, Pamela, m.1999; Capt, Mal. b 24 Sep 72

BANFIELD, Stephen (Quincy, MA, 1978); Lt-Col, USA Nat. b 17 Mar 53. BA (Psych); with
BANFIELD, Janet (née Anderson) m 1976; Lt-Col, USA Nat. b 27 Apr 55. Served in USA E.

BARKAT, Samuel (Thal, 1973); Maj, Pak.
b 7 Aug 51; with
SAMUEL, Margaret m 1971; Maj, Pak.
b 7 Aug 52.

BARNARD, Rodney (Norwood, 1982); Lt-Col,
Aus S. b 7 Apr 49; with
BARNARD, Jennifer (née Rowe) m 1970;
Lt-Col, Aus S. b 5 Nov 50. Served in UK.

BARR, John M. (Ian) (Saltcoats, 1972);
Lt-Col, UK. b 10 Aug 50. BD (Hons), MA
Cert Ed. Served at ITC. m 1974; Lt-Col
Christine, ret 2009.

BATE, Alastair (Central Citadel, NY, USA E,
1990); Lt-Col, USA E. b 9 Jan 63; BS; and
BATE, Carole (née Voisey, Hempstead, NY,
USA E, 1989); Lt-Col, USA E. b 12 Mar 67.
Served in EET (CS/TSWM).

BATEMAN, David (Lower Hutt, 1988);
Maj, NZ. b 17 Dec 60. Dip Bus, Cert Mgmt
(NZIM); with
BATEMAN, Margaret (née Allott) m 1983;
Maj, NZ. b 19 Nov 58. BN, RGON.

BECKMAN, Elisabeth (née Sundström)
(Stockholm Temple, 2006); Capt, Swdn,
b 18 Jan 65.

BELL, Donald C. (Spokane, WA, USA W, 1978);
Comr, TC, NZ. b 12 Oct 49. BA (Econ & Hist),
JD (Law);
BELL, Debora K. (née Perry) (Hobbs, NM,
1977) m 1979; Comr, TPWM, NZ. b 6 Feb 56.
Served at USA Nat, in USA W (CS/TSWM)
and NZ (CS/TSWM).

BELL, Mark (Hagerstown, MD, 1977); Lt-Col,
USA S. b 27 Mar 51; with
BELL, Alice (née Armendariz) m 1975;
Lt-Col, USA S. b 26 Sep 54.

BERG, Gro (née Egeland) (Stavanger, 1985);
Maj, Nor. b 11 Oct 62.

BERG, Odd (Harstad, 1969); Lt-Col, Nor.
b 4 Mar 47; with
BERG, Grethe (née Knetten) (Ski, 1969)
m 1971; Lt-Col, Nor. b 12 May 48. Served in
Nor, UK, Den and Ger (CS/TSWM).

BERNAO, Raul (Trelew,1983); Maj, S Am E.
b 11 Oct 61; and
BERNAO, Lidia (née Lopez) (Santiago del
Estero, 1981) m 1984; Maj, S Am E.
b 20 Feb 59.

BERRY, Donald E. (Kearny, NJ, 1976); Maj,
USA E. b 9 Jun 49; with
BERRY, Vicki (née Van Nort) m 1970;
Maj, USA E. b 15 Jan 50. BA (Engl),
MA (Strategic Comms & Ldrshp).

BEZZANT, Ivan (Wellington South, 1981);
Maj, NZ. b 3 Sep 58; and

BEZZANT, Glenda (nee Mills) (Wellington
South, 1982) m 1982; Maj, NZ. b 9 Jan 59.

BIAKLIANA, S. (Hnahthial, 1981); Maj,
Ind E. b 15 Feb 56; and
BIAKMAWII (Dolchera, 1982) m 1982;
Maj, Ind E. b 10 Aug 62.

BLOMBERG, Sonja (née Waern) (Kristinehamn
1994); Maj, Swdn. b 1 May 56;
and
BLOMBERG, Christer (Kristinehamn 1994)
Maj, Swdn. b 16 Jul 54.

BLOOMFIELD, Glenn C. (Philadelphia NE,
PA, 1971); Maj, USA E. b 25 Feb 50; and
BLOOMFIELD, Carol (née Thompson)
(Cleveland Temple, OH, 1971) m 1972;
Maj, USA E. b 1 Jun 48.

BOADU, Stephen (Topremang 1985); Maj, Gha.
b 17 Jul 61; with
BOADU, Cecilia (née Ofori) m 1983; Maj,
Gha. b 4 Apr 63.

BODE, William H. (Alliance, OH, 1970);
Maj, USA E. b 6 Sep 49, and
BODE, Joan I. (née Burke) (Brooklyn 8th
Ave, NY, 1969) m 1971; Maj, USA E.
b 30 Aug 48.

BODDU GNANA Prakash Rao (Bhogapuram,
1987); Maj, Ind C. b 24 May 66, with
BODDU, Annamani m 1985; Maj, Ind C. b
20 July 68.

BONAZEBI, Philippe (Makaka, 1992); Maj,
Con (Braz). b 14 Sep 63; with
BONAZEBI, Julie Rose (née Kouba)
m 1988; Maj, Con (Braz). b 15 Jul 70.

BOND, Linda (St James, Winnipeg, Can, 1968);
General (see page 16).

BOOTH, Patrick (Paris-Central, Frce, 1989);
Maj, IHQ. b 12 Jan 55; with
BOOTH, Margaret (née Miaglia) m 1983;
Maj, IHQ. b 31 Jul 61. Served in Frce
UK and S Afr.

BOSCHUNG, Franz (Basle 2, 1977); Comr,
TC, Switz. b 21 Feb 49; with
BOSCHUNG, Hanny (née Abderhalden)
m 1971; Comr, TPWM, Switz. b 7 Apr 50.
Served in Con (Braz).

BOUZIGUES, Ricardo (Colegiales, 1976);
Col, TC, Mex. b 12 Sep 52. BA (Pract Theol),
MA (Theol); and
BOUZIGUES, Sonia (née Alvez) (Cordoba,
1979) m 1979; Col, TPWM, Mex. b 12 Nov 54.
Served in S Am E (CS/TSWM).

BOWERS, Thomas M. (Moline, IL, 1978);
Maj, USA C. b 19 Sep 55; with
BOWERS, Jacalyn G. (née Thorson)
m 1975; Maj, USA C. b 20 Mar 55. AA (Soc).

BOWLES, Marsha-Jean (née Wortley) (Woodstock, ON, Can, 1990); Lt-Col, CS, Ger. b 2 Mar 62; with
BOWLES, David m 1981; Lt-Col, Ger. b 20 Jul 60. Served in Can.

BRAUND, James (Peterborough Temple, ON, 1987); Maj, Can. b 12 Nov 60. B Sc; and
BRAUND, Ann (née Hennessey) (Picton, ON, 1983) m1987; Maj, Can. b 12 Apr 61.

BREKKE, Birgitte (née Nielsen) (Copenhagen Temple, 1980); Comr, IHQ (IS Eur). b 17 Sep 54. SRN. Served in Nor, Sri Lan, Ban (CPWO), UK, E Eur, Pak (TPWM) and Den (TC, TPWM). Ww Col Bo, pG 2007.

BROWN, Rosemarie (Kingston Central, Jamaica, 1978); Maj, Carib. b 17 Oct 57. BA (Theol) Served at ICO.

BUCKINGHAM, Lyndon (Whangarei, 1988); Lt-Col, CS, Sing. b 13 Feb 62; with
BUCKINGHAM, Bronwyn (née Robertson) m 1986; Lt-Col, TSWM, Sing. b 21 Jun 65. Served in Can and NZ.

BUEYA, Nsoki Joseph (Kavwaya, 1981); Lt-Col, DR Con. b 12 Jul 48; with
BUEYA, Germaine (née Nkenda Mbuku) m 1978; Lt-Col, DR Con. b 10 Jun 52.

BUKIEWICZ, Ralph (Milwaukee West, WI, 1980); Lt-Col, USA C. b 3 Mar 60; and
BUKIEWICZ, Susan (née Cunard) (Dearborn Heights, MI, 1981) m 1981; Lt-Col, USA C. b 9 May 58.

BUNGAY, Wayne (Fortune, NL, 1984); Maj, Can. b 16 Oct 1960. BA, BRS, with
BUNGAY, Deborah (née Loveless) m 1981; Maj, Can. b 4 May 1963. Served in Carib.

BURAVA, Vari (Lebogoro, 1987); Maj, PNG. b 1 Jan 62. Ww Capt Nellie, pG 2011.

BURN, Margaret (née Cain) (Lincoln Citadel, 1966); Lt-Col, UK. b 12 Nov 46.

BURNS, Alan (Harlow, 1976); Lt-Col, UK. b 1 May 54. BSc (Hons), MA (Evan); and
BURNS, Alison (née Hitchin) (Regent Hall, 1979) m 1981; Lt-Col, UK. b 8 Oct 52. Served at IHQ.

BURR, W. Howard (Lexington, KY, 1973); Lt-Col, USA E. b 8 Nov 47. BA (Psych), MS (Ed Adm); with
BURR, Patricia (née Stigleman) m 1970; Lt-Col, USA E. b 29 Jun 51.

C

CACHELIN, Hervé (Biel, 1979); Maj, Switz. b 16 Feb 57; and
CACHELIN, Deborah (née Cullingworth) (Catford, UK, 1981) m 1983; Maj, Switz.

b 2 Jul 57. Served in Aus E and UK.

CAFFULL, Michael (Worthing, 1978) Lt-Col, UK. b 20 Dec 55. MA (Miss Ldrshp); and
CAFFULL, Wendy (née Hart) (Southend Citadel, 1977) m 1978; Lt-Col, UK. b 24 Mar 57. BA (Pastoral Care with Psych). Served at IHQ.

CAIRNS, Philip (Campsie, 1982); Lt-Col, Aus E. b 5 Feb 51. Dip Mus Ed, Dip Min, MTh; with
CAIRNS, Janice (née Manson) m 1972; Lt-Col, Aus E. b 7 Oct 48. ATCL, LTCL, Grad Dip Chrstn Counselling.

CALDWELL, Bradley J. (Shreveport, LA, USA S, 1993); Maj, E Eur. b 31 Aug 64. MA (Div). BA (Phil); with
CALDWELL, Anita Maye (née Howard) m 1989; Maj, E Eur. b 1 Dec 56. BA (Rel). Served in USA S.

CALLANDER, Ian (Fairfield, Aus S, 1977); Lt-Col, Aus S. b 7 Aug 55. BTh; and
CALLANDER, Vivien (née Wiseman) (Adelaide Congress Hall, Aus S, 1977) m 1978; Lt-Col, Aus S. b 7 May 53. Dip Tech Physio, Grad Cert HR Mgmt. Served in E Eur.

CALVO, Esteban (Concepcion de Rios, 1987); Maj, L Am N. b 23 Jan 63; and
CALVO, Ileana (née Jimenez) (Concepcion de Rios, 1986) m 1989; Maj, L Am N. b 5 Jun 66.

CAMARGO, Iolanda (Niterói, Brz, 1969); Maj, Asst TSWM, Brz. b 6 Aug 49.

CAMARILLO, Luís (Mexico City 1, 2001); Capt, Mex. b 25 Apr 73; with
CAMARILLO, Nohemí (née Martínez) m 1999; Capt, Mex. b 20 May 73. BA (Adm).

CAMPBELL, Mark T. (Wollongong, 1985); Maj, Aus E. b 4 May 60. MA Th, BAL; with
CAMPBELL, Julie A. (née Woodbury) m 1983; Maj, Aus E. b 17 Sep 59.

CAMPOS Manuel (Mexicali, 1980); Maj, Mex. b 14 Jun 58; with
CAMPOS Ana (née Flores) m 1978; Maj, Mex. b 26 Jul 57.

CANNING, Joan (Moncton, NB, Can, 1983); Lt-Col, USA Nat. b 27 Sep 62. BA (Bib and Theol) MA (Theol). Served in Can and at IHQ.

CAPSEY, Mary (Leeds Central, UK, 1984); Lt-Col, IHQ. b 10 Mar 59. SRN, SCM, MSc (Health Ed & Prom). Served in UK, Gha, Belg, Con (Braz) and Zimb.

CAREY, Graham (Southend Citadel, 1972) Maj, E Eur. b 28 Nov 50 and
CAREY, Hélène (née Paulus) (Liege, Belg, 1972) m 1975; Maj, E Eur. b 24 Dec 50. Served in Belg, Frce and UK.

CAREY, Roderick (Dunedin Fortress, 1984); Maj, NZ. b 19 Mar 58. Dip BRS, BTh; with **CAREY, Jennifer** (née Cross) m 1980; Maj, NZ. b 5 Feb 61. Served Aust E.

CARLSON, William (Staten Island Port Richmond, NY, 1971); Col, CS, USA E. b 9 Jan 48. BA (Soc Studies); and **CARLSON, Marcella** (née Brewer) m 1971; Col, TSWM, USA E. b 18 Sep 49.

CASTILLO, Luis (Antofagasta, S Am W, 1977); Lt-Col, OC, Sp. b 7 Jan 48; and **CASTILLO, Aída** (Quinta Normal, 1968) m 1972; Lt-Col, CPWM, Sp. b 5 Nov 49. Served in S Am W (CS/TSWM), Mex (CS/TSWM) and S Am E (CS/TSWM).

CASTOR, Onal (Aquin, Haiti, 1979); Col, TC, Carib. b 20 Jul 55; and **CASTOR, Edmane** (née Montoban) (Duverger, Haiti, 1980) m 1980; Col, TPWM, Carib. b 1 Oct 57. Served in USA S, Con (Kin) and Carib (CS/TSWM).

CAVANAGH, David (Catania, It, 1992); Maj, GS, It. b 15 Jan 65; and **CAVANAGH, Elaine** (née Piercy) (Southport, UK, 1992) m 1992; Maj, CSWM, It. b 28 Sep 62. Served in UK.

CENECIRO, Joel (Manila, 1989); Maj, Phil. b 23 May 66. BA (Biblical Studies), MA (Chrstn Studies); and **CENECIRO, Susan** (née Pudpud) (Tondo, 1989); Maj, Phil. b 31 Oct 66. B Min.

CEREZO, Josué (Monterrey, Mex, 1985); Lt-Col, CS, L Am N. b 16 May 57; with **CEREZO, Ruth** (née Garcia) m 1983; Lt-Col, TSWM, L Am N. b 22 Oct 60. Served in Mex (CS/TSWM).

CESAR, Danièle (née Polrot) (La Villette, 1983) m 1979, Maj, TSWM, Frce and Belg. b 26 Aug 58.

CHAGAS, Edgar (São Paulo Central, 1988); Maj, Brz. b 24 Feb 58. BA (Phys) MA (Sci); with **CHAGAS, Sara** (née Parker) m 1982; Maj, Brz. b 26 Aug 60. BA (Psychol).

CHALWE, Frazer (Chikumbi, 1989); Lt-Col, Zam. b 25 Jan 65; with **CHALWE, Rodinah** (née Mukunkami) m 1986; Lt-Col, Zam. b 8 May 68.

CHAMNESS, John M. (Seattle Temple, WA 1989); Maj, USA W. b 7 Jan 63; and **CHAMNESS, Martie (Lani) L.** (née Abella) (Pasadena Tabernacle, CA 1989) m 1990; Maj USA W. b 5 Feb 60.

CHAMPLIN, David A. (Oneonta, NY, 1981); Maj, USA E. b 22 Dec 50. BA (Mgmt), CERT (Finance); with

CHAMPLIN, Eunice (née Schmidt) m 1972; Maj, USA E. b 11 Nov 52. BA (Christian Edu), MA (Ldrshp & Min).

CHANG, Man-Hee (San Francisco Korean, CA, 1993); Maj, USA W. b 31 Mar 58. BA (Bus Adm), MBA (Bus Adm); with **CHANG, Stephanie** (née Shim) m 1983; Maj, USA W. b 1 Jun 59. BA (Math).

CHARAN, Samuel (Rampur, Ind N, 1978); Comr, TC, Ind SW. b 1 Apr 53; with **CHARAN, Bimla Wati** m 1974; Comr, TPWM, Ind SW. Served in Ind N, Ind SW (CS/TSWM) and Ind E (CS/TSWM, TC/TPWM).

CHAUHAN, Jashwant Soma (Tarapur, 1979); Maj, Ind W. b 20 Feb 52; with **CHAUHAN, Indiraben** m 1976; Maj, Ind W. b 8 Jun 56.

CHAWNGHLUNA, Chhangte (Sawleng 1983); Maj, Ind E. b 13 Apr 59. BA, BTh; and **KHAWLHRING Chhuanmawii** (Bethlehem 1986); m 1986; Maj, Ind E. b 14 Jun 65.

CHELLA Wycliff (Murukondapadu, Ind C, 1994) .b 6 Jan 65; with **CHELLA Chinnammaye** m 1990; Maj, Ind C. b 5 Jan 71.

CHELLAIYAN, Anbayan (Perai, 1982); Maj, Ind SE. b 9 Apr 55. BA, BD; and **DITCH, Saroja Bai Anbayan** (Vannioor, 1984) m 1984; Maj, Ind SE. b 31 May 61.

CHELLIAH, Moni (Osaravillai, 1976); Lt-Col, CS, Ind SW. b 18 May 55. MA; and **MALLIKA, Moni** (Alady, 1978) m 1978; Lt-Col, TSWM, Ind SW. b 6 Mar 57. Served in Ind SE.

CHELLIAH, Swamidhas (Kannankulam, 1977); Maj, Ind SE. b 21 Apr 55; and **JOICEBAI, Swamidhas** (Kaliancaud, 1973) m 1977; Maj, Ind SE. b 16 Feb 53.

CHENDA, Joster (Matero, 1981); Maj, Zam. b 10 Jun 57; and **CHENDA, Christine** (née Chingala) (Libala, 1983) m 1983; Maj, Zam. b 3 Mar 62.

CHEPKURUI, Stephen (Cheptais, Ken, 1982); Col, TC, Zam. b 22 Feb 58; and **CHEPKURUI, Grace** (née Madolio) (Vigeze, Ken, 1980) m 1985; Col, TPWM, Zam. b 15 May 55. Served in E Afr, Tanz (GS/CSWM) and Rwa (RC/RPWM, OC/CPWM).

CHEPSIRI, Harun (Toroso, 1995) Capt, Ken W. b 20 Sep 65; with **CHEPSIRI, Beatrice** (née Cherop) m 1992; Capt, Ken W. b 6 Jul 68.

CHIGARIRO, Vinece (Gunguwe, 1975); Comr, TC, TPWM, Ken E. b 7 Mar 54. Served in Tanz (GS) Zam (TC) and Zimb (TC,TPWM).

CHIKOONDO, Clifford (Nangogwe, 1995);
Maj, Zam. b 12 Jul 62; with
CHIKOONDO, Moudy (Mweemba)
m 1986; Major, Zam. b 11 Mar 68.

CHILYABANYAMA, Metson (Chitumbi,
1987); Lt-Col, Zam. b 30 Oct 55; with
CHILYABANYAMA, Rosemary (née
Mboozi) m 1982; Lt-Col, Zam. b 8 Aug 61.

CHIMIMBA, Gerald (Migowi, 1986); Maj,
Mal. b 31 Jul 56; with
CHIMIMBA, Ellen m 1983; Maj, Mal. b 4 Apr 60.

CHINYEMBA, Casman (Chimbumu, 1989);
Maj, Zimb. b 7 Jan 62; with
CHINYEMBA, Martha (née Gomo) m
1988; Maj, Zimb. b 16 Oct 63. Served in Tanz.

CHISENGELE, Bernard (Monze, 1983); Maj,
Zam. b 1 Jan 51; and
CHISENGELE, Dorothy (née Mweemba)
(Kaumba, 1985) m 1985; Maj, Zam. b 14 Nov 59.

CHITANDA, Sheila (née Mvere) (Kwekwe,
1992); Maj, Zimb. b 15 Oct 68; and
CHITANDA, Henry (Chinhoyi, 1991) m 1992;
Maj, Zimb. b 6 Apr 66.

CHOO, Seung-chan (Yung Deung Po, 1980);
Lt-Col, Kor. b 15 Jun 50; with
LEE, Ok-hee m 1978; Lt-Col, Kor. b 2 Aug 54.

CHRISTIAN, Gabriel Ibrahim (Muktipur,
Ind W, 1983); Lt-Col, CS, Ind SE. b 24 Dec
59. BA (Eng) BD and
CHRISTIAN, Indumati (née Samual Macwan)
(Petlad Central, 1985) m 1986; Lt-Col, TSWM,
Ind SE. b 30 Aug 62; BD. Served in Ind W.

CHRISTIAN, Prabhudas Jetha (Sihunj,
1978); Maj, Ind W. b 23 Jan 52 and
CHRISTIAN, Persis (née Zumal) (Jholod
1978) m 1978 Maj, Ind W. b 5 Apr 48.

CHRISTURAJ, Rajamani (Elappara, 1983);
Maj, Ind SW. b 27 Dec 61; and
CHRISTURAJ, Mary (née Mathew)
(Elampally, 1983) m 1983; Maj, Ind SW.
b 11 May 59.

CHRISTIAN, Rasik Paul (Chunel, 1988); Maj,
Ind W. b 7 Sep 65; and
CHRISTIAN, Ramilaben (née Samuel)
(Piplag, 1990) m 1990; Maj, Ind W. b 17 Apr 68.

CHRISTIAN, Yusuf Daud (Finav, 1982); Maj,
Ind W. b 27 Feb 59, and
CHRISTIAN, Suhasini (Pandoli, 1989); m
1989 Maj, Ind W. b 10 Apr 68

CHUN, Joon-hung (Yong Dong, 1978);
Lt-Col, Kor. b 20 Jun 48; with
SHIN, Myung-ja m 1976; Lt-Col, Kor.
b 28 Sep 49.

CHUNG, Edmund L. (Manhattan Citadel,
USA E, 1976); Lt-Col, IHQ. b 8 Aug 48.
BS (Chem), MS (Management); and

CHUNG, Carolynne J. (née Wiseman)
(Lexington, KY, USA E, 1976) m 1977. BA,
MA (Org Ldrshp); Lt-Col, IHQ. b 28 Jul 46.
Served in USA E, USA Nat and UK.

CLÉNAT, Jean Aurore (Aquin, Haiti, Carib,
2001); Capt, GS, Rwa. b 8 Oct 73; and
CLÉNAT, Elianese (née Pierre) (Gros Morne,
Haiti, Carib, 1998) m 2002; Capt, CSWM,
Rwa. b 22 May 68. Served in Carib.

CLINCH, Ronald (Launceston, Aus S, 1986);
Lt-Col, Aus S. b 6 Sep 54. BEd; with
CLINCH, Robyn (née Mole) m 1982; Lt-Col,
Aus S. b 8 Nov 60. Served in Phil (CS/TSWM).

COCHRANE, William (Barrhead, Scot, 1975);
Comr, IHQ (IS to CoS). b 7 Sep 54.
Served in UK (CS).

COLA, Iliesa (Raiwai, 1995); Maj, NZ.
b 7 Nov 55; with
COLA, Litiana (née Vuidreketi) m 1982;
Maj, NZ. b 8 Mar 62.

COLEMAN, Michael T. (Kwinana, Aus S,
1986); Maj, RC, Tai. b 4 Nov 54; with
COLEMAN, Annette (née Willey) m 1976;
Maj, RPWM, Tai. b 23 Oct 55. BSc. Served
in Aus S.

CONDON, James (Shoalhaven, Aus E, 1971),
Comr, TC, Aus E. b 29 Nov 49; and
CONDON, Jan (née Vickery) (Uralla,
Aus E, 1971) m 1972; Comr, TPWM, Aus E.
b 25 Jan 47. Served in UK, PNG (CS/TSWM)
Aus E (CS/TWSM) and at IHQ (IS/ZSWM).

CONRAD, Keith (Matroosfontein, S Afr,
1988); Lt-Col, IHQ. b 31 Mar 62; with
CONRAD, Yvonne (née Jansen) m 1984; Lt-Col,
IHQ. b 13 Mar 63. Served in NZ and S Afr.

COOPER, Raymond, III (Garland, TX,
USA S, 1984); Maj, USA Nat. b 12 Jun 61.
Served in USA S.

COTTERILL, Anthony (Regent Hall, 1984);
Lt-Col, UK. b 9 Dec 57. BA (Hons); with
COTTERILL, Gillian (née Rushforth)
m 1979; Lt-Col, UK. b 15 Sep 57. SRN.

COWDERY, Colin (Eastleigh, UK, 1980);
Maj, Pak. b 7 Dec 49. BA; with
COWDERY, Rosemary (née Thomas)
m 1966; Maj, Pak. b 4 Oct 49. Served in UK
S Afr and Zam.

COWLING, Alison (Maclean, Aus E, 1978);
Maj, Asst CS, Can. b 10 Feb 50. Served in
Aus E and at IHQ.

COX, André (Geneva 1, Switz, 1979); Comr,
IHQ (CoS). b 12 Jul 54; with
COX, Silvia (née Volet) m 1976; Comr, IHQ
(WPWM). b 18 Nov 55. Served in Switz,
Zimb, Fin (TC/TPWM) S Afr (TC/TPWM)
and UK (TC/TPWM).

CRAIG, Heather (née Mackay) (Parramatta, Aus E, 1986); Maj, Gha. b 31 Dec 57; and
CRAIG, Graeme (Rockhampton, Aus E, 1984) m 1986; Maj, Gha. b 10 Feb 56. Served in Aus E.

CRITCH, Shawn (La Scie, NL, 1990); Maj, Can. b 26 Jun 67. CGA; and
CRITCH, Brenda (née Cooper) (St John's Temple, NL, 1990) m 1991; Maj, Can. b 25 Jul 63. BSc N.

CUMBERBATCH, Emmerson (Spice Town, Barbados, 1988); Maj, Carib. b 5 Jan 54; and
CUMBERBATCH, Carolinda (nee White) (San Fernando, Trinidad, 1987) m 1988; Maj, Carib. b 19 Nov 62.

D

DALI, Peter (Ebushibungo, Ken, 1978); Lt-Col, Ken W. b 2 Mar 52; and
DALI, Jessica (née Kavere) (Masigolo, Ken, 1978) m 1979; Lt-Col, Ken W. b 25 Dec 55. Served in Ken, Tanz, at IHQ, in Gha (CS/TSWM), Zim (CS/TSWM) and Lib (OC/CPWM).

DALY, Gordon (Wellington South, NZ, 1977), Lt-Col, OC, Port. b 5 Mar 54; and
DALY, Susan (née Crump) (Te Aroha, NZ, 1976) m 1977; Lt-Col, CPWM, Port. b 22 Oct 54. L Th. Served in NZ, Carib, S Am W and Sing.

DALVI, Vijay Ramchandar (Kudgaon 1978); Maj, Ind W. b 13 Aug 54 and
DALVI, Rajani (Kherdi 1982); m 1981 Maj, Ind W. b 30 Sep 62.

DAMOR, Nicolas Maganlal (Jalpa, 1979); Maj, Ind W. b 1 Jun 55; and
DAMOR, Flora (née David) (Dilsar, 1980) m 1980; Maj, Ind W. b 26 Apr 58.

DANIEL, Washington (Khanewal, 1997); Maj, Pak. b 25 Nov 56; and
WASHINGTON, Azra (née Zakar) m 1990; Maj, Pak b 2 Feb 62.

DANIELSON, Douglas (El Paso, TX, USA W, 1987); Lt-Col, CS, Mex. b 19 Aug 58. BSc (Cmptr Sci), MA(Missiology). Ww Lt-Col Rhode, pG 2010. Served in USA W, S Am E, L Am N (CS) and at IHQ.

DANSO, Isaac (Asene, 1991); Lt-Col, Gha. b 22 Feb 1960; with
DANSO, Eva (née Amoah) m 1988; Lt-Col, Gha. b 1 Jul 61.

DASARI Daniel Raju (Arul Nagar, 1991); Major, Ind C. b 24 Feb 65; with
DASARI Baby Sarojini m 1989; Maj, Ind C. b 26 Jan 63.

DASARI, John Kumar (Pathamupparru, 1991); Maj, Ind C. b 7 Jan 61; with

DASARI, Mani Kumari m 1986; Maj, Ind C. b 3 May 66. BTh, MA.

DAVID, K. C. (Puthuchira, Ind SW, 1978); Lt-Col, CS, Ind W. b 5 Jan 53. BA; and
DAVID, Gracy Marykutty (Thevalapuram, Ind SW, 1981) m 1981; Lt-Col, TSWM, Ind W. b 12 Nov 55. Served in Ind SW and at Ind Nat.

DAVIDSON, Daniel (Trivandrum Central, 1985); Maj, Ind SW. b 6 May 53. BA; with
DAVIDSON, M.V. Estherbai m 1984, Maj, Ind SW. b 1 Jun 61.

DAWNGLIANA, C. (Chhilngchip, 1981); Maj, Ind E. b 1 Oct 55; and
H. MANTHANGI (Champhai, 1982) m 1982; Maj, Ind E. b 20 Sep 61.

DEFIBAUGH, Sandra (Staunton, VA, 1978); Lt-Col, USA Nat. b 19 Jan 51. Served in USA S.

DENGI, Michael (Tent City, 1996); Capt, PNG. b 8 May 65; with
DENGI, Giam (née Benjain); Capt, PNG. b 13 Jun 69.

DEN HOLLANDER, Johannes A. (Treebeek, 1990); Lt-Col, Neth. b 21 Nov 56, with
DEN HOLLANDER, Annetje C. (née Poppema) m 1978; Lt-Col, Neth. b 4 May 57.

DEVASUNDARAM, Samuel Raj (Vadasery, 1974); Maj, Ind SE. b 21 Sep 54; and
KANAGAMONY, Samuel Raj (Brahmmapuram, 1978) m 1978; Maj, Ind SE. b 5 Feb 52.

DIAKANWA, Wante Emmanuel (Kintambo, 1985); Maj, DR Con. b 23 Dec 50; with
DIAKANWA, Madeleine (née Sitwakemba Luzizila) m 1974; Maj, DR Con. b 11 Nov 55.

DIAZ, Evelyn (Oakbrook Terrace, IL, 1981); Maj, USA C. b 1 Jun 60. AA (Pract Min). Served in Swdn.

DICKINSON, William Jr (Seattle Temple, WA 1993); Maj, USA W. b 10 Nov 63. BS (Bus Admin); with
DICKINSON, Lisa (née Schmidt) m 1984; Maj, USA W. b 25 Sep 63.

DIKALEMBOLOVANGA, Eugene (Kinshasa, 1981); Lt-Col, Gha, b. 30 Apr 52; with
DIKALEMBOLOVANGA, Odile (née Luasu) m 1980; Lt-Col, Gha, b. 2 Mar 58.

DLAMINI, Thomas (Mbabane, Swaz 1992); Maj, Swaz. b 23 Feb 65; and
DLAMINI, Doris (née Mvelase) (Mathunjwa 1992) m 1992; Maj, S Afr. b 14 Dec 68.

DONALDSON, Robert (Dunedin South, NZ, 1987); Lt-Col, CS, S Afr. b 8 Jul 61. BSc, LTh. PG Dip Bus Admin; with
DONALDSON, Janine (née Hamilton) m 1983, Lt-Col, TSWM, S Afr. b 23 Sep 62.

Served in NZ and Zamb.

DONZÉ, Jacques (St Aubin, 1988); Maj, Switz. b 16 Feb 64; with
DONZÉ, Claude-Evelyne (née Roth) m 1983; Maj, Switz. b 5 Feb 63. Served in Belg.

DOUGHTY, Victor (Seattle Temple, WA, 1984); Lt-Col, USA W. b 25 Mar 54. BA (Soc Anthr), MSW (Soc Wk), CERT (Soc Wk); with
DOUGHTY, Joan (née Ritchie) m 1980; Lt-Col, USA W. b 7 May 55.

DOUNIAMA, Jean Pierre (Gamboma, 1988); Maj, Con (Braz). b 25 Dec 67; and
DOUNIAMA, Odile (née Ando) (Gamboma, 1988) m 1988; Maj, Con (Braz). b 8 Jun 69.

DOWNER, Gillian (Great Yarmouth, UK, 1977); Col, Sing (TC, TPWM). b 18 Mar 54. Served in UK, Phil, Vietnam, HK, Tai, Sing (GS and CS) and at IHQ.

DREW, Marion (Boscombe, 1979); Lt-Col, UK. b 12 Jan 49. BA (French & Law), Dip Inst Linguists. Served at ICO.

DUHU, Imanuel (Surabaya 2, 1992); Maj, Indon. b 1 Aug 63; and
DUHU, Henny (Tumpaan, 1990) m 1995; Maj, Indon. b 2 Jul 67.

E

EDGAR, Samuel (Londonderry, 1969); Maj, UK. b 26 Feb 49. Served at ITC and in Ger.

EGGER, Paulette (Vallorbe, 1977); Maj, Switz. b 22 Nov 55.

ELIASEN, Torben (Bosque, Brz, 1983); Comr, IHQ, (IS Am & Carib) . b 28 Nov 60; and
ELIASEN, Deise Calor (née de Souza) (Rio Comprido, Brz, 1985) m 1985; Comr, IHQ, (ZSWM Am & Carib). b 22 Feb 66. BA (Jrnlsm). Served in Brz (CS) and Moz (TC/TPWM)

ELLIS, Stephen R. (Atlanta Temple, GA, 1989); Maj, USA S. b 25 Oct 62. BA (Eng), MA (Div), MBA; with
ELLIS, Susan (née Kennedy) m 1984; Maj, USA S. b 27 Apr 62. ABJ (PR). Served in Ger.

EMMANUEL, Muthu Yesudhason (Neduvaazhy, Ind SE, 1974); Comr, TC, Ind C. b 8 May 51; and
REGINA, Chandra Bai (Valliyoor, Ind SE, 1978) m 1978; Comr, TPWM, Ind C. b 3 Mar 55. Served in Ind SE, Ind N (CS/TSWM) and Ind E (TC/TPWM).

EVANS, Stuart (Dubbo, 1994) Maj, Aus E. b 24 Nov 58. BA Econ, MA Bus; with
EVANS, Donna (née Hutchinson) m 1979; Maj, Aus E. b 2 Feb 58. Dip Ed, BA.

EXANTUS, Vilo (Arcahaie, Haiti, 1984); Maj. Carib. b 12 May 57 and

EXANTUS, Yvrose (née Benjamin) (Arcahaie, Haiti, 1985) m 1986; Maj. Carib. b 17 Jan 58. Served in L Am N.

EZEKIEL, Mathai (Thottamon, Kangazha, 1975); Maj, Ind SW. b 12 Dec 48; and
EZEKIEL, Kunjamma (Kottarakara Central, 1980) m 1979; Maj, Ind SW. b 10 Nov 54.

EZEKWERE, Chika Boniface (Umuchu, 1978); Maj, Nig. b 1 Jan 49; with
EZEKWERE, Virginia Ete m 1976; Maj, Nig. b 1 Jan 54.

F

FARTHING, Peter (Dundas Outpost, 1976) Maj, Aus E. b 8 Jun 51. BSS, Dr Min; and
FARTHING, Kerrie (née Gale) (Wollongong, 1976) m 1978; Maj, Aus E, b 31 Aug 52. Served at IHQ.

FERGUSON, Lester (Nassau, Bahamas, 1988); Maj, Carib. b 1 Sep 65. BA (Bible and Theol), MA (Chrstn Ed), MDiv; and
FERGUSON, Beverely (née Armstrong) (Bridgetown Central, Barbados, 1999) m 1999; Capt, Carib. b 12 Dec 64.

FERNANDEZ, Ricardo J. (Caparra Temple, PR, 1996); Lt-Col, CS, S Am E. b 3 Jun 60; with
FERNANDEZ, Mirtha N. (née Benitez) m 1979; Lt-Col, TSWM, S Am E. b 4 Jan 57. Served in USA E

FERNANDO, Newton (Handugala, 1981); Maj, Sri Lan. b 30 Aug 60; and
FERNANDO Ajantha (née Marasinghalage) (Talampitiya, 1984) m 1984; Maj, Sri Lan. b 8 Jun 61.

FERREIRA, Jorge Alberto (Cordoba, S Am E, 1972); Comr, TC, S Am W. b 24 Jun 53; and
FERREIRA, Adelina (née Solorza) (Lauis, S Am E, 1974) m 1979; Comr, TPWM, S Am W. b 19 Sep 55. Served in S Am E (CS/TSWM) and L Am N (TC/TPWM).

FINCHAM, Melvin (Croydon Citadel, 1981); Lt-Col, UK. b 20 May 56; and
FINCHAM, Suzanne (née Kenny) (Stockport Citadel, 1981) m 1981; Lt-Col, UK. b 19 Jan 59.

FINGER, Raymond (Hawthorn, 1974); Comr TC, Aus S. b 11 Jul 51; and
FINGER, Aylene (née Rinaldi) (Maylands, 1976) m 1976; Comr, TPWM, Aus S. b 17 Apr 53. Served in Aus S (CS/TSWM).

FLEEMAN, W. Paul (Royal Oak, MI, 1976); Maj, USA C. b 23 Dec 48. BA (Psychol), MA (Relig), MDiv (Counselling/Ed); with
FLEEMAN, Paula (née Cloyd) m 1973; Maj, USA C. b 14 Jun 54.

311

FLORES, Eliseo (Cochabamba, 1977); Maj, S Am W. b 28 Jul 56; and
FLORES, Remedios (née Gutiérrez) (Oruro, 1977) m 1978; Maj, S Am W. b 6 Apr 55.

FLÜCKIGER, Jean-Marc (Vevey, 1994); Maj, Switz. b 13 Dec 1963; with
FLÜCKIGER, Nathalie (née Pellaton) m 1987; Maj, Switz. b 13 Mar 1967.

FOLEY, Timothy (Concord, CA 1982); Maj, USA W. b 7 May 59. MA (Theology); and
FOLEY, Cynthia (née Hill) (Pendleton, OR, 1985) m 1985; Maj USA W. b 23 May 63.

FOURNEL, Bernard (Lyon, 1980) Maj, Frce and Belg. b 4 Oct 56; and
FOURNEL, Claire-Lise (née Naud) (Paris-Montparnasse, 1979) m 1981; Maj, Frce & Belg. b 27 Nov 52.

FOREMAN, Ronald R. (Concord, NH, 1978); Maj, USA E. b 17 Sep 1952. BA (Socio) MSW (Soc Wk), EJD (Gen Law); with
FOREMAN, Dorine (née Long); m 1972; Maj, USA E. b 6 Apr 1955. BSW (Soc Wk), MSW (Soc Wk). Served at USA Nat.

FORREST, Peter (Blackpool Citadel, UK, 1984); Maj, IHQ. b 24 Jun 1960; MA; and
FORREST, Julie (née Raine) (Chester-le-Street, UK, 1987); m 1987; Maj, IHQ. b 26 Feb 1965. MSc. Served in UK and IHQ (ICO).

FORSTER, Malcolm (St Helier, UK, 1971); Lt-Col, S Afr. b 26 Mar 51; and
FORSTER, Valerie (née Jupp) (Croydon Citadel, UK, 1978) m 1979; Lt-Col, S Afr. b 5 Jun 55. Served in UK, at ITC, in Zam & Mal, Gha & Lib, Mal (OC/CPWM) and Tanz (OC/CPWM).

FOSEN, Jan Peder (Haugesund, 1976); Col, CS, Nor. b 18 Nov 55; and
FOSEN, Birgit (née Taarnesvik) (Trondheim, 1981) m 1979; Col, TSWM, Nor. b 27 Aug 49.

FREIND, John (Floreat Park, 1981); Maj, Aus S. b 11 Dec 55; with
FREIND, Wendy (née Morris) m 1977; Maj, Aus S. b 5 Aug 53.

FUGE, Walter J. (Anacortes, WA, USA W, 1972); Lt-Col, IHQ. b 18 Aug 52. MBA (Bus Adm), BS (Bus & Mngmnt), CERT (Data Analyst) (Internal Audit); and
FUGE, Ardis (née Muus) (Monterey, CA, USA W, 1974) m 1974; Lt-Col, IHQ. b 31 Jan 53. Served in USA W.

FUJII, Kenji (Kyobashi, 1982); Lt-Col, CS, Jpn. b 25 Feb 60; and
FUJII, Chiaki (née Inoue) (Kiyose, 1981) m 1987; Lt-Col, TSWM, Jpn. b 17 Nov 59.

G

GABRIEL, Michael (Faisalabad, 1995); Maj, Pak. b 14 Aug 61; and
MICHAEL, Shamim (née Riaz) m 1981; Maj, Pak. b 26 Dec 62.

GABRIEL, K. M. (Kaithaparambu, 1981); Lt-Col, Ind SW. b 15 Nov 55; and
GABRIEL, Molamma (Vappala, 1986) m 1986; Lt-Col, Ind SW. b 10 May 67.

GALVÁN, Guadalupe (Savo Loredo, 1975); Maj, Mex; b 28 Mar 51.
Served in USA S and L Am N.

GARCÍA, Angela (née Sanguinetti) (Lima, 1982); Maj, S Am W. b 15 Oct 1953; and
GARCÍA, Víctor (Trujillo, 1982) m 1983; Maj, S Am W. b 21 Jan 1955. Served in USA C and L Am N.

GARCÍA, Humberto (Monterrey, 1990); Maj, Mex. b 19 Jan 57. LLM; with
GARCÍA, Leticia (née Castañeda) m 1981; Maj, Mex. b 9 Mar 59. BA (Primary Ed).

GARRAD, Rob, (Skegness, UK, 1971); Lt-Col, IHQ. b 16 Jan 52.
Served in UK and Rus.

GAYMO, Ben (Trodian Corps, 1991); Maj, Lib. b 12 Jun 57; with
GAYMO Etta (née Gargar) m 1989; Maj, Lib. b 27 May 60.

GENABE, Alexander (Cebu, 1981); Maj, Phil. b 27 Mar 58; and
GENABE, Jocelyn (née Willy) (Baguio, 1993) m 1993; Maj, Phil. b 10 Feb 60. BSN, BSSW.

GEORGE, N. J. (Moncotta, 1978); Maj, Ind SW. b 24 Dec 51; and
RUTH, M. C. (Moncotta, 1977) m 1979, Maj, Ind SW. b 23 Apr 48.

GERA, Thomas (EBLH, Bapatla, Ind C. 1988); Lt-Col, Ind N. b 12 Jul 65; with
GERA, Sion Kumari m 1984; Lt-Col, Ind N. b 9 Oct 67. Served in Ind C.

GHULAM, Haroon (Khanewal, 1989); Maj, Pak. b 25 July 63; with
HAROON, Jennifer (née John) m 1992; Capt, Pak. b 25 Feb 69.

GHULAM, Yousaf (Lahore, 1975); Lt-Col, CS, Pak. b 4 Jan 55; and
YOUSAF, Rebecca (née Charn Masih) (Shantinagar, 1976) m 1976; Lt-Col, TSWM, Pak. b 6 May 56.

GIBBS, Raelton (Regent Hall, 1984) Maj, Sing. b 22 Jul 59; with
GIBBS, Lynn (née Baxter) m 1980, Maj, Sing. b 29 May 60. Served in UK and at IHQ.

GILL, Daniel (Alidullapur, 1980); Maj, Ind N. b 5 Apr 57; and

GILL, Parveen Daniel (Mukerian 1981)
m 1981; Maj, Ind N. b 3 Apr 62.

GITANG'ITA, James (Kitagutiti, 1994), Maj,
Tanz. b 8 Oct 68; with
GITANG'ITA, Yustina m 1990; Maj, Tanz.
b 8 May 74.

GITONGA, Isaac (Kangoro, Embu 1992) Maj,
Tanz. b. 27 May 1966; with
GITONGA, Enacy M. m 1988; Maj, Tanz.
b 27 Mar 69. Served in Ken E.

GIUSTI, Rafael (Tucuman, 1991); Maj,
S Am E. b 24 Oct 68; and
GIUSTI, Karina (née Acosta) (Tucuman,
1992) m 1993; Maj, S Am E. b 26 Feb 72.

GJERULDSEN, Frank (Brevik, 1981); Maj,
Nor. b 21 Jan 58; and
GJERULDSEN, Tone (née Olsen) (Templet,
Oslo, 1984) m 1983; Maj, Nor.
b 11 Feb 1959.

GLUYAS, Miriam (Wauchope, 1981); Lt-Col,
CS, PNG. b 3 Jun 59. Dip Min. Dip Bus.
Served in Aus E.

GNANADASAN, Daniel (Anakotoor, 1981);
Maj, Ind SW. b 10 Sep 55; and
D. I. SOSAMMA, Gnanadasan (Kottoor,
1980) m 1982; Maj, Ind SW. b 24 Oct 52.

GOA, Christian (Lae, 1994); Maj, PNG.
b 9 Feb 69; with
GOA, Tilitah (née Shong); Maj, PNG.
b 6 Apr 69.

GODKIN, David J. (Parramatta, 1986); Lt-Col,
Aus E. b 14 Aug 59. Dip Min; with
GODKIN, Sandra F. (née Press) m 1982;
Lt-Col, Aus E. b 20 Apr 62. Dip Min.

GONÇALVES, Adão (Pelotas, 1997); Maj, Brz.
b 3 Sep 65; and
GONÇALVES, Vilma (née Rosa) (Bosque,
1996) m 1986; Maj, Brz. b 8 Nov 51. BA (SocS).

GONI, Widajati (Bandung 1, 1993); Maj,
Indon. b 27 May 69; and
GONI, Banjamin (Palembang, 1993) m 2000;
Maj, Indon. b 5 Jul 69.

GOWER, Ross R. (Christchurch City, 1980);
Col, NZ. b 15 Dec 50; with
GOWER, Annette (née Knight) m 1972;
Col, NZ. Served in NZ, UK, Indon
(CS/TSWM) and at IHQ.

GRAVES, Lee (Tillsonburg, ON, 1983);
Lt-Col, Can. b 8 Aug 61. MBA; with
GRAVES, Deborah (née Smith) m 1984;
Lt-Col, Can. b 24 Feb 1960. BA, BSW.

GREENIDGE, Brenda (Sea View, Barbados,
1980): Maj, Carib. b 25 Dec 57.

GRIFFIN, Stanley (St John's, Antigua, 1979);
Maj, Carib. b 20 Feb 54; and

GRIFFIN, Hazel (née Whyte) (St John's,
Antigua, 1980) m 1981; Maj, Carib.
b 23 Sep 57. Served in L Am N.

GROVES, Jennifer (Wellington South, NZ,
1990); Lt-Col, IHQ. b 25 Sep 64. Served in
NZ and Port.

GUIAMBA, João (Conguiana, Moz, 1997)
Capt, Moz. b 2 Apr 66; and
GUIAMBA, Graça (née Rozicene) m 1992;
Capt, Moz. b 17 April 74.

GUTIERREZ, Hugo (Bahia Blanca, S Am E,
1986) Maj, Moz. b 14 Dec 59; and
GUTIERREZ, Maria (née Lopez) (Laplata
S Am E, 1987) m 1988; Maj, Moz. b 20 Jul
62. Served in S Am E.

H

HAGEN, Eli (née Nodland) Maj, Nor. b 25
Mar 57; with
HAGEN, Jan Harald m 1976 (Templet,
Oslo, 1980); Maj, Nor. b 12 Feb 54.

HAGGAR, Kerry (née Geers) (Rockdale, 1982);
Lt-Col, Aus E, b 30 Nov 59. BComm, MAL;
and
HAGGAR, Colin (Rockdale 1983) m 1983;
Lt-Col, Aus E. b 16 Mar 59. BE, ATh.

HAN, Sea-jong (Kwachun, 1996); Maj, Kor. b
22 Sep 65; with
KIM, Ok-young; m 1991, Maj, Kor. b 1 Jul 68.

HANGOMA, Donald (Munali, 1995); Capt,
Zam. b 15 Jan 70; and
HANGOMA, Patricia (née Michelo) (1993);
Maj, Zam. b 19 Mar 70.

HARFOOT, William (Detroit Brightmoor, MI,
1977); Col, Nat CS, USA Nat. b 6 Sep 48. BS
(Ed), MA (Relig); with
HARFOOT, Susan (née Stange) m 1969;
Col, NSWM, USA Nat. b 21 Oct 48. AA.
Served in USA E and USA W.

HARMER, Bruce (Sydney Congress Hall,
1989) Maj, Aus E. b 31 May 65. Ass TH; and
HARMER, Carolyn (née Walker) m 1992
(Brisbane City Temple, 1990) Maj, Aus E. b
14 Nov 64.

HARTLEY, Curtiss (Peoria [Citadel] Illinois,
1981); Maj, PNG . b 29 Aug 59; and
HARTLEY, Sandy (née Zarfas) (Omaha
[Citadel] Nebraska, USC, 1983) m 1983;
Maj, PNG. b 16 Nov 59. Served in USA C.

HARTVEIT, Jørg Walter (Langesund, 1971);
Lt-Col, Nor. b 22 Jun 47. m 1971; Lt-Col
Rigmor, ret 2006.

HAUGHTON, Devon (Port Antonio, Jamaica,
1981); Maj, Carib. b 22 Jul 59; and
HAUGHTON, Verona Beverly (née Henry)

(Havendale, Jamaica, 1976) m 1982; Maj, Carib. b 15 Apr 54. BA (Guidance and Counselling).

HAUPT, Gary W. (New Orleans, LA, USA S, 1982); Lt-Col, E Eur. b 27 Nov 53. BS (Bus Adm); with
HAUPT, Suzanne H. (née Hogan); m 1979; Lt-Col, E Eur. b 3 May 56. BS (Ed). Served in USA S and at USA Nat.

HAWKINS, Kenneth (Maidenhead, 1985); Maj, Zam. b 28 Mar 58; B Div, M Th; and
HAWKINS, Ann (née Tupling) (Maltby, 1984) m 1985; Maj, Zam. b 24 Jan 60. Served in UK.

HEATWOLE, Merle (Milwaukee Citadel, WI, 1984); Col, CS, USA C. b 7 Jan 60. BS (Maths); with
HEATWOLE, Dawn (née Lewis) m 1981; Col, TSWM, USA C. b 26 Nov 62. AA (Pract Min).

HEDGREN, R. Steven (Chicago Mont Clare, IL, USA C, 1978); Comr, USA S. b 7 Mar 50. BS (Bus Adm); with
HEDGREN, Judith Ann (née White) m 1975; Comr, USA S. b 14 Feb 49. AS (Bus). Served in USA C and USA E (CS/TSWM, TC/TPWM).

HEELEY, William (Rock Ferry, 1974); Lt-Col, UK. b 6 May 48; and
HEELEY, Gillian (née Lacey) (Rock Ferry, 1975) m 1975; Lt-Col, UK. b 18 Apr 52.

HEFFORD, Douglas (Buchans, NL, 1972); Maj, Can. b 13 Feb 51. BRe, MDiv; with
HEFFORD, Jean (née Bowering) m 1973; Maj, Can b 11 Aug 51.

HENNE, Ingrid Elisabeth (Bergen 1, 1982); Lt-Col, Nor. b 6 Sep 52.

HENRY, Samuel A. (Atlanta Temple, GA, 1983); Lt-Col, USA S. b 28 Nov 48; with
HENRY, Nancy (née Southwood) m 1969; Lt-Col, USA S. b 13 Apr 47.

HERRING, Alistair Chapman (Wellington City, NZ, 1975); Comr, IHQ, (IS, SPEA). b 4 Mar 51. DipSW; with
HERRING, Verna Astrid (née Weggery) m 1971; Comr, IHQ (ZSWM, SPEA). b 29 Oct 51. Served in NZ and E Eur (CS/TSWM)

HETTIARACHCHI, Nihal (Colombo, 1985); Lt-Col, Sri Lan. b 20 Jun 64; and
HETTIARACHCHI, Rohini Swarnalatha (née Wettamuni) (Colombo Central, 1994) m 1994; Lt-Col, Sri Lan. b 18 Oct 64.

HIGHTON, Michael (Hinckley, 1985); Maj, UK. b 27 May 53; with
HIGHTON, Lynn (née Edwards) m 1975; Maj, UK. b 10 Mar 53.

HIGUCHI, Kazumitsu (Nagoya, 1976); Maj, Jpn. b 9 Apr 51; and
HIGUCHI, Aiko (née Kutomi) (Shibuya, 1979) m 1982; Maj, Jpn. b 25 Sep 53. BA (Eng Lit).

HILL, Edward (Pasadena Tabernacle, CA 1993); Maj, USA W. b 7 Nov 59. BA (History), MA (Chrstn Ed); with
HILL, Shelley (née Chandler) m 1985; Maj, USA W. b 11 Jul 63.

HILL, Martin (Northampton Central, 1984); Maj, UK. b 3 Jul 55. BA (Hons) (Soc Sci), MTh (Ap Theol).

HINTON, David (Blackheath, 1975); Col, CS, UK. b 28 Oct 53; and
HINTON, Sylvia (née Brooks) (Bedlington, 1975) m 1977; Col, TSWM, UK. b 2 Dec 53.

HOBGOOD, W. Edward (Greenville, NC, 1983); Lt-Col, IHQ. b 6 Apr 58; with
HOBGOOD, M. Kathryn (née Hathaway) m 1978; Lt-Col, IHQ. b 12 Jun 54. Served in USA S.

HODDER, Kenneth G. (Pasadena Tabernacle, CA, USA W, 1988); Comr, TC, Ken W. b 16 Jun 58. BA (Hist), JD (Law); with
HODDER, Jolene (née Lloyd) m 1982; Comr, TPWM, Ken W. b 30 Jul 61. BA (Home Econ). Served in USA W, USA S, Ken (CS/TLWM) Ken E (CS/TLWM) and at IHQ (IS Int Pers, Legal & Constitutional Advisor to the General/Assoc IS Int Pers).

HOFER, Allan (Sissach Basel, Switz, 1986); Maj, USA S. b 30 Mar 61; and
HOFER, Fiona (née Pressland) (Barking, UK, 1987) m 1987; Maj, USA S, b 15 Apr 64. Served in Switz, Port, UK and Brz.

HOOD, George (Hamilton, OH, USA W, 1968); Maj, USA Nat. b 31 Jan 47. BS (Mgmt), MS (Mgmt); and
HOOD, Donna (née Morrison) (Newport, KY, USA W, 1969); m 1969; Maj, USA Nat. b 25 Oct 47. BS (Org Mgmt), MA (Theol). Served in USA E and W.

HORWOOD, S. Edward (Ted) (Monterey, CA, USA W, 1992); Maj, GS, Ang. b 1 Feb 61. BA (Eng), MA (Intercultural Studies); with
HORWOOD, Deborah (née Haynes) m 1987; Maj, CSWM, Ang. b 22 Mar 66. Served in USA W, Zamb & Mal and at IHQ.

HOSTETLER, Donald D. (Cincinnati Citadel, OH, 1972); Maj, USA E. b 2 Jan 49. BA (Socio), MA (Public Admin); with
HOSTETLER, Arvilla J. (née Marcum) m 1969; Maj, USA E. b 14 Aug 50. BA (Org Psych). Served in USA W.

HOWARD, Steven (Hamilton, OH, 1983); Col, USA E. b 21 May 57. BS, MSc; with

HOWARD, Janice (née Collopy) m 1979; USA E. b 18 Mar 59. BS (Bus Ed). Served at ICO and in Ken E (CS/TLWM).

HOWELL, Willis (Hyattsville, MD, 1985); Maj, USA S. b 3 Mar 56; with
HOWELL, Barbara (née Leidy) m 1978; Maj, USA S. b 3 Apr 57.

HUDSON, David E. (Portland Tabernacle, OR, 1975); Col, CS, USA W. b 28 Jun 54. BS (Bus Mgmt); and
HUDSON, Sharon (née Smith) (Santa Ana, CA, 1975) m 1976; Col, TSWM, USA W. b 14 Jun 52.

HULSMAN, Everdina (Nijverdal, 1975); Lt-Col, Neth. b 21 Dec 47.

HUTSON, Ian (Spreydon, 1984); Maj, NZ. b 26 Nov 54; Grad Dip Soc Work, Cert Bus; with
HUTSON, Lynette (née Collett) m 1974; Maj, NZ. b 20 Jul 54; Grad Dip Soc Work, MA (Soc Work). Served in Can.

HUNTER, Barbara (née Booth) (Tucson, AZ, USA W, 1968); Lt-Col, USA E. b 17 Mar 47. BS (Org Mgmt). Served in USA W and Rus (CSWO). Ww Lt-Col R. William, pG 2001.

HWANG, Kyu-hong (Chun An, 2000); Capt, Kor. b 15 Jan 68; with
MA, Jin-young; m 1995, Capt Kor. b 6 Jul 71.

HWANG, Sun-yup (Ah Hyun, 1985); Lt-Col, Kor. b 28 Dec 55; with
CHOI, Myung-soon m 1982; Lt-Col, Kor. b 9 Sep 59. Served in USA S and UK.

HYNES, Junior (Happy Valley, NL, 1971); Lt-Col, Can. b 6 Jan 51; and
HYNES, Verna (née Downton) (Windsor, NL, 1971) m 1973; Lt-Col, Can. b 27 Aug 50. Served in UK.

I

IGHOTY, Christopher (Kamenge, 1996); Maj, Tanz. b 10 Nov 70; with
IGHOTY, Mary (née Elinazi) m 1993; Maj, Tanz. b 1 Jan 73.

IGLEHEART, Kelly (Owensboro, KY, 1992); Lt-Col, USA S. b 29 Oct 61; with
IGLEHEART, Donna (née Vincent) m 1981; Lt-Col, USA S. b 30 Apr 62.

IP KAN, Ming-chun Connie (Kwai Chung, 1985); Maj, CSWM, HK. b 16 Jul 62.

IQBAL, Safdar (Qasroor,1996); Capt. Pak b 25 Dec 69; and
SAFDAR, Asia (née Kala) m 1993; Capt, Pak b 22 Nov 72.

ILUNGA, Bidwaya Clément (Salle Centrale, 1987); Maj, DR Con. b 16 Nov 62; with
ILUNGA, Béatrice (née Kalenga Monga) m 1988; Maj, DR Con. b 12 Sep 60.

IMMANUEL, Sam (Thulickal, 1984); Maj, Ind SW. b 27 May 59; with
IMMANUEL, Rachel P. C. m 1982; Maj, Ind SW. b 15 Jun 57.

INDURUWAGE, Malcolm (Colombo Central, Sri Lan, 1977); Comr, TC, Sri. b 24 Sep 50; and
INDURUWAGE, Irene (née Horathalge) (Colombo Central, Sri Lan, 1977) m 1977; Comr, TPWM, Sri. b 29 Nov 55. Served in Sri Lan and Phil (CS/TSWM, TC/TPWM).

IP KAN, Ming-chun Connie (Kwai Chung, 1985); Maj, CSWM, HK. b 16 Jul 62.

IRVING, Ray (Shiremoor, 1989) m 1989; Maj, UK. b 20 Apr 51. MVA, MCMI; Maj Angela ret 2012.

ISRAEL, Betty A. (née Sheinfeldt) (Waltham, MA, USA E, 1971); Maj, USA Nat. b 6 Jan 47. BA (Sociol), MA (Counselling/Human Services), PG Dip. Served in USA E and at IHQ. Ww Capt James, pG 1988.

ISRAEL, Mark H. (Warner Robbins, GA, USA S, 1982); Lt-Col, USA S. b 8 May 58. BA (Bible), MA (Theol Studies); and
ISRAEL, Carolee J. (née Zarfas) (Des Moines Citadel, IA, USA C, 1981); m 1982; Lt-Col, USA S. b 30 Mar 58. BS (Pract Min). Served at USA Nat.

IUNG, Ricardo (São Paulo Central, 1999); Capt, Brz. b 29 Nov 70. BA (Admin); with
IUNG, Cindy (née Meylan) m 1995; Capt, Brz. b 13 Feb 77. Served in Switz.

J

JACKSON, David (Romford, 1976); Maj, UK. b 10 Nov 52. Served at IHQ.

JAMES, M. C. (Monkotta, Ind SW, 1979); Comr, TC, Ind SE. b 20 Oct 54. MA Soc; and
SUSAMMA, James (Pothencode, Ind SW, 1983) m 1983; Comr, TPWM, Ind SE. b 1 Mar 61. Served in Ind SW, Ind N and Ind C (CS/TSWM, TC/TPWM).

JANOWSKI, Achim (Freiburg im Breisgau 1995); Maj, Ger. b 3 Dec 66. Soc Pedagogue; and
JANOWSKI, Anette (née Stoll) (Freiburg, 96) m 1996; Maj, Ger. b 23 Jan 65.

JAYARATNASINGHAM, Packianathan (Jaffna, 1973); Maj, Sri Lan. b 4 Nov 52; and
JAYARATNASINGHAM, Delankage Chandralatha (née Delankage) (Siyambalangamua, 1979) m 1980; Maj, Sri Lan. b 28 Oct 59. Served at IHQ.

JEBAMONY, Jayaseelan (Maharajaduram 1982); Maj, Ind SE. b 20 May 57; and
GNANASELVI, Jayaseelan (Nattalam, 1985) m 1980; Maj, Ind SE. b 30 Dec 57.

Biographical Information

JEYARAJ, Daniel Jebasingh Raj (Booth Tucker Hall, Nagercoil, 1987); Maj, Ind SE. b 10 Jun 61. BA (Eng), MA (Social), BTh, BD, MTh and
RAJAM, Daniel Jebasingh Raj (Kuzhikalai, 1992) m 1992; Maj, Ind SE. b 12 Mar 64. BA (Eng), MA (History), BTh PM, MTh PM. Served in Ind SE and at Ind Nat.

JEYARAJ, Samraj (Booth Tucker Hall, Nagercoil, 1982); Maj, Ind SE. b 14 Aug 58. BSc, MA (Sociol), MA (JMC), PGDHM; and
JESSI, Thayammal Samraj (Gnaniahpuram, 1986) m 1986; Maj, Ind SE. b 21 Oct 63. MusB. Served at Ind Nat.

JEFFREY, David (Morgantown, WV, USA S, 1973); Comr, TC, USA S. b 2 Aug 51. BS, MA (Relig); and
JEFFREY, Barbara (née Garris) (Morgantown, WV, USA S, 1966) m 1969; Comr TPWM, USA S. b 1 Jul 46. Served in USA S (CS/TSWM) and at USA Nat (Nat CS/NSWM).

JERA, Onai (Marowa, 1992); Maj, Zimb. b 10 Sep 67; and
JERA, Deliwe (née Gasa) (Gunguhwe, 1992) m 1994; Maj, Zimb. b 18 Jun 68.

JEWETT, Vernon Wayne (Atlanta Temple, GA, 1980); Lt-Col, USA S. b 11 Dec 47. BA, MA; with
JEWETT, Martha Gaye (née Brewer) m 1975; Lt-Col, USA S. b 22 Oct 52. BA.

JOB, William (Manalikarai, 1981); Maj, Ind SE. b 8 Dec 51. BA; and
DAIZY, Bai William (Poottetty, 1982) m 1982; Maj, Ind SE. b 17 Apr 59.

JOHN, Rajan K. (Parayankerry, 1979); Maj, Ind SW. b 26 Mar 52; with
RAJAN, Susamma m 1977; Maj, Ind SW. b 17 Oct 52.

JOHN, Samuel (Faisalabad, 1997) Maj, Pak. b 5 Jul 69; and
SAMUEL, Rebecca (née William) m 1993; Maj, Pak b 11 Mar 72.

JOHNSON, Kenneth (Charlotte Temple, NC, USA S, 1984); Col, TC, E Eur. b 10 Aug 56. BS (Bus Mgmt); with
JOHNSON, Paula (née Salmon) m 1981; Col, TPWM, E Eur. b 23 Nov 62. Served in USA S.

JOHNSON, Rex (Auckland Congress Hall, NZ, 1973); Maj, PNG. b 24 May 48; and
JOHNSON, Geraldine (née Stratton) (Dunedin Fortress, NZ, 1976) m 1976; Maj, PNG. b 6 Mar 1954. Served in NZ.

JOHNSTONE, Wendy (London South, ON,

Can, 1980); Maj, S Am E. b 31 Oct 57. Served in Can and at IHQ.

KASAEDJA, Jones (Kulawi, 1982); Lt-Col, CS, Indon. b 22 Jun 68; and
KASAEDJA, Mariyam (née Barani) (Salupone, 1982) m 1989; Lt-Col, TSWM, Indon. b 10 Oct 54.

KASBE, Devdan (Ahmednagar Central, 1970); Maj, Ind W. b 9 Feb 49; and
KASBE, Marya B. (née Devhe) (Dapodi, 1972) m 1972; Maj, Ind W. b 16 Oct 52.

KATHURI, Gabriel (Mombasa, 1982); Col, IHQ (Principal, SALT Afr.). b 13 Jan 51; with
KATHURI, Monica (née Minoo) m 1977; Col, IHQ. b 22 Feb 54. Served in Ken E (CS/TSWM).

KATSUCHI, Jiro (Hamamatsu, 1984); Comr, TC, Jpn. b 3 May 49; and
KATSUCHI, Keiko (née Munemori) (Nagoya, 1969) m 1986; Comr, TPWM, Jpn. b 30 Jun 47.

KELLY, David E. (Cincinnati, OH, 1980); Maj, USA E. b 30 Nov 59. AS (Bus Adm), MA (Ldrshp & Min); and
KELLY, Naomi R. (née Foster) (Tonawanda, NY, 1977) m 1981; Maj, USA E. b 14 Sep 56. BA (Org Mgmt).

KHAIZADINGA (Bukpui, 1974); Lt-Col, Ind E. b 20 Jan 50; with
RAMTHANMAWII m 1970; Lt-Col, Ind E. b 23 Nov 53.

KHAMALISHI, Fredrick (Masera, Ken 1989); Maj, Ken W. b 22 Feb 63; with
KHAMALISHI, Jesca (née Masera) m 1988; Maj, Ken W. b 12 Apr 65.

KHAYUMBI, Luka (Musudzuu, Ken, 1994); Maj, S Afr. b 5 Nov 66; with
KHAYUMBI, Rasoa (née Inyangala) m 1990; Maj. S Afr. b 3 Oct 70. Served in Ken E.

KHOLOWA, Paul, (Migowi, 1997); Capt, Mal. b 1 Jan 70; and
KHOLOWA, Doreen (née Mwaitanda) m 2003; Lt, Mal. b 5 Jan 82

KHOZA, Jabulani (Mbabane, 1985); Lt-Col, S Afr. b 8 Jun 62; and
KHOZA, Fikile (née Mkhize) (Ezakheni, 1986) m 1986; Lt-Col, S Afr. b 28 Aug 66.

KIBOTI, Ndombasi Théophile (Kavwaya, 1987); Lt-Col, Dem Rep Con. b 2 Apr 58; with
KIBOTI, Simone (née Kodi Kisala) m 1985; Lt-Col, Dem Rep Con. b 12 Feb 66

KIMASWOCH, Patrick (Kaptel, Ken 1998); Capt, Mal. b 4 Apr 70; with
KIMASWOCH, Frida (née Indusa) m 1996; Capt, Mal. b 11 Sep 70. Served in Ken W.

KIM, Byoung-moo (San Kok, 1990); Maj,
Kor. b 2 Oct 60; with
LEE, Joo-young m 1987; Maj, Kor.
b 10 Mar 61.

KIM, Jong-koo (Chin Chook, 1980); Maj, Kor.
b 22 Nov 51; with
KIM, Kye-suk (Chun Yun, 1980); m 1978;
Maj, Kor. b 10 May 56.

KIM, Jong-sun (Suh Chun An, 1997); Maj,
Kor. b 23 May 63; with
CHUNG, In-ok (Suh Chun An, 1997)
m 1988; Maj, Kor. b 4 April 57. Served in
Phil and USA W.

KIM, Nam-sun (Ah Hyun, 1983); Maj, Kor.
b 11 Sep 54.

KIM, Pill-soo (Yung Deung Po, 1985); Maj,
Kor. b 2 Jan 55; with
CHOI, Sun-hee m 1982; Maj, Kor. b 28 Sep 57.

KIM, Un-ho (Eum Am, 1979); Lt-Col, Kor.
b 31 Jan 52; with
LEE, Ok-kyung (Duk Am, 1979) m 1977;
Lt-Col, Kor. b 9 Jun 53.

KIM, Young-tae (Chin Chook, 1986); Maj, Kor.
b 23 Mar 56. BAdm, MBA; with
PYO, Choon-yun m 1977; Maj, Kor. b 30 Aug 53.

KITHOME, Lucas (Mwala, 1986); Maj, Ken E.
b 10 Feb 59; with
KITHOME, Agnes (née Nduku) m 1984;
Maj, Ken E. b 15 Jan 63.

KITONYI, Joshua (Kathiani, 1990); Maj,
Ken E. b 8 Oct 65; and
KITONYI, Edith (née Mbogo) m 6 Nov 93;
Maj, Ken E. b 30 Mar 66. Served in Ken W.

KIVINDYO, Isaac (Kanzalu, 1982); Lt-Col,
Ken E. b 1 Aug 56; with
KIVINDYO, Naomi (née Loko) m 1970;
Lt-Col, Ken E. b 1 May 60. Served in Ken W.

KLARENBEEK, Elsje (Amsterdam Zuid,
1979); Maj, Neth. b 2 Jun 52.

KLEMAN, Johnny (Boras, Swdn, 1982);
Col, TC, Fin. b 29 Jul 59. BTh; and
KLEMAN, Eva (née Hedberg) (Motala,
Swdn, 1981) m 1982; Col, TPWM, Fin. b 6
Sep 1960. Served in Swdn (CS/TSWM).

KLEMANSKI, Guy (Lewiston-Auburn, ME,
1971); Lt-Col, USA E. b 21 Nov 50; and
KLEMANSKI, Henrietta (née Wallace)
(Cleveland, West Side, OH, 1970) m 1972;
Lt-Col, USA E. b 27 Jul 47.

KNAGGS, James (Philadelphia Roxborough,
PA, USA E, 1976); Comr, TC, USA W.
b 5 Dec 50. MPS (Urban Min); with
KNAGGS, Carolyn (née Lance) m 1972;
Comr, TPWM, USA W. b 19 Sep 51.
Served in USA E (CS/TSWM) and Aus S
(TC/TPWM).

KNEDAL, Jan Øystein (Templet, Oslo, 1974);
Lt-Col, Nor. b 25 Aug 52; and
KNEDAL, Brit (née Kolloen) (Templet, Oslo,
1976) m 1978; Lt-Col, Nor. b 27 Apr 58.

KOMBO, Blaise (Makelekele, 1996); Capt,
Con (Braz). b 15 Oct 68. MA Psych; with
KOMBO, Evelynne (née Missamon)
(Sangolo, 1996) m 1992; Capt, Con (Braz).
b 6 Jan 75.

KORNILOW, Petter (Parkano, 1981); Maj,
Fin. b 21 Aug 53; and
KORNILOW, Eija Hellevi (née Astikainen)
(Tampere Kaleva, 1981) m 1981; Maj, Fin.
b 28 Jun 56.

KROMMENHOEK, Dick (Amsterdam
Congress Hall, Neth, 1983); Comr, TC, Nor.
b 18 Jun 52. MA (Music); with
KROMMENHOEK, Vibeke (née Schou
Larsen) m 1978; Comr, TPWM, Nor.
b 27 Nov 56. MA (Theol). Served in Neth,
Den (TC/TPWM), Frce (TC/TPWM),
Fin (TC/TPWM) and at IHQ.

KUMARAVEL, Felix, (Colombo 2003);
Capt, Sri Lan. b 18 Jan 80.

KUMAR BABU, K. Y. Raj (Kahjipalem, 1981);
Maj, Ind C. b 11 Jun 55; with
KRUPA, Bai m 1976; Maj, Ind C. b 6 Jan 55.

KUMAR, K. Y. Dhana (Khajipalem, Bapatla,
1980); Maj, Ind C. b 21 Sep 57. BCom; with
KUMAR, Yesamma (née Dasari) m 1978;
Maj, Ind C. b 18 May 1961.

KUMAR, Raj (Nawanpind, Mukerian, 1989);
Maj, Ind N. b 7 Aug 64. BA, BD; with
RAJKUMAR Mohinder m 1987; Maj,
Ind N. b 5 May 64.

KWENDA, Peter (Mutondo, 1976);
Lt-Col, Zimb. b 10 Apr 57; and
KWENDA, Norma (née Nyawo) (Dombwe-
Makonde, 1977) m 1977; Lt-Col, Zimb. b 10
Jul 55. Served in Nig.

KYEI, Edward (Fomena, 1979); Maj, Gha,
b. 2 Jun 60; with
KYEI, Catherine (née Adjeiwah); m 1979;
Maj, Gha, b. 23 Nov 1963.

KYEREMEH, Samuel (Nkawkaw, 1991); Maj,
Gha. b 18 Feb 60; with
KYEREMEH, Juliana (née Boakye) m 1987;
Maj, Gha. b 11 May 63.

L

LABOSSIERE, James P. (Cambridge Citadel,
MA, 1985); Maj, USA E. b 21 Feb 60. BS
(Comm Min), MS (Org Ldrshp); with
LABOSSIERE, Patricia (née Levesque)
m 1982; Maj, USA E. b 28 Nov 60. BS
(Church Mgmt).

LAHASE, Kashinath V. (Chapadgaon, Ind W, 1972); Comr, TC, Ind N. b 1 Nov 49; with **LAHASE, Kusum K.** m 1970; Comr, TPWM, Ind N. b 7 Jun 49. Served in Ind W, Ind SW and Ind N (CS/TSWM).

LALAC, Valery (Dubossary, Moldova, 1999); Capt, E Eur. b 10 May 59; with **LALAC, Victoria** (née Pocotilo) m1986; Capt, E Eur, b 9 May 67.

LAITHANMAWIA (Ratu, 1981); Maj, Ind E. b 15 Mar 56 with **LALBIALTLUANGI** (Darlawn 1982); Maj, Ind E. b 20 Aug 60.

LALBULLIANA (Serchip, 1987); Lt-Col, Ind E. b 20 Sep 64; and **LALBULLIANA, Lalnunhlui** (Thingsulthliah, Ind E, 1990) m 1990; Lt-Col, Ind E. b 12 Dec 65. Served in Ken E.

LALHMINGLIANA (Chaltlang, 1994); Maj, Ind E. b 29 Sep 71. BA (Hons) (Hist); and **LALHLIMPUII** (Bethel, 1994) m 1994; Maj, Ind E. b 28 Oct 71. Served at IHQ.

LALKIAMLOVA (Kahrawt, 1971); Comr, IHQ (IS S Asia). b 7 Mar 49. BA; and **LALHLIMPUII** (Saitual, 1973) m 1973; Comr, IHQ (ZSWM S Asia). b 25 Sep 53. Served in Ind E, Ind SW (CS/TSWO) and Ind C (TC/TPWM).

LALNGAIHAWMI, Naomi (Aizawl Central, 1978); Col, TC, TPWM, Ind E. b 1 Jan 54. MA. Served at Ind Nat

LALRAMHLUNA (Chaltlang, 1981); Lt-Col, CS, Ind E. b 9 May 51; with **KAWLRAMTHANGI** m 1972; Lt-Col, TSWM, Ind E. b 14 Nov 52.

LALRAMLIANA, Hnamte (Govt Complex, Aizawl, Ind E, 1996); Maj, Ind Nat. b 3 Jan 67. BA, BD; with **C. LALHRIATPUII** m 1994; Maj, Ind Nat. b 15 Sep 69. Served in Ind E.

LALZAMLOVA (Tuinu, Ind E, 1986); Col, TC, Phil. b 1 Feb 62. BA; with **NEMKHANCHING (Nu-i)** m 1984; Col, TPWM, Phil. b 23 Feb 63. Served in Ind E, Ind N and Phil (TC/TPWM).

LAMARTINIERE, Lucien (Petit Goave, Haiti, 1992); Lt-Col, CS, DR Con. b 13 Jun 57; with **LAMARTINIERE, Marie** (née Bonhomme) m 1980; Lt-Col, TSWM, DR Con. b 26 May 57. Served in Can and Carib.

LANCE, Donald W. (Philadelphia Roxborough, PA, 1980); Lt-Col, USA E. b 7 Feb 53. BA (Bus), MPA (Non-Profit Mgmt); and **LANCE, Renee** (née Hewlett) (Scranton, PA, 2002) m 2003; Lt-Col, USA E. b 3 Jun 53. RN (Nursing).

LANGA, William (Witbank, 1977); Comr, TC, S Afr. b 15 Jul 49; with **LANGA, Thalitha** (née Themba) m 1973; Comr, TPWM, S Afr. b 1 Sep 50. Served as CS/TSWM.

LASUT, Ernie (Bandung 1, 1986); Maj, Indon. b 4 Sep 61.

LAUKKANEN, Arja (Turku 2, 1975); Lt-Col, CS, Fin. b 29 Apr 46.

LAWS, Peter (Wauchope, 1973); Lt-Col, Aus E. b 23 Oct 1950. BAL, MBA; with **LAWS, Jan** (née Cook) m 1970; Lt-Col, Aus E. b 18 Jun 50.

LEAVEY, Wendy (Street, UK, 1980); Lt-Col, IHQ. b 17 Feb 53. SRN, SCM. Served in UK and Gha.

LECOCQ, Noélie (Quaregnon,1973), Maj, RO, Frce and Belg, b 29 Feb 48.

LEE, Ki-yong (Chun Yun, Seoul 1982); Maj, Kor. b 9 Aug 52; and **KIM, Sun-ho** (Eum Am, 1985); m 1985; Maj, Kor. b 19 Jan 54.

LEE, Kong Chew (Bob) (Balestier, 1983); Lt-Col, CS, Phil. b 8 Oct 57. BDiv; and **LEE, Teoh Gim Leng (Wendy)** (Penang, 1983) m 1982; Lt-Col, TSWM, Phil. b 24 Aug 57. Served in Sing (CS/TSWM).

LEEDOM, Darryl (Freemont, NE, USA C, 1989); Maj, USA Nat. b 11 Jul 65. BS (Pract Min), MSW; and **LEEDOM, Donna** (née Horton) (Ft Dodge, IA, USA C, 1989); m 1989; Maj, USA Nat. b 2 Dec 66. Served in USA C.

LEMPID, I. Sadia (Polonia, 1989); Maj, Indon. b 13 Dec 64; and **LEMPID, Syastiel** (née Haku) (Semarang 3, 1996) m 1996; Maj, Indon. b 9 Oct 72.

LESCANO, Lee R. (San Diego Citadel, CA, 1988); Maj, USA W. b 14 Jul 52. MA , BA , CERT (Elementary Ed); with **LESCANO, Michele** (née Meyer) m 1985; Maj, USA W. b 3 Oct 55. BA (Bib and Theol).

LESLIE, Victor A. (Port-of-Spain, 1980); Lt-Col, CS, Carib. . b 5 Nov 56. BA (Mgmt), MA (Relig Studies), CERT (Chem Dpndnce), JD (Law), MBA (Mgmt); and **LESLIE, Rose-Marie** (née Campbell) (Lucea, 1977) m 1980; Lt-Col, TSWM, Carib. b 15 Aug 57. BS (Soc Wk), AS (Nursing), RN (Nursing), BS (Nursing), CERT (Public Health Nurse). Served in USA W.

LEVIS, Linda (Harrow, UK, 1980); Maj, Tanz. b 2 Nov 49. BA (Hons), PGCE. Served in UK and at ITC.

LIANHLIRA (Ratu, 1979); Maj, Ind E. b 28 Apr 51, with **THANZUALI** m 1975; Maj, Ind E. b 20 Jan 57.

LIGT de, Cornelis (Nieuwegein, Neth, 1990)
Maj, Ban. b 23 Sep 61; and.
LIGT de, Jacoba (née Oosterheerd)
(Nieuwegein, Neth, 1987) m 1988; Maj, Ban.
b 24 Apr 58. Served in Neth, E Afr, Ken E
and Ken W.

LIM, Hun-taek (Kunsan, 1979); Lt-Col, Kor.
b 24 Aug 50; with
CHUN, Soon-ja m 1977; Lt-Col, Kor.
b 9 Mar 50. Served in Aus S.

LIM, Young-sik (Shin An, 1975); Lt-Col, Kor.
b 26 Jun 49; with
YEO, Keum-soo (Mokpo, 1975); m 1972;
Lt-Col, Kor. b 14 Dec 50.

LIVIALA, Isaack (Londiana, Ken 1985); Maj,
Ken W. b 15 Jan 59 with
LIVIALA, Rose (nee Kagena) m 1984; W.
b 12 Dec 1963.

LÖFGREN, Kehs David (Norrköping, 1968);
Col, Swdn. b 8 Nov 45; and
LÖFGREN, Edith (née Sjöström) (Borlänge,
1974) m 1977; Col, Swdn. b 2 Mar 51.
Served in UK and Nor (CS/TSWO).

LOMAX, Denis (Prescot, 1974); Maj, UK.
b 26 Jan 53. Dip RS; and
LOMAX, Olive (née Baird) (Prescot, 1974)
m 1974; Maj, UK. b 15 Jan 55.

LOROT, Ibrahim (Lokitaung, 1994), Maj, Ken
W. b 4 Dec 61; with
LOROT, Anne (née Edung) m 4 Aug 1984;
Maj, Ken W. b 13 Mar 65. Served in Ken E.

LOSSO, Mesak (Jakarta 2, 1968); Lt-Col,
Indon. b 12 Nov 45; and
LOSSO, Mona (née Warani) (Turen, 1971)
m 1972; Lt-Col, Indon. b 13 Jun 44.

LOUBACKY, Urbain (Bakongo, 1992);
Maj, Con (Braz), b 20 Dec 64; with
LOUBACKY, Judith (née Bikouta) m 1989;
Maj, Con (Braz). b 16 Apr 68

LOUZOLO Dieudonné (Nzoko, 1992); Maj,
Con (Braz). b 20 Apr 67. BA Lang; with
LOUZOLO Edith (née Boudzoumou)
m 1990; Maj, Con (Braz). b 25 Jul 69.

LUFUMBU, Enock (Londiani, Nakuru, 1982);
Maj, Ken E. b 10 Feb 52; with
LUFUMBU, Beatrice (née Kageha) m 1978;
Maj, Ken E. b 22 Feb 57.

LUKAU, Joseph (Kimbanseke 1, Con (Kin),
1977); Col, TC, Con (Braz). b 18 Sep 53;
with
LUKAU, Angélique (née Makiese) m 1975;
Col, TPWM, Con (Braz). b 1 Sep 54. Served
in Con (Kin), Frce (CS/TPWM) and at IHQ.

LUTHER, Lise (Harstad, 1992); Maj, Nor.
b 20 May 65.

LUYK, Kenneth E. (Columbus, GA, 1985);

Lt-Col, USA S. b 2 Oct 55. MA (Relig); with
LUYK, Dawn M. (née Busby) m 1981; Lt-
Col, USA S. b 5 Jun 60. BA (Chrstn Min).

M

MABASO, Timothy John (Witbank, S Afr,
1988); Lt-Col, Ken W. b 18 May 60.
BA (Bus Adm); with
MABASO, Zakithi (née Zulu) m 1983;
Lt-Col, Ken W. b 16 Dec 57. Served in S Afr.

MABUTO, Christopher (Chaanga, Zam, 1979);
Lt-Col, CS, Zam. b 2 Jan 54; with
MABUTO, Anne (née Hamayobe) m 1974;
Lt-Col, TSWM, Zam. b 25 Feb 58. Served in
Zam & Mal, Ken W and Tanz.

MABWIDI, Malonga Philippe (Salle Centrale,
1985); Maj, DR Con. b 25 Jan 53; with
MABWIDI Marie-Thérèse (née Biyela
Lukimwena), m 1986; Maj, DR Con. b 13 Mar 63.

MACWAN, Paul Vahalji (Palaj, 1982); Maj,
Ind W. b 7 Jul 54; and
MACWAN, Shalomi Paul (Shevgaon, 1986)
m 1991; Maj, Ind W. b 20 Apr 60.

MACWAN, Punjalal Ukabhai (Lingda, 1980);
Maj, Ind W. b 8 Jul 51; with
MACWAN, Margaret m 1975; Maj, Ind W.
b 17 May 55.

MACWAN, Yakub Gala (Dabhan 1983); Maj,
Ind W. b 3 Jul 59; and
MACWAN, Sophia (Vaso 1983); m 1981,
Maj, Ind W. b 7 Sep 62.

McCLIMONT, Graeme, (Brighton, 1977);
Maj, Aus S. b 29 Jan 48. B Soc Wel, B Beh Sc;
with
McCLIMONT, Helen (née Clee) m 1969;
Maj, Aus S. b 1 Dec 49. Served in UK and PNG.

McLAREN, Phillip (Shortland, 1975); Maj,
Aus E. b 25 Apr 48; with
McLAREN, Nancy (née Bramble) m 1969;
Maj, Aus E. b 27 Aug 49.

McMILLAN, Susan (Montreal Citadel, Can,
1979); Col, S Am E, TC, TPWM. b 20 Oct 54.
BAS, MBA, CGA. Served in Can, Mex and
Cent Am, S Am W (CS) and at IHQ.

MADOKI, Japhael (Ilembo, 1982) Maj, Tanz.
b. 7 Jan 61; with
MADOKI, Aliyinza (nee) m 1981; Maj, Tanz
b. 1 Jan 61.

MADYANENZARA, Joseph, (Alaska Mine,
1986); Maj, Zimb. b. 25 Dec 56; with
MADYANENZARA, Molly; Maj, Zimb. b.
25 May 58.

MAFUTA, Mavana Denis (Kamina, 1993);
Capt, DR Con. b 18 Oct 54; with
MAFUTA Modestine (née Lumwanga
Ngoy); Maj, DR Con. b 18 Oct 1962.

MAGAIGWA, Musa (Kitaguti, 1992) Maj, Tanz. b 26 Sep 1965; with
MAGAIGWA, Esther m. 1991; Maj, Tanz. b 1 Jan 61.

MAGANLAL, Paul (Vaso, 1979); Maj, Ind W. b 7 Jan 54; with
MAGANLAL, Febiben m 1973; Maj, Ind W. b 11 Jun 52.

MAGAR, Bhausaheb J. (Dahiphal, 1977); Maj, Ind W. b 2 Jun 53; and
MAGAR, Pushpa (née Gajbhiv) (Dahiphal, 1978) m 1979; Maj, Ind W. b 2 Jun 54.

MAGAYA, Jessie (née Milambo) (Chitumbi, 1981); Maj, TSWM, Zam. b 20 Sep 63; with
MAGAYA, Bexter m 1979; Maj, Zam. b 29 Jan 56.

MAHIDA, Jashwant D. (Vishrampura, 1984); Maj, Ind W. b 12 Jun 60; and
MAHIDA, Ruth (née Maganlal) (Anand Central, 1990) m 1990; Maj, Ind W. b 12 Nov 67.

MAHLANGU, Solomon (Brits, 1983); Maj, S Afr. b 29 Oct 60; and
MAHLANGU, Mercy (née Razwinani) (Khubvi, 1983) m 1985; Maj, S Afr. b 30 Jun 63. BA Soc Studies. Served at IHQ.

MAHLOBO, Themba (Vryheid, 2001); Capt, S Afr. b 1 Nov 76 with
MAHLOBO, Nokuthula (née Mabaso) (Estill, 2001) m 2002; Capt, S Afr. b 26 Jun 81

MAIN, Gordon (Moonah, 1995); Maj, Aus S. b 19 Mar 52; with
MAIN, Dianne (née Grice) m 1972; Maj, Aus S. b 9 May 51.

MAIN, Paul (Rutherglen, 1986) Maj, UK. b 11 Aug 64; and
MAIN, Jenine (née Hixon) (Basingstoke, 1986) m 1986; Maj, UK. b 12 Dec 60. BA.

MAINO, Andrew (Lealea, 2000); Capt, PNG. b 3 Mar 61. Ww Capt Morea, pG 2011.

MALABI, Joash (Mulatiwa, Ken, 1984); Comr, IHQ (IS, Afr). b 17 May 55; and
MALABI, Florence (née Mutindi) (Webuye, Ken, 1988) m 1988; Comr, IHQ (ZSWM, Afr). b 26 Jun 64. Served in E Afr, Rw (RC/RPWM), S Afr (CS/TSWM) and Ken W (TC/TLWM).

MALINS, Stephen (Johannesburg City Corps, 1997); Capt, S Afr. b 7 Sep 62. Bth with;
MALINS, Theresa (née Lotter) m 1985; Capt, S Afr. b 27 May 65

MAMBO, Tineyi (Seke Materera, 1989); Maj, Zimb. b 23 Jan 67; and
MAMBO, Rumbidzai (Mungate, 1989) m 1991; Maj, Zimb. b 29 May 67.

MANDGULE Ashok (Nasarapur 1982); Maj, Ind W. b 4 May 59 and
MANDGULE Sheela (Fariabagh 1983); Maj, Ind W. b 14 Sep 64.

MANGIWA, Indra (Bandung 2, 1976), Maj, Indon. b 14 Mar 52; and
MANGIWA, Helly (née Salainti) (Surabaya, 1977) m 1982; Maj, Indon. b 16 Jun 56.

MANHARDT, Linda (Pasadena Tabernacle, USA W, 1978); Maj, Phil. b 11 Apr 52. MA.

MANKOMBA, Elisha (Choma, 1989); Maj, Zam. b 22 Mar 53 with
MANKOMBA, Alice (née Mutinta) m 1983, Maj, Zam, b 4 Jun 64.

MANOHARAN, Yesudian (Nantikuzhy, Ind SE, 1987); Maj, Ind SE. b 14 May 64. MCom, M Min; and
MANOHARAN, Vethamony (Ettamadai, Ind SE, 1987) m 1987; Maj, Ind SE. b 20 Mar 64. Served in Ind N and Tanz.

MANULAT, Edward (San Jose Antique, 1983); Maj, Phil. b 1 Dec 59. and
MANULAT, Arlene (née Nicor) (Pandanan, 1984) m 1984, Maj, Phil. b. 10 Aug 59.

MÁRQUEZ, Manuel (La Esperanza, 1995) Maj, S Am W. b 12 Feb 1971; and
MÁRQUEZ, Paulina (née Condori) (Viacha, 1987) m 1997; Maj, S Am W. b 2 Mar 1964.

MARSEILLE, Gerrit W. J. (Ribe, Den, 1978); Comr, IHQ. b 8 Jun 51. MSc, MLP; with
MARSEILLE, Eva (née Larsen) m 1976; Comr, IHQ. b 18 Jun 52. Cand Odont. Served in Neth, Zai, Den, S Afr and Con (Braz) (CS/TSWM).

MARTI, Paul William (Templet, Oslo, 1980), Maj, Nor. b 24 Jan 61; and
MARTI, Margaret Saue (née Saue) (Voss, 1980) m 1983, Maj, Nor. b 29 Aug 58. Served in Switz.

MARTIN, August (Biel, 1977); Maj, Switz. b 24 Oct 52; with
MARTIN, Ruth (née Beyeler) m 1974; Maj, Switz. b 22 Oct 51.

MARTIN, Larry (Edmonton Northside, AB, 1980); Maj Can. b 31 Jul 1950. BA, MA, MTS; with
MARTIN, Velma (née Ginn) m 1972; Maj Can. b 4 Oct 1950. Served in UK.

MARZAN, Jorge L. (San Juan, PR, 1977); Maj, USA E. b 3 Nov 56. Cert (Database); and
MARZAN, Limaris (née Negron) (Ponce, PR, 2002) m 2001; Capt, USA E. b 10 Sep 75. BA (Soc Wk).

MASANGO, Frederick (Mangula, 1971); Maj, Zimb. b 24 Jul 49; and

320

MASANGO, Rosemary (née Handiria) (Karambazungu, 1981) m 1981; Maj, Zimb. b 13 Feb 56.

MASIH, Edwin (Bareilly, Ind N, 1979); Lt-Col, CS, Ind C. b 6 Oct 57; and
MASIH, Sumita (Gurdaspur, Ind N, 1983) m 1983; Lt-Col, TSWM, Ind C. b 9 Oct 63. Served in Ind N and Carib.

MASIH, Gurnam (Kaler Kalan, 1991); Maj, Ind N. b 7 Jan 68; and
MASIH, Razia (Durangla, 1987); m 1992; Maj, Ind N. b 1 Apr 65.

MASIH, Joginder (Bhoper, 1982); Lt-Col, Ind N. b 13 Jul 58; with
MASIH, Shanti m 1980; Lt-Col, Ind N. b 15 May 59. Served in Ban (GS/CSWM).

MASIH, Makhan (Shahpur Guraya, 1990); Maj, Ind N. b 30 Mar 68; and
MASIH, Sunila Makhan (City Corps, Amritsar, 1992) m 1992; Maj, Ind N. b 5 May 66.

MASIH, Manga (Bhandal, 1979); Maj, Ind N. b 1 May 54; and
MASIH, Roseleen (Batala Central, 1980) m 1980; Maj, Ind N. b 2 Jun 59.

MASIH, Manuel (Amritsar, 1994); Maj, Ind N. b 1 Apr 64; with
MASIH, Anita m 1991; Maj, Ind N. b 22 Apr 62.

MASIH, Parkash (Khunda, 1984); Lt-Col, Ind N. b 10 Mar 58; with
MASIH, Mariam Parkash m 1981; Lt-Col, Ind N. b 2 Apr 62.

MASIH, Piara (Kathane, 1982); Maj, Ind N. b 3 Mar 61; with
MASIH, Grace (Babri Jiwanwal, 1984) m 1985; Maj, Ind N. b 6 Feb 64.

MASIH, Salamat (Chamyari, 1979); Maj, Ind N. b 2 Jan 59; and
MASIH, Snehlata (Chamyari, 1987) m 1981; Maj, Ind N. b 18 May 61.

MASIH, Salamat (Shantinagar, 1989); Maj, Pak. b 12 Aug 64; with
SALAMAT, Grace (née Sardar) m 1987; Maj, Pak. b 18 Apr 64.

MASIH, Sulakhan (Dina Nagar 1988); Maj, Ind N. b 15 Apr 64, and
MASIH, Sheela (Hayat Nagar 1984) m 1988; Maj, Ind N. b 5 Apr 64.

MASIH, Yaqoob (Chamroua 1986); Maj, Ind N. b 6 Jun 62; with
MASIH, Sumitra m 1980; Maj, Ind N. b 6 Jan 63.

MASILAMONY, Stalin (Nettancode, 1997); Maj, Ind SE. b 27 May 71; with
KEZIAL, Stalin m 1995; Maj, Ind SE. b 9 Apr 70.

MASON, Winsome (née De Lisser) (Montego Bay, 1967) m 1969; Lt-Col, Carib b 19 Feb 49. Served in USA E, and Can. Lt-Col Raphael ret 2012.

MASON, Winsome (Burnie, Aus S 1987); Maj, Pak. b 2 Feb 1958. Served in UK and Aus S.

MASSIÉLÉ, Antoine (Yaya, 1982); Maj, Con (Braz). b 20 Feb 53; with
MASSIÉLÉ, Marianne (née Ngoli) m 1978; Maj, Con (Braz). b 2 Jan 50.

MATA, Mayisilwa Jean-Baptiste (Kisenso, 1983); Lt-Col, DR Con. b 21 Oct 51; with
MATA Marie (née Mundele Kisokama), m 1981; Lt-Col. DR Con. b 22 Mar 58.

MATHANGI, Daniel Raju (M.R. Nagaram, Ind C, 1984); Lt-Col, CS, Ind N. b 20 Jun 54. MA (Econ); with
MATHANGI, Rachel (nee Kondamudi) m 1982; Lt-Col, TSWM, Ind N. b 15 Jun 62. Served in Ind C.

MATONDO, Gracia Victor (Kimpese, 1985); Lt-Col, DR Con. b 23 May 60; with
MATONDO, Isabel (née Lydia) m 1982; Lt-Col, DR Con. b 8 Sep 1962.

MATONDO, Isidore Mayunga (Boma, 1989); Maj, DR Con. b 6 Jul 56; with
MATONDO, Marthe (née Nlandu Luzoladio) m 1987; Maj, DR Con. b 7 Dec 62.

MATSIONA, Pascal (Sangolo, 1992); Maj, Con (Braz.) b 5 Jun 57; and
MATSIONA Adèle (née Mibenzibandoki) m 1989; Maj, Con (Braz.), b 21 Jul 55

MAVOUNA, Nkouka François (Nzoko, 1988); Maj, Con (Braz). b 15 Mar 60; with
MAVOUNA, Louise (née Matondo) m 1986; Maj, Con (Braz). b 11 Dec 62.

MAXAM, Byron (Savanna-la-mar, Jamaica, 1971): Maj, Carib. b 31 Aug 50; and
MAXAM, Joycelyn (nee Jonas) (St Johns, Antigua, 1970) m 1994: Maj, Carib. b 4 Sep 48.

MAXWELL, Philip (Orange, NSW, Aus E, 1984); Maj, PNG. b 21 Apr 62. B Bus, MBA; and
MAXWELL, Deslea (née Pethybridge) (Campsie, NSW, Aus E, 1984) m 1984; Maj, PNG. b 23 Feb 62. Served in Aus E.

MAXWELL, Wayne (Canberra City Temple, 1984); Col, CS, Aus E. b 31 May 58. DipMin, BMin, MAL; with
MAXWELL, Robyn (née Alley) m 1980; Col, TSWM, Aus E. b 14 Feb 60. Dip Pastoral Counselling.

MAYASI, Mabasa Alphonse (Mbanza-Nzundu, 1985); Maj, DR Con. b 12 Nov 60, and
MAYASI, Bernadette (née Makwiza Nlandu) m 1992; Maj, DR Con. b 10 Jul 63.

MAYNOR, Kenneth (Cleveland South, OH, 1980); Lt-Col, USA E. b 1 Feb 59. BS (Org Mgmt); with
MAYNOR, Cheryl Ann (née Staaf) m 1977; Lt-Col, USA E. b 27 Sep 58. BS (Church Mgmt).

MAYORGA, Max (Central, Costa Rica, 1989); Maj, L Am N. b 1 Feb 62; with
MAYORGA, Julia (née Obando); m 1981; Maj, L Am N. b 23 Oct 61.

MBAGWU, Joseph (Kano, 1994); Maj, Nig. b 21 Oct 64; with
MBAGWU, Ngozi m 1992; Maj, Nig. b 17 Sep 68.

MBAJA, Tiras Atulo (Kibera, 1986); Maj, Ken W. b 13 Jul 54; with
MBAJA, Mebo (née Mukiza) m 1983; Maj, Ken W. b 25 Mar 60.

MBALA, Lubaki Sébastien (Kifuma, 1987); Maj, DR Con. b 23 Jun 58, and
MBALA, Godette Mboyo (née Moseka) (Kintambo, 1987) m 1988; Maj, DR Con. b 26 Sep 62.

MBAKAYA, Herman (Nairobi Central, 1986), Maj, Ken W. b 11 Jan 57; with
MBAKAYA, Lucia (née Manduu) m 1992; Maj, Ken W. b 13 Oct 67.

MBIZI, Gabin (Ouenze, 1988); Maj, Con (Braz). b 30 Jan 63; with
MBIZI, Philomene (née Nkounkou) m 1986; Maj, Con (Braz). b 22 Aug 67.

MBUNGU, Joyce (Kagumo,1978); Maj, Ken E. b 4 Feb 56.

MBUTHU, Simon (Kilembwa, 1984); Maj, Ken E. b 14 Nov 60; and
MBUTHU, Zipporah (née Mwikali), (Makadara, 1996), m 1996; Capt, Ken E. b 26 Jul 73.

MEITEI, Shamu (Leizhangphai Manipur, 1988); Maj, Ind E. b 1 Jan 61. BCom; with
HOIHNIANG m 1983; Maj, Ind E. b 10 Jun 59.

MEITROTT, Claranne (née Griffith) (Reading, PA 1975) Maj, USA E. b 20 Jan 52. BA (Adv Chrstn Min); with
MEITROTT, Bernard W. m 1970; Maj, USA E. b 18 Jun 48.

MENDES, Marcio (Belo Horizonte, 1980); Maj, Brz. b 24 Feb 57. BA (Theol); and
MENDES, Jurema (née Mazzini) (Quarai, 1979) m 1981; Maj, Brz. b 4 Aug 57. BA (Ed).

MENDEZ, Jorge (El Faro, 1988); Maj, L Am N. b 5 Oct 51; with
MENDEZ, Idali (née Jiminez) m 1973; Maj, L Am N. b 24 Aug 52.

MENIA, Virgilio (Asingan, 1990); Lt-Col, Phil. b 2 Jun 61. BSCE (Civil Engr); and
MENIA, Ma Luisa (née Araneta) (Negros Occ, 1984) m 1990; Lt-Col, Phil. b 7 Jan 62.

MERAS, Marja (Turku 2, 1977); Maj, Fin. b 6 Sep 49.

MERRETT, Kelvin (Renown Park, 1983); Maj, Aus S. b 6 Sep 58. ADipTh; and
MERRETT, Winsome (née Morris) (Kempsey, 1987) m 1987; Maj, Aus S. b 21 Sep 58. MA; BSpTher; DipTh; AMusA.

MEYNER, Marianne (née Stettler) (Basle 2, 1983); Maj, Switz. b 14 Apr 57; with
MEYNER, Urs m 1978; Maj, Switz. b 30 Jan 51.

MGBEBUIHE, Benson (Amauzari, 1990); Maj, Nig. b 1 Aug 64; with
MGBEBUIHE, Celine m 1988; Maj, Nig. b 1 Aug 66.

MGBEBUIHE, Obed (Amauzari, 1988); Maj, Nig. b 20 Dec 58, with
MGBEBUIHE, Violet m 1986; Maj, Nig. b 6 May 69.

MHASVI, Evan (Shirichena, 1977); Lt-Col, Zimb. b 1 Feb 55. Served in Zam and Mal. Ww Lt-Col Henry pG 2006.

MHEMBERE, Isaac (Mukwenya 1989); Maj, Zimb. b 5 May 69; and
MHEMBERE, Charity (née Muchapondwa) (Muchapondwa, 1990) m 1991; Maj, Zimb. b 2 Jan 67.

MILAMBO, Saraphina (née Shikawala) (Kafue, 1989); Maj, TSWM, Zam. b 1 Feb 55. Ww Maj Vincent, pG 2007.

MILLAR, Ronald (Winnipeg Cit, Can, 1978); Maj, Can. b 22 Oct 50. BA, BEd, MTS, MBA; with
MILLAR, Donna (née Barkwell) m 1973; Maj, Can. b 12 Dec 51. BA. Served in Aus E and Carib.

MKAMI, Samuel Chacha (Kitagutiti, 1988); Lt-Col, CS, Mal. b 16 Apr 65; with
MKAMI, Mary (née Kibera) m 1985; Lt-Col, TSWM, Mal. b 20 Jul 66. Served in Tanz.

MNYAMPI, Benjamin (Mgulani, Tanz, 1985), Col, TC, Uga. b 1 Mar 54; with
MNYAMPI, Grace (née Sage) m 1984; Col, TPWM, Uga. b 3 Jun 63. Served in E Afr, Rwa, Zimb, Tanz (CS/TSWM) and Ken W (CS/TSWM).

MOCKABEE, William (Anniston, AL, USA S, 1975); Lt-Col, CS, Sri Lan. b 1 Nov 54; and
MOCKABEE, Debra (née Salmon) (Oklahoma City, OK, USA S, 1976) m 1976; Lt-Col, TSWM, Sri Lan. b 9 Sep 54. Served in USA S.

MORAN, Peter (Bradford West Bowling, 1979); Maj, UK. b 11 Feb 51; with
MORAN, Sandra (née Clapham) m 1971; Maj, UK. b 16 Jul 49.

MORENO, Julio (Santiago de Cuba, Cuba, 2005) Capt, L Am N. b 7 Aug 52; and **MORENO, Leyanis (née González)** m 1991; Capt, L Am N. b 23 Dec 67.

MORRIS, STEPHEN P. (Tampa, FL, 1993); Maj, USA S. b 15 Oct 65. BA (Psych); with **MORRIS, WENDY J.** (née Laxton) m 1990; Maj, USA S. b 28 Aug 65. BA (Bus Mngmt).

MOTSI, Isiah (Tomlinson, 1989); Maj, Zimb. b 9 Sep 68. Ww Maj Leah, pG 2010.

MOUKOKO, Daniel (Bacongo, Con (Braz), 1990); Lt-Col, CS, Con (Braz). b 2 Dec 60; with **MOUKOKO, Arschette** (née Nguitoukoulou) m 1988; Lt-Col, TSWM, Con (Braz). b 30 Oct 62. Served in Rwa and S Afr.

MOYA, Danton (Lo Valledor, 1989); Maj, S Am E. b 17 Jun 58; with **MOYA, Juana** (neé Balboa) m 1979, Maj, S Am E. b 24 Jun 60. Served in S Am W.

MPAKULA, Dickson (Nansolola,1999); Capt, Mal. b 13 Oct 72; with **MPAKULA, Chricy,** (neé Lankeni Phiri) (Gooke, 2003) m 2003; Capt, Mal. b 26 Jan 80

MPANZU, Manu Emmanuel (Kimbanseke 1, 1979); Maj, DR Con. b 20 Jul 54; with **MPANZU, Albertine** (née Luzayadio Yema) m 1977; Maj, DR Con. b 27 Dec 58.

MSONGWE, Yohana (Ilembo, 1985); Maj, Zimb. b 1 Jan 62; with **MSONGWE, Jesinala** m 1985; Maj, Zimb. b 15 Jun 64. Served in Tanz.

M'TETU, Sarah (Gichiche, 1986); Maj, Ken E. b 27 Jan 61. Served in Ken W.

MUBAIWA, Final (Nyarukunda, 1990); Maj, Zimb. b 29 June 60, with **MUBAIWA, Pfumisai** (née Ngwenya) m 1988; Maj, Zimb. b 12 May 69.

MUIKKU, Aino (Turku II, Fin, 1985); Lt-Col, Fin. b 3 May 56. Served in Den (CS).

MUKOKO, Mamfweni Pierre (Mbanza-Nsundi, 1979); Maj, DR Con. b 3 Feb 49; with **MUKOKO, Marie-José** (née Sansa Mundele) m 1981; Maj, DR Con. b 25 Feb 59.

MUKONGA, Julius (Kwa Kyambu, 1978); Lt-Col, Ken E. b 10 Mar 53; with **MUKONGA, Phyllis** (née Mumbua) m 1976; Lt-Col, Ken E. b 28 Mar 57.

MÜNCH, Joan (née Nielsen) (Paris, Frce, 1991); Maj, Den. b 12 Nov 65. Served in Frce.

MUNN, Richard (Lexington, KY, USA E, 1987); Col, IHQ (Principal, ICO). b 16 Jan 56. BA (Ed), MDiv (Theol), DM (Chrstn Ldrshp); with **MUNN, Janet** (née White) m 1980; Col, IHQ. b 22 Oct 60. BA (Psych/Spanish), MA (Ldrshp & Min). Served in USA E.

MUPUKUTA, Taviringwa (Mashuma, 1997); Capt, Zim, b 14 Sep 68 with **MUPUKUTA, Emmaculate** m 1996; Capt, Zim, b 26 Aug 73.

MUNYEKHE, Boniface (Kithituni, 1977); Maj, Ken E. b 21 Mar 50; with **MUNYEKHE, Esther** (née Mumbe) m 1973; Maj, Ken E. b 12 May 52.

MUSYOKI, David (Mweani, 1999); Capt, Mal. b 5 Jan, 68; with **MUSYOKI, Grace,** m. 1996. Capt, Mal. b 5 Dec 72.

MUTUNGI, William (Kawethi, Kenya, 1990) Maj Lib b 3 Nov 62; with **MUTUNGI, Florence** (née Mbithe) m 1988; Maj, Lib. b 12 Dec 66. Served in Ken E and Ken W.

MUZORORI, Trustmore, (Alaska Mine, 1987); Maj, Zimb. b 4 Mar 66; and **MUZORORI, Wendy** (Mutukwa, 1989); m 1989 Maj, Zimb. b 16 Feb 68. Served in Kenya and Uga.

MWALUKANI, Wilson (Maendeleo, 1984); Maj, Tanz. b 1 Aug 59; with **MWALUKANI, Tamali** (née Sanya) m 1983; Maj, Tanz. b 1 Jan 63.

MWANGI, Samson (Maragwa, 1994); Maj, Ken E. b 31 Dec 68; with **MWANGI, Mary** (née Macharia) m 1991; Capt, Ken E. b 14 Aug 70.

MWEEMBA, Richard (Choma, Zam, 1989); Maj, Ken E. b 24 Feb 54; with **MWEEMBA, Eunice** (née Chiyalamanza) m 1975; Maj, Ken E. b 15 Apr 60. Served in Zam.

N

NABISWA, Eliud (Butemulani, Uganda 1986); Maj, Uganda. b 8 June 58 with **NABISWA, Aidah;** m 1982; Maj, Uganda. b 4 April 60

NAKO, Gideon (Mwambaisyuko, Ken E 1994); Maj, Ken E. b 30 Oct 65; with **NAKO, Lucy** (née Mbuta 94) m 20 Feb 89; Maj, Ken E. b 28 Feb 70.

NALLATHAMBI, Edwin Sathyadhas (Kolvey, 1981); Maj, Ind SE. b 10 Aug 55; with **GNANA, Jessibell Edwin Sathyadhas** m 1980; Maj, Ind SE. b 15 Jun 57

NANGI, Masamba Henri (Kinzadi, 1979); Lt-Col, DR Con. b 21 May 53; with **NANGI, Josephine** (née Nsimba Babinga); Lt-Col, DR Con. b 30 Dec 53.

NANLABI, Priscilla (San Jose, Phil, 1980); Lt-Col, Phil. b 15 Nov 58. Served in HK (GS).

NATHANIEL, Alladi (Bhogapuram, 1980);
Lt-Col, Ind C. b 9 Dec 52. BA; with
NATHANIEL, Rajeswari (née Yesu)
m 1971; Lt-Col, Ind C. b 6 Jul 55.

NAUD, Daniel (Paris-Montparnasse, Frce, 1979);
Lt-Col, OC, It. b 8 Mar 54; and
NAUD Eliane (née Volet) (Strasbourg, Frce,
1980) m 1980; Lt-Col, CPWM, It. b 3 Apr 60.
Served in Frce & Belg and It & Gr.

NAUD, Patrick (Paris Villette, Fra, 1987);
Col, TC, Ger. b 15 Mar 58; and
NAUD, Anne-Dore (nèe Kaiser)
(Hamburg, 1987) m 1987; Col, TPWM, Ger.
b 26 Nov 59. Served in Fra and Belg.

NAYAK, Baldev (Penagoberi, 1990); Maj,
Ind N. b 12 Feb 65; and
NAYAK, Chandrika (Sartaguda, 1994)
m 1994; Maj, Ind N. b 5 Jul 74.

NAYAK, Philip (Angul, 1986); Maj, Ind N. b 1
Aug 68; and
NAYAK, Nayami; (Penagoberi Phulbani
Orissa, 1989) m 1989; Maj, Ind N. b 15 Jan 66.

NCUBE, Dubayi (Ndola, 1972); Lt-Col, Zimb.
b 8 Jun 52; and
NCUBE, Orlipha (née Ndlovu)
(Mpopoma, 1976) m 1976; Lt-Col, Zimb.
b 25 Dec 54.

NGCOBO, Herbert (Imbali, 1981); Maj,
S Afr. b 28 Jun 57 with
NGCOBO, Elizabeth (née Magali)
(Nkondweni 1978) m 1982, Maj, S Afr.
b 11 Jun 55.

NEEDHAM, John (Atlanta, GA, 1977); Maj,
USA S. b 11 Aug 51. BS, MTS; with
NEEDHAM, Marthalynn (née Ling) m 1973;
Maj, USA S. b 5 Jun 52. Served in UK.

NHELENHELE, Manuel (Mavalane, Moz,
1995) Lt-Col, CS, Moz. b Sep 55; with
NHELENHELE, Irene (née Sevene)
m 1981; Lt-Col, TSWM, Moz. b April 60

NESTERENKO, Alex (Vitarte, 1986); Lt-Col,
CS, Braz. b 13 Dec 63; and
NESTERENKO, Luz (née Henríquez)
(Santiago Central, 1990) m 1991;
Lt-Col, TSWM, Braz. b 10 May 67. Served in
Rus and S Am W.

NGOY, Wa Mande Hubert (Kamina, 1989);
Lt-Col, DR Con. b 5 Jul 60; with
NGOY, Mbayo Célestine (née Mbayokidi)
m 1983; Lt-Col, DR Con. b 21 Nov 62.
Served in Tanz.

NGWANGA, Kakinanatadiko Madeleine
(Matadi, 1979); Comr, TC and TPWM,
DR Con. b 25 Nov 55. Served in DR Con
(CS and TSWM).

NICOLASA, Pablo (Buenos Aires Central,
1989); Maj, S Am E. b 20 Feb 61; with
NICOLASA, Estela (née Ocampo) m 1984;
Maj, S Am E. b 4 Jul 60.

NIELSEN, JOSTEIN (Stavanger 1976) Maj
Nor. b 2 Jul 56 and
NIELSEN, MAGNA VÅJE (née Våje) m
1978, Maj Nor, b 23 Sep 57. Served in E. Eur.

NIEMAND, Garth (Kensington, Port Elizabeth, 1999); Capt, S Afr. b 22 Dec 1969;
with
NIEMAND, Patricia (née Nel) m 1990;
Capt, S Afr. b 8 Mar 1972.

NIETES, Allain (Murcia, 1987); Maj, Phil.
b 20 Nov 65. BS (Accountancy); and
NIETES, Marialyn (Bacolod, 1990)
m 1990; Maj, Phil. b 16 Feb 65.

NJIRU, Nahashon (Mombasa, 1984); Lt-Col,
Ken E. b 30 Apr 53; with
NJIRU, Zippora (née Ndeleve) m 1976;
Lt-Col, Ken E. b 22 Feb 56.

NILES, Allie Laura (Pasadena Tabernacle, CA,
1985); Maj, USA W. b 24 Oct 56. BA (Psych),
BA (Soc Wk).

NISHIMURA, Tamotsu (Azabu, 1995); Maj,
Jpn. b 2 August 65. BA (Social).

NKANU, Bintoma Norbert (Kavwaya, 1981);
Maj, DR Con. b 29 Jun 54, with
NKANU, Hèléne (née Makuiza Lutonadio)
m 1978; Maj, DR Con. b 18 Nov 61.

NKHOMA, Sammy (Zhombe, 1990); Maj, Zimb.
b 7 Jul 61; with
NKHOMA, Ellen (née Mandizvidza) m 1987;
Maj, Zimb. b 27 Sep 66.

NKOMO, Bigboy (Vumangwe, 1993); Maj,
Zimb. b 6 Aug 70; and
NKOMO,Winnet; (Mt Hampden, 1990)
m 1995; Maj, Zimb. b 22 May 69

NOAKES, David (Edendale, 1980); Maj, NZ.
b 21 Sep 53. BA, DipTchg, DipGrad,
PG DipTh; with
NOAKES, Vyvyenne (née Melhuish) m 1974;
Maj, NZ. b 16 Mar 53. DipTchg (ECE).

NORDENBERG, Kenneth (Hisingskåren 1973);
Lt-Col, Swdn. b 3 Jan 47; with
NORDENBERG, Ewa (née Landström);
Lt-Col, Swdn. b 1 Sep 49.

NORDENBERG, Mattias (Vårby Gård 1998);
Capt, Swdn. b 11 Dec 73

NTEMBI, Lukombo Esaïe (Mvuila, 1987);
Maj, DR Con. b 15 Sep 57; and
NTEMBI, Marie-José (née Yoka
Nzakimuena) m 1983; Maj, DR Con.
b 6 Oct 62.

NTOYA, Kapela (Kinshasa IV, Con, 1985);
Maj, RC,Ml. b 2 Apr 55. BA; and

324

NTOYA, Rose-Nicole (née Makuena) (Kinshasa IV, Con, 1983); m 1983; Maj, RPWM, Ml. b 21 Nov 60. Served in Con (Kin) and at IHQ.

NTSHANGASE, Shadrack (Peart Memorial, 1992) Maj, S Afr. b 27 Feb 61; and
NTSHANGASE, Rosannah (née Shabangu) (Emangweni, Komatipoort, 1994) m 2003 Maj, S Afr. b 16 Sept 1970.

NYAGAH, Henry Njagi (Kagaari, Ken E, 1986); Comr, TC, Zimb. b 21 Feb 54; with
NYAGAH, Catherine (née Njoki) m 1984; Comr, TPWM, Zimb. b 3 Sep 59. Served in E Afr, Ken W (CS/TSWM) and Mal (TC/TPWM).

NYAMBALO, Francis (Migowi, 1982); Lt-Col, OC, Rwa . b 15 Aug 51; with
NYAMBALO, Jamiya (née Khumani) m 1970; Lt-Col, CPWM, Rwa. b 14 Aug 56. Served in Zam and Mal (GS/CSWM).

NYARUBERU, Tomson (Murereka, 1987); Major, Zimb. b 15 Aug 67 and
NYARUBERU,Crisia m 1990; (née Dube) (Rutendo, 1987); Maj, Zimb, b 17 Feb 68.

NYERERE, Josephat (Izumbwe, 1999); Capt, Tanz. b 1 Jan 70 with
NYERERE Sisita m 1993; Capt, Tanz. b. 1 Dec 73.

NYBO, Thorgeir (Sandefjord, 1981); Lt-Col, Nor. b 4 Sep 59; and
NYBO, Marianne (née Østensen) (Sandefjord, 1981) m 1981; Lt-Col, Nor. b 19 Jul 59.

NYEREYEMHUKA, Funny (Dombwe, 1973); Lt-Col, Zimb. b 15 Dec 50; and
NYEREYEMHUKA, Ellen (née Mpofu) (Gandiwa Society, 1978) m 1978; Lt-Col, Zimb. b 9 Jul 55.

NZILA, Luyeye Barthélemy (Lemba-Ngaba, 1987); Capt, DR Con. b 16 Mar 61; and
NZILA, Bibisky (née Ntombo Nsosa) m 1985; Capt, DR Con. b 6 Oct 66.

NZINGOULA, Victor (Loussala, 1988); Maj, Con (Braz). b 27 Mar 63; with
NZINGOULA, Emma (née Malonga) m 1986; Maj, Con (Braz). b 27 Apr 68.

O

OALANG, David (Sta Barbara, 1995); Maj, Phil. b 20 Feb 66. BSc (Bus Adm); and
OALANG, Elsa (née Gallna) (Quezon City 1, 1988) m 1995; Maj, Phil. b 25 May 62. BSc (Mass Comm), MA (Theol).

ÖBERG, Leif (Centrumkåren, 1986); Maj, Swdn. b 17 Dec 60; and
ÖBERG, Helena (née Gezelius); Maj, Swdn. b 25 May 61.

O'BRIEN, Douglas G. (San Francisco Citadel, 1976); Lt-Col, USA W. b 1 Aug 49. BA (Speech), MA (Relig); and
O'BRIEN, Diane (née Lillicrap) (Staines, UK, 1975) m 1988; Lt-Col, USA W. b 8 Nov 50. FTCL, GTCL. Served in UK.

ODURO, Godfried (Kyekyewere, 1981); Maj, Gha. b 17 Jul 54; with
ODURO, Felicia (née Obeng) m 1978; Maj, Gha. b 25 Jun 60.

ODURO, James (Achiase, 1983); Lt-Col, Gha, b 21 Jun 59, with
ODURO, Elizabeth (née Nimfah) m 1980: Lt-Col, Gha. b 13 Jul 61. Served in Lib

ODURO, Rockson (Kwao Nartey, 1993); Maj, Gha. b 29 Jan 63; with
ODURO, Emelia (née Lamtei) m 1991; Maj, Gha. b 12 Mar 64.

ODURO-AMOAH, Peter (Achiase, 1989); Maj, Gha. b 26 Aug 58; with
ODURO-AMOAH, Grace (née Fosua) m 1984; Maj, Gha. b 11 Feb 64.

OGUNDAHUNSI, Raphael (Ogbagi, 1986); Maj, Nig. b 10 Jul 59; with
OGUNDAHUNSI, Esther m 1984; Maj, Nig. b 13 Apr 64.

OKLAH, Samuel Kwao (Accra Newtown, 1983); Lt-Col, CS, Gha. b 5 Mar 58; and
OKLAH, Philomina (née Addo) (Tema, 1985) m 1985; Lt-Col, TSWM, Gha. b 21 Dec 62. Served in Mal.

OLATUNDE, Michael (Apatere, 1994); Maj, Nig. b 1 Oct 60. BSc (Soc Sci); with
OLATUNDE, Sarah m 1984; Maj, Nig. b 22 Oct 63.

OLEWA, John (Mukhombe, 1986); Maj, Ken W. b 12 Nov 54; with
OLEWA, Mary (née Kadzo) m 1982; Maj, Ken W. b 19 Sep 1960. Served in Ken E

OLORUNTOBA, Festus (Supare, Nig, 1976); Lt-Col, OC, Lib. b 7 Jul 55. Ww Lt-Col Gloria, pG 2009. Served in Nig (CS).

OLUBWAYO, Jacob, (Bukura, Shigomere, 1988) Maj, Ken W b. 16 May 62; with
OLUBWAYO, Mary (née Okwambitsa) m. 1988; Maj, Ken W. b. 17 Jan.66.

ON, Dieu-Quang (Altona, Aus S, 1983) Maj, GS, HK. b 9 Apr 55. Served in Aus S.

OMUZEE, Fredrick, (Nahururu, 1993) Maj, Kenya W. b 13 Dec 64 with
OMUZEE, Leah (née Chebet) m 1990; Maj Ken W. b 29 Dec 68

ONYEKWERE, Paul (Umuogo, 1984); Lt-Col, Nig. b 27 Jul 58; with

ONYEKWERE, Edinah; Lt-Col, Nig.
b 29 Oct 61.

ORASIBE, Patrick (Akokwa, 1988); Maj, Nig.
b 9 Oct 58; with
ORASIBE, Blessing (née Chituru) Maj, Nig.
b 5 Dec 58.

ORD, Norman (Peterborough Citadel, 1992);
Maj, UK. b 28 Sep 55. MA (Hons) (French
and Music), PGCE, CDRS. Ww Capt
Christine, pG 2009 and
ORD, Margaret (née Read) (Nunhead,
1975); Maj, UK. b 4 Aug 55. Ww Maj
Graham Grayston 2008; m 2012.

ØRSNES, Bernt Olaf (Bergen 1, Nor, 1983);
Lt-Col, Carib. b 22 Apr 59; and
ØRSNES, Hildegard (née Anthun) (Bergen 1,
Nor, 1984) m 1986; Lt-Col, Carib.
b 29 Sep 61. Served in Nor.

OTA, Haruhisa (Hamamatsu, 1973); Maj, Jpn.
b 30 Jan 50; and
OTA, Hiromi (née Nakatsugawa) (Hamamatsu,
1973) m 1976; Maj, Jpn. b 21 Jun 48.

OWEN, Graham (Nuneaton, 1977); Lt-Col, UK.
b 8 Jul 53; and
OWEN, Kirsten (née Jacobsen)
(Copenhagen Temple, Den, 1977) m 1978;
Lt-Col, UK. b 2 May 56. Served in Den
(CS/THQ).

P

PALLANT, Dean (Bromley, UK, 1993); Maj,
IHQ. b 23 Nov 64. BSoc Sc, Dip LR, PG Dip
(Theol), DTh; and
PALLANT, Eirwen (née Lowther) (Leeds
Central, UK, 1992) m1993; Maj, IHQ.
b 9 May 62. BSc (Hons), MB ChB, DTM&H,
MRCGP. Served in UK and Zam.

PANDORANTE, Marthen (Surabaya 4, 1989);
Maj, Indon. b 6 Oct 64; and
PANDORANTE, Yulien (née Ganna)
(Bandung 2, 1984) m 1981; Maj, Indon.
b 22 Jun 61.

PAONE, Massimo (Naples, It, 1977); Col, TC,
Frce. b 8 Jun 52; and
PAONE, Elizabeth Jane (née Moir)
(Nunhead, UK, 1982) m 1982; Col, TPWM,
Frce. b17 Dec 58. BA (Hons). Served in UK,
It (OC/CPWM) and Frce (CS/TLWM).

PARDO, Zoilo B. (Hollywood, CA, 1989);
Lt-Col, USA W. b 9 Dec 53. BA (Acct); with
PARDO, Magali (née Pacheco) m 1980;
Lt-Col, USA W. b 20 Apr 56. BA (Gen Ed),
BA (Acct). Served in Mex and L Am N (CS/
TSWM).

PAREDES, Tito E. (La Paz, S Am W, 1976);
Col, TC, L Am N. b 14 Aug 54; and

PAREDES, Martha (née Nery) (Cochabamba,
S Am W, 1976) m 1977; Col, TPWM, L Am N.
b 3 Jun 54. Served in S Am W, USA E and
L Am N (CS/TSWM).

PARK, Chong-duk (Pupyung, 1977); Col,
CS, Kor. b 22 May 50. ThM, DipMin; with
YOON, Eun-sook m 1975; Col, TSWM, Kor.
b 23 Oct 50. Served in Aus S.

PARK, Man-hee (Chung Ju, 1975); Comr,
TC, Kor. b 11 Aug 47; with
KIM, Keum-nyeo m 1973; Comr, TPWM,
Kor b 13 Jun 51. Served in Kor (CS/TSWM).

PARKER, Michael (Hucknall, 1977);
Comr, TC, Indon. b 28 Jul 50; with
PARKER, Joan (née Brailsford) m 1971;
Comr, TPWM, Indon. b 16 Jan 52. Served at
ITC, in UK and Indon (CS/TSWM).

PARMAR, Kantilal K. (Ode, 1983); Maj,
Ind W. b 1 Jun 53. BA, BEd; and
PARMAR, Eunice K. (née Gaikwad)
(Mohmedwadi, 1977) m 1983; Maj, Ind W.
b 30 Oct 52.

PASWERA, Effort, (Gororo, Zim 1993) Maj,
Mal. b 26 Apr 70 with
PASWERA, Annet, m. 1998; Maj,Mal.
b 17 Nov 70.

PATHARE Gulab Yohan (Shevgaon 1982);
Maj, Ind W. b 1 June 58 with
PATHARE Meena (Kherdi 1982); m 1980;
Maj, Ind W. b June 62

PAWAR, Suresh S. (Ahmednagar Evangeline
Booth Hall, Ind W, 1981); Maj, IHQ. b 10 Feb
60; and
PAWAR, Martha (née Shirsath) (Ahmednagar
Central, Ind W, 1981) m 1981; Maj, IHQ.
b 17 Nov 63. Served in Ind W.

PAYNE, Godfrey (Goff) (Tunbridge Wells, UK,
1980); Lt-Col, CS, Nig. b 15 Oct 51; with
PAYNE, Diane (née Harris) m 1975; Lt-Col,
TSWM, Nig. b 28 Dec 52. Served in UK,
E Afr, Zam & Mal, Uga (OC/CPWM) and Mal
(OC/CPWM).

PEDDLE, Brian (Dildo/New Harbour, NL,
Can, 1977); Comr, TC, Can. b 8 Aug 57; and
PEDDLE, Rosalie (née Rowe) (Carbonear,
NL, Can, 1976) m 1978; Comr, TPWM, Can.
b 17 Jan 56. Served in NZ and UK (CS/TSWM).

PERINBANAYAGAM, Suthanathadhas
(Booth Tucker Hall, Nagercoil, 1986); Maj,
Ind SE. b 14 Oct 56. MA, HACDP; and
ESTER, Evangelin Suthananthadhas
(Attoor, 1986) m 1986; Maj, Ind SE.
b 18 Apr 63. BSc.

PETRUS, I. Made (Den Pasar, Bali, 1983);
Maj, Indon. b 12 Jul 60; and
PETRUS, Margaretha (née Pinontoan)

Biographical Information

(Ambon/Bandung 2, 1975) m 1984; Maj, Indon. b 15 Mar 53.

PETTERSEN, Per Arne (Sarpsborg, 1969); Maj, Nor. b 20 Mar 47; and
PETTERSEN, Lillian (née Madsø) (Namsos, 1969) m 1971; Maj, Nor. b 5 Jun 45.

PHILIP, Alister, (Colombo, 1988) Lt-Col, Sri Lan. b 11 Oct 61; and
PHILIP, Nilanthi, (Colombo, 1987) m 1988; Lt-Col, Sri Lan. b 24 May 67

PHILIP, P. K. (Thottamon, 1975); Maj, Ind SW. b 12 Dec 48; and
PHILIP, Rachel (Kottarakara Central, 1980) m 1979; Maj, Ind SW. b 10 Nov 54.

PHO, Samuel (Altona, Aus S, 1983); Lt-Col, OC, HK. b 17 Jun 57. BTh; and
PHO, Donni (née Kkuu) (Altona, Aus S, 1985) m 1985; Lt-Col, CPWM, HK. b 30 May 58.

PILKINGTON, George A. (Lamberhead Green, 1972); Lt-Col, UK. b 11 Apr 50. SRN. Served at ITC. m 1974; Maj Vera, ret 2007.

PIZZIRUSSO, Hugo (Arroyito, 1989); Maj, S Am E. b 7 Nov 66; and
PIZZIRUSSO, Elsa (née Coppeto) (Nueva Chicago, 1989) m 1991; Maj, S Am E. b 3 Feb 67.

POA, Selly Barak (Jakarta, 1979); Lt-Col, Indon. b 25 Sep 55; and
POA, Anastasia (née Djoko Slamet) (Surakarta 2, 1984) m 1985; Lt-Col, Indon. b 29 Jun 62.

POLSLEY, Randall (Omaha, NE, 1993); Maj, USA C. b 22 Sep 61. BA; with
POLSLEY, Charlene (née Sniffen) m 1989; Maj, USA C. b 7 Dec 67.

PONNAPPAN, Yesuvadian (Nantikuzhy, 1991) Maj, India SE b 2 Mar 57; with
PUSHPAM, Ponnappan m 1984; Maj, Ind SE, b 25 Feb 56.

POSADAS, Leopoldo (Dagupan City, Phil, 1981); Maj, GS, Ban. b 18 Aug 58. BBA Mgmnt; and
POSADAS, Evelyn (née Felix) (Hermoza, Phil, 1982) m 1982; Maj, CSWM, Ban. b 2 Aug 57. Served in Phil.

POSILLICO, Joseph E. (Los Angeles Lincoln Heights, CA, 1972); Lt-Col, USA W. b 29 Dec 50; and
POSILLICO, Shawn L. (née Patrick) (San Francisco, CA, 1984) m 1988; Lt-Col, USA W. b 3 Aug 57. BS (Bus Econ).

POWELL, Charles (New Bern, NC, 1984); Maj, USA S. b 26 Aug 58. BA, with
POWELL, Paula V. (née Johnson) m 1985; Maj, USA S. b 12 Jul 51.

PRASAD, P. C. (Annavaram, 1981); Maj, Ind C. b 9 Sep 58; with

PRASAD, Krupamma m 1979; Maj, Ind C. b 4 Jun 59.

PREUSS, Annette (née Klein) (Siegen, 1979) m 1981; Maj, Ger. b 11 Sept 54

PRITCHETT, Wayne (Deer Lake, NL, 1970); Lt-Col, Can. b 13 Aug 46. BA, BEd, MTS; and
PRITCHETT, Myra (née Rice) (Roberts Arm, NL, 1969) m 1972; Lt-Col, Can. b 19 Jun 50. BRE, MTS. Served at IHQ.

PULULU, Celestino Pepe (Makala, DR Con, 1985), Lt-Col, OC, Ang. b 15 Oct 52; with
PULULU, Veronica Lukombo (née Nkenge) m 1978; Lt-Col, CPWM, Ang. b 4 Dec 57. Served in Con (Kin) and Moz (CS/TSWM).

PUOTINIEMI, Tella (née Juntunen) (Helsinki IV, 1983); Maj, Fin. b 17 Oct 52; and
PUOTINIEMI, Antero (Oulu, 1981) m 1983; Maj, Fin. b 15 Oct 48.

R

RAINES, Timothy (Mt Vernon, NY, 1971); Lt-Col, USA E. b 30 Dec 47. BS (Org Mgmt); and
RAINES, Lynda Lou (née Swingle) (Zanesville, OH, 1969) m 1969; Lt-Col, USA E. b 23 Aug 48. BS (Org Mgmt).

RAJU, K. Samuel (Kakulapadu, 1980); Maj, Ind C. b 5 May 58; and
RAJU, K. Raja (née Kumari) (Pedaparapudi, 1980) m 1981; Maj, Ind C. b 3 May 64.

RALTE LALLIANKUNGA (Bilkhawthlir 1992); Maj, Ind E. b 3 Jan 69. BA, BD; with
ZONUNSANGI (Khatla 1994) m 1994; Maj, Ind E. b 5 Feb 64.

RAMDINTHARI VARTE (Chaltlang 2001); Capt Ind E. b 1 May 77

RAM LAL, Samuel (Rajpura, 1981); Maj, Ind N. b 31 Oct 62; and
RAM LAL, Sunila (Moradabad, 1983) m 1984; Maj, Ind N. b 10 Jun 64.

RAMOS, Hugo (Salto Central, 1991);Maj, S Am E. b 22 Mar 64; and
RAMOS, María del Luján (née León Gularte) m 1984; Maj, S Am E. b 21 Aug 65.

RAMOS, Jocabet (née Martínez) (San Luis Potosí, 1993); Maj, Mex. b 7 Oct 66; with
RAMOS, Marco m 1990; Maj, Mex. b 9 Oct 67.

RANDIVE Benjamin B. (Shevgaon 1981); Maj, Ind W. b 11 Jan 60 ; and
RANDIVE Ratnamala (née Teldhune) (Shevgaon Central, 1981) m 1981; Maj, Ind W. b 17 Aug 62.

RANGI, Gidion (Kulawi, 1990), Maj, Indon. b 7 Aug 60; with
RANGI, Lidia (née Norlan) m 1985; Maj, Indon. b 25 Nov 65.

RAO, S. Jayananda (Madras Central, 1981); Maj, Ind C. b 29 Oct 52; with
RAO, S. Christiansen m 1976; Maj, Ind C. b 22 Dec 60.

RASELALOME, Johannes (Seshego, 1982); Maj, S Afr. b 3 May 60; and
RASELALOME, Veliswa Atalanta (née Mehu) (Tshoxa, 1982) m 1985; Maj, S Afr. b 16 Jul 62.

RATHAN, P. Samuel (Mandavalli, 1974); Maj, Ind C. b 3 May 51; with
KUMARI, P. Ananda m 1976; Maj, Ind C. b 1 Oct 57.

RAYMER, RONNIE L. (Tampa, FL 1982); Maj, USA S. b 2 Jun 58 with
RAYMER, SHARON L. (née Wright) m 1979; Maj, USA S. b 19 Jun 60.

READ, Alan (Newcastle Byker, UK, 1980); Lt-Col, IHQ. b 10 Apr 58. MSc, FCIS; and
READ, Janet (née Rumble) (Redhill, UK, 1977) m 1982; Lt-Col, IHQ. b 22 Mar 55. BA (Hons), MA (Rel Stds). Served in UK.

REDDISH, Graeme John (Thames, 1974); Col, CS, NZ. b 28 Aug 49. Ww Maj Nola, pG 2002; and
REDDISH, Wynne (née Jellyman) (Miramar, 1982) m 2005; Col, TSWM, NZ. b 22 Apr 57. Dip BRS, BBus, Dip Mgmt (NZIM). Served at IHQ.

REES, David H. (Rockdale, 1976); Lt-Col, Aus E. b 29 Jun 47; with
REES, Christine F. (née Cairns) m 1969; Lt-Col, Aus E. b 11 Apr 49. Served in Sri Lan and at IHQ.

REES, John (Ipswich, 1974); Maj, Aus E. b 29 Jun 47; with
REES, Narelle (née Lehmann) m 1969; Maj, Aus E. b 27 Jun 48. Served in PNG and Rus.

RETNAM, Aruldhas (Alady, Nagercoil, 1988); Maj, Ind SE. b 17 Apr 66 and
Saradha Aruldhas (Layam, Azagiapandipuram, 1988) m 1988; Maj, Ind SE. b 7 May 65.

REYNOLDS, James (Canton Citadel, OH, 1976); Lt-Col, USA E. b 2 Jun 48. BS (HRM); with
REYNOLDS, Blanche Louise (née Labus) m 1972; Lt-Col, USA E. b 16 Dec 49.

RICE, Sandra (Roberts Arm, NL, 1980); Lt-Col, Can. b 16 Feb 58. BEd, BA, MTS.

RICHARDSON, Lonneal (Bloomington, IN, 1983) Maj, USA C. b 3 Mar 59. BA (Bus Adm); and
RICHARDSON, Patty (née Barton) (Omaha South, NE, 1979) m 1983; Maj, USA C. b 30 Jan 57. BA (Bus Adm), MA (Org Ldrshp).

RIGLEY, Graeme (Norwood, 1988); Maj, Aus S. b 10 Aug 54. BMd, BS; with
RIGLEY, Karyn (née Whitehead) m 1981; Maj, Aus S. b 8 Apr 59.

RILEY, Douglas F. (Pasadena Tabernacle, CA, 1995); Lt-Col, USA W. b 6 Feb 59. BS (Fin), MBA (Bus Adm), MA (Theol); with
RILEY, Colleen R. (née Hogan) m. 1991; Lt-Col, USA W. b 14 Aug. 68.

ROBERTS, Jonathan (Leicester Central, UK, 1986); Lt-Col, IHQ. b 20 Feb 62. BA (Theol), BA (Econ), MTh; and
ROBERTS, Jayne (née Melling) (Southend Citadel, UK, 1985) m 1986; Lt-Col, IHQ. b 23 Apr 58. BA (Eng Lit) PGCE. Served in UK.

ROBERTS, William A. (Detroit Citadel, MI, USA C, 1971); Comr, NC, USA Nat. b 26 Feb 46; BS, MA; with
ROBERTS, Nancy Louise (née Overly) m 1968; Comr, NPWM, USA Nat. b 27 Oct 43. BS, MA. Served in USA C, S Am E (TC/TPWM), at IHQ (IS Bus Adm/Sec for Staff Dev) and in Ken W (TC/TPWM).

ROBERTSON, Laurie (Broken Hill, 1980); Lt-Col, Aus E. b 26 Sep 55; Dip Min; and
ROBERTSON, Simone (née Riley) (Manly, 1980) m 1980; Lt-Col, Aus E. b 16 Nov 59. Served in Aus S and at IHQ.

RODWELL, Heather (Dunedin South, 1990); Maj, NZ. b 24 Sep 55.

ROWE, Dennis (Norwood, 1971); Maj, Aus S. b 25 Jun 48; and
ROWE, Patricia (née Muir) (Woodville Gardens, 1970) m 1972; Maj, Aus S. b 18 Mar 48. Served in HK and Tai.

ROWE, Lindsay (Chance Cove, NL, Can, 1972); Col, CS, Tanz. b 21 Sep 51. BA, MDiv; and
ROWE, Lynette (née Hutt) (Winterton, NL, Can, 1971) m 1974; Col, TSWM, Tanz. b 13 Feb 52. Served in Can, S Afr and Carib (CS/TSWM).

S

SABIR, Imran (Tank, 1996); Capt, Pak b 16 May 66, and
IMRAN, Nighat (née Daniel) m 1994; Capt, Pak b 28 Aug 69.

SÁENZ, Jannette (Chihuahua, 1993); Maj, Mex. b 27 Nov 70.

SAKAMESSO, Jean-Aléxis (Ouenze, 1979); Lt-Col, Con (Braz). b 25 May 50; with
SAKAMESSO, Pauline (née Louya) m 1976; Lt-Col, Con (Braz). b 19 Jan 56.

SAMHIKA, Bishow (Chigango, Zim, 1995) Maj, Moz. b Nov 75; and

SAMHIKA, Pamela (née Ncube) (Nanga, Zim, 1994) m 1997; Maj, Moz. b Oct 74.

SAMRAJ, Babu (Ettamadai Corps, Ind SE 1997); Maj. Ind N. b 11 May 66. MA (Eng), MA(JMC), MBA; with
BABU, Santhi m1995; Maj, Ind N; b 6 May 69. Served in Ind SE.

SAMUEL, John (Trivandrum Central, 1984); Maj, Ind SW. b 22 May 53. Ww Maj Annamma, pG 2007.

SAMUEL, M. (Central, Kottarakara, 1974); Maj, Ind SW. b 15 Dec 51; and
SAMUEL, K. Thankamma (Ommanoor, 1977) m 1976; Maj, Ind SW. b 15 Oct 53.

SANCHEZ, Oscar (Lima Central, S Am W, 1982); Comr, TC, Brz. b 21 Nov 56; and
SANCHEZ, Ana Rosa (née Limache) (Huayra K'assa, S Am W, 1985) m 1987; Comr, TPWM, Brz. b 12 Jun 60. Served in Sp, S Am W, USA W and L Am N (TC/TPWM).

SANTIAGO, José (Guayama, PR, USA E, 1987); Maj, L Am N. b 8 Aug 50; with
SANTIAGO, Hilda (née Amill); m 1975; Maj, L Am N. b 15 Nov 53.

SATHIYASEELAN, D. (Kanacode, 1974); Maj, Ind SW. b 10 May 51; and
SATHIYASEELAN, Aleyamma (Adoor Central,1975) m 1980; Maj, Ind SW. b 29 Jun 50.

SATTERLEE, Allen (Lakeland, FL, USA S, 1975); Maj, USA Nat,b 21 Apr 53. BS (Psych) MTS; and
SATTERLEE, Esther (née Sands) (Laurel, MS, USA S, 1979); m 1982; Maj, USA Nat. b 9 Mar 55. BS (Admin). Served in USA S, Caribbean, Papua New Guinea.

SAYUTI, Yohannes (Surabaya 2, 1975); Lt-Col, Indon. b 28 Jul 51; and
SAYUTI, Asya (née Tonta) (Bandung 3, 1974) m 1979; Lt-Col, Indon. b 5 Jan 51.

SCHMID, Fritz (Adelboden/Thun, 1980); Maj, Switz. b 20 Nov 53; and
SCHMID, Margrit (née Dössegger) (Seon, 1981) m 1981; Maj, Switz. b 4 Dec 52.

SCHOLTENS, Teunis (Zwolle, 1980); Maj, Neth. b 28 Aug 52; with
SCHOLTENS, Hendrika (née Stuurop) m 1977; Maj, Neth. b 28 May 56.

SEDLAR, Deborah (Philadelphia [Roxborough], PA, USA E, 1987); Maj, IHQ. b. 6 Mar 59. Served in USA Eastern.

SEILER, Paul R. (Hollywood Tabernacle, CA, USA W, 1981); Comr, TC, USA C. b 23 May 51. MBA, BS (Bus Adm); with
SEILER, Carol (née Sturgess) m 1978; Comr, TPWM, USA C. b 6 Apr 52. RN, BS

(Nursing), MPH, MS (Nursing). Served in USA W and USA C (CS/TSWM).

SEMENO, Thataetsile Piet (Stilfontein, 1999); Capt, S Afr. b 11 Aug 75; with
SEMENO, Noluntu (née Mampemvini) (Ethembeni Eastern Cape, 1999); m 2000; Capt, S Afr. b 14 April 76

SENARATNE Ranjith (Siyambalangamuwa, 1994) Maj, Sri Lan. b 7 Jan 68; and
SENARATNE Vijayashri (née Kandasamy) (Jaffna, 1994) m 1995; Maj, Sri Lan. b 3 Oct 70.

SERÈM, Alberto (Lisbon Central, Port, 1985), Maj, Brz. b 27 Nov 56; and
SERÈM, Maria José (née Leitão) (Picheleira, Port, 1977) m 1980; Maj, Brz. b 13 Dec 52. Served in UK, It and Port (OC/CPWM).

SEVAK, David Keshav (Sokhada, 1981); Maj, Ind W. b 15 Nov 50; and
SEVAK, Vimalaben (Bharoda, 1983) m 1983; Maj, Ind W. b 5 Jun 63.

SEYMOUR, Geanette (Belmore, Aus E, 1973); Col, IHQ. b 20 Feb 50. BA (Soc Wk). Served in Aus E (CS)

SHAKESPEARE, David (Catford, UK, 1981); Lt-Col, UK. b 8 Oct 59; and
SHAKESPEARE, Karen (née Grainger) (Catford, UK, 1980) m 1981; Lt-Col, UK. b 2 Aug 54. BEd (Hons), MA (Pastoral Theol), MA (Adult Ed with Theol Reflection), PrD. Served at IHQ and in Ken E.

SHAROVA, Svetlana (née Blagodirova) (Chisinau Botannica, 1999); Capt, E Eur. b 18 Jun 65; with
SHAROV, Alexander m 1986; Capt, E Eur. b 6 Jul 57.

SHAVANGA, Edward (Matunda, Ken W, 1982); Lt-Col, Zam. b 9 Mar 58; with
SHAVANGA, Florence (née Vulehi) m 1979; Lt-Col, Zam. b 11 Oct 60. Served in E Afr and Ken.

SHAVANGA, Moses (Musudzuu, 1984); Maj, Ken W. b 10 Jun 57; with
SHAVANGA, Gladys (née Sharia) m 1982; Maj, Ken W. b 18 Mar 61. Served in Tanz.

SHEKWA, Albert Zondiwe (Emangweni, 1974); Maj, S Afr. b 12 Mar 51; and
SHEKWA, Peggy (née Maimela) (Louis Trichardt, 1974) m 1974; Maj, S Afr. b 3 Jun 54.

SHIN, Jae-kook (Un Po, 1983); Maj, Kor. b 27 Dec 57; with
CHO, Hwa-soon m 1981; Maj, Kor. b 20 Jul 58.

SHIROMA, Lawrence (San Francisco Citadel, CA, 1979); Maj, USA W. b 10 Mar 49. MSSW, BA (Sociol); with

SHIROMA, Victoria. (née Sorrano) (Salinas, CA, 1975) m. 1977; Maj, USA W. b 14 Sep 52. M Ed, BA.

SIAMOYA, Margaret (Loubomba, Zam, 1991) Maj, Zimb. b 15 Jul 65. Ww Maj Siamoya, pG 2010.

SICHILOMBA, Casson (Nakambala, Zam, 1993); Maj, Zam. b 1 Jan 59; and **SICHILOMBA, Mary** (née Kalikenka) m 1984; Maj, Zam. b 24 Mar 65.

SIDEROV, Vitali (Petrozavodsk, 2004) Capt, E Eur. b 16 Sep 73; with **SIDEROVA, (née Borisnova)** Capt, E Eur, b 26 May 73.

SIJUADE, Michael A. (Ife Ife, 1992); Maj, Nig. b 13 Jun 64; with **SIJUADE, Comfort** m 1990; Maj, Nig. b 11 Nov 67.

SIMON, T. J. (Perumpetty, 1977); Maj, Ind SW. b 15 Nov 52; and **SIMON, Ammini** (Pulickal, 1980) m 1979; Maj, Ind SW. b 1 Feb 60.

SINGH, Dilip (Simultala, 1990); Maj, Ind N. b 4 Nov 68; and **SINGH, Nivedita** (née Christian) (Fatapukur, 1992) m 1992; Maj, Ind N. b 14 Sep 71.

SJOGREN, Daniel (St Paul [Temple], MN, USA C, 1972); Lt-Col, CS, Swdn. b 12 Nov 51; and **SJOGREN, Rebecca** (née Nefzger) (Hibbing, MN, USA C, 1973) m 1973; Lt-Col, TSWM, Swdn. b 11 Jun 53. Served in USA C

SMARTT, HOWARD (Petersham, 1984) Maj, Aus E. b 3 Jan 57. BA Ed, MA and **SMARTT, ROBYN** (née MacKay) m 1986 (Parramatta, 1982) Maj, Aus E. b 31 Dec 57. BA Ed, MA (Counselling). Served in Can.

SMITH, Charles (Kansas City (Blue Valley), MO, 1978); Maj, USA C. b 22 Aug 57; with **SMITH, Sharon** (née Cockrill) m 1975; Maj, USA C. b 7 Mar 54.

SMITH, Jeffrey (Flint Citadel, MI, 1986); Lt-Col, USA C. b 19 Jan 54. BA (Bible), MRE; with **SMITH, Dorothy R.** (née Kumpula) m 1974; Lt-Col, USA C. b 22 Oct 54. BA (Psychol/ Sociol), MSW, MPC (Pastoral Counselling).

SMITH, Judith E. (Monterey Peninsula, CA, 1988); Lt-Col, USA W. b 4 Aug 49. BS (Ed). Served at IHQ.

SMITH, Paul (Lansing Citadel, WI, 1985); Maj, USA C. b 23 Jun 56. BA (Psychol), MA (Theatre), MA (Org Ldrship); and **SMITH, Renea** (née Bonifield) (Grand Rapids Centennial Temple, MI, 1984) m 1985; Maj, USA C. b 16 Nov 57. BS (Ed).

SMITH, Stephen C. (Renton, WA, 1988); Lt-Col, USA W. b 12 Jun 58. MA (Music Comp), BA (Music Perf); with **SMITH, Marcia** (née Harvey), m 1981, Lt-Col, USA W. b 12 Jan 59. BS (Chrstn Ldshp).

SOLOMON, K.M. (Ooramana, Alwaye, 1978); Lt-Col, Ind SW. b 3 Jun 55, and **SOLOMON, Elizabeth** (Brahmapuram, Alwaye, 1982) m 1982; Lt-Col, Ind SW. b 5 Nov 56.

SONDA, Jean-Pierre (Mahita, 1990); Lt-Col, Con (Braz). b 28 Nov 56; with **SONDA, Jeannette** (née Ndoudi) m 1988; Lt-Col, Con (Braz). b 25 Jan 67.

SOPER, SHELLEY (nee Woods) (Shortland,1983); Maj, Aus E. b 5 Sep 52 with **SOPER, DAVID** m 1972; Maj, Aus E. b 31 Jan 53.

SOUZA, Maruilson (Petrolina, 1987); Maj, Brz. b 6 May 64. BA (Acct), BA (Admin), BA (Theol), MA (Theol), PhD (Theol); with **SOUZA, Francisca** (née Rodrigues) m 1982; Maj, Brz. b 15 Oct 66.

STARRETT, Daniel L. (Roswell, NM, USA W, 1973); Lt-Col, USA W. b 1 Jun 52. BS (Appl Bus & Mgmt), MBA; and **STARRETT, Helen** (née Laverty) (San José, CA, USA W, 1973) m 1974; Lt-Col, USA W. b 20 Jul 48. Served at IHQ and USA Nat.

STEELE, Hubert S. III (Middletown, OH, 1981); Maj, USA E. b 24 Mar 59; and-**STEELE, Kathleen** (née Fleming) (Ithaca, NY, 1980) m 1981; Maj, USA E. b 19 Dec 54. BS (Music Ed).

STEVENS, Bruce (Moreland, 1992); Maj, Aus S. b 24 Oct 58. BBus (Acc); DipTh; DipMin; with **STEVENS Debra** (née Booth) m 1980; Maj, Aus S. b 19 Aug 61.

STRASSE, Wilson S. (Rio Grande, 1988); Maj, Brz. b 20 Jul 63; with **STRASSE, Nara** (née Charão) m 1985; Maj, Brz. b 12 Feb 68.

STREET, Robert (Stotfold, UK, 1968); Comr, IHQ (IS Eur). b 24 Feb 47; with **STREET, Janet** (née Adams) m 1967; Comr, IHQ (ZSWM Eur). b 19 Aug 45. Served in UK, Aus E (CS/TSWM) and at IHQ (IS to CoS/WSWM, IS/ZSWM SPEA).

STRINGER, Beverly, (née Barker) (Yiewsley, 1991); Maj, UK. b 20 Apr 64. with **STRINGER, Adrian,** m 1983; Maj, UK. b 7 July 61. Served in Czechoslovakia.

STRISSEL, Dennis L. (St Louis Northside, MO, USA C, 1974); Col, USA C. b 4 Mar 52; and **STRISSEL, Sharon** (née Olson) (Sioux City,

330

IA, USA C, 1974) m 1975; Col, USA C. b 7
Oct 51. Served in USA C, S Afr and Gha
(TC/TPWM).

SUAVE, Jackson (Lae, 2001); Capt, PNG.
b 10 Oct 65; with
SUAVE, Lenny (née Malo) m 1988;
Capt, PNG. b 23 Sep 70.

SUNDARAM, Motchakan (Aramboly, 1974);
Maj, Ind SE. b 17 Mar 50; and
SELVABAI, Motchakan (Kaliancaud, 1974)
m 1975; Maj, Ind SE. b 2 May 50.

SUSEELKUMAR, John (Pallickal, 1978);
Lt-Col, Ind SW. b 11 Oct 51, Ww Maj
Aleyamma, pG 2007.and
THANKAMMA SUSEELKUMAR
(Pookkottumannu, Malabar, 1987) m 2010,
Lt-Col, Ind SW. b 6 Jan 60

SWANSBURY, Charles (Croydon Citadel, UK,
1983); Col, TC, Gha. b 7 Dec 52. BA, MBA;
with
SWANSBURY, Denise (née Everett) m 1974;
Col, TPWM, Gha. b 9 Nov 53. BA. Served in
UK, Zim, Lib (GS/CSWM) and at IHQ.

SWANSON, Barry C. (Chicago Mt
Greenwood, IL, USA C, 1978); Comr, TC,
USA E. b 22 Apr 50. BS (Marketing); with
SWANSON, E. Sue (née Miller) m 1975;
Comr, TPWM, USA E. b 13 Aug 50. BA
(Soc Work). Served in USA C (CS/TSWM,
TC/TPWM), at USA Nat (Nat CS/NSWM)
and at IHQ (IS/ZSWM Am and Carib,
CoS/WSWM,WPWM).

T

TADI, Patrick (Bimbouloulou, 1984); Maj,
Con (Braz). b 17 Apr 59; with
TADI, Clémentine (née Bassinguinina)
m 1982; Maj, Con (Braz). b 4 Apr 58.

TAMPAI, Yusak (Turen, 1993); Maj, Indon.
b 25 Mar 66; and
TAMPAI, Widiawati (Anca, 1995) m 1997;
Maj, Indon. b 19 Apr 73. Served at ICO.

TANAKA, Chieko (née Hirose) (Nishinari,
1977); Maj, Jpn. b 22 Apr 48. BA; and
TANAKA, Teiichi (Omori, 1983) m 1984;
Maj, Jpn. b 19 Feb 52. MA (Econ).

TANDAYAG, Susana (née Organo) (Santiago
Isabela, 1989); Maj, Phil. b 26 Feb 60.
BSc (Home Tech), BSSW; and
TANDAYAG, Miguel (Pasig, 1980) m 1982;
Capt, Phil. b 30 Sep 58.

TARI, Samuel (Shantinagar, 1970); Maj, Pak.
b 7 Sep 49; and
SAMUEL, Victoria (née Khurshid) (Khanewal,
1971) m 1973; Maj, Pak. b 15 Oct 52.

TATY, Daniel (Pointe-Noire, 1982), Maj,
Con (Braz). b 14 Feb 54; with
TATY, Angèle (née Louya) m 1980; Maj,
Con (Braz). b 6 Dec 56.

TAVARES, Verónica (née Espinosa) (Mexico
City Corps #1, 1990); Maj, Mex. b 1 Aug 61.
BS (Nursing); with
TAVARES, Marcos m 1986; Maj, Mex. b 2
May 55. BS (Architecture), MA (Ed Admin).
Served in L Am N.

TELFER, Ivor (Clydebank, 1984); Lt-Col, UK.
b 26 May 54. MSc, FCMI; with
TELFER, Carol (née Anderson) m 1980;
Lt-Col, UK. b 26 Aug 59. RGN, SCM.
Served in Pak and Can & Ber.

TEMINE, David (Lembina, 1992); Maj, PNG.
b 3 Sep 73; and
TEMINE, Doreen (née A'o) (Kamila, 1999) m
2002; Capt, PNG. b 24 Feb 73.

THAMALAPAKULA, Raj Paul (Rajah-
mundary, Ind C, 1996); Capt, Ind Nat. b 4
Aug 68; with
JAYA, Santha Kumari m 1993; Capt, Ind
Nat. b 28 Jan 73. Served in Ind C.

THARMAR, Alfred (Arumanai, 1977); Maj,
Ind SE. b 23 May 54; and
RAJABAI, Alfred (Pottetty, 1975) m 1977;
Maj, Ind SE. b 16 Apr 53.

THEODORE, Sinous (Luly, Haiti, 1981); Maj,
Carib. b 20 Oct 52; and
THEODORE, Marie Lourdes (née Doralus)
(Port-au-Prince, Haiti, 1981) m 1982; Maj,
Carib. b 22 Sep 57.

THEU, Chatonda (Migowi, Mal, 1987); Maj,
Zimb. b 3 Mar 59; with
THEU, Joyce (née Banda) m 1986; Maj,
Zimb. b 5 Mar 65. Served in Mal.

THOMAS, Darrell (Southend Citadel, UK,
1975); Maj, UK. b 28 Jun 53; and
THOMAS, Katrina (née Lagunowitsch)
(Royston, UK, 1976) m 1976; Maj, UK.
b 27 Sep 51. Served in Sing.

THOMSON, Robert E. (Evansville Asplan
Citadel, IN, 1971); Maj, USA C. b 20 Nov 50.
BS (Soc Wk), MSW;
with
THOMSON, Nancy (née Philpot) m 1972;
Maj, USA C. b 4 May 50.

THUMATI, Vijayakumar (Denduluru, Ind C,
1970); Col, TC, Ind W. b 10 Jun 49; and
**THUMATI, Keraham Manikyam
Vijayakumar** (née Karuhu) (Denduluru,
Ind C, 1970) m 1971; Col, TPWM, Ind SE.
b 17 Apr 53. Served in Ind C, Ban
(GS/CSWM), Ind SE (CS/TSWM), Ind Nat.

TIDD, Floyd (Sudbury, ON, 1986); Col, CS, Can. b 11 Mar 61. BSc, MTS; with
TIDD, Tracey (née Blacklock) m 1982; Col, TSWM, Can. b 9 Jan 61.

TILLSLEY, Mark W. (East Northport, NY, 1987); Lt-Col, USA E. b 20 Nov 57. BA (Psych/Socio), MSW; with
TILLSLEY, Sharon (née Lowman) m 1979; Lt-Col, USA E. b 21 Jun 57. BS (Nursing).

TOKUNAGA, Kojiro (Kanda, 1984); Maj, Jpn. b 27 Apr 57. BSc (Engin); and
TOKUNAGA, Yumi (née Ryugo) (Tsuruhashi, 1977) m 1986; Maj, Jpn. b 28 Dec 55.

TOLLERUD, Douglas (Santa Ana, CA, 1983); Maj, USA W. b 16 Mar 57; with
TOLLERUD, Sheryl (née Smith) m 1978; Maj, USA W. b 12 Jan 59. BS (Org Mngmnt).

TONI, Belo Kiangangu Antoine (Kinsuka, 1973); Maj, DR Con. b 30 Oct 50; and
TONI, Bernadette (née Yuta Lusakweno) m 1977; Maj, DR Con. b 15 Jul 52.

TRIBHUVAN Jagannath (Khopadi 1978); Maj, Ind W. b 12 Apr 56 and
TRIBHUVAN Kusum m 1977; (Samangaon 1977); Maj, Ind W. b 8 Oct 53.

TURNER, John E. (St. Louis, Maplewood, MO 1988); Maj, USA C. b 12 Aug 55. AA (Pract Min); with
TURNER, Theresa (née Rutter) m 1976; Maj, USA C. b 24 Nov 58. AA (Pract Min).

TURSI, Massimo (Naples, 1983); Lt-Col, CS, Switz. b 14 Nov 57; and
TURSI, Anne-Florence (née Cachelin) (Bern 1, Switz, 1983) m 1983; Lt-Col, TSWM, Switz. b 25 Mar 59. Served in Ger and It (GS/CSWM).

TVEDT, Hannelise (Copenhagen Temple, Den, 1976); Col, CS, TSWM, Neth. b 13 Dec 55. MSc (Psych), MA (Psych). Served in Den, Nor and UK.

U

UNICOMB, CHRISTINE (nee Mawson) (Mt Gravatt, 1981) Maj. Aus E. b27 Jun 54. BA Med, MA Soc Science. Served in Zimb; and
UNICOMB, BRIAN (Hurstville, 1982) m 1984; Maj, Aus E. b 1 Dec 53.

URBIEN Elnora (Manila Central, 1980); Lt-Col, Phil. b 4 Apr 50. BSc (Element Ed). Served in PNG.

UWAK, Udoh (Ikot Obio Inyang, 1992); Maj, Nig. b 2 Oct 66; with
UWAK, Esther m 1990; Maj, Nig. b 12 Dec 73.

V

VALDÉS, Victor (Piedras Negras, 1973); Maj,

Mex. b 28 Oct 53; and
VALDÉS, Marie (née Clara) (Reynosa Temple, 1976) m 1977; Maj, Mex. b 14 Oct 56. Served in USA S.

VAN DUINEN, Susan (née Jewers) (Mississauga, ON, 1978); Lt-Col, Can. b 11 Mar 50. BA, MDiv, DMin; with
VAN DUINEN, Dirk m 1970; Lt-Col. b 13 Jun 49. Served Ger and Cze Rep.

VAN VLIET, Johan C. J. (Baarn, 1975); Comr, TC, Neth. b 17 Jul 52. DSocS Admin; with
VAN VLIET, Maria (néé de Ruiter) m 1971; Comr, TPWM, Neth. b 9 May 51. Served in PNG (CS/TSWM).

VANDER WEELE, Richard E. (Kalamazoo, MI, 1976); Lt-Col, USA C. b 19 May 48. BS (Soc), MSW, Cert ACSW.

VARGHESE, Davidson (Trivandrum Central, Ind SW, 1986); Lt-Col, Ind Nat. b 13 Dec 58. BA, MA; and
DAVIDSON, Mariamma (née Chacko) (Adoor Central, Ind SW, 1985) m 1988; Lt-Col, Ind Nat. b 1 May 65. Served in Ind SW and Zam.

VARUGHESE, Wilfred (Trivandrum Central, Ind SW, 1985); Col, CS, Zim. b 25 Mar 58. BSc, BTS; and
WILFRED, Prema (née Prema) (Anayara, Ind SW, 1987) m 1987; Col, TSWM, Zim. b 25 May 60. BA, BD. Served in Ind SW and at Ind Nat.

VELE, David (Hohola, 1997); Capt, PNG . b 9 May 66; with
VELE, Rita (née Pisin) m 1994; Capt, PNG. b 26 Sep 73.

VENABLES, Brian (Ottawa Citadel, 1991); Maj, Can. b 10 Feb 56; with
VENABLES, Anne (née Kelly) m 1977; Maj, Can. b 4 Oct 57.

VENTER, Alistair (Cape Town Citadel, 1981); Lt-Col, OC, Ban. b 19 Aug 58. ThA; BTh; and
VENTER, Marieke (née van Leeuwen) (Benoni, 1988) m 1987; Lt-Col, CPWM, Ban. b 31 Dec 62, BCur, MTh. Served in S Afr.

VERA, Facundo (Tampico, 1970); Maj, Mex. b 27 Nov 48; and
VERA, Bersabé (née Hernández) (Coatzacoalcos, 1969) m 1971; Maj, Mex. b 12 Oct 49.

VERU, Zarena (Bhogiwal, 1973); Lt-Col, Pak. b 1 Jan 52.

VYLE, Bruce (Hamilton City, 1995); Maj, NZ. b 5 Jun 46. MA, BA, DipT; with
VYLE, Elaine (née French) m 1968; Maj,

NZ. b 9 Jul 48.

W

WAINWRIGHT, John (Reading Central, UK, 1979); Comr, IHQ. b 13 Mar 51; with **WAINWRIGHT, Dorita** (née Willetts) m 1976; Comr, IHQ, (ZSWM, Eur). b 19 Oct 51. Served in UK, E Afr, Zimb, Zam (TC/TPWM) and Ken E (TC/TPWM).

WALKER, Peter (Morley, 1982); Col, CS, Aus S. b 2 Mar 54. BA (Soc); with **WALKER, Jennifer** (née Freind) m 1975; Col, TSWM, Aus S. b 26 Feb 56. BEd, Dip Teach, Dip RE. Served in Mlys.

WALTERS, Rodney (Bundamba, Aus E, 1983); Lt-Col, CS, E Eur,. b 9 Jan 59. BAL; and **WALTERS, Wendy** (née Woodbury) (Wollongong, Aus E, 1983) m 1985; Lt-Col, TSWM, E Eur. b 15 May 61. Served in Rus and Aus E.

WALZ, Reinhold (Reutligen, 1975); Maj, Ger. b 10 Sep 52; and **WALZ, Ruth** (née Beckschulte) (Nuremberg, 1987) m 1987; Maj, Ger. b 10 Jul 56.

WANDULU, Moses (Bumbo, Uga, 1986); Col, TC, Mal. b 5 Aug 60; with **WANDULU, Sarah** (née Rwolekya) m 1986; Col, TPWM, Mal. b 30 Aug 1964. Served in E Afr and Uga (OC/CPWM).

WANJARE, Sanjay (Vithalwadi, 1994); Capt, Ind W. b 10 Oct 67. Ww Capt Sunita, pG 2010.

WANYAMA, Sarah (Wabukhonyi, Ken E, 1978); Lt-Col, Ken W. b 3 Mar 56. Served in Ken E.

WARD, Robert (Brock Avenue, TO, Can, 1970); Col, TC, Pak. b 22 Feb 48. MHSc (Health Mgmt), BA (Adm); and **WARD, Marguerite** (née Simon) (Swift Current, SK, Can, 1970) m 1971; Col, TPWM, Pak. b 13 May 48. Served in Can, S Afr, Zimb (CS/TSWM) and USA C.

WARNER, John (Bromley, 1971); Maj, UK b19 Dec 50. MSc (Charity Finance), FCIS, FAIA. Served in S Afr and at IHQ. m 1974; Maj Gwen, ret 2009

WATT, Neil (Montreal Citadel, 1977); Lt-Col, Can. b 4 Nov 48. BTh. Served in UK. m 1968; Lt-Col Lynda, ret 2011.

WATTERS, Alan (Cape Town Citadel, S Afr/ Brighton East, 1987); Maj, UK. b 2 May 53. BD; with **WATTERS, Linda** (née Farrier) m 1980; Maj, UK. b 13 Nov 56. Served in S Afr.

WATTS, Gavin (Carina, 1994); Maj, Aus E. b 30 Oct 69. Dip Min, Dip Bus; with **WATTS, Wendy** (née Wallis) m 1990; Maj, Aus E. b 27 Apr 68. DipTeach, DipMin.

Served in NZ.

WEBB, Geoff (Ulverstone, 1984); Maj, Aus S. b 18 Jan 59. DTh, BD, BEd and **WEBB, Kalie** (née Down) (Box Hill, 1997) m 1993; Maj, Aus S. b. 8 Jul 69. BTh Served in Pak.

WEBB, Neil (Nottingham New Basford, UK, 1983); Col, TC, PNG. b 6 Sep 58; and **WEBB, Christine** (née Holdstock) (Bromley, UK, 1983) m 1983; Col, TPWM, PNG. b 1 Mar 55. BA, Dip RS. Served in UK and PNG (CS/TSWM).

WEBER, Stephan (Nuremberg, 1987); Maj, Ger. b 5 Jul 59; with **WEBER, Andrea** (née Mueller) m 1982; Maj, Ger. b 21 Mar 63.

WELANDER, Knud David (Copenhagen Temple, Den/Oslo Temple, Nor, 1984); Col, TC, Den. b 20 May 61. BSc (Bus Admin); and **WELANDER, Lisbeth** (née Wederhus) (Florø, 1984) m 1984; Col, TPWM, Den. b 29 Nov 63. Served in Nor and Phil.

WESTMORELAND, Bobby (Hattiesburg, USA S, 1996) Maj, E Eur. b 23 Apr 71. BS; and **WESTMORELAND, Anne** (nee Edelbo) (Copenhagen Temple, Den, 2003) Capt, E Eur b 28 Jul 73. BA, MA (Th).

WESTRUPP, Andrew (Dunedin South, 1980); Maj, NZ. b 4 Oct 54; with **WESTRUPP, Yvonne** (née Medland) m 1974; Maj, NZ. b 13 Jul 54.

WHITE, Charles (Owensboro, KY, 1967); Lt-Col, USA S. b 7 May 46; with **WHITE, Shirley** (née Sanders) m 1962; Lt-Col, USA S. b 24 Apr 43.

WICKINGS, Margaret (Welling, UK, 1976); Lt-Col, IHQ. b 15 Apr 51. BEd, MTh. Served in UK, Zam, E Afr and Gha.

WIDYANOADI, Wayan (Semarang 2, 1990); Lt-Col, Indon. b 2 Jan 68; and **WIDYANOADI, Herlina** (née Ayawaila) (Bandung, 1995) m 1995; Lt-Col, Indon. b 30 Jan 65.

WILKINSON, Darrell (Long Bay, Barbados, 1985); Maj, Carib. b 1 Apr 55; and **WILKINSON, Joan** (née Marshall) (Carlton, Barbados, 1985) m 1986; Maj, Carib. b 18 Sep 58.

WILLERMARK, Marie (Göteborg 1, 1980); Comr, TC, TPWM, Swdn. b 18 Jun 54. Served in Den and E Eur.

WILLIAMS, John (Murukondapadu, 1991); Maj, Ind C. b 7 May 66. Ww Capt K. Mary Rani; and **WILLIAMS, Ratna Sundari** (Murukondapadu, 2000) m 1999; Capt, Ind C. b 22 Nov 67.

WIMMERS, Anne (Amsterdam Zuid, 1984); Maj, Neth. b 18 April 57.

WITTWER, Bernhard (Brienz, 1988); Maj, Switz. b 1 Feb 61; with
WITTWER, Regina (née Mäder) m 1983, Maj, Switz. b 22 May 63.

WOLAYO, Johnstone (Sikata, Ken 1991); Lt-Col, CS, Ken W. b 17 Jan 64; and
WOLAYO, Linnet (nee Nabila) m 1991; Lt-Col, TSWM, Ken W. b 25 May 69.

WOODALL, Ann (Croydon Citadel, UK, 1969); Comr, IHQ (IS Bus Adm). b 3 Feb 50. MA, MSc, FCCA, PhD. Served in Con, Zam, Zaï and UK.

WOODWARD, Cecil (Coorparoo, 1969); Maj, Aus E. b 3 Jun 46. BSW (Hons), MSWAP, MBA; and
WOODWARD, Catherine (née Lucas) (Miranda, 1969) m 1970; Maj, Aus E. b 20 Jan 48.

WYLES, Russell (Hillingdon, UK 1986); Maj, UK. b 14 Mar 64. MA; and
WYLES, Catherine (née Dolling) m 1986; (Hillingdon, UK 1986); Maj, UK. b 29 Dec 63

Y

YANDERAVE, Borley (Lembina, 1991); Maj, PNG. b 7 Oct 58; with
YANDERAVE, Iveme (née John) m 1985; Maj, PNG. b 25 Oct 66.

.**YESUDAS, Kancherla** (Pedapalli, 1984); Maj, Ind C. b 13 Apr 54. BA (Econ); with
YESUDAS, Hemalatha (née Devi) m 1979; Maj, Ind C. b 16 Jul 58.

YOHANNAN, C. S. (Kaithaparambu, 1975); Maj, Ind SW. b 8 Jan 54; and
YOHANNAN, L. Rachel (Pathanapuram, 1979) m 1978; Maj, Ind SW. b 31 Jul 55.

YOSHIDA, Tsukasa (Shibuya, 1982); Maj, Jpn. b 26 Nov 54; and
YOSHIDA, Kyoko (née Tsuchiya) (Kiyose, 1980) m 1982; Maj, Jpn. b 13 Oct 53.

YOUSAF, Javed (Amritnagar, 1990); Maj, Pak b 2 Nov 66; and
JAVED, Surriya (née Zafar Masih) m 1987; Maj, Pak b 18 May 69.

Z

ZIPINGANI, Langton (Pearson, 1987); Lt-Col, Zimb. b 22 Nov 61. MBA; and
ZIPINGANI, Beauty (née Chimunda) (Mutonda, 1987) m 1989; Lt-Col, Zimb.

b 2 Aug 66.

ZOLA, Ambroise (Kingudi, DR Con, 1979); Col, TC, Moz. b 6 Sep 52; with
ZOLA, Alphonsine Kuzoma (née Nsiesi) m 1976; Col, TPWM, Moz. b 2 Jan 57. Served in Con (Kin), Con (Braz) (CS/TSWM) and Ang (OC/CPWM).

ZOTHANMAWIA (Lamka Churachandpur 1992); Maj, Ind E.b 29 Sept 63; with
VANLALNUNGI; Maj, Ind E. b 3 Oct 64.

334

Retired Generals and Commissioners

A

ADIWINOTO, Lilian E. (Malang, Indon, 1954); Comr b 31 Jul 27. Served in UK, Indon (TC) and at IHQ.

ANZEZE, Hezekiel (Naliava, Kenya, 1980); Comr.b 15 Mar 49. Ww Comr Clerah, pG 2005. Served in Ken E, TC; m Margaret 2011.

ASANO, Hiroshi (Shizuoka, Jpn, 1950); Comr b 5 May 27; and Mrs Comr **Tomoko** (née Ohara) (Kyoto, 1953) m 1955. Served in Jpn (TC/TPWO).

B

BAILLIE, Kenneth (Warren, USA E, 1966); Comr b 3 Nov 42. BA (Soc); with Comr **Joy M.** (née Gabrielsen) m 1962; b 30 May 41. BA (Biochem). Served in Can, USA E, E Eur (OC/CPWO) and USA C (TC/TPWM).

BANKS, Keith (Wokingham, UK, 1963); Comr b 5 Nov 42. Served in UK, PNG (OC), Jpn (CS) and at IHQ (IS Int Per). Ww Comr Pauline, pG 2008.

BASSETT, W. Todd (Syracuse Citadel, NY, USA E, 1965); Comr b 25 Aug 39. BEd; with Comr **Carol A.** (née Easterday) m 1960; b 10 Dec 40. BEd. Served in USA E, at IHQ (IS to CoS/Mission Res Sec) and at USA Nat (NC/NPWM).

BATH, Vida (née McNeill) (Moree, Aus E, 1945); Mrs Comr. Served in Sri Lan, Ind W, Ind NE, Ind SW, at IHQ and in Aus E. Ww Comr Robert, pG 2006.

BAXENDALE, David A. (Pittsburgh, PA, USA E, 1954); Comr b 23 Apr 30. MA (Col), BSc (Sprd); with Mrs Comr **Alice** (née Chamberlain); BMus Ed (Syra). Served in USA E, USA W (CS/THLS), Carib (TC/TPWO), S Am W (TC/TPWO), at ICO (Principal) and IHQ (IS/SWO Am and Carib).

BIMWALA, Zunga Mbanza Etienne (Kinshasa 1, Zaï, 1959); Comr b 29 Sep 32. Served in Zaï (TC) and Switz. Ww Mrs Comr Alice, pG 2004.

BIRD, Patricia (Fulham, UK, 1958); Comr b 7 Aug 35. Served in Nig, UK, Zam (TC) and at IHQ (IS Fin, IS Afr).

BOSH, Larry (Mansfield, OH, USA E, 1966); Comr b 9 Jun 46. BS (Acct), MBA; and Comr **Gillian** (née Reid) (Akron Citadel, OH, USA E, 1960) m 1967; b 4 Dec 40. Served at USA Nat (Nat CS/NSWM, NRVAVS), in USA E (CS/TSWM) and at IHQ (IS/ZSWM Am and Carib).

BOVEN van, Johannes (The Hague, Neth, 1955); Comr b 9 Jan 35; and Comr **Klazina** (née Grauwmeijer) (Rotterdam, 1959) m 1960; b 22 Sep 35. Served in Neth (TC/TPWO).

BRAUN, Françoise (née Volet) (Vevey, Frce, 1968); Comr b 8 Dec 43. Served in Frce and Switz. Ww Comr Edouard, pG 2010.

BRINGANS, David (Albion, NZ, 1970); Comr b 25 May 47; with Comr **Grace** (née Palmer) m 1968; b 21 Sep 46. Served in NZ, HK, Vietnam, Tai (RC/RPWM), Sing (GS/CSWO, TC/TPWM) and Mex (TC/TPWM).

BUCKINGHAM, Lorraine (née Smith) (Waimate, NZ, 1960); Comr. Served in Aus S, NZ and Aus E. Ww Comr Hillmon, pG 2009.

BURGER, Kurt (Los Angeles Congress Hall, CA, USA W, 1972); Comr b 26 Aug 46. BS (Bus Adm), BA (Psych), MBA (Bus Adm), Cert CPA; and Comr **Alicia** (née Pedersen) (San Bernardino, CA, USA W, 1976) m 1988; b 6 Jul 46. Served in USA W and Switz (TC/TPWM).

BURROWS, Eva Evelyn General (1986-1993) (see page 15).

BUSBY, John A. (Atlanta Temple, GA, USA S, 1963); Comr b 14 Oct 37. BA (Asbury); with Comr **Elsie Louise** (née Henderson) m 1958; b 11 Jun 36. Served in Can (CS/TSWO), USA S (TC/TPWO) and USA Nat (NC/NPWM).

C

CACHELIN, Genevieve (née Booth) (Paris Central, Frce, 1947); Mrs Comr. MA. Served in Switz, Belg, Frce, Ger, BT and at IHQ. Ww Comr Francy, pG 2007.

CAIRNS, Alistair G. (West End, Aus E, 1942); Comr b 12 Dec 16. AM, Order of Australia (1996). Served in Kor, Aus E (CS), at ITC and in S Afr (TC). Ww Mrs Comr Margery, pG 2006.

CAIRNS, Beulah (née Harris) (Parramatta, Aus E, 1959); Mrs Comr. Served in Aus E and at IHQ. Ww Comr William, pG 2008.

CALVERT, Ruth (Port Hope, ON, 1955); Mrs Comr b 8 Feb 35. Served in Aus E. Ww Comr Roy, pG 1994.

CAMPBELL, Donald (Highgate, Aus S, 1945); Comr b 31 Oct 23. Served in NZ (TC) and Aus S (TC). Ww Comr Crystal, pG 2008.

CHANG, Peter Hei-dong (Seoul Central, Kor, 1960); Comr b 12 May 32. BD, STm (Union, NY), BTh MEd (Columbia, NY); and Comr **Grace Eun-Shik** (née Chung) (Seoul, Kor, 1963) m 1963. BA, BMus (Seoul Nat).

Served in UK, Sing, HK, USA E, Kor (CS/THLS, TC/TPWO), USA W (TC/TPWO) and at IHQ.

CHARLET, Horst (Berlin-Neukölln, 1969); Comr b 1 May 46. Dip SW, Dip Soc Pedagogue; with Comr **Helga** (née Werner); Comr b 18 Oct 48. Served in Ger (CS/TSWM, TC/TPWM).

CHEVALLY, Simone (née Gindraux) (Lausanne 1, Switz, 1947); Mrs Comr. Served in Switz and at IHQ. Ww Comr Robert, pG 1989.

CHIANGHNUNA (Ngupa, Ind W, 1951); Comr b 10 Jun 29; and Mrs Comr **Barbara** (née Powell) (Ware, UK, 1948) m 1968. Served in Ind N (CS/THLS), Ind E (CS/THLS) and Ind W (TC/TPWO).

CHUN, Kwang-pyo (Duk Am, Kor, 1971); Comr b 15 Sep 41; with Comr **Yoo, Sung-ja** m 1969; b 11 Jan 41. Served in Kor (CS/ TSWM) (TC/TPWM).

CLAUSEN, Siegfried (Catford, UK, 1958); Comr b 4 Mar 38; and Comr **Inger-Lise** (née Lydholm) (Valby, 1958) m 1961; b 1 Oct 39. Served in UK, S Am W, Sp (OC/CPWO), L Am N (TC/TPWO), Ger (TC/TPWO) and at IHQ (IS/SWM Am and Carib).

CLIFTON, Shaw General (2006-2011), (see p16). Ww Comr Helen pG 2011.

CLINCH, John H. (Fairfield, Aus S, 1956); Comr b 30 Nov 30; with Comr **Beth** (née Barker). Served in Aus S, Aus E (CS/THLS), at IHQ (IS/SWO SPEA) and in Aus S (TC/TPWO).

COLES, Alan C. (Harrow, UK, 1953); Comr b 2 Feb 25. ACIB. Ww Heather, pG 1978; and Mrs Comr **Brenda** (née Deeming) (Tipton, UK, 1959) m 1980. Served in Zimb (TC) and at IHQ.

COLES, Dudley (North Toronto, ON, Can, 1954); Comr b 22 Mar 26; and Mrs Comr **Evangeline** (née Oxbury) (Powell River, BC, Can, 1954) m 1956. Served in Can, Ind Audit, Ind W, Sri Lan (TC/TPWO) and at IHQ (IS/SWO S Asia).

COOPER, Raymond A. (Washington Georgetown, DC, USA S, 1956); Comr b 24 May 37; and Comr **Merlyn S.** (née Wishon) (Winston Salem Southside, NC, USA S, 1957) m 1959; b 2 Sep 36. Served in USA C and USA S (TC/TPWO).

COX, Hilda (née Chevalley) (Geneva, 1949); Mrs Comr. Served in UK, Zam, Zimb, Frce, Neth and at IHQ (WSHL). Ww Comr Ron, pG 1995.

CUTMORE, Ian (Tamworth, Aus E, 1954); Comr b 27 Sep 33; and Comr **Nancy** (née

Richardson) (Atherton, Aus E, 1957). Served in Aus E, PNG, UK (CS/TSWO), ICO (Principal) and NZ (TC/TPWO).

D

DAVIS, Douglas E. (Moreland, Aus S, 1960); Comr b 12 Feb 37; with Comr **Beverley J.** (née Roberts) m 1958; b 23 Feb 38. Served in NZ, UK (CS/TSWO) and Aus S (TC/TPWO).

DELCOURT, France (née Bardiaux) (Lyon 1, Frce, 1943); Mrs Comr. Served in BT and Frce. Ww Comr Raymond A., pG 2010.

DEVAVARAM, Prathipati (New Colony, Ind C, 1964); Comr b 15 Nov 46. MBBS, BSc; and Comr **P. Victoria** (Bapatla Central, Ind C, 1970) m 1974; b 25 Nov 49. BSc, BEd, BLSc. Served in Ind C, at Ind Nat, in Ind E and Ind SE (TC/TPWM).

DIAKANWA, Mbakanu (Poste Francais, Kin, Zaï, 1949); Comr b 1923. Officier de l'Ordre du Leopard (1981). Served in Zaï (TC). Ww Comr Situwa, pG 1998.

DITMER, Anne (née Sharp) (Dayton Central, OH, USA E, 1957) Mrs Comr. Served in USA S, USA C and USA E. Ww Comr Stanley, pG 2003.

DUNSTER, Robin (Dulwich Hill Temple, Aus E, 1970); Comr b 12 Jan 44. SRN, SCM, RPN, RMN, IPPF (Ed). Served in Aus E, Zimb (CS), Con (Kin) (TC, TPWO), Phil (TC, TPWM) and at IHQ (CoS).

DU PLESSIS, Paul (Salt River, S Afr, 1968); Comr b 3 Jul 41. MB ChB, MRCP, DTM&H; with Comr **Margaret** (née Siebrits); m 1964; b 17 Jul 42. BSoc Sc. Served in Zam, Ind C (TC/TPWO), S Afr (TC/TPWO) and at IHQ.

DURMAN, Vera (née Livick) (South Croydon, UK, 1942) Mrs Comr. Served in UK, Ind W and at IHQ. Ww Comr David, pG 2010.

DWYER, June M. (Windsor, NS, Can, 1952); Comr. b 28 Aug 32. Served at USA Nat, in S Afr (CS) and at IHQ (IS Admin).

E

EDWARDS, David (New Market Street, Georgetown, Guyana, Carib, 1962); Comr b 15 May 41; and Comr **Doreen** (née Bartlett) (Wellington St, Barbados, Carib, 1957) m 1966; b 4 Mar 35. Served in USA E, Carib (TC/TPWO), at IHQ (IS/SWO Am and Carib) and in USA W (TC/TPWO).

ELIASEN, Carl S. (Gartnergade, Den, 1951); Comr b 28 Mar 32. Served in Port (OC), Brz (TC), S Am W (TC) and at IHQ (IS Americas). Ww Comr Maria, pG 2003.

EVANS, Willard S. (Greenville, SC, USA S, 1949), Comr b 2 Sep 24. BA (Bob Jones Univ); with Mrs Comr **Marie** (née Fitton). Served in USA S, USA E (CS/THLS) and USA W (TC/TPWO).

F

FEENER, Maxwell (Port Leamington, NL, Can, 1966); Comr b 5 Jul 45, with Comr **Lenora** (née Tippett) m 1967; Comr b 26 Dec 45. Served in Can, S Afr (CS/TSWM) and USA S (CS/ TSWM, TC/TPWM).

FORSYTH, Robin W. (Edinburgh Gorgie, UK, 1968); Comr b 30 Aug 1946; with Comr **Shona** (née Leslie) m 1966; Comr b 25 Mar 1948. Served in Aus S, Mex, UK, L Am N (TC/ TPWM), NZ (CS/TSWM) and at IHQ (IS Prog Res/ Chaplain).

FRANCIS, William (Paterson, NJ, USA E, 1973); Comr b 5 Mar 44. BA (Mus/Hist), MDiv, Hon DD; with Comr **Marilyn** (née Burroughs) m 1965; Comr, TPWM, Can. b 3 Feb 43. BA (Mus), MA. Served in USA E (CS/TSWM), Can (TC/TPWM) and at IHQ (IS/SWM Am and Carib).

FRANS, Roy (Surabaya 4, Indon, 1977); Comr. b 30 Oct 50; and Comr **Arda** (née Haurissa) (Jakarta 1, Indon, 1978) m 1978; Comr. b 10 May 44. Served in Indon, Aus E, Sing, Ban, Sri Lan (TC/TPWM), at IHQ (IS/ ZSWM SPEA, Rep to UN, SPEA) and in Neth (TC/TPWM).

FREI, Werner (Rorbas, Switz, 1965); Comr b 6 Mar 40; and Comr **Paula** (née Berweger) (Heiden, Switz, 1965) m 1967; b 19 Mar 36. Served in Switz (CS/TSWO) and Ger (TC/TPWM).

FULLARTON, Frank (Bromley, UK, 1955); Comr b 3 Mar 31. BSc, DipSoc; and Comr **Rosemarie** (née Steck) (Croydon Citadel, UK, 1958) m 1959. BEd (Hons), MITD. Served at IHQ (CS to CoS, IS/SWO Eur), Soc S (GBI) (Ldr) and in Switz (TC/TPWO).

G

GAITHER, Israel L. (New Castle, PA, USA E, 1964); Comr b 27 Oct 44. Hon LHD, Hon DD; and Comr **Eva D.** (née Shue) (Sidney, OH, USA E, 1964) m 1967; b 9 Sep 43. Served in USA E (CS/TSWO) (TC/TPWM), S Afr (TC/ TPWO), at IHQ (CoS/WSWM) and USA Nat (NC/NPWM, USA).

GAUNTLETT, Marjorie (née Markham) (Wood Green, UK, 1952); Mrs Comr. Served at ITC, in Zimb, Frce, Ger, Switz and at IHQ (WSHL). Ww Comr Caughey, pG 2009.

GOODIER, William Robert (Atlanta Temple, GA, USA S, 1941); Comr b 23 May 16. Served in USA S (CS), at USA Nat (CS), in Aus S (TC) and USA E (TC). Ww Mrs Comr Renee pG 2012.

GOWANS, John General (1999-2002) (see page 16); and Comr **Gisèle** (née Bonhotal) (Paris Central, Frce, 1955) m 1957. Served in USA W, Frce (TPWO), Aus E (TPWO), UK (TPWO) and at IHQ (WPWM).

GRIFFIN, Joy (née Button) (Tottenham Citadel, UK, 1957); Mrs Lt-Comr. Served in BT. Ww Lt-Comr Frederick, pG 1990.

GRINSTED, Dora (née Bottle) (Sittingbourne, UK, 1950); Mrs Comr. Served in UK, Zam, Zimb, Jpn and at IHQ. Ww Comr David Ramsay, pG 1992.

GULLIKSEN, Thorleif R. (Haugesund, Nor, 1967); Comr b 26 Apr 40; with Comr **Olaug** (née Henriksen) m 1962; b 25 Jan 38. Served in Nor, Neth (TC/TPWO) and at IHQ (IS/SWM Eur).

H

HANNEVIK, Anna (Bergen 2, Nor, 1947); Comr b 9 Aug 25. Served in Nor, UK (Ldr SocS), Swdn (TC) and at IHQ (IS Eur). Paul Harris Medal (1987), Commander of the Royal Order of the Northern Star (Sweden).

HANNEVIK, Edward (Oslo 3, Nor, 1954); Comr b 6 Dec 32; and Comr **Margaret** (née Moody) (Newfield, UK, 1956) m 1958. Served in UK, Den (TC/TPWO), Nor (TC/ TPWO) and at IHQ (IS/SWO Eur).

HARITA, Nozomi (Shibuya, Jap, 1966); Comr b 10 May 39. BA (Mus); and Comr **Kazuko** (née Hasegawa) (Shibuya, Jap, 1966) m 1969; b 19 Dec 37. BA (Ed). Served in Aus E and Jap (TC/TPWM).

HARRIS, Bramwell Wesley (Cardiff Stuart Hall, UK, 1948); Comr b 25 Nov 28; and Mrs Comr **Margaret** (née Sansom) (Barking, UK, 1949), m 1955. Served in UK, at IHQ, in Aus S (CS/THLS), Scot (TC/THLP), NZ (TC/TPWO) and Can (TC/TPWO).

HEDBERG, Lennart (Nykoping, Swdn, 1954); Comr b 12 Oct 32; and Comr **Ingvor** (née Fagerstedt) (Nykoping, Swdn, 1955) m 1956. Served in Den, Swdn (TC/TPWO) and at IHQ (IS/SWO Eur).

HINSON, Harold D. (High Point, NC, USA S, 1955); Comr b 7 Sep 35; and Comr **Betty M.** (née Morris) (New Orleans, LA, USA S, 1955); b 1 Jun 35. Served in USA S (CS/THLS) and USA C (TC/TPWO).

HODDER, Kenneth L. (San Francisco Citadel, CA, USA W, 1958); Comr b 30 Oct 30. BA (Richmond), DSS (Hons) (Richmond), JD (California); and Comr **Marjorie J.** (née Fitton) (San Francisco Citadel, CA, USA W, 1958). Served in USA W, USA C, Aus S (CS), USA S (TC/TPWO) and at USA Nat (Nat Commander/NPWM).

HOLLAND, Louise (née Cruickshank) (Invercairn, UK, 1958); Mrs Comr. Served in UK, E Afr, Nig, Gha, Pak and at IHQ. Ww Comr Arthur, pG 1998.

HOOD, H. Kenneth (Denver Citadel, CO, USA W, 1954); Comr b 27 Jan 33; and Comr **Barbara** (née Johnson) (Pasadena, CA, USA W, 1952) m 1957. Served in USA W (CS/THLS), at USA Nat (CS/Asst NPWO) and in USA S (TC/TPWO).

HOUGHTON, Raymond (Woodhouse, UK, 1967); Comr b 12 Apr 44. MCMI; with Comr **Judith** (née Jones) m 1965; b 15 Nov 45. Served in UK (CS/TSWO), at IHQ (IS to CoS/Mission Resources Sec) and in Carib (TC/TPWM).

HOWE, Norman (Dartford, UK, 1957); Comr b 13 Aug 36; and Comr **Marian** (née Butler) (Boscombe, UK, 1953) m 1959; b 9 Feb 30. Cert Ed. Served in UK, at ITC (Principal), in Aus S (CS) and Can (TC/TPWO) and at IHQ (IS Prog Res/SWO Eur, General's Travelling Representative).

HUGHES, Alex (Paisley West, UK, 1960); Comr b 29 Jan 42; and Comr **Ingeborg** (née Clausen) (Catford, UK, 1964) m 1971; b 2 Jan 42. Served in L Am N, S Am E (CS/THLS, TC/TPWO), S Am W (TC/TPWO), at IHQ (IS/SWO Am and Carib) and in UK (TC/TPWM).

HUGUENIN, Willy (Le Locle, Switz, 1954); Comr b 22 Sep 31; and Mrs Comr **Miriam** (née Luthi) (La Chaux-de-Fonds, Switz, 1953) m 1955. Served in Zaï (GS), Con (TC/TPWO), Switz (TC/TPWO) and at IHQ (IS/SWO Afr).

I

IRWIN, Ronald G. (Philadelphia, PA, USA E, 1957); Comr b 4 Aug 33. BS (Rutgers), MA (Columbia); and Comr **Pauline** (née Laipply) (Cincinnati, OH, USA E, 1953) m 1967. Served in USA W (CS/THLS) and USA E (TC/TPWO).

ISRAEL, Jillapegu (Peralipadu, Ind N, 1957); Comr b 31 May 32. BA, BEd; with Comr **Rachel** (née Amarthaluri); Served in Ind M & A (CS/THLS), Ind N (TC/TPWO) and Ind SW (TC/TPWO).

K

KALAI, Andrew (Koki, 1981); Comr b 18 Jan 56. BA (Psych). Ww Capt Napa, pG 1994; Ww Col Julie, pG 2006. Served in UK and PNG (TC).

KANG, Sung-hwan (Noh Mai Sil, Kyung Buk, Kor, 1973); Comr b 15 Dec 39; with Comr **Lee, Jung-ok** m1970; b 10 Nov 49. Served in Aus S and Kor (TC/TPWM).

KARTODARSONO, Ribut (Surakarta, 1975); Comr b 13 Dec 49. BA (Relig Ed), MA (Relig Ed & Public Societies); and Comr **Marie** (née Ticoalu) (Bandung 3, 1975) m 1979; b 30 Nov 52. Served in UK and Indon (CS/TSWM, TC/TPWM).

KELLNER, Paul S. (Miami Citadel, FL, USA S, 1963); Comr b 1 Sep 35. BMus; with Comr **Jajuan** (née Pemberton); b 23 Feb 39. Served in USA S, Carib, Con (Braz) and Zimb (TC/TPWO).

KENDREW, K. Ross (Sydenham, NZ, 1962); Comr b 7 Dec 38; and Comr **M. June** (née Robb) (Wanganui, NZ, 1961) m 1964; b 8 Oct 39. Served in NZ (TC/TPWO) and Aus S (TC/TPWM).

KERR, Donald (Vancouver Temple, BC, Can, 1955); Comr b 25 Oct 33; and Comr **Joyce** (née Knaap) (Mt Dennis, ON, 1955) m 1957; b 12 Jan 35. Served in UK (CS) and Can (TC/TPWO).

KIM, Suk-tai (Choon Chun, Kor, 1957); Comr b 23 Jan 26. ThB, BA, MSoc; and **Lim, Jung-sun** (Sudaemun, Kor, 1969) m 1975. BMus. Served in Kor (TC/TPWO).

KING, Margaret (née Coull) (Fairview, S Afr, 1936); Mrs Comr. Served in S Afr. Ww Comr Hesketh, pG 1990.

KJELLGREN, Hasse (Östra Kåren, Swdn, 1971); Comr b 1 Nov 45. BSc; and Comr **Christina** (née Forssell) (Hisingskaren, Swdn, 1971) m 1971; b 21 May 47. Served in S Am E (TC/TPWO), Switz (TC/TPWM), Swdn (TC/TPWM) and at IHQ (IS/ZSWM Eur).

L

LALTHANNGURA (Ratu, Ind E, 1963); Comr b 15 Sep 38. BA; with **Kaphliri**; b 9 Sep 43. Served in Ind C (CS/THLS) and Ind E (TC/TPWM).

LANG, Ivan B. (Auburn, Aus S, 1967); Comr b 18 Jul 40. AM, Order of Australia (2007), with Comr **Heather C.** (née Luhrs) m 1961;

338

b 8 Dec 42. Served in Sing (OC/CPWO), Aus E (CS/TSWO), at IHQ (IS/SWM SPEA) and in Aus S (TC/TPWM).

LARSSON, John General (2002-2006) (see page 16); and Comr **Freda** (née Turner) (Kingston-upon-Thames, UK, 1964) m 1969. Served in S Am W (THLS), at ITC, in UK (TPWO), NZ (TPWO), Swdn (TPWO) and at IHQ (WSWM, WPWM).

LEE, Sung-duk (Cho Kang, Kor, 1963); Comr b 10 Jun 35. Served in Kor (TC). Ww Comr Cho, In-sun. pG 2011.

LIM, Ah Ang (Balestier Rd, Sing, 1954); Comr b 30 May 32; and Comr **Fong Pui Chan** (Singapore Central, 1954) m 1958. Served in Sing, HK (OC/CPWO), Phil (TC/TPWO) and at IHQ (IS/SWO SPEA).

LINDBERG, Ingrid E. (Norrköping, Swdn, 1951); Comr b 12 Dec 25. Served in Swdn, Zimb, Phil (OC), Den (TC) and Fin (TC).

LINNETT, Merle (née Clinch) (Hindmarsh, Aus S, 1947); Mrs Comr. Served in NZ, at IHQ, ITC, ICO and in Aus S. Ww Comr Arthur, pG 1986.

LOVATT, Olive (née Chapman) (Doncaster, UK, 1949); Mrs Comr. Served in UK, Aus S, Aus E & PNG and at IHQ. Ww Comr Roy, pG 2000.

LUDIAZO, Jean Bakidi (Salle Centrale, Kinshasa, Con (Kin), 1971); Comr b 19 Nov 45; with Comr **Véronique** (née Lusieboko Lutatabio) m 1970; b 26 Sep 53. Served in Con, Can, Con (Kin) (TC/TPWM) and Nig (TC/TPWM).

LUTTRELL, Bill (Greeley, CO, USA W, 1958); Comr b 4 Jul 38. BA Soc; and Comr **Gwendolyn** (née Shinn) (Long Beach, CA, USA W, 1961) m 1962; b 3 Sep 38. BA Soc. Served at IHQ (IS/SWO Am and Carib) and in Can (TC/TPWM) and USA W (CS/TSWO, TC/TPWM).

LYDHOLM, Carl A. S. (Gartnergade, Den, 1966); Comr b 14 Nov 45; and Comr **Gudrun** (née Arskog) (Odense, Den, 1967) m 1967; b 5 Aug 47. MTh. Served in Den, UK, Rus/CIS (GS/CSWM), Fin (TC/TPWM) and Nor (TC/TPWM).

LYSTER, Ingrid (Valerenga, Nor, 1947); Comr b 7 Apr 22. BA (S Afr). Served in Nig, Zimb, Nor (CS) and at ICO (Principal).

M

MABENA, William (Bloemfontein, S Afr, 1959); Comr b 23 May 40; and Comr **Lydia** (née Lebusho) (Bloemfontein, S Afr, 1959)

m 1960; b 25 Jun 39. Served in UK, S Afr (CS/THLS, TC/TPWM), Gha (TC/TPWO) and at IHQ (IS/SWO Afr).

MacMILLAN, M. Christine (North York, Can, 1975); Comr b 9 Oct 47. Served in UK, Aus E, PNG (TC, TPWM), Can (TC, TPWM) and at IHQ.

MAILLER, Georges (Neuchatel, Switz, 1961); Comr b 9 Nov 36. BTh; with Comr **Muriel** (née Aeberli) m 1959; b 15 Apr 35. Served at ESFOT, in Frce and Switz (TC/TPWO).

MAKINA, Amos (Gwelo, Zimb, 1971); Comr, b 28 Jun 47; and Comr **Rosemary** (née Chinjiri) (Mutonda, Zimb, 1973) m 1973; b 8 Aug 52. Served in Gha, Zimb (TC/TPWM) and at IHQ (IS/ZSWM Afr).

MAKOUMBOU, Antoine (Bacongo, Con (Braz), 1968); Comr b 2 Mar 40; with Comr **Véronique** (née Niangui) m 1967; b 30 Aug 46. Served in Con (Braz) (TC/ TPWM).

MANNAM, Mrs Comr **Ruby** (née Manuel) (Leyton Citadel, UK, 1953) m 1975. Served in Ind M & A (TPWO), Ind W (TPWO), Ind SW (TPWO), Ind E (TPWO) and Ind N (TPWO). Ww Comr Samuel pG 2011.

MASIH, Mohan (Khundi, Ind W, 1961); Comr b 29 Sep 39; with Comr **Swarni** m 1958; b 14 Mar 42. Served in Ind N (CS/THLS), Ind C (TC/TPWO), Ind SW (TC/TPWO) and Ind W (TC/TPWM).

MATEAR, John (Whifflet, 1978); Comr b 26 Apr 47; and Comr **Elizabeth** (née Kowbus) (Greenock Citadel, 1977) m 1978; b 16 Aug 52. Dip Youth, Commun and Soc Wk, Emp Law. Served in Carib (TC/TPWM) and UK (TC/TPWM).

MAXWELL, Earle Alexander (Orange, Aus E, 1954); Comr b 8 Jul 34. FCIS, ASA, CPA; and Comr **Wilma** (née Cugley) (Camberwell, Aus S, 1956) m 1957. Served in Aus E, Sing (OC/CPWO), Phil (TC/TPWO), NZ (TC/ TPWO) and at IHQ (CoS/WSWO).

McKENZIE, Garth (Wellington City, NZ, 1975); Comr b 19 Feb 44; with Comr **Merilyn** (née Probert) m 1968; b 20 Jul 46. Served in Aus S and NZ (TC/TPWM).

MILLER, Mrs Comr **Joan** (née Hackworth) (Hamilton, OH, USA E, 1945) m 1946. Hon LHD (Wesley Biblical Seminary, MS). Served in USA E, USA C (THLS), USA S (TPWO) and at USA Nat (NPWO). Ww Comr Andrew S. pG 2011.

MORETZ, Lawrence R. (Sunbury, PA, USA E, 1964); Comr b 22 Jul 43; and Comr **Nancy A.** (née Burke) (Kingston, NY, USA E, 1964) m 1965; b 29 Nov 44. Served in S Am W (TC/TPWO), USA C (TC/TPWM) and USA E (TC/TPWM).

MORGAN, K. Brian (Bairnsdale, Aus S, 1958); Comr b 5 Oct 37; and Comr **Carolyn** (née Bath) (Melville Park, Aus S, 1958) m 1961; b 5 Mar 38. Served in Rus/CIS (CS/TSWO), Aus S (CS/TSWO) and Aus E (TC/TPWM).

MORRIS, Louise (née Holmes) (Charleston, W VA, USA S, 1953) Comr. Served in USA S and Jpn. Ww Comr Ted, pG 2004.

MOYO, Selina (née Ndhlovu) (Bulayao Central, 1951); Mrs Comr. Served in Zimb. Ww Comr David, pG 2005.

MUNGATE, Stuart (Mabvuku, Zimb, 1970); Comr, b 15 Nov 46. BA, Grad Cert Ed, Dip Bus Admin; and Comr **Hope** (née Musvosvi) (Mucherengi, Zimb, 1974) m 1974; b 23 Mar 53. Dip Journ. Served in Zimb, Con (Kin) (CS/TSWM, TC/TPWM), Nig (TC/TPWM) and DR Con (TC/TPWM).

MUTEWERA, Stanslous (Sinoia, Zimb, 1970); Comr b 25 Dec 47; and Comr **Jannet** (née Zinyemba) (Tsatse, Zimb, 1973) m 1973; b 11 Nov 52. Served in UK and Zimb (TC/TPWM).

N

NEEDHAM, Philip D. (Miami Citadel, USA S, 1969); Comr b 5 Dec 40. BA (Rel), MDiv, ThM, DMin; with
Comr **Keitha** (née Holz)
m 1963; b 9 Oct 41. BA (Ed). Served at ICO (Principal), in USA W and USA S (TC/TPWM).

NELSON, John (Victoria Citadel, BC, Can, 1952); Comr b 19 Aug 32; and Comr **Elizabeth** (née McLean) (Chatham, Ont, Can, 1953) m 1956. Served in Can, at IHQ (IS/SWO S Asia), in Carib and Pak (TC/TPWO).

NELTING, George L. (Brooklyn, Bushwick, NY, USA E, 1942); Comr b 20 Jun 18. Ww Mrs Kathleen (née McKeag), pG 1976; and Mrs Comr **Juanita** (née Prine) (Cincinnati Cent, OH, USA E, 1962) m 1977. Served in USA E, at USA Nat (CS), Neth (TC/TPWO), at IHQ (IS/SWO Afr and IS Far East) and in USA C (TC/TPWO).

NILSON, Birgitta K. (Boone, IA, USA C, 1964); Comr. b 2 Oct 37. AB (Chicago), MSW (Loyola). Served in USA C, Swdn (TC) and at IHQ (IS Eur).

NILSSON, Sven (Vansbro, Swdn, 1940); Comr b 27 Jul 19. King's Medal (12th size)

Sweden (1983). Served in Nor (CS), Den (TC) and Swdn (TC). Ww Mrs Comr Lisbeth, pG 2007.

NOLAND, Joseph J. (Santa Ana, CA, USA W, 1965); Comr b 17 Jul 37. BA, MS; and Comr **Doris** (née Tobin) (Los Angeles Congress Hall, CA, USA W, 1965) m 1966. RN. Served in USA W, Aus E and USA E (TC/TPWO).

NTUK, Patience (née Ekpe) (Ibadan, 1969); Comr. Served in Nig. Ww Comr Joshua, pG 2007.

O

ØDEGAARD, B. Donald (Oslo 3, Nor, 1966); Comr b 18 Dec 40. Cand Mag; and Comr **Berit** (née Gjersøe) (Tønsberg, Nor, 1964) m 1967; b 27 Sep 44. SRN. Served in Zimb, S Afr, Nig (TC/TPWO), E Afr (TC/TPWO), Nor (TC/TPWM) and at IHQ (IS Prog Resources/'Sally Ann' Coordinator).

OLCKERS, Roy (Uitenhage, S Afr, 1952); Comr b 16 Jul 29; and Mrs Comr **Yvonne** (née Holdstock) (Fairview, S Afr, 1952) m 1955. Served in S Afr (TC/TPWO).

ORD, John (Easington Colliery, UK, 1948); Comr b 7 Sep 29; and Mrs Comr **Lydie** (née Deboeck) (Brussels, Belg, 1951) m1953. Served in Frce, Belg (OC/OPWO), at ITC, at ICO, in UK and Nor (TC/TPWO).

ORSBORN, Amy (née Webb) (Adelaide North, Aus S, 1951); Mrs Comr. Served in Aus S, NZ, UK, Swdn and Aus E. Ww Comr Howard, pG 2008.

OSBORNE, James (Washington 3, DC, USA S, 1947); Comr b 3 Jul 27; with Mrs Comr **Ruth** (née Campbell). Served in USA W (CS), USA S (TC) and at USA Nat (NC).

P

PARKINS, May (née Epplett) (Seattle Citadel, WA, USA W, 1951); Mrs Lt-Comr. Served in USA E, USA S and USA W. Ww Lt-Comr William, pG 1990.

PATRAS, Gulzar (Punjgarian, 1973); Comr b 19 Aug 47; and Comr **Sheila** (née John) (Amritnagar, Pak, 1973) m 1973; b 22 Sep 46. Served in Pak (TC/TPWM).

PATTIPEILOHY, Blanche (née Sahanaja) (Djakarta 1, Indon, 1955); Mrs Comr. Served in Indon. Ww Comr Herman G., pG 2000.

PEARCE, Lynette J. (Parkes, Aus E, 1971); Comr b 13 Jan 45. BA. Served in Aus E, at ICO and IHQ (IS Int Pers, WSWM).

PENDER, Winifred (née Dale) (Godmanchester, UK, 1954); Comr. Served in NZ, S Afr, Scot,

at IHQ, in Aus S and UK. Ww Comr
Dinsdale, pG 2006.

POBJIE, Barry R. (Paddington, Aus E, 1965);
Comr b 25 Jan 45. Served in PNG. Ww Capt
Ruth, pG 1978; and Comr **Raemor** (née
Wilson) (Port Kembla, Aus E, 1971) m 1980;
b 22 Sep 48. Served in NZ, Aus E, Rus (GS/
CSWO), E Eur (OC/CPWM, TC/TPWM) and
at IHQ (IS/ZSWM SPEA) (IS/ZSWM Eur).

POKE, Victor (Burnie, Aus S, 1968); Comr
b 8 Jan 46; and Comr **Roslyn** (née Pengilly)
(Maylands, Aus S, 1968) m 1970; b 20 Jun 45.
Served in Aus S, UK (CS/ TSWM) and Swdn
(TC/TPWM).

PRATT, Mrs Comr **Kathleen** (née Lyons)
(Harlesden, UK, 1948) m 1949. Served at
IHQ, in BT, USA W (TPWO) and Can
(TPWO). Ww Comr William pG 2011.

R

RADER, Paul A. General (1994-1999) (see page
15); with Comr **Kay F.** (née Fuller) (Cincinnati,
OH, USA E, 1995) m 1956. BA (Asbury), Hon
DD (Asbury Theol Seminary), Hon LHD
(Greenville), Hon DD (Roberts Wesleyan).
Served in Kor (THLS), USA E (THLS), USA W
(TPWO) and at IHQ (WPWO).

RAJAKUMARI, P. Mary (née Desari)
(New Colony, Bapatla, Ind C, 1978); Comr.
MA (Engl), MA (Hist). Served in Ind M &
A, at IHQ, at Ind Cent Off, in Ind W, Ind N
and Ind SE (TPWM). Ww Comr P. D. Krupa
Das, pG 2007.

RANGEL, Paulo (Rio Comprido, Brz, 1968);
Comr b 19 Nov 41. Hon DD; and Comr
Yoshiko (née Namba) (São Paulo, Brz, 1967) m
1969; b 1 Sep 44. Served in Brz (TC/ TPWM).

READ, Harry (Edinburgh Gorgie, UK, 1948);
Comr b 17 May 24. Served in UK, at IHQ, ITC
(Principal), in Can (CS), Aus E (TC) and BT
(Brit Comr). Ww Mrs Comr Winifred, pG 2007.

REFSTIE, Peder R. (Mandal, Nor, 1965);
Comr, b 13 Jul 43; and Comr **Janet M.** (née
Dex) (Bedford, UK, 1966) m 1969; b 7 Jul 43.
Served in UK, S Am W, Port, Nor, Sp (OC/
CPWM), at IHQ, in S Am E (TC/TPWM) and
Brz (TC/TPWM).

RIGHTMIRE, Robert S. (Cincinnati, OH,
USA E, 1946); Comr b 23 Jun 24; and Comr
Katherine (née Stillwell) (Newark Citadel,
USA E, 1942) m 1947. Served in USA E,
S Afr (CS), Jpn (TC/TWPWO, Kor (TC/
TPWO) and USA C (TC/TPWO).

RIVERS, William (Hadleigh Temple, UK,
1952); Comr b 22 Dec 27; and Mrs Comr

Rose (née Ross) (Aberdeen Torry, UK, 1956)
m 1957. Served in UK and at IHQ (IS Admin).

ROBERTS, William H. (Detroit Brightmoor,
MI, USA C, 1943); Comr b 27 May 22; and
Mrs Comr **Ivy** (née Anderson) (Marshalltown,
IA, USA C, 1943) m 1945. BA (Wayne State).
Served in USA C, Aus S (CS) and at IHQ
(IS Am and Carib, IS for Dev).

ROOS, Rolf (Uppsala, Swdn, 1962); Comr
b 13 Nov 40; and Comr **Majvor** (née
Ljunggren) (Uppsala, Swdn, 1964) m 1965;
b 15 Sep 38. Served in Fin (TC/TPWO) and
Swdn (TC/ TPWM).

RUTH, Fred L. (Shawnee, OK, 1955); Comr
b 21 Aug 35. BA (Georgia State), Dip Ed, MA
(Counselling and Psychol Studies) (Trinity).
Served in Kor, USA W, USA S, at USA Nat
and at IHQ (IS SPEA). Ww Mrs Col Sylvia,
pG 1990.

S

SAUNDERS, Robert F. (Philadelphia Pioneer,
PA, USA E, 1962); Comr b 16 Jan 37.
C Th (Fuller); and Comr **Carol J.** (née Rudd)
(Seattle Temple, WA, USA W, 1966) m 1967;
b 10 Sep 43. Served in Carib, USA E, USA W,
Kor (CS/TSWO), Phil (TC/TPWO) and at
IHQ (IS/SWO SPEA).

SCHURINK, Reinder J. (Zutphen, Neth,
1947); Comr b 2 Dec 27. Officer Order of
Orange Nassau (1987). Ww Mrs Capt
Henderika (née Hazeveld), pG 1961. Served
in Ger (CS), Neth (TC) and Rus (Cmndr).
Ww Mrs Comr Wietske (née Kloosterman),
pG 1997. m Lt-Col Dora Verhagen, 1998.

SCOTT, Albert P. (Lawrence, MA, USA E,
1941); Comr b 15 Oct 18. Ww Mrs Dorothy,
pG 1970; and Mrs Comr **Frances O.** (née
Clark) (Concord, NH, USA E, 1953)
m 1971. Served in USA E (CS) and at IHQ
(IS Am and Carib, and IS Development).

SHIPE, Tadeous (Mukakatanwa, Zimb, 1969);
Comr b 13 Jul 43. Served in Zimb, Zam &
Mal (TC/TPWM) and Zam (TC/TPWM).
Ww Comr Nikiwe, pG 2008.

SHOULTS, Harold (St Louis Tower Grove,
MO, USA C, 1949); Comr b 6 Mar 29; and
Mrs Comr **Pauline** (née Cox) (St Louis Tower
Grove, MO, USA C, 1951) m 1952. Served in
USA E (CS/TSWO), USA N (CS/Asst NPWO)
and USA C (TC/TPWO).

SKINNER, Verna E. (West End, Aus E,
1957); Comr b 5 May 36. Served in Aus E,
HK, Sri Lan (TC), Aus S (CS), at IHQ
(IS Resources) and in E Afr (TC).

SMITH, Wilma, (née Cherry) (Portland Citadel, OR 1937). Mrs Comr. Served in NZ, at IHQ and in USA W. Ww Comr Lawrence, pG 2009.

STRONG, Leslie J. (Kalbar, Aus E, 1965); Comr. b 5 Apr 43. BAL; and Comr **Coral** (née Scholz) (Kalbar, Aus E, 1966) m 1967; b 30 Mar 44. Served in Aus S (CS/TSWM) and Aus E (TC/TPWM).

SUNDARAM, Thota Gnana (Denduluru, Ind SE, 1963); Comr b 1 Oct 35; with Comr **Suseela** m 1955; b 16 Apr 36. Served in Ind C, Ind SE (TC/TPWO) and Ind W (TC/TPWO).

SUTHERLAND, Margaret (Sleaford, UK, 1968); Comr b 22 Jul 43. MA, ARCO. Served in Zam, UK, Zimb (CS), at IHQ (IS Afr) and at ICO (Principal).

SWINFEN, John M. (Penge, UK, 1955); Comr b 24 Jan 31. BA, Cert Ed, Chevalier de l'Ordre du Merite Exceptionnel (Congo); with Comr **Norma** (née Salmon). Served in Zimb, at ITC, in UK, E Afr (CS/THLS), Con (TC/TPWO) and at IHQ (IS/SWO Afr).

SWYERS, B. Gordon (Atlanta Temple, GA, USA S, 1959); Comr b 25 Jul 36. BBA (Georgia State); and Comr **Jacqueline** (née Alexander); b 25 Dec 29. Served in USA S and at IHQ (IS Admin/SWO SPEA).

SWYERS, Philip W. (Dallas Temple, TX, USA S, 1968); Comr b 22 Apr 44. BBA; and Comr **Patricia L.** (née Lowery) (Charlotte, NC, USA S, 1962); b 26 Aug 41. Served in USA C (CS/TSWM), USA S (CS/TSWM) and USA W (TC/TPWM).

T

TAYLOR, Margaret (née Overton) (Aylsham, UK, 1962); Comr b 13 Feb 40. Served in UK, E Afr (THLS), Pak (TPWO), and at IHQ (SWO SAsia, SWO Afr, IS Prog Resources). Ww Comr Brian E., pG 2004.

TAYLOR, Orval (Seattle Citadel, WA, USA W, 1940); Comr b 21 May 19; and Mrs Comr **Muriel** (née Upton) (Long Beach, USA W, 1937) m 1943. Served in USA W, USA S, USA N (CS/TSWO), Carib (TC/TPWO), at IHQ (IS Plan & Dev) and USA E (TC/TPWO).

THOMPSON, Arthur T. (Croydon Citadel, UK, 1961); Comr b 23 Dec 32. BSc, PhD, PGCE, Freeman of City of London; and Comr **Karen** (née Westergaard) (Camberwell, UK, 1961) m 1962. BA, PGCE. Served in Zimb, Zam, UK, NZ (CS/THLS) and at IHQ (IS Admin/IS Resources, SWO Eur).

THOMSON, Robert E. (Racine, WI, USA C, 1951); Comr b 21 Feb 28. BM (St Olaf); with Mrs Comr **Carol** (née Nielsen); BA (St Olaf). Served at USA Nat, in USA C (CS/TSWO), at IHQ (IS/SWO Am and Carib) and in USA E (TC/TPWO).

TILLSLEY, Bramwell Howard General (1993-1994) (see page 15); with Mrs General **Maud** (née Pitcher). Served in Can, at ITC, in USA S, Aus S (TPWO) and at IHQ (WSWO,WPWO).

TONDI, Roos (née Mundung) (Sonder, Indon, 1958); Comr. Served in Aus S and Indon. Ww Comr Victor, pG 2002.

TUCK, Trevor M. (Kensington Citadel, S Afr, 1969); Comr b 11 Sep 43; and Comr **Memory** (née Fortune) (Benoni, S Afr, 1965) m 1968; b 28 Apr 45. Served in PNG (TC/TPWM) and S Afr (CS/TSWM, TC/TPWM).

V

VAN DER HARST, Willem (Scheveningen, Neth, 1966); Comr b 13 Mar 44. Ww Capt Suzanne, pG 1985; and Comr **Netty** (née Kruisinga) (Amsterdam Congress Hall, Neth, 1984) m 1985; b 15 Feb 58. Served in Cze R, Neth (TC/TPWM) and E Eur (TC/TPWM).

VERWAAL, Sjoerdje (née Zoethout) (Zaandam, Neth, 1947); Mrs Comr. Served at IHQ and in Neth. Ww Comr Cornelis, pG 2002.

W

WAGHELA, Chimanbhai Somabhai (Ratanpura, Ind W, 1968); Comr b 1 Jun 47; with Comr **Rahelbai** m 1972; b 1 May 52. Served in Ind W, Ind SE (CS/TSWO), Ind E (CS/TSWO) and Ind SW (TC/TPWM).

WAHLSTRÖM, Maire (née Nyberg) (Helsinki 1, Fin, 1944); Mrs General. Served in Fin (TPWO), Swdn (TPWO), Can (TPWO) and at IHQ (WPWO). Ww General Jarl Wahlström, pG 1999.

WALTER, Alison (née Harewood) (Calgary Citadel, AB, Can, 1955); Mrs Comr. Served in Zimb, E Afr, Can, S Afr and at IHQ. Ww Comr Stanley, pG 2004.

WATERS, Margaret (née Eastland) (Niagara Falls, Can, 1953); Comr b 1 Mar 34. Served in Can and at IHQ. Ww Comr Arthur W., pG 2002.

WATILETE, Johannes G. (Bandung 3, Indon, 1963); Comr b 9 Sep 41. BA, MTh, DTh, DMin (HC); and Comr **Augustina** (née Sarman) (Bandung 3, Indon, 1962) m 1966; b 16 Aug 39. Served in Sing (GS/CHLS), Phil (CS/THLS and TC/TPWO) and Indon (TC/TPWM).

WATSON, Robert A. (Philadelphia Pioneer, PA, USA E, 1955); Comr b 11 Aug 34; and Comr **Alice** (née Irwin) (Philadelphia Pioneer, PA, USA E, 1956) m 1957. Served in USA E (CS/THLS) and at USA Nat (NC/NPWO).

WICKBERG, Eivor (née Lindberg) (Norrköping 1, Swdn, 1946); Mrs General. Ww General Erik Wickberg, pG 1996.

WILLIAMS, Harry William (Wood Green, UK, 1934); Comr b 13 Jul 13. OF, OBE, FRCS (Edin), FICS. Served in Ind W, Ind NE, Ind S (TC), NZ (TC), Aus E (TC) and at IHQ (IS Am, IS Australasia, IS Plan & Dev). Ww Mrs Comr Eileen M., pG 2002.

Y

YOHANNAN, Paulose (Kalayapuram, Ind SW, 1974); Comr b 1 Dec 45. MA (Sociol), DD, PhD; with Comr **Kunjamma** (née Jesaiah) m 1966; b 15 Jun 47. Served in Ind SW, Ind E, Ind SE (TC/TPWM) and Ind N (TC/TPWM).

YOSHIDA, Makoto (Shibuya, 1969); Comr b 7 Dec 45. BSc (Engin); and Comr **Kaoru** (née Imamura) (Omori, 1971) m 1974; b 13 Jan 45. Served in Jpn (CS/TSWM, TC/TPWM) and at IHQ (IS/ZSWM SPEA).

Retirements from Active Service

AUSTRALIA EASTERN

Capt Ron Anderson from Chaplain, Rural Fire Service, NSW on 18 Sep 2011

Capt Carol Anderson from Family Support Officer, Rural Fire Service, NSW on 18 Sep 2011

Maj Bruce Hodges from Chaplain for Retired Officers on 31 Dec 2011

Capt Trevor Friend from Red Shield Defence Services on 31 Dec 2011

Maj Marina Randall from Chaplain, Employment Plus, NSW on 21 Jan 2012

Lt-Col John Hodge from Booth College (Principal) on 31 Jan 2012

Lt-Col Pamela Hodge from THQ on 31 Jan 2012

Maj Diane Maxwell from DHQ, Sydney East and Illawara on 26 Feb 2012

Capt Keith Atkinson from Grafton, NSW on 1 Mar 2012

Maj Heather Gill from Papua New Guinea on 1 Mar 2012

Maj Mavis Humphreys from Booth College on 30 Mar 2012

Maj Colin Hopper from Brisbane, Qld on 31 Mar 2012

Majs William and Judy Hutley from Nambour, Qld on 1 Apr 2012

AUSTRALIA SOUTHERN

Capt Colin Abram from Kalgoorlie, W Aus on 11 Jan 2012

Majs Samuel and Evelyn Hancock from Playford, S Aus on 11 Jan 2012

Maj Cilla Bone from THQ on 1 Feb 2012

Capt Christine Haig from Barrington Lodge, Tas on 1 Feb 2012

Maj Dorothy Poke from Kardinia Network, W Vic on 1 Feb 2012

Lt-Cols Frank and Yvonne Daniels from THQ and Melbourne Central Division on 1 May 2012

Maj Hubert Hicks from Centennial Court, on 1 May 2012

Maj Dennis McMillin from Chaplain, Melbourne Magistrates' Court on 1 Jul 2012

Maj Peter Power from W Aus Division on 1 Jul 2012

BRAZIL

Majs Celso Alves and Margaret England Batista from Natal on 31 Dec 2011

CANADA AND BERMUDA

Maj Margaret Bailey from Chilliwack, BC on 1 Feb 2012

Capts Inhee and Heather Cheon from Toronto on 1 Apr 2012

Majs Douglas and Elizabeth Lewis from Toronto on 1 Jul 2012

Majs Eric and Donna Bond from Winnipeg, MAN on 1 Jul 2012

Majs Ivan and Pauline Budgell from Whitby on 1 Jul 2012

Majs Larry and Phyllis Fudge from Triton Brighton, NL on 1 Jul 2012

Maj Katie Bungay from St John's, NL on 1 Jul 2012

Maj Richard Mouland from Point Leamington, NL on 1 Jul 2012

Maj Agnes MacDonald from Ottawa on 1 Jul 2012

Maj Barbara Champ from Toronto on 1 Aug 2012

Majs Harold and Christine Aitkenhead from Calgary, AB on 1 Sep 2012

Majs Max and Doreen Sturge from Toronto on 1 Nov 2012

CARIBBEAN

Lt-Col Raphael Mason from THQ on 7 Jul 2012

Majs Keith and Molvie Graham from THQ on 12 Jul 2012

Majs Maxene and Avis Jean Louis from Jamaica Eastern Division on 12 Jul 2012

Maj Sheila Booth from Jamaica Eastern Division on 12 Jul 2012

CONGO (BRAZZAVILLE)

Majs Jerome and Jeanne Nzita from Louingui Division on 30 Oct 2011

FINLAND AND ESTONIA

Maj Paulo Franke from Hämeenlinna on 1 Nov 2011

Maj Pirjo Laaksonen from Helsinki on 1 Nov 2011

Maj Antero Puotiniemi from Helsinki on 1 Dec 2011

FRANCE AND BELGIUM

Majs Jean Michel and Danièle Garcia Abelan from Valence on 1 Nov 2011

Maj Anne Rose Muller Boenle from THQ on 1 May 2012

Retirements from Active Service

Majs Maurice and Ariane Alègre Mollet from Dieppe on 1 Jul 2012

Maj Geneviève Caudron Chanon from Belfort on 1 Jul 2012

HONG KONG AND MACAU

Maj Annette Choi Ling Li from Mongkok on 1 Nov 2011

INDIA CENTRAL

Maj E. Jayamma from EBH, Nidubrolu on 6 June 2011

Comr P. Rajakumari from India Central THQ (TC) on 30 Aug 2011

Majs Chelli Samuel and Esther Rani from Eluru on 31 Aug 2011

Majs G.V. Ratnam and G. Rajakumari from Hyderabad DHQ on 30 Apr 2012

Majs N. Jeevaratnam and N. Nireekshana Kumari from Bapatla on 1 May 2012

Majs V. Prabhudas and V. Ratnakumari from Nalgonda on 1 May 2012

NDIA EASTERN

Majs Thankiamlova and Vanrammawii on 26 Feb 2012

Lt-Cols Ralte Thanhlira and Hluando Thantluangi on 29 Feb 2012

Majs Ralte Sangthangdula and Ralte Malsawmi on 1 Jul 2012

INDIA NORTHERN

Lt-Cols Paul and Anandiben Christian from THQ (CS/TSWM) on 30 Sep 2011

Majs Gian and Salima Masih from Chandigarh DHQ on 1 Oct 2011

Majs Peter and Dharmi Masih from Mukerian DHQ on 1 Nov 2011

Majs Tarsem and Mohinder Masih from Amritsar on 1 May 2012

Majs Shaukat and Vilot Masih from Batala on 1 May 2012

Majs Umed and Sheela Masih from Bareilly on 1 May 2012

Majs Ajit and Bimla Masih from Pathankot on 1 May 2012

Majs Peter and Rashidan Masih from Amritsar on 1 May 2012

INDIA SOUTH EASTERN

Maj S. Esther Rani from CBH, Nagercoil on 31 Dec 2011

Majs S. Pauliah and Grace from Dennispuram on 30 Apr 2012

Majs M. Thairiyam and Perinbam from Atchankulam on 30 Apr 2012

Maj R. Kannimariyal from CBH, Nagercoil on 30 Apr 2012

Maj A. Joicebai from Girls' Home, Marthandam on 1 May 2012

Maj A. Asirbai from CBH, Nagercoil on 31 May 2012

Maj M. Chellam from Tucker Girls' Home, Nagercoil on 31 May 2012

Majs S. James and Nesabai from Tuticorin District on 31 May 2012

INDIA SOUTH WESTERN

Maj Chinnamma Vijayadas on 1 Jun 2011

Majs J. Samuel and Moni on 1 Nov 2011

Maj D. Daisy Gnanaprasad on 31 Dec 2011

Majs P.K. Philip and M. Rachel Philip on 31 Dec 2011

Majs L. Mathew and S. Mary Mathew on 31 Dec 2011

Majs P.J. Yohannan and O.J. Annamma Yohannan on 31 Dec 2011

Aux-Capts K.M. John and Rachel John on 1 Feb 2012

Majs Lazer Mathew and Mariamma Mathew on 1 May 2012

INDIA WESTERN

Majs Gaikwad Benjamin Yacob and Sudina Benjamin from THQ on 1 Oct 2011

Maj Phulen W. Macwan from EBH, Ahmednagar on 1 Oct 2011

Majs Kasbe Devdan and Kasbe Maria from Ahmednagar DHQ on 29 Feb 2012

Maj Shardaben Maganlal from Vadodara School on 1 May 2012

Maj Jayanti William from Joyland Home, Anand on 1 May 2012

Maj Emmanuel Paul from Emery Hospital, Anand on 1 May 2012

Maj Asha Kamble from EBH, Ahmednagar on 1 May 2012

Majs P.V. Macwan and Salomi P. Macwan from Emery Hospital, Anand on 1 Jun 2012

INDONESIA

Maj Soeparmin from Semarang on 1 Jul 2011

Majs Kaleb and Yeni Lindjaua from Joonoge on 1 Jul 2012

Majs Aman and Elsye Mantaely from Pantolobete on 1 Jul 2011

Comrs Roy and Arda Frans from Jakarta (IHQ UN reps) on 31 Jul 2011

Retirements from Active Service

Majs Albert and Dientje Tawaang from Semarang on 1 Sep 2011

Majs Habil and Hana Taringolu from Kulawi on 1 Oct 2011

Maj Egnius Sango from Manusi Ampera on 1 Jul 2012

Maj Edith Singara from Bandung on 1 Jul 2012

Majs Jonathan and Carolina Kudje from Sibowi on 1 Jul 2012

JAPAN

Lt-Cols Naoshi and Seiko Hiramoto from THQ (CS/TSWM) on 31 Oct 2011

Maj Ayako Kawaguchi from Hamamatsu on 28 Mar 2012

Maj Kimiko Tateishi from Nishinari on 28 Mar 2012

Maj Yasuo Soga from Kyoto on 31 Mar 2012

KENYA EAST

Majs Daniel and Tabitha Nziu from Itetani on 8 Dec 2011

Majs Jairus and Jannate Njagi from Mutuyu on 8 Dec 2011

KENYA WEST

Majs Isaac and Alice Barechi from Saboti on 30 Jun 2011

KOREA

Maj Park, Nai-hoon and Maj Kil, Soon-boon from Choong Chung DHQ on 31 Oct 2011

Lt-Col Yang, Tae-soo and Lt-Col Chun, Ok-kyung from Seoul DHQ on 29 Feb 2012

Maj Kwon, Sung-dal and Maj Kim, Moon-ok from Choong Saw DHQ on 30 Apr 2012

LATIN AMERICA NORTH

Capts Gabino and Caridad Rodríguez from Cuba on 29 Dec 2011

MEXICO

Majs Daniel and Teresa Guerra from Monterrey on 31 Dec 2011

Majs Manuel and Carmen Padilla from Guadalajara on 31 Jan 2012

Maj Luis Flores from Alvarado on 31 Mar 2012

Majs Marcos and Lucía Villarreal from Mexico City on 30 Jun 2012

Capts Erasmo and Ofelia Vargas from Tijuana on 30 Jun 2012

THE NETHERLANDS AND CZECH REPUBLIC

Maj Gerben Barkmeijer from Gouda on 1 Aug 2011

Maj Joke Valster from Ede on 1 Sep 2011

Lt-Col Ine Voorham from THQ on 2 Sep 2011

Maj Corrie Jongejans from CWZW, Central Region on 4 Oct 2011

Lt- Col Jaap Kanis from THQ on 12 Oct 2011

Maj Mieke Schiedon from Valleistreek on 1 Jan 2012

Maj Johan Staal from Hilversum on 14 March 2012

Maj Diny Veenendaal from Zeist on 3 May 2012

Maj Wil van Pelt from CWZW, Flevoland Region on 4 May 2012

Lt-Col Theo Wolterink from THQ on 16 Jun 2012

NEW ZEALAND, FIJI AND TONGA

Majs Ray and Jocelyn Gordon from Porirua on 30 Sep 2011

Maj Darrell Leque from Christchurch on 31 Oct 2011

Lt-Col Ethne Flintoff from Bangladesh on 30 Nov 2011

Maj Raewyn Chisholm from Levin on 12 Jan 2012

Majs Malcolm and Laurel Herring from Lower Hutt on 12 Jan 2012

Majs Mata'afa and Kalo Fohe from Otahuhu on 31 Jan 2012

Majs Campbell and Gay Roberts from THQ on 29 Feb 2012

Comrs David and Grace Bringans from Mexico (TC/TPWM) on 30 Jun 2012

NIGERIA

Majs Christian and Felicia Amasiatu on 31 Dec 2011

Majs Chika B. and Virginia Ezekwere on 31 Jan 2012

Maj Ekereobong Udoh on 31 May 2012

Majs Edwin and Agnes Okoruogo on 31 Jul 2012

Maj Ime Udongwo on 31 Jul 2012

Majs Luke and Victoria Ezennaka on 31 Aug 2012

Majs Stephen and Edi Uzoho on 30 Sep 2012

NORWAY, ICELAND AND THE FÆROES

Maj Inger Hille Ytterdahl from THQ on 31 Dec 2011

Maj Ann Elise Breivik from Social Services on 30 Jun 2012

Maj Lillian Pettersen from DHQ on 30 Jun 2012

Retirements from Active Service

PAKISTAN
Maj Musaraf Walter from Jaranwala DHQ on
31 Mar 2012
Majs Jacob Banta Ram and Angelina Jacob
from Ghung on 31 Mar 2012
Majs Ayub John and Parveen Ayub from
Gujjar on 31 Mar 2012

PAPUA NEW GUINEA
Majs Ian and Dana Zaio from Sogeri on
19 Nov 2011
Majs Steven and Eva'aso Nehaya from
North Eastern DHQ on 10 Dec 2011
Aux-Capts Manki and Yaferi Oyena from
Lembina on 18 Dec 2011
Majs Areka and Joe Nato from THQ on
1 Apr 2012

SINGAPORE, MALAYSIA AND MYANMAR
Lt-Cols Tan, Thean Seng and Loo, Lay Saik
on 31 Jul 2012

SOUTH AMERICA WEST
Majs Franklin and Gladys Abasto from
Temuco, Chile on 1 Mar 2012
Maj Dalia Almendras from THQ on
1 Mar 2012

SOUTHERN AFRICA
Majs Jeffry and Leah Ngwane on
3 Jul 2011
Lt-Cols Barry and Anja Schwartz on
29 Nov 2011
Maj Thandi Nxumalo on 31 Dec 2011
Maj Margaret Strydom on 31 Dec 2011
Maj Agnes Mkhasibe on 31 Dec 2011
Cols Hezekiel and Mirriam Mavundla from
THQ (CS/TPWM) on 31 Jan 2012

SRI LANKA
Maj Shelton P. and Grace Hemalatha
Fernando from Southern Section on
27 Oct 2011
Maj K.R.T. Kumarasinghe from Matale on
19 Nov 2011
Maj Shanthimala R. Kumarasinghe from
Matale on 19 Nov 2011

SWEDEN AND LATVIA
Maj Anita Ahlström from THQ on
30 Sep 2011
Maj Marie Hallsten from Kumla on
31 Oct 2011
Maj Per Åke Ekman from Sundbyberg on
1 May 2012

SWITZERLAND, AUSTRIA AND HUNGARY
Maj Elisabeth Moser from Langnau on
30 Apr 2012
Maj Vreni Keller from Bern DHQ on
30 Apr 2012
Maj Ruth Vaterlaus from THQ on
31 May 2012
Maj Vreni Eggenberger from Ost-Division
DHQ on 30 Jun 2012
Maj Samuel Winkler from THQ on
31 Aug 2012
Maj Pierre Alain Droz from THQ on
30 Sep 2012

UNITED KINGDOM WITH THE REPUBLIC OF IRELAND
Maj Carol Ainsworth from THQ on
1 Sep 2011
Maj Catherine Knott from Lochgelly on
1 Sep 2011
Maj David Jepson from Christchurch on
1 Oct 2011
Maj Ann Mahy from East Midlands DHQ on
1 Oct 2011
Maj Margaret Wicker from THQ on
1 Oct 2011
Maj Gillian Andrews from Ealing on 1 Nov 2011
Maj Elizabeth Ackroyd from Heathrow
Airport Chaplaincy on 1 Nov 2011
Maj Mary Bullock from Jarrett Community
Project SSC on 1 Nov 2011
Maj Ralph Chambers from Bury St Edmunds
on 1 Nov 2011
Maj Alan Green from South and Mid Wales
DHQ on 1 Nov 2011
Capt Jacqueline Parker from Eccles on
1 Nov 2011
Maj Henry Silcock from Chaplain, Bramwell
House Lifehouse on 1 Nov 2011
Maj Enid Leeder from Sunbury Court
Conference Centre on 1 Dec 2011
Maj David Pickard from Administrator,
Hopetown Lifehouse SSC on 1 Dec 2011
Lt-Col Michael Williams from THQ on
1 Jan 2012
Maj Olga Rainford from THQ on 1 Feb 2012
Maj Sylvia Walters from Glasgow West on
1 Feb 2012
Maj Howard Webber from THQ on
1 Feb 2012
Maj Richard Cook from Rothwell on
1 Mar 2012
Majs David and Susan Hall from Wimbledon
on 1 Mar 2012

Retirements from Active Service

Majs Robert and Zena Peppiatt from Nottingham William Booth Memorial Halls on 1 Apr 2012

Comrs John and Elizabeth Matear from THQ (TC/TPWM) on 1 May 2012

Majs Edward and Freda Benneyworth from Derby Central on 1 Jun 2012

Lt-Col David Burrows from IHQ on 1 Jun 2012

Maj Colin Edwin from Chaplain, Eden Villa Lifehouse, Leamington Spa and Lincoln Street Lifehouse, Coventry on 1 Jun 2012

Majs Ian and Irene Kerrison from Maltby on 1 Jun 2012

Maj Roy Milner from Booth House, Swindon on 1 Jun 2012

Maj Michael Sebbage from THQ on 1 Jun 2012

Maj John Thompson from Central South DHQ on 1 Jun 2012

Maj Angela Irving from THQ on 1 Jul 2012

Majs David and Marian Lewis from South Shields on 1 Jul 2012

Majs Brian and Janis Lowndes from West Cornforth on 1 Jul 2012

Majs Denise and Robert Barham-Hall from Driffield ORC on 1 Aug 2012

Maj Sheila Biddle from Alnwick and Chaplain, Cedar House on 1 Aug 2012

Maj Glenis Bonsell from Darlaston and Chaplain, Shepherds Green House on 1 Aug 2012

Maj Wendy Chambers from Bury St Edmunds on 1 Aug 2012

Maj Antony Clifton from Swadlincote on 1 Aug 2012

Maj Gwen Cox from Gatwick Airport Chaplaincy on 1 Aug 2012

Maj Robert Davies from Newbiggin by the Sea on 1 Aug 2012

Maj Heather Durrant from Bourne on 1 Aug 2012

Majs Brenda and John Irvine from King's Lynn on 1 Aug 2012

Maj Graham Kinsley from THQ on 1 Aug 2012

Majs Iris and Peter Leech from Worthing and WBC on 1 Aug 2012

Maj Carol Lockhart from Newquay on 1 Aug 2012

Capt Harry McMillan from Enniskillen on 1 Aug 2012

Maj Peter Mylechreest from Boscombe on 1 Aug 2012

Majs Georgina and Sidney Pinches from Haverhill on 1 Aug 2012

Maj Margaret Prescott from Lockerbie on 1 Aug 2012

Majs Robert and Violet Smart from Wisbech on 1 Aug 2012

Maj Sylvia Watts from Swindon Citadel on 1 Aug 2012

Maj Barry Willson from Lowestoft Citadel on 1 Aug 2012

USA CENTRAL

Maj Shirley Espersen from NHQ on 1 Oct 2011

Majs Manuel and JoAnn Madrid from Northern DHQ on 1 Oct 2011

Maj Marie Ellsworth from THQ on 1 Dec 2011

Majs Geoffrey and Marian Allan from THQ on 1 Mar 2012

Maj Phyllis Blinks from Kansas and Western Missouri DHQ on 1 Jul 2012

Maj Kathleen Hovelman from CFOT on 1 Jul 2012

Maj Gloria Stepke from THQ on 1 Jul 2012

Majs John and Margaret Crampton from LaPorte, IN on 1 Aug 2012

Majs Richard and Judy Forney from Grandview, MO on 1 Aug 2012

Majs Maxim and Betty Grindle from Holland, MI on 1 Aug 2012

Majs James and Mary Hoskin from THQ on 1 Aug 2012

USA EASTERN

Maj Margaret Allen from Pittsburgh, PA ARC on 1 Oct 2011

Majs Edward and Darlene Russell from THQ on 1 Oct 2011

Majs Edward and Judi Pritchard from New Castle, PA on 1 Nov 2011

Maj Betty Sharp from THQ on 1 Nov 2011

Majs Edward and Florence Forster from NHQ on 1 Dec 2011

Maj Kathleen Bearcroft from THQ on 1 Feb 2012

Majs Clinton E. and Marjorie Foster from Carnegie, PA DHQ on 1 Feb 2012

Majs Ernest and Mary Jane Koenemund from THQ on 1 Feb 2012

Majs Paul and Evelyn Merriam from THQ on 1 Feb 2012

Lt-Cols Gary and Pearl Asperschlager from THQ on 1 May 2012

Majs Richard A. and Olivia Gulley from Cincinnati, OH DHQ on 1 May 2012

Majs James J. and Mary Smith from Oneonta, NY on 1 May 2012

Majs Philip E. and Constance DeMichael from Wilmington, DE on 1 Jun 2012

Majs John R. and Kathleen Foster from Columbus, OH on 30 Jun 2012

Comrs Larry and Gillian Bosh from IHQ (IS/ZSWM for the Americas) on 1 Jul 2012

Maj Beatrice E. Connell from Scranton, PA on 1 Aug 2012

Maj Sandra Shutt from THQ on 1 Aug 2012

Majs Ronald A. and Donna Wendt from THQ on 1 Aug 2012

Maj Florence M. Townsend from THQ on 1 Sep 2012

USA SOUTHERN

Capts Bobby and Sandy Mullins from Huntington, WV on 1 Sep 2011

Capts Gary and Patricia Steward from FLA DHQ on 1 Sep 2011

Maj Denny Hewitt from FLA DHQ on 1 Nov 2011

Maj Elda Flores from NCV DHQ on 1 Nov 2011

Maj Joyce Bergen from Clarksville, TN on 7 December 2011

Majs William and Rita Sue Cundiff from Doraville, GA on 1 Jan 2012

Majs Michael and Gloria Reagan from THQ on 1 Jan 2012

Maj Nancy Jean Reyes from San Antonio, TX on 18 Jan 2012

Majs Ernest and Starr Branscum from Garland, TX on 1 Apr 2012

Maj Cynthia Wise from Florence, SC on 1 Jun 2012

Majs Francisco and Carolyn Zuniga from West Volusia County, FL on 1 Jul 2012

Capts Cedric and Evelyn Middleton from Ft Worth, TX on 1 Jul 2012

Maj Hilda Howell from THQ on 1 Aug 2012

USA WESTERN

Maj Charleen Bradley from Long Beach, CA on 1 Oct 2011

Majs Peter and Estelle Clack from Phoenix, AZ on 1 Oct 2011

Majs Samuel and Carol Southard from Happy Valley, OR on 1 Dec 2011

Majs Douglas and Leslie Peacock from Long Beach, CA on 1 Jan 2012

Maj Lanell Washington from Seattle, WA on 1 Feb 2012

Majs Hendrik and Susan Aalders from Denver, CO on 1 Jul 2012

Majs George W. and Julie Beauchamp from Oakland, CA on 1 Jul 2012

Lt-Col Eda Hokom from Happy Valley, OR on 1 Jul 2012

Majs Daniel and Verna Hughes from El Sobrante, CA on 1 Jul 2012

Majs Maynard F. and Kathleen Sargent from Seattle, WA on 1 Jul 2012

Maj Carolyn F. Storey from Fresno, CA on 1 Sep 2012

ZAMBIA

Lt-Cols Bislon and Melody Hanunka from THQ (CS/Asst TPWM) in Jun 2011

Majs Berrington and Christine Mbiri on 6 Nov 2011

Majs Willy and Annah Bankombo on 13 Nov 2011

ZIMBABWE

Maj Michael Bridge on 25 Sep 2011

WORDS OF LIFE

THE Salvation Army's international Bible reading plan, *Words of Life*, is an invaluable aid to daily devotional study. The readings cover a wide selection of Scripture and the comments give opportunity to build a lasting library for further study and reflection. Points for prayer and praise are a further enrichment to personal devotion. Major Beverly Ivany (Canada and Bermuda Territory) continues her term as writer of *Words of Life* with the January–April 2013 edition. Subscriptions are available through Salvationist Publishing and Supplies, UK Territory.

Promotions to Glory

AUSTRALIA EASTERN
Maj Cec Hall on 23 Sep 2011
Mrs Capt Betty Fullerton on 23 Oct 2011
Maj Mervyn Hopper on 26 Oct 2011
Col Bram Lucas on 1 Nov 2011
Maj Lila Pearse on 11 Nov 2011
Envoy Kay Henderson on 27 Nov 2011
Maj Jessie Rablin on 20 Dec 2011
Maj Allan Armstrong on 27 Dec 2011
Maj Hazel Coker on 11 Feb 2012
Aux-Capt Isabel Tite on 28 Mar 2012
Maj Rodney Towerton on 30 Mar 2012
Lt-Col Peggy Stephens on 17 Apr 2012

AUSTRALIA SOUTHERN
Brig Isabel Kowalick on 3 Jul 2011
Lt-Col Lorna Clee on 27 Jul 2011
Maj Marjorie Bywaters on 13 Oct 2011
Lt-Col Garnet Clee on 19 Dec 2011
Lt-Col Walter Hull on 19 Jan 2012
Maj Norma Betty Cassidy on 12 Feb 2012
Maj Elizabeth Gowlett on 10 Mar 2012
Maj June Webb on 15 Mar 2012
Maj Joyce Guy on 23 Mar 2012
Maj Allan Parish on 11 Apr 2012
Maj Ivy Ruth Bennett on 30 Apr 2012
Maj Kenneth Peeke on 12 May 2012
Maj Phyllis Duck on 9 Jul 2012
Maj Joy Daddy (A) from Moe on 20 Jul 2012
Maj Jean Langmead on 27 Jul 2012

BRAZIL
Maj Adelaide Campos on 1 Jan 2012

CANADA AND BERMUDA
Mrs Comr Gladys Pindred on
  6 Jun 2011.
Maj David Goulding on 8 Jun 2011
Brig Thomas Smith on 10 Jul 2011
Maj Charles Smith on 2 Aug 2011
Maj Grace Williams on 12 Aug 2011
Mrs Brig Gertrude Frayn on 8 Sep 2011
Lt-Col Helen Morrison on 25 Sep 2011
Capt William Udell on 6 Oct 2011
Maj Lawrence Spragg on 2 Nov 2011
Lt-Col Ellen Ratcliffe on 6 Nov 2011
Maj Shirley Pond on 7 Nov 2011
Capt Mrs Hazel Townsend on 21 Nov 2011
Col Joyce Tutton on 6 Dec 2011
Maj Beryl Price on 18 Dec 2011

Col Calvin Ivany on 19 Dec 2011
Aux-Capt Douglas Knee on 29 Jan 2012
Maj Lynne Sullivan on 1 Feb 2012
Lt-Col George Oystryk on 8 Feb 2012
Maj Joanne Guenther on 10 Feb 2012
Col Earl Robinson on 11 Feb 2012
Maj Solomon Jewer on 12 Feb 2012
Capt Mary Wray on 1 Mar 2012
Lt-Col Beulah Craig on 12 Mar 2012
Capt John Fredborg on 1 Apr 2012
Lt-Col Raymond Homewood on 26 Apr 2012
Maj Allan Hicks on 30 Apr 2012
Brig Gordon Holmes on 7 May 2012
Maj Edward Hayden (A) from Strathroy,
  Ontario on 8 May 2012
Maj Eric Brown on 15 May 2012
Maj Douglas Burry on 28 May 2012
Maj Naomi Duke on 1 Jun 2012

CARIBBEAN
Maj Frances Batson on 15 Sep 2011
Maj Thelma John on 17 Dec 2011
Col Sybil Morris on 7 Mar 2012
Maj Clifton Anglin on 9 Mar 2012
Maj Margaret Emmanuel on 3 Jun 2012

DEMOCRATIC REPUBLIC OF CONGO
Capt Antoine Mbuyu (A) from Rwashi Corps
  on 18 Nov 2011
Capt Abraham Nani Wambote (A) from
  Makai II Corps on 5 Apr 2012

EASTERN EUROPE
Capt Boris Shulyansky (A) from Taganka
  Corps, Moscow on 7 Nov 2011

FINLAND AND ESTONIA
Maj Irene Pankka on 14 Nov 2011
Maj Irene Nieminen on 5 Mar 2012
Maj Maijaliisa Manninen on 26 May 2012
Maj Maiju Mäkinen on 30 Jul 2012

FRANCE AND BELGIUM
Maj Marguerite Lautier on 27 Sept 2011
Col Raymond Yarde on 1 Nov 2011
Lt-Col Juliette Vanderkham-Bonhotel
  (Belgium) on 12 Dec 2011
Lt-Col Lucienne Chatelain on 20 Jan 2012
Maj Julie Allard on 4 May 2012
Maj Mireille Bordas on 8 May 2012

GERMANY AND LITHUANIA
Lt-Col Eva-Maria Alisch on 9 Sep 2011
Maj Willi Kothe on 2 Jan 2012
Maj Liselotte Gross on 30 Apr 2012

GHANA
Maj Margaret Bannor on 18 Oct 2011
Capt Grace Abremkkaw on 23 Oct 2011
Aux-Capt Samuel Dadzie on 8 Nov 2011
Envoy Ernestina Abagna on 11 Nov 2011
Lt-Col Moses Obiri on 30 Jan 2012
Maj Stephen Borbor on 12 Mar 2012

INDIA CENTRAL
Maj B. Lilliamma on 29 Apr 2011
Maj B. Gurupadam on 6 Aug 2011
Lt-Col P. Zachariah on 26 Aug 2011
Lt-Col R. Aseervadam on 1 Sep 2011
Maj Mathangi Ermia (A) from Eluru on
    24 Sep 2011
Maj K. Surya Rao on 30 Sep 2011
Maj K. Santhoshamma on 30 Sep 2011
Maj G. Padma (A) from Stuartpuram
    on 13 Nov 2011
Maj K. Evabayamma on 24 Nov 2011
Maj P. Suvarna Kumari on 9 Jan 2012
Maj Vimala Ratnam on 1 Apr 2012
Maj B. Sanjeevarao on 2 May 2012
Maj Chellia Mariyamma on 17 May 2012
Maj Babuji Rao (A) from Guntur on
    29 May 2012

INDIA EASTERN
Maj Kamsavunga on 1 Jun 2011
Col Parte Sawichhunga OF on 3 Jun 2012

INDIA NORTHERN
Maj Zeenath Sardar Masih on 9 Jan 2012
Maj Nasreen Kaleb Masih (A) from Lehal
    Corps, Gurdaspur on 9 Jan 2012
Maj Lazar Masih (A) from William Booth
    School, Bareilly on 28 Mar 2012
Maj Dalbir Masih (A) from Beas DHQ on
    15 Aug 2012

INDIA SOUTH EASTERN
Lt-Col Elisie Selvaraj on 15 Sep 2011
Maj Joseph on 8 Dec 2011
Brig Nesammal Asirvatham on 25 Dec 2011
Maj D.D. Abel on 5 Jan 2012
Lt-Col Sugumary Sundaram on 25 Feb 2012
Maj S. Murial Joice (A) from CB Hospital,
    Nagercoil on 26 Mar 2012

Maj Kamalam Yesudhas on 20 Apr 2012
Maj Rosammal Sundaram on 22 Apr 2012
Maj Leyal Yesuretnam on 27 Apr 2012
Maj Jebamony Daniel on 10 May 2012
Capt Santham Asirvatham on 22 May 2012
Maj M. Yesudhas on 28 May 2012
Lt-Col A. Ayyapillai on 3 Jun 2012
Maj Packiam Muthuraj on 22 Jun 2012
Maj V. Manuel on 26 Jun 2012

INDIA SOUTH WESTERN
Maj Jacob Gnanaprasad (A) on 25 Aug 2011
Maj Maj D. Thankayyan on 2 Oct 2011
Maj Y. Yesumathy (A) on 15 Oct 2011
Lt-Col P.C. Jacob on 2 Jan 2012
Maj K.J. Mathai on 11 Jan 2012
Maj S. Devanesam on 29 Jan 2012
Maj P.C. Annamma Mathai on 8 May 2012

INDIA WESTERN
Maj Swarthabai D. Shendge on 19 Feb 2012
Capt Jolif Paul (A) from Riyapura Ahmedabad
    Corps on 3 Mar 2012
Maj Petrus Ghadge on 17 Mar 2012
Capt Khima Damor (A) from Abhalod Corps
    on 4 Apr 2012
Maj Yadhav Muktikar on 23 Apr 2012
Brig Dinaben Ashirwad on 30 Apr 2012

INDONESIA
Maj Suparmi Soeparmin (A) on
    18 Jun 2011
Maj Matsari Utniel on 17 Aug 2011
Maj Rebekka Benjamin on 21 Nov 2011
Maj Pfitzer Sango (A) on 17 Apr 2012
Maj Andrianus Panie (A) on 21 Apr 2012

JAPAN
Maj Toru Asaka on 17 Oct 2011
Maj Yoshitatsu Iizuka on 13 Jan 2012
Brig Hokichi Yamakawa on 13 Mar 2012
Maj Ritsuko Imamura on 4 Apr 2012

KENYA EAST
Maj Pilisca Kibuga on 30 Oct 2011
Maj Jane Murungi on 13 Dec 2011
Maj Joseph Nako on 18 Apr 2012
Comr Joshua Ngugi OF on 2 May 2012

KENYA WEST
Maj Haron Wangila on 8 Dec 2011
Maj Solomon Lihanda (A) from Mukhombe
    on 26 Jan 2012

Maj Isaac Juma Musieni (A) from Saosi Corps on 6 Feb 2012
Maj Peter Musamili Wakhungu (A) from Matunda Corps on 5 May 2012

KOREA
Maj Lee, Wohl-ae on 17 Mar 2012
Maj Hong, Bong-yoo on 2 Jun 2012
Maj Lee, Jung-hoon on 17 Aug 2012

LATIN AMERICA NORTH
Maj Shirla Gonsalves on 10 Jun 2012

MEXICO
Capt David Yépez Delgado on 26 Nov 2011
Maj José Luis López Esparza on 13 Feb 2012

THE NETHERLANDS AND CZECH REPUBLIC
Brig Christina Walraven on 15 Jun 2011
Brig Christina Dekker on 8 Jul 2011
Lt-Col Hendrika Noorlander on 26 Sep 2011
Maj Johannes van Doorn on 23 Apr 2012

NEW ZEALAND, FIJI AND TONGA
Lt-Col Melvin Taylor on 10 Jan 2012
Maj Dean Fairhurst (A) from Oamaru Corps on 19 Feb 2012
Maj Dorothy Lord on 22 Feb 2012
Lt-Col Moira Wright on 7 Mar 2012
Brig Enid Parsons on 12 Mar 2012
Brig Olive Sampson on 14 Mar 2012
Maj Claude Williams on 22 Mar 2012
Brig Alice Adams on 2 Apr 2012
Capt Lindsay West on 12 Apr 2012
Maj Joan Hutson on 25 May 2012

NIGERIA
Maj Rachel Omole on 22 Sep 2011
Maj Etim Udoh on 16 Nov 2011
Lt-Col Martins Ebiwonjumi on 27 Dec 2011
Maj Grace Akpaah on 2 Jan 2012
Maj Benson Erhunmwunsee on 10 Mar 2012

NORWAY, ICELAND AND THE FÆROES
Maj Kjell Arnfinn Nilsen on 29 Sep 2011
Maj Inga Kinserdal on 26 Oct 2011
Lt-Col Ragnhild Hagen on 5 Nov 2011
Maj Anlaug Tellefsen on 24 Nov 2011
Capt Kirsten Andersen on 9 Dec 2011
Lt-Col Astrid Hansen on 5 Jan 2012
Maj Gerd Mortensen Lindstad on 19 Feb 2012
Maj Ada Cecilie Vang on 5 Mar 2012
Maj Kristine Sandaaker on 2 Apr 2012

Maj Margrethe Fjelde on 2 Jun 2012
Comr Karsten A Solhaug on 26 Aug 2012

PAKISTAN
Maj John Iqbal on 17 Sep 2011
Maj Walter Emmanuel (A) from Jaranwala DHQ on 6 Dec 2011
Maj Parveen Yousaf (A) from Islamabad on 24 Apr 2012
Maj Martha David on 23 May 2012
Maj Hanzal Masih on 16 Jun 2012
Brig Barkat Masih on 17 Jul 2012
Maj Majidan Bashir on 17 Jul 2012

PAPUA NEW GUINEA
Capt Maino Morea (A) from THQ on 26 Nov 2011

SOUTH AMERICA WEST
Maj Ramiro Ponce (A) from DHQ and Men's Home, La Paz, Bolivia on 7 Apr 2012
Maj Irmas Salinas on 9 Jun 2012.
Maj Luz Nuñez (A) from Peru DHQ on 24 Jul 2012
Lt-Col Edelmira Miranda de Lalut on 16 Sep 2012

SRI LANKA
Maj P.V. Rupasinghe (A) from Kotte Corps on 6 Jun 2012

SWEDEN AND LATVIA
Brig Mildred Andersson on 22 Jul 2011
Envoy Irma Jerdung on 22 Jul 2011
Envoy Karl-Erik Sand on 23 Jul 2011
Lt-Col Inger Lundin on 29 Jul 2011
Maj Ulla Pettersson on 29 Jul 2011
Brig Malte Persson on 30 Jul 2011
Lt-Col Ann-Mari Person on 23 Aug 2011
Envoy Alva Jönebro on 15 Oct 2011
Capt Kerstin Nilsson on 1 Feb 2012
Maj Kenneth Karlsson (A) from THQ on 5 Apr 2012
Mrs Col Carin Larsson on 25 Apr 2012

SWITZERLAND, AUSTRIA AND HUNGARY
Maj Alice Dill on 2 Mar 2011
Brig Gertrud Schudel on 17 Jun 2011
Comr Verena Egger-Halbenleib on 2 Aug 2011
Brig Rosa Künzib on 24 Aug 2011
Col Germaine Fivaz on 25 Dec 2011
Maj Erwin Saugy on 19 Jan 2012

Maj **Rosa Zünd** on 2 Apr 2012
Maj **Oscar Iselin** on 1 May 2012
Maj **Anne-Marie Dorthe** on 27 May 2012
Maj **Liliane Poget** on 30 May 2012

UNITED KINGDOM WITH THE REPUBLIC OF IRELAND

Mrs Brig **Annie Thompson** on 5 May 2011
Maj **George Thomas** on 6 May 2011
Maj **Colin Johnson** on 9 May 2011
Maj **Gordon Howard** on 15 May 2011
Mrs Maj **Sarah Sunter** on 23 May 2011
Maj **Roberta Fraser** on 4 Jun 2011
Mrs Maj **Mary Holliday** on 13 Jun 2011
Brig Mrs **Elizabeth Groves** on 15 Jun 2011
Maj **Dennis Padfield** on 18 Jun 2011
Capt **Edith Wilkins** on 24 Jun 2011
Maj **David Moffat** on 1 Jul 2011
Mrs Lt-Col **Chrissie Barnes** on 10 Jul 2011
Comr **William Pratt** on 14 Jul 2011
Mrs Maj **Gwynneth Smith** on 16 Jul 2011
Maj **Joan Bell** on 19 Jul 2011
Mrs Maj **Vera Pettit** on 24 Jul 2011
Mrs Lt-Col **Bathenia Bolton** on 25 Jul 2011
Maj Mrs **Clare Cloutt** on 25 Jul 2011
Mrs Maj **Annabella Haylett** on 28 Jul 2011
Brig Mary **Aspden** on 30 Jul 2011
Mrs Maj **Mary Hollowell** on 4 Aug 2011
Maj **Beatrice Bailey** on 13 Aug 2011
Lt-Col **Laurence Sutton** on 25 Aug 2011
Mrs Lt-Col **Emmie Bailey** on 28 Aug 2011
Maj **Philip Perry** on 31 Aug 2011
Maj **Joyce Edwards** on 31 Aug 2011
Brig **William Evans** on 5 Sep 2011
Maj **Isabella Cumming** on 5 Sep 2011
Maj **Michael Crookes** on 14 Sep 2011
Maj **Douglas Neale** on 17 Sep 2011
Maj **Arthur Keepin** on 21 Sep 2011
Maj **Stanley Richardson** on 24 Sep 2011
Mrs Lt-Col **Kathleen Tucker** on 25 Sep 2011
Maj **Frances Lake** on 1 Oct 2011
Capt **Miriam Irwin (A)** from Newtownards on 21 Oct 2011
Mrs Brig **Olive Patton** on 23 Oct 2011
Mrs Brig **Marjorie Whybrow** on 29 Oct 2011
Maj **Stanley Cleaves** on 7 Nov 2011
Mrs Brig **Charlotte Daniel** on 21 Nov 2011
Brig **John Thompson** on 24 Nov 2011
Mrs Brig **Annie Hagelstein** on 30 Nov 2011
Maj **Evelyn Andrew** on 1 Dec 2011
Lt-Col Mrs **Martha Osborne** on 5 Dec 2011
Maj **Margaret Shead** on 6 Dec 2011
Maj **Patricia Roberts** on 12 Dec 2011
Mrs Comr **Mary Hawkins** on 14 Dec 2011

Col **Maurice Griffiths** on 17 Dec 2011
Mrs Maj **Irene Sherratt** on 17 Dec 2011
Mrs Maj **Iris Keepin** on 18 Dec 2011
Maj **David Ireland** on 22 Dec 2011
Mrs Lt-Col **Doris Baker** on 25 Dec 2011
Maj **Joan Welch** on 25 Dec 2011
Brig **Clifford Honeyball** on 31 Dec 2011
Mrs Maj **Grace Whittingham** on 2 Jan 2012
Maj **Alma Harlow** on 3 Jan 2012
Maj **Margaret Taylor** on 6 Jan 2012
Maj **Reginald Scott** on 6 Jan 2012
Mrs Maj **Alice Strike** on 14 Jan 2012
Maj **Ivy Roberts** on 15 Jan 2012
Mrs Maj **Gweneth Griffin** on 19 Jan 2012
Mrs Aux-Capt **Marjorie Fry** on 31 Jan 2012
Mrs Col **Irene Durman** on 4 Feb 2012
Maj **Norina Staples** on 4 Feb 2012
Brig Mrs **Isabel Jackson** on 5 Feb 2012
Mrs Brig **Phyllis Warne** on 11 Feb 2012
Mrs Lt-Col **May Ripley** on 14 Feb 2012
Aux-Capt **Florence Jardine** on 22 Feb 2012
Mrs Maj **Lucy Butcher** on 24 Feb 2012
Maj **Margaret Stewart** on 27 Feb 2012
Mrs Brig **Norah Reid** on 27 Feb 2012
Maj **Sheila Martin** on 2 Mar 2012
Maj **William Davies** on 7 Mar 2012
Maj **Phyllis Allsop** on 10 Mar 2012
Maj **Florence Atherton** on 12 Mar 2012
Mrs Maj **Kathleen Scarborough** on 12 Mar 2012
Lt-Col **Lincoln Parkhouse** on 16 Mar 2012
Maj **Louis Kinsey** on 21 Mar 2012
Aux-Capt **Isobel Tite** on 28 Mar 2012
Mrs Maj **Rosina Wall** on 1 Apr 2012
Maj **Jane Woodhouse** on 14 Apr 2012
Maj **John Birch** on 14 Apr 2012
Mrs Brig **Pauline Ham** on 16 Apr 2012
Brig Mrs **Dorothy Evans** on 18 Apr 2012
Maj **Ethel Hall** on 18 Apr 2012
Maj **Muriel Foster** on 23 Apr 2012
Maj **Albert Stevens** on 23 Apr 2012
Brig **Gladys Byatt** on 24 Apr 2012
Maj **Patricia Yon** on 27 Apr 2012

USA CENTRAL

Mrs Maj **Marion Stickley** on 7 Aug 2011
Maj **C. Vernon Jewett** on 5 Dec 2011
Maj **Carl C. Amick** on 14 Dec 2011
Maj **Anna Thomas** on 16 Dec 2011
Mrs Maj **Ida MacNichol** on 10 Jan 2012
Maj **VaLeta Mae Merritt** on 13 Feb 2012
Maj **Paul E. Thompson** on 4 Apr 2012
Maj **(Evelyn) Joyce Baer** on 12 Apr 2012
Maj **Robert Geddis** on 8 May 2012
Maj **Jennette Stern** on 30 May 2012

USA EASTERN

Mrs Brig Florence A. Squibb on 4 Jun 2011
Maj Paul E. Hodges on 5 Jun 2011
Brig Mrs Miriam E. Jeffris on 29 Jul 2011
Brig G. Newton McClements on 31 Jul 2011
Mrs Brig Miriam G. Seaver on 2 Aug 2011
Maj Frederick C. Damery on 1 Sep 2011
Maj Eunice Blackie on 5 Sep 2011
Mrs Maj Doris Baker on 20 Sep 2011
Maj Donna Marie Ginter (A) from Buffalo Citadel, NY on 21 Sep 2011
Maj Harden H. White on 7 Oct 2011
Maj Karen Ann Wetzel (A) from Carlisle, PA on 20 Oct 2011
Mrs Brig Elizabeth Henry on 26 Oct 2011
Maj David L. Hathorn on 22 Nov 2011
Lt-Col Ralph E. Joyce on 26 Nov 2011
Lt-Col Betty J. Lyons on 27 Nov 2011
Maj Dorothy E. Breen on 7 Jan 2012
Mrs Brig Alice M. Svenson on 8 Jan 2012
Brig Walter G. Hooper on 12 Jan 2012
Brig Thelma L. Peirce on 13 Jan 2012
Maj Betty Bartlebaugh (A) from Hartford, CT DHQ on 25 Jan 2012
Brig Flora L. Snow on 2 Feb 2012
Mrs Maj Elverna R. Borror on 2 Feb 2012
Maj Kenneth M. Williams on 31 Mar 2012

USA SOUTHERN

Mrs Maj Lily Edna Russell on 2 Sep 2011
Mrs Maj Janice Faye Bovender on 10 Oct 2011
Maj Emory McGowing Frierson on 13 Oct 2011
Maj James Craig Greenham (A) from Ada, OK on 29 Oct 2011

Maj Dora Virginia McDilda Garthwaite on 31 Oct 2011
Maj Robert Hilton Boyce on 5 Nov 2011
Maj James Amburgey on 12 Nov 2011
Maj Ronald C. Greene on 3 Dec 2011
Maj John H. Tharp on 9 Dec 2011
Mrs Comr Renee Goodier on 2 Feb 2012
Maj Preston Leonard on 3 Mar 2012
Capt Pinkney Thompson on 9 Mar 2012
Maj Derek Farmer on 17 Apr 2012
Mrs Maj Margaret Oelschaeger on 9 May 2012
Maj James G. Carleton Jr on 2 Jun 2012

USA WESTERN

Maj Harold Wells on 13 Dec 2011
Maj Lola Bacon on 20 Jan 2012
Maj Clarence Orion on 30 Jan 2012
Capt Maria Espinoza (A) from Redwood City, CA on 11 Feb 2012
Maj Richard Taba on 17 Feb 2012
Brig Therma C. Cline on 9 Apr 2012
Lt-Col Elnora McIntyre on 21 Apr 2012
Maj Sven (Oscar) Youngquist on 21 Apr 2012
Maj Marjorie Helen Akin on 24 Apr 2012
Maj Esther A. Ruml on 17 May 2012

ZIMBABWE

Maj Alec Tengemhare on 4 Oct 2011
Maj Martha Siyawareva on 31 Dec 2011
Maj Misheck Nyandoro on 2 Jan 2012
Lt-Col Stella Nyakotyo on 9 Feb 2012
Maj Elizabeth Moyo on 24 Apr 2012
Lt-Col Jerinah Gorejena on 17 May 2012

PROMOTED TO GLORY

THERE are many descriptions to soften the harshness of the word 'death' but one of the most radical is the Army's phrase, 'promoted to Glory'. It sounds a triumphant, positive note in support of the Army's belief in Heaven and an unending life in Glory with the Father. It declares that death is not the end, but the beginning of a new and glorious experience for those redeemed by the blood of Jesus Christ.

The term was first used in *The War Cry* of 14 December 1882, at a time when many other military phrases were being introduced following the advent of the name 'The Salvation Army' four years earlier and soon entered common usage.

It was also consistent with the Founder's dislike of sombre black clothing as a sign of mourning. He believed that, while Christ sympathises with sorrow, he desires to make personal tragedy a stepping stone to greater faith by seeing death as a victory.

INDEX

A

Adams, Comr Clive, 191, 250
Adams, Comr Marianne, 191, 291, 252
Africa Development Centre, 35
Akpan, Comr Ime, 187, 188
Akpan, Comr Mfon, 187
All the World, 17, 22, 32, 343
Alley, Maj Kelvin, 43
Andaman and Nicobar Islands, 123
Andersen, Lt-Col Henrik, 87
Andersen, Lt-Col Lisbeth, 88
Angola, 18, 24, 41-43, 83
Antigua, 18, *see also* Caribbean, 74-78
Appeateng, Lt-Col Janet, 246
Appeateng, Lt-Col Seth, 245
Argentina, 18, *see also* South America
    East, 215-218
Arnal, Lt-Col Sylvie, 97
Australia, 5, 13, 17, 18, 23, 27, 40, 43, 44, 50
    National Secretariat, 43
    Eastern, 2, 5-6, 28, 29, 44-49
    Southern, 29, 50-57, 244
Australian Agency for International
    Development (AusAID), 40

B

Bahamas, The 18, *see also* Caribbean, 74-78
Bailey, Col Bradford, 272
Bailey, Col Heidi, 273
Bamanabio, Lt-Col Brigitte, 249
Bamanabio, Lt-Col Eugene, 248
Bamford, Lt-Col Lorraine, 220
Bamford, Lt-Col William, 219
Bangladesh, 18, 58-60
Barbados, 18, 8 *see also* Caribbean, 74-78
Belgium, 18, 8 *see also* France and
    Belgium, 97-101
Belize, 18, *see also* Caribbean, 74-78
Bell, Comr Debora, 182, 184
Bell, Comr Donald, 182
Bermuda, 18, *see also* Canada and
    Bermuda, 65-73

Bolivia, 18, *see also* South America
    West, 219-224
Bond, General Linda, 1, 5, 16, 17, 28, 30,
    66, 92, 94, 98, 127, 131, 165, 175, 192,
    215, 218, 230, 235, 239, 257, 265
Booth, Bramwell, 11, 12, 18, 106, 298
    Catherine, 11, 298
    Evangeline, 13, 298
    William, 2, 5, 11, 12, 13, 17, 27, 34
        97, 250, 251, 252, 257, 298ff
Boschung, Comr Franz, 238
Boschung, Comr Hanny, 239
Bosh, Comr Gillian, 74, 220
Bosh, Comr Larry, 74
Botswana, 18, 292
Bouzigues, Col Ricardo, 169
Bouzigues, Col Sonia, 170
Bowles, Lt-Col Marsha-Jean, 102
Brazil, 18, 61-64
Brekke, Col Birgitte, 32
Brengle, Samuel Logan, 24, 74, 88
British Guiana, 299
British Honduras, 300
Brown, General Arnold, 12, 14
Buckingham, Lt-Col Bronwyn, 212
Buckingham, Lt-Col Lyndon, 211
Burma, 18, 211, *see also* Myanmar
Burrows, General Eva, 12, 15, 23, 51, 53
Burundi, 17, 18, *see also* Rwanda and
    Burundi, 208-210

C

Canada, 2, 13, 14, 15, 16, 17, 18, 26
Canada and Bermuda, 14, 15, 22, 65-73, 166
Canadian International Development Agency
    (CIDA), 40
Canary Islands, *see* Spain 229-230
Caribbean, 17, 22, 23, 38, 39, 74-78
Carlson, Col Marcella, 265
Carlson, Col William, 264
Carpenter, General George, 12, 13, 29

Index

Carpenter, Mrs General Minnie, 26
Castillo, Lt-Col Aída, 229, 230
Castillo, Lt-Col Luis, 229
Castor, Col Edmane, 74, 75
Castor, Col Onal, 74, 75
Cavanagh, Maj David, 142
Cavanagh, Maj Elaine, 143
Celebes, 230
Cerezo, Lt-Col Josué, 158
Cerezo, Lt-Col Ruth, 159
Chandra Bai, Comr T. Regina, 115, 116
Channel Islands, 298, see also United
   Kingdom, 250-256
Charan, Comr Bimla, 131, 132
Charan, Comr Samuel, 131, 132
Chepkurui, Maj Grace, 288, 289
Chepkurui, Maj Stephen, 288
Chigariro, Comr Vinece, 147, 148, 293
Chile, 18, 300, see also South
   America West, 219-224
China, 18, see also Hong Kong and Macau,
   109-113
Christian, Lt-Col Gabriel, 127
Christian, Lt-Col Indumati, 128
Christian Mission, The, 31, 250, 298
Clénat, Capt Elianese, 209
Clénat, Capt Jean, 208
Clifton, General Shaw, 12, 16, 23, 24
Cochrane, Comr William, 31, 37
Coleman, Maj Annette, 243, 244
Coleman, Maj Michael, 243
Colombia, 301 see also Latin
   America North, 158-162
Community Care Ministries, 26
Community Development Projects, 40
Condon, Comr James, 44, 45
Condon, Comr Jan, 44, 45
Congo (Brazzaville), 18, 22, 31, 79-82
Congo (Kinshasa) and Angola, 18, 22,
   41, 42, 83-86
Costa Rica, 18, see also Latin America
   North, 158-162
Coutts, General Frederick, 12, 14
Cox, Comr André, 30, 226

Cox, Comr Silvia, 32, 226
Cuba, 19, 300, see also Latin America
   North, 158-162
Curacao, 177, 298
Czech Republic (Czechoslovakia), 18, 23,
   38, 39, 178, see also Netherlands, The,
   and Czech Republic, 177-181, 300

D

Daly, Lt-Col Gordon, 206
Daly, Lt-Col Susan, 205, 206, 207
Danielson, Lt-Col Douglas, 169
David, Lt-Col K.C., 134
David, Lt-Col Marykutty, 135
Democratic Republic of Congo, 17, 18,
   22, 41 79, 83-86
Denmark, 18, 22, 87-89
Devil's Island (French Guiana), 298
Dikalembolovanga, Lt-Cols, 167
Doctrines of The Salvation Army, 10, 298
Dominican Republic, 18, 301,
   see also Latin America North, 158-162
Donaldson, Lt-Col Janine, 226
Donaldson, Lt-Col Robert, 225
Downer, Col Gillian, 211, 212

E

East Africa, 300, 245, 248
Eastern Europe, 17, 22, 24, 90-93
Ecuador, 18, 301, see also South America
   West, 219-224
Egypt, 301
Eliasen, Col Deise, 165, 175
Eliasen, Col Torben, 165, 175
El Salvador, 18, 302, see also Latin
   America North, 158-162
Emmanuel, Comr Muthu Yesudhason,
   115, 116
England, see United Kingdom, 250-256
Estonia, 18, 38, 39, see also Finland and
   Estonia, 94-96

F

Færoes, The, 18, 300, see also Norway,

Index

Iceland and The Færoes, 191-194
Fellowship of the Silver Star, 25, 205
Fernández, Lt-Col Mirtha, 216
Fernández, Lt-Col Ricardo, 215
Ferreira, Comr Adelina, 219, 220
Ferreira, Comr Jorge, 219
Fiji, 17, 19, 38, 39, see also New Zealand,
   Fiji and Tonga, 182-186
Finger, Comr Aylene, 50, 52
Finger, Comr Raymond, 50, 51
Finland, 18, 22, 24, 94
Finland and Estonia, 31, 33, 46, 105-107
Forsyth, Comr Robin, 184
Fosen, Col Birgit, 191, 193
Fosen, Col Jan Peder, 191
France, 97, 298
France and Belgium, 22, 38, 97-101
French Guyana, 18, see also Caribbean,
   74-78
Fujii, Lt-Col Kenji, 144
Fujii, Lt-Col Chiaki, 145

G

General's Consultative Council, The, 31
Georgia, 17, 18, see also Eastern Europe,
   90-93
Germany, 18, 38, 39, 299
Germany and Lithuania, 18, 22, 24, 38,
   39, 102-105
Ghana, 18, 22, 24, 38, 39, 106-108
Ghulam, Lt-Col Yusaf, 195
Gibraltar, 299
Gluyas, Lt-Col Miriam, 199
Gowans, General John, 12, 16
Greece, 18, see also Italy, 142-143
Greenland, 17, 18, 89
Grenada, 18, 300, see also Caribbean, 74-78
Grinsted, Maj Heather, 173, 174
Grinsted, Maj Stewart, 173
Guam, 257, 302, see also USA Western,
   278-287
Guatemala, 18, see also Latin America
   North, 158-162
Guernsey, 19

Guyana, 19, 299 see also Caribbean, 74-78

H

Haiti, 18, 73 see also Caribbean, 74-78
Harfoot, Col Susan, 258
Harfoot, Col William, 257
Hawaii/Hawaiian Islands, 4, 278, 299
Heatwole, Col Dawn, 261
Heatwole, Col Merle, 259
Hedgren, Comr R. Steven, 264
Herring, Comr Alistair, 41, 109, 138, 200,
   203
Herring, Comr Astrid, 41, 109, 138, 200,
   203
Higgins, General Edward J., 12, 13
High Council, 12, 13, 300, 301, 302, 303
Hinton, Col David, 37, 250
Hinton, Col Sylvia, 252
Hodder, Comr Jolene, 150, 151
Hodder, Comr Kenneth, 37, 150
Home League, 11, 25
Honduras, 18, see also Latin America
   North, 158-162
Hong Kong, 19, 22, 109
Hong Kong and Macau, 19, 22, 38,
   39, 109-113
Horwood, Maj Deborah, 42
Horwood, Maj Edward (Ted), 41
Howard, Comr Henry, 27
Huson, Col David E., 127, 278
Howard, Col Sharron, 127, 280
Hungary, 17, 18, 39, see also Switzerland,
   Austria and Hungary, 238-242

I

Iceland, 19, 299, see also Norway, Iceland
   and The Faeroes, 191-194
India, 19, 114-137
   National Secretariat, 22, 24, 39, 114
   Central, 22, 38, 39, 115-119
   Eastern, 22, 38, 39, 120-122
   Northern, 22, 38, 39, 123-126
   South Eastern, 22, 24, 38, 39 127-130
   South Western, 22, 24, 38, 39, 131-133

Index

Western, 22, 38, 39, 134-137
Indonesia, 17, 18, 22, 38, 39, 138-141, 177
Induruwage, Comr Irene, 231, 232
Induruwage, Comr Malcolm, 59, 231
International College for Officers, 34, 300, 301
International College for Officers and Centre for Spiritual Life Development, 17, 34, 36
International Conference of Leaders, 17
International Doctrine Council, 17, 31
International Emergency Services, 7-9, 32, 249
International Headquarters, 2, 12, 13, 14, 16, 17, 22, 23, 27, 30-40, 299
  Administration Department, 31
  Administrative Structure, 46
  Business Administration Department, 32
  International Management Council, 31
  Programme Resources Department, 32
  Zonal Departments, 32-33
International Health Services, 32
International Heritage Centre, 253
International Literature Programme, 24, 32
International Moral and Social Issues Council (IMASIC), 17, 31, 33
International Projects and Development Services, 7-9, 32, 40
International Self-Denial Fund, 38
International Social Justice Commission, 31, 33
International Staff Band, 251, 252, 259, 298
International Staff Songsters, 252, 301
International Training College, 14, 15, 16, 300
Ireland, Republic of, 13, 19, 298 see also United Kingdom 250-256
Isle of Man, 19, 298, see also United Kingdom, 250-256
Italy, 18, 22, 24, 38-39, 142
Italy and Greece, 142-143

J

Jamaica, 19, 299 see also Caribbean, 74-78

James, Comr Susamma, 127, 128
James, Comr M.C., 127
Japan, 18, 22, 24, 38, 39, 144-146, 153, 154
Java, 299, 300, see also Indonesia, 138-141
Jeffrey, Comr Barbara, 272, 273
Jeffrey, Comr David, 272
Jersey, 19
Johnson, Col Kenneth, 90, 104
Johnson, Col Paula, 90, 103, 104

K

Kalai, Comr Andrew, 199
Kartodarsono, Comr, 138
Kathuri, Lt-Col Gabriel, 35
Kathuri, Lt-Col Monica, 35
Kasaedja, Lt-Col Jones, 138
Kasaedja, Lt-Col Mariyam, 139
Katsuchi, Comr Jiro, 144
Katsuchi, Comr Keiko, 144, 145
Kawlramthangi, Lt-Col, 120
Kenya, 17, 19, 35
Kenya East, 22, 25, 38, 39, 147-149, 150, 151
Kenya West, 22, 24, 38, 39, 148, 150-152
Kim, Comr Keum-nyeo, 153, 155
Kitching, General Wilfred, 12, 13
Kleman, Col Eva, 94, 95
Kleman, Col Johnny, 94
Knaggs, Comr Carolyn, 202, 278
Knaggs, Comr James, 202, 278, 279
Korea, 15, 19, 23, 24, 38, 39, 153-157
Korea, Democratic People's Republic of, 153
Krommenhoek, Comr Dick, 191
Krommenhoek, Comr Vibeke, 191, 193
Kuwait, 19, 173-174

L

Lahase, Comr Kashinath, 123, 124
Lahase, Comr Kusum, 123, 124
Lalhlimpuii, Comr, 41, 72, 120, 123 131
Lalkiamlova, Comr, 41, 45, 72, 120, 123, 131, 134
Lalngaihawmi, Col, 120, 121

Index

Lalramhluna, Lt-Col, 120
Lalzamlova, Col, 202, 203
Lamartiniere, Lt-Col Lucien, 83
Lamartiniere, Lt-Col Marie, 84
Langa, Comr Thalitha, 225, 226
Langa, Comr William, 225, 226
Larsson, General John, 12, 16
Latin America North, 23, 38,39, 158-162
Latvia, 19, 24, 39, 300, 302, *see also*
   Sweden and Latvia, 234-237
Laukkanen, Lt-Col Arja, 94
League of Mercy, 26
Lee, Lt-Col Bob, 202
Lee, Lt-Col Wendy, 203
Leslie, Lt-Col Rose-Marie, 75
Leslie, Lt-Col Victor, 74, 75
Lesotho, 19, 301, *see also* Southern Africa,
   225-228
Liberia, 19, 38, 39, 163-164
Lithuania, 19, *see also* Germany and
   Lithuania, 102-105
Lukau, Col Angélique, 79, 80
Lukau, Col Joseph, 79, 80

M

Mabuto, Lt-Col Annah, 288, 289
Mabuto, Lt-Col Christopher, 288
Macau, 19, *see also* Hong Kong and
   Macau, 109-113
MacMillan, Comr M. Christine, 66, 98,
   139, 200
McMillan, Col Susan, 215, 216
Makina, Comr Amos, 37, 107, 168, 188,
   209, 249, 288
Makina, Comr Rosemary, 188, 209, 249,
   289
Malabi, Comr Florence, 150
Malabi, Comr Joash, 150, 151
Malawi, 19, 38, 39, 165-166, 176, 288
Malaysia, 19, 38, 39, *see also* Singapore,
   Malaysia and Myanmar, 211-214
Mali, 19, 39, 167-168, 187
Mallorca, *see* Spain, 229-230
Manikyam, Col Keraham, 135
Marseille, Comr Eva, 32, 79

Marseille, Comr Gerrit, 32, 79, 249
Marshall Islands, 257, 301, *see also*
   USA Western, 278-287
Masih, Lt-Col Edwin, 115
Masih, Lt-Col Sumita, 116
Mathangi, Lt-Col Daniel Raju, 123
Mathangi, Lt-Col Rachel, 124
Maxwell, Col Robyn, 45
Maxwell, Col Wayne, 44
Mexico, 19, 23, 38, 39, 169-172
Micronesia, Federated States of, 19,
   see also USA Western, 278-287
Middle East, 39, 173-174
Mkami, Lt-Col Mary, 166
Mkami, Lt-Col Samuel, 165
Mockabee, Lt-Col Debra, 232
Mockabee, Lt-Col William, 231, 248
Moldova, 19, *see also* Eastern Europe,
   90-93
Mongolia, 303, *see also* Korea, 153-157
Moni, Lt-Col Chelliah, 131
Moni, Lt-Col Mallika, 132
Moukoko, Lt-Col Daniel, 79
Moukoko, Lt-ColArschette, 79, 80
Mozambique, 18, 21, 28, 32, 46, 47, 165,
   175-176
Mumford, Catherine, 13, 298
Munn, Col Janet, 31, 34, 121, 279
Munn, Col Richard, 31, 34, 279
Myanmar, 19, 38, 38, *see also*
   Singapore, Malaysia and Myanmar,
   211-214
Mynampi, Col Benjamin, 248
Mynampi, Col Grace, 247, 248, 249

N

Namibia, 19, *see also* Southern Africa,
   225-228
Naud, Col Anne-Dore, 102, 104
Naud, Lt-Col Daniel, 141, 142
Naud, Lt-Col Eliane, 141, 142, 143
Naud, Col Patrick, 102
Nemkhanching, Col Nu-i, 203
Nepal, 19, 303
   see also India Eastern, 120-122

Index

Nesterenko, Lt-Col Alex, 61

Nesterenko, Lt-Col Luz, 62

Netherlands, The, 19, 28, 38, 39, 40, 209, 299

Netherlands, The, and Czech Republic, 22, 24, 38, 39, 177-181

Newfoundland, 15, 298
   see also Canada and Bermuda, 65-73

New Zealand, 13, 19, 298

New Zealand, Fiji and Tonga, 16, 17, 18, 19, 23, 38, 39, 182-186

Ngwanga, Comr Madeleine, 83, 84

Nhelenhele, Lt-Col Irene, 176

Nhelenhele, Lt-Col Manuel, 175, 176

Nicaragua, 19 *see also* Latin America North, 158-162

Nigeria, 17, 19, 22, 24, 38, 39, 187-190

Nijiru, Lt-Col Nahashon, 147

Nijiru, Lt-Col Zipporah, 148

NORAD (Norway), 40

Norway, 19, 23, 38, 39, 40, 92, 191, 299

Norway, Iceland and The Færoes, 19, 22, 24, 38, 39, 40, 91,163, 191-194

Ntoya, Maj Kapela, 167

Ntoya, Maj Rose-Nicole, 167, 168

Nyagah, Comr Catherine, 292, 293

Nyagah, Comr Henry, 292

Nyambalo, Lt-Col Francis, 208

Nyambalo, Lt-Col Jamiya, 208, 209

O

Officer, The, 22, 32

Oklah, Lt-Col Philomina, 107

Oklah, Lt-Col Samuel, 106

Oloruntoba, Lt-Col Festus, 163

On, Maj Dieu-Quang, 109

Order of Distinguished Auxiliary Service, 29, 301

Order of the Founder, 27-28, 300

Orsborn, General Albert, 12, 13, 34

P

Pakistan, 19, 22, 38, 39, 195-198, 299

Panama, 19, *see also* Latin America North, 158-162

Paone, Col Jane, 97, 99

Paone, Col Massimo, 97, 98

Papua New Guinea, 16, 17, 19, 22, 38, 39, 45, 199-201

Paraguay, 19, *see also* South America East, 215-218

Paredes, Col Martha, 158, 159

Paredes, Col Tito, 158

Park, Col Chong-duk, 153

Park, Comr Man-hee, 153

Parker, Comr Joan, 138, 139

Parker, Comr Michael, 138

Payne, Lt-Col Diane, 188

Payne, Lt-Col Godfrey, 187

Peddle, Comr Brian, 65, 66, 166

Peddle, Comr Rosalie, 65, 66, 67

Peru, 19, *see also* South America West, 219-224

Philippines, 17, 19, 23, 38, 39, 201-205

Pho, Lt-Col Donni, 109, 110

Pho, Lt-Col Samuel, 109, 110

Poland, 19, 39, *see also* Germany and Lithuania, 102-105

Portugal, 19, 38, 39, 206-207, 301

Portuguese East Africa, 300

Posadas, Maj Evelyn, 59

Posadas, Maj Leopoldo, 58

Puerto Rico, 19, 257, *see also* USA Eastern, 264-270

Pululu, Lt-Col Celestino Pepe, 41

Pululu, Lt-Col Veronica, 41, 42

R

Rader, General Paul A., 12, 15, 259

Rader, Comr Kay, 259

Reddish, Col Graeme, 182

Reddish, Col Wynne, 184

Reliance Bank Ltd, 37, 299

Revive, 17, 22, 32

Roberts, Comr Nancy, 257, 258

Roberts, Comr William, 257, 258

Romania, 19, *see also* Eastern Europe, 90-93

Rowe, Col Lindsay, 245

Rowe, Col Lynette, 246

Index

Russia (Russian Federation), 19, 300, 302,
 see also Eastern Europe, 90-93
Rwanda, 17, 38, 39, 208
Rwanda and Burundi, 208-210

S

Sabah (East Malaysia), 302
St Helena, 19, *see also* Southern Africa,
 225-228
St Kitts, 19, *see also* Caribbean, 74-78
St Lucia, 19, *see also* Caribbean, 74-78
St Maarten, 19, *see also* Caribbean, 74-78
St Vincent, 19, *see also* Caribbean, 74-78
'Sally Ann' Trading Programme, 59, 196
Salvation Army
 International Trustee Company, 37
 Leadership Training College of Africa
  (SALT College), 35, 39
 Medical Fellowship, 26, 301
Salvation Army Act 1931, 12, 300
Salvation Army Act 1980, 12, 301
Salvation Army Song Book Project, 31
Salvation Army World Service Office
 (SAWSO), 38, 40, 258
Sanchez, Comr Ana Rosa, 61, 62
Sanchez, Comr Oscar, 61
Scotland, 13, 14, 15, 16, 298 *see also*
 United Kingdom 250-256
Seiler, Comr Carol, 2, 3, 259, 261
Seiler, Comr Paul, 259
Seymour, Col Geanette, 31, 33, 220
Sierra Leone, 19, 303, *see also* Liberia,
 163-164
Singapore, 19, 38, 39, 300
Singapore, Malaysia and Myanmar, 19, 23,
 210-214
Sjogren, Lt-Col Daniel, 234
Sjogren, Lt-Col Rebecca, 235
Solomon Islands, 17, 45, 48, 57, 199
Soper, Capt Florence, 11
South Africa, 19, 23, 38, 39, *see*
 also Southern Africa, 225-228
South America East, 23, 38, 39, 215-218
South America West, 23, 24 38, 39,
 219-224

South Asia (Zone), 9, 32, 58, 115, 120,
 123, 127, 131, 134, 173, 195, 231
South Pacific and East Asia (SPEA Zone),
 9, 33, 39, 44, 50, 109, 138, 144, 153,
 182, 199, 202, 211, 243
Southern Africa, 22, 38, 39, 225-228
Spain, 19, 38, 39, 229-230, 301
Sri Lanka, 19, 23, 38,39, 231-233, 299
Street, Comr Janet, 32, 95, 98, 102, 142,
 192, 206, 229
Street, Comr Robert, 32, 24, 95, 98,102,
 142, 192, 206, 229
Sumatra, 300
Sunbury Court, 13, 254
Suriname, 19, 300, *see also* Caribbean
 74-78
Swansbury, Col Charles, 106
Swansbury, Col Denise, 106, 107
Swanson, Comr Barry C., 91, 141, 143,
 147, 183, 205, 219, 225, 234, 264
Swanson, Comr Sue, 25, 91, 141, 143,
 147, 183, 219, 225, 234, 264, 265, 293
Swaziland, 19, *see also* Southern Africa
 225-228
Sweden, 13, 14, 15, 19, 38, 39
Sweden and Latvia, 19, 23, 38, 40,
 234-237, 299
Switzerland, 14, 19, 40, 1102, 299
Switzerland, Austria and Hungary, 22, 38,
 39, 154, 238-239

T

Taiwan, 19, 23, 38, 39, 110, 243-244, 301
Tanzania, 19, 38, 39, 208, 245-247, 300
Theu, Maj Chatonda, 163
Theu, Maj Joyce, 164
Tidd, Col Floyd, 65
Tidd, Col Tracey, 67
Tillsley, General Bramwell H., 12, 15
Tobago, 19, *see also* Caribbean, 74-78
Togo, 19, 106, 108, 303
Tonga, 19, 301 *see also* New Zealand, Fiji
 and Tonga, 182-186
Trinidad, 19, 299, *see also* Caribbean,
 74-78

Index

Turks and Caicos Islands, The, 19, *see also* Caribbean 74-78
Tursi, Lt-Col Anne-Florence, 239
Tursi, Lt-Col Massimo, 238
Tvedt, Col Hannelise, 177, 178

U

Uganda, 17, 19, 23, 38, 39, 248-249, 300
Ukraine, 17, 19, *see also* Eastern Europe, 90-93
United Arab Emirates, 19, 173-174
United Kingdom with the Republic of Ireland, 16, 19, 23, 24, 38, 39, 226, 250-256, 272, 302
United Nations, 33
United States of America, 2, 17, 19, 26, 40, 65, 257-287
  National, 23, 40, 257-258
  Central, 4, 22, 38, 116, 202, 259-263
  Eastern, 23, 24, 38, 264-270
  Southern, 23, 38, 248, 272-277
  Western, 23, 38, 278-287
Uruguay, 19, 299, *see also* South America East, 215-218
USAID, 40

V

Van Vliet, Comr Hans, 139, 177, 178, 179, 180
Van Vliet, Comr Marja, 139, 177, 178
Varghese, Lt-Col Davidson, 114
Varguhese, Col Prema, 293
Varguhese, Col Wilfred, 292
Venezuela, 19, *see also* Latin America North, 158-162
Venter, Lt-Col Alistair, 58, 59
Venter, Lt-Col Marieke, 58, 59
Vijayakumar, Lt-Col Thumati, 134
Virgin Islands, 19, 257, *see also* USA Eastern, 264-270

W

Wahlström, General Jarl, 12, 15, 23
Wainwright, Comr Dorita, 32, 165
Wainwright, Comr John, 32, 165

Wales, 298, *see also* United Kingdom, 250-256
Walker, Col Jennifer, 52
Walker, Col Peter, 50
Walters, Lt-Col, Rodney, 90
Walters, Lt-Col, Wendy, 92
Wandulu, Lt-Col Moses, 165
Wandulu, Lt-Col Sarah, 165, 166
Ward, Col Marguerite, 9, 195, 196
Ward, Col Robert, 195
Webb, Col Christine, 199, 200
Webb, Col Neil, 199
Welander, Col Knud David, 87
Welander, Col Lisbeth, 87, 88
Wickberg, General Erik, 12, 14, 23
Willermark, Comr Marie, 234, 235
William Booth College (UK), 18, 39, 259
Wiseman, General Clarence, 12, 14
Wolayo, Lt-Col Johnstone, 150
Wolayo, Lt-Col Linnet, 151
Women's Ministries, 25, 32
Woodall, Comr Ann, 32, 37
Woodland, Lt-Col Donald, 28, 45
Words of Life, 23, 32, 349

Y

Yoon, Col, Eun-sook, 155
Yousaf, Lt-Col Rebecca, 196
Yugoslavia, 300

Z

Zambia, 19, 38, 39, 154, 175, 288-291
Zimbabwe, 19, 23, 38, 39, 292-294
Zola, Lt-Col Alphonsine, 175, 176
Zola, Lt-Col Ambroise, 175, 176
Zululand, 225, 299

Notes

Notes

Notes

Notes

TERRITORIES (T), COMMANDS (C) AND REGIONS (R) WITHIN EACH ZONE

AFRICA
Angola (C)
Congo (Brazzaville) (T)
Democratic Republic of Congo (T)
Ghana (T)
Kenya East (T)
Kenya West (T)
Liberia (C)
Malawi (T)
Mali (R)
Mozambique (T)
Nigeria (T)
Rwanda and Burundi (C)
Southern Africa (T)
Tanzania (T)
Uganda (T)
Zambia (T)
Zimbabwe (T)

AMERICAS AND CARIBBEAN
Brazil (T)
Canada and Bermuda (T)
Caribbean (T)
Latin America North (T)
Mexico (T)
South America East (T)
South America West (T)
USA Central (T)
USA Eastern (T)
USA Southern (T)
USA Western (T)

EUROPE
Denmark (T)
Eastern Europe (T)
Finland and Estonia (T)
France and Belgium (T)
Germany and Lithuania (T)
Italy and Greece (C)
The Netherlands and Czech
    Republic (T)
Norway, Iceland and The Færoes (T)
Portugal (C)
Spain (C)
Sweden and Latvia (T)
Switzerland, Austria and Hungary (T)
United Kingdom with the Republic
    of Ireland (T)

SOUTH ASIA
Bangladesh (C)
India Central (T)
India Eastern (T)
India Northern (T)
India South Eastern (T)
India South Western (T)
India Western (T)
Middle East (R)
Pakistan (T)
Sri Lanka (T)

SOUTH PACIFIC AND EAST ASIA
Australia Eastern (T)
Australia Southern (T)
Hong Kong and Macau (C)
Indonesia (T)
Japan (T)
Korea (T)
New Zealand, Fiji and Tonga (T)
Papua New Guinea (T)
The Philippines (T)
Singapore, Malaysia and
    Myanmar (T)
Taiwan (R)